PARADISE LOST

Milton at sixty-two, engraving by William Faithorne
from the frontispiece to Milton's *History of Britain* (1670).

JOHN MILTON

PARADISE LOST

Edited by William Kerrigan,
John Rumrich,
and Stephen M. Fallon

THE MODERN LIBRARY

NEW YORK

2008 Modern Library Paperback Edition

Copyright © 2007 by Random House, Inc.

Published in the United States by Modern Library,
an imprint of The Random House Publishing Group,
a division of Random House, Inc., New York.

MODERN LIBRARY and the TORCHBEARER Design are registered
trademarks of Random House, Inc.

Originally published as part of *The Complete Poetry and Essential Prose
of John Milton* in hardcover in the United States by Modern Library,
an imprint of The Random House Publishing Group, a division of
Random House, Inc., in 2007.

Illustration credits can be found on page vii.

LIBRARY OF CONGRESS CATALOGING-IN-PUBLICATION DATA
Milton, John, 1608–1674.
Paradise lost/by John Milton; edited by William Kerrigan, John
Rumrich, and Stephen M. Fallon.
p. cm.
Taken from The complete poetry and essential prose
of John Milton. 2007.
Includes bibliographical references (p.   ) and index.
ISBN: 978-0-375-75796-9 (trake pbk.: alk. paper)
1. Bible. O.T. Genesis—History of Biblical events—Poetry.
2. Adam (Biblical figure)—Poetry.   3. Eve (Biblical figure)—Poetry.
4. Fall of man—Poetry.   I. Kerrigan, William,   II. Rumrich, John
Peter   III. Fallon, Stephen M.   IV. Complete poetry and essential
prose of John Milton.   V. Title.
PR3560 2008
821'.4—dc22   2008009709

Printed in the United States of America

www.modernlibrary.com

CONTENTS

PARADISE LOST

List of Illustrations

All illustrations are used with permission.

INTRODUCTION

Milton became entirely blind in 1652, just a short while before the death of his first wife, Mary Powell Milton, followed six weeks later by the death of their infant son, John. He married again in 1656. In 1658 Katharine Woodcock Milton died of complications arising from child-birth, again followed about six weeks later by the death of their infant daughter, Katharine. The political cause to which Milton had devoted two decades of his life suffered a resounding defeat with Charles II's ascent to the throne in 1660. Through this time of loss and reversal, Milton kept busy on various prose projects, including his theological treatise *Christian Doctrine,* a Latin thesaurus, and his *History of Britain.* He translated a group of Psalms in 1653. He wrote the occasional sonnet. Then, probably before the Restoration, he shook off potential depression, concentrated his powers, and began composing the greatest long poem in the English language. "His great works," Samuel Johnson declared, "were performed under discountenance, and in blindness, but difficulties vanished at his touch; he was born for whatever is arduous" (Thorpe 88).

Though Edward Phillips did not mention these dates in his life of Milton, he told John Aubrey that the poem was begun "about 2 years before the king came in, and finished about three years after the king's restoration" (lxvi). Although Milton associated literary creativity with the temperate Mediterranean climate that had nurtured Homer and Vergil, he himself composed *Paradise Lost* only during the winter, from the autumnal to the vernal equinox. Various secretaries copied it down. Milton's habit was to rise early in the morning with "ten, twenty, or thirty verses" (Darbishire 73) ready for dictation. If his amanuensis happened to be late, he had a little joke ready, and "would complain, saying *he wanted to be milked*" (Darbishire 33).

A major poem had long been his chief ambition. As early as *At a Vacation Exercise* in 1628, the nineteen-year-old undergraduate had magically suspended the expectations of a humorous ritual occasion to evoke the highest raptures of epic, "where the deep transported mind may soar/Above the wheeling poles, and at Heav'n's door/Look in," and "sing of secret things that came to pass/When beldam Nature in her cradle was." For a time, as references in *Manso* and *Epitaph for Damon* reveal, he considered a specifically British poem shaped from Arthurian materials. Such a work would be "doctrinal and exemplary to a nation" (*RCG* in *MLM* 841). We do not know precisely why Milton abandoned this plan. He might have come to feel that a patriotic epic was simply too provincial, or that the choice of an early British king for a hero would commit the work to some degree of monarchism; then, too, he might have realized as maturity settled on him that he could admire Spenser without trying to duplicate his achievement.

The first plans for a work on the Fall of man in the Garden of Eden appear in four outlines for a tragic drama in the Trinity College manuscript (*CMS*), probably drafted in the early 1640s. The third of these is called "Paradise Lost." Adam and Eve do not take the stage until after the Fall, presumably because their "first naked glory" (*PL* 9.1115) could not be accommodated in a fallen theater. In the fourth and final version, which shifts from the outline format to narrative prose, Milton roughs in some features of *Paradise Lost*. Satan has a new prominence. The work will end with the expelling angel showing Adam a pageant about the fallen world he is soon to enter.

THE BOOK

Paradise Lost was published in 1667 by the bookseller Samuel Simmons, whose London shop was near Aldersgate. The Pierpont Morgan Library in New York possesses a manuscript of Book 1 of the poem in the hand of a copyist, and corrected by as many as five other hands, that was used to set the type for this edition (see Darbishire 1931 for a photographic facsimile). The contract stipulated that Milton was to be paid five pounds for the manuscript, another five pounds upon the sale of a first edition of thirteen hundred copies, and yet another five pounds upon the sale of a second edition of the same size. The earliest title page of the 1667 quarto identifies Paradise Lost as "A POEM Written in TEN BOOKS By *JOHN MILTON*." Sales were apparently sluggish. Through 1668 and 1669, the edition was issued with four more title pages, as Simmons added Milton's note on unrhyming verse and his prose arguments summarizing the action of the poem book by book. When the first printing finally sold out in April 1669, Milton was paid a second five pounds.

It was perhaps Dryden's announcement in April 1674 that he would transform *Paradise Lost* into a heroic opera (this "never acted" opera was published as *The State of Innocence* in 1677) that led Simmons to print a second and octavo edition of the epic in July 1674. This book contained prefatory poems by Samuel Barrow (in Latin) and Andrew Marvell (in English). The epic was "amended, enlarged, and differently disposed as to the number of books, by his own hand, that is by his own appointment [by someone acting as his agent]" (Edward Phillips in Darbishire, 1932, 75). The shift from ten to twelve books meant dividing the original Book 7 into the new Books 7 and 8, with the addition of four new lines at the beginning of Book 8; the long Book 10 of the first edition was divided into Books 11 and 12, with five new lines at the beginning of Book 12. There were four other major revisions (the reworking of 1.5104–5, the expansion at 5.636–41, the addition of 11.485–87, the alteration of 11.551). The authority of the second edition cannot be doubted in these matters. An unwell Milton made an oral will on or about July 20, 1674, two weeks after the second publication of *Paradise Lost*, and died on November 9, 1674. The second edition of *Paradise Lost* was the last printing over which he exerted control.

There are thirty-seven substantive differences between the two editions. In thirteen of these, the quarto text supplies the superior reading; in only eight is the octavo text superior; editors differ over the remaining sixteen (Moyles 22–26). It would seem from this evidence that editors should not, as many have claimed to do, adopt the 1674 octavo as a copy text and automatically follow it with regard to the accidentals of spelling and punctuation (Moyles 28). There are over eight hundred variants of this kind between the two editions. We have treated each as a separate case rather than defer to the rule of the copy text.

Simmons published a third edition in 1678. A printer named Brabazon Aylmer purchased the poem from Simmons in 1680, then sold half of it to a young entrepreneur named Jacob Tonson. He was

Dryden's chief publisher and would become known for his beautiful editions of Shakespeare and Spenser. But Milton was his great love and, happily enough for a businessman, his great moneymaker too. He and Aylmer printed a folio-size fourth edition of the epic in 1688, adding illustrations, a frontispiece portrait of Milton, and an epigram by Dryden in which Milton is said to be the union of Homer and Vergil. Tonson purchased Aylmer's half of the poem in 1691. He also obtained from Aylmer the manuscript of Book 1 now owned by the Pierpont Morgan Library. For the sixth edition, of 1695, Tonson added 321 pages of explanatory notes by Patrick Hume; no other English poem had ever been so lavishly annotated. Tonson and his family would print *Paradise Lost*, and other works by Milton, in various configurations again and again throughout the eighteenth century. When asked which poet had brought him the greatest financial profit, Tonson without hesitation replied "Milton" (Lynch 126). He had his portrait painted holding a copy of *Paradise Lost*.

In 1732 a cantankerous, seventy-year-old academic named Richard Bentley, then England's foremost classicist and a specialist in textual emendation, published a notorious edition of *Paradise Lost*. Believing that he had purified textual corruption in classical authors such as Manilius, Bentley brought the same methods to Milton's modern epic. Blind, Milton was unable to correct wayward copyists. But Bentley, suspecting a more deliberate and insidious errancy, posited the existence of a "phantom" editor. Befuddled by Milton's learning and linguistic precision, this unknown person rewrote the text to suit his own imbecility. Today the Bentley edition seems a work of glaring subjectivity. Truths about the epic, such as the immense thoughtfulness manifest in its details, do not break into the editor's awareness because his attention is devoted wholly to his own theory and method. It was hardly a compliment to Milton to suppose that *Paradise Lost* as readers knew it was a work of genius systematically effaced by the work of a moron. But modern critics such as William Empson, Christopher Ricks, and John Leonard have been inspired by Bentley's scrutiny of the minutiae of Milton's style. Textual emendation became the rage in Shakespeare studies in the eighteenth century and is still widely practiced today. The aberration of Bentley's *Paradise Lost* aside, it never caught on among Milton's editors.

The next notable edition was Thomas Newton's beautiful two-volume variorum of 1749. Its copious and often unequaled annotations were mostly reprinted, with the addition of many new ones, in the 1826 variorum of Milton's entire poetic works assembled by Reverend Henry Todd. Anyone who becomes seriously curious about the meaning of a particular word or passage in Milton will want to go back to Todd and Newton, and behind them to the first of Milton's annotators, Patrick Hume. They will also want to explore works such as Jonathan Richardson's *Explanatory Notes and Remarks on Milton's Paradise Lost* (1734) and James Paterson's *A Complete Commentary with Etymological, Explanatory, Critical and Classical Notes on Milton's "Paradise Lost"* (1744). There are many subtleties, exactitudes, and points of information in these notes for which we, like other modern editors, have simply found no room.

Among the editions of the last century or so, we were most surprised to discover the sustained elucidation of A. W. Verity, who is largely forgotten today; besides the excellence of their commentary, his notes teem with examples of Romantic and Victorian imitation of Milton and will prove useful in future studies of that subject. In working on this edition, we came to think of Verity as the unknown god of Milton annotation. We also paid especially close attention to the thoughtful notes of Alastair Fowler and John Leonard, and consulted Merritt Hughes, Douglas Bush, Scott Elledge, and Roy Flannagan, among others.

COSMOS

Heaven sits atop Milton's cosmos. Beneath it lies Chaos. We sense that both of these realms have, so to speak, been around forever. It would be a nice point in Milton's theology to ask whether Chaos precedes Heaven or vice versa, since the very existence of God seems to require an abode, and therefore a Heaven of some sort, while on the other hand Chaos appears to be the precondition of all creations, including those of the Son, the angels, and Heaven. As the poem begins, these two established cosmic areas have been joined by two new spaces. At the bottom of Chaos stands Hell, the elder of the new realms. Between Heaven and Chaos, suspended on a golden chain affixed to Heaven (2.1004–6), lies the most recent of God's creations: our Earth, including the planets and stars surrounding it.

Readers of the poem are usually familiar with dualistic visions of Heaven, in which the realm of the divine is carefully separated from such imperfect earthly things as body and alteration. But Milton's universe is monistic. Everything stems from "one first matter" (5.472). Instead of excluding materiality, pleasure, pain, appetite, sexuality, and time from Heaven, Milton welcomes them in. As on Earth, day and night alternate in Heaven; Heaven's night is not the darkness of Earth's but rather comparable to earthly twilight (5.627–29, 645–46, 685–86). Beneath the very Mount of God is a cave "Where light and darkness in perpetual round/Lodge and dislodge by turns, which makes through Heav'n/Grateful vicissitude, like day and night" (6.6–8). Milton's God, satisfying an appetite for vicissitude, resides on time.

Angels live large in a Heaven that is vast but not infinite. When Satan leaves the military camp near the deity, he and his followers retreat to the "palace of great Lucifer" in north Heaven (5.760). Apparently, on the model of the court and the country, angels live in estates various distances from the mountainous throne of God. Buildings designed by angelic architects, radiant with gems and precious metals, grace the realm. The orders of angels (Seraphim, Cherubim, Thrones, Dominations, Virtues, Powers, Principalities, Archangels, Angels) were strictly hierarchical in traditional Christian thought. At times in Milton, the terms carry their old hierarchical force, but often they are used interchangeably, as a pool of synonyms for the generic angel. Milton is rather insistent on the point that while likenesses between Heaven and Earth may be necessary fictions, they could also be ontologically sound (5.571–76). "O Earth, how like to Heav'n!" Satan exclaims (9.99). Heaven has vales, streams, breezes, trees, flowers, and vines. The vegetation produces ambrosial food, "the growth of Heaven" (5.635). Heaven and Earth, like spirit and matter or men and angels, differ "but in degree, of kind the same" (5.490).

Although Chaos can be studied in terms of antecedents in classical literature and philosophy (Chambers 1963), its appearance in the epic owes its problematic character to Milton's theology. Chaos is infinite, and filled by a ubiquitous God who has nonetheless withdrawn his creative will from chaotic matter (7.168–73). None of the categorical binaries established during the creation of Genesis inhere in Chaos. It is neither this nor that, "neither sea, nor shore, nor air, nor fire,/But all these in their pregnant causes mixed/Confus'dly" (2.912–14); therefore

Satan, as he traverses this indeterminate space, confusedly mixes loco-motions, "And swims or sinks, or wades, or creeps, or flies" (2.950). The "embryon atoms" (2.900) of Chaos are "the womb of Nature" (2.911), the pure potential that the Son first circumscribes with golden compasses when creating our universe (7.225–31) and will doubtless use again in creating new worlds (2.915–16). Chaos cannot be good until God has infused it with creative order. It is at least morally neutral, at best thoroughly praiseworthy, as a part of the process by which God makes and sustains all things.

But alongside the language of atomism, Milton gives us a mythic Chaos, personified as the ruler of his realm, or rather its "Anarch" (2.988), since Chaos is by definition without rule. This Chaos, speaking for his consort, Night, and for a shadowy pack of Hesiodic creatures and personifications (2.963–67), expresses his resentment over recent losses (the creations of Hell and our universe) and supports Satan's mission on the assumption that "Havoc and spoil and ruin are my gain" (2.1009). We thus arrive at paradox. Theologically, Chaos is neutral or better. Mythically, in terms of the epic narrative, Chaos is the ally of Satan.

Jewish and Christian theologians have sometimes distinguished the Bible from other Mesopotamian creation myths in which the god-hero defeats a chaos monster, out of whose slain body the world is made; in Genesis, by contrast, the world is initially good, and God affirms its goodness on every day of the creation. Evil appears with the fall of man (Ricoeur 172, 175–210), though of course the enigmatic presence of the snake promises a backstory of some kind. For Ricoeur the matter at stake here is whether religious symbols are recessive, and must always point backward to the defeat of Chaos, or whether they can look toward novel futures, as is apparently the case with the messianic and eschatological strands of Judaism and Christianity. Regina Schwartz, defending Milton's mythic Chaos, argues that the separation of evil from the Creation is not really true of the Bible, and is patently untrue of *Paradise Lost*, where Chaos gives Satan his nod of approval. All of God's revelations, all of Satan's subsequent defeats, echo the initial triumph over Chaos, and redemption itself is but a repetition of that original victory (Schwartz 8–39; see also Leonard 2000, xx–xxi).

John Rumrich, defending the theological Chaos, notes that the irony of Chaos's expression of solidarity with Satan lies in the old Anarch's failure to understand that Satanic evil is rigid, not anarchic, a fixed posture of defiance and disobedience (1995, 1035–44). We see this in Book 10, where Sin and Death are building a bridge through Chaos to link Earth and Hell, and a double-crossed Chaos seethes at this new incursion into his realm:

> On either side
> Disparted Chaos overbuilt exclaimed,
> And with rebounding surge the bars assailed,
> That scorned his indignation. (10.415-18)

Chaos, Rumrich maintains, is "a part of the deity, arguably feminine, over which the eternal father does not exercise control, from which, in other words, the father is absent as an active, governing agent" (1995, 1043; see also Danielson 32–57).

Expelled from Heaven, the rebel angels fall for nine days and nights through Chaos to Hell (6.871), which "Yawning received them whole, and on them closed" (6.875). They land on a burning sulfurous lake. After spending another nine days and nights stretched out dazed or unconscious on this lake (1.50–53), they awaken to the baleful prospect of Hell. Milton famously describes it as "darkness visible" (1.63), a place where fire burns without giving off light. Its purpose is not clear to the fallen angels. Among the first topics addressed in Hell is whether the Hell is for punishment or confinement (1.146–52).

In Milton's day the idea of Hell and its eternal torments was just entering a period of declining popularity among educated Europeans (Walker). Americans in particular, remembering such figures as Jonathan Edwards, tend to associate Puritanism with resistance to this trend. Milton exposes the simplicity of this view. His narrator introduces Hell as a "dungeon" for "torture without end" (1.61–69). But beyond the nine days in burning sulfur, we do not observe much in the way of punishment. To be sure, there are the more or less classical touches of the devils' periodic exposure to the extremes of ice and fire (2.596–603); the frustrating waters of Lethe, which shrink from seekers of oblivion (2.604–14); the terrifying monsters bred in Hell (2.622–28); the annual metamorphosis of the demons into serpents (10.572–77). But nothing here approaches the individualized tortures inflicted over and over on the inmates of Dante's Hell. Perhaps the difference lies in the fact that

Milton's Hell is inhabited by fallen angels only, whereas Dante's is peopled. But there is no direct allusion in *Paradise Lost* to tortures awaiting the damned in the future. William Empson, a critic acutely attuned to the idea of God as torturer, found no evidence of this despicable notion in *Paradise Lost:* "Milton's God is not interested in torture, and never suggests that he uses it to improve people's characters" (273). For Milton, one has the impression, exile from God is the primal punishment, and all others merely the flash points of low imaginations.

As for confinement, the only exit from Hell is through a locked gate. But the key has been entrusted to Sin (2.774–77, 850–53, 871–89). She alone can unlock the gate, and does, and is incapable of closing it. At the end of time, Hell may indeed become a dungeon of torment (10.629–37), the universe's vacuum-cleaner bag, but in the meantime devils will possess the fallen earth, especially its air. Milton's Hell is more importantly a spiritual condition. "The mind is its own place," Satan declares, "and in itself/Can make a Heav'n of Hell, a Hell of Heav'n" (1.254–55). It can certainly do the second, as we see in the birth of Sin from the mind of Satan. Out of the "darkness" of a painful headache, "flames thick and fast" appear (2.754): a precise echo of Hell's "darkness visible." Even in Heaven, Satan has Hell within him, "nor from Hell/One step no more than from himself can fly/By change of place" (4.21–23).

The first half of *Paradise Lost* begins with Milton's search for a Heavenly Muse who was present at the Creation, "and with mighty wings outspread/Dove-like sat'st brooding on the vast abyss" (1.20–21). Only with this Muse illuminating what is dark in him, raising and supporting what is low in him, can Milton create the poem. The second half of *Paradise Lost* begins in Book 7 with a direct and expanded account of this miracle. It is the perfect fit between inspiration and subject matter: the metaphorical creation of the poem now recounts the actual Creation. This world, the handiwork of God, was the single greatest stimulus to Milton's imagination.

We find many examples of this literary excitement in Milton's treatment of astronomy. He met the blind Galileo in 1638 or 1639, when the Inquisition had confined him to his villa outside of Florence. The "Tuscan artist" is the only contemporary mentioned in the epic. There are three explicit references (1.287–91, 3.588–90, 5.261–63). To these must be added passages that allude to one or another of Galileo's discoveries, such as newly sighted stars (7.382–84), the nature of the Milky Way (7.577–81), the phases of Venus (7.366), the moons of Jupiter (8.148–52), and the freshly detailed description of the moon (7.375–78, 8.145–48). This fascination extends to other matters concerning the new astronomy of the seventeenth century. Milton returns four times to the question of whether there has been from the beginning, or may be in the future, a plurality of inhabited worlds (2.912, 7.191, 7.621–22, 8.148–52). He leaves open debated matters such as whether the earth rotates on its axis (4.591–95). When he writes of the "three different motions" of the earth (8.130), we can infer a somewhat detailed knowledge of Copernicus (Babb 81–82), the champion of the heliocentric universe, who wrote at length about the three motions (daily rotation, annual revolution about the sun, and the slow movement about the ecliptic, or "trepidation," causing the precession of the equinoxes).

On the large question of whether to prefer the modern "Copernican" heliocentric model or the ancient "Ptolemaic" geocentric model of the universe, Milton has Raphael, Adam's first angelic educator, insist on the undecidability of such matters (8.66–178). But it would have been impossible to represent cosmic space with any precision without making a choice, and in point of fact the design of the poem's universe is Ptolemaic. Earth is the still point of the turning world. The spheres of the moon, sun, Mercury, Venus, Mars, Jupiter, and Saturn turn about a central Earth. Beyond them is the eighth sphere of the fixed stars, so called because they do not appear to change their positions with regard to one another. The ninth is the so-called crystalline sphere, whose vibrations cause the "trepidation" (3.483). Finally, the primum mobile, the outer circle moved directly by God, encases this entire mesh of spheres within spheres.

Did Milton see the heavens through a telescope? Might he, to broach the most exciting thought of all, have looked through Galileo's telescope? Such speculations, common in the discipline of Milton studies, are inspired by his epic's unprecedented aesthetics of space. If Milton ultimately sided with the ancients in universe design, his rendering of the great vistas both seen and traversed by space-traveling angels opens a whole new area in modern literary sublimity. "Milton's canvas in *Paradise Lost* is the vastest used by an English artist" (Nicolson 1960, 187). Dante's universe is finished. Milton's is a work in progress. The novelties of Earth and Hell have reorganized space itself;

more novelties can be anticipated. Novelty in the representation of space is a conscious literary feature of the epic, and stands for its modernity. When Satan throws his shield over his back, Milton interposes, between our mental sight and its object, the "optic glass" of Galileo:

> the broad circumference
> Hung on his shoulders like the moon, whose orb
> Through optic glass the Tuscan artist views
> At evening from the top of Fesole,
> Or in Valdarno, to descry new lands,
> Rivers or mountains in her spotty globe. (1.286–91)

Homer had compared the brightness of Achilles' shield to the moon. Milton switches the focus from brightness, so crucial in Greek poetics, to size, so crucial in his poetics, and relocates the old simile inside the circle of Galileo's telescope. This invention, he implies, is the only modern device to expand the imaginative range of poetry, to provide a worldly conceptualization of what it means to describe immortals and inquire into the ways of God. Notice how, once Galileo is introduced, the passage forgets Satan and the narrative line of the poem to celebrate the wandering curiosity of Galileo's viewing and descrying eye. For Milton, the Tuscan artist represents curiosity rewarded: despite Catholic dogmatism, Galileo wanted to see, and he did see, which is what the blind narrator of *Paradise Lost* seeks in his invocation to light at the opening of Book 3.

Many of the poem's best sidereal effects derive from what Alastair Fowler calls "an entire fictive astronomy," whose implications Milton works out "with ingenuity reminiscent of science fiction" (35). Before the Fall, Milton postulates, the path of the sun never deviates from the equator. The axis of the earth is perfectly parallel to the axis of the sun. The sun is always in Aries. There is no precession of equinoxes. Day and night are always of equal duration. There are no seasons. Within the beautiful simplicity of this system, Milton arranges the various journeys and arrivals of his poem. An extraordinary number of important things happen at the four cardinal points of the day, dawn and dusk, noon and midnight (Cirillo 1962).

Allusions to the zodiac and the constellations are often both realistic and symbolic. Milton rarely underlines, rarely sticks an elbow in our ribs. When Satan leaves our world in Book 10, "Betwixt the Centaur and the Scorpion steering/His zenith, while the Sun in Aries rose" (328–29), the author expects a very great deal of his reader. She must know that the constellation Anguis, the body of the serpent held by Ophiuchus, lies between the Centaur and the Scorpion. She must recall that, some 5,833 lines ago, Satan entered our world (3.555–61), and Milton described his view in such a way that he must have been gazing out from the head of Anguis. A reader able to put all this together realizes that Satan enters through the head and exits from the tail of the serpent. She appreciates a scatological joke. She is reminded of eating and digestion, which is rather a serious matter in *Paradise Lost*. She recalls with a dawning sense of complexity that Satan in Eden possesses the serpent through its mouth. And so on. As one of the finest of Milton's eighteenth-century commentators put it, "A reader of Milton must be always upon duty; he is surrounded with sense, it rises in every line, every word is to the purpose. . . . All has been considered, and demands and merits observation" (Richardson in Darbishire 1932, 315).

It will not surprise close students of Milton to learn that there is a passage in the poem that apparently calls into question everything we have said about the energy, originality, and sublimity of his cosmos. For what are we to make of Raphael's dismissive rebuke to the ambitions of astronomers (8.66–178)? God will laugh at their attempts to divulge his secrets. Adam is advised to leave the heavens to their own workings: "be lowly wise" (173). The speech is not, as it has sometimes been taken to be, an all-out attack on the new learning that elsewhere seems to intrigue and inspire the poet. God is in fact pictured laughing at the old Ptolemaic astronomers, adding orbits within orbits and strange counterpressures ("build, unbuild") in order to make the model fit the appearances (Babb 88):

> perhaps to move
> His laughter at their quaint opinions wide
> Hereafter, when they come to model heav'n
> And calculate the stars, how they will wield
> The mighty frame, how build, unbuild, contrive
> To save appearances, how gird the sphere
> With centric and eccentric scribbled o'er,
> Cycle and epicycle, orb in orb. (8.77–84)

The angel also insists that man is not the only being who must discipline his curiosity; the workings of the universe have been kept secret from "man or angel" (see also 7.122–24). And no doubt Raphael has a point in maintaining that the correctness of this or that celestial picture makes no difference to life on Earth, which must be the focus of our wisdom.

Still, censuring a desire to understand the heavens seems directly contrary in spirit to the passage on Satan's shield, with its excited shift of focus to the knowledge-hungry eyes of Galileo surveying the moon. Perhaps Nicolson was right in supposing that there were "two persistent aspects of Milton's personality, one satisfied with proportion and limitation, the other revelling in the luxuriant and the unrestrained" (1960, 186). Then again, it is possible that the dismissal of astronomy belongs not to a conflict between contentment and aspiration but to the structure of aspiration. This divine disapproval could be viewed as a scientific expression of the general sense of trespass Milton encounters when approaching God. "May I express thee unblamed" (3.3)? He cannot reach the heights without taking liberties.

THEOLOGY

Milton's theology is systematic, Christian, Protestant, and for the most part quite standard. That much is evident from his epic argument, which incorporates the familiar locales, actors, and events of Christian orthodoxy: Heaven, Hell, an almighty and all-knowing deity, hateful rebel angels, benevolent unfallen angels, Adam and Eve, a garden Paradise on Earth, the Fall, Original Sin, the penalty of mortality, and, in prospect, satisfaction of that penalty through sacrifice of God's only-begotten Son. Indeed, this large conformity has permitted generations of Milton scholars to downplay or ignore his unorthodoxy. Yet, despite the substantially ordinary Christianity of *Paradise Lost*, Milton did endorse various theological opinions deemed heretical, some criminally so in the view of seventeenth-century civil and ecclesiastical authorities.

A few of these unorthodox beliefs figure crucially in *Paradise Lost*. Most do not. On the one hand, Milton's advocacy of adult baptism by immersion, for example, and his rejection of obligatory Sabbath observation, though significant enough in the religious politics of the seventeenth century, do not bear on his epic. Vitalist monism and insistence on creation *ex deo*, on the other hand, are grand generative heresies foundational to the fictional world imagined by Milton—its spiritual-natural ground rules, as detailed in the preceding section. The three great religious debates of seventeenth-century England, and the heresies that correspond to them, are even more overtly pertinent, especially to the declared intention of the epic narrative to "justify the ways of God to men." The first of these controversies concerns the means of salvation (soteriology); the second, church government (ecclesiology); and the third, the status of the Son of God (Christology).

Most Christians in a relatively tolerant age would deem Milton's theological opinions as they relate to the first two of these controversies unremarkable and, in any case, his own business. But his opinions concerning the Son of God still register as heretical according to most Christian sects. They have also been a focus of sometimes heated scholarly controversy for nearly two centuries, since the manuscript of his theological treatise, *Christian Doctrine,* was discovered in 1823. The longest chapter of the treatise criticizes the orthodox doctrine of the Trinity as a logical impossibility devoid of scriptural authority and depicts the Son as a distinctly lesser God: the first of all creatures, begotten in time, and variously inferior to his father. That Milton's arguments should therefore be classified as Arian and contrary to Nicene formulations ("true God from true God . . . of one essence with the Father") was the seemingly inescapable conclusion endorsed by theologically informed Milton scholars from the time of Bishop Sumner, the original translator of the treatise, through the era of C. S. Lewis and Maurice Kelley in the mid–twentieth century. Orthodox believers who saw Milton as a bulwark of traditional Christianity were discomfited, the unorthodox heartened. Thus in 1826 the American Unitarian clergyman William Ellery Channing, a forerunner of Transcendentalism, enthusiastically grouped Milton with other celebrated seventeenth-century antitrinitarians: "our Trinitarian adversaries are perpetually ringing in our ears the names of Fathers and Reformers. We take MILTON, LOCKE, and NEWTON, and place them in our front, and want no others to oppose to the whole army of great names on the opposite side. Before these intellectual suns, the stars of self-named orthodoxy 'hide their diminished heads'" (35–36).

Readers who found *Paradise Lost* nonetheless orthodox comforted themselves with the often repeated observation that before the discovery of the treatise readers better informed theologically than their twentieth-century counterparts failed to suspect Milton's epic of heresy. C. S. Lewis reasoned that Milton when he composed his epic must have deliberately set aside his theological eccentricities in order to appeal to the majority of Christian readers (90–91). This surmise segued into the still current argument that because the theological treatise is inconsistent with the epic, the former should not be relied on as a guide to understanding the latter (Patrides; Campbell et al. 110).

Such claims simply do not hold water. John Toland, writing Milton's life in 1698, declined to defend *Paradise Lost* "against those people who brand [it] with heresy" (128), indicating that such complaints were fairly common even before the discovery of the treatise. Unlike Toland, Jonathan Richardson, writing in 1734, says he cannot in good conscience "pass over in silence another conjecture which some have made, . . . that Milton was an Arian; and this is built on certain passages in *Paradise Lost*" (xlix). Theologically acute readers like Daniel Defoe (1660–1731) objected to Milton's account of the Son's exaltation (5.600–615) for laying, in Defoe's words, a "foundation for the corrupt doctrine of Arius" (75). A century later, shortly after *Christian Doctrine* was published, Thomas Macaulay remarked that "we can scarcely conceive that any person could have read *Paradise Lost* without suspecting him of [Arianism]" (3). Suspicion falls short of conviction, however, and unsupported by the evidence of the theological treatise, the Arianism of the epic is "no other than a conjecture" (Richardson, xlix). The muteness of the epic's heretical account of the Son has been persuasively attributed to Milton's discretion in an intolerant age and the narrative disposition of epic (Rajan 23–31). Milton's main goal in *Paradise Lost* is to tell a story, not to argue doctrine.

The challenge to this commonsense observation mounted by W. B. Hunter, C. A. Patrides, and J. H. Adamson was complicated, recondite, and, to the embarrassment of Milton scholarship, highly successful. Hunter originally argued that Milton's version of the godhead exemplified a not always unorthodox strain of early church opinion, called "subordinationism," which conceived of the Christian Trinity in terms of Platonic hypostases. Ralph Cudworth does in 1678 use the key term *subordination* in explaining the beliefs of the "Platonic Christian" and in asserting that such beliefs were consistent with those of "the generality of Christian doctors for the first three hundred years after the apostles' times" (2:417). This claim is not controversial, but it has no bearing on Milton's alleged orthodoxy. Like Arius before him, Milton was not a Platonic theologian, not when it came to his insistence on the absolute singularity of infinite God or on the finite existence of the Son. And even if Milton had been one of Cudworth's Platonic Christians, by the seventeenth century the Platonist version of the Christian Trinity did qualify as heretical. The subordinationism attributed to Milton is in short, per Michael Bauman's definitive formulation, "not orthodox, and Milton does not teach it" (133). Despite these flaws, Hunter's argument prevailed for an entire generation, so that in scholarship from the 1970s and '80s one generally finds the evasive and misleading label "subordinationist" in discussions of Milton's depiction of the Son.

Less controversial by far are Milton's opinions on how salvation occurs, perhaps because these opinions are now predominant among orthodox Christians and because Milton's God himself details them in a plain theological exposition difficult to misconstrue (3.173–202). During Milton's lifetime the Calvinist theory of salvation, and predestination as its distinctive tenet, reigned in England and especially in the Puritan culture that nurtured the young poet. Opposed to Calvinist orthodoxy was Arminianism, so called after the Dutch clergyman Jacobus Arminius (1560–1609), whose deviations from determinist doctrine were condemned at the grand Calvinist council of the early seventeenth century, the Synod of Dort (1618–19). According to articles endorsed at Dort, neither the blessed nor the damned can influence their respective fates. For the sake of his glory, God extends saving grace to a few utterly depraved sinners, thereby expressing his mercy. Also for his glory's sake, but additionally to exemplify divine justice, God consigns the rest of humanity (a large majority) to eternal torment. As for human liberty, even unfallen Adam and Eve were never free to obey, as Calvin insists: "God foreknew what end man was to have before he created him, and consequently foreknew because he so ordained by his decree" (3.23.7).

Arminians, by contrast, held that human beings are created free and, once fallen, receive sufficient grace to effect salvation, provided that they embrace the opportunity rather than reject it. The dependence of such a moral framework on human choice seems to have struck Calvin as a self-evident slight to divine omnipotence, as if "God ordained nothing except to treat man according to his own deserts" (3.23.7). The notion that the deity would leave individual human beings to determine their own fates roused Calvin's indignation. Four main claims distinguish the Arminians' "barren invention," as he called it (3.23.7). First, God's grace is universal, extended to all humanity. Second, this grace is not irresistible, which is to say, as an anti-Calvinistic Thomas Jefferson insists in his summary of Arminian beliefs, "man is always *free* and at liberty to receive or reject grace." Third, as Jefferson continues, divine justice "would not permit [God] to punish men for crimes they are predestinated to commit" (1:554). And last, foreknowledge and causation are distinct, even in a time line created, governed, and immutably foreseen by an omnipotent and omniscient God.

In England before the 1640s, clergy who held Arminius's heterodox opinions regarding salvation tended to be high-ranking and conservative, adhering to and even embellishing sacramental ritual and set liturgical forms that to Puritan sensibilities smacked of Roman Catholicism. This religiously and politically conservative English clergy presided over a top-down episcopal hierarchy whose regime complemented and reinforced the Stuart monarchy's civil sway—hence the so-called "thorough" government of church and state during the 1630s, when king and bishop sought to rule without Parliamentary interference. Continental followers of Arminius, by contrast, remained largely Calvinist in devotional culture and practice. Their deviations from Calvinist orthodoxy, moreover, were republican and not authoritarian in their political implications, as Jefferson's enthusiastic assessment suggests. Yet Arminian English bishops were oblivious to any such implications and, though in the minority, used their power to institute and enforce their cultural and governmental preferences, even when doing so meant outraging consciences or ruthlessly punishing dissent. Such impositions grated on the Puritans, who, regardless of their views on salvation, deplored episcopal pomp, debunked most sacraments, and endorsed plain spontaneity in worship.

During the 1640s, the defeat of the high-church, anti-Calvinist elite and the ready resort of the now predominant Presbyterian faction to its own coercive policies seem to have freed Milton to argue explicitly in behalf of rational choosing and free will. For all his support of the Presbyterian faction against the prelates, Milton had never endorsed predestination. His Arminian tendencies become unmistakable in the divorce tracts and in *Areopagitica*'s exaltation of rational choice, toleration, and individual accountability. Milton insists that God created man free, and if Adam had not been free, he might as well have been a puppet: "a mere artificial Adam, such an Adam as he is in the motions" (*MLM* 944). By the end of the 1640s, Milton's contention that the English have every right to try and execute King Charles rests on an anti-Presbyterian first premise, all the more provocative for being presented as a self-evident truth: "No man who knows aught can be so stupid [as] to deny that all men naturally were born free, being the image and resemblance of God himself" (*TKM* in *MLM* 1028). At this distance, it seems clear that Milton's breach with the Presbyterians rests on differing conceptions of the dignity of the human subject. By the time he comes to write his epic, choice and responsibility are for Milton the very stuff of human morality and of human desert (Danielson; S. Fallon 1998). Most Presbyterians, by contrast, deemed the ethical categories of choice and responsibility meaningless or wickedly delusional.

In *Paradise Lost*, it is only to the characterization of Satan and his followers that the language of predestination applies. Hell is thus described as a "prison ordained" to which they have been eternally "decreed,/Reserved and destined" (1.71, 2.160–61). Like stereotypical Calvinists, certain devils spend vast stretches of time debating "of providence, foreknowledge, will and fate/Fixed fate, free will, foreknowledge absolute"—i.e., "in wand'ring mazes lost" (2.559–61). Fate is their preferred ideological fiction as they persistently elide their responsibility for rebelling against the only divine right monarch whose legitimacy Milton ever acknowledged. When they debate policy and strategy, they do so in "synods," a term historically associated with the determinist doctrinal pronouncements of Calvinist and Presbyterian assemblies (2.391).

Even the narrative and dramatic stress placed on Satan's role and character, which some have deemed disproportionate, is an indicator of Milton's distance from the determinist tenets of the Presbyterians. The serpent's temptation is beside the point in Calvinist theology, as indeed is any agency outside God. The Fall is divinely ordained.

Calvin's deity was a volitional black hole, obviating the need for a malevolent opponent who sparks evil. For Milton, by contrast, temptation is an ethical state crucial to theodicy, permitting merit to the creature, as in the case of Abdiel, while at the same time justifying the redemption of humanity: unlike the irreversibly damned rebel angels, "man falls deceived/By the other first" (3.130–31). Most important, the freedom and accountability presumed by temptation prevent humanity's recriminations against God "as if predestination overruled/Their will" (3.114–15). The justification of God's ways to men turns out to be largely an Arminian response to the Calvinist insistence on the bondage of the will. Foreknowledge does not predetermine; the choices of unfallen humanity are free: "authors to themselves in all/Both what they judge and what they choose; for so/I formed them free" (3.122–24). As Perez Zagorin observes, Milton's "loyalty to the principle of liberty as he understood it was absolute" (114). It was a matter of doing justice to man and God.

To God more than to man, however. Liberty is a state that we ordinarily associate with human beings, but from Milton's highly theocentric and theodical perspective, freedom is primarily and definitively a quality essential to the nature of God. Only because the human race is created in the image of God is it self-evident that humanity is born free. The only necessity that applies to God is that he not involve himself in contradiction. Any action he takes must therefore conform to the good, goodness being definitive of divine identity rather than a limitation on his freedom. Though raised in the highly Calvinist culture of seventeenth-century London, Milton insists on the freedom allowed humanity in Arminian theology because his God must not be held liable for the sins of humanity, as Calvin's was. The necessity that God's deeds be good ones does not wed God to any particular action, however; his "goodness" remains "free/To act or not" (7.171–72). Such freedom holds true even concerning the generation of the Son. God is under no necessity to beget a second divinity; he freely chooses to do so. The Son, in his turn, freely offers himself as a sacrifice on behalf of humanity (3.236–65). Adam and Eve echo and also mediate the praiseworthy choices of the Father and Son when they decide to procreate and so begin the line that will produce their redeemer (10.867–1096). So the theodicy comes full circle, with goodness remaining free at every juncture to act or not.

GENRE

"The greatest writer who has ever existed of a limited genre"—that is how T. S. Eliot in 1926 described Milton. The initial superlative hints at a magnanimous finish, but Eliot instead concludes by demeaning genre and diminishing his praise: "Instead of poetry, you get *genres* of poetry" (201). Centuries earlier, Thomas Rymer had also denied the authenticity of Milton's poetry, snidely describing *Paradise Lost* as a work that "some are pleased to call a poem" (1678, 143). He even omits it from a summary of English heroic poetry that culminates instead with Davenant's *Gondibert* (1651) and Cowley's *Davideis* (1656) (1694, preface). Rymer condemns Milton for not being sufficiently generic, whereas Eliot criticizes him for being excessively generic. Their shared disdain may owe less to Milton's artistic fraudulence than to the not uncommon tendency of lesser artists to mitigate the achievements of greater ones. Rymer is more easily cleared from that suspicion. True to his name, he scorned unrhymed narrative verse as prose, an arbitrary genre distinction but one general at the time as the note on verse affixed to the first edition attests. By contrast, Eliot's dedication to the proposition that genre is an ersatz proxy for true poetry remains a head-scratcher, even in its historical context.

According to the *OED*, the term *genre* did not enter English usage until the nineteenth century. The concept of literary kind had by then already been debated for millennia, however, energetically so during the European Renaissance, when genre was held in very high esteem, not least by Milton himself. His ideal curriculum includes prosody as a necessary technical study, but far above it in real dignity he places the "sublime art" that teaches "the laws" governing "true" poems, whether epic, dramatic, or lyric (*Of Ed* in *MLM* 977–78). The reverential diction is telling. Taken together with the related claim that Scripture offers the most perfect instances of the major genres (*RCG* in *MLM* 841), it suggests that for Milton, as for Sir Philip Sidney before him, literary genres were divinely authorized modes of mimesis, corresponding to the Creator's arrangement of reality. Compared with any individual poem, genre was the more real thing, and indeed "the first thing the reader needs to know about *Paradise Lost*," according to C. S. Lewis (1).

Eliot's low regard for genre may have stemmed from discomfort with prescriptive rules for poetry. Milton does insist on "laws" for poems, after all. But his neoclassicism is distinct from the neoclassicism that prevailed in England after the Restoration, Rymer being one of its chief proponents. Through the sixteenth and well into the seventeenth century, Italy was the center of cultural authority in Europe. Its cities "swarmed with critics," according to Rymer, but as "swarmed" suggests, the Italian critical hegemony lacked uniformity or a common national focus. During the first half of the seventeenth century, the individualism of the Italian swarm gradually gave way to the regimentation of the French. "From Italy, France took the cudgels," the pugnacious Rymer put it, tracing French ascendancy to Cardinal Richelieu's amalgamation of cultural with political authority at the increasingly absolutist French court (1694, A2r–v). Milton, however, never acknowledged the cultural turn away from his beloved Italy. His ambitions as an epic poet crystallized during his visit to Italy (1638–39), and his disdain for France was quite general and persistent. His masterworks of the Restoration display a sublime if studied indifference to Gallic dictates, and his conception of literary genre, epic specifically, owes a great deal to the formative influence of sixteenth-century Italians, Torquato Tasso most prominently.

Milton refers to Tasso repeatedly in poems composed during his visit to Italy (see, e.g., *Manso*), and when in *The Reason of Church Government* he discusses epic, Tasso alone is named in the company of Homer and Vergil (*MLM* 840–41). It was Tasso who originally argued that the "laws of poetry" are divinely established realities, "essential and fixed by the very nature and law of things" (Kates 36). A poet did not need to conform to fixed rules derived from authoritative precedent but could instead embody the objectively based laws of poetry according to the judgment of natural reason, judgment informed not only by subjective experience and the efforts of precursors but also by, most crucially for a Christian poet, scriptural revelation. Milton may have adored Homer above all other poets, but to fulfill his own poetic vocation in the genre that Homer epitomized, Milton characteristically believed himself morally obliged to manifest the epic genre on his own terms, taking full advantage of his access to Christian doctrine. In short, the heroic poem as Milton conceived it was more adaptable to the individual poet's conception of truth than a rote critic like Rymer could stomach.

English critics nursed on Gallic canons early on censured *Paradise*

Lost for its wantonness. John Dennis in 1704 described it as "the most lofty but most irregular poem that has been produced by the mind of man" (bv), and unlike Dennis, who ultimately judges *Paradise Lost* above the critical law, subsequent neoclassical critics typically laud Milton's loftiness and rue his irregularities. Milton's idiosyncratic version of epic defies standard definitions because it is unusually inclusive, almost all-encompassing. Northrop Frye calls it "the story of all things," yet even that broad rubric seems inadequate (3). The reach of *Paradise Lost* extends far beyond creation, affording local habitation and a name even to the uncreated realm of the Anarch Chaos and comprising the infinite and eternal together with the finite and fleeting. In its "diffuse" form, epic is the only genre that Milton discusses in *The Reason for Church Government* for which he cites no scriptural precedent. This tantalizing omission may in part suggest that Milton did not consider any book in the Bible, not even Genesis, both unified and ample enough to qualify.

In her magisterial study of Milton and genre, Barbara Lewalski tracks Milton's use of virtually every subgenre recognized by Renaissance rhetoricians and deems *Paradise Lost* "an encyclopedia of literary forms" (125). Jonathan Richardson makes much the same point in defending Milton's masterwork as "a composition ... not reducible under any known denomination," "the quintessence of all that is excellent in writing" (cxlv, clii). If in its encompassing formal plenitude *Paradise Lost* violates the "limited genre" defined by neoclassical critics, its promiscuity is nonetheless profoundly classical in spirit. Aristotle himself distinguishes epic from other genres by its capacity to assimilate within a single narrative other modes, such as the dramatic or lyric, and their various subgenres (26). Book 4 illustrates Milton's singular gift for subduing such multiplicity under a unified narrative arc. The basic story line—Satan's intrusion into Paradise leading ultimately to his apprehension and expulsion—occasions, among other genre variations, authorial apostrophe, Satanic soliloquy, landscape poetry with features of the country house tradition, various love lyrics, metamorphic tales of origin, evening prayer, and confrontational martial dialogue. Nor was epic originally confined to what Voltaire in his *Essai sur la poésie épique* defined as "narratives in verse of warlike adventures" (331), which Milton scorned as "tedious havoc" (*PL* 9.30).

Deriving from the Greek word for "story" or "story-related," *epic* seems to have been a broader category for the early Greeks, virtually indistinguishable from what is now meant by narrative in general. Aristocratic martial and amorous encounters are undeniably the stuff of Homeric epic, and of mock epic (Homer is supposed to have composed one of those, too), but Hesiod's overtly didactic narratives also qualified, as did Orphic poems celebrating religious mysteries. In each case, the bard tells a story meant to epitomize and even justify the supernaturally shaped course of human events. Milton observes the familiar trappings and formal insignia of epic: invocations, extended similes, catalogs, epithets, and the rest. But he does so idiosyncratically, in line with his highly individual Christian faith. The invocations exemplify this characteristic willingness to interpret the "laws" of epic according to his own situation. Embracing and expanding on a liberty asserted previously by Tasso, he uses the invocations as occasions to speak not simply in his own voice but to an unprecedented extent of himself and his anxious situation, "in darkness, and with dangers compassed round" (7.27).

When Aristotle described epic as an inclusive, composite form, he was distinguishing it from drama, the genre that shows rather than tells and brooks no authorial narration. By contrast, the authorial voice in epic sometimes withdraws in favor of storytelling characters involved in dramatic dialogue or lyrical self-expression. Aristotle thought drama the nobler genre, not only purer in mode but also more disciplined in plot than sprawling epic (26). Early modern theorists, however, focused on the magnitude of solitary authorial effort rather than on the purity of the form or concentrated efficiency of the action. The actors in a drama, furthermore, "share the poet's praise," as Dryden says (1800, 1:436). Such critics were nearly unanimous in accounting epic, precisely because it is vast, complicated, and solitary in execution, as "the greatest work which the soul of man is capable to perform" (Dryden 1800, 1:425). Milton, of course, as if to satisfy classical as well as modern standards of preeminence, composed both a capacious epic and a stringent classical tragedy (one never designed for staging or actors' shares). Still, the most momentous and defining artistic decision he ever made came down to a choice between these two great genres.

When he originally conceived the story of the Fall as the subject of a tragedy, Milton honored the long-standing critical consensus that unhappy events are best reserved for dramatic presentation—an affinity of form and subject acknowledged in the epic's most genre-conscious moment, the invocation to Book 9. As if to signal this anomaly formally, the same invocation fails to do what invocations by their very name promise they will do: invoke. Acknowledging his dependence on the Muse only in the last line, Milton devotes this "invocation" instead to justifying his deviation from mainline epic into tragedy. For, despite his concessions, Milton clearly thought that in choosing to tell this sad story in the grandest narrative genre, he had made a good trade-off. The story of the Fall allows him, as he indicates in the invocation, to redefine heroism in accordance with his Christian faith (9.13–41). More important, if "an epic poem must either be national or mundane," as Coleridge claimed, once an author has chosen the mundane, the goal must be to tell a story "common to all mankind" (1886, 240). This is a tall order, but in a Christian culture, the story of Adam and Eve, though tragic, more than fills the bill. Not simply the greatest story ever told, it is every story ever told: Milton's "Adam and Eve are all men and women inclusively," as Coleridge observed (240). If he could not claim to invent the epic mode, as Homer had, Milton could reinvent it in light of Christian revelation and aspire to include all other epics, all other narratives of any kind.

The other main advantage of arranging the story of man's first disobedience as a narrative and not a tragic drama was the chance to exploit the single most definitive formal requirement of an epic narrative—that it begin in the midst of things. Milton made much of this opportunity: a titanic Satan and his followers, first rolling in hell-fire and then debating revenge, followed by the farsighted judgment of a Zeus-like God and his obsequious adherents in Heaven. Indeed, the opening books are so striking that they have largely determined the poem's reception in modern times. These books address received traditions of heroic poetry overtly and extensively, and they also contain, according to many readers, the most poetic energy and the thematic designs crucial to the work as a whole.

To revive a thesis that originated in the early eighteenth century and fell out of fashion in the twentieth, we think it likely that Milton's inspiration for making Satan weltering in Hell his "midst of things" was the pre-Norman, English tradition of biblical poetry, especially the Old English *Genesis B,* long attributed to Caedmon. No one denies that Milton had opportunity to become acquainted with this and other works in the Caedmon manuscripts, discovered in 1651 by the philologist Franciscus Junius, then residing in London. If Milton was given access to the manuscripts while he was still sighted, he probably took note of the illustrations, including one of the rebel angels plunging headlong into the jaws of Leviathan (below). Scholars have argued, not without evidence, that Milton's competency in Old English was at best slight and that any acquaintance he might have had with the Caedmon poems, whether in manuscript or in print, would therefore have been superficial and inconsequential. Yet even a superficial acquaintance would have left him aware that *Genesis B* begins, as *Paradise Lost* does, with Satan and his thanes rallying in Hell. Furthermore, as French Fogle's introduction to Milton's *History of Britain* observes, Milton's access to freshly published Old English texts and translations was extensive (Yale 5: xxxvi–xxxvii). The conception of Christ prevalent in England until the Conquest, "which views the cross from the perspective of world history and emphasizes its victorious aspect, the conquest of Satan," was far more amenable to him than the later emphasis on the sufferings of Christ (Huttar 242).

"Him the Almighty Power / Hurled headlong
flaming from th' ethereal sky" (1.44–45).

While Milton dismissed the monks who wrote the early history of Britain as "ill gifted with utterance" (Yale 5:288), it does not follow that he would have disdained the Anglo-Saxon language. His schoolmaster at St. Paul's, Alexander Gill, was an advocate of the English vernacular and demonstrably knowledgeable about Old English (Fletcher 1:185). The common complaint that *Paradise Lost* is replete with Latinisms, an English estranged from its vernacular roots, is unjustified, as Fowler's edition repeatedly observes. On the contrary, Milton's English is generally idiomatic. When in 1807 James Ingram translated the first fifteen lines of *Paradise Lost* into Old English, he left the syntax virtually untouched and required substitutes for ten loan words only (47–48). We think it not only fitting but probable that the catalyst for Milton's choice of epic subject once he had abandoned the British theme was the coincidental discovery in the 1650s of a native tradition of biblical poetry written before the Conquest.

PROSODY AND STYLE

Paradise Lost is written in unrhymed pentameter lines, or blank verse. Early in the sixteenth century, the Earl of Surrey adopted this form for his partial translation of Vergil's *Aeneid*, and toward the end of that century it became the conventional medium of Elizabethan drama. Shakespeare's plays are primarily written in blank verse. But Spenser had not used it. Milton's choice of blank verse was a daring one, for at that time there was no long blank-verse poem of much distinction in English or any other language. It was largely because of Milton's precedent that blank verse established itself as early as James Thomson's *Seasons* (1726–30) as the preferred metrical form for long and ambitious English poems. Wordworth's *The Prelude;* Keats's *Hyperion;* Tennyson's *The Princess, Enoch Arden,* and *The Idylls of the King;* Browning's *The Ring and the Book;* Arnold's *Empedocles on Etna;* the long narratives of Edwin Arlington Robinson; sections of Crane's *The Bridge;* Stevens's *Sunday Morning* and *Notes toward a Supreme Fiction;* Frost's *Home Burial;* and Betjeman's *Summoned by Bells* are all written in blank verse.

Milton organized his narrative into verse paragraphs, within which he devised syntactical patterns famous for their length and lucidity.

Having freed himself from the ancient bondage of rhyme, he created musical effects with consonance, dissonance, alliteration, repetition, and even the occasional internal rhyme. He particularly excelled in the "turn of words," as it was called in the seventeenth and eighteenth centuries—repeating the same words in a reversed or modified order. Dryden tells us that he once looked for these turns in Milton but failed to find them (*Essays* 2:108–9). In fact the effect is everywhere, as in "though fall'n on evil days,/On evil days though fall'n" (7.25–26), which reminded Emerson of "the reflection of the shore and trees in water" (R. Richardson 318). When the Father announces the forthcoming creation in Book 7, "Glory they sung to the most high" (182), then "Glory to him" (184), the Son who has just defeated the rebel angels, and finally, with a turn of words, "to him/Glory and praise" (186–87). Through creation the Son will "diffuse" the glory of the Father "to worlds and ages infinite" (190–91), and in this very passage we feel that glory has been squeezed from the word *glory* and diffused from clause to clause. Some of the best-known turns include Eve's initial infatuation with her image in the pool ("Pleased I soon returned,/. . . Pleased it returned as soon") at 4.460–65, and Eve's great love lyric enclosed by the brackets of "Sweet is" and "is sweet" (4.641–56); inside them she lists the same natural beauties twice, once as sweet, once again as not sweet. Addison thought this last "one of the finest turns of words that I have ever seen" (Shawcross 1:142).

Distinguished achievement in sound effects is an excellence that no one has ever seriously denied to Milton. His verse has few rivals in what Hazlitt termed "the adaptation of the sound and movement of the verse to the meaning of the passage" (Thorpe 104). Sometimes the adaptations are relatively simple, like certain film scores. As Satan struggles through Chaos, the verse also seems to have trouble making headway: "So he with difficulty and labor hard/Moved on, with difficulty and labor he" (2.1021–22). When he hears "a universal hubbub wild/Of stunning sounds" (2.951–52), it is clear that *universal* and *wild* are ways of defining what the word *hubbub,* all meaning aside, delivers to us purely through its sound. *Stunning sounds* echoes the chaotic crack of *hubbub,* as if sounds had indeed been stunned. Sometimes the adaptation of sound to meaning is wittier, more conceptual. When Satan departs from Pandaemonium, the philosophical devils "reasoned high/Of providence, foreknowledge, will and fate,/Fixed fate, free will, Foreknowledge absolute,/And found no end, in wand'ring mazes lost" (2.558–61). Milton makes the catalog of philosophical concepts into a little semantic labyrinth in which "foreknowledge, will and fate" enough resemble "Fixed fate, free will, foreknowledge absolute" to make us wonder how they are alike, how not alike. Have we really gone anywhere in moving from one line to the next?

When the poem introduces a distinction, the difference is likely to be taken up, explored, and often complicated by the verse. In Book 4, for example, the narrator reads gender differences from the naked bodies of Adam and Eve, and the result is the greatest politically incorrect passage in English poetry. "For contemplation he and valor formed,/For softness she and sweet attractive grace" (297–98). We can see immediately that alliteration serves Eve. The poetry is already indicating its willingness to interfere with the passage's legalism, but for now there is no time to explore the bond between Eve and poetic beauty. The law must be pronounced. Adam is formed for God, she for God in him. His forehead and eye "declared/Absolute rule" (300–301).

At this point Milton begins to describe their differing hair treatments, Adam's first:

> Hyacinthine locks
> Round from his parted forelock manly hung
> Clust'ring, but not beneath his shoulders broad. (301–3)

The two run-on lines imitate the fall of his hair (*Hyacinthine* implies that it is black), while the strong end-stop of line 303 puts a limit to its hanging down. *But not* has an almost corrective force, as if things might have been getting out of hand. They immediately do. Eve's blond tresses introduce four straight run-on lines, followed by four more end-stopped lines:

> She as a veil down to the slender waist
> Her unadornèd golden tresses wore
> Disheveled, but in wanton ringlets waved
> As the vine curls her tendrils, which implied
> Subjection, but required with gentle sway,
> And by her yielded, by him best received,

> Yielded with coy submission, modest pride,
> And sweet reluctant amorous delay. (304–11)

He the cluster, she the vine. He words in their stable sense, words as law, words that set limits; she words as their sense is in transit, disheveled, drawn out variously from line to line, creeping and curling with wanton implication. Syntax flows across the unit of the line. Milton's verse becomes femalelike in describing femaleness, then arrives at the key word *Subjection* in line 308, which mates with all the verbs to come. Enjambment stops. We have returned to the matter of the law, but in, so to speak, another semantic universe. Subjection is what is *required,* what is *yielded,* what is *best received,* and again what is *yielded.* It is their bond, and also their sexual spark. He requires and receives it; she yields and yields it. Lacking compulsion, it is no longer "subjection" in the usual sense but rather her free consent.

This passage begins with the law of gender difference, yet by its end we find that law realized in amorous love and artistic excitement. Eve yields her subjection with "coy submission, modest pride," both phrases being oxymorons, and the first of them of particular richness in Renaissance love poetry (Kerrigan and Braden 204–18). An oxymoron naturally requires two words, a plus and a minus, a point and a counterpoint. The last line, with Eve-like luxuriance, doubles the oxymoron quotient with four perfect words, oxymoronic in various ways: *reluctant* crosses *amorous, amorous* crosses *delay, delay* crosses *reluctant.* But all of them and their nest of contradictory combinations are *sweet,* the very word that Eve will turn so memorably a few hundred lines later, enclosing the couple's love and their lapsing days of Paradise in its embrace. They will not make love until the end of the day. Eve's *sweet . . . delay* is an oxymoronic union of desire and control, consent and refusal, passion and rule, profusion and limit, fusing the various contraries of the passage. Adam also participates in this knot of contraries. *Gentle sway* is the first oxymoron of the passage, and links to *delay* through a delayed rhyme. Of "Yielded with coy submission, modest pride,/And sweet reluctant amorous delay," Walter Savage Landor remarked, "I would rather have written these two lines than all the poetry that has been written since Milton's time in all the regions of the earth" (Thorpe 368–69).

Milton's style marries male and female, "which two great sexes animate the world" (8.151). There is male law. There are requirements, fixed meanings, ripe clusters of sense. But there is energy as well, and the energy in this poetry is female, vinelike, curling here and then back, various in its repetition, paradoxical, nurturing underbrushes of implication that modify and even revise the abstract fixities of law.

DICTION

Johnson proclaimed that Milton "wrote no language, but has formed what Butler calls a Babylonish Dialect" (Thorpe 86). Yet his strictures on Milton are almost always wrong or exaggerated. A recent study such as John Hale's *Milton's Languages* is from the outset friendlier toward the multilingual characteristics of Milton's style than would have been possible in the confines of Johnson's linguistic patriotism. Modern statistical studies have demonstrated that the style of *Paradise Lost* is neither as archaic nor as Latinate as some of its critics have imagined (Boone). Milton is a learned author, to be sure, but a student determined to appreciate at least some of the learning in his language will be not be led away from the genius of ordinary English. T. S. Eliot, writing in the Johnson tradition, emphasized "the remoteness of Milton's verse from ordinary speech" (Thorpe 321). But in fact Milton's poetry enriches ordinary speech in new and surprising ways.

Now and then Milton will use a word in its classical or etymological sense, waving aside its derived meaning in English. In "There went a fame in Heav'n" (1.651), *fame* has its Roman sense of "word spoken." An imperial Milton banishes the English sense. Similarly, *succinct* in "His habit fit for speed succinct" (3.643) has the Latin meaning of "tucked under, tight-fitted." Christopher Ricks has shown that Milton will sometimes insist on the etymological sense when naming an unfallen world in which words with definitions involving immorality are not yet appropriate (109–17). At their creation the rivers of the earth run "with serpent error wand'ring" (7.302), but *error* in the Latin sense of "wandering" contains no taint of crime or mistake. Words too have their original innocence. In order to grasp this last example, a reader must see that the Latin definition is in meaningful dialogue with the derived sense, and that the rejection of the ordinary English meaning, far from being arbitrary, belongs to the larger significance of the passage.

Milton "was not content," Walter Raleigh observed, "to revive the exact classical meaning in place of the vague or weak English acceptation; he often kept both senses, and loaded the word with two meanings at once" (1900, 209). When the hair of the angel Uriel falls "Illustrious on his shoulders" (3.627), Milton refers at once to the luster or brightness of the hair and the august reputation of the angel. As it approaches Eve in Book 9, the snake is "voluble" (436). In its classical sense, the word denotes the coiling motion of the snake, but in its newer English sense, it announces the serpent's forthcoming talkativeness (Ricks 108). Beelzebub refers to Chaos as "the vast abrupt" (2.409), where *abrupt* seems first of all to retain its Latin sense of "broken off, precipitous." The rebel angels have fallen through Chaos and have some idea of what it means to traverse this abyss of indefiniteness. Whoever enters Chaos breaks off from the stabilities of Heaven and Hell. But the English meanings seem also in play when we note that Milton has transformed an adjective into a noun. Chaos itself will be a constant sequence of abrupt changes, a place where interruption is not a surprise but the norm.

There is a fund of linguistic peculiarities in *Paradise Lost.* Milton, for example, likes the sequence adjective + noun + adjective, as in *universal hubbub wild* or *vast profundity obscure.* He was not the first to try this sequence, but it is a good bet that, wherever we encounter it in subsequent English verse, Milton is probably on the author's mind; Arnold's "vast edges drear" in "Dover Beach" hopes to remind us of the seething Chaos of *Paradise Lost.* F. T. Prince (112–29) discussed Milton's interest in a related sequence found in Italian verse as early as Dante: adjective + noun + and + adjective, as in "Sad task and hard" (5.564) or "Sad resolution and secure" (6.541). Does the second adjective come in as an afterthought? The *task,* let us say, is primarily *sad,* so much so that one forgets for a moment that it is *hard* as well. Or does the second adjective bear the main emotion? A *sad* task would be burden enough, but this one is, more important, *hard.* Milton enjoyed playing with this scheme. He experimented, for example, with distancing the adjectives: "pleasing was his shape,/And lovely" (9.503–4) or "For many are the trees of God that grow/In Paradise, and various" (9.618–19). In place of adjective + noun + and + adjective, he tried noun + verb + and +

noun, as in "he seemed/For dignity composed and high exploit" (2.110–11). The poet did not invent a "Babylonish Dialect." He wrote English with a high degree of originality, and his original poetry sublime unleashes a number of effects that had never been tried before in English verse.

THREE CONTROVERSIES

Attacks on Milton's verse early in the twentieth century by Ezra Pound, Herbert Read, F. R. Leavis, T. S. Eliot, and A. J. A. Waldock sparked a debate that eventually came to be known as the Milton Controversy (Murray 1–12). Although the notion of Milton's artistic greatness had never before been questioned so systematically, this was hardly an isolated incident. Historically Milton is by some measure the most controversial of the great English poets. He has given rise to an inordinate number of critical debates, altogether too many, in fact, for us to suppose that his poetry is itself innocent of contentiousness. Certainly in his prose Milton liked to mix it up. He was among the greatest controversialists of the day. The decades he spent fighting the wars of truth, Coleridge suggested, added a "controversial spirit" to his youthful character (Thorpe 91). But the early poems are also imbued with the love of argument. When Milton in the first invocation to *Paradise Lost* refers to "this great argument," the word *argument* primarily means "plot," as in the prose "Argument" or plot summary attached to each book of the epic. Yet the great argument of the plot is wed to an "argument" of another kind, a rational contention, since Milton vows that "to the highth of this great argument" he will, if inspired, "assert eternal providence,/And justify the ways of God to men" (1.24–26).

Emerson wrote that no man in literary history, perhaps in all history, excelled Milton in the power to inspire: "Virtue goes out of him to others" (*Early Lectures* 1:148). No doubt some of the controversies about Milton have not demonstrated much of the poet's own idealism, but the generally high quality of Milton debates over the centuries is arguably the finest of the poet's gifts to our culture, as Christopher Ricks has pointed out. It is for good reason that Milton is "the most argued-about poet in English." He brings out the serious and passionate advocate in us:

> Of the needs to which he ministers, one of the greatest is our need to commit ourselves in passionate argument about literature. Not as part of the academic industry, but because literature is a supreme controversy concerning "the best that has been thought and said in the world" (to adopt the words which Matthew Arnold applied to culture). By the energy and sincerity of his poetry, Milton stands—as no other poet quite does—in heartening and necessary opposition to all aestheticisms, old and new. (xi)

Milton's argumentative art refuses to stay within aesthetic boundaries, however they may be drawn. Virtue goes out of him to his readers. His arguments come to life, and participating in them both pleases and elevates us.

One of the oldest of the Milton debates swirls about the character of Satan. Is he the hero of the epic? Is he so attractive as to upset the standard moral balance of Christianity? The first of these questions is the more easily answered. Early in the poem, Milton deliberately places Satan in the roles occupied by classical epic heroes. He founds a civilization in Hell. He undertakes a long and arduous journey. Compared to Odysseus, Addison observed, Satan "put in practice many more wiles and stratagems, and hides himself under a greater variety of shapes and appearances" (Shawcross 1:152). To some extent, Milton uses his Satan as a diagnostic test of the moral health of classical epic.

In the beginning of the poem especially, Satan exudes glamour. His appearance—huge, ruined, thunder-scarred, darkened, but still able to evoke the memory of his former luminescence in Heaven—makes a tremendous impression. The Satan glimpsed in Tasso's *Jerusalem Liberated* has, like the cheap special-effects devils of modern supernatural thrillers, massive horns, red eyes, a huge beard, an open mouth filthy with red blood and spewing rancid fumes (4.6–7). As William Hazlitt put it, the Satan of *Paradise Lost* "has no bodily deformity to excite our loathing or disgust. The horns and tail are not there.... Milton was too magnanimous and open an antagonist to support his argument by the bye-tricks of a hump and cloven foot" (Thorpe 109; see also Newton in Shawcross 2:154). Satan is proud, obstinate, the rebel of rebels. He speaks thrillingly of his "unconquerable will." For Milton, part of giving the devil his due is having the devil give God his due. Satan several times concedes the omnipotence of his foe. When he finds himself cursing the "free love" God gave to all the angels because it did not prevent him from falling, Satan fiercely, and in the name of truth, recoils on himself: "Nay cursed be thou; since against his thy will / Chose freely what it now so justly rues" (4.71–72).

William Blake took the romantic exaltation of Satan to an extreme in *The Marriage of Heaven and Hell*: "The reason Milton wrote in fetters when he wrote of Angels & God, and at liberty when of Devils & Hell, is, because he was a true poet and of the Devil's party without knowing it." Blake was something of a Gnostic, for whom Milton's God the Father was an evil and inferior God, and his satanic opposition the force of true deity (Nuttall 224). But readers whose imaginations remain responsive to the ordinary polarities of Christianity will probably not leave the poem with the favorable impression of Satan with which they began. As the work continues, they realize that Satan's cannonlike recoils inevitably issue in a fatalistic resolve to go on being himself and fulfill his initial plan of corrupting mankind. His speeches remake the same decision over and over again. Readers come to understand that conceding the omnipotence of God, far from being magnanimous, is the only way Satan can reconcile his pride with his defeat. Heroic resistance begins to look like habitual stubbornness. Satan would desperately like to believe that he is self-created. But his image of his own greatness is also his enemy, the uncreated Father. Satan sits in "God-like imitated state" (2.511). Declaring that evil is his good, he dreams of sharing "divided Empire with Heav'n's King" (4.111)—in other words, of being the equal of God in a Manichaean universe.

But Satan's true God is his own will. Milton always maintained that tyrants were self-enslaved. An unconquerable will sacrifices the willer and everyone under his sway. Most readers, their infatuation with Satan having run its course, savor his final comeuppance in the poem, as his triumphant return to Hell becomes the first of countless annual reenactments of the wicked self-harming travesty he is doomed to think a victory. The attractions of Satan are real, and beguiling, but in the end not so profound as his degradation.

Satan's heroism, though felt in its highest form by the Romantics, did not die with them and remains a main source of argument in modern Milton criticism. It is crucial, for example, to the middle period of Harold Bloom's work, which begins with *The Anxiety of Influence* (1973). Hazlitt noted that Milton showed no signs of alarm over a vast literary indebtedness that would have stymied many a lesser poet: "Milton has borrowed more than any other writer, and exhausted every source of imitation, sacred or profane; yet he is perfectly distinct from every other writer.... The quantity of art in him shows the strength of his genius: the weight of his intellectual obligations would have oppressed any other writer. Milton's learning has the effect of intuition" (Thorpe 101).

Bloom points to a great subtext in *Paradise Lost* concerning the apparent ease with which Milton masters the anxiety of being belated, preceded, and preempted. Satan is the modern poet (20). God is "cultural history, the dead poets, the embarrassments of a tradition grown too wealthy to need anything more" (21). Everything has been done. The world created, the Bible written, the classical epics finished, the romance versions of them already penned by Ariosto and Spenser. What is there to do? To rally what remains, to salvage all creative impulses that are not infected by devotion, while trying to fend off the knowledge that nothing remains, that one will wind up in one God-like imitated state or another. Wallace Stevens's famous aphorism "The death of Satan was a tragedy/For the imagination" ("Esthétique du Mal") seems pertinent here. Assuming that his death has occurred, or may soon occur, this reading of *Paradise Lost* shows the dimensions of the tragedy. For Satan *is* imagination. Bloom transformed the Satan controversy into a neo-Romantic fable for modern poets.

The arguments set forth in Stanley Fish's influential *Surprised by Sin: The Reader in Paradise Lost* (1967) are also to a large extent responses to the traditional Satan controversies. The author, a born Miltonist, loves to argue. Fish maintains that it is all right for the most serious readers, for readers in search of the author's intentional meaning, to allow heroic images of Satan to form in their minds, provided they are willing to sacrifice those images when the intentional meaning of the poem requires it (as it always will). Satan's attractiveness is not an unconscious or unintended effect of some sort. Milton wanted his readers to entertain false ideas of Satan's virtue. He deliberately and repeatedly trapped them into doing so, only to correct them in the next phrase or line or passage. Blake responded to attractive cues but refused to obey the corrective cues, and wound up losing touch with the poem. Milton himself is the creator of, and ultimate manager of, the Satan controversy. Fish's most impressive examples are of course drawn from the glamorous treatments of Satan in the first two books of the epic. The spasmodic self-corrections of his model reader uncannily resemble the recoils of Satan.

While impressed with the neatness of this argument, and the energy with which Fish has defended it, other critics have wondered at the infinite gullibility of Fish's model reader, who goes through the same experience again and again without learning his lesson, as if reading were less a process of illumination than an obsessive-compulsive ritual. They doubt Fish's implicit view of Milton as a dogmatist unable to admit to mixed feelings about the devil. They question whether great poetry could be as Pavlovian in its didacticism as Fish implies (Kerrigan 1974, 180n, 1983, 98–99; Rumrich 1996, 2–4, 7–11, 60–64; Pritchard; Leonard 2002).

A related and comparably venerable controversy concerns Milton's portrait of God. Pope observed that "God the Father turns a School-Divine" ("The First Epistle of the Second Book of Horace Imitated"). The word *school-divine* appears in many subsequent discussions of this issue. It means "a medieval scholastic theologian, of the sort that was taught in European universities," and was not usually a derogatory word, though it does appear to have pejorative charge for Pope. He seems to be referring primarily to God's speeches during the Heavenly Council at the opening of Book 3, where the Father explains the relationship between freedom and foreknowledge, and the doctrine of the Atonement, in a language compounded of standard theological terminology and statements from Scripture. Some have answered with Addison that in Book 3 the central mysteries of Christianity and the "whole dispensation of Providence with respect to man" are defined with admirable clarity and concision (Shawcross 1:178). Some have maintained that Milton went wrong in the very decision to assign speech to deity, since this procedure will inevitably bring God down to a human level (Wilkie in Shawcross 2:240–43).

But the deeper issue here is not whether God should speak at all and if he must in what vocabulary. Milton's God, foreseeing the development of human philosophy and theology, anticipates being held responsible for the sins of Adam and Eve. This forethought irritates him:

> so will fall
> He and his faithless progeny: whose fault?
> Whose but his own? Ingrate, he had of me
> All he could have; I made him just and right,
> Sufficient to have stood, though free to fall. (3.95–99)

The speech implies that man's theodical attacks continue the faithless-ness of the Fall itself. If someone maintains that God did not make him in such a way that he could be responsible for the Fall, he manifests in-gratitude. He wants to have been given more from God than mere free-dom. He deems his divine endowment not "sufficient." With regard to the poem's readers, God is provocative and ill-tempered. "Go on," he seems to be saying, "blame me. Doing so can only show your fallenness, your faithlessness, your ingratitude, and your utter lack of responsibility."

The same sort of provocation, daring his audience to disagree or dis-obey, marks the Father's words when he is exalting the Son in Heaven. He demands that the angels kneel and "confess him [the Son] Lord":

> Him who disobeys
> Me disobeys, breaks union, and that day
> Cast out from God and blessed union, falls
> Into utter darkness, deep engulfed, his place
> Ordained without redemption, without end. (5.611–15)

It is difficult not to be reminded, as we contemplate such a passage, that Milton hated the bullying ways of earthly monarchs. Why did he make the Father, at times, into a threatening king?

Milton would probably have replied that because God is a king, almighty and eternal, no one else can be. For all others sit in God-like imitated state, aspiring to godhead like Satan himself. God's legiti-macy through merit, not birthright, renders all other monarchies ille-gitimate, all other monarchs pretenders. This helps to explain why a republican like Milton can have a king for a God, but not why his God should be angry and threatening. God is not always that, to be sure, and at one point amuses the Son by acting the role of some chronicle-history Henry IV worried about usurping northern lords (5.721–32). His aims are merciful, and he praises the Son for seizing upon those aims and guaranteeing their future realization (3.274–343). When pretending that Adam does not need a mate, God seems playful, and appreciative of a creature whose freedom and rational self-confidence permit him to disagree with his creator (8.357–448). But as we have seen, Milton's God has a tough side.

This much can be said. Today we are somewhat embarrassed to think about God in terms of human emotions, unless the emotion in question is love. But the idea of God having in any sense a character—with exasperation, anger, jealousy, and wrath to go along with his love, mercy, and playfulness—probably seems childish or simplistic or even (though we have grown suspicious of this word) primitive. As Milton saw things, however, the portrait of God in the Bible was full of anthropomorphism. No form of divine symbolism can represent God as he is. But in the Bible, God delivered the metaphors through which he wished us to know him. There can be no shame in taking him at his word. "Why does our imagination shy away from a notion of God which he himself does not hesitate to promulgate in unambiguous terms?" (*CD* 1.2 in *MLM* 1148). Milton had little interest in the sort of God we sometimes associate with philosophers and mystics, known to us through some esoteric and reason-humbling symbolism. By the same token, he was relatively unexcited by the thought of contemplating the *visio dei*. His angels seem happiest, like Milton himself, when performing a divinely assigned task.

Both the God and the Satan Controversies animate William Empson's striking *Milton's God* (1960). In the process of indicting Christianity, this book invents a new way to praise Milton, albeit one that he himself would surely have deplored. Christianity, for Empson, is intractably evil. In any telling of the story of the Fall of man, God will in some manner be revealed as the responsible party. Milton was a Christian of uncommon moral sensitivity, and he did virtually all that one could do to improve the faith. There is, as we have noted, no torture. The Crucifixion, though recounted briefly (12.411–19), is hardly the centerpiece of Milton's religion. Temptation, the act of free moral decision, takes its place. Satan is more sympathetic than ever before. But God the Father is still provocative, still threatening. This portrait, far from being the failure it was conventionally assumed to be on one side of the God Controversy, shows Milton's honesty. His God manifests the dark impulse to rule, to wield power purely and simply, that the many attractive aspects of *Paradise Lost* conceal from our view. Dennis Danielson's aptly titled *Milton's Good God* (1982) defends Milton and Christianity against some of the main arguments in *Milton's God*.

The third of our controversies, about the character of Eve, first appeared in the feminist criticism of the twentieth century. "For the Romantics," Mary Nyquist and Margaret Ferguson wrote in 1987, "it was Satan who was oppressed by the author's consciously held beliefs. In our time it tends to be Eve" (xiv). Satan was the controversy of another day. Feminism has arrived, and it wants to argue about Eve.

Traditionally Milton had received mostly high marks for his characterizations of Adam and Eve. Coleridge thought the love of Adam and Eve was "removed from everything degrading," the creation of two people who give each other what is most permanent in them and achieve "a completion of each in the other" (Thorpe 96). Their love unfolds without flattery or falsehood. Hazlitt told of some men's club wit who maintained that Adam and Eve enjoyed only the least interesting of the pursuits of human life, the relations between man and wife. Hazlitt replied with a long catalog of the furniture of fallen life (wars, riches, contracts, et cetera) missing from the supreme pleasures of Eden: "Thank Heaven, all these were yet to come" (Thorpe 111). Extending Hazlitt's idea that Milton had the power to think "of nobler forms and nobler things than those he found about him" (Thorpe 98), Emerson praised the poet for giving us a new human ideal: "Better than any other he has discharged the office of every great man, namely, to raise the idea of Man in the minds of his contemporaries and of posterity. . . . Human nature in these ages is indebted to him for its best portrait" (*Early Lectures* 149).

But there was information of diverse sorts suggesting that Milton might have had a grudge against womankind. During the time that he was deserted by his first wife, Mary Powell, Milton wrote four pamphlets arguing in favor of divorce on the grounds of spiritual incompatibility. Mary's daughters did not get along with his subsequent wives. Now and then the daughters were asked to read to their blind father in languages they could not understand (Darbishire 177, 277). And there were also a few passages in the poetry cataloging domestic unhappinesses with a somewhat unbalanced fervor. Samuel Johnson brought all of these factors together in a memorably pithy sentence: "There appears in his books something like a Turkish contempt of females, as subordinate and inferior beings" (*Lives* 1:193).

But through the eighteenth, the nineteenth, and much of the twentieth centuries, Milton's misogynistic streak was usually considered an eccentricity, not a malign preoccupation at the center of his being. At the dawn of the feminist period, Sandra Gilbert and Susan Gubar, in their groundbreaking *The Madwoman in the Attic*, maintained that Milton's patriarchal version of Genesis had from the beginning intimidated and oppressed female writers. He taught that a divine Father and Son had created everything, that Sin was a cursed mother, that Eve was supposed to be obedient to Adam ("He for God only, she for God in him") but instead was corrupted by the devil (Gilbert 368–82; later in Gilbert and Gubar 187–212). Philip Gallagher objected immediately (Gallagher and Gilbert 319–22) and later expanded his views in the fervently argued *Milton, the Bible, and Misogyny* (1990).

Joseph Wittreich's *Feminist Milton* (1987) showed that, Gilbert and Gubar to the contrary, many women down through the years had been empowered by Milton's portrait of Eve. Early commentators on *Paradise Lost* were well aware that a passage such as Adam's enumeration of marital woes to come at 10.896–908 was forced and gratuitous, since Adam "could not very naturally be supposed at that time to foresee so very circumstantially the inconvenience attending our *straight conjunction with this sex*, as he expresses it" (Thyer, cited in Todd 3.321). A few passages on a pet peeve were not too high a price to pay for great literature. Most poets had bees in their bonnets. Shakespeare himself never had a good word for dogs and cats. But feminists feared that Milton, whether consciously or not, was the agent of patriarchy or logocentrism or bourgeois individualism—whatever its name, a large conspiracy of overlapping ideological commitments hostile to women and progressive civilization alike.

The main positions in feminist Milton studies are essentially the same as those adopted in Shakespeare studies, and no doubt in other literary disciplines. Some interpreters found that Milton's poetry, if read sympathetically, yields meanings surprisingly favorable to women (McColley 1983; Woods). Others of this persuasion explored the possibility that Milton was not primarily threatened by women but in fact identified with them in profound ways (Kerrigan 1983, 184–86, 188–89, and 1991; S. Davies; Turner 65–71, 142–48; Lieb 83–113). Some, by contrast, agreed with Gilbert and Gubar that Milton is irredeemably an obstruction and will have to be cleared away (Froula). There were also those evenhanded souls contending that Milton is pretty much all right so far as he goes, but does not go far enough. James Turner in *One Flesh* found Milton's Eden erotically liberating; yet the poem has "two quite different models of the politics of love: one is drawn from the experience of being in love with an equal, . . . the other from the hierarchical arrangement of the universe, and the craving for male supremacy" (285). Mary Nyquist conceded that Milton seemed progressive in championing companionate marriage based on conversational partnership but warned that a woman content with such by-products of individualism would be settling for too little. The "blear illusion" (*Masque* 155) of these bourgeois goods prevents women from appreciating the higher truths to their left (99–100, 115–24).

This is still a young tradition. Up to now it has no doubt been too caught up in the barren chore of ideological grading. But the arguments have begun.

References and Abbreviations

Most of the many editions, books, and articles cited in the introduction and notes can be found, alphabetized by author, in the Works Cited bibliography at the end of this volume. Where an author's surname is given without a date, it means that only one of this author's works has been cited in the edition. Where a name is coupled with a date, it means that at least two works by this author have been cited in the edition. Multiple entries in Works Cited are arranged chronologically.

We use these abbreviations for works by John Milton:

1667	*Paradise Lost. A Poem Written in Ten Books* (1667).
1671	*Paradise Regained. A Poem in IV Books. To which is added Samson Agonistes* (1671).
1674	*Paradise Lost. A Poem in Twelve Books. The Second Edition . . .* (1674).
CMS	Manuscript of poems by Milton at Trinity College, Cambridge.
MLM	*The Complete Poetry and Essential Prose of John Milton*, ed. William Kerrigan, John Rumrich, and Stephen M. Fallon. Modern Library edition: New York, 2007.
Yale	*Complete Prose Works of John Milton*, ed. Don M. Wolfe *et al.* (8 vols., Yale Univ. Press, 1953–80).
Anidmad	*Animadversions on the Remonstrant's Defense*
Apology	*An Apology for Smectymnuus*
Areop	*Areopagitica*
CD	*Christian Doctrine*
Damon	*Epitaph for Damon*
DDD	*The Doctrine and Discipline of Divorce*

Eikon	*Eikonoclastes*
Il Pens	*Il Penseroso*
L'All	*L'Allegro*
Lyc	*Lycidas*
Masque	*A Masque Presented at Ludlow Castle*
Nat Ode	*Nativity Ode*
Of Ed	*Of Education*
Of Ref	*Of Reformation*
PL	*Paradise Lost*
PR	*Paradise Regained*
RCG	*The Reason of Church Government Urged Against Prelaty*
REW	*The Ready and Easy Way to Establish a Free Commonwealth*
SA	*Samson Agonistes*
TKM	*The Tenure of Kings and Magistrates*
1Def	*Pro Populo Anglicano Defensio* (*A Defense of the English People*)
2Def	*Defensio Secunda* (*Second Defense of the English People*)

Citations to Milton's prose refer either to the Modern Library Milton (*MLM*) or, for passages not included in the Modern Library Milton, to the volume and page number of the Yale edition.

We use the following abbreviations for works by Shakespeare:

ADO	*Much Ado About Nothing*
ANT	*Antony and Cleopatra*
COR	*Coriolanus*
HAM	*Hamlet*
1H4	*The First Part of King Henry the Fourth*
2H4	*The Second Part of King Henry the Fourth*
H5	*King Henry the Fifth*
JC	*Julius Caesar*
LLL	*Love's Labor's Lost*
LR	*King Lear*
MAC	*Macbeth*
MM	*Measure for Measure*
MND	*A Midsummer Night's Dream*
OTH	*Othello*
R2	*King Richard the Second*
R3	*King Richard the Third*

ROM	*Romeo and Juliet*
TMP	*The Tempest*
TN	*Twelfth Night*
TRO	*Troilus and Cressida*

Unless otherwise indicated, we quote the Bible from the *AV* (King James Version), and use standard abbreviations when referring to its books; we sometimes cite *Geneva* (*The Geneva Bible,* 1588). Poetry in English, except where otherwise indicated, we cite from the Oxford authors series. Classical works are cited from the Loeb Classical Library unless otherwise noted, with standard abbreviations, such as, prominently, *Il.* and *Od.* for Homer's *Iliad* and *Odyssey, Ec.* and *Aen.* for Vergil's *Eclogues* and *Aeneid,* and *Her.* and *Met.* for Ovid's *Heroides* and *Metamorphoses.*

We also use these abbreviations:

Torquato Tasso,	*GL*	*Gerusalemme Liberata*
Ludovico Ariosto,	*OF*	*Orlando Furioso*
Edmund Spenser,	*FQ*	*The Faerie Queene*

A Chronology of Milton's Life

1608   (December 9) John Milton born on Bread Street in London.

1615   (November 24?) Brother Christopher born.

1620   (?) Enters St. Paul's School under the headmastership of Alexander Gill, Sr. Begins his friendship with Charles Diodati. Thomas Young tutors Milton at home.

1625   (February 12) Admitted to Christ's College, Cambridge.

1629   (March 26) Receives his B.A. degree. In December writes *On the Morning of Christ's Nativity*.

1632   (July 3) Receives his M.A. degree. Retires to his father's country house at Hammersmith for continued study.

1634   (September 29) *A Masque* performed at Ludlow Castle in Wales.

1635 or '36   Moves with his parents to Horton.

1637   *A Masque* published (dated 1637 but possibly published in 1638). Mother, Sara, dies in Horton on April 3. *Lycidas* written in November and published the next year.

1638–9   Milton tours the Continent from April or May 1638 to July or August 1639. Charles Diodati dies in August 1638.

1639   Settles in London, where he makes his living as a tutor.

1641   Earliest antiprelatical tracts—*Of Reformation* (May), *Of Prelatical Episcopacy* (June or July), *Animadversions on the Remonstrant's Defense* (July)—published.

1642   Publishes *The Reason of Church Government* (January or February) and *An Apology for Smectymnuus* (April). Marries Mary Powell in June or July. In August she leaves him and the Civil War begins.

1643   *The Doctrine and Discipline of Divorce* published in August.

1644   The second edition of *The Doctrine and Discipline of Divorce* published in February; *Of Education* in June; *The Judgment of Martin Bucer* in August; *Areopagitica* in November.

1645 Two more divorce pamphlets, *Tetrachordon* and *Colasterion*, published in March. Reconciles with Mary in July or August and moves to a larger house in Barbican in September.

1646 *Poems of Mr. John Milton* published in January, dated 1645. Daughter Anne born July 29.

1647 (March 13) On or about this date his father dies, leaving Milton the Bread Street house and a moderate estate. (September–October) Moves to a smaller house in High Holborn.

1648 (October 25) Daughter Mary born.

1649 (January 30) Charles I executed. *Eikon Basilike* published a week later. (February 13) *The Tenure of Kings and Magistrates* published, with a second edition in September. (March 15) Appointed Secretary for Foreign Tongues and ordered to answer *Eikon Basilike*. (May 11) Salmasius's *Defensio Regia* arrives in England. (October 6) *Eikonoklastes* published, answering *Eikon Basilike*.

1651 (February 24) The *Pro Populo Anglicano Defensio* (*A Defense of the English People*) published, answering Salmasius. (March 16) Son John born.

1652 (February or March) Total blindness descends. Daughter Deborah born May 2. Wife Mary dies on May 5. Son John dies in June.

1653 Duties as Secretary for Foreign Tongues are reduced by the addition of an assistant. Cromwell installed as Protector in December.

1654 *Defensio Secunda* (*Second Defense of the English People*) published in May.

1655 Milton is pensioned in April and though he continues to work for the Protectorate, devotes more time to private studies. *Pro Se Defensio* (*Defense of Himself*) published in August.

1656 (November 12) Marries Katharine Woodcock.

1657 (October 19) Daughter Katharine born.

1658 Probably begins work on *Paradise Lost*. Wife Katharine dies on February 3. Daughter Katharine dies on March 17. Cromwell dies in September, succeeded by his son Richard.

1659 *A Treatise of Civil Power* published in February. Richard

Cromwell resigns in May. *Considerations Touching the Likeliest Means to Remove Hirelings out of the Church* published in August.

1660   *The Ready and Easy Way to Establish a Free Commonwealth* published in February, with a second edition in April. Charles II proclaimed king in May. Milton arrested and imprisoned between September and November and released in December.

1663   (February 24) Marries Elizabeth Minshull. Moves to a house in Artillery Walk, near Bunhill Fields.

1665   Around June, moves to Chalfont St. Giles to avoid the London plague.

1667   (October or November) *Paradise Lost* published as a poem in ten books.

1670   (Around November 1) *History of Britain* published.

1671   *Paradise Regained* and *Samson Agonistes* published.

1672   *Artis Logicae* (*The Art of Logic*) published.

1673   *Of True Religion* published. An enlarged edition of *Poems* published, also including *Of Education.*

1674   *Epistolae Familiarum* (*Familiar Letters*) published, including his *Prolusions. Paradise Lost. A Poem in Twelve Books* published around July 1. Milton dies November 9 or 10 and is buried in St. Giles, Cripplegate.

Minutes of the Life of Mr. John Milton

John Aubrey

There are several seventeenth-century Milton biographers, including the anonymous biographer (most likely Milton's friend Cyriack Skinner), the Oxford historian Anthony à Wood, Milton's nephew and former student Edward Phillips, and the deist John Toland. One can find their works in Helen Darbishire's *The Early Lives of Milton* (1932), which attributes the anonymous biography to Edward Phillips's brother, John. We choose to print the biographical notes gathered by the antiquarian John Aubrey, which are notable for their author's extraordinary attention to personal details and efforts to verify his information by consulting those who knew Milton well, including the poet's widow, his brother, and some of his friends.

Aubrey's manuscript notes are loosely organized, partly chronologically and partly by the person interviewed. Our text follows the chronologically arranged version established by Andrew Clark (2:62–72). Those wanting to identify the sources of individual comments may consult Clark's edition or Darbishire's. We have reproduced Clark's interpolated headings, but we have in some places made different choices in our inclusions and exclusions. We have also modernized the text, changing punctuation and spelling. Aubrey's notes are peppered with ellipses, where he leaves blanks to be filled in should further information appear. Bracketed ellipses in our text indicate places where we omit material found in Clark's edition; otherwise the ellipses are Aubrey's.

[HIS PARENTAGE]

His mother was a Bradshaw.

Mr. John Milton was of an Oxfordshire family.

His grandfather, ..., (a Roman Catholic), of Holton, in Oxfordshire, near Shotover.

His father was brought up in the University of Oxon, at Christ Church, and his grandfather disinherited him because he kept not to the Catholic religion (he found a Bible in English in his chamber). So thereupon he came to London, and became a scrivener (brought up by a friend of his; was not an apprentice) and got a plentiful estate by it, and left it off many years before he died. He was an ingenious man; delighted in music; composed many songs now in print, especially that of *Oriana*.[1]

I have been told that the father composed a song of fourscore parts for the Landgrave of Hesse, for which [his] highness sent a medal of gold, or a noble present. He died about 1647; buried in Cripplegate church, from his house in the Barbican.

[HIS BIRTH]

His son John was born in Bread Street, in London, at the Spread Eagle, which was his house (he had also in that street another house, the Rose, and other houses in other places).

He was born Anno Domini ... the ... day of ..., about ... o'clock in the ...

(John Milton was born the 9th of December, 1608, *die Veneris*,[2] half an hour after 6 in the morning.)

---

1. *Oriana:* Milton's father contributed a song, "Fair Orian," to *The Triumphs of Oriana* (1601), a volume of songs dedicated to Queen Elizabeth I.
2. *die Veneris:* Venus's Day, i.e., Friday.

Portrait of Milton at age ten,
by Cornelius Janssen.

[His precocity]

Anno Domini 1619, he was ten years old, as by his picture; and was then a poet.

[School, college, and travel]

His schoolmaster then was a Puritan, in Essex, who cut his hair short.

He went to school to old Mr. Gill, at Paul's School. Went at his own charge only to Christ's College in Cambridge at fifteen, where he stayed eight years at least. Then he traveled into France and Italy (had Sir H. Wotton's commendatory letters). At Geneva he contracted a great friendship with the learned Dr. Diodati of Geneva (*vide* his poems). He was acquainted with Sir Henry Wotton, ambassador at Venice, who delighted in his company. He was several years <*Quaere,* how many? *Resp.,* two years> beyond sea, and returned to England just upon the breaking out of the civil wars.

From his brother, Christopher Milton: When he went to school, when he was very young, he studied very hard and sat up very late, commonly till twelve or one o'clock at night, and his father ordered the maid to sit up for him; and in those years (10) composed many copies of verses which might well become a riper age. And was a very hard student in the university, and performed all his exercises there with very good applause. His first tutor there was Mr. Chapell; from whom receiving some unkindness <whipped him>; he was afterwards (though it seemed contrary to the rules of the college) transferred to the tuition of one Mr. Tovell,[3] who died parson of Lutterworth.

He went to travel about the year 1638 and was abroad about a year's space, chiefly in Italy.

[RETURN TO ENGLAND]

Immediately after his return he took a lodging at Mr. Russell's, a tailor, in St. Bride's churchyard, and took into his tuition his [Milton's] sister's two sons, Edward and John Phillips, the first 10, the other 9 years of age; and in a year's time made them capable of interpreting a Latin author at sight, etc., and within three years they went through the best of Latin and Greek poets: Lucretius and Manilius <and with him the use of the globes and some rudiments of arithmetic and geometry> of the Latins; Hesiod, Aratus, Dionysius Afer, Oppian, Apollonii *Argonautica,* and Quintus Calaber. Cato, Varro, and Columella *De re rustica* were the very first authors they learned. As he was severe on the one hand, so he was most familiar and free in his conversation to those to whom most sour in his way of education. N.B. he made his nephews songsters, and sing, from the time they were with him.

3. I.e., Nathaniel Tovey.

[First wife and children]

He married his first wife, Mary Powell of Fosthill,[4] at Shotover, in Oxonshire, Anno Domini . . . ; by whom he had four children. [He] hath two daughters living: Deborah was his amanuensis (he taught her Latin, and to read Greeke to him when he had lost his eyesight, which was anno Domini . . .).

[Separation from his first wife]

She went from him to her mother's at . . . in the king's quarters, near Oxford, anno Domini . . . ; and wrote the *Triplechord* about divorce.[5]

Two opinions do not well on the same bolster. She was a . . . Royalist, and went to her mother to the King's quarters, near Oxford. I have perhaps so much charity to her that she might not wrong his bed: but what man, especially contemplative, would like to have a young wife environed and stormed by the sons of Mars, and those of the enemy party?

His first wife (Mrs. Powell, a Royalist) was brought up and lived where there was a great deal of company and merriment <dancing, etc.>. And when she came to live with her husband, at Mr. Russell's in St. Bride's churchyard, she found it very solitary; no company came to her; oftentimes heard his nephews beaten and cry. This life was irksome to her, and so she went to her parents at Fosthill. He sent for her, after some time; and I think his servant was evilly entreated: but as for manner of wronging his bed, I never heard the least suspicions; nor had he, of that, any jealousy.

[Second wife]

He had a middle wife, whose name was Katharine Woodcock. No child living by her.

---

4. I.e., Forest Hill.
5. **Triplechord** *about divorce:* most likely *Tetrachordon* (four strings).

[THIRD WIFE]

He married his second [sic] wife, Elizabeth Minshull, anno ... (the year before the sickness): a gentle person, a peaceful and agreeable humor.

[HIS PUBLIC EMPLOYMENT]

He was Latin secretary to the Parliament.

[HIS BLINDNESS]

His sight began to fail him at first upon his writing against Salmasius, and before 'twas full completed one eye absolutely failed. Upon the writing of other books after that, his other eye decayed.

His eyesight was decaying about 20 years before his death. His father read without spectacles at 84. His mother had very weak eyes, and used spectacles presently after she was thirty years old.

[WRITINGS AFTER HIS BLINDNESS]

After he was blind he wrote these following books, viz.: *Paradise Lost, Paradise Regained, Grammar, Dictionary* (imperfect).

I heard that after he was blind that he was writing a Latin dictionary (in the hands of Moses Pitt). *Vidua affirmat*[6] she gave all his papers (among which this dictionary, imperfect) to his nephew, a sister's son, that he brought up ... Phillips, who lives near the Maypole in the Strand. She has a great many letters by her from learned men, his acquaintance, both of England and beyond the sea.

[HIS LATER RESIDENCES]

He lived in several places, e.g., Holborn near Kingsgate. He died in Bunhill, opposite the Artillery-garden wall.

---

6. **Vidua affirmat:** His widow maintains.

[His death and burial]

He died of the gout, struck in the 9th or 10th of November, 1674, as appears by his apothecary's book.

He lies buried in St. Giles Cripplegate, upper end of the chancel at the right hand, *vide* his gravestone. Memorandum: his stone is now removed, for about two years since (now 1681) the two steps to the communion table were raised. I guess John Speed[7] and he lie together.

[Personal characteristics]

His harmonical and ingenious soul did lodge in a beautiful and well-proportioned body—*"In toto nusquam corpore menda fuit,"* Ovid.[8]

He was a spare man. He was scarce so tall as I am, [...] of middle stature.

He had auburn hair. His complexion exceeding fair—he was so fair that they called him *the Lady of Christ's College.* Oval face. His eye a dark gray.

He had a delicate tuneable voice, and had good skill. His father instructed him. He had an organ in his house; he played on that most.

Of a very cheerful humor. He would be cheerful even in his goutfits, and sing.

He was very healthy and free from all diseases: seldom took any physic (only sometimes he took manna):[9] only towards his latter end he was visited with the gout, spring and fall.

He had a very good memory; but I believe that his excellent method of thinking and disposing did much to help his memory.

He pronounced the letter R <*littera canina*[10]> very hard (a certain sign of a satirical wit—from John Dryden.).

---

7. ***John Speed:*** author of *The History of Great Britain,* he is buried in St. Giles, as is John Foxe, author of *The Book of Martyrs* and *Acts and Monuments.*
8. 1 *Amores* 5.18: "There was not a blemish on her body."
9. ***manna:*** a mild laxative.
10. **littera canina:** dog letter, so called because making a continuous *r* sound resembles a dog's growl when threatening attack.

[Portraits of him]

Write his name in red letters on his pictures, with his widow, to preserve.[11]

His widow has his picture, drawn very well and like, when a Cambridge-scholar, which ought to be engraven; for the pictures before his books are not *at all* like him.

[His habits]

His exercise was chiefly walking.

He was an early riser <*scil.* at 4 a clock *manè*[12]>; yea, after he lost his sight. He had a man read to him. The first thing he read was the Hebrew bible, and that was at 4 h. *manè*, 1/2 h. plus. Then he contemplated.

At 7 his man came to him again, and then read to him again and wrote till dinner; the writing was as much as the reading. His (2nd) daughter, Deborah, could read to him in Latin, Italian and French, and Greek. [She] married in Dublin to one Mr. Clarke <sells silk, etc.>; very like her father. The other sister is Mary, more like her mother.

After dinner he used to walk 3 or 4 hours at a time (he always had a garden where he lived); went to bed about 9.

Temperate man, rarely drank between meals.

Extreme pleasant in his conversation and at dinner, supper, etc; but satirical.

[Notes about some of his works]

From Mr. E. Phillips:—All the time of writing his *Paradise Lost,* his vein began at the autumnal equinoctial, and ceased at the vernal or thereabouts (I believe about May); and this was 4 or 5 years of his doing it. He began about 2 years before the king came in, and finished about three years after the king's restoration.[13]

---

11. A note to himself.
12. **Scil. . . . manè**: It is well known (*scilicet*) . . . in the morning.
13. I.e., Milton composed his epic between 1658 and 1663.

In the 4th book of *Paradise Lost* there are about six verses of Satan's exclamation to the sun, which Mr. E. Phillips remembers about 15 or 16 years before ever his poem was thought of, which verses were intended for the beginning of a tragedy which he had designed, but was diverted from it by other business.

Whatever he wrote against monarchy was out of no animosity to the king's person, or out of any faction or interest, but out of a pure zeal to the liberty of mankind, which he thought would be greater under a free state than under a monarchial government. His being so conversant in Livy and the Roman authors, and the greatness he saw done by the Roman commonwealth, and the virtue of their great commanders induced him to.

From Mr. Abraham Hill:—Memorandum: his sharp writing against Alexander More, of Holland, upon a mistake, notwithstanding he had given him by the ambassador all satisfaction to the contrary: viz. that the book called *Clamor* was writ by Peter du Moulin. Well, that was all one; he having writ it,[14] it should go into the world; one of them was as bad as the other.

Memorandum:—Mr. Theodore Haak. Regiae Societatis Socius, hath translated half his *Paradise Lost* into High Dutch in such blank verse, which is very well liked of by Germanus Fabricius, Professor at Heidelberg, who sent to Mr. Haak a letter upon this translation: *"incredibile est quantum nos omnes affecerit gravitas styli, et copia lectissimorum verborum,"*[15] etc.—*vide* the letter.

Mr. John Milton made two admirable panegyrics, as to sublimity of wit, one on Oliver Cromwell, and the other on Thomas, Lord Fairfax, both which his nephew Mr. Phillips hath. But he hath hung back these two years, as to imparting copies to me for the collection of mine [...]. Were they made in commendation of the devil, 'twere all one to me:

---

14. Milton published his *Second Defense of the English People* (1654), with its attack on More as the author of the *Cry of the King's Blood* (*Regii Sanguinis Clamor*), even after learning that another had written the book.

15. "It is incredible how much the dignity of his style and his most excellent diction have affected all of us."

'tis the ὕψος[16] that I look after. I have been told that 'tis beyond Waller's or anything in that kind.[17] [...]

[HIS ACQUAINTANCE]

He was visited much by learned [men]; more than he did desire.

He was mightily importuned to go into France and Italy. Foreigners came much to see him, and much admired him, and offered to him great preferments to come over to them; and the only inducement of several foreigners that came over into England was chiefly to see Oliver Protector and Mr. John Milton; and would see the house and chamber where he was born. He was much more admired abroad than at home.

His familiar learned acquaintance were Mr. Andrew Marvell, Mr. Skinner, Dr. Pagett, M.D.

Mr. . . . [Cyriack] Skinner, who was his disciple.

John Dryden, Esq., Poet Laureate, who very much admires him, and went to him to have leave to put his *Paradise Lost* into a drama in rhyme. Mr. Milton received him civilly, and told him *he would give him leave to tag his verses.*[18]

His widow assures me that Mr. T. Hobbes was not one of his acquaintance, that her husband did not like him at all, but he would acknowledge him to be a man of great parts, and a learned man. Their interests and tenets did run counter to each other, *vide* Mr. Hobbes' *Behemoth.*

---

16. ὕψος: loftiness, altitude.

17. We omit here a catalog of Milton's works.

18. John Dryden's *The State of Innocence, and Fall of Man: An Opera Written in Heroique Verse,* based on *Paradise Lost,* was published in 1677. A *tag* was an ornamental, metal-tipped lace or string that dangled from a garment.

A Note on the Text

This text of *Paradise Lost* is based on the second edition of 1674, the last edition published in Milton's lifetime and the last over which he exerted some degree of control. The qualifier "some degree" is necessary because Renaissance publishers normally introduced their own habits of orthography and punctuation into printed texts. Milton, who is usually assumed to have resisted this practice more than other authors of the period, by no means had his own way in these matters, as we know from the fact that the Pierpont Morgan Library manuscript of Book I of *Paradise Lost* is more lightly punctuated than the printed version. We have assessed significant variations found in this manuscript, in the first edition of 1667, and in editions subsequent to 1674 on a case-by-case basis, and discussed them in our notes. The virtues of an eclectic approach to editing Milton have been ably set forth by John Creaser (1983, 1984).

We have sought to ease the journey of modern readers. Most of Milton's capitalizations, italics, and contractions have been removed. Quotation marks came into vogue some years after the death of Milton, and they do not appear in the first two editions of his epic. We have added them. His spelling has been modernized and Americanized; "brigad" becomes "brigade," and "vigour" becomes "vigor." But there are important exceptions to these preferences. Our efforts at modernization have been checked by a desire to preserve whenever possible the sound, rhythm, and texture of the poem. We have therefore left archaic words and some original spellings intact; "enow" does not become "enough," and "highth" does not become "height." In cases where Milton's contractions indicate that a syllable voiced in the modern pronunciation of a word is to be elided, as with "flow'ry" at 9.456 or "heav'nly" at 9.457, we have left them alone. Sometimes the final *-ed*

Another ſide, umbrageous Grots and Caves
Of coole receſs, o're which the mantling vine
Layes forth her purple Grape, and gently creeps
Luxuriant ; mean while murmuring waters fall
Down the ſlope hills, diſperſt, or in a Lake,
That to the fringed Bank with Myrtle crownd,
Her chryſtal mirror holds, unite thir ſtreams.
The Birds thir quire apply ; aires, vernal aires,
Breathing the ſmell of field and grove, attune
The trembling leaves, while Univerſal *Pan*
Knit with the *Graces* and the *Hours* in dance
Led on th' Eternal Spring. Not that faire field
Of *Enna*, where *Proſerpin* gathering flours
Her ſelf a fairer Floure by gloomie *Dis*
Was gatherd, which coſt *Ceres* all that pain
To ſeek her through the world; nor that ſweet Grove
Of *Daphne* by *Orontes*, and th' inſpir'd
Caſtalian Spring, might with this Paradiſe
Of *Eden* ſtrive ; nor that *Nyſeian* Ile
Girt with the River *Triton*, where old *Cham*,
Whom Gentiles *Ammon* call and *Lybian Jove*,
Hid *Amalthea* and her Florid Son
Young *Bacchus* from his Stepdame *Rhea's* eye ;
Nor where *Abaſſin* Kings thir iſſue Guard,
Mount *Amara*, though this by ſom ſuppos'd
True Paradiſe under the *Ethiop* Line
By *Nilus* head, encloſd with ſhining Rock,
A whole days journy high, but wide remote
From this *Aſſyrian* Garden, where the Fiend
Saw undelighted all delight, all kind
Of living Creatures new to ſight and ſtrange :
Two of far nobler ſhape erect and tall,
Godlike erect, with native Honour clad
In naked Majeſtie ſeemd Lords of all,

And

in words such as "fixed" is not voiced, as in "Of Godhead fixed forever firm and sure" (7.586). Where *-ed* is a voiced syllable, as in "His fixèd seat" (3.669), we have placed an accent mark slanting down from left to right.

Punctuation offers especially complex choices for modernizers. For punctuation, or "pointing" as it was called in Milton's day, serves two purposes at least. It displays the logic of the syntax, aiding a reader in the basic chore of construing sense. But especially in a poetic text, and more especially still in the poetic text of the seventeenth century, punctuation also indicates rhythmic pauses. It is generally assumed, perhaps without much evidence, that a semicolon points to a longer pause than a comma, a colon to a longer pause than a semicolon, and a period to the most pronounced pause of all. Milton's punctuation is difficult to update for modern readers in both of its functions. For his syntax is not packaged in the modern unit of the sentence. The grammatical shoots of *Paradise Lost* twist and turn like wanton vines. His verbs can refer back to subjects introduced some ten or more lines before, and what seem at first to be subordinate clauses will often develop complex syntactical lives of their own. On the rhythmic side, many of the commas and semicolons that look superfluous by modern standards could well indicate the sound-patterns of his verse. Some readers would argue that, whenever the two functions of punctuation come into conflict, sound must be sacrificed to sense. But in poetry, as in good prose, sound-patterns *are*, above and beyond their inherent beauty, meaning-patterns. Countless works of criticism have demonstrated that sound effects in literary language have the power to bear meaning, and we see no reason to doubt these results. Milton, moreover, is widely judged to be a supreme master of this aspect of literary craftsmanship.

Given these concerns, we have sought within a general framework of modernization to respect the punctuation schemes developed by Milton and his publishers. We remove a number of commas. Some are changed to semicolons and periods for the sake of readability. But in places where marking the rhythm seems paramount (see 2.315), we reproduce either closely or exactly the pointing of 1674.

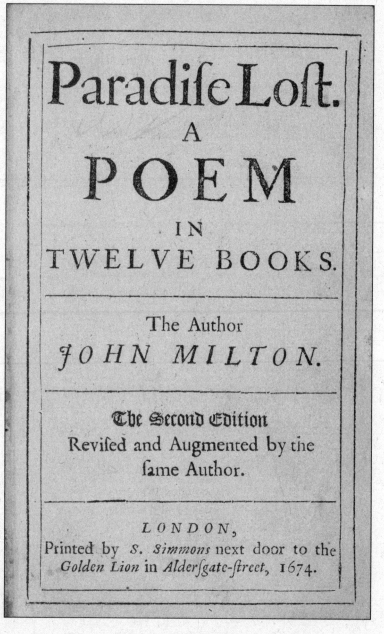

Paradise Loſt.
A
POEM
IN
TWELVE BOOKS.

The Author
JOHN MILTON.

𝕿𝖍𝖊 𝕾𝖊𝖈𝖔𝖓𝖉 𝕰𝖉𝖎𝖙𝖎𝖔𝖓
Reviſed and Augmented by the
ſame Author.

LONDON,
Printed by *S. Simmons* next door to the
Golden Lion in *Alderſgate-ſtreet,* 1674.

Title page to the second edition of *Paradise Lost* (1674).

INTRODUCTION TO PREFATORY POEMS

These laudatory poems first prefaced *Paradise Lost* in 1674. The Latin verses by Samuel Barrow concentrate on the expulsion of Satan and his followers from Heaven and its classical precedents, the defeat and punishment of the Titans and Giants. Given the literary triumph of this section of *Paradise Lost*, Barrow confidently welcomes Milton onto the stage of world poetry (where he has been ever since). The English verses by Andrew Marvell assert the religious propriety and superior artistry of Milton's achievement, stressing its capaciousness and aesthetic excellence by invoking the cramped neoclassical canons that prevailed after the Restoration. Aware of Dryden's desire to rewrite *Paradise Lost* as a drama in heroic couplets, Marvell detects traces of divine inspiration even in Milton's blank verse prosody, created like the world itself "in number, weight, and measure."

Barrow was noted for his affection for Charles I, had been much involved with the political maneuvering of the late 1650s leading to the Restoration, and yet had also been linked with Cromwell. Appointed a physician to Charles II in 1660, he was a discreet, well-connected man of science and a great admirer of Milton. Marvell had a similar history of shifting political allegiance and a well-deserved reputation for discretion. Like Barrow a Royalist sympathizer at the beginning of the English Revolution, he must have adopted the Republican cause by 1653, when Milton recommended him for a position in Cromwell's government. (He was not appointed until 1657.) After the Restoration, he served ably as member of Parliament for Hull and was widely respected. The participation of Barrow and Marvell in the second edition seems to have been orchestrated as a broad-based appeal to judicious men of learning and affairs on behalf of a poet much maligned for his political crimes. Marvell had earlier come to the aid of the embattled Milton. Immediately after the Restoration, he helped protect the defender of regicide against his enemies and was instrumental in clearing Milton of a supposed debt to the sergeant at arms after his imprisonment in 1660. A decade later, in *The Rehearsal Transpos'd,* he championed Milton against the scurrilous attack of Samuel Parker.

IN PARADISUM AMISSAM SUMMI POETAE IOHANNIS MILTONI

[*On the Supreme Poet John Milton's* Paradise Lost]

Qui legis Amissam Paradisum, grandia magni
  Carmina Miltoni, quid nisi cuncta legis?
Res cunctas et cunctarum primordia rerum
  Et fata et fines continet iste liber.
5 Intima panduntur magni penetralia mundi,
  Scribitur et toto quicquid in orbe latet:
Terraeque tractusque maris coelumque profundum
  Sulphureumque Erebi flammivomumque specus;
Quaeque colunt terras pontumque et Tartara caeca,
10 Quaeque colunt summi lucida regna poli;
Et quodcunque ullis conclusum est finibus usquam,
  Et sine fine chaos et sine fine Deus,
Et sine fine magis, si quid magis est sine fine,

You who read *Paradise Lost,* great Milton's grand poem, what do you read but everything? This book contains all things, and the origins of all things, and their fates and their ends. The innermost secrets of the great universe are displayed, and whatever in the whole world is hidden is written out: the lands and the expanses of the sea and deep heaven and the sulfurous and flame-vomiting cave of Erebus; and those things that inhabit the lands and the sea[9] and blind Tartarus, and those that inhabit the bright realms of highest heaven; and whatever anywhere is enclosed within any boundaries, and boundless Chaos, and boundless God; and more

---

9. **pontumque:** "portumque" (harbor) in the 1674 *Paradise Lost.*

In Christo erga homines conciliatus
  amor.
15 Haec qui speraret quis crederet esse
  futurum?
  Et tamen haec hodie terra Britanna legit.
  O quantos in bella duces, quae protulit
  arma!
  Quae canit et quanta praelia dira tuba!
  Coelestes acies, atque in certamine
  coelum,
20 Et quae coelestes pugna deceret agros!
  Quantus in aetheriis tollit se Lucifer
  armis,
  Atque ipso graditur vix Michaele minor!
  Quantis et quam funestis concurritur iris
  Dum ferus hic stellas protegit, ille rapit!
25 Dum vulsos montes ceu tela reciproca
  torquent
  Et non mortali desuper igne pluunt,
  Stat dubius cui se parti concedat Olympus
  Et metuit pugnae non superesse suae.
  At simul in coelis Messiae insignia
  fulgent,
30 Et currus animes armaque digna Deo,
  Horrendumque rotae strident, et saeva
  rotarum
  Erumpunt torvis fulgura luminibus,
  Et flammae vibrant, et vera tonitrua rauco
  Admistis flammis insonuere polo,
35 Excidit attonitis mens omnis et impetus
  omnis,

boundless—if anything is more boundless—Christ's love directed toward men. Who would have believed there would come someone who would aspire to such things?—and yet today the land of Britain reads them. How many chieftains he brought to war, and what weaponry! What battles he sings, and with what a trumpet!— battlelines in Heaven, and Heaven in conflict, and fighting that befits the fields of Heaven! What a Lucifer lifts himself to ethereal warfare, and strides scarcely lower than Michael himself! With what great and fatal rage the fight is joined while one in his fierceness protects the stars, the other assaults them! While they hurl uprooted mountains as retaliatory weapons and they rain down from above with no mortal fire, Olympus stands unsure to which side to yield, and fears it will not survive its own battle. But as soon as the Messiah's standards shine out in Heaven and you rouse his chariot and the arms worthy of God, and the wheels shriek horrifyingly and savage lightning breaks from the wheels with grim flashes, and flames shake and true thunderclaps resound with a mixture of flames in the clangorous sky, all consciousness falls from those who have been struck, and

Et cassis dextris irrita tela cadunt.
Ad poenas fugiunt, et ceu foret Orcus
    asylum
Infernis certant condere se tenebris.
Cedite romani scriptores, cedite Graii
40 Et quos fama recens vel celebravit anus.
Haec quicunque leget tantum cecinisse
    putabit
Maeonidem ranas, Virgilium culices.
                      S.B. M.D.

all strength, and their use-less weapons drop from their empty hands. They flee to punishment, and as if the underworld were asy-lum they strive to settle themselves in the infernal shades. Yield, Roman writ-ers, yield, Greeks, and those whom recent or ancient fame has celebrated; who-ever reads this will think Homer just sang of frogs, Vergil of gnats.

                S[amuel] B[arrow]

ON MR. MILTON'S *PARADISE LOST*

When I beheld the poet blind, yet bold,
In slender book his vast design unfold,
Messiah crowned, God's reconciled decree,
Rebelling angels, the Forbidden Tree,
5 Heav'n, Hell, Earth, Chaos, all; the argument
Held me a while misdoubting his intent,
That he would ruin (for I saw him strong)
The sacred truths to fable and old song,
(So Samson groped the temple's posts in spite)
10 The world o'erwhelming to revenge his sight.
    Yet as I read, soon growing less severe,
I liked his project, the success did fear;
Through that wide field how he his way should find
O'er which lame Faith leads Understanding blind,
15 Lest he perplexed the things he would explain,
And what was easy he should render vain.
    Or if a work so infinite be spanned,

---

5. **argument:** the plot or subject matter.
9. Marvell appears to have read *Samson Ago-nistes,* first published in 1671. But the pri-

mary allusion is to Judges 16.28, a passage that Milton does *not* represent in *SA.*
15. **perplexed:** complicated unnecessarily.

Jealous I was that some less skilful hand
(Such as disquiet always what is well,
20 And by ill imitating would excel)
Might hence presume the whole Creation's day
To change in scenes and show it in a play.
    Pardon me, mighty poet, nor despise
My causeless, yet not impious, surmise.
25 But I am now convinced that none will dare
Within thy labors to pretend a share.
Thou hast not missed one thought that could be fit,
And all that was improper dost omit:
So that no room is here for writers left,
30 But to detect their ignorance or theft.
    That majesty which through thy work doth reign
Draws the devout, deterring the profane.
And things divine thou treat'st of in such state
As them preserves, and thee, inviolate.
35 At once delight and horror on us seize,
Thou sing'st with so much gravity and ease;
And above human flight dost soar aloft,
With plume so strong, so equal, and so soft.
The bird named from that paradise you sing
40 So never flags, but always keeps on wing.
    Where couldst thou words of such a compass find?
Whence furnish such a vast expense of mind?
Just heaven thee, like Tiresias, to requite,
Rewards with prophecy thy loss of sight.
45   Well might'st thou scorn thy readers to allure
With tinkling rhyme, of thine own sense secure;

18. **some less skilful hand:** Dryden, who asked Milton if he could make a rhymed drama of *Paradise Lost.* "Mr. Milton received him civilly, and told him he would give him leave to tag his verses" (Aubrey, p. lxviii).

30. **detect:** expose.

39. **bird named from that paradise:** Birds of Paradise were thought to live entirely in the air, never touching ground.

43. **Tiresias:** The legendary seer, mentioned in *PL* 3.36, was given prophetic vision in recompense for his blindness.

46. **tinkling rhyme:** Cp. Milton's "jingling sound of like endings" in his remarks on "The Verse" of *PL*.

While the *Town-Bays* writes all the while and spells,
And like a pack horse tires without his bells.
Their fancies like our bushy points appear:
50 The poets tag them; we for fashion wear.
I too transported by the mode offend,
And while I meant to *praise* thee must *commend*.
Thy verse created like thy theme sublime,
In number, weight, and measure, needs not rhyme.

47. **Town-Bays:** In Buckingham's play *The Rehearsal*, Dryden is lampooned in the character of Bayes. The name alludes to the laurel used to crown poets, which by synecdoche refers to all fame-seeking versifiers.

49. **bushy points:** Points attached the hose to the doublet. They were either tasseled (*bushy*) or gathered together, like modern shoelaces, in a metal *tag*. Tagging bushy laces is here a metaphor for introducing regular end-rhyme in Milton's flowing blank verse.

54. **In number, weight, and measure:** See Wisdom 11:20: "thou hast ordered all things in measure, and number, and weight."

PARADISE LOST

THE PRINTER TO THE READER[1]

Courteous Reader, there was no argument at first intended to the book, but for the satisfaction of many that have desired it, I have procured it, and withal a reason of that which stumbled many others, why the poem rhymes not. S. Simmons

THE VERSE

The measure is English heroic verse without rhyme, as that of Homer in Greek, and of Vergil in Latin; rhyme being no necessary adjunct or true ornament of poem or good verse, in longer works especially, but the invention of a barbarous age, to set off wretched matter and lame meter; graced indeed since by the use of some famous modern poets, carried away by custom, but much to their own vexation, hindrance, and constraint to express many things otherwise, and for the most part worse than else they would have expressed them. Not without cause therefore some both Italian and Spanish poets of prime note have rejected rhyme both in longer and shorter works, as have also long since our best English tragedies, as a thing of itself, to all judicious ears, trivial and of no true musical delight; which consists only in apt numbers, fit quantity of syllables, and the sense variously drawn out from one verse into another, not in the jingling sound of like endings, a fault avoided by the learned ancients both in poetry and all good oratory.

---

1. The defense of blank verse and the prose arguments summarizing each book "procured" by Milton's printer, Samuel Simmons, were inserted in bound copies of the first edition beginning in 1668, with this brief note.

This neglect then of rhyme so little is to be taken for a defect, though it may seem so perhaps to vulgar readers, that it rather is to be esteemed an example set, the first in English, of ancient liberty recovered to heroic poem from the troublesome and modern bondage of rhyming.

Book I

The Argument

This first book proposes, first in brief, the whole subject, man's disobedience, and the loss thereupon of Paradise wherein he was placed: then touches the prime cause of his fall, the serpent, or rather Satan in the serpent, who revolting from God, and drawing to his side many legions of angels, was by the command of God driven out of Heaven with all his crew into the great deep. Which action passed over, the poem hastes into the midst of things, presenting Satan with his angels now fallen into Hell, described here, not in the center (for heaven and earth may be supposed as yet not made, certainly not yet accursed) but in a place of utter darkness, fitliest called Chaos. Here Satan with his angels lying on the burning lake, thunder-struck and astonished, after a certain space recovers, as from confusion, calls up him who next in order and dignity lay by him. They confer of their miserable fall. Satan awakens all his legions, who lay till then in the same manner confounded; they rise, their numbers, array of battle, their chief leaders named, according to the idols known afterwards in Canaan and the countries adjoining. To these Satan directs his speech, comforts them with hope yet of regaining Heaven, but tells them lastly of a new world and new kind of creature to be created, according to an ancient prophecy or report in Heaven; for that angels were long before this visible creation was the opinion of many ancient Fathers. To find out the truth of this prophecy, and what to determine thereon, he refers to a full council. What his associates thence attempt. Pandaemonium the palace of Satan rises, suddenly built out of the deep. The infernal peers there sit in council.

Of man's first disobedience, and the fruit
Of that forbidden tree, whose mortal taste
Brought death into the world, and all our woe,
With loss of Eden, till one greater man
5 Restore us, and regain the blissful seat,
Sing Heav'nly Muse, that on the secret top
Of Oreb, or of Sinai, didst inspire
That shepherd, who first taught the chosen seed,
In the beginning how the heavens and earth
10 Rose out of Chaos: or if Sion hill
Delight thee more, and Siloa's brook that flowed
Fast by the oracle of God, I thence

1. The first line's introduction of an exemplary man recalls the epics of Homer and Vergil. Milton's theme, however, is neither martial nor imperial but spiritual: humanity's disastrous failure to obey God counterpoised by the promise of redemption. **Of man's:** The proper name *Adam* is also the Hebrew word for generic man or humankind. He is both an individual male and, with Eve, the entire species: "so God created man . . . ; male and female he created them" (Gen. 1.27). *Of man* translates the Hebrew for "woman" (Gen. 2.23). **fruit:** Its dual meanings (outcome, food) are put in play by enjambment, a primary formal device by which Milton draws out sense "from one verse into another" (*The Verse*).

4. **one greater man:** Jesus, second Adam (1 Cor. 15.21–22; Rom. 5.19). Cp. *PR* 1.1–4.

5. **blissful seat:** translates Vergil's epithet for Elysium, *Aen.* 6.639.

6. **Sing Heav'nly Muse:** the verb and subject of the magnificently inverted sixteen-line opening sentence. By invoking a Muse, Milton follows a convention that dates from Homer. Yet Milton's Muse is not the muse of classical epic (Calliope) but the inspiration of Moses, David, and the prophets (cp. 17–18n). **secret:** set apart, not common. When the Lord descends to give Moses the law, thick clouds and smoke obscure the mountaintop, and the people are forbidden on pain of death to cross boundaries around the mountain (Exod. 19.16, 23).

8. **shepherd:** The vocation of shepherd is a key vehicle for Milton's integration of classical and scriptural traditions. Moses encounters God while tending sheep on Mount Horeb (*Oreb*) and later receives the law on *Sinai*, a spur of Horeb (Exod. 3; 19). (Or the doubling of names may simply acknowledge the inconsistency of Exod. 19.20 and Deut. 4.10.)

9. **In the beginning:** opening phrase of Genesis and the Gospel of John.

10. **Chaos:** classical term for the primeval state of being out of which God creates, also referred to as "the deep" (as in Gen. 1.2) and "the abyss" (as in l. 21). **Sion hill:** Mount Zion, site of Solomon's Temple, "the house of the Lord" (1 Kings 6.1, 13). Adding to the persistent doubleness of the invocation, Milton requests inspiration from two scriptural sites associated with God's presence and prophetic inspiration. Both sites receive dual designations: Mount Horeb/Sinai and Mount Zion/Siloa's brook.

11–12. **Siloa's brook . . . God:** spring whose waters flowed through an underground aqueduct, supplied a pool near (*Fast by*) Solomon's Temple, and irrigated the

Invoke thy aid to my advent'rous song,
That with no middle flight intends to soar
15   Above th' Aonian mount, while it pursues
Things unattempted yet in prose or rhyme.
And chiefly thou, O Spirit, that dost prefer
Before all temples th' upright heart and pure,
Instruct me, for thou know'st; thou from the first
20   Wast present, and with mighty wings outspread
Dove-like sat'st brooding on the vast abyss
And mad'st it pregnant: what in me is dark
Illumine, what is low raise and support,
That to the highth of this great argument
25   I may assert eternal providence,
And justify the ways of God to men.

---

king's lush garden (cp. 4.225–30). Jerome says it ran directly beneath Mount Zion (A. Gilbert 1919, 269). Scripturally, it symbolizes David's monarchical line (Isa. 7–8, esp. 8.6). In opening the eyes of the man born blind, Jesus sends him to wash his eyes with its waters (John 9). Cp. 3.30–31. **oracle of God:** the holiest place in the Temple, the tabernacle of the Ark of the Covenant (1 Kings 6.19). The classical Muses haunt a spring (Aganippe) on Helicon (cp. 15n), "the sacred well, / That from beneath the seat of Jove doth spring" (*Lyc* 15–16). In identifying the spring near the "Holy of Holies" as similarly a site of inspiration, Milton again links scriptural and classical prophetic and poetic traditions.

14. **no middle flight:** Milton will go beyond middle air, whose upper boundary is as high as the peaks of tall mountains, and soar to the highest Empyrean, the abode of God. His soaring ambition recalls the myth of Icarus, whose failure to follow a *middle flight* caused him to tumble into the sea (cp. 7.12–20).

15. **Aonian mount:** Helicon, Greek mountain favored by the Muses (cp. 11–12n). Hesiod says that while he tended sheep on Helicon (like Moses on Horeb), the

Muses called him to sing of the gods (*Theog.* 22).

16. Translates the opening of *Orlando Furioso* (1.2) and is reminiscent of *Masque* 43–45; cp. similar claims by Lucretius (*De Rerum Nat.* 1.925–30) and Horace (*Odes* 3.1.2–4).

17–18. 1 Cor. 3.16–17, 6.19. The *Spirit* is the Holy Spirit (l. 21). In Milton's theology, the diverse functions of the Holy Spirit derive from "the virtue and power of God the Father," in this case "the force or voice of God, in whatever way it was breathed into the prophets" (*CD* 1.6, p. 1194). The site of revelation progresses from Horeb/Sinai to Sion hill/Siloa's brook to, finally, the individual human heart.

21. **brooding:** Milton thus renders the Hebrew word translated as "moved" in the *AV* (Gen. 1.2) but as *incubabat* (brooded) in St. Basil and other Latin patristic authors (see also 7.235). Cp. Sir Thomas Browne, *Religio Medici:* "This is that gentle heat that brooded on the waters, and in six days hatched the world" (73).

24. **argument:** subject matter; cp. 9.28.

25. **assert:** take the part of, champion.

26. **justify:** vindicate; cp. Pope, *Essay on Man:* "Laugh where we must, be candid where we can,/But vindicate the ways of God to

Say first, for Heav'n hides nothing from thy view
Nor the deep tract of Hell, say first what cause
Moved our grand parents in that happy state,
30   Favored of Heav'n so highly, to fall off
From their Creator, and transgress his will
For one restraint, lords of the world besides?
Who first seduced them to that foul revolt?
Th' infernal serpent; he it was, whose guile
35   Stirred up with envy and revenge, deceived
The mother of mankind, what time his pride
Had cast him out from Heav'n, with all his host
Of rebel angels, by whose aid aspiring
To set himself in glory above his peers,
40   He trusted to have equaled the Most High,
If he opposed; and with ambitious aim
Against the throne and monarchy of God
Raised impious war in Heav'n and battle proud
With vain attempt. Him the Almighty Power
45   Hurled headlong flaming from th' ethereal sky
With hideous ruin and combustion down
To bottomless perdition, there to dwell
In adamantine chains and penal fire,

---

man" (1.15–16). Milton's word order permits dual readings: either "justify (the ways of God to men)" or "justify (the ways of God) to men." Cp. *SA:* "Just are the ways of God,/And justifiable to men" (293–94).

27–28. Milton introduces the narrative with a query, an epic convention; cp. "Tell me, O Muse, the cause" (Vergil, *Aen.* 1.8). Homer also depicts the Muses as all-knowing: "Tell me now, ye Muses that have dwellings on Olympus—for ye are goddesses and are at hand and know all things" (*Il.* 2.484–85).

29. **grand:** great, original, all-inclusive; cp. line 122.

30. **fall off:** deviate, revolt (as in l. 33).

33. Cp. *Il.* 1.8.

36. **what time:** when; cp. *Masque* 291, *Lyc* 28.

44–49. **Him . . . arms:** "God spared not the angels that sinned, but cast them down to hell and delivered them into chains of darkness" (2 Pet. 2.4; cp. Jude 6).

45. "I beheld Satan as lightning fall from heaven" (Luke 10.18); cp. Homer's Hephaestus "hurled . . . from the heavenly threshold . . . headlong" (*Il.* 1.591–92).

46. **ruin:** a fall from a great height, from the Latin *ruina;* cp 6.867–68.

48. **adamantine:** unbreakable (Gk.); cp. Aeschylus's Prometheus, clamped "in shackles of binding adamant that cannot be broken" (*Prom.* 6). The myth of adamant persists today; the indestructible claws of the Marvel Comics hero Wolverine are made of "adamantium."

Who durst defy th' Omnipotent to arms.
50 Nine times the space that measures day and night
    To mortal men, he with his horrid crew
    Lay vanquished, rolling in the fiery gulf
    Confounded though immortal: but his doom
    Reserved him to more wrath; for now the thought
55 Both of lost happiness and lasting pain
    Torments him; round he throws his baleful eyes
    That witnessed huge affliction and dismay
    Mixed with obdurate pride and steadfast hate:
    At once as far as angels ken he views
60 The dismal situation waste and wild,
    A dungeon horrible, on all sides round
    As one great furnace flamed, yet from those flames
    No light, but rather darkness visible
    Served only to discover sights of woe,

---

49. **durst:** dared.

50–52. The rebel angels regain consciousness after nine days falling from Heaven (6.871) and nine days *rolling in the fiery gulf.* Hesiod's Titans fall nine days from heaven to earth and another nine from earth to Tartarus (*Theog.* 720–25). Milton, like many Christian mythographers, deemed the Titans' rebellion a pagan analogue for Satan's fall.

53. **Confounded:** destroyed. Combined with *though immortal,* it neatly defines the Christian concept of damnation.

54. **Reserved:** "And the angels which kept not their first estate, but left their own habitation, he hath reserved in everlasting chains under darkness unto the judgment of the great day" (Jude 6; cp. 2 Pet. 2.4). In *CD,* Milton cites these verses and others to show that "bad angels are kept for punishment" (1.9 in *MLM* 1218).

56. **baleful:** Of Old English origin, *baleful* signifies evil in both its active and its passive aspects. Satan's eyes thus brim with his own suffering and with malice toward others.

57. **witnessed:** Like *baleful,* active and passive. Satan's eyes express spite and woe and also observe it in the surrounding scene.

59. **ken:** "are able to see." Possessive apostrophes do not appear in early modern texts, so that *ken* here could also mean "visual range" of angels. The word is used both as a verb and as a noun elsewhere in *PL* (5.265, 11.379).

63. **darkness visible:** Judged "difficult to imagine" by T. S. Eliot, the paradox has scriptural and classical precedents. See the description in Job of the realm of the dead, "where the light is as darkness" (10.22) or, in Euripides' *Bacchae,* Pentheus's command to imprison Dionysus "so that he may see only darkness" (510). Milton previously flirted with the paradox in *Il Pens* (79–80). Cp. Keats's marginalia: "It can scarcely be conceived how Milton's blindness might here aid the magnitude of his conceptions, as a bat in a large gothic vault" (Lau 74).

65   Regions of sorrow, doleful shades, where peace
     And rest can never dwell, hope never comes
     That comes to all; but torture without end
     Still urges, and a fiery deluge, fed
     With ever-burning sulfur unconsumed:
70   Such place eternal justice had prepared
     For those rebellious, here their prison ordained
     In utter darkness, and their portion set
     As far removed from God and light of Heav'n
     As from the center thrice to th' utmost pole.
75   O how unlike the place from whence they fell!
     There the companions of his fall, o'erwhelmed
     With floods and whirlwinds of tempestuous fire,
     He soon discerns, and welt'ring by his side
     One next himself in power, and next in crime,
80   Long after known in Palestine, and named
     Beëlzebub. To whom th' Arch-Enemy,
     And thence in Heav'n called Satan, with bold words
     Breaking the horrid silence thus began.
          "If thou beest he; but O how fall'n! How changed

66–67. **And rest . . . all:** The inscription above the gate to Dante's Hell reads, "Abandon every hope, who enter here" (*Inf.* 3.9). Cp. Euripides, *Trojan Women* (681–82).

67–68. **but . . . urges:** "The devil that deceived them was cast into the lake of fire and brimstone . . . and shall be tormented day and night for ever and ever" (Rev. 20.10). **Still:** constantly.

70. Cp. "the everlasting fire, prepared for the devil and his angels" (Matt. 25.41). Dante similarly depicts the inferno as an artifice of divine justice (*Inf.* 3.4).

72. **utter darkness:** destination of those excluded from the kingdom of Heaven (Matt. 8.12, 22.13, 25.30). The *AV* has "outer" instead of "utter"; cp. 3.16. The Geneva gloss on Matt. 8.12 explains, "there is nothing but mere darkness out of the kingdom of heaven."

73–74. Homer, Hesiod, and Vergil precede Milton in expressing as a ratio distances between heaven, earth, and the pit of hell (*Il.* 8.16; *Theog.* 722–25; *Aen.* 6.577–79).

74. **center:** the earth, at the center of the Ptolemaic cosmos; **pole:** the point on the outside of the cosmic sphere closest to heaven.

78. **welt'ring:** rolling on waves; cp. *Lyc* 13.

81. **Beëlzebub:** Phoenician god at Ekron consulted by King Ahaziah (2 Kings 1.2). The name in Hebrew means "Lord of Flies." In the Gospels, he is called "prince of the devils"; he was often identified with Satan (Matt. 12.24; cp. *CD* 1.9 in *MLM* 1219).

82. **Satan:** Hebrew word for adversary or enemy, first applied to Satan after his rebellion (5.658). He ultimately glories in the title (10.386–87).

84. **If . . . fall'n:** "How art thou fallen from heaven, O Lucifer, son of the morning!" (Isa. 14.12; cp. Vergil, *Aen.* 2.274). The appearance of the rebel angels is altered for

85 From him, who in the happy realms of light
    Clothed with transcendent brightness didst outshine
    Myriads though bright: if he whom mutual league,
    United thoughts and counsels, equal hope
    And hazard in the glorious enterprise,
90 Joined with me once, now misery hath joined
    In equal ruin: into what pit thou seest
    From what highth fall'n, so much the stronger proved
    He with his thunder: and till then who knew
    The force of those dire arms? Yet not for those,
95 Nor what the potent victor in his rage
    Can else inflict, do I repent or change,
    Though changed in outward luster; that fixed mind
    And high disdain, from sense of injured merit,
    That with the mightiest raised me to contend,
100 And to the fierce contention brought along
    Innumerable force of spirits armed
    That durst dislike his reign, and me preferring,
    His utmost power with adverse power opposed
    In dubious battle on the plains of Heav'n,
105 And shook his throne. What though the field be lost?
    All is not lost; the unconquerable will,
    And study of revenge, immortal hate,
    And courage never to submit or yield:
    And what is else not to be overcome?
110 That glory never shall his wrath or might
    Extort from me. To bow and sue for grace
    With suppliant knee, and deify his power,
    Who from the terror of this arm so late
    Doubted his empire, that were low indeed,

---

the worse. They are also bereft of names
(ll. 361–65). Hence Satan persists in the
conditional salutation (l. 87).
98. **high disdain:** noble scorn. A relatively
common reaction in an aristocratic era
(Kerrigan 2000), it is characteristic of
Satan (cp. 4.50, 82, 180).

103–5. Satan's account differs from Ra-
phael's; cp. 6.832–34, 853–55.
107. **study:** pursuit.
109. "And what else does it mean 'not to be
overcome'?"
114. **Doubted:** feared for.

115 That were an ignominy and shame beneath
This downfall; since by fate the strength of gods
And this empyreal substance cannot fail,
Since through experience of this great event
In arms not worse, in foresight much advanced,
120 We may with more successful hope resolve
To wage by force or guile eternal war
Irreconcilable, to our grand foe,
Who now triumphs, and in th' excess of joy
Sole reigning holds the tyranny of Heav'n."

125 So spake th' apostate angel, though in pain,
Vaunting aloud, but racked with deep despair:
And him thus answered soon his bold compeer.

"O Prince, O chief of many thronèd powers,
That led th' embattled Seraphim to war
130 Under thy conduct, and in dreadful deeds
Fearless, endangered Heav'n's perpetual King,
And put to proof his high supremacy,
Whether upheld by strength, or chance, or fate,
Too well I see and rue the dire event,

---

115. **ignominy:** can be pronounced "ig-no-min-y" or "ig-no-my" (as it was often spelled). In the former case, the terminal *y* would coalesce with *and*. Cp. 2.207, 6.383.

116. **fate:** Satan makes fate the ultimate authority, distinct from the deity, as in Homer. God later defines fate as what he wills, 7.173; cp. *CD* 1.2 in *MLM* 1145–46. The portrayal of fate as an independent governing principle is a feature of Stoic philosophy specifically criticized by Jesus in *PR* (4.313–18). **gods:** "Anyone can observe throughout the whole of the Old Testament . . . that angels often take upon them as their own the name . . . of God" (*CD* 1.5 in *MLM* 1185). God himself refers to the angels as gods (3.341). Cp. Herrick, *Of Angels:* "Angels are called gods; yet of them, none / Are gods, but by participation" (1–2).

117. **empyreal substance:** fiery essence, like the substance of Heaven; cp. 2.771. Heaven (the empyrean) and Hell both are based on the element of fire: in Hell it possesses only its destructive properties, in Heaven only its salutary ones. See 63n.

123. **triumphs:** Emphasis on the second syllable stresses a plosive-fricative fusion, as in *harumph*. It was common to accent the word thus.

125–27. Cp. Vergil's depiction of the seemingly optimistic Aeneas after he has rallied his distressed comrades: "So spake his tongue; while sick with weighty cares he feigns hope on his face, and deep in his heart stifles the anguish" (*Aen.* 1.208–9).

128–29. **powers . . . Seraphim:** Thrones and Powers, like *Seraphim*, are angelic orders. The phrase *thronèd powers* invokes no specific order of angel, however. It instead indicates the dignity and spiritual nature of those led by Satan, including the *Seraphim*.

134. **event:** outcome.

135   That with sad overthrow and foul defeat
      Hath lost us Heav'n, and all this mighty host
      In horrible destruction laid thus low,
      As far as gods and Heav'nly essences
      Can perish: for the mind and spirit remains
140   Invincible, and vigor soon returns,
      Though all our glory extinct, and happy state
      Here swallowed up in endless misery.
      But what if he our conqueror (whom I now
      Of force believe almighty, since no less
145   Than such could have o'erpow'red such force as ours)
      Have left us this our spirit and strength entire
      Strongly to suffer and support our pains,
      That we may so suffice his vengeful ire,
      Or do him mightier service as his thralls
150   By right of war, whate'er his business be
      Here in the heart of Hell to work in fire,
      Or do his errands in the gloomy deep;
      What can it then avail though yet we feel
      Strength undiminished, or eternal being
155   To undergo eternal punishment?"
      Whereto with speedy words th' Arch-Fiend replied.
        "Fall'n cherub, to be weak is miserable
      Doing or suffering: but of this be sure,

---

141. **glory:** effulgence or brilliant, radiant light (see 63n, 117n). *Glory* is a word with a broad range of meaning in the poem (cp. in Book i, ll. 39, 110, 239, 370, 594, 612; see Rumrich 1987, 3–52). **extinct:** (be) put out, extinguished.

144. **Of force:** perforce; cp. 4.813.

147. **support:** endure.

148. **suffice:** satisfy.

149–50. **thralls/By right of war:** slaves by conquest. "The effects and consequences of this right are infinite so that there is nothing so unlawful but the lord may do it to his slaves . . . there are no torments but what may with impunity be imposed on them, nothing to be done but what

they may be forced to do by all manner of rigor and severity." (Grotius, *Rights* 481; cp. *CD* i.11).

152. **deep:** chaos; see 10n.

153–55. The question crystallizes Satan and Beëlzebub's developing awareness of their plight: what possible advantage is there in being a mighty entity eternally sustained only to absorb eternal punishment?

158. **Doing or suffering:** The Stoic counterpoise of suffering and doing was a literary commonplace, with suicide sometimes seeming the active option. So Hamlet ponders whether it is nobler "to suffer/ The slings and arrows of outrageous

To do aught good never will be our task,
160 But ever to do ill our sole delight,
As being the contrary to his high will
Whom we resist. If then his providence
Out of our evil seek to bring forth good,
Our labor must be to pervert that end,
165 And out of good still to find means of evil;
Which ofttimes may succeed, so as perhaps
Shall grieve him, if I fail not, and disturb
His inmost counsels from their destined aim.
But see the angry victor hath recalled
170 His ministers of vengeance and pursuit
Back to the gates of Heav'n: the sulfurous hail
Shot after us in storm, o'erblown hath laid
The fiery surge, that from the precipice
Of Heav'n received us falling, and the thunder,
175 Winged with red lightning and impetuous rage,
Perhaps hath spent his shafts, and ceases now
To bellow through the vast and boundless deep.
Let us not slip th' occasion, whether scorn,
Or satiate fury yield it from our foe.
180 Seest thou yon dreary plain, forlorn and wild,
The seat of desolation, void of light,
Save what the glimmering of these livid flames
Casts pale and dreadful? Thither let us tend
From off the tossing of these fiery waves,
185 There rest, if any rest can harbor there,
And reassembling our afflicted powers,
Consult how we may henceforth most offend
Our enemy, our own loss how repair,

---

fortune / Or to take arms against a sea of
troubles" (3.1.56–58). The antithesis is reg-
ularly and variously invoked in the first
two books (see, e.g., 2.199) and later ap-
proaches personification in the characters
of the aggressively suicidal Moloch and
the craven Belial.
167. **fail:** err.

172. **o'erblown hath laid:** having blown over
(or, having blown down from above) has
calmed.
178. **slip:** neglect, miss.
182. **livid:** black and blue, like a bruise; furi-
ous.
186. **afflicted:** struck down, routed.

How overcome this dire calamity,
190 What reinforcement we may gain from hope,
If not what resolution from despair."
    Thus Satan talking to his nearest mate
With head uplift above the wave, and eyes
That sparkling blazed, his other parts besides
195 Prone on the flood, extended long and large
Lay floating many a rood, in bulk as huge
As whom the fables name of monstrous size,
Titanian, or Earth-born, that warred on Jove,
Briareos or Typhon, whom the den
200 By ancient Tarsus held, or that sea beast
Leviathan, which God of all his works
Created hugest that swim th' ocean stream:
Him haply slumb'ring on the Norway foam
The pilot of some small night-foundered skiff,
205 Deeming some island, oft, as seamen tell,
With fixèd anchor in his scaly rind
Moors by his side under the lee, while night
Invests the sea, and wishèd morn delays:
So stretched out huge in length the Arch-Fiend lay
210 Chained on the burning lake, nor ever thence
Had ris'n or heaved his head, but that the will

196. **rood:** a measure of length that varies from 5.5 to 8.0 yards (5.0 to 7.3 meters); a measure of land equal to a quarter acre, or 40 square rods (0.1 hectare).

198–99. **Titanian . . . Typhon:** In Greek myth the Titans, children of Heaven (Uranus) and Earth (Gaia), were of the generation before the Olympian gods. The Giants, monstrous and huge, were also *Earth-born*. The Titans and Giants *warred* against the Olympian gods on separate occasions, but the two battles were often confused. See 50–52n. *Briareos* was a Titan with a hundred hands; *Typhon*, a hundred-headed Giant, "the Earth-born dweller of the Cilician caves," in Aeschylus's phrase (*Prom.* 353–54; cp. Homer, *Il.* 2.783, Pindar, *Pyth.* 1.15).

200. **Tarsus:** the capital of ancient Cilicia.

201. **Leviathan:** gigantic sea beast, symbolic of God's creative power (Job 41), but in Isa. 27.1 a target of divine judgment, identified as Satan by commentators. Cp. 7.412–16.

203–8. Tales of enormous sea creatures and of mariners who mistook them for islands were common, as were moral applications of such stories.

204. **night-foundered:** sunk in night.

207. **lee:** the side away from the wind and thus sheltered from it.

208. **Invests:** cloaks.

210–15. **Chained . . . damnation:** Cp. lines 239–41. Some readers regard this providential logic with disapproval. See Tennyson's response, as recorded by his son

And high permission of all-ruling Heaven
Left him at large to his own dark designs,
That with reiterated crimes he might
215 Heap on himself damnation, while he sought
Evil to others, and enraged might see
How all his malice served but to bring forth
Infinite goodness, grace and mercy shown
On man by him seduced, but on himself
220 Treble confusion, wrath and vengeance poured.
Forthwith upright he rears from off the pool
His mighty stature; on each hand the flames
Driv'n backward slope their pointing spires, and rolled
In billows, leave i' th' midst a horrid vale.
225 Then with expanded wings he steers his flight
Aloft, incumbent on the dusky air
That felt unusual weight, till on dry land
He lights, if it were land that ever burned
With solid, as the lake with liquid fire,
230 And such appeared in hue, as when the force
Of subterranean wind transports a hill
Torn from Pelorus, or the shattered side
Of thund'ring Etna, whose combustible
And fueled entrails thence conceiving fire,
235 Sublimed with mineral fury, aid the winds,

Hallam: "I hope most of us have a higher idea in these modern times of the Almighty than this" (881).

224. **horrid**: bristling, spiky (as *pointing spires* suggests).

226. **incumbent**: pressing with his weight (cp. *recumbent*); cp. Spenser's description of the dragon's flight, *FQ* 1.11.18.

230. **hue**: not simply color but also form or aspect. Cp. Shakespeare, *Sonnets* (20.7).

230–35. **as . . . winds**: Milton's account of Etna erupting echoes Vergil in diction (*thund'ring, entrails*), but unlike Vergil, he describes a geological process rather than trace the eruption to a pent-up giant (*Aen.* 3.571–77). The seismic violence attributed to wind trapped underground is similarly described by Ovid (*Met.* 15.296–306) and Lucretius (*On the Nature of Things* 6.535–607). Cp. 6.195–98; *SA* 1647–48.

232. **Pelorus**: Cape Faro, promontory of northeastern Sicily, near Etna.

234. **fueled . . . fire**: combustible interior (*entrails*) igniting from the force of the wind and spreading.

235. Vaporized (*sublimed*) by the intense heat of burning rock, the fuel-laden interior becomes hot mineral gas that augments the wind expelled from the *shattered side* of the mountain.

And leave a singèd bottom all involved
With stench and smoke: such resting found the sole
Of unblest feet. Him followed his next mate,
Both glorying to have scaped the Stygian flood
240 As gods, and by their own recovered strength,
Not by the sufferance of supernal power.
 "Is this the region, this the soil, the clime,"
Said then the lost Archangel, "this the seat
That we must change for Heav'n, this mournful gloom
245 For that celestial light? Be it so, since he
Who now is sov'reign can dispose and bid
What shall be right: farthest from him is best
Whom reason hath equaled, force hath made supreme
Above his equals. Farewell happy fields
250 Where joy for ever dwells: hail horrors, hail
Infernal world, and thou profoundest Hell
Receive thy new possessor: one who brings
A mind not to be changed by place or time.
The mind is its own place, and in itself
255 Can make a Heav'n of Hell, a Hell of Heav'n.
What matter where, if I be still the same,
And what I should be, all but less than he
Whom thunder hath made greater? Here at least
We shall be free; th' Almighty hath not built

239. **Stygian flood:** body of water like the river Styx; the *fiery gulf* (52).

240–41. Satan and Beëlzebub contradict the narrator's explanation (ll. 210–15). Cp. Homer's Aias, who, having been saved from the sea by Poseidon, "declared that it was in spite of the gods that he had escaped the great gulf" (*Od.* 4.504). Poseidon immediately kills him.

244. **change:** exchange.

252. **possessor:** one who occupies without ownership (a legal term).

253. Cp. Horace, "the sky not the mind changes in one who crosses the sea" (*Epist.* 1.11.27). Young Milton adopted this as his motto (Hanford 98).

254–56. The chiasmus concluding line 255 epitomizes Satan's claim for the mind's constitutive power. Cp. *Hamlet:* "There is nothing either good or bad, but thinking makes it so" (2.2.249–50). That Satan's condition is a function of his own unchanging psyche is later borne out, ironically and to his dismay; see 4.75, 9.118–23.

257. **all but less than:** This puzzling phrase is usually glossed as a combination of "only less than" and "all but equal to." Satan is not conceding inequality, however, but asserting parity. He is anything but less than God, who triumphed because of superior armament—"his only dreaded bolt" (6.491).

260 Here for his envy, will not drive us hence:
     Here we may reign secure, and in my choice
     To reign is worth ambition though in Hell:
     Better to reign in Hell, than serve in Heav'n.
     But wherefore let we then our faithful friends,
265 Th' associates and copartners of our loss
     Lie thus astonished on th' oblivious pool,
     And call them not to share with us their part
     In this unhappy mansion, or once more
     With rallied arms to try what may be yet
270 Regained in Heav'n, or what more lost in Hell?"
          So Satan spake, and him Beëlzebub
     Thus answered. "Leader of those armies bright,
     Which but th' Omnipotent none could have foiled,
     If once they hear that voice, their liveliest pledge
275 Of hope in fears and dangers, heard so oft
     In worst extremes, and on the perilous edge
     Of battle when it raged, in all assaults
     Their surest signal, they will soon resume
     New courage and revive, though now they lie
280 Groveling and prostrate on yon lake of fire,
     As we erewhile, astounded and amazed,
     No wonder, fallen such a pernicious highth."
          He scarce had ceased when the superior fiend
     Was moving toward the shore; his ponderous shield

263. Cp. Plutarch's account of Caesar riding past a sorry barbarian village, "I would rather be first here than second at Rome" (*Lives* 469) or the sentiments of Euripides' Eteocles, "When I can rule, shall I be this man's slave?" (*Phoe.* 520). Satan's specific preference has plentiful precedent, typically to the contrary: "I should choose . . . to serve as the hireling . . . of some portionless man . . . rather than to be lord over all the dead" (*Od.* 11.489–91); "I had rather be a doorkeeper in the house of my God, than to dwell in the tents of wickedness" (Ps. 84.10). See Abdiel's similar declaration, 6.183–84.

265. **copartners:** equal participants (coheirs) in an inheritance.
266. **astonished:** shocked, thunderstruck; **oblivious:** producing oblivion; cp. 2.74.
268. **mansion:** abode; cp. John 14.2: "In my father's house are many mansions."
276. **edge:** critical moment; battle line (as at 6.108). Shakespeare's Henry IV calls it "the edge of war" (*1H4* 1.1.17).
281. **erewhile:** some time ago; **amazed:** stunned; a stronger term in Milton's era than in ours.
284. **Was moving:** began to move; a classical use of the imperfect tense.

285 Ethereal temper, massy, large and round,
    Behind him cast; the broad circumference
    Hung on his shoulders like the moon, whose orb
    Through optic glass the Tuscan artist views
    At evening from the top of Fesole,
290 Or in Valdarno, to descry new lands,
    Rivers or mountains in her spotty globe.
    His spear, to equal which the tallest pine
    Hewn on Norwegian hills, to be the mast
    Of some great ammiral, were but a wand,
295 He walked with to support uneasy steps
    Over the burning marl, not like those steps
    On Heaven's azure, and the torrid clime
    Smote on him sore besides, vaulted with fire;
    Nathless he so endured, till on the beach
300 Of that inflamèd sea, he stood and called
    His legions, angel forms, who lay entranced
    Thick as autumnal leaves that strow the brooks
    In Vallombrosa, where th' Etrurian shades

288–91. **Tuscan . . . globe:** Galileo is *the Tuscan artist*, the only contemporary to whom Milton in *PL* overtly alludes or names (5.262). *Artist* here signifies one skilled in a science. In *Areopagitica*, Milton claims that he visited Galileo while touring Tuscany (*MLM* 950). Galileo was by 1638 already blind or nearly so, making it unlikely that Milton witnessed him using his telescope (*optic glass*) to view the moon. Yet the poet was obviously fascinated by the new technology and the vistas it opened to imagination (Nicolson). *Fesole* overlooks the Arno river valley (*Valdarno*) and the city of Florence—a landscape and a society that Milton idolized. Galileo describes the moon's surface as mountainous in *Sidereal Messenger*.

292–94. Homer's Polyphemos, the Cyclops, wields "a staff . . . as large as is the mast of a black ship of twenty oars" (*Od.* 9.322). After he is blinded, "a lopped pine guides and steadies his steps" (Vergil, *Aen.* 3.659). Milton extends Homer's comparison into a ratio that renders a great ship's mast inadequate to indicate the size of Satan's spear.

294. **ammiral:** obsolete spelling of *admiral;* a vessel carrying an admiral, flagship.

296. **marl:** rich, crumbly soil.

298. **vaulted:** The heavens are commonly described as an arched structure, or vault, like the ceiling of a cathedral. In Hell, even the sky is on fire.

299. **Nathless:** nonetheless.

302. **autumnal leaves:** Comparison of the dead to fallen leaves is commonplace; cp. Homer, *Il.* 6.146; Vergil, *Aen.* 6.309–10; Dante, *Inf.* 3.112–15. Milton's description is distinctly echoed in Dryden's 1697 translation of Vergil: "thick as the leaves in autumn strow the woods" (*Aen.* 6.428).

303. Milton likely visited the heavily wooded valley of *Vallombrosa* in the fall of 1638. The Italian place name literally means

High overarched embow'r; or scattered sedge
305 Afloat, when with fierce winds Orion armed
Hath vexed the Red Sea coast, whose waves o'erthrew
Busiris and his Memphian chivalry,
While with perfidious hatred they pursued
The sojourners of Goshen, who beheld
310 From the safe shore their floating carcasses
And broken chariot wheels. So thick bestrown
Abject and lost lay these, covering the flood,
Under amazement of their hideous change.
He called so loud, that all the hollow deep
315 Of Hell resounded. "Princes, potentates,
Warriors, the flow'r of Heav'n, once yours, now lost,
If such astonishment as this can seize
Eternal spirits; or have ye chos'n this place
After the toil of battle to repose
320 Your wearied virtue, for the ease you find
To slumber here, as in the vales of Heav'n?
Or in this abject posture have ye sworn
To adore the conqueror, who now beholds
Cherub and Seraph rolling in the flood
325 With scattered arms and ensigns, till anon
His swift pursuers from Heav'n gates discern
Th' advantage, and descending tread us down

"shady valley." Note its somber aural combination with *autumnal, strow, brooks,* and *embow'r.* Etruria: classical name for the Tuscan region. *Shades* is a metonymy for trees as well as a name for spirits of the dead.

304. sedge: botanical transition from the autumnal leaves of Vallombrosa to the Red Sea of Exodus. The Hebrew name for the Red Sea means "Sea of Sedge."

305. Orion armed: constellation of a hunter with sword and club. Orion rising was associated with stormy weather.

307. Busiris: mythical Egyptian king often identified as an oppressor of the Hebrews but here as the scriptural Pharaoh whose

army is engulfed after it pursues the Hebrews into the parted Red Sea (Exod. 14). Memphian chivalry: Memphis was the ancient capital of Egypt; *chivalry* refers to armed forces (cp. *PR* 3.344).

309. sojourners of Goshen: Hebrews fleeing Egypt, the land of Goshen (Gen. 47.27).

320. virtue: strength, valor.

324. Seraph: singular of *seraphim* (on the model of *cherub/cherubim*).

325. anon: straightaway, instantly (not "in a little while").

327. tread us down: trample us in triumph; cp. 2.79.

Thus drooping, or with linkèd thunderbolts
Transfix us to the bottom of this gulf?

330 Awake, arise, or be for ever fall'n."
    They heard, and were abashed, and up they sprung
Upon the wing, as when men wont to watch
On duty, sleeping found by whom they dread,
Rouse and bestir themselves ere well awake.

335 Nor did they not perceive the evil plight
In which they were, or the fierce pains not feel;
Yet to their general's voice they soon obeyed
Innumerable. As when the potent rod
Of Amram's son in Egypt's evil day

340 Waved round the coast, up called a pitchy cloud
Of locusts, warping on the eastern wind,
That o'er the realm of impious Pharaoh hung
Like night, and darkened all the land of Nile:
So numberless were those bad angels seen

345 Hovering on wing under the cope of Hell
'Twixt upper, nether, and surrounding fires;
Till, as a signal giv'n, th' uplifted spear
Of their great sultan waving to direct
Their course, in even balance down they light

350 On the firm brimstone, and fill all the plain;
A multitude, like which the populous north
Poured never from her frozen loins, to pass
Rhene or the Danaw, when her barbarous sons
Came like a deluge on the south, and spread

355 Beneath Gibraltar to the Libyan sands.
Forthwith from every squadron and each band

---

337. The construction *obey to* is unusual but not unprecedented; see Shakespeare's *Phoenix:* "to whose sound chaste wings obey" (4); cp. Rom. 6.16.

339. **Amram's son:** Moses, who with his rod calls a black (*pitchy*) cloud of locusts to afflict Egypt (Exod. 10.12–15; cp. 12.185–86).

341. **warping:** floating and swarming.

345. **cope:** covering, vault, like that of the sky; cp. l. 298, 4.992.

348. **sultan:** ruler, despot, or tyrant.

351–55. Alludes to barbarian hoards (Goths, Huns, Vandals) who from the third to fifth centuries poured into the southern Roman Empire. The Vandals crossed from Spain (*Beneath Gibraltar*) into Northern Africa (*Libyan sands*).

353. **Rhene . . . Danaw:** Rhine, Danube.

The heads and leaders thither haste where stood
Their great commander; godlike shapes and forms
Excelling human, princely dignities,
360 And Powers that erst in Heaven sat on thrones;
Though of their names in Heav'nly records now
Be no memorial, blotted out and razed
By their rebellion, from the Books of Life.
Nor had they yet among the sons of Eve
365 Got them new names, till wand'ring o'er the Earth,
Through God's high sufferance for the trial of man,
By falsities and lies the greatest part
Of mankind they corrupted to forsake
God their Creator, and th' invisible
370 Glory of him that made them to transform
Oft to the image of a brute, adorned
With gay religions full of pomp and gold,
And devils to adore for deities:
Then were they known to men by various names,
375 And various idols through the heathen world.
Say, Muse, their names then known, who first, who last,
Roused from the slumber on that fiery couch,
At their great emperor's call, as next in worth
Came singly where he stood on the bare strand,
380 While the promiscuous crowd stood yet aloof?
The chief were those who from the pit of Hell
Roaming to seek their prey on earth, durst fix
Their seats long after next the seat of God,
Their altars by his altar, gods adored

---

363. **Books:** On God's condemnation as erasure (*razed*) from the roll of eternal life, see Exod. 32.32–33 and Rev. 22.5. The fallen angels' previous identities no longer exist; cp. 84n.

372. **gay:** gaudy, wanton; cp. 4.942.

373. That pagan gods were fallen angels was a Christian commonplace rooted in classical and scriptural thought, as Verity details (672–74). Cp. *Nat Ode* 173–228, *PR* 2.121–26.

376. The catalog is conventional, as is the request of the Muse to supply it; cp. Homer, *Il.* 5.703; Vergil, *Aen.* 9.664. Invocation of the Muse, a pagan deity, may seem jarring here, though in the invocations to Books 1 and 7 Milton identifies his Muse with inspiration from God.

380. **promiscuous:** random, diverse.

385   Among the nations round, and durst abide
       Jehovah thund'ring out of Sion, throned
       Between the Cherubim; yea, often placed
       Within his sanctuary itself their shrines,
       Abominations; and with cursèd things
390   His holy rites, and solemn feasts profaned,
       And with their darkness durst affront his light.
       First Moloch, horrid king besmeared with blood
       Of human sacrifice, and parents' tears,
       Though for the noise of drums and timbrels loud
395   Their children's cries unheard, that passed through fire
       To his grim idol. Him the Ammonite
       Worshipped in Rabba and her wat'ry plain,
       In Argob and in Basan, to the stream
       Of utmost Arnon. Nor content with such
400   Audacious neighborhood, the wisest heart
       Of Solomon he led by fraud to build
       His temple right against the temple of God
       On that opprobrious hill, and made his grove
       The pleasant valley of Hinnom, Tophet thence

386–87. Sion . . . Cherubim: Zion is the site of Solomon's Temple, which houses the Ark of the Covenant. The throne of God's invisible presence stands on top of the Ark between images of cherubim; see 10n.

389. Abominations: scripturally, causes of pollution, especially idols of false gods; objects that excite disgust and hatred in true believers.

392–96. Moloch . . . idol: *Moloch,* whose name is Hebrew for "king," was an Ammonite god represented by an idol "of brass, having the head of a calf . . . with arms extended to receive the miserable sacrifice [an infant], seared to death with his burning embracements. For the idol was hollow within, filled with fire. And lest their lamentable shrieks should sad the hearts of their parents, the priests of Moloch did deaf their ears with the continual clang of trumpets and timbrels"

(Sandys 1637, 186). Victims were said to be *passed through fire* to Moloch (2 Kings 23.10).

397–99. Rabba: Ammonite capital, the "city of waters" (2 Sam. 12.27); *Argob* was Ammonite territory in *Basan* (on the Eastern side of the Jordan). *Arnon* is the name of a river erroneously supposed to flow near Rabba.

400–405. Moloch dares induce worship among the Ammonites, whose realm bordered on Israel. Even more impudently, he leads Solomon to build him a temple opposite God's temple.

404. Hinnom, Tophet thence: valley sacred to Moloch, south of Jerusalem. The Greek for *Gehenna* ("valley of Hinnom") is in the *AV* translated as Hell (e.g., Matt. 23.33). *Hinnom* was thought to derive from the Hebrew for "outcry," referring to the screams of sacrificial babies; *Tophet* from the Hebrew for "timbrel," the instrument

405 And black Gehenna called, the type of Hell.
Next Chemos, th' obscene dread of Moab's sons,
From Aroar to Nebo, and the wild
Of southmost Abarim; in Heseboñ
And Horonaim, Seon's realm, beyond
410 The flow'ry dale of Sibma clad with vines,
And Eleale to th' Asphaltic Pool.
Peor his other name, when he enticed
Israel in Sittim on their march from Nile
To do him wanton rites, which cost them woe.
415 Yet thence his lustful orgies he enlarged
Even to that hill of scandal, by the grove
Of Moloch homicide, lust hard by hate;
Till good Josiah drove them thence to Hell.
With these came they, who from the bord'ring flood
420 Of old Euphrates to the brook that parts
Egypt from Syrian ground, had general names
Of Baälim and Ashtaroth, those male,
These feminine. For spirits when they please
Can either sex assume, or both; so soft
425 And uncompounded is their essence pure,
Nor tied or manacled with joint or limb,
Nor founded on the brittle strength of bones,

---

used to drown the screams (Selden 314). Post-exile Jews made the valley a dump where corpses of animals and criminals were burned. It thence symbolized the place of eternal punishment.

406–17. **Chemos:** god of the Moabites (*Moab's sons*); a Priapus-like idol also called Baal-Peör (412). See Selden 46–65. The scriptural place names in lines 407–11 demarcate Moabite territory on the east shore of the Dead Sea (*Asphaltic Pool*). During the Exodus, wandering Hebrews participated in his *wanton rites* and were punished with a plague (*woe*); see Num. 25, which Milton in *CMS* cites as the basis for a future work. Later, Solomon built a temple to Chemos on the mount (*hill of scandal*) where Moloch's temple also

stood (1 Kings 11.7; see 400–405n). The fertility cult of Chemos practiced ritual sex; Moloch's worshipers burned babies: hence, *lust hard by hate.*

418. **Josiah:** King of Judah admired by Reformers because he destroyed idols and defiled their sites of worship; see 2 Kings 23.10–14.

419–21. **from . . . ground:** I.e., the land of Israel or Canaan, distinguished by rivers that mark its northeastern and southwestern boundaries (Gen. 2.14).

422. **Baälim and Ashtaroth:** collective titles for Canaanite fertility gods and goddesses (sing. Baal, Ashtoreth—as at l. 438), often worshiped by ancient Israelites.

425. **uncompounded:** not differentiated into anatomical parts or systems.

Like cumbrous flesh; but in what shape they choose
Dilated or condensed, bright or obscure,
430 Can execute their airy purposes,
And works of love or enmity fulfill.
For those the race of Israel oft forsook
Their Living Strength, and unfrequented left
His righteous altar, bowing lowly down
435 To bestial gods; for which their heads as low
Bowed down in battle, sunk before the spear
Of despicable foes. With these in troop
Came Astoreth, whom the Phoenicians called
Astarte, Queen of Heav'n, with crescent horns;
440 To whose bright image nightly by the moon
Sidonian virgins paid their vows and songs,
In Sion also not unsung, where stood
Her temple on th' offensive mountain, built
By that uxorious king, whose heart though large,
445 Beguiled by fair idolatresses, fell
To idols foul. Thammuz came next behind,
Whose annual wound in Lebanon allured
The Syrian damsels to lament his fate
In amorous ditties all a summer's day,
450 While smooth Adonis from his native rock
Ran purple to the sea, supposed with blood
Of Thammuz yearly wounded: the love-tale
Infected Sion's daughters with like heat,
Whose wanton passions in the sacred porch

433. **Living Strength:** epithet for God (cp. 1 Sam. 15.29).

438–41. Phoenician version of the Assyrian Istar and the Greek Aphrodite, called *Astarte.* Her image had the body of a woman and the head of a horned bull, representing the crescent moon; cp. *Nat Ode* 200 and *Masque* 1002. Jeremiah (7.18) titles her the *Queen of Heaven. Sidon* was a chief Phoenician seaport. See Selden 141–71.

444–46. **uxorious . . . foul:** The king is Solomon, who to please foreign wives (*fair idolatresses*) erects temples on the Mount of Olives (*th' offensive mountain*) to Moloch, Chemos, and Ashtoreth (2 Kings 11.1–8). Cp. lines 403, 416. Solomon's *large heart* refers to his intellectual capacity (1 Kings 3.9–12). His *uxorious* idolatry appears in *CMS* among subjects for future works.

446–52. **Thammuz . . . wounded:** Thammuz is beloved of Astarte, who precedes him in the catalog. He is the Phoenician (Syrian) original of Adonis, which is also the

455   Ezekiel saw, when by the vision led
      His eye surveyed the dark idolatries
      Of alienated Judah. Next came one
      Who mourned in earnest, when the captive ark
      Maimed his brute image, head and hands lopped off
460   In his own temple, on the grunsel edge,
      Where he fell flat, and shamed his worshippers:
      Dagon his name, sea monster, upward man
      And downward fish: yet had his temple high
      Reared in Azotus, dreaded through the coast
465   Of Palestine, in Gath and Ascalon
      And Accaron and Gaza's frontier bounds.
      Him followed Rimmon, whose delightful seat
      Was fair Damascus, on the fertile banks
      Of Abbana and Pharphar, lucid streams.
470   He also against the house of God was bold:
      A leper once he lost and gained a king,
      Ahaz his sottish conqueror, whom he drew
      God's altar to disparage and displace
      For one of Syrian mode, whereon to burn
475   His odious off'rings, and adore the gods

---

name of a river in Lebanon that runs red after the summer solstice, purportedly with blood from Thammuz's mortal wound. The river's source lies in a rocky coastal mountain range; hence its *native rock*. Adonis is a sun god whose annual death and revival signifies the changing of the seasons. See Sandys 1637, 20; Selden 239–49. Milton alludes to the familiar myth often, e.g., *Nat Ode* 204, *Manso* 11, and *Eikon*, where he scorns hypocritical mourning for the beheaded Charles (Yale 3:365).

455. Ezekiel: Like other prophets, he condemned idolatrous observances in Israel, among them "women weeping for Thammuz" (Ezek. 8.14).

457–66. Next . . . bounds: During the era of Judges, the Philistines captured the Ark of the Covenant (see 386–87n) and set it in the temple of their god, *Dagon*. His idol then fell before the Ark onto the temple threshold (*grunsel*) and broke (1 Sam. 5). Lines 464–66 name the chief cities of the Philistines. *Dag* is Hebrew for "fish." See Selden 173–89.

467–69. Rimmon: Syrian deity worshiped in Damascus, which lies between the rivers *Abbana* and *Pharphar.*

471. A leper once he lost: Elisha told the Syrian leper Naaman to cleanse himself in the Jordan. Naaman proclaimed the superiority of the rivers of Damascus but ultimately humbled himself, washed in the Jordan, and was cured (2 Kings 5.8–19).

471–76. gained . . . vanquished: King Ahaz of Judah defeated the Syrians but, returning to Jerusalem, erected an altar to Rimmon and worshiped him (2 Kings 16.10–16).

472. sottish: stupid.

Whom he had vanquished. After these appeared
A crew who under names of old renown,
Osiris, Isis, Orus and their train
With monstrous shapes and sorceries abused
480 Fanatic Egypt and her priests, to seek
Their wand'ring gods disguised in brutish forms
Rather than human. Nor did Israel scape
Th' infection when their borrowed gold composed
The calf in Oreb: and the rebel king
485 Doubled that sin in Bethel and in Dan,
Lik'ning his Maker to the grazèd ox,
Jehovah, who in one night when he passed
From Egypt marching, equaled with one stroke
Both her first born and all her bleating gods.
490 Belial came last, than whom a spirit more lewd
Fell not from Heaven, or more gross to love
Vice for itself: to him no temple stood
Or altar smoked; yet who more oft than he
In temples and at altars, when the priest

478–82. Osiris ... human: Ovid reports that when Typhon attacked Olympus (cp. 198–200n), some gods fled and wandered Egypt disguised as beasts (*Met.* 5.319–31). *Isis* and *Osiris* are Egyptian gods represented as having the heads of a cow and a bull. Plutarch wrote influentially about them, and their myth had a hold on Milton's imagination; see *Areop,* p. 955. Falcon-headed *Orus* was their son.

484–89. While Moses received the law on Mount Horeb (see 8n), the Hebrews pressured Aaron to forge a calf to worship (Exod. 12.35–36). It was made of Egyptian gold, *borrowed* by the Hebrews just before the Exodus (Deut. 9.8–21; Exod. 31.18, 32).

484–86. rebel . . . ox: Jeroboam, who rebelled against Solomon's son Rehoboam, *doubled* the sin at Horeb (see previous note) by repeating the former idolatry and by making two golden calves instead of one (2 Kings 12.12–23). "Thus they changed their glory into the similitude of an ox that eateth grass" (Ps. 106.20).

487–89. Refers to the Hebrews' departure from Egypt, when Jehovah smites "all the first born in the land of Egypt, both man and beast" and executes judgment "against all the gods of Egypt" (Exod. 12.12).

488. equaled: Jehovah with *one stroke* ends (and so proves equal to) many lives.

490. Belial: The Hebrew for *Belial* is not a proper noun, much less the name of a god, but refers to anyone opposing established authority, civil or religious. In English translations it became "worthless fellow" or "vile scoundrel." A Rabbinical etymology derives it from a verb meaning "throws off the yoke"; the Septuagint accordingly translates *Belial* with terms that signify lawlessness (*anomia* or *paranomos*). Milton with characteristic bite links Belial to organized religion and the court (cp. *PR* 2.182–83).

495   Turns atheist, as did Eli's sons, who filled
        With lust and violence the house of God.
        In courts and palaces he also reigns
        And in luxurious cities, where the noise
        Of riot ascends above their loftiest tow'rs,
500   And injury and outrage: and when night
        Darkens the streets, then wander forth the sons
        Of Belial, flown with insolence and wine.
        Witness the streets of Sodom, and that night
        In Gibeah, when the hospitable door
505   Exposed a matron to avoid worse rape.
        These were the prime in order and in might;
        The rest were long to tell, though far renowned,
        Th' Ionian gods, of Javan's issue held
        Gods, yet confessed later than Heav'n and Earth
510   Their boasted parents; Titan Heav'n's first born
        With his enormous brood, and birthright seized
        By younger Saturn, he from mightier Jove
        His own and Rhea's son like measure found;
        So Jove usurping reigned: these first in Crete
515   And Ida known, thence on the snowy top

---

495. **Eli's sons:** For the lechery and sacrilege of Eli's sons, see 1 Sam. 2.12–24.

502. **flown:** filled to excess (obsolete past participle of *flow*).

503–4. **Sodom . . . Gibeah:** biblical cities in which gangs of men clamor at hosts' doors to rape male guests and are offered women instead—Lot's daughters in *Sodom* and the visiting Levite's concubine in *Gibeah* (Gen. 19, Judg. 19). 1667 reads "when hospitable doors / Yielded their matrons to prevent worse rape." 1674 concentrates on Gibeah, where the concubine, unlike Lot's daughters, actually is assaulted and in the morning deposited lifeless at the door where she had been *exposed*.

505. **matron:** Her Hebrew title is translated by "concubine," but Milton's diction is not prudish. In polygamous Hebrew culture, concubines were secondary wives, owed the same respect from other men as the primary wife.

508. **Javan's issue:** Noah's grandson Javan was deemed (*held*) the ancestor of the Ionian Greeks; his name in the Septuagint is a version of Ionia (Gen. 10.2). Cp. *SA* 715–16.

509–14. **Gods . . . reigned:** Uranus and Gaea (*Heav'n* and *Earth*) beget the Greek gods. According to the Roman republican poet Ennius Quintus (239–170 B.C.E.), Titan's younger brother, Saturn, took Titan's *birthright* (cited by Lactantius, *Divine Institutes* 1.14). *Jove*, Saturn's son by *Rhea*, usurped his father's throne.

515. **Ida:** mountain in *Crete* where Jove was born (cp. *Il Pens* 29).

Of cold Olympus ruled the middle air
Their highest heav'n; or on the Delphian cliff,
Or in Dodona, and through all the bounds
Of Doric land; or who with Saturn old
520 Fled over Adria to th' Hesperian fields,
And o'er the Celtic roamed the utmost isles.
All these and more came flocking; but with looks
Downcast and damp, yet such wherein appeared
Obscure some glimpse of joy, to have found their chief
525 Not in despair, to have found themselves not lost
In loss itself; which on his count'nance cast
Like doubtful hue: but he his wonted pride
Soon recollecting, with high words, that bore
Semblance of worth, not substance, gently raised
530 Their fainting courage, and dispelled their fears.
Then straight commands that at the warlike sound
Of trumpets loud and clarions be upreared
His mighty standard; that proud honor claimed
Azazel as his right, a cherub tall:
535 Who forthwith from the glittering staff unfurled
Th' imperial ensign, which full high advanced
Shone like a meteor streaming to the wind
With gems and golden luster rich emblazed,
Seraphic arms and trophies: all the while

516. **Olympus:** snowcapped peak where the Greeks supposed the gods resided; **middle air:** cooler region of the atmosphere, extending to the mountaintops. Milton makes it the postlapsarian possession of Satan and his followers (*PR* 1.44–46).

517. **Delphian cliff:** on the southern slope of Mount Parnassus, the seat of the oracle of Apollo.

518. **Dodona:** town in Epirus, where Zeus had an oracle.

519. **Doric land:** Greece.

520–21. Saturn and his followers flee west from Greece, over the Adriatic Sea to Italy (*Hesperian fields*), to France (*the Celtic*), and finally to northwestern is-

lands, including Britain (*the utmost isles*); cp. *Masque* 59–61.

523. **damp:** dejected; cp. 11.293.

528. **recollecting:** remembering, reassembling; cp. 9.471.

532. **clarions:** "small shrill treble trumpet" (Hume).

534. **Azazel:** variously construed, but the Hebrew name suggests rugged strength. Cabbalistic lore made him one of Satan's standard-bearers, as Milton could have known from various sources (West 155ff).

537. **meteor:** comet.

538–39. **emblazed . . . trophies:** lit up or decorated with heraldic devices (*arms*) and memorials (*trophies*). Cp. 5.592–93.

540 Sonorous metal blowing martial sounds:
At which the universal host upsent
A shout that tore Hell's concave, and beyond
Frighted the reign of Chaos and old Night.
All in a moment through the gloom were seen
545 Ten thousand banners rise into the air
With orient colors waving: with them rose
A forest huge of spears: and thronging helms
Appeared, and serried shields in thick array
Of depth immeasurable: anon they move
550 In perfect phalanx to the Dorian mood
Of flutes and soft recorders; such as raised
To highth of noblest temper heroes old
Arming to battle, and instead of rage
Deliberate valor breathed, firm and unmoved
555 With dread of death to flight or foul retreat,
Nor wanting power to mitigate and swage
With solemn touches, troubled thoughts, and chase
Anguish and doubt and fear and sorrow and pain
From mortal or immortal minds. Thus they
560 Breathing united force with fixèd thought
Moved on in silence to soft pipes that charmed
Their painful steps o'er the burnt soil; and now
Advanced in view they stand, a horrid front
Of dreadful length and dazzling arms, in guise
565 Of warriors old with ordered spear and shield,

540. **Sonorous metal:** synecdoche referring to the trumpets and clarions of line 532.
542. **tore Hell's concave:** carried through Hell's vaulted roof; see 8.242–44.
543. **reign:** realm; for *Chaos* and *Night* see 2.894–909, 959–1009. Their reaction is prophetic; Satan's activity will encroach on their realm; cp. 10.415–18.
546. **orient:** lustrous like a pearl; rising like the sun in the east.
548. **serried:** in close order.
550. **Dorian:** Plato would allow "manly" Dorian music in his ideal state because it

inspires, in Aristotle's words, "a moderate and settled temper" (*Rep.* 3.398–99; *Pol.* 8.5). Cp. *Areop* in *MLM* 943; *Of Ed* in *MLM* 979. Thucydides' account (5.70) of the Spartans in unbroken *phalanx*, calmly marching into battle to the sound of flutes, lies behind lines 549–62.
556. **swage:** assuage.
563. **horrid:** bristling (with spears).
565. **warriors old:** from the reader's perspective only; humanity has not yet been created.

Awaiting what command their mighty chief
Had to impose: he through the armèd files
Darts his experienced eye, and soon traverse
The whole battalion views, their order due,
570 Their visages and stature as of gods,
Their number last he sums. And now his heart
Distends with pride, and hard'ning in his strength
Glories: for never since created man,
Met such embodied force, as named with these
575 Could merit more than that small infantry
Warred on by cranes: though all the giant brood
Of Phlegra with th' heroic race were joined
That fought at Thebes and Ilium, on each side
Mixed with auxiliar gods; and what resounds
580 In fable or romance of Uther's son
Begirt with British and Armoric knights;
And all who since, baptized or infidel,
Jousted in Aspramont or Montalban,

567–68. **files . . . traverse:** He looks down and across the lines of warriors.

571. **Their number last he sums:** David orders a census to count the warriors he might deploy, as Satan does here; God punishes Israel for David's presumption and implicit lack of faith (2 Sam. 24).

573. **since created man:** since man was created.

575. **small infantry:** pygmies, mentioned by Homer (*Il.* 3.3–6). Addison was "afraid" that Milton intended the pun on *infant* (*Spectator* 297, Feb. 9, 1712).

577. **Phlegra:** In Greek myth, the Olympian gods defeated the giants on their breeding ground at Phlegra (Pallene), the westernmost prong of the Chalcidicean peninsula in the Aegean. The place name derives from the Greek for fire (cp. *Phlegethon* 2.581–82), so called because of the volcanic soil. Some later writers claimed that the battle culminated in Italy, where Jupiter blasts the giants on

similar turf—the Phlegraean plains near Vesuvius—and then imprisons them beneath regional volcanoes (*Diodorus* 4.21.5).

578. Thebes and Troy (*Ilium*) are main sites of Greek epic and tragedy.

579. **auxiliar:** In classical epic, the gods aid their mortal kin and other favorites.

580–81. King Arthur (*Uther's son*) and his knights, some from Brittany (*Armoric*). For Milton's fascination with Arthur, see *Damon* 166–68.

583–84. **Aspramont . . . Trebisond:** Fighting against the Saracens, Roland wins honor at the castle of *Aspramont*, an episode often mentioned in Italian epic (see Ariosto, *OF* 17.14). *Montalban* is the site of the castle of Rinaldo, the hero to whom Tasso assigns victory in the battle for Jerusalem (*GL*). *Damasco, Marocco,* and *Trebisond* are also sites associated with great warriors and battles between Christian and Saracen.

Damasco, or Marocco, or Trebisond,
585 Or whom Biserta sent from Afric shore
When Charlemagne with all his peerage fell
By Fontarabia. Thus far these beyond
Compare of mortal prowess, yet observed
Their dread commander: he above the rest
590 In shape and gesture proudly eminent
Stood like a tow'r; his form had yet not lost
All her original brightness, nor appeared
Less than Archangel ruined, and th' excess
Of glory obscured: as when the sun new ris'n
595 Looks through the horizontal misty air
Shorn of his beams, or from behind the moon
In dim eclipse disastrous twilight sheds
On half the nations, and with fear of change
Perplexes monarchs. Darkened so, yet shone
600 Above them all th' Archangel: but his face
Deep scars of thunder had intrenched, and care
Sat on his faded cheek, but under brows
Of dauntless courage, and considerate pride
Waiting revenge: cruel his eye, but cast
605 Signs of remorse and passion to behold
The fellows of his crime, the followers rather

---

585. **Biserta:** Tunisian seaport from which Saracens embarked to invade Spain.

586–87. **Charlemagne . . . Fontarabia:** According to the Spanish Jesuit historian and noted advocate of tyrannicide Juan de Mariana (1536–1624), *Charlemagne* fell—that is, suffered ruinous defeat—at *Fontarabia* (1699). The historical incident is the basis for the epic tale of the death of Roland and his twelve paladins at nearby Roncesvalles.

588. **observed:** heeded, reverenced. Though it exceeds the greatest historical and legendary human armies combined, Satan's army acknowledges the still greater excellence of its leader.

594. **glory:** a coronalike brilliance; see 14n.

596. **Shorn:** an allusion to Samson, whose name derives from the Hebrew word for "sun."

596–99. **from . . . monarchs:** Charles II's censor objected to these lines, presumably because the king himself had been born on the day of an eclipse in 1630, a coincidence later construed "as a portent of the interregnum" (Leonard).

599. **Perplexes:** torments, a stronger term in seventeenth-century usage than now; see, e.g., *OTH* 5.2.346.

601. **intrenched:** cut into.

603. **considerate:** thoughtful, deliberate.

605. **passion:** suffering or affliction, in contrast with *cruel*, disposed to inflict suffering.

(Far other once beheld in bliss) condemned
For ever now to have their lot in pain,
Millions of spirits for his fault amerced
610　Of Heav'n, and from eternal splendors flung
For his revolt, yet faithful how they stood,
Their glory withered. As when heaven's fire
Hath scathed the forest oaks or mountain pines,
With singèd top their stately growth though bare
615　Stands on the blasted heath. He now prepared
To speak; whereat their doubled ranks they bend
From wing to wing, and half enclose him round
With all his peers: attention held them mute.
Thrice he assayed, and thrice in spite of scorn,
620　Tears such as angels weep burst forth: at last
Words interwove with sighs found out their way.
　　"O myriads of immortal spirits, O powers
Matchless, but with th' Almighty, and that strife
Was not inglorious, though th' event was dire,
625　As this place testifies, and this dire change
Hateful to utter: but what power of mind
Foreseeing or presaging, from the depth
Of knowledge past or present, could have feared,
How such united force of gods, how such
630　As stood like these, could ever know repulse?

609. **amerced:** from the French for "at the mercy of"; a law term meaning "fined at the court's discretion." Milton's unidiomatic construction suggests that he had in mind a similar Greek verb used by Homer to explain the blindness of the bard Demodokos: "Of his sight [the Muse] deprived [*ámerse*] him" (*Od.* 8.64).

615. **blasted heath:** Cp. *MAC* 1.3.77.

620. **Tears . . . forth:** According to Raphael, angels digest food and make love. Here it seems that they also have the capacity to shed tears after their fashion (cp. 5.407–39, 8.622–29, 10.23–25). It was commonly supposed that males weep because they are born of women. Milton rejects this theory (see 10.1101–2, 11.494–97) and had precedent for presenting angels capable of weeping; see, e.g., Shakespeare, *MM* 2.2.879, *OTH* 3.3.371. In context, Satan's tears suggest those of the Persian tyrant Xerxes before his invasion of Greece. Reviewing his vast army, he was overcome by consciousness of his soldiers' mortality "at the time when he was hastening them to their fate, and to the intended destruction of the greatest people in the world, to gratify his own vain glory" (Newton). Cp. 10.307–11.

624. **event:** outcome.

For who can yet believe, though after loss,
That all these puissant legions, whose exile
Hath emptied Heav'n, shall fail to reascend
Self-raised, and repossess their native seat?
635 For me be witness all the host of Heav'n,
If counsels different, or danger shunned
By me, have lost our hopes. But he who reigns
Monarch in Heav'n, till then as one secure
Sat on his throne, upheld by old repute,
640 Consent or custom, and his regal state
Put forth at full, but still his strength concealed,
Which tempted our attempt, and wrought our fall.
Henceforth his might we know, and know our own
So as not either to provoke, or dread
645 New war, provoked; our better part remains
To work in close design, by fraud or guile
What force effected not: that he no less
At length from us may find, who overcomes
By force, hath overcome but half his foe.
650 Space may produce new worlds; whereof so rife
There went a fame in Heav'n that he ere long
Intended to create, and therein plant
A generation, whom his choice regard
Should favor equal to the sons of Heav'n:

632. **puissant:** powerful.

641. **still:** invariably.

642. **tempted our attempt:** Milton's propensity for paronomasia—close repetition of similar-sounding words distinct in meaning—has long been derided as "jingling": "like marriages between persons too near of kin, to be avoided" (Hume). It is a figure distinctive of Hebrew Scripture, however, and one found in late Latin writers and Renaissance Italian poets. Milton often uses it in expressions of derision; see lines 666–67, 4.286, 5.869, 9.11, 9.648, 11.627, 12.78.

646. **close:** covert.

650. **Space may produce:** a notably active construction for a state commonly regarded as a passive locale or empty setting. By *worlds* Milton means what we would call "universes." The one that Satan proceeds to mention is our own, which "may be supposed as yet not made" (Argument; cp. 8.229–36).

651. **fame:** rumor; cp. 2.345–53, 830–35, 10.481–82.

653. **generation:** race; **choice regard:** selective estimation or judgment. *Regard* may also mean "purpose" or "intention," as in the description of Shakespeare's Henry V: "The King is full of grace, and fair regard" (1.2.22).

655 Thither, if but to pry, shall be perhaps
    Our first eruption, thither or elsewhere:
    For this infernal pit shall never hold
    Celestial spirits in bondage, nor th' abyss
    Long under darkness cover. But these thoughts
660 Full counsel must mature: peace is despaired,
    For who can think submission? War then, war
    Open or understood must be resolved."
        He spake: and to confirm his words, out flew
    Millions of flaming swords, drawn from the thighs
665 Of mighty Cherubim; the sudden blaze
    Far round illumined Hell: highly they raged
    Against the Highest, and fierce with graspèd arms
    Clashed on their sounding shields the din of war,
    Hurling defiance toward the vault of Heav'n.
670   There stood a hill not far whose grisly top
    Belched fire and rolling smoke; the rest entire
    Shone with a glossy scurf, undoubted sign
    That in his womb was hid metallic ore,
    The work of sulfur. Thither winged with speed
675 A numerous brigade hastened. As when bands
    Of pioneers with spade and pickax armed
    Forerun the royal camp, to trench a field,
    Or cast a rampart. Mammon led them on,
    Mammon, the least erected spirit that fell

---

656. **eruption:** outbreak; the diction seems suggestive of "hell's volcanoes" (Leonard), but according to the *OED* the association of *eruption* with volcanic activity is not current in England until well into the eighteenth century.

672. **scurf:** any incrustation upon the surface of a body (especially diseased or scabbed skin); here a sulfurous deposit.

673. **womb:** belly or cavity.

674. **work of sulfur:** "the offspring and production of sulfur, . . . the subterranean fire [that] concocts and boils up the crude and undigested earth into a more profitable consistence, and by its innate heat, hardens and bakes it into metals" (Hume).

676. **pioneers:** soldiers who do demolition or construction for siege or defense.

678. **Mammon:** like *Belial,* a common noun. Derived from the Arabic for "riches," it means "wealth"; cp. Matt. 6.24. By medieval times, Mammon had been personified as a Christian version of Pluto. See Spenser, *FQ* 2.7.

679. **erected:** upright in posture, lofty in character.

680　From Heav'n, for ev'n in Heav'n his looks and thoughts
　　　Were always downward bent, admiring more
　　　The riches of Heav'n's pavement, trodden gold,
　　　Than aught divine or holy else enjoyed
　　　In vision beatific: by him first
685　Men also, and by his suggestion taught,
　　　Ransacked the center, and with impious hands
　　　Rifled the bowels of their mother Earth
　　　For treasures better hid. Soon had his crew
　　　Opened into the hill a spacious wound
690　And digged out ribs of gold. Let none admire
　　　That riches grow in Hell; that soil may best
　　　Deserve the precious bane. And here let those
　　　Who boast in mortal things, and wond'ring tell
　　　Of Babel, and the works of Memphian kings,
695　Learn how their greatest monuments of fame,
　　　And strength and art are easily outdone
　　　By spirits reprobate, and in an hour
　　　What in an age they with incessant toil
　　　And hands innumerable scarce perform.
700　Nigh on the plain in many cells prepared,
　　　That underneath had veins of liquid fire
　　　Sluiced from the lake, a second multitude
　　　With wondrous art founded the massy ore,
　　　Severing each kind, and scummed the bullion dross:

---

682. **Heav'n's pavement:** see Rev. 21.21.

684. **vision beatific:** literally, the "happy-making sight" (*On Time* 18); viewing God.

686. **center:** the earth's interior.

686–88. **impious . . . hid:** a commonplace that originates in Ovid's account of a maternally abusive degeneration from the original "golden" age of justice and temperance (*Met.* 1.137–40). See Spenser, *FQ* 2.7.16, for a similar association of Mammon with such impiety. Cp. Comus's reversal of the theme, 718–36.

688–90. **Soon . . . gold:** The diction anticipates the production of Eve at 8.463ff.

690. **ribs:** veins of ore; **admire:** wonder.

694. The Tower of Babel (see 12.43–62) and the Egyptian pyramids.

700–704. The *massy ore* (gold is dense) extracted by the pioneers is melted (*founded*) in prepared *cells* heated from below by a second group of fallen angels, who use *liquid fire* conveyed from the burning lake in sluices (*Sluiced*). Smelting the metals separates (*severing*) the heavy gold from the less dense matter (*dross*), which rises to the top and is skimmed off (*scummed*), leaving pure gold in the cells. In line 703, 1674 prints *found out* instead of *founded* (1667).

705   A third as soon had formed within the ground
      A various mold, and from the boiling cells
      By strange conveyance filled each hollow nook,
      As in an organ from one blast of wind
      To many a row of pipes the soundboard breathes.
710   Anon out of the earth a fabric huge
      Rose like an exhalation, with the sound
      Of dulcet symphonies and voices sweet,
      Built like a temple, where pilasters round
      Were set, and Doric pillars overlaid
715   With golden architrave; nor did there want
      Cornice or frieze, with bossy sculptures grav'n;
      The roof was fretted gold. Not Babylon,
      Nor great Alcairo such magnificence
      Equaled in all their glories, to enshrine
720   Belus or Serapis their gods, or seat
      Their kings, when Egypt with Assyria strove

705–9. *A various mold* (hollow form or matrix) has been shaped by yet another crew, which fills it with molten gold transported from the cells *by strange conveyance.* This process is compared to an intricate musical composition taking audible form from *one blast of wind* into an organ.

710. **fabric:** fabrication.

711–12. Structural principles of music (e.g., Pythagoras' golden section) were deemed basic to architecture and other plastic arts, including, as Milton later presents it, cuisine (see *5.333–49*). Athenians played music at the dedication of temples like the Parthenon.

711. **exhalation:** vapor emitted by the earth.

713–17. **Built . . . gold:** The edifice looks like a pagan temple, with features that recall the Roman Pantheon (e.g., golden roof), though the satirical Milton presumably also has St. Peter's Basilica in mind.

713. **pilasters round:** square columns built into the wall; *round* modifies *set.*

714. **Doric:** the least ornamented style of Greek column; like the laconic music of line *550.*

715. **architrave:** the "master beam" or basis of the upper section of a classical temple; it sits on top of the columns (hence *overlaid*).

716. **Cornice or frieze:** The *frieze* is a band that sits on the architrave and is often, as in the case of the Parthenon, decorated with sculptures that stand out in relief, as if embossed (*bossy*). The *cornice* caps the frieze and is also often ornamented.

717. **fretted gold:** gold wrought with ornamental designs, as in the Pantheon.

718. **Alcairo:** Memphis, ancient capital of Egypt, near modern Cairo.

720. **Belus:** name for Baal in Babylon, where he had a celebrated temple, described by Ralegh (1621, 183); **Serapis:** Ptolemaic amalgamation of Hades and Osiris, with splendid temples in Memphis and Alexandria.

In wealth and luxury. Th' ascending pile
Stood fixed her stately highth, and straight the doors
Op'ning their brazen folds discover wide
725 Within, her ample spaces, o'er the smooth
And level pavement: from the archèd roof
Pendant by subtle magic many a row
Of starry lamps and blazing cressets fed
With naphtha and asphaltus yielded light
730 As from a sky. The hasty multitude
Admiring entered, and the work some praise
And some the architect: his hand was known
In Heav'n by many a towered structure high,
Where sceptered angels held their residence,
735 And sat as princes, whom the supreme King
Exalted to such power, and gave to rule,
Each in his hierarchy, the orders bright.
Nor was his name unheard or unadored
In ancient Greece; and in Ausonian land
740 Men called him Mulciber; and how he fell
From Heav'n, they fabled, thrown by angry Jove
Sheer o'er the crystal battlements; from morn
To noon he fell, from noon to dewy eve,
A summer's day; and with the setting sun
745 Dropped from the zenith like a falling star,
On Lemnos th' Aegean isle: thus they relate,

722–23. **ascending pile / Stood fixed:** After rising like a vapor out of the ground, the magnificent building achieved its finished state.

728. **cressets:** iron baskets suspended from the ceiling, containing flaming pitch (*asphaltus*).

729. **naphtha:** liquid pitch, supplies the lamps.

739. **Ausonian land:** Greek name for a district of Italy.

740. **Mulciber:** smelter; another name for Vulcan, Roman counterpart to the Greek Hephaestus, god of fire and crafts. Homer mentions palaces he erects on Olympus (*Il.* 1.605–8), and Hesiod says he forged Pandora (cp. 688–90n; 4.714–19n).

740–48. **Men . . . before:** Homer's Hephaestus tells how Zeus threw him from Olympus to punish him for siding with Hera (*Il.* 1.591–95). Milton closely imitates that account but then corrects it.

745. **zenith:** (1) upper region of the sky, where vaporous meteorological phenomena such as *falling stars* were thought to ignite; (2) the highest point above the

Erring; for he with this rebellious rout
Fell long before; nor aught availed him now
To have built in Heav'n high tow'rs; nor did he scape
750 By all his engines, but was headlong sent
With his industrious crew to build in Hell.
Meanwhile the wingèd heralds by command
Of sov'reign power, with awful ceremony
And trumpets' sound throughout the host proclaim
755 A solemn council forthwith to be held
At Pandaemonium, the high capital
Of Satan and his peers: their summons called
From every band and squarèd regiment
By place or choice the worthiest; they anon
760 With hundreds and with thousands trooping came
Attended: all access was thronged, the gates
And porches wide, but chief the spacious hall
(Though like a covered field, where champions bold
Wont ride in armed, and at the soldan's chair
765 Defied the best of paynim chivalry
To mortal combat or career with lance)
Thick swarmed, both on the ground and in the air,
Brushed with the hiss of rustling wings. As bees
In springtime, when the sun with Taurus rides,

observer's horizon attained by a celestial
body (the sun in this case).

750. **engines:** contrivances (it shares a com-
mon Latin root with *invention*); cp. 4.17.

756. **Pandaemonium:** Greek for "place of all
the demons."

759. **By place or choice:** by virtue of rank or
election.

764. **Wont** were wont (accustomed) to; **sol-
dan's:** sultan's (see 348n).

765. **paynim:** pagan.

766. **career:** short gallop at full speed, as in
jousting.

767–75. **swarmed . . . affairs:** Bee similes
occur frequently in classical literature,
and the phrasing here variously echoes

precursors (cp. Homer, *Il.* 2.87–90; Vergil,
Aen. 1.430–36; 6.707–9, and especially *Georg.*
4.149–227). Bees are usually presented as
exemplary creatures, beneficial to hu-
manity. Milton bends the tradition so that
the inaugural scene of *state affairs* in
Satan's palace anticipates the final one,
when the fallen angels are straitened into
swarms of hissing serpents (cp. 10.508ff).
Note the predominance of sibilants in
both passages. When Milton was in Rome,
the seemingly ubiquitous insignia of
Pope Urban VIII was a bee, and his fol-
lowers were called bees.

769. **Taurus:** The sun stays in the astrologi-
cal sign of Taurus from April 20 till May

770 Pour forth their populous youth about the hive
    In clusters; they among fresh dews and flowers
    Fly to and fro, or on the smoothèd plank,
    The suburb of their straw-built citadel,
    New rubbed with balm, expatiate and confer
775 Their state affairs. So thick the airy crowd
    Swarmed and were straitened; till the signal giv'n,
    Behold a wonder! They but now who seemed
    In bigness to surpass Earth's giant sons
    Now less than smallest dwarfs, in narrow room
780 Throng numberless, like that pygmean race
    Beyond the Indian mount, or faerie elves
    Whose midnight revels, by a forest side
    Or fountain some belated peasant sees,
    Or dreams he sees, while overhead the moon
785 Sits arbitress, and nearer to the earth
    Wheels her pale course, they on their mirth and dance
    Intent, with jocund music charm his ear;
    At once with joy and fear his heart rebounds.
    Thus incorporeal spirits to smallest forms
790 Reduced their shapes immense, and were at large,
    Though without number still amidst the hall
    Of that infernal court. But far within
    And in their own dimensions like themselves

20, the period immediately after Aries, the sign under which the world was created and would have persisted had the Fall not occurred.

774. **expatiate:** (1) walk about; (2) speak at length. Bees communicate by moving their legs in view of other bees, relaying directions to the best sites for pollen. Although such entomological discoveries are relatively recent, beekeepers have long recognized that allowing bees to "walk about" each other augments the harvest of honey; hence the "suburban" plank laid outside the hive for that purpose.

778. **Earth's giant sons:** See 198–200n.

780–81. **Throng . . . mount:** The legendary Pygmies were commonly thought to live beyond the Ganges in secluded mountainous regions where the Cranes that they battle lay their eggs (cp. 575n).

783–84. **belated . . . he sees:** The phrasing is generally taken as a borrowing from Vergil, when Aeneas thinks he glimpses Dido's shade. But vacillation between seeing and dreaming and mention of a *belated peasant* make reminiscence of *MND* equally likely (4.1.204–14).

785. **arbitress:** observer and judge.

The great Seraphic lords and Cherubim
795 In close recess and secret conclave sat
A thousand demigods on golden seats,
Frequent and full. After short silence then
And summons read, the great consult began.

---

795. **close recess:** enclosed, secluded place; **conclave:** literally, "lockable room"; in the Catholic Church, it denotes the meeting held to select a new pope, so called from the secure room in which the meeting occurs.

797. **Frequent:** numerous.

798. **consult:** In seventeenth-century usage, the term is associated with secret meetings for plotting insurgency.

Book II

The Argument

The consultation begun, Satan debates whether another battle be to be hazarded for the recovery of Heaven: some advise it; others dissuade. A third proposal is preferred, mentioned before by Satan: to search the truth of that prophecy or tradition in Heaven concerning another world and another kind of creature, equal or not much inferior to themselves, about this time to be created; their doubt who shall be sent on this difficult search. Satan their chief undertakes alone the voyage, is honored and applauded. The council thus ended, the rest betake them several ways and to several employments, as their inclinations lead them, to entertain the time till Satan return. He passes on his journey to Hell gates, finds them shut, and who sat there to guard them: by whom at length they are opened and discover to him the great gulf between Hell and Heaven; with what difficulty he passes through, directed by Chaos, the power of that place, to the sight of this new world which he sought.

High on a throne of royal state, which far
Outshone the wealth of Ormus and of Ind,
Or where the gorgeous East with richest hand
Show'rs on her kings barbaric pearl and gold,

---

2. **Ormus:** Hormuz, famously wealthy island town ideally situated in the Persian Gulf for trade in spices and jewels. Ships of the British East India Company helped the Dutch take it from the Portuguese in 1622. For acquiescing in the unauthorized aggression, King James and the Duke of Buckingham pocketed large bribes. **Ind:** India, celebrated for precious stones; cp. *Masque* 606.

4. **barbaric:** Greek for "foreign," primarily used of Asia or *the gorgeous East*. Classical authors depict Asian rulers as profligate despots; hence Vergil describes the doors of Priam's palace as "proud with the spoils of barbaric gold" (*Aen.* 2.504).

"High on a throne of royal state . . ." (2.1).

5   Satan exalted sat, by merit raised
    To that bad eminence; and from despair
    Thus high uplifted beyond hope, aspires
    Beyond thus high, insatiate to pursue
    Vain war with Heav'n, and by success untaught
10   His proud imaginations thus displayed.
       "Powers and Dominions, deities of Heav'n,
    For since no deep within her gulf can hold
    Immortal vigor, though oppressed and fall'n,
    I give not Heav'n for lost. From this descent
15   Celestial Virtues rising, will appear
    More glorious and more dread than from no fall,
    And trust themselves to fear no second fate.
    Me though just right, and the fixed laws of Heav'n
    Did first create your leader, next, free choice,
20   With what besides, in counsel or in fight,
    Hath been achieved of merit, yet this loss
    Thus far at least recovered, hath much more
    Established in a safe unenvied throne
    Yielded with full consent. The happier state
25   In Heav'n, which follows dignity, might draw
    Envy from each inferior; but who here
    Will envy whom the highest place exposes
    Foremost to stand against the Thunderer's aim
    Your bulwark, and condemns to greatest share
30   Of endless pain? Where there is then no good

---

5. **merit:** desert, good or bad.

9. **success:** outcome; like *merit,* ironically complicated by its more usual positive sense.

11. **Powers and Dominions:** two kinds of angels (Col. 1.16).

14. **I . . . lost:** "I refuse to concede the loss of Heaven."

15. **Virtues:** efficacious qualities (not moral virtues); also, members of a rank of angels.

18–21. **Me . . . merit:** The tortuous syntax makes Stoic principles—*just right* and *fixed laws*—agents of Satan's creation as leader. The direct object (*Me*) begins the clause. His created status, Satan says, has been confirmed by the *free choice* of his followers and by his own deeds.

24–25. **happier . . . dignity:** Satan claims that in Heaven, the higher one's rank, the happier one's existence, and that in Hell the reverse holds true, which should deter envy and promote unity.

28. **Thunderer:** classical epithet for Jove.

For which to strive, no strife can grow up there
From faction; for none sure will claim in Hell
Precedence, none, whose portion is so small
Of present pain, that with ambitious mind
35   Will covet more. With this advantage then
To union, and firm faith, and firm accord,
More than can be in Heav'n, we now return
To claim our just inheritance of old,
Surer to prosper than prosperity
40   Could have assured us; and by what best way,
Whether of open war or covert guile,
We now debate; who can advise, may speak."
    He ceased, and next him Moloch, sceptered king,
Stood up, the strongest and the fiercest spirit
45   That fought in Heav'n, now fiercer by despair.
His trust was with th' Eternal to be deemed
Equal in strength, and rather than be less
Cared not to be at all; with that care lost
Went all his fear: of God, or Hell, or worse
50   He reck'd not, and these words thereafter spake.
    "My sentence is for open war. Of wiles,
More unexpert, I boast not: them let those
Contrive who need, or when they need, not now.
For while they sit contriving, shall the rest,
55   Millions that stand in arms and longing wait
The signal to ascend, sit ling'ring here
Heav'n's fugitives, and for their dwelling place
Accept this dark opprobrious den of shame,
The prison of his tyranny who reigns
60   By our delay? No, let us rather choose
Armed with Hell flames and fury all at once
O'er Heav'n's high tow'rs to force resistless way,

---

43. **Moloch:** Hebrew for "king"; see I.392n;
  sceptered king: translates Homer's for-
  mulaic epithet for kings (e.g., *Il.* 1.279).
50. **reck'd:** heeded; cared.

51. **sentence:** judgment. Cp. line 291.
52. **More unexpert:** less knowledgeable or
  experienced.

Turning our tortures into horrid arms
Against the Torturer; when to meet the noise
65 Of his almighty engine he shall hear
Infernal thunder, and for lightning see
Black fire and horror shot with equal rage
Among his angels; and his throne itself
Mixed with Tartarean sulfur, and strange fire,
70 His own invented torments. But perhaps
The way seems difficult and steep to scale
With upright wing against a higher foe.
Let such bethink them, if the sleepy drench
Of that forgetful lake benumb not still,
75 That in our proper motion we ascend
Up to our native seat: descent and fall
To us is adverse. Who but felt of late
When the fierce foe hung on our broken rear
Insulting, and pursu'd us through the deep,
80 With what compulsion and laborious flight
We sunk thus low? Th' ascent is easy then;
Th' event is feared. Should we again provoke
Our stronger, some worse way his wrath may find
To our destruction, if there be in Hell
85 Fear to be worse destroyed. What can be worse
Than to dwell here, driv'n out from bliss, condemned

63. **horrid:** bristling (*with Hell flames*).

65. **engine:** instrument of war (cp. 4.17); here, God's lightning and thunder.

69. **Tartarean:** infernal; horrible. Tartarus confines the rebellious Titans, according to Homer and Hesiod (*Il.* 14.278; 8.478–91; *Theog.* 713–45). **strange fire:** "Nadab and Abihu died because they offered strange fire before the Lord" (Num. 26.61; cp. Lev. 10.1). The Geneva Bible glosses *strange fire* as fire "not taken of the altar"—that is, unholy or illicit fire.

73. **drench:** dose; douse. Cp. *Animad* (Yale 1:685).

74. **forgetful:** causing a state of oblivion; cp. "oblivious pool" (1.266).

79. **Insulting:** springing upon scornfully; trampling in triumph. Cp. 1.327.

81. For Fowler, Moloch's claim is "belied by the allusion to *Aen.* 6.126–29": "easy is the descent to Avernus . . . but to recall thy steps and pass out to the upper air, this is the task, this the toil!" Cp. *PL* 2.432–33, 3.20–21. Unlike Aeneas, however, the rebels are spiritual beings: "bodies compounded and elemented of Earth do naturally descend; but to spirits, those divine, airy, agile beings, as our poet well observes, . . . all motion downward seems forced and contrary" (Hume).

82. **event:** outcome.

In this abhorrèd deep to utter woe;
Where pain of unextinguishable fire
Must exercise us without hope of end
90 The vassals of his anger, when the scourge
Inexorably, and the torturing hour
Calls us to penance? More destroyed than thus
We should be quite abolished and expire.
What fear we then? What doubt we to incense
95 His utmost ire? Which to the highth enraged,
Will either quite consume us and reduce
To nothing this essential, happier far
Than miserable to have eternal being:
Or if our substance be indeed divine,
100 And cannot cease to be, we are at worst
On this side nothing; and by proof we feel
Our power sufficient to disturb his Heav'n,
And with perpetual inroads to alarm,
Though inaccessible, his fatal throne:
105 Which if not victory is yet revenge."
     He ended frowning, and his look denounced
Desperate revenge, and battle dangerous
To less than gods. On th' other side up rose
Belial, in act more graceful and humane;
110 A fairer person lost not Heav'n; he seemed

---

89. **exercise:** a range of meanings applies, from "agitate" or "vex" to the more common "train" or "cause to undergo a physical regimen or ascetic discipline."

90. **vassals:** slaves (see *PR* 4.133).

91. **torturing hour:** Shakespeare's Theseus seeks entertainment "to ease the anguish of a torturing hour"—the time between the marriage rite and its consummation (*MND* 5.1.37). The fallen angels will also pursue diversions from pain (ll. 458–62, 523–27), not least that of endlessly frustrated desire (4.508–11).

94. **doubt we:** makes us hesitate.

97. **essential:** essence or being (adj. for noun). On the active disposition to suicide represented by Moloch, see 1.158n.

100–101. **we . . . nothing:** "we could not be in a worse state than we are now." Cp. *PR* 3.204–11.

101. **proof:** experience, trial; also, testing artillery by firing a heavy charge (see 6.584–99).

104. **fatal:** allotted by fate; cp. 1.133.

106. **denounced:** threatened.

109. **Belial:** "Belial . . . taketh the form of a beautiful angel; he speaketh fair" (Scot 15.2). See 1.158n and 1.490n.

For dignity composed and high exploit:
But all was false and hollow; though his tongue
Dropped manna, and could make the worse appear
The better reason, to perplex and dash
115   Maturest counsels: for his thoughts were low;
To vice industrious, but to nobler deeds
Timorous and slothful: yet he pleased the ear,
And with persuasive accent thus began.
    "I should be much for open war, O peers,
120   As not behind in hate, if what was urged
Main reason to persuade immediate war,
Did not dissuade me most, and seem to cast
Ominous conjecture on the whole success:
When he who most excels in fact of arms,
125   In what he counsels and in what excels
Mistrustful, grounds his courage on despair
And utter dissolution, as the scope
Of all his aim, after some dire revenge.
First, what revenge? The tow'rs of Heav'n are filled
130   With armèd watch, that render all access
Impregnable; oft on the bordering deep
Encamp their legions, or with obscure wing
Scout far and wide into the realm of Night,
Scorning surprise. Or could we break our way
135   By force, and at our heels all Hell should rise
With blackest insurrection, to confound
Heav'n's purest light, yet our great enemy
All incorruptible would on his throne
Sit unpolluted, and th' ethereal mold
140   Incapable of stain would soon expel

113. **manna:** divinely provided food, sweet like honey (Exod. 16.31). So Homer describes the oratory of Nestor: "from whose tongue flowed speech sweeter than honey" (1.249). The ability to *make the worse appear / The better reason* defines sophistry and is a charge brought against Socrates (*Apology* 19b), as Milton observes: "that he ever made the worse cause seem the better" (*Tetrachordon* in *MLM* 989).
123. **conjecture:** doubt; **success:** outcome.
124. **fact:** deed, feat. *Fact of arms* translates an idiom common in French and Italian.
127. **scope:** object, end.
139. **mold:** material substance; for celestial beings, light or pure fire (see Ps. 104.4).

Her mischief, and purge off the baser fire
Victorious. Thus repulsed, our final hope
Is flat despair: we must exasperate
Th' almighty Victor to spend all his rage,
145 And that must end us, that must be our cure,
To be no more. Sad cure; for who would lose,
Though full of pain, this intellectual being,
Those thoughts that wander through eternity,
To perish rather, swallowed up and lost
150 In the wide womb of uncreated Night,
Devoid of sense and motion? And who knows,
Let this be good, whether our angry foe
Can give it, or will ever? How he can
Is doubtful; that he never will is sure.
155 Will he, so wise, let loose at once his ire,
Belike through impotence, or unaware,
To give his enemies their wish, and end
Them in his anger, whom his anger saves
To punish endless? 'Wherefore cease we then?'
160 Say they who counsel war, 'we are decreed,
Reserved and destined to eternal woe;
Whatever doing, what can we suffer more,
What can we suffer worse?' Is this then worst,
Thus sitting, thus consulting, thus in arms?
165 What when we fled amain, pursued and strook
With Heav'n's afflicting thunder, and besought
The deep to shelter us? This Hell then seemed
A refuge from those wounds. Or when we lay

Cp. Comus's claim that he and his band
are of "purer fire" than agents of morality
(111).

141. **Her mischief:** the harm intended her
(i.e., the *ethereal mold* of l. 139).

149–50. **swallowed . . . Night:** Satan will re-
iterate this fear (ll. 438–41, 10.476–77).

152. **Let this be good:** "were we to concede
that nonexistence is desirable."

156. As if through lack of self-control, or un-

wittingly. The astute Belial ironically
registers God's omnipotence and omni-
science.

160. **they who:** "Belial avoids naming
Moloch, who is in any case nameless"
(Leonard). Naming a previous speaker is
prohibited by Parliamentary rules of de-
bate.

165. **amain:** at full speed.

Chained on the burning lake? That sure was worse.
170 What if the breath that kindled those grim fires
Awaked should blow them into sevenfold rage
And plunge us in the flames? Or from above
Should intermitted vengeance arm again
His red right hand to plague us? What if all
175 Her stores were opened, and this firmament
Of Hell should spout her cataracts of fire
Impendent horrors, threat'ning hideous fall
One day upon our heads; while we perhaps
Designing or exhorting glorious war,
180 Caught in a fiery tempest shall be hurled
Each on his rock transfixed, the sport and prey
Of racking whirlwinds, or for ever sunk
Under yon boiling ocean, wrapped in chains;
There to converse with everlasting groans,
185 Unrespited, unpitied, unreprieved,
Ages of hopeless end. This would be worse.
War therefore, open or concealed, alike
My voice dissuades; for what can force or guile
With him, or who deceive his mind, whose eye
190 Views all things at one view? He from Heav'n's highth
All these our motions vain, sees and derides;
Not more almighty to resist our might
Than wise to frustrate all our plots and wiles.
Shall we then live thus vile, the race of Heav'n

170. "The breath of the Lord, like a stream of brimstone, doth kindle [hellfire]" (Isa. 30.33). Cp. the story of King Nebuchadnezzar, who fires his furnace "seven times more than it was wont" to incinerate his prisoners (Dan. 3.19). According to the *Geneva* gloss, angry tyrants exercise their wits by "inventing strange and cruel punishments."

173. **intermitted:** discontinued temporarily.

174. **red right hand:** translates Horace's account of Jove's *rubente dextera* (*Odes* 1.2.3–4.). Horace evokes Rome's panic at a catastrophic flood threatened by Jove's thunder. Belial conjures up a vision of Hell similarly inundated, but with fire.

175. **Her:** Hell's.

176. **cataracts:** heavy downpours.

180–82. **Caught . . . whirlwinds:** Cp. Pallas' vengeance on Ajax: "him, as with pierced breast he breathed forth flame, she caught in a whirlwind and impaled on a spiky crag" (Vergil, *Aen.* 1.44–45).

187–93. Belial offers impeccable theological rationale against either alternative on Satan's agenda (l. 41; cp. 1.661–62).

188. **what can force or guile:** "what can force or guile accomplish."

195   Thus trampled, thus expelled to suffer here
      Chains and these torments? Better these than worse
      By my advice; since fate inevitable
      Subdues us, and omnipotent decree,
      The victor's will. To suffer, as to do,
200   Our strength is equal, nor the law unjust
      That so ordains: this was at first resolved,
      If we were wise, against so great a foe
      Contending, and so doubtful what might fall.
      I laugh, when those who at the spear are bold
205   And vent'rous, if that fail them, shrink and fear
      What yet they know must follow, to endure
      Exile, or ignominy, or bonds, or pain,
      The sentence of their conqueror. This is now
      Our doom; which if we can sustain and bear,
210   Our supreme foe in time may much remit
      His anger, and perhaps thus far removed
      Not mind us not offending, satisfied
      With what is punished; whence these raging fires
      Will slacken, if his breath stir not their flames.
215   Our purer essence then will overcome
      Their noxious vapor, or inured not feel,
      Or changed at length, and to the place conformed
      In temper and in nature, will receive
      Familiar the fierce heat, and void of pain;

197–99. **since . . . will:** Belial's theological clarity persists as he accurately links *fate, omnipotent decree,* and *the victor's will* (cp. 5.602, 7.173).

199. **To suffer, as to do:** Editors since Newton cite Livy's quotation of the legendary Mutius Scaevola ("left-handed"), who earned his name by burning off his own right hand in response to captors' threats: "The strength of Rome is to do and also to suffer" (2.12). Cp. 1.158n and *PR* 3.195. Belial, by contrast—nameless on account of his crimes and already engulfed in flames—recommends passivity to reduce

suffering (ll. 208–14). In the narrator's terms, he seeks *ignoble ease* through *peaceful sloth* (l. 227).

200–208. **Our strength . . . conqueror:** The *law* to which Belial refers is the law of conquest or right of war, which Milton in *CD* cites to justify the death sentence imposed on all of Adam and Eve's descendants (1.11 in *MLM* 1238). Cp. 1.149–50n.

213. **what is punished:** the punishment already inflicted.

213–19. **whence . . . pain:** "If God were to stop stoking the fire, the purity of our native substance might overcome it. Or, we

220 This horror will grow mild, this darkness light,
     Besides what hope the never-ending flight
     Of future days may bring, what chance, what change
     Worth waiting, since our present lot appears
     For happy though but ill, for ill not worst,
225 If we procure not to ourselves more woe."
          Thus Belial with words clothed in reason's garb
     Counseled ignoble ease, and peaceful sloth,
     Not peace: and after him thus Mammon spake.
          "Either to disenthrone the King of Heav'n
230 We war, if war be best, or to regain
     Our own right lost: him to unthrone we then
     May hope when everlasting Fate shall yield
     To fickle Chance, and Chaos judge the strife:
     The former vain to hope argues as vain
235 The latter: for what place can be for us
     Within Heav'n's bound, unless Heav'n's Lord supreme
     We overpower? Suppose he should relent
     And publish grace to all, on promise made
     Of new subjection; with what eyes could we
240 Stand in his presence humble, and receive
     Strict laws imposed, to celebrate his throne
     With warbled hymns, and to his Godhead sing
     Forced hallelujahs; while he lordly sits
     Our envied Sov'reign, and his altar breathes

---

might grow accustomed to a less intense
fire and not notice it. Or perhaps our
physiology and substance will adapt, so
that hellfire will feel natural to us." Be-
lial's first alternative fits with his rejection
of Moloch's plan; cp. lines 139–42. The
last alternative anticipates Mammon's
proposal—that they adapt themselves to
Hell (ll. 274–78). On God as the bellows
infuriating hellfire, see 170n.

220. **light:** Possible meanings include the
overtly paradoxical "illumination," as
well as less obviously contradictory ad-

jectival senses, such as "luminous" and
"less harsh." "The rhyme at 220–21 offers a
suitably jingling accompaniment to the
cheerful fantasy" (Fowler).

223–24. **since . . . worst:** "Insofar as happi-
ness is concerned, our current situation is
certainly a bad one, but for a bad situa-
tion, it is not the worst."

228. **Mammon:** See 1.678n.

243. **hallelujahs:** songs of praise; in Hebrew,
hallelujah means "praise God."

244. **breathes:** exhales or emanates, as a fra-
grance; cp. 5.482.

245 Ambrosial odors and ambrosial flowers,
     Our servile offerings. This must be our task
     In Heav'n, this our delight; how wearisome
     Eternity so spent in worship paid
     To whom we hate. Let us not then pursue
250 By force impossible, by leave obtained
     Unacceptable, though in Heav'n, our state
     Of splendid vassalage, but rather seek
     Our own good from our selves, and from our own
     Live to our selves, though in this vast recess,
255 Free, and to none accountable, preferring
     Hard liberty before the easy yoke
     Of servile pomp. Our greatness will appear
     Then most conspicuous, when great things of small,
     Useful of hurtful, prosperous of adverse
260 We can create, and in what place soe'er
     Thrive under evil, and work ease out of pain
     Through labor and endurance. This deep world
     Of darkness do we dread? How oft amidst
     Thick clouds and dark doth Heav'n's all-ruling Sire
265 Choose to reside, his glory unobscured,
     And with the majesty of darkness round
     Covers his throne; from whence deep thunders roar
     Must'ring their rage, and Heav'n resembles Hell?
     As he our darkness, cannot we his light
270 Imitate when we please? This desert soil
     Wants not her hidden luster, gems and gold;
     Nor want we skill or art, from whence to raise
     Magnificence; and what can Heav'n show more?
     Our torments also may in length of time
275 Become our elements, these piercing fires

---

245. **Ambrosial:** divinely fragrant; classically, ambrosia is divine nourishment.

256. **easy yoke:** "who best / Bear his mild yoke, they serve him best" (*Sonnet 19* 10–11).

263–68. **How oft . . . Hell?:** "The Lord hath said that he would dwell in the thick darkness" (2 Chron. 6.1; see also Ps. 18.11–13).

271. **Wants not:** does not lack.

275. **elements:** components, habitats (cp. *Il Pens* 93–94); Belial makes a similar conjecture at lines 217–18.

As soft as now severe, our temper changed
Into their temper; which must needs remove
The sensible of pain. All things invite
To peaceful counsels, and the settled state
280 Of order, how in safety best we may
Compose our present evils, with regard
Of what we are and where, dismissing quite
All thoughts of war: ye have what I advise."
　　He scarce had finished, when such murmur filled
285 Th' assembly, as when hollow rocks retain
The sound of blust'ring winds, which all night long
Had roused the sea, now with hoarse cadence lull
Seafaring men o'erwatched, whose bark by chance
Or pinnace anchors in a craggy bay
290 After the tempest: such applause was heard
As Mammon ended, and his sentence pleased,
Advising peace: for such another field
They dreaded worse than Hell: so much the fear
Of thunder and the sword of Michael
295 Wrought still within them; and no less desire
To found this nether empire, which might rise
By policy, and long process of time,
In emulation opposite to Heav'n.
Which when Beëlzebub perceived, than whom,
300 Satan except, none higher sat, with grave
Aspect he rose, and in his rising seemed
A pillar of state; deep on his front engraven
Deliberation sat and public care;
And princely counsel in his face yet shone,

278. **sensible**: what is felt; sensation (adj. for noun).
281. **Compose**: adjust to (by becoming part of); calm.
282. **where**: 1667; "were" in 1674.
288. **o'erwatched**: sleep deprived.
288–89. **bark, pinnace**: small sailing ships.
292. **such another field**: another battle such as they fought in Heaven.
297. **policy**: statecraft; in Milton's era, *policy* often implies Machiavellian cunning.
　　process of time: Cp. Adam and Eve's prospects for improvement, "by tract of time" (5.498).
302. **front**: brow, face.

305 Majestic though in ruin: sage he stood
With Atlantean shoulders fit to bear
The weight of mightiest monarchies; his look
Drew audience and attention still as night
Or summer's noontide air, while thus he spake.

310   "Thrones and imperial Powers, offspring of Heav'n,
Ethereal Virtues; or these titles now
Must we renounce, and changing style be called
Princes of Hell? For so the popular vote
Inclines, here to continue, and build up here

315 A growing empire; doubtless; while we dream,
And know not that the King of Heav'n hath doomed
This place our dungeon, not our safe retreat
Beyond his potent arm, to live exempt
From Heav'n's high jurisdiction, in new league

320 Banded against his throne, but to remain
In strictest bondage, though thus far removed,
Under th' inevitable curb, reserved
His captive multitude: for he, be sure
In highth or depth, still first and last will reign

325 Sole king, and of his kingdom lose no part
By our revolt, but over Hell extend
His empire, and with iron scepter rule

306. **Atlantean:** Atlas-like; Zeus doomed
Atlas, a rebel Titan, to uphold the sky (cp.
4.987n). Statesmen were often compared
to Atlas or to Hercules relieving Atlas of
his burden. See Cowley's praise of King
Charles: "On whom (like Atlas shoulders)
the propped state/(As he were the *Pri-
mum Mobile* of fate)/Solely, relies" (*On his
Majesty's Return out of Scotland*).

312. **style:** official name or title. The fallen an-
gels' original titles indicated their author-
ity, the defense of which Satan cited as
cause for their initial rebellion (see, e.g.,
5.772–802). Beëlzebub invokes these titles
to ask if they are indeed willing to forsake
their Heavenly identities, as Mammon has
suggested. Cp. 10.460–62, *PR* 2.121–25.

315. We retain from 1674 the semicolons
bracing *doubtless,* which seem intended to
indicate deliberate pauses for rhetorical
effect.

321. In reply to Belial's conjecture at lines
209–13.

324. **first and last:** Cp. the persistent account
of God in Isaiah (41.4, 27; 43.10; 44.6; 48.12)
and of the Son in Revelation (1.11, 17; 2.8;
21.6; 22.13).

327–28. **iron, golden:** The association of iron
with severity and gold with mercy distin-
guishes between the regime of God in
Hell and in Heaven. Cp. Ps. 2.9 and Esther
4.11. See also the iron and golden keys of
St. Peter in *Lyc* 110–11.

Us here, as with his golden those in Heav'n.
What sit we then projecting peace and war?
330 War hath determined us, and foiled with loss
Irreparable; terms of peace yet none
Vouchsafed or sought; for what peace will be giv'n
To us enslaved, but custody severe,
And stripes, and arbitrary punishment
335 Inflicted? And what peace can we return,
But to our power hostility and hate,
Untamed reluctance, and revenge though slow,
Yet ever plotting how the Conqueror least
May reap his conquest, and may least rejoice
340 In doing what we most in suffering feel?
Nor will occasion want, nor shall we need
With dangerous expedition to invade
Heav'n, whose high walls fear no assault or siege,
Or ambush from the deep. What if we find
345 Some easier enterprise? There is a place
(If ancient and prophetic fame in Heav'n
Err not) another world, the happy seat
Of some new race called Man, about this time
To be created like to us, though less
350 In power and excellence, but favored more
Of him who rules above; so was his will
Pronounced among the gods, and by an oath,

---

329. **What:** why; **projecting:** scheming; devising.

330. **determined us:** settled our course. Cp. 11.227.

334. **stripes:** marks left by a whip.

337. **reluctance:** resistance, opposition.

338–40. **how . . . feel?:** "how to mitigate God's victory and pleasure in tormenting us?" These challenging lines initiate the figure of God as a reaper seeking to maximize his yield (cp. 4.983) and cap the debate's running concern with the balance of *suffering* and *doing* (see 199n).

349. **like to us:** a comparison indicative of

the fallen angels' egocentrism, or antitheocentrism. Resemblance between humans and angels derives from their reflection of the same creator (cp. 3.100–128, 4.567).

349–51. **To be . . . above:** "Thou hast made him a little lower than the angels, and hast crowned him with glory and honor" (Ps. 8.5).

352–53. Fowler observes that the precedent for God's Heaven-shaking oath is both biblical and classical. See Isa. 13.12–13 and especially Heb. 6.17 (a crucial verse for *Lycidas* also); Homer, *Il.* 1.528–30, and Vergil, *Aen.* 9.104–6.

That shook Heav'n's whole circumference, confirmed.
Thither let us bend all our thoughts, to learn
355 What creatures there inhabit, of what mold,
Or substance, how endued, and what their power,
And where their weakness, how attempted best,
By force or subtlety: though Heav'n be shut,
And Heav'n's high arbitrator sit secure
360 In his own strength, this place may lie exposed
The utmost border of his kingdom, left
To their defense who hold it: here perhaps
Some advantageous act may be achieved
By sudden onset, either with Hell fire
365 To waste his whole creation, or possess
All as our own, and drive as we were driven,
The puny habitants, or if not drive,
Seduce them to our party, that their God
May prove their foe, and with repenting hand
370 Abolish his own works. This would surpass
Common revenge, and interrupt his joy
In our confusion, and our joy upraise
In his disturbance, when his darling sons
Hurled headlong to partake with us, shall curse
375 Their frail original, and faded bliss,

355. **mold:** form. Cp. line 139. The sense "constitutive substance" (in humanity's case, earth) is secondary here because *substance* follows. See Rumrich 1987, 53–69.

357. **attempted:** attacked or tempted. The options are elaborated through line 376.

367. **puny:** from the French *puis né*, later born.

368. **God:** "The first time in *PL* that any devil has spoken the name" (Leonard).

369–70. **May . . . works:** "And the Lord said, I will destroy man . . . for it repenteth me that I have made them" (Gen. 6.7). Following the Calvinist interpretive practice known as "accommodation," the Geneva Bible explains that "God doeth never repent, but he speaketh after our capacity."

Milton refuses to go along: "God would [not] have said anything . . . about himself unless he intended that it should be a part of our conception of him. . . . Let us believe that he did repent" (*CD* 1.2 in *MLM* 1147).

374. **Hurled headlong:** repeats 1.45, the account of the rebel angels' expulsion. Beëlzebub assumes that God will be consistent in punishing rebellion; hence *partake* (share) *with us.*

375. **original:** 1667 reads "originals." The meaning includes "parentage" but also the prelapsarian state of bliss (see 10.731–42). Cp. *RCG:* "run questing up as high as Adam to fetch their original" (Yale 1:762).

Faded so soon. Advise if this be worth
Attempting, or to sit in darkness here
Hatching vain empires." Thus Beëlzebub
Pleaded his devilish counsel, first devised
380 By Satan, and in part proposed: for whence,
But from the author of all ill could spring
So deep a malice, to confound the race
Of mankind in one root, and Earth with Hell
To mingle and involve, done all to spite
385 The great Creator? But their spite still serves
His glory to augment. The bold design
Pleased highly those infernal States, and joy
Sparkled in all their eyes; with full assent
They vote: whereat his speech he thus renews.
390   "Well have ye judged, well ended long debate,
Synod of gods, and like to what ye are,
Great things resolved, which from the lowest deep
Will once more lift us up, in spite of fate,
Nearer our ancient seat; perhaps in view
395 Of those bright confines, whence with neighboring arms
And opportune excursion we may chance
Re-enter Heav'n; or else in some mild zone
Dwell not unvisited of Heav'n's fair light
Secure, and at the bright'ning orient beam
400 Purge off this gloom; the soft delicious air,
To heal the scar of these corrosive fires
Shall breathe her balm. But first whom shall we send
In search of this new world, whom shall we find
Sufficient? Who shall tempt with wand'ring feet
405 The dark unbottomed infinite abyss

---

377. **to sit in darkness here:** "Such as sit in darkness and in the shadow of death, being bound in affliction and iron; Because they rebelled against the words of God and condemned the counsel of the most High" (Ps. 107.10–11).

379–80. **first devised/By Satan:** See 1.650–56.

383. **one root:** Adam and Eve, the genealogical root of humanity.

387. **States:** representatives, dignitaries.

391. **Synod:** meeting, assembly (usually of clergy or church elders); cp. 6.156, 11.67.

404. **tempt:** make trial of, test.

405. **abyss:** Greek for "bottomless"; translates "the deep" in the Septuagint.

And through the palpable obscure find out
His uncouth way, or spread his airy flight
Upborne with indefatigable wings
Over the vast abrupt, ere he arrive
410 The happy isle; what strength, what art can then
Suffice, or what evasion bear him safe
Through the strict senteries and stations thick
Of angels watching round? Here he had need
All circumspection, and we now no less
415 Choice in our suffrage; for on whom we send,
The weight of all and our last hope relies."
      This said, he sat; and expectation held
His look suspense, awaiting who appeared
To second, or oppose, or undertake
420 The perilous attempt: but all sat mute,
Pondering the danger with deep thoughts; and each
In other's count'nance read his own dismay
Astonished: none among the choice and prime
Of those Heav'n-warring champions could be found
425 So hardy as to proffer or accept
Alone the dreadful voyage; till at last
Satan, whom now transcendent glory raised
Above his fellows, with monarchal pride
Conscious of highest worth, unmoved thus spake.
430   "O progeny of Heav'n, empyreal Thrones,

---

406. **palpable obscure:** tangible dark. Cp.
the "darkness which may be felt" inflicted
by God on Egypt (Exod. 10.21) and the
threat of "thick and palpable clouds of
darkness" invoked in the prefatory epistle
to the *AV.*
407. **uncouth:** unknown, strange, unpleas-
ant.
409. **abrupt:** chasm.
410. **happy isle:** the universe of this world,
hung in the sea of chaos (ll. 1011, 1051). The

phrasing recalls the Islands of the Blessed
in Greek mythology.
412. **senteries:** sentries. The meter requires
the three-syllable form, a variation com-
mon in the seventeenth century.
413. **had:** would have.
415. **Choice in our suffrage:** judgment in
arriving at a consensus.
418. **suspense:** attentive, in suspense, as is
appropriate for personified *expectation.*
430–66. Cp. Satan's corresponding speech at
PR 1.44–105.

With reason hath deep silence and demur
Seized us, though undismayed: long is the way
And hard, that out of Hell leads up to light;
Our prison strong, this huge convex of fire,
435 Outrageous to devour, immures us round
Ninefold, and gates of burning adamant
Barred over us prohibit all egress.
These past, if any pass, the void profound
Of unessential night receives him next
440 Wide gaping, and with utter loss of being
Threatens him, plunged in that abortive gulf.
If thence he scape into whatever world,
Or unknown region, what remains him less
Than unknown dangers and as hard escape.
445 But I should ill become this throne, O Peers,
And this imperial sov'reignty, adorned
With splendor, armed with power, if aught proposed
And judged of public moment, in the shape
Of difficulty or danger could deter
450 Me from attempting. Wherefore do I assume
These royalties, and not refuse to reign,
Refusing to accept as great a share
Of hazard as of honor, due alike
To him who reigns, and so much to him due

432–33. **long . . . light:** Satan echoes the warning of Vergil's Sibyl to Aeneas before his trip to the underworld (*Aen.* 6.126–29; cp. 8.111, 3.20–21).

434. **convex:** hemisphere or domelike vault, seen from the outside.

435. **Outrageous to devour:** fierce enough to destroy rapidly and completely.

436. **adamant:** from the Greek for "unbreakable."

438. **void profound:** translates Lucretius' *inane profundum* (*On the Nature of Things* 1.1108).

439. **unessential:** lacking essence; without entity. Cp. "unoriginal" (10.477), "unsubstantial" (*PR* 4.399). Satan proceeds to re-

visit Belial's fear (ll. 149–51), as he will again when he returns to Hell (10.476–77).

441. **abortive:** threatening *utter loss of being* (as at l. 440), as if one had never been born. The sense "preventive" may also apply because, by swallowing Satan, the preexistent womb of chaos would end his mission before it begins; see lines 932–38.

443. **remains:** awaits.

444. Beginning with Edition 4 (1688), editors often supply a question mark after *escape*. The sentence may be construed as interrogative in form, but Satan is not asking a question.

448. **moment:** consequence.

452. **Refusing:** "if I refuse."

455 Of hazard more, as he above the rest
High honored sits? Go therefore mighty Powers,
Terror of Heav'n, though fall'n; intend at home,
While here shall be our home, what best may ease
The present misery, and render Hell
460 More tolerable; if there be cure or charm
To respite or deceive, or slack the pain
Of this ill mansion: intermit no watch
Against a wakeful foe, while I abroad
Through all the coasts of dark destruction seek
465 Deliverance for us all: this enterprise
None shall partake with me." Thus saying rose
The monarch, and prevented all reply,
Prudent, lest from his resolution raised
Others among the chief might offer now
470 (Certain to be refused) what erst they feared;
And so refused might in opinion stand
His rivals, winning cheap the high repute
Which he through hazard huge must earn. But they
Dreaded not more th' adventure than his voice
475 Forbidding; and at once with him they rose;
Their rising all at once was as the sound
Of thunder heard remote. Towards him they bend
With awful reverence prone; and as a god
Extol him equal to the highest in Heav'n:
480 Nor failed they to express how much they praised,
That for the general safety he despised
His own: for neither do the spirits damned
Lose all their virtue; lest bad men should boast

457. **intend at:** attend to.
461. **respite or deceive:** relieve or beguile, parallel to *cure or charm* (460).
467. **prevented:** forestalled.
468. **raised:** buoyed, uplifted (by Satan's resolve); modifies *Others* (469).
478. **With awful reverence prone:** For Leonard, the phrase implies respect; for Fowler, groveling submission. The former reading suits the republican strain of Hell's polity, the latter its affinity with Asian tyranny. Cp. *CD* 2.13: "We nowhere read of obeisance being made to kings in any other way than by a low bow. Yet this same mark of respect was frequently used by one private individual to another" (*Yale* 6:651); also *PL* 4.958–60, 5.357–60.
483–85. **lest . . . zeal:** "to prevent bad men

Their specious deeds on earth, which glory excites,
485 Or close ambition varnished o'er with zeal.
Thus they their doubtful consultations dark
Ended rejoicing in their matchless chief:
As when from mountain tops the dusky clouds
Ascending, while the north wind sleeps, o'erspread
490 Heav'n's cheerful face, the louring element
Scowls o'er the darkened lantskip snow, or show'r;
If chance the radiant sun with farewell sweet
Extend his ev'ning beam, the fields revive,
The birds their notes renew, and bleating herds
495 Attest their joy, that hill and valley rings.
O shame to men! Devil with devil damned
Firm concord holds, men only disagree
Of creatures rational, though under hope
Of heavenly grace: and God proclaiming peace,
500 Yet live in hatred, enmity, and strife
Among themselves, and levy cruel wars,
Wasting the earth, each other to destroy:
As if (which might induce us to accord)
Man had not Hellish foes enow besides,
505 That day and night for his destruction wait.
　　　The Stygian Counsel thus dissolved; and forth
In order came the grand infernal Peers:
Midst came their mighty Paramount, and seemed
Alone th' antagonist of Heav'n, nor less
510 Than Hell's dread Emperor with pomp supreme,
And God-like imitated state; him round

---

from boasting about actions that appear virtuous but are really motivated by fame or hidden ambition cloaked with enthusiasm."

489. **while the north wind sleeps:** "what time the might of the north wind sleepeth" (Homer, *Il.* 5.524).

490. **louring element:** threatening (thus "lowering") sky; the *element* is air.

491. **lantskip:** landscape (old spelling).

496–502. "There is more amity among serpents than among men" (Juvenal, *Satire* 15.159). According to Rusca, devils maintain harmony to tempt humanity more effectively (Hughes).

504. **enow:** archaic plural of "enough."

511–13. The imitation of God's *state* (ceremonial pomp) is slavish in detail. As in the scriptural account of God on his throne (Isa. 6.1–7), Satan is surrounded by a host

A globe of fiery Seraphim enclosed
With bright emblazonry, and horrent arms.
Then of their session ended they bid cry
515 With trumpets' regal sound the great result:
Toward the four winds four speedy Cherubim
Put to their mouths the sounding alchemy
By herald's voice explained: the hollow abyss
Heard far and wide, and all the host of Hell
520 With deaf'ning shout, returned them loud acclaim.
Thence more at ease their minds and somewhat raised
By false presumptuous hope, the rangèd powers
Disband, and wand'ring, each his several way
Pursues, as inclination or sad choice
525 Leads him perplexed, where he may likeliest find
Truce to his restless thoughts, and entertain
The irksome hours, till this great chief return.
Part on the plain, or in the air sublime
Upon the wing, or in swift race contend,
530 As at th' Olympian Games or Pythian fields;
Part curb their fiery steeds, or shun the goal
With rapid wheels, or fronted brigades form.
As when to warn proud cities war appears

---

of *Seraphim* in a compact band (*globe;* cp. *PR* 4.581). Recent editors (Fowler, Leonard) cite the Hebrew verb "to burn" as the source of *Seraphim* (hence *fiery Seraphim*). But the *Jewish Encyclopedia* cites the Hebrew noun for "fiery flying serpents" (Num. 21.6–9; Deut. 8:15).

513. **emblazonry:** heraldic devices decorating shields; **horrent:** bristling, dreadful.

517. **alchemy:** goldlike alloy, "alchemy gold"; here, a synecdoche for trumpets.

526. **entertain:** occupy. See 9in.

528–69. Classical precedents abound for the diversions of the fallen angels. Cp. the Myrmidons' exercises during Achilles' absence from battle (*Il.* 2.774–79) or Horace's list of pursuits favored by various men (*Odes* 1.1). Milton's specific choice of

model is ironic; see Vergil's inventory of the activities of the blessed dead in Elysium (*Aen.* 6.642–78).

528. **sublime:** aloft, uplifted; cp. *PR* 4.542.

530. **Pythian fields:** Delphi; site of games instituted by Apollo after he slew the Python.

531. **shun the goal:** go tightly around the turning post, without touching it. Cp. "the turning post cleared with glowing wheel" (Horace, *Odes* 1.1.4–5).

532. **fronted:** directly opposed, front to front.

533–34. **As when . . . sky:** Cloudy apparitions preceded the fall of Jerusalem, writes Josephus (*The Wars of the Jews* 6.5.3), and atmospheric conditions at the time of Caesar's assassination also warned of strife, according to many authors. Portentous

Waged in the troubled sky, and armies rush
535 To battle in the clouds, before each van
Prick forth the airy knights, and couch their spears
Till thickest legions close; with feats of arms
From either end of heav'n the welkin burns.
Others with vast Typhoean rage more fell
540 Rend up both rocks and hills, and ride the air
In whirlwind; Hell scarce holds the wild uproar.
As when Alcides from Oechalia crowned
With conquest, felt th' envenomed robe, and tore
Through pain up by the roots Thessalian pines,
545 And Lichas from the top of Oeta threw
Into th' Euboic Sea. Others more mild,
Retreated in a silent valley, sing
With notes angelical to many a harp
Their own heroic deeds and hapless fall
550 By doom of battle; and complain that fate
Free virtue should enthrall to force or chance.
Their song was partial, but the harmony
(What could it less when spirits immortal sing?)
Suspended Hell, and took with ravishment

---

weather was similarly observed "about the time of [the] Civil Wars" in England (Hume). Milton persistently likens fallen angels to ominous or deceptive meteorological phenomena, in line with his account of airy angelic substance and the rebels' authority as "powers of air" (*PR* 1.44).

535. **van:** front line of a battle formation.

536. **Prick forth:** spur forward; **couch:** lower into position for attack.

538. **welkin:** sky.

539. **Typhoean:** Identified with Etna's volcanic power, Typhon was deemed father of the winds and is also an English word meaning *whirlwind* (l. 541). See 1.197–99.
fell: of cruel or vicious character.

542–46. **As when . . . Euboic Sea:** Homeward bound after sacking *Oechalia*, Hercules asks *Lichas* to fetch a ceremonial robe. Hercules' unwitting wife supplies an *envenomed* garment, which fastens to his flesh and burns unrelentingly. Uprooting trees in blind fury (*pines* is Milton's detail), Hercules hurls Lichas into the *Euboic Sea* from atop Mount *Oeta* in southern Thessaly. Sophocles dramatizes the story in *Trachiniae,* and Seneca in *Hercules Oetaeus.* But Milton mainly follows Ovid (*Met.* 9.134–272, *Her.* 9).

552. **partial:** biased; "silent as to the corrupt motive of their conduct, and dwelt only on the sad consequences of it" (Cowper). The ensuing contrast with *harmony* suggests that "in parts" or "polyphonic" is not the intended sense.

554. **Suspended:** The *OED* cites this line to exemplify the sense "riveted the attention of," and recent editors agree. The more likely meaning, however, is "to bring

555 The thronging audience. In discourse more sweet
    (For eloquence the soul, song charms the sense)
    Others apart sat on a hill retired,
    In thoughts more elevate, and reasoned high
    Of providence, foreknowledge, will, and fate,
560 Fixed fate, free will, foreknowledge absolute,
    And found no end, in wand'ring mazes lost.
    Of good and evil much they argued then,
    Of happiness and final misery,
    Passion and apathy, and glory and shame,
565 Vain wisdom all, and false philosophy:
    Yet with a pleasing sorcery could charm
    Pain for a while or anguish, and excite
    Fallacious hope, or arm th' obdurèd breast
    With stubborn patience as with triple steel.
570 Another part in squadrons and gross bands,
    On bold adventure to discover wide
    That dismal world, if any clime perhaps

---

about the temporary cessation" (of a condition). The parenthesis implies this sense by interrupting the syntax and deferring the verb, as Newton observed. Cp. the effect on Satan of the Garden's beauty (4.356, 9.462–66). Classical antecedents include Orpheus' suspension of Hell (Vergil, *Georg.* 4.481–84) and the effect of Alcaeus's music on the tormented Titans, "beguiled of their sufferings by the soothing sound" (Horace, *Odes* 2.13.38). **took:** charmed, enchanted (cp. l. 556).

558–69. Though well versed in classical philosophy and scholastic argument, Milton in later works includes passages critical of them (cp. *PR* 4.286–321, *SA* 300–306). God later makes his way through the mazy discourse of free will versus predestination (3.96–119); so does Milton in his theological treatise (*CD* 1.3, 4).

564. **apathy:** impassivity; signature virtue of Stoicism, one that Milton did not endorse. Cp. *CD* 2.10: "Sensibility to pain,

and complaints or lamentations, are not inconsistent with true patience" (*Yale* 6:740); also, *PR* 4.300–18. Orthodox theology makes God the paragon of this virtue, denoted by the term *impassibility*. But Milton insists that we should deem God to be as passionate as Scripture says (see 369–70n).

568. **obdurèd:** hardened, especially in sinfulness; stubborn and unyielding, sometimes by divine intercession. See 6.785. Elledge cites *obdurèd* as an example of prolepsis, a figure in which the adjective describes a state yet to be produced by the action of the verb. If it is God who renders the rebels obdurate, however, the figure instead expresses a coincidence common in seventeenth-century theologies: the damned creature's philosophical appropriation of God's sentence; cp. 1.211–12, 240–41.

570. **gross:** dense, closely packed.

Might yield them easier habitation, bend
Four ways their flying march, along the banks
575 Of four infernal rivers that disgorge
Into the burning lake their baleful streams;
Abhorrèd Styx the flood of deadly hate,
Sad Acheron of sorrow, black and deep;
Cocytus, named of lamentation loud
580 Heard on the rueful stream; fierce Phlegeton
Whose waves of torrent fire inflame with rage.
Far off from these a slow and silent stream,
Lethe the river of oblivion rolls
Her wat'ry labyrinth, whereof who drinks,
585 Forthwith his former state and being forgets,
Forgets both joy and grief, pleasure and pain.
Beyond this flood a frozen continent
Lies dark and wild, beat with perpetual storms
Of whirlwind and dire hail, which on firm land
590 Thaws not, but gathers heap, and ruin seems
Of ancient pile; all else deep snow and ice,
A gulf profound as that Serbonian Bog
Betwixt Damiata and Mount Casius old,
Where armies whole have sunk: the parching air
595 Burns frore, and cold performs th' effect of fire.
Thither by harpy-footed Furies haled,

575–81. The account of each river is a translation of its Greek name; e.g., *Cocytus* derives from *kokutos,* Greek for "wailing" or *lamentation loud.*

591. **pile:** vast building.

592–94. **A gulf . . . sunk:** Surrounded by hills of sand, Lake Serbonis lay between *Mount Casius* and *Damiata,* at the center of a notorious morass on the lower Egyptian coast. Diodorus Siculus (1.30) and Sandys (1637, 137) describe the fatally deceptive locale and report it swallowing *whole armies.* Apollonius makes it, not Etna, Zeus's prison for Typhon (2.1210–15). Related similes appear at 939–40 and 9.634–42.

595. **frore:** frosty. "When the cold north wind bloweth, and the water is congealed into ice, it . . . clotheth the water as with a breastplate. It . . . burneth the wilderness and consumeth the grass as fire" (*Ec.* 43.20–21). That Hell's torments include ice as well as fire was a commonplace; see Dante, *Inf.* 3.86–87, and Shakespeare, *MM* 3.1.121–22.

596. **harpy-footed:** with hooked claws, like a raptor. In Greek culture, Harpies were wind spirits thought to snatch people from this world and deliver them to the Furies (with whom they were sometimes confounded). They are particularly identified with sweeping storm winds (hence

At certain revolutions all the damned
Are brought: and feel by turns the bitter change
Of fierce extremes, extremes by change more fierce,
600 From beds of raging fire to starve in ice
Their soft ethereal warmth, and there to pine
Immovable, infixed, and frozen round,
Periods of time, thence hurried back to fire.
They ferry over this Lethean sound
605 Both to and fro, their sorrow to augment,
And wish and struggle, as they pass, to reach
The tempting stream, with one small drop to lose
In sweet forgetfulness all pain and woe,
All in one moment, and so near the brink;
610 But fate withstands, and to oppose th' attempt
Medusa with Gorgonian terror guards
The ford, and of itself the water flies
All taste of living wight, as once it fled
The lip of Tantalus. Thus roving on
615 In confused march forlorn, th' advent'rous bands
With shudd'ring horror pale, and eyes aghast
Viewed first their lamentable lot, and found
No rest: through many a dark and dreary vale
They passed, and many a region dolorous,
620 O'er many a frozen, many a fiery alp,
Rocks, caves, lakes, fens, bogs, dens, and shades of death,

---

the power to carry away). 1667 and 1674 have "hailed," not "haled." The spellings were interchangeable in Milton's time, and the superimposed senses of wind-driven precipitation, of being summoned, and of being dragged are likely intended.
600. **starve:** die a lingering death from the cold.
604. **Lethean sound:** the river of forgetfulness, Lethe (see l. 583).
611. **Medusa:** "snaky-headed Gorgon" (*Masque* 447), the most notorious of three

terrifying sisters. All who beheld Medusa were literally petrified.
613. **wight:** creature.
614. **Tantalus:** Homer depicts him in Tartarus, where he suffers perpetual thirst and appetite while standing chin deep in a lake that flees his lips, under boughs of fugitive fruit (*Od.* 11.582–92; see also Horace, *Satires* 1.68). Cp. 4.325–36, 10.556–70.
621. The variation of iambic rhythm in the first six monosyllables is shocking, maybe unique. It describes the unrelenting variety of a uniformly deathly landscape.

A universe of death, which God by curse
Created evil, for evil only good,
Where all life dies, death lives, and nature breeds,
625 Perverse, all monstrous, all prodigious things,
Abominable, inutterable, and worse
Than fables yet have feigned, or fear conceived,
Gorgons and Hydras, and Chimeras dire.
　　Meanwhile the Adversary of God and man,
630 Satan with thoughts inflamed of highest design,
Puts on swift wings, and towards the gates of Hell
Explores his solitary flight; sometimes
He scours the right hand coast, sometimes the left,
Now shaves with level wing the deep, then soars
635 Up to the fiery concave tow'ring high.
As when far off at sea a fleet descried
Hangs in the clouds, by equinoctial winds

628. **Hydra:** a venomous serpent with multiple, regenerative heads; **Chimera:** a fire-breathing mix of lion, goat, and serpent (*Il.* 6.180–82). *Prolusion 1* presents these monsters as the horrors of a guilty conscience (*MLM* 792). On *Gorgons*, see 611n. Cp. 10.524: "Scorpion and asp, and amphisbaena dire."

629. **Adversary:** See 1.82n.

632. **Explores:** makes trial of, reconnoiters.

633–34. **scours . . . shaves:** "moves quickly over . . . skims the surface of." As suggested by *explores*, Satan both makes a test flight and inspects the bounds of his new realm. The contact and coverage implied by *scours* and *shaves* is characteristic of the way Satan marks territory; cp. 9.63–66.

636–37. **As . . . clouds:** Sailing ships seen from afar (*descried*) appear suspended in air; Greek authors termed them *meteorous*, "hanging" or "aloft" (see Thucydides 1.48.3).

637–42. **by . . . pole:** The comparison is to merchant ships, sailing either from Ben-

gal (*Bengala*) in northeastern India or from *Ternate* and *Tidore*, "spice islands" in the East Indies. For the association of Satan's regime with the region, see 2n, 4n.

637. **equinoctial:** usually and incorrectly glossed as "at the equator" on the authority of the *OED*. The rest of the simile indicates that the *winds* in question are not the light and shifting breezes at the equator but monsoons. They dominate the climate of the Indian Ocean (*the wide Ethiopian*), reversing direction at the equinoxes (hence *equinoctial*), thus determining the schedule for shipping spices to Europe along the established commercial course (*trading flood*). During the southern winter (April to October), the monsoon blows to the northeast, out of Southern Africa. A fleet bent on sailing toward the *Cape* (of Good Hope) against that prevailing wind would set a course southwest, as *close* to the eye of the wind as possible, and tack repeatedly (*ply*).

Close sailing from Bengala, or the isles
Of Ternate and Tidore, whence merchants bring
640 Their spicy drugs: they on the trading flood
Through the wide Ethiopian to the Cape
Ply stemming nightly toward the pole. So seemed
Far off the flying Fiend: at last appear
Hell bounds high reaching to the horrid roof,
645 And thrice threefold the gates; three folds were brass,
Three iron, three of adamantine rock,
Impenetrable, impaled with circling fire,
Yet unconsumed. Before the gates there sat
On either side a formidable shape;
650 The one seemed woman to the waist, and fair,
But ended foul in many a scaly fold
Voluminous and vast, a serpent armed
With mortal sting: about her middle round
A cry of Hell-hounds never ceasing barked
655 With wide Cerberean mouths full loud, and rung
A hideous peal: yet, when they list, would creep,
If aught disturbed their noise, into her womb,
And kennel there, yet there still barked and howled,
Within unseen. Far less abhorred than these

642. **stemming ... pole:** Ships bound for the Cape would alter course *nightly*, making headway (*stemming*) directly to the south (*toward the pole*), to avoid shallow coastal waters. In the southern winter, the higher the latitude, the longer the night.

647. **impaled:** surrounded, enclosed.

650–59. **The one . . . unseen:** Milton's allegory of Sin comes out of the Spenserian tradition: cp. Spenser's Error (*FQ* 1.1.14–15), Phineas Fletcher's Hamartia (*Purple Island* 12.27–31) and Sin (*Apollyonists* 1.10–12). Classical sources include Hesiod's Echidna (half woman, half snake) (*Theog.* 300–25). See also Vergil's Scylla (*Aen.* 3.426–32) and Ovid's story of her origin (*Met.* 14.50–67), to which Milton al-

ludes at 659–61 (see note); cp. *Masque* 257–58.

652. **Voluminous:** winding or coiling, like a serpent.

653. **mortal sting:** "The sting of death is sin" (1 Cor. 15.56).

654. **cry:** pack; group noun for hounds.

655. **Cerberean:** In Greek myth, Cerberus is a many-headed guard dog at the entrance to Hades.

658. Cp. the complaint of Shakespeare's Margaret to the Duchess of York: "From forth the kennel of thy womb hath crept / A hell-hound that doth hunt us all to death" (*R3* 4.4.47–48).

659–61. Circe poisons the sheltered coastal pool in which Scylla bathes. According to

660 Vexed Scylla bathing in the sea that parts
Calabria from the hoarse Trinacrian shore:
Nor uglier follow the night-hag, when called
In secret, riding through the air she comes
Lured with the smell of infant blood, to dance
665 With Lapland witches, while the laboring moon
Eclipses at their charms. The other shape,
If shape it might be called that shape had none
Distinguishable in member, joint, or limb,
Or substance might be called that shadow seemed,
670 For each seemed either; black it stood as night,
Fierce as ten Furies, terrible as Hell,
And shook a dreadful dart; what seemed his head
The likeness of a kingly crown had on.
Satan was now at hand, and from his seat
675 The monster moving onward came as fast
With horrid strides; Hell trembled as he strode.
Th' undaunted Fiend what this might be admired,
Admired, not feared; God and his Son except,
Created thing naught valued he nor shunned;

Ovid, she wades in up to her waist and "sees her loins disfigured with barking monster shapes . . . gaping dogs' heads, such as a Cerberus might have" (*Met.* 14.60–65). She then preys on sailors from a cave on the Sicilian (*Trinacrian*) coast near Messina, opposite the southern tip of the Italian mainland (*Calabria*). Milton may deem the shore along the Strait of Messina *hoarse* because of nearby Etna's frequent roaring.

662. **night-hag:** probably Hecate, the only Titan left at large by Zeus. The Greeks associated her with, among other things, infernal powers, the moon, and witchcraft. Howling dogs signaled her approach. See *Masque* 535, *MAC* 3.5.

664–66. **Lured . . . charms:** Witches were thought to use infant blood in their rites. Hence seventeenth-century authorities suspected midwives of practicing witchcraft and serving Satan by infanticide

(Baillie 63, Ehrenreich and English). *Laboring* evokes the process of childbirth.

665. **Lapland:** northernmost portion of the Scandinavian peninsula. Hume records the common reputation of the inhabitants: "their diabolical superstitions, and vindictive natures, added to their gross stupidity, and the malicious imaginations of melancholy, have made them infamous for witchcraft and conjuration." **laboring:** That magic could afflict the moon, causing it to labor in its movement, was an old and widespread belief. One meaning of the Latin *laborare* is "to undergo eclipse."

673. Milton's representation of Death with a *kingly crown* may reflect his antimonarchical views. Cp. Shakespeare's *R2*: "Within the hollow crown/That rounds the mortal temples of a king/Keeps Death his court" (3.2.160–62).

677. **admired:** wondered.

678–79. **God . . . shunned:** "When God was

680 And with disdainful look thus first began.
      "Whence and what art thou, execrable shape,
    That dar'st, though grim and terrible, advance
    Thy miscreated front athwart my way
    To yonder gates? Through them I mean to pass,
685 That be assured, without leave asked of thee:
    Retire, or taste thy folly, and learn by proof,
    Hell-born, not to contend with spirits of Heav'n."
      To whom the Goblin full of wrath replied,
    "Art thou that traitor angel, art thou he,
690 Who first broke peace in Heav'n and faith, till then
    Unbroken, and in proud rebellious arms
    Drew after him the third part of Heav'n's sons
    Conjured against the highest, for which both thou
    And they outcast from God, are here condemned
695 To waste eternal days in woe and pain?
    And reckon'st thou thyself with spirits of Heav'n,
    Hell-doomed, and breath'st defiance here and scorn,
    Where I reign king, and to enrage thee more,
    Thy king and lord? Back to thy punishment,
700 False fugitive, and to thy speed add wings,
    Lest with a whip of scorpions I pursue
    Thy ling'ring, or with one stroke of this dart

---

except (past participle, *OED* 3b: 'ex-cluded'), no basis for value remained" (Fowler). Although this gloss may seem strained, the more common reading—"of all creation Satan values or shuns only God and the Son"—has a nodding Milton imply that God is created.
681. In asking his opponent's origin, Satan speaks in the manner of Achilles, though to ironically comic effect (cp. *Il.* 21.150).
683. **miscreated front:** ugly face.
686. **taste:** learn by experience or *proof,* a figurative usage crucial to the epic action.
692. "[The dragon's] tail drew the third part of the stars of heaven, and did cast them to the earth" (Rev. 12.4). Satan tends to overstate his faction as "well nigh half"

(9.141). The precise ratio had long been a point of scholastic controversy.
693. **Conjured:** sworn together (stress on the second syllable).
697. **Hell-doomed:** retort to Satan's scornful *Hell-born* (l. 687). Raphael's narrative of the rebellion (5.563ff) confirms Death's summary, which is oddly well informed and free from the infernal bias prevalent for most of the first two books.
701. Cp. Solomon's son Rehoboam to the Is-raelites: "My father hath chastised you with whips, but I will chastise you with scorpions" (1 Kings 12.11). The allusion suggests that God (Satan's punisher) is also Death's father, though we are about to learn otherwise.

Strange horror seize thee, and pangs unfelt before."
   So spake the grisly terror, and in shape,
705 So speaking and so threat'ning, grew tenfold
More dreadful and deform: on th' other side
Incensed with indignation Satan stood
Unterrified, and like a comet burned,
That fires the length of Ophiucus huge
710 In th' Arctic sky, and from his horrid hair
Shakes pestilence and war. Each at the head
Leveled his deadly aim; their fatal hands
No second stroke intend, and such a frown
Each cast at th' other, as when two black clouds
715 With heav'n's artillery fraught, come rattling on
Over the Caspian, then stand front to front
Hov'ring a space, till winds the signal blow
To join their dark encounter in mid air:
So frowned the mighty combatants, that Hell
720 Grew darker at their frown, so matched they stood;
For never but once more was either like
To meet so great a foe: and now great deeds
Had been achieved, whereof all Hell had rung,
Had not the snaky sorceress that sat
725 Fast by Hell gate, and kept the fatal key,
Ris'n, and with hideous outcry rushed between.
   "O father, what intends thy hand," she cried,

705–11. **So speaking . . . war:** Cp. Satan's confrontation with Gabriel (4.985ff).

708–11. **Unterrified . . . war:** Vergil and Tasso, among others, precede Milton in comparing warriors to comets (*Aen.* 10.272–73; *GL* 7.52). They were since ancient times believed to presage pestilence, war, and change of kingdoms.

709. **Ophiucus:** serpent bearer; a large constellation that Milton associates with Satan, located in the Northern (hence *Arctic*) Hemisphere.

710. **horrid hair:** Another example of Milton's etymologically instructive wordplay. *Comet* derives from the Greek *kometes*,

"long-haired." *Horrid* means "bristling" and derives from the same root as *hirsute* ("hairy").

714–18. Boiardo's Orlando and Agricane are similarly opposed like *two black clouds* (*Orlando Innamorato* 1.16.10). Satan, whose realm will be "mid air" (*PR* 1.44–46), is persistently linked to meteorological phenomena.

716. **Caspian:** region commonly associated with storms (see, e.g., Horace, *Odes* 2.9.2–3).

722. **foe:** the Son of God. See 1 Cor. 15.25–26 and Heb. 2.14.

"Against thy only son? What fury O son,
Possesses thee to bend that mortal dart
730 Against thy father's head? And know'st for whom;
For him who sits above and laughs the while
At thee ordained his drudge, to execute
Whate'er his wrath, which he calls justice, bids,
His wrath which one day will destroy ye both."

735 　　She spake, and at her words the Hellish pest
Forbore, then these to her Satan returned:
　　"So strange thy outcry, and thy words so strange
Thou interposest, that my sudden hand
Prevented spares to tell thee yet by deeds
740 What it intends; till first I know of thee,
What thing thou art, thus double-formed, and why
In this infernal vale first met thou call'st
Me father, and that phantasm call'st my son?
I know thee not, nor ever saw till now
745 Sight more detestable than him and thee."
　　T' whom thus the portress of Hell gate replied:
"Hast thou forgot me then, and do I seem
Now in thine eye so foul, once deemed so fair
In Heav'n, when at th' assembly, and in sight
750 Of all the Seraphim with thee combined
In bold conspiracy against Heav'n's King,
All on a sudden miserable pain
Surprised thee, dim thine eyes, and dizzy swum
In darkness, while thy head flames thick and fast
755 Threw forth, till on the left side op'ning wide,
Likest to thee in shape and count'nance bright,
Then shining Heav'nly fair, a goddess armed

---

746. **portress:** "The *Porter* to th' infernal gate
is *Sin*" (P. Fletcher, *Apollyonists* 1.10.1).
748. "This is a very just and instructive part
　of the allegory. . . . Sin, pleasant in con-
　templation and enjoyment, is foul in ret-
　rospect" (Cowper).
752–53. **All . . . thee:** Sin's narrative and
　Raphael's later narrative offer distinct ex-

planations of Satan's first experience of
pain; cp. 6.327ff, 432ff.
754–58. **while . . . sprung:** The general
amazement at the cephalic delivery of Sin
full-blown, as *a goddess armed*, recalls the
account of Athena's birth in *Homeric
Hymn* 28.

Out of thy head I sprung: amazement seized
All th' host of Heav'n; back they recoiled afraid
760 At first, and called me Sin, and for a sign
Portentous held me; but familiar grown,
I pleased, and with attractive graces won
The most averse, thee chiefly, who full oft
Thyself in me thy perfect image viewing
765 Becam'st enamored, and such joy thou took'st
With me in secret, that my womb conceived
A growing burden. Meanwhile war arose,
And fields were fought in Heav'n; wherein remained
(For what could else) to our almighty foe
770 Clear victory, to our part loss and rout
Through all the empyrean: down they fell
Driv'n headlong from the pitch of Heaven, down
Into this deep, and in the general fall
I also; at which time this powerful key
775 Into my hand was giv'n, with charge to keep
These gates for ever shut, which none can pass
Without my op'ning. Pensive here I sat
Alone, but long I sat not, till my womb
Pregnant by thee, and now excessive grown
780 Prodigious motion felt and rueful throes.
At last this odious offspring whom thou seest
Thine own begotten, breaking violent way
Tore through my entrails, that with fear and pain
Distorted, all my nether shape thus grew
785 Transformed: but he my inbred enemy

760. Critics preoccupied with postmodern semiotics belabor the proximity of *Sin* and *sign,* near homophones.

768. **fields:** battles; cp. 1.105.

771. **empyrean:** highest part of Heaven, where pure fire or light subsists.

772. **pitch:** pinnacle, height.

774–77. **at which time . . . op'ning:** Citing these lines, Fowler (746n) dismisses Empson's concern over God's choice of Sin and Death as guards. An allegory in which a personification of sin is expected to obey God's command is nonetheless perplexing.

778–87. **till . . . destroy:** "Then when lust hath conceived, it bringeth forth sin: and sin, when it is finished, bringeth forth death" (James 1.15). Cp. Shakespeare, *Sonnet 129.* As with the birth of Sin (754–58n), the delivery of Death echoes the discharge of Satan's artillery (6.586–90).

Forth issued, brandishing his fatal dart
Made to destroy: I fled, and cried out 'Death';
Hell trembled at the hideous name, and sighed
From all her caves, and back resounded 'Death.'
790 I fled, but he pursued (though more, it seems,
Inflamed with lust than rage) and swifter far,
Me overtook his mother all dismayed,
And in embraces forcible and foul
Engend'ring with me, of that rape begot
795 These yelling monsters that with ceaseless cry
Surround me, as thou saw'st, hourly conceived
And hourly born, with sorrow infinite
To me, for when they list into the womb
That bred them they return, and howl and gnaw
800 My bowels, their repast; then bursting forth
Afresh with conscious terrors vex me round,
That rest or intermission none I find.
Before mine eyes in opposition sits
Grim Death my son and foe, who sets them on,
805 And me his parent would full soon devour
For want of other prey, but that he knows
His end with mine involved; and knows that I
Should prove a bitter morsel, and his bane,
Whenever that shall be; so fate pronounced.
810 But thou O father, I forewarn thee, shun
His deadly arrow; neither vainly hope
To be invulnerable in those bright arms,
Though tempered Heav'nly, for that mortal dint,
Save he who reigns above, none can resist."
815   She finished, and the subtle Fiend his lore

---

789. Vergil similarly describes the sound
produced by a spear thrown into the side
of the Trojan horse: "With the womb's re-
verberation the vaults rang hollow, send-
ing forth a moan" (*Aen.* 2.52–53).

795–802. The description of this hourly
cycle suggests a nightmarish clock mech-
anism. Postlapsarian time consciousness

is also consciousness of death; cp. 4.266–
68; *On Time*.

809. **so fate pronounced:** Leonard cites
Milton's theological treatise: "fate or
fatum is only what is *fatum*, spoken, by
some almighty power" (*MLM* 1146).

813. **dint:** blow, stroke.

Soon learned, now milder, and thus answered smooth.
   "Dear daughter, since thou claim'st me for thy sire,
And my fair son here show'st me, the dear pledge
Of dalliance had with thee in Heav'n, and joys
820 Then sweet, now sad to mention, through dire change
Befall'n us unforeseen, unthought of, know
I come no enemy, but to set free
From out this dark and dismal house of pain,
Both him and thee, and all the Heav'nly host
825 Of spirits that in our just pretenses armed
Fell with us from on high: from them I go
This uncouth errand sole, and one for all
Myself expose, with lonely steps to tread
Th' unfounded deep, and through the void immense
830 To search with wand'ring quest a place foretold
Should be, and, by concurring signs, ere now
Created vast and round, a place of bliss
In the purlieus of Heav'n, and therein placed
A race of upstart creatures, to supply
835 Perhaps our vacant room, though more removed,
Lest Heav'n surcharged with potent multitude
Might hap to move new broils: be this or aught
Than this more secret now designed, I haste
To know, and this once known, shall soon return,
840 And bring ye to the place where thou and Death
Shall dwell at ease, and up and down unseen
Wing silently the buxom air, embalmed
With odors; there ye shall be fed and filled
Immeasurably, all things shall be your prey."

---

825. **pretenses:** claims; the meaning "false claims" was equally current in Milton's time.

827. **uncouth errand sole:** unknown mission alone; cp. line 407.

829. **unfounded:** bottomless, unestablished.

833. **purlieus:** outskirts. "A French word (as most of our law terms are) of *pur* pure and *lieu* a place, and denotes the ground adjoining to, and being accounted part of any forest, by Henry II and other Kings, was ... separated again from the same and adjudged *Purlieu*, that is pure and free from the Laws of the Forest" (Hume).

836. **surcharged:** overburdened.

837. **broils:** tumults, riots. Without once mentioning God, Satan insinuates that humanity's location outside Heaven is a security measure aimed at crowd control.

842. **buxom:** pliant, yielding (cp. 5.270); em-

845   He ceased, for both seemed highly pleased, and Death
       Grinned horrible a ghastly smile, to hear
       His famine should be filled, and blessed his maw
       Destined to that good hour: no less rejoiced
       His mother bad, and thus bespake her sire.
850   "The key of this infernal pit by due,
       And by command of Heav'n's all-powerful King
       I keep, by him forbidden to unlock
       These adamantine gates; against all force
       Death ready stands to interpose his dart,
855   Fearless to be o'ermatched by living might.
       But what owe I to his commands above
       Who hates me, and hath hither thrust me down
       Into this gloom of Tartarus profound,
       To sit in hateful office here confined,
860   Inhabitant of Heav'n, and Heav'nly-born,
       Here in perpetual agony and pain,
       With terrors and with clamors compassed round
       Of mine own brood, that on my bowels feed:
       Thou art my father, thou my author, thou
865   My being gav'st me; whom should I obey
       But thee, whom follow? Thou wilt bring me soon
       To that new world of light and bliss, among
       The gods who live at ease, where I shall reign
       At thy right hand voluptuous, as beseems
870   Thy daughter and thy darling, without end."
         Thus saying, from her side the fatal key,

---

balmed: balmy, aromatic; also, "preserved with balm and precious spices, as princes and great persons are at their death, a word well applied to caress the ugly phantom" (Hume).

861–62. Sin's plight is echoed in Milton's account of his situation at the Restoration (7.25–28).

868. **gods who live at ease**: translates Homer's epithet for the Olympian gods (*Il.* 6.138).

869–70. Milton has Sin prophesy in phrases burlesquing the Nicene Creed ("Christ... sits on the right hand of the father... [his] kingdom shall have no end"). Milton scorned prescribed statements of faith and thought the doctrine of the Trinity articulated in the Nicene Creed especially contemptible. In his epic, the closest thing to the orthodox Trinity is the incestuous unity and variety of Satan, Sin, and Death.

Sad instrument of all our woe, she took;
And towards the gate rolling her bestial train,
Forthwith the huge portcullis high up drew,
875 Which but herself not all the Stygian powers
Could once have moved; then in the key-hole turns
Th' intricate wards, and every bolt and bar
Of massy iron or solid rock with ease
Unfastens: on a sudden open fly
880 With impetuous recoil and jarring sound
Th' infernal doors, and on their hinges grate
Harsh thunder, that the lowest bottom shook
Of Erebus. She opened, but to shut
Excelled her power; the gates wide open stood,
885 That with extended wings a bannered host
Under spread ensigns marching might pass through
With horse and chariots ranked in loose array;
So wide they stood, and like a furnace mouth
Cast forth redounding smoke and ruddy flame.
890 Before their eyes in sudden view appear
The secrets of the hoary deep, a dark
Illimitable ocean without bound,
Without dimension, where length, breadth, and highth,
And time and place are lost; where eldest Night

872. **all our woe:** repeats 1.3. Sin provides the instrument that permits Satan to seduce humanity to the *first disobedience* (1.1).

876–79. **then . . . Unfastens:** Cp. Homer's description of Penelope opening the door to the storeroom where Odysseus's bow is kept: "Straightaway she quickly loosed the thong from the handle and thrust in the key, and with sure aim shot back the bolts . . . quickly they flew open before her" (*Od.* 21.46–50).

877. **wards:** corresponding ridges or grooves in a lock and key.

880–82. **With . . . thunder:** "Grating on harsh, jarring hinges, the infernal gates open" (*Aen.* 6.873–74).

883. **Erebus:** darkness, the underworld.

889. **redounding:** surging, rolling upward in superabundance.

891. **secrets:** places, parts, or causes unknown, perhaps intentionally concealed; cp. 3.707. The realm of Chaos and Night is described as a womb (see l. 911, 10.476–77), impregnated by the Spirit during creation (1.21–22). Satan's trespass could thus be construed as sexual prying or a violation of the maternal (cp. 1.684–88, 2.785ff). **hoary:** white-haired and thus old or ancient.

894–910. **where . . . all:** Milton describes *eldest Night* as *eternal*, like the *anarchy* over which she and *Chaos* preside (e.g., l. 150, 3.18, 10.477). His presentation of Chaos is indebted to Ovid and Lucretius (*Met.* 1.5–20; *On the Nature of Things* 2). Com-

895 And Chaos, ancestors of Nature, hold
    Eternal anarchy, amidst the noise
    Of endless wars, and by confusion stand.
    For Hot, Cold, Moist, and Dry, four champions fierce
    Strive here for mast'ry, and to battle bring
900 Their embryon atoms; they around the flag
    Of each his faction, in their several clans,
    Light-armed or heavy, sharp, smooth, swift or slow,
    Swarm populous, unnumbered as the sands
    Of Barca or Cyrene's torrid soil,
905 Levied to side with warring winds, and poise
    Their lighter wings. To whom these most adhere,
    He rules a moment; Chaos umpire sits,
    And by decision more embroils the fray
    By which he reigns: next him high arbiter
910 Chance governs all. Into this wild abyss,
    The womb of Nature and perhaps her grave,
    Of neither sea, nor shore, nor air, nor fire,
    But all these in their pregnant causes mixed

---

menting on Ovid, Sandys objects that "by not expressing the original, he seems to intimate the eternity of his *Chaos*" (1632, 49). Only God is eternal. The attribution of eternal being to Chaos and Night thus renders Milton's account of primordial matter heretical in one of two ways: either Chaos represents a realm distinct from God and, like him, eternal and existentially independent, or Chaos represents an aspect of eternal God himself. The discussion of matter in *Christian Doctrine* indicates that Milton endorsed the latter heresy (1.7). Cp. 915–16n.

898. **Hot, Cold, Moist, and Dry:** These had long been considered the four fundamental qualities that combine to constitute all created phenomena: humors, elements, planets, or bodies in general. Thus, earth was dry and cold, water moist and cold, air moist and hot, fire dry and hot, et cetera.

900–903. **embryon atoms ... unnumbered:** indivisible units of primal matter, undeveloped and unformed; cp. line 913. The relative weights, shapes, motions, and textures of these countless (*unnumbered*) "seeds of things," the *semina rerum* of Lucretian atomist philosophy, account for the phenomenal variety of the world (*On the Nature of Things* 2.62–833).

904. **Barca or Cyrene's:** desert region of Northern Africa notorious for sandstorms.

906. **To whom these:** The referents of *whom* are the *four champions fierce* of line 898; *these* refers to the atoms.

907–10. **Chaos ... all:** On the rule of *Chaos* and *Chance* in relation to fate and God's will, cp. lines 232–33, 915–16, and 7.172–73.

911. Except for the insertion of *perhaps*, the line loosely translates Lucretius's portrayal of the Earth (*On the Nature of Things* 5.259).

Confus'dly, and which thus must ever fight,
915 Unless th' Almighty Maker them ordain
His dark materials to create more worlds,
Into this wild abyss the wary Fiend
Stood on the brink of Hell and looked a while,
Pondering his Voyage; for no narrow frith
920 He had to cross. Nor was his ear less pealed
With noises loud and ruinous (to compare
Great things with small) than when Bellona storms,
With all her battering engines bent to raze
Some capital city; or less than if this frame
925 Of heav'n were falling, and these elements
In mutiny had from her axle torn
The steadfast Earth. At last his sail-broad vans
He spreads for flight, and in the surging smoke
Uplifted spurns the ground, thence many a league
930 As in a cloudy chair ascending rides
Audacious, but that seat soon failing, meets
A vast vacuity: all unawares
Flutt'ring his pennons vain plumb down he drops
Ten thousand fathom deep, and to this hour
935 Down had been falling, had not by ill chance
The strong rebuff of some tumultuous cloud

915–16. Milton allows that God could use the *dark materials* of chaos to create more worlds (universes, not simply planets), provoking the complaint that Milton heretically "supposes the Deity to have needed means with which to work . . . [though] the very word *creation* implies existence given to something which never before existed" (Cowper). As Milton recognized, however, the Hebrew verb *create* implies the opposite of what Cowper claimed it does (*CD* 1.7; see 894–910n).

919. **frith**: firth, channel.

920. **pealed**: assailed, rung.

921–22. **to compare . . . small**: Cp. 6.310–11, 10.306; *PR* 4.563–64, where Milton uses the same formula, borrowed from Vergil (*Ec.* 1.24, *Georg.* 4.176).

922. **Bellona**: Roman goddess of war, sister to Mars.

924. **frame**: that which supports the sky. Cp. Horace's admiration of "the man tenacious of his purpose in a righteous cause": "Were the vault of heaven to break and fall upon him, its ruins would smite him undismayed" (*Odes* 3.3.1, 7–8).

927. **vans**: wings. Milton persists in linking Satan to a sailing ship.

930. **cloudy chair**: car formed of clouds.

933. **pennons**: pinions, wings.

935–38. **Down . . . aloft**: Satan's escape from oblivion owes to the *rebuff* (counterblast) of a cloud *instinct with* (moved or impelled by) *fire and niter*, ingredients of gunpowder, Satan's signature invention from chaotic materials (see 6.478–83,

Instinct with fire and niter hurried him
As many miles aloft: that fury stayed,
Quenched in a boggy Syrtis, neither sea,
940 Nor good dry land: nigh foundered on he fares,
Treading the crude consistence, half on foot,
Half flying; behooves him now both oar and sail.
As when a gryphon through the wilderness
With wingèd course o'er hill or moory dale,
945 Pursues the Arimaspian, who by stealth
Had from his wakeful custody purloined
The guarded gold: so eagerly the Fiend
O'er bog or steep, through strait, rough, dense, or rare,
With head, hands, wings or feet pursues his way,
950 And swims or sinks, or wades, or creeps, or flies:
At length a universal hubbub wild
Of stunning sounds and voices all confused
Born through the hollow dark assaults his ear
With loudest vehemence: thither he plies,
955 Undaunted to meet there whatever power
Or spirit of the nethermost abyss
Might in that noise reside, of whom to ask
Which way the nearest coast of darkness lies
Bordering on light; when straight behold the throne
960 Of Chaos, and his dark pavilion spread

511–15). Phenomena like shooting stars, comets, and lightning were attributed to the atmospheric ignition of such vapors. Cp. other instances of Satan's luck (4.530; 9.85, 421–23).

939. **Syrtis:** The Syrtes are two shallow gulfs (Sidra and Cabes) off the north coast of Libya, a region dreaded for its quicksands (e.g., Acts 27.17). Milton echoes Lucan's *Pharsalia* (9.364ff) in describing it as neither sea nor land.

942. **both oar and sail:** all possible force, might and main. Galley ships when pressed used both oars and sails; cp. *Aen.* 3.563.

943–45. **gryphon . . . Arimaspian:** The *gryphon* (or griffin) is a mythical guardian

of gold, with the upper half of an eagle and lower of a lion. It can thus speed over varied terrain *with wingèd course* (with wings and feet) in pursuit of the *Arimaspian,* legendary one-eyed people who steal the guarded gold. See Herodotus 3.116; 4.13, 27.

948–49. The extended series of disjointed monosyllables and breakdowns in iambic meter express the difficulty of negotiating the helter-skelter of chaos.

951–54. **universal hubbub . . . vehemence:** Cp. the curse of Babel, 12.53–62.

954. **vehemence:** mindlessness; **plies:** alters course, tacks (see 637–42n).

960–61. **Of Chaos . . . deep:** "He made

Wide on the wasteful deep; with him enthroned
Sat sable-vested Night, eldest of things,
The consort of his reign; and by them stood
Orcus and Ades, and the dreaded name
965   Of Demogorgon; Rumor next and Chance,
And Tumult and Confusion all embroiled,
And Discord with a thousand various mouths.
      T' whom Satan turning boldly, thus. "Ye Powers
And Spirits of this nethermost abyss,
970   Chaos and ancient Night, I come no spy,
With purpose to explore or to disturb
The secrets of your realm, but by constraint
Wand'ring this darksome desert, as my way
Lies through your spacious empire up to light,
975   Alone, and without guide, half lost, I seek
What readiest path leads where your gloomy bounds
Confine with Heav'n; or if some other place
From your dominion won, th' Ethereal King
Possesses lately, thither to arrive
980   I travel this profound, direct my course;
Directed, no mean recompense it brings

---

darkness pavilions round about him, dark waters, and thick clouds of the skies" (2 Sam. 22.12; cp. Ps. 18.11).

961. **wasteful:** vast, desolate. Milton is prone to repetition of initial *w* sounds, and especially to alliterative compounds with *wide*. See 1.3, 2.1007, 6.253, 8.467, 11.121, 487; *Nat Ode* 51, 64; *Il Pens* 75, *Lyc* 13; *Sonnet 19* 2.

962. **sable-vested Night:** translates Euripides' epithet for Night, *Ion* 1150 (literally, "black-robed Night"). She and Chaos preside over a court of accessory personifications.

964. **Orcus and Ades:** Latin and Greek for the underworld and its ruler (the Greek word is usually spelled *Hades*).

965. **Demogorgon:** Boccaccio copied the *dreaded name* from a medieval manuscript's gloss of an allusion in Statius (*Thebiad* 4.516). The reference is to a deity

whose name alone terrifies infernal powers. Boccaccio applied it to the primeval deity in his *Genealogy of the Gods.* Subsequent authors followed suit and often made Demogorgon master of the Fates. See, e.g., Spenser, *FQ* 1.1.37, 4.2.47. Cp. Milton's *Prolusion 1* in *MLM* 787.

967. Milton transfers to *Discord* a trait ordinarily found in personifications of fame or rumor, as when Shakespeare has *Rumor* "painted full of tongues" speak the prologue to *2H4.* In *PL,* rumor seems to originate in God and is aligned with prophecy, though it does inspire conflict (see, *e.g.,* ll. 345–53, 831, 1.651, 10.481–82).

977. **Confine with:** border on.

980. **this profound:** the deep (adj. for noun). The punctuation and dodgy syntax of lines 980–86 suggest that Satan is improvising as he speaks.

To your behoof, if I that region lost,
All usurpation thence expelled, reduce
To her original darkness and your sway
985 (Which is my present journey) and once more
Erect the standard there of ancient Night;
Yours be th' advantage all, mine the revenge."
    Thus Satan; and him thus the Anarch old
With falt'ring speech and visage incomposed
990 Answered. "I know thee, stranger, who thou art,
That mighty leading angel, who of late
Made head against Heav'n's King, though overthrown.
I saw and heard, for such a numerous host
Fled not in silence through the frighted deep
995 With ruin upon ruin, rout on rout,
Confusion worse confounded; and Heav'n gates
Poured out by millions her victorious bands
Pursuing. I upon my frontiers here
Keep residence; if all I can will serve,
1000 That little which is left so to defend,
Encroached on still through our intestine broils
Weak'ning the scepter of old Night: first Hell
Your dungeon stretching far and wide beneath;
Now lately heaven and Earth, another world
1005 Hung o'er my realm, linked in a golden chain
To that side Heav'n from whence your legions fell:

---

982. **behoof:** advantage.

982–87. **if I . . . revenge:** Satan is setting up a double cross. Cp. 10.399–418.

988. **Anarch:** anarchy's head of state.

989. **incomposed:** without composure or orderly arrangement; cp. "increase" (3.6).

993–98. **I saw . . . Pursuing:** Cp. 6.871–74.

1001. **our:** In light of lines 908–9, some editors substitute "your," construing *our intestine broils* as a reference to the War in Heaven rather than to the constitutional strife of chaos. Cp. Henry IV's account of the "intestine shock / And furious close of civil butchery" involving opponents

"all of one nature, of one substance bred" (*1H4* 1.1.11–13).

1004. **heaven:** not the abode of God and the angels, as in line 1006, but the sky. The *world* of which Chaos speaks is in modern usage called the "universe."

1005. **golden chain:** Homer's Zeus boasts that the combined strength of the other gods could not prevent him from pulling them and the world up to heaven by a golden chain (*Il.* 8.18–27). Milton endorsed the traditional interpretation of this chain as a symbol of cosmic design and order (*Prolusion 2*, Yale 1:236).

If that way be your walk, you have not far;
So much the nearer danger; go and speed;
Havoc and spoil and ruin are my gain."

1010   He ceased; and Satan stayed not to reply,
But glad that now his sea should find a shore,
With fresh alacrity and force renewed
Springs upward like a pyramid of fire
Into the wild expanse, and through the shock
1015   Of fighting elements, on all sides round
Environed wins his way; harder beset
And more endangered, than when Argo passed
Through Bosporus betwixt the jostling rocks:
Or when Ulysses on the larboard shunned
1020   Charybdis, and by th' other whirlpool steered.
So he with difficulty and labor hard
Moved on, with difficulty and labor he;
But he once passed, soon after when man fell,
Strange alteration! Sin and Death amain
1025   Following his track, such was the will of Heav'n,
Paved after him a broad and beaten way
Over the dark abyss, whose boiling gulf
Tamely endured a bridge of wondrous length
From Hell continued reaching th' utmost orb
1030   Of this frail world; by which the spirits perverse
With easy intercourse pass to and fro

1007. **walk:** distance to be covered; course of conduct or action.

1008. **danger:** As with much of what Chaos says, the meaning is difficult to pin down. Is Satan approaching danger, or is danger, in the person of Satan, approaching the world?

1013. "The pyramid is the solid which is the original element and seed of fire" (Plato, *Timaeus* 56b). In sharp contrast to the anarchy of *embryon atoms* (l. 900), Satan through sheer force of will launches himself toward creation in the atomic form of his own element (Kerrigan 1983, 138–39).

1017. **Argo:** the ship of Jason and his crew (Argonauts). They encounter the clashing (*jostling*) rocks of the *Bosporos* (the Strait of Constantinople) (Apollonius 2.552–611).

1019. **larboard:** left side of a vessel, port.

1020. **Charybdis:** dreaded whirlpool in the Strait of Messina, just opposite man-eating Scylla (see 659–61n). Ulysses avoided the total destruction that *Charybdis* threatened by sailing nearer to Scylla (Homer, *Od.* 12.234–59).

1024–30. **Sin . . . world:** For construction of this *broad and beaten way* (cp. Matt. 7.13), see 10.293–305.

1024. **amain:** in full force, numbers.

To tempt or punish mortals, except whom
God and good angels guard by special grace.
But now at last the sacred influence
1035 Of light appears, and from the walls of Heav'n
Shoots far into the bosom of dim Night
A glimmering dawn; here Nature first begins
Her farthest verge, and Chaos to retire
As from her outmost works a broken foe
1040 With tumult less and with less hostile din,
That Satan with less toil, and now with ease
Wafts on the calmer wave by dubious light
And like a weather-beaten vessel holds
Gladly the port, though shrouds and tackle torn;
1045 Or in the emptier waste, resembling air,
Weighs his spread wings, at leisure to behold
Far off th' empyreal Heav'n, extended wide
In circuit, undetermined square or round,
With opal tow'rs and battlements adorned
1050 Of living sapphire, once his native seat;
And fast by hanging in a golden chain
This pendant world, in bigness as a star
Of smallest magnitude close by the moon.
Thither full fraught with mischievous revenge,
1055 Accursed, and in a cursèd hour he hies.

1033. **special grace:** Cp. 3.183–84. See *Masque* 36–42, 216–20, 453–63.

1034. **sacred influence:** Light is inseparable from God himself (3.1–6). Its influence, whether sunlight or starlight, is the chief agent of creative growth; see 4.661–73, 6.476–81, 9.107, 192.

1039. **her outmost works:** Nature's *works* are fortifications against the tumult of chaos.

1043. **holds:** maintains heading for.

1044. **shrouds and tackle:** rigging on a sailing ship; cp. *SA* 198–200, 717.

1046. **Weighs:** holds steady.

1048. **undetermined:** The expanse of Heaven is so vast that one cannot tell whether it is circular or square.

1050. **living:** in its native condition and site, unlike Satan, whose connection with his *native seat* and the source of his being lies irretrievably in the past. The walls are also, like everything in Heaven, living in the literal sense (6.860–61, 878–79).

1052. **pendant world:** the entire universe, hanging like a jewel on a chain.

1055. **hies:** hastens. "Milton begins Book 3 with the same alliteration" (Leonard).

Book III

The Argument

God sitting on his throne sees Satan flying towards this world, then newly created; shows him to the Son who sat at his right hand; foretells the success of Satan in perverting mankind; clears his own justice and wisdom from all imputation, having created man free and able enough to have withstood his tempter; yet declares his purpose of grace towards him, in regard he fell not of his own malice, as did Satan, but by him seduced. The Son of God renders praises to his Father for the manifestation of his gracious purpose towards man; but God again declares that grace cannot be extended towards man without the satisfaction of divine justice; man hath offended the majesty of God by aspiring to Godhead, and therefore with all his progeny devoted to death must die, unless someone can be found sufficient to answer for his offense, and undergo his punishment. The Son of God freely offers himself a ransom for man: the Father accepts him, ordains his incarnation, pronounces his exaltation above all names in Heaven and Earth, commands all the angels to adore him. They obey, and hymning to their harps in full choir, celebrate the Father and the Son. Meanwhile Satan alights upon the bare convex of this world's outermost orb; where wandering he first finds a place since called the Limbo of Vanity; what persons and things fly up thither; thence comes to the gate of Heaven, described ascending by stairs, and the waters above the firmament that flow about it: his passage thence to the orb of the sun; he finds there Uriel the regent of that orb, but first changes himself into the shape of a meaner angel; and pretending a zealous desire to behold the new creation and man whom God had placed here, inquires of him the place of his habitation, and is directed; alights first on Mount Niphates.

Hail holy light, offspring of Heav'n first-born,
Or of th' Eternal coeternal beam
May I express thee unblamed? Since God is light,
And never but in unapproachèd light
5   Dwelt from eternity, dwelt then in thee,
Bright effluence of bright essence increate.
Or hear'st thou rather pure ethereal stream,
Whose fountain who shall tell? Before the sun,
Before the heavens thou wert, and at the voice
10 Of God, as with a mantle didst invest
The rising world of waters dark and deep,
Won from the void and formless infinite.
Thee I revisit now with bolder wing,
Escaped the Stygian pool, though long detained
15 In that obscure sojourn, while in my flight
Through utter and through middle darkness borne

1–55. This passage of transition from Hell and Chaos to Heaven, known as "the invocation to light," is at once the most speculative and intimate of the poem's four invocations (at the openings of Books 1, 3, 7, and 9). The meaning of the light addressed has often been debated. Some identify *holy light* with physical light, the first of created things (Kelley 91–94), while others think that light here symbolizes some aspect of the Godhead, usually the Son (Hunter et al., 149–56). In the second case, however, Milton in lines 1–8 would be uncertain whether the Son was created in time, whereas elsewhere in the poem (3.384, 5.603), as in his prose (*CD* 1.5), he is definite on the Son's createdness. See 6n.

2. Or the beam coeternal with the Father (and therefore not *first-born*).

3–6. Since . . . increate: These lines expand on the likelihood that light, being the dwelling of God, is eternal.

3. express: describe, invoke; unblamed: without being judged blasphemous or im-

proper; God is light: quoted from 1 John 1.5.

4. unapproachèd light: See 1 Tim. 6.16. Even angels shade their eyes with their wings when approaching the *dazzling* Father (ll. 375–82).

6. effluence: flowing out; essence: deity, the divine essence of the Father; increate: uncreated, without origin.

7. hear'st thou rather: do you prefer to be called; ethereal: composed of ether, the lightest and most subtle element, ubiquitous in the heavens; see 7.244n.

8. Whose fountain who shall tell: whose beginning is unknown and unknowable; see Job 38.19.

10. invest: clothe, wrap; see Ps. 104.2.

12. void and formless infinite: Chaos is void of form, not matter; on its infinity, see 7.168–71n.

14. Stygian pool: classical synecdoche for Hell; long detained: for Book 1 and nearly all of Book 2.

15. sojourn: place of temporary stay.

16. utter . . . middle darkness: *Utter darkness* is Hell; *middle darkness* is Chaos.

With other notes than to th' Orphean lyre
I sung of Chaos and eternal Night,
Taught by the Heav'nly Muse to venture down
20 The dark descent, and up to reascend,
Though hard and rare: thee I revisit safe,
And feel thy sov'reign vital lamp; but thou
Revisit'st not these eyes, that roll in vain
To find thy piercing ray, and find no dawn;
25 So thick a drop serene hath quenched their orbs,
Or dim suffusion veiled. Yet not the more
Cease I to wander where the Muses haunt
Clear spring, or shady grove, or sunny hill,
Smit with the love of sacred song; but chief
30 Thee Sion and the flow'ry brooks beneath
That wash thy hallowed feet, and warbling flow,
Nightly I visit: nor sometimes forget
Those other two equaled with me in fate,
So were I equaled with them in renown,
35 Blind Thamyris and blind Maeonides,

17. **other notes:** Orpheus sang before Pluto in order to secure his wife's release from death. Milton's song is not Orphean because he has not sought to charm or bargain with the ruler of Hell. Milton might also be deflating the obscure, pseudomystical night worship found in a poem ("Hymn to Night") often ascribed to Orpheus.

19. **Heav'nly Muse:** See 1.6, 7.1, 9.21.

20–21. **up . . . rare:** another echo of the Sybil's advice to Aeneas in *Aen.* 6.126–29; see 2.432–33n.

23–24. **roll . . . ray:** Milton told his Athenian correspondent Leonard Philaras that "upon the eyes turning" he saw in the mist of his blindness "a minute quantity of light as if through a crack" (*MLM* 780).

25. **drop serene:** an English translation of the Latin *gutta serena*, a medical term for complete blindness whose cause is not visible to the physician's eye. It was thought to result from normally airy spir-

its and humors congealing into obstructing tumors in the optical nerves. A main cause of the congealing was the body's inability to rid itself of vapors produced by digestion. See Banister, sec. 9, chap. 1. **quenched:** put out the sight of; in Milton's case, the spirits necessary for sight could not, because of the tumors, pass through his eyes. **orbs:** eyeballs.

26. **dim suffusion:** translates the Latin *suffusio nigra* or *obscura*, another medical term for blindness.

27. **where the Muses haunt:** Mount Helicon, here a symbol of classical literature itself.

30. **Sion:** the biblical equivalent of Helicon, and a symbol of Hebrew poetry. See *PR* 4.346–47 on the preference for Hebrew poetry.

34. "Would that I were their equal in fame."

35. **Thamyris:** A Thracian poet mentioned in Homer, *Il.* 2.594–600. After he boasted that he could outsing the Muses, they

And Tiresias and Phineus prophets old.
Then feed on thoughts, that voluntary move
Harmonious numbers; as the wakeful bird
Sings darkling, and in shadiest covert hid
40   Tunes her nocturnal note. Thus with the year
Seasons return, but not to me returns
Day, or the sweet approach of ev'n or morn,
Or sight of vernal bloom, or summer's rose,
Or flocks, or herds, or human face divine;
45   But cloud instead, and ever-during dark
Surrounds me, from the cheerful ways of men
Cut off, and for the book of knowledge fair
Presented with a universal blank
Of Nature's works to me expunged and razed,
50   And wisdom at one entrance quite shut out.
So much the rather thou celestial light
Shine inward, and the mind through all her powers
Irradiate, there plant eyes, all mist from thence
Purge and disperse, that I may see and tell
55   Of things invisible to mortal sight.
        Now had th' Almighty Father from above,

---

blinded him and deprived him of the ability to sing. **Maeonides:** Homer; his father's name was Maeon.

36. **Tiresias:** the blind Theban sage, best known from *Oedipus Rex*. Among the explanations for his blindness is the anger of Athena, whom he spied bathing. **Phineus:** Thracian king blinded for revealing the gods' will in accurate prophecies.

37. **voluntary move:** of themselves utter (without a further act of volition). The idea is that these thoughts need not be turned into poetry because they *are* poetry and naturally arrange themselves in harmonious verse.

38. **numbers:** verse; **wakeful bird:** the nightingale, who appears often in Milton's early poetry and also in *PL* (4.602–3, 7.435–36).

39. **darkling:** in the dark. The word, become poetic diction, appears in Keats's "Ode on a Nightingale," Arnold's "Dover Beach," and Hardy's "The Darkling Thrush."

47. **book of knowledge:** the book of Nature. "There are two books from whence I collect my divinity; besides that written one of God [the Bible], another of his servant Nature, that universal and public manuscript that lies expansed unto the eyes of all" (Browne, 1.16)—but not to the blind eyes of Milton.

48. **blank:** a white or blank page.

49. **expunged and razed:** "The Romans *expunged* writing on wax tablets by covering it with little pricks, or *razed* it by shaving the tables clean" (Leonard).

56–417. The dialogue between Father and Son is comparable to the "Parliament in Heaven" scene found in medieval mystery and morality plays (Lewalski 1985,

From the pure empyrean where he sits
High throned above all highth, bent down his eye,
His own works and their works at once to view:
60   About him all the sanctities of Heaven
Stood thick as stars, and from his sight received
Beatitude past utterance; on his right
The radiant image of his glory sat,
His only Son; on Earth he first beheld
65   Our two first parents, yet the only two
Of mankind, in the happy Garden placed,
Reaping immortal fruits of joy and love,
Uninterrupted joy, unrivaled love
In blissful solitude; he then surveyed
70   Hell and the gulf between, and Satan there
Coasting the wall of Heav'n on this side Night
In the dun air sublime, and ready now
To stoop with wearied wings and willing feet
On the bare outside of this world, that seemed
75   Firm land embosomed without firmament,
Uncertain which, in ocean or in air.
Him God beholding from his prospect high,
Wherein past, present, future he beholds,
Thus to his only Son foreseeing spake.
80   "Only begotten Son, seest thou what rage
Transports our Adversary, whom no bounds
Prescribed, no bars of Hell, nor all the chains
Heaped on him there, nor yet the main abyss

118–21). The four "daughters of God" (Mercy, Truth, Righteousness, and Peace) debated the fate of sinful man, with Truth and Righteousness opposing Mercy and Peace. After a thorough search to find a substitute for man, the Son's offer to redeem mankind resolved the debate in favor of Mercy and Peace.

60. **sanctities:** angels.
62. **on his right:** as in Heb. 1.2–3.
71. **this side Night:** the side of Chaos (the realm of Night) closest to Heaven.

72. **dun air sublime:** Satan is *sublime* (aloft) in the *dun* (dusky) air between Chaos and our world.
74. **this world:** not Earth but all creation.
74–76. **seemed . . . air:** Viewed from the outside, the universe appeared to be a solid sphere with no sky, surrounded by either air or water.
81. **Transports:** both "drives" and "bears."
83. **main abyss:** Chaos.

Wide interrupt can hold; so bent he seems
85   On desperate revenge, that shall redound
    Upon his own rebellious head. And now
    Through all restraint broke loose he wings his way
    Not far off Heav'n, in the precincts of light,
    Directly towards the new-created world,
90   And man there placed, with purpose to assay
    If him by force he can destroy, or worse,
    By some false guile pervert; and shall pervert;
    For man will hearken to his glozing lies,
    And easily transgress the sole command,
95   Sole pledge of his obedience: so will fall
    He and his faithless progeny: whose fault?
    Whose but his own? Ingrate, he had of me
    All he could have; I made him just and right,
    Sufficient to have stood, though free to fall.
100   Such I created all th' ethereal Powers
    And spirits, both them who stood and them who failed;
    Freely they stood who stood, and fell who fell.
    Not free, what proof could they have giv'n sincere
    Of true allegiance, constant faith or love,
105   Where only what they needs must do, appeared,
    Not what they would? What praise could they receive?
    What pleasure I from such obedience paid,
    When will and reason (reason also is choice)
    Useless and vain, of freedom both despoiled,
110   Made passive both, had served necessity,
    Not me. They therefore as to right belonged,
    So were created, nor can justly accuse
    Their Maker, or their making, or their fate,
    As if predestination overruled

---

84. **Wide interrupt:** widely breached. Editors usually construe *interrupt* as a past participle rather than as a noun made from a verb; it indicates the interval between Hell and the realms of light.

90. **assay:** test.

93. **glozing:** falsely flattering.

99. As Satan admits at 4.63–68. See also 5.525–43; *CD* 1.3.

108. **reason also is choice:** "For reason is but choosing" (*Areop* in *MLM* 944). Cp. Aristotle, *Ethics* 3.2.

115   Their will, disposed by absolute decree
     Or high foreknowledge; they themselves decreed
     Their own revolt, not I: if I foreknew,
     Foreknowledge had no influence on their fault,
     Which had no less proved certain unforeknown.
120   So without least impulse or shadow of fate,
     Or aught by me immutably foreseen,
     They trespass, authors to themselves in all
     Both what they judge and what they choose; for so
     I formed them free, and free they must remain,
125   Till they enthrall themselves: I else must change
     Their nature, and revoke the high decree
     Unchangeable, eternal, which ordained
     Their freedom; they themselves ordained their fall.
     The first sort by their own suggestion fell,
130   Self-tempted, self-depraved: man falls deceived
     By the other first: man therefore shall find grace,
     The other none: in mercy and justice both,
     Through Heav'n and Earth, so shall my glory excel,
     But mercy first and last shall brightest shine."
135   Thus while God spake, ambrosial fragrance filled
     All Heav'n, and in the blessèd spirits elect
     Sense of new joy ineffable diffused:
     Beyond compare the Son of God was seen
     Most glorious, in him all his Father shone
140   Substantially expressed, and in his face
     Divine compassion visibly appeared,
     Love without end, and without measure grace,

---

119. **had . . . unforeknown:** because fore-knowledge, "since it exists only in the mind of the foreknower, has no effect on its object" (*CD* 1.3 in *MLM* 1175). Leonard's description of the passage as inconsistent with *Christian Doctrine* and symptomatic of a breakdown in Milton's theodicy is confused.
120. **impulse:** instigation.

129. **The first sort:** the rebel angels; **suggestion:** temptation; see 5.702.
135. **fragrance:** synesthesia; God's words smell rather than resound.
140. **Substantially:** In *CD* 1.5, Milton argues that the Father transferred "divine substance," but not "the whole essence," to the Son.
141. **visibly:** See 6.681–82.

Which uttering thus he to his Father spake.
    "O Father, gracious was that word which closed
145 Thy sov'reign sentence, that man should find grace;
For which both Heav'n and Earth shall high extol
Thy praises, with th' innumerable sound
Of hymns and sacred songs, wherewith thy throne
Encompassed shall resound thee ever blest.
150 For should man finally be lost, should man
Thy creature late so loved, thy youngest son
Fall circumvented thus by fraud, though joined
With his own folly? That be from thee far,
That far be from thee, Father, who art judge
155 Of all things made, and judgest only right.
Or shall the Adversary thus obtain
His end, and frustrate thine, shall he fulfill
His malice, and thy goodness bring to naught,
Or proud return though to his heavier doom,
160 Yet with revenge accomplished and to Hell
Draw after him the whole race of mankind,
By him corrupted? Or wilt thou thyself
Abolish thy creation, and unmake,
For him, what for thy glory thou hast made?
165 So should thy goodness and thy greatness both
Be questioned and blasphemed without defense."
    To whom the great Creator thus replied.
    "O Son, in whom my soul hath chief delight,
Son of my bosom, Son who art alone
170 My Word, my wisdom, and effectual might,
All hast thou spoken as my thoughts are, all
As my eternal purpose hath decreed:
Man shall not quite be lost, but saved who will,

---

143. **uttering:** making exterior, bringing out (as in the *utter*—exterior—darkness of line 16).

152. **circumvented:** entrapped.

153–54. See Abraham's plea for the Sodomites (Gen. 18.25).

166. **blasphemed:** defamed.

168. Cp. Matt. 3.17.

170. **My Word:** In the New Testament "word" (Gk. *logos,* Lat. *verbum*) is a title of the Son (Rev. 19.13); **effectual might:** the means by which the Father exercises power, as at the Creation; see John 1.1–3.

Yet not of will in him, but grace in me
175 Freely vouchsafed; once more I will renew
His lapsèd powers, though forfeit and enthralled
By sin to foul exorbitant desires;
Upheld by me, yet once more he shall stand
On even ground against his mortal foe,
180 By me upheld, that he may know how frail
His fall'n condition is, and to me owe
All his deliv'rance, and to none but me.
Some I have chosen of peculiar grace
Elect above the rest; so is my will:
185 The rest shall hear me call, and oft be warned
Their sinful state, and to appease betimes
Th' incensèd Deity, while offered grace
Invites; for I will clear their senses dark,
What may suffice, and soften stony hearts
190 To pray, repent, and bring obedience due.
To prayer, repentance, and obedience due,
Though but endeavored with sincere intent,
Mine ear shall not be slow, mine eye not shut.
And I will place within them as a guide
195 My umpire conscience, whom if they will hear,
Light after light well used they shall attain,
And to the end persisting, safe arrive.
This my long sufferance and my day of grace
They who neglect and scorn, shall never taste;
200 But hard be hardened, blind be blinded more,

174. This line might seem to state the Calvinist position that people cannot contribute to their salvation, but see lines 187–90, 302.

183. **peculiar grace**: grace given uniquely to some extraordinary souls. See S. Fallon 1998, 95–97.

186. **betimes**: in time.

187–90. The language carefully indicates that God's *offered grace* is not irresistible. It only *invites*, and *may suffice* rather than "will suffice." The Protestant belief in conditional election and resistable grace is called Arminianism, after the Dutchman Jacobus Arminius (1560–1609), who tried to introduce free will into Calvin's deterministic theology.

189. **stony hearts**: See Ezek. 11.19.

197. **persisting**: remaining steadfast; **safe arrive**: attain salvation in the end.

200–202. In *CD* 1.8, Milton argues that when God blinds or hardens a sinner, "he is not the cause of sin" (*MLM* 1213).

That they may stumble on, and deeper fall;
And none but such from mercy I exclude.
But yet all is not done; man disobeying,
Disloyal breaks his fealty, and sins
205　Against the high supremacy of Heav'n,
Affecting Godhead, and so losing all,
To expiate his treason hath naught left,
But to destruction sacred and devote,
He with his whole posterity must die,
210　Die he or Justice must; unless for him
Some other able, and as willing, pay
The rigid satisfaction, death for death.
Say Heav'nly powers, where shall we find such love,
Which of ye will be mortal to redeem
215　Man's mortal crime, and just th' unjust to save,
Dwells in all Heaven charity so dear?"
　　He asked, but all the Heav'nly choir stood mute,
And silence was in Heav'n: on man's behalf
Patron or intercessor none appeared,
220　Much less that durst upon his own head draw
The deadly forfeiture, and ransom set.
And now without redemption all mankind
Must have been lost, adjudged to death and Hell
By doom severe, had not the Son of God,
225　In whom the fullness dwells of love divine,
His dearest mediation thus renewed.
　　"Father, thy word is past, man shall find grace;
And shall grace not find means, that finds her way,

---

204. **fealty:** allegiance.
208. **sacred and devote:** absolutely doomed; the words are near synonyms, with *sacred* meaning "dedicated to a deity for destruction" and *devote* meaning "given to destruction as by a vow."
212. The idea that the Atonement satisfied justice originated with Anselm's *Cur Deus Homo* I.II–16, 19–21.
215. **just:** in that he is "able" and "willing" to

"pay / The rigid satisfaction, death for death" (ll. 211–12).
219. **Patron:** advocate.
221. **ransom set:** put down the ransom price, which is a life.
224. **doom:** judgment.
226. **mediation:** One of the Son's traditional titles is mediator between God and man (and in Milton's poem, between God and angel as well).

The speediest of thy wingèd messengers,
230   To visit all thy creatures, and to all
Comes unprevented, unimplored, unsought,
Happy for man, so coming; he her aid
Can never seek, once dead in sins and lost;
Atonement for himself or offering meet,
235   Indebted and undone, hath none to bring:
Behold me then, me for him, life for life
I offer, on me let thine anger fall;
Account me man; I for his sake will leave
Thy bosom, and this glory next to thee
240   Freely put off, and for him lastly die
Well pleased, on me let Death wreck all his rage;
Under his gloomy power I shall not long
Lie vanquished; thou hast giv'n me to possess
Life in myself forever, by thee I live,
245   Though now to Death I yield, and am his due
All that of me can die, yet that debt paid,
Thou wilt not leave me in the loathsome grave
His prey, nor suffer my unspotted soul
Forever with corruption there to dwell;
250   But I shall rise victorious, and subdue
My vanquisher, spoiled of his vaunted spoil;
Death his death's wound shall then receive, and stoop
Inglorious, of his mortal sting disarmed.
I through the ample air in triumph high
255   Shall lead Hell captive maugre Hell, and show
The powers of darkness bound. Thou at the sight
Pleased, out of Heaven shalt look down and smile,

---

231. **unprevented:** unanticipated (that is to say, not prayed for).

233. **dead in sins:** See Col. 2.13.

234. **meet:** adequate.

236–38. **me . . . me . . . me . . . me:** The self-emphasis of the repetition is perhaps balanced by the humility of *me* being in all four cases an unstressed syllable. *Me* is both repeated and stressed in the battlefield oration of 6.812–18.

241. **on me:** Here at last *me* occurs in the stressed position (see previous note); **wreck:** give vent to.

244. Cp. John 5.26.

247–49. "Thou will not leave my soul in hell; neither wilt thou suffer thine Holy One to see corruption" (Ps. 16.10).

253. **his mortal sting disarmed:** 1 Cor. 15.55: "O death, where is thy sting?" See 12.432.

255. **maugre:** in spite of; **show:** to the Father.

While by thee raised I ruin all my foes,
Death last, and with his carcass glut the grave:
260 Then with the multitude of my redeemed
Shall enter Heaven long absent, and return,
Father, to see thy face, wherein no cloud
Of anger shall remain, but peace assured,
And reconcilement; wrath shall be no more
265 Thenceforth, but in thy presence joy entire."
    His words here ended, but his meek aspect
Silent yet spake, and breathed immortal love
To mortal men, above which only shone
Filial obedience: as a sacrifice
270 Glad to be offered, he attends the will
Of his great Father. Admiration seized
All Heav'n, what this might mean, and whither tend
Wond'ring; but soon th' Almighty thus replied:
    "O thou in Heav'n and Earth the only peace
275 Found out for mankind under wrath, O thou
My sole complacence! Well thou know'st how dear
To me are all my works, nor man the least
Though last created, that for him I spare
Thee from my bosom and right hand, to save,
280 By losing thee a while, the whole race lost.
Thou therefore whom thou only canst redeem,
Their nature also to thy nature join;
And be thyself man among men on earth,
Made flesh, when time shall be, of virgin seed,
285 By wondrous birth: be thou in Adam's room
The head of all mankind, though Adam's son.
As in him perish all men, so in thee

258. **ruin:** hurl down.
259. **Death last:** 1 Cor. 15.26: "The last enemy that shall be destroyed is death." **glut the grave:** gratify to the full the appetite of the grave. For the commonplace metaphor of the hungry grave, see Shakespeare's *ROM* 5.3.45–48.
270. **attends:** awaits.

271. **Admiration:** wonder.
276. **complacence:** pleasure.
281–82. "Therefore join your nature to the nature of those whom only you can redeem."
285. **room:** place, stead.
287–88. "As in Adam all die, even so in Christ shall all be made alive" (1 Cor. 15.22).

As from a second root shall be restored,
As many as are restored, without thee none.
290   His crime makes guilty all his sons, thy merit
Imputed shall absolve them who renounce
Their own both righteous and unrighteous deeds,
And live in thee transplanted, and from thee
Receive new life. So man, as is most just,
295   Shall satisfy for man, be judged and die,
And dying rise, and rising with him raise
His brethren, ransomed with his own dear life.
So Heav'nly love shall outdo Hellish hate,
Giving to death, and dying to redeem,
300   So dearly to redeem what Hellish hate
So easily destroyed, and still destroys
In those who, when they may, accept not grace.
Nor shalt thou by descending to assume
Man's nature, lessen or degrade thine own.
305   Because thou hast, though throned in highest bliss
Equal to God, and equally enjoying
God-like fruition, quitted all to save
A world from utter loss, and hast been found
By merit more than birthright Son of God,
310   Found worthiest to be so by being good,
Far more than great or high; because in thee
Love hath abounded more than glory abounds,
Therefore thy humiliation shall exalt
With thee thy manhood also to this throne;
315   Here shalt thou sit incarnate, here shalt reign
Both God and man, Son both of God and man,
Anointed universal King; all power

290–91. **thy merit/Imputed:** Christ's merit is imputed, "attributed vicariously," to saved human beings. Cp. 12.407–10; *CD* 1.22.

299. **Giving:** submitting.

300. **dearly:** both "lovingly" and "expensively."

301. **still:** always.

306. **Equal to God:** applies to *throned in highest bliss*, not to the Son's divine nature.

307. **fruition:** enjoyment; **quitted:** both "left" (in becoming incarnate) and "paid, redeemed" (man's debt of sin).

317–18. **all power/I give thee:** "All power is given to me" (Matt. 28.18).

I give thee, reign forever, and assume
Thy merits; under thee as Head Supreme
320 Thrones, Princedoms, Powers, Dominions I reduce:
All knees to thee shall bow, of them that bide
In Heaven, or Earth, or under Earth in Hell;
When thou attended gloriously from Heav'n
Shalt in the sky appear, and from thee send
325 The summoning Archangels to proclaim
Thy dread tribunal: forthwith from all winds
The living, and forthwith the cited dead
Of all past ages to the general doom
Shall hasten, such a peal shall rouse their sleep.
330 Then all thy saints assembled, thou shalt judge
Bad men and angels, they arraigned shall sink
Beneath thy sentence; Hell, her numbers full,
Thenceforth shall be for ever shut. Meanwhile
The world shall burn, and from her ashes spring
335 New Heav'n and Earth, wherein the just shall dwell,
And after all their tribulations long
See golden days, fruitful of golden deeds,
With joy and love triumphing, and fair truth.
Then thou thy regal scepter shalt lay by,
340 For regal scepter then no more shall need,
God shall be all in all. But all ye gods,
Adore him, who to compass all this dies,
Adore the Son, and honor him as me."

318–19. **assume/Thy merits:** echoes Horace's *Odes* 3.30.14–15.

320. The line lists the four orders of angels found in Col. 1.16; see also 5.840.

321–22. "At the name of Jesus every knee should bow, of things in heaven, and things in earth, and things under the earth" (Phil. 2.10). See Satan's resentment of this "knee-tribute" at 5.782.

326. **all winds:** all quarters of the compass.

327. **cited:** summoned.

328. **doom:** judgment.

329. Cp. *Nat Ode* 155–56.

330. **saints:** righteous worshipers.

331. **arraigned:** accused.

334. **The world shall burn:** See 2 Pet. 3.10–13.

340. **need:** be necessary. The regal conception of deity will in the end be abandoned.

341. **God shall be all in all:** See 1 Cor. 15.28.

342. **compass:** accomplish, but perhaps anticipating the compasses of 7.225.

343. **as me:** If this phrase means "as you do me," God is simply prescribing rites of adoration, but if it means "as if me" he is sharing or even handing over his kingship. Cp. John 5.23.

No sooner had th' Almighty ceased, but all
345 The multitude of angels with a shout
Loud as from numbers without number, sweet
As from blest voices, uttering joy, Heav'n rung
With jubilee, and loud hosannas filled
Th' eternal regions: lowly reverent
350 Towards either throne they bow, and to the ground
With solemn adoration down they cast
Their crowns inwove with amarant and gold,
Immortal amarant, a flow'r which once
In Paradise, fast by the Tree of Life
355 Began to bloom, but soon for man's offense
To Heav'n removed where first it grew, there grows,
And flow'rs aloft shading the fount of life,
And where the river of bliss through midst of Heav'n
Rolls o'er Elysian flow'rs her amber stream;
360 With these that never fade the spirits elect
Bind their resplendent locks inwreathed with beams,
Now in loose garlands thick thrown off, the bright
Pavement that like a sea of jasper shone
Impurpled with celestial roses smiled.
365 Then crowned again their golden harps they took,
Harps ever tuned, that glittering by their side
Like quivers hung, and with preamble sweet
Of charming symphony they introduce
Their sacred song, and waken raptures high;
370 No voice exempt, no voice but well could join
Melodious part, such concord is in Heav'n.
Thee Father first they sung omnipotent,
Immutable, immortal, infinite,
Eternal King; thee Author of all being,
375 Fountain of light, thyself invisible
Amidst the glorious brightness where thou sitt'st

---

348. **jubilee:** jubilation; **hosannas:** from the Hebrew "Save, we pray."
353. **amarant:** a legendary immortal flower; see 11.78n, *Lyc* 149.
357. **fount of life:** See Rev. 7.17, 22.1–2.

359. **amber:** clear.
363. **sea of jasper:** See Rev. 21.11.
367. **preamble:** musical prelude.
370. **exempt:** excluded.

Throned inaccessible, but when thou shad'st
The full blaze of thy beams, and through a cloud
Drawn round about thee like a radiant shrine,
380   Dark with excessive bright thy skirts appear,
Yet dazzle Heav'n, that brightest Seraphim
Approach not, but with both wings veil their eyes.
Thee next they sang of all creation first,
Begotten Son, divine similitude,
385   In whose conspicuous count'nance, without cloud
Made visible, th' Almighty Father shines,
Whom else no creature can behold; on thee
Impressed the effulgence of his glory abides,
Transfused on thee his ample spirit rests.
390   He Heav'n of Heav'ns and all the Powers therein
By thee created, and by thee threw down
Th' aspiring Dominations: thou that day
Thy Father's dreadful thunder didst not spare,
Nor stop thy flaming chariot wheels, that shook
395   Heav'n's everlasting frame, while o'er the necks
Thou drov'st of warring angels disarrayed.
Back from pursuit thy Powers with loud acclaim
Thee only extolled, Son of thy Father's might,
To execute fierce vengeance on his foes,
400   Not so on man; him through their malice fall'n,
Father of mercy and grace, thou didst not doom
So strictly, but much more to pity incline:
No sooner did thy dear and only Son
Perceive thee purposed not to doom frail man
405   So strictly, but much more to pity inclined,

---

377. **but:** except.
381. **that:** so that.
382. **veil their eyes:** See Isa. 6.2.
383. **of all creation first:** The phrase has biblical precedent (Rev. 3.14, Col. 1.15–17), but for Milton such verses were not, as they were for believers in the orthodox Trinity, metaphorical. On Christ as the first creation, see *CD* 1.5, and, on Milton's Arianism, Bauman 1987.

387. **Whom . . . behold:** See Exod. 33.18–20; John 1.18, 14.9.
388. **effulgence:** radiance.
392. **Dominations:** usually one of the nine angelic orders, but here apparently, by synecdoche, a name for all of the nine orders.
397. **powers:** angels.

He to appease thy wrath, and end the strife
Of mercy and justice in thy face discerned,
Regardless of the bliss wherein he sat
Second to thee, offered himself to die
410 For man's offense. O unexampled love,
Love nowhere to be found less than divine!
Hail Son of God, Savior of men, thy name
Shall be the copious matter of my song
Henceforth, and never shall my harp thy praise
415 Forget, nor from thy Father's praise disjoin.
    Thus they in Heav'n, above the starry sphere,
Their happy hours in joy and hymning spent.
Meanwhile upon the firm opacous globe
Of this round world, whose first convex divides
420 The luminous inferior orbs, enclosed
From Chaos and th' inroad of darkness old,
Satan alighted walks: a globe far off
It seemed, now seems a boundless continent
Dark, waste, and wild, under the frown of Night
425 Starless exposed, and ever-threat'ning storms
Of Chaos blust'ring round, inclement sky;
Save on that side which from the wall of Heav'n
Though distant far some small reflection gains
Of glimmering air less vexed with tempest loud:
430 Here walked the fiend at large in spacious field.
As when a vulture on Imaüs bred,
Whose snowy ridge the roving Tartar bounds,
Dislodging from a region scarce of prey
To gorge the flesh of lambs or yeanling kids

412–15. The promise to devote future songs to the praise of a god was conventional in classical hymns. See Callimachus, *Hymns* 3.137.

418. **opacous:** opaque.

419. **first convex:** the outer sphere or *primum mobile* of our universe.

429. **vexed:** tossed about.

430. **at large:** freely.

431. **Imaüs:** mountains that were believed to stretch from Afghanistan to the Arctic.

432. **roving Tartar:** nomadic inhabitants of central Asia, "a people the most barbarous, bloody, and fierce of all mankind … the scourges of God on the civilized world" (Hume). *Tartar* is also a shortened form of *Tartarus,* or hell.

434. **yeanling:** newborn.

435　On hills where flocks are fed, flies toward the springs
　　　Of Ganges or Hydaspes, Indian streams;
　　　But in his way lights on the barren plains
　　　Of Sericana, where Chineses drive
　　　With sails and wind their cany wagons light:
440　So on this windy sea of land, the Fiend
　　　Walked up and down alone bent on his prey,
　　　Alone, for other creature in this place
　　　Living or lifeless to be found was none,
　　　None yet, but store hereafter from the earth
445　Up hither like aërial vapors flew
　　　Of all things transitory and vain, when Sin
　　　With vanity had filled the works of men:
　　　Both all things vain, and all who in vain things
　　　Built their fond hopes of glory or lasting fame,
450　Or happiness in this or th' other life;
　　　All who have their reward on Earth, the fruits
　　　Of painful superstition and blind zeal,
　　　Naught seeking but the praise of men, here find
　　　Fit retribution, empty as their deeds;
455　All th' unaccomplished works of Nature's hand,
　　　Abortive, monstrous, or unkindly mixed,
　　　Dissolved on Earth, fleet hither, and in vain,
　　　Till final dissolution, wander here,
　　　Not in the neighboring moon, as some have dreamed;
460　Those argent fields more likely habitants,

435. **the springs:** Both the *Ganges* and the *Hydaspes* (the modern Jhelum) have their *springs*, or sources, in the Himalayas.

438. **Sericana:** China; *Chineses* was the standard seventeenth-century plural form.

439. **With sails and wind:** Peter Heylyn, *Cosmography* (1620), notes that the Chinese "have carts and coaches driven with sails" (867); **cany:** made of cane or bamboo.

444. **store:** plenty.

444–97. Milton's Paradise of Fools has its seed in Ariosto's *OF* 34, where the English knight Astolfo goes to the Limbo of Vanity on the moon in search of his lost wits. Milton may also have been influenced by Ovid's House of Fame (*Met.* 12.52–61).

449. **fond:** foolish.

452. **painful:** painstaking.

454. **empty:** The Latin for *empty* is *vanus*, the etymological root of *vanity* (447).

455. **unaccomplished:** unfinished, lacking.

456. **Abortive:** fruitless, useless; **unkindly:** unnaturally.

457. **fleet:** glide away.

459. **some:** Ariosto for one (*OF* 34.73ff).

Translated saints or middle spirits hold
Betwixt th' angelical and human kind:
Hither of ill-joined sons and daughters born
First from the ancient world those giants came
465   With many a vain exploit, though then renowned:
The builders next of Babel on the plain
Of Sennaär, and still with vain design
New Babels, had they wherewithal, would build:
Others came single; he who to be deemed
470   A god, leaped fondly into Etna flames,
Empedocles, and he who to enjoy
Plato's Elysium, leaped into the sea,
Cleombrotus, and many more too long,
Embryos and idiots, eremites and friars
475   White, black and gray, with all their trumpery.
Here pilgrims roam, that strayed so far to seek
In Golgotha him dead, who lives in Heav'n;
And they who to be sure of Paradise
Dying put on the weeds of Dominic,
480   Or in Franciscan think to pass disguised;
They pass the planets seven, and pass the fixed,

---

461. **Translated saints:** righteous men such as Enoch and Elijah, who were taken from Earth without having to die (cp. 11.670–71).

464. **giants:** sired by the Sons of God (fallen angels in one tradition) on human women (Gen. 6.4). See 11.573–627; *PR* 2.178–81.

467. **Sennaär:** Vulgate form of Shinar (Gen. 11.2).

470. **fondly:** foolishly.

471. **Empedocles:** a philosopher who threw himself into Etna to hide his mortality. The volcano threw back one of his sandals. See Horace, *De Arte Poetica* 464–66.

473. **Cleombrotus:** A philosopher who drowned himself after reading of Elysium in Plato's *Phaedo.* See Callimachus, *Epigrams* 25.

474. **Embryos:** beings in an unrealized state; **eremites:** hermits; **friars:** Franciscan friars taught that idiots and unbaptized in-

fants went not to Heaven but to a limbo above the earth; Milton in a satirical gesture puts the friars in his Paradise of Fools along with *embryos and idiots.*

475. The Carmelites wore a white mantle, the Dominicans a black, and the Franciscans a gray. **trumpery:** religious ornaments.

476–77. The pilgrims to Golgotha repeat the error of the Apostles before learning of the Resurrection: "Why seek ye the living among the dead? He is not here, but is risen" (Luke 24.5).

478–80. It was not uncommon for dying Roman Catholics to disguise themselves as members of religious orders to ease their passage to Heaven.

481–83. This depiction of the Ptolemaic cosmos includes *seven* planetary spheres, the sphere of the *fixed* stars (the eighth), the

And that crystalline sphere whose balance weighs
The trepidation talked, and that first moved;
And now Saint Peter at Heav'n's wicket seems
485   To wait them with his keys, and now at foot
Of Heav'n's ascent they lift their feet, when lo
A violent crosswind from either coast
Blows them transverse ten thousand leagues awry
Into the devious air; then might ye see
490   Cowls, hoods and habits with their wearers tossed
And fluttered into rags, then relics, beads,
Indulgences, dispenses, pardons, bulls,
The sport of winds: all these upwhirled aloft
Fly o'er the backside of the world far off
495   Into a limbo large and broad, since called
The Paradise of Fools, to few unknown
Long after, now unpeopled, and untrod;
All this dark globe the fiend found as he passed,
And long he wandered, till at last a gleam
500   Of dawning light turned thitherward in haste
His traveled steps; far distant he descries
Ascending by degrees magnificent

---

crystálline sphere (ninth), and the *primum mobile* or *that first moved* (tenth). The crystalline sphere was a late and controversial insertion, invented to account for precession of the equinoxes and a perceived oscillation of the starry sphere, i.e., *the trepidation talked*. The poles of this hypothetical crystalline orb were thought to correspond to the equinoctial opposites of Aries and Libra in the eighth. The *balance* that measures (*weighs*) the trepidation may thus refer to Libra ("the balance") (Fowler). Or it may refer to the librating axis of the crystalline sphere, which imparts (*weighs*) irregular motions as it moves back and forth like a beam holding scales. Cp. "trepidation of the spheres" in Donne's "A Valediction Forbidding Mourning."

484. **wicket:** a small door made in, or placed beside, a large one.
485. **keys:** the keys of the kingdom of Heaven given to Peter (Matt. 16.19). Cp. *Lyc* 108–11.
489. **devious:** off their main course.
491. **beads:** rosaries.
492. For Protestants, sale of *indulgences* granting released time from Purgatory was a main Catholic abuse. *Dispenses* or dispensations voided obligations. *Pardons* absolved from offenses. *Bulls* were papal edicts.
494. **backside of the world:** the dark side of the *primum mobile,* farthest from Heaven.
495. **limbo:** fringe region.
496. **Paradise of Fools:** a proverbial phrase; see Shakespeare, *ROM* 2.4.163.
501. **traveled:** punning on "travailed, wearied."
502. **degrees:** steps, stairs.

Up to the wall of Heaven a structure high,
At top whereof, but far more rich appeared
505   The work as of a kingly palace gate
With frontispiece of diamond and gold
Embellished; thick with sparkling orient gems
The portal shone, inimitable on Earth
By model, or by shading pencil drawn.
510   The stairs were such as whereon Jacob saw
Angels ascending and descending, bands
Of guardians bright, when he from Esau fled
To Padan-Aram, in the field of Luz
Dreaming by night under the open sky,
515   And waking cried, "This is the gate of Heav'n."
Each stair mysteriously was meant, nor stood
There always, but drawn up to Heav'n sometimes
Viewless, and underneath a bright sea flowed
Of jasper, or of liquid pearl, whereon
520   Who after came from Earth, sailing arrived,
Wafted by angels, or flew o'er the lake
Rapt in a chariot drawn by fiery steeds.
The stairs were then let down, whether to dare
The fiend by easy ascent, or aggravate
525   His sad exclusion from the doors of bliss.
Direct against which opened from beneath,
Just o'er the blissful seat of Paradise,
A passage down to th' Earth, a passage wide,

---

506. **frontispiece:** ornamental pediment above an entranceway.

507. **orient:** lustrous as pearl.

510–15. See Gen. 28.10–17.

513. The 1667 and 1674 editions have no comma after *Padan-Aram* but include one after *Luz.* We insert the first and omit the second to avoid geographical confusion. Jacob's vision occurs in the vicinity of *Luz,* or Bethel, just north of Jerusalem. He sleeps there en route to *Padan-Aram* in northwest Mesopotamia.

516. **mysteriously:** symbolically, as an allegorical figure.

518. **Viewless:** unseen.

518–19. **bright sea . . . pearl:** The Argument identifies this *bright sea* as "waters above the firmament that flow about [the gate of Heaven]." Cp. 7.619.

521. **Wafted:** gently floated, as Lazarus was (Luke 16.22).

522. **Rapt:** carried away or caught up, as Elijah was (2 Kings 2.11; cp. *PR* 2.16–17).

526–28. **Direct . . . Earth:** At the bottom of the stairway, precisely above Paradise, a wide passage opened down to Earth.

Wider by far than that of aftertimes
530 Over Mount Sion, and, though that were large,
Over the Promised Land to God so dear,
By which, to visit oft those happy tribes,
On high behests his angels to and fro
Passed frequent, and his eye with choice regard
535 From Paneas the fount of Jordan's flood
To Beërsaba, where the Holy Land
Borders on Egypt and the Arabian shore;
So wide the op'ning seemed, where bounds were set
To darkness, such as bound the ocean wave.
540 Satan from hence now on the lower stair
That scaled by steps of gold to Heaven gate
Looks down with wonder at the sudden view
Of all this world at once. As when a scout
Through dark and desert ways with peril gone
545 All night; at last by break of cheerful dawn
Obtains the brow of some high-climbing hill,
Which to his eye discovers unaware
The goodly prospect of some foreign land
First seen, or some renowned metropolis
550 With glistering spires and pinnacles adorned,
Which now the rising sun gilds with his beams.
Such wonder seized, though after Heaven seen,
The spirit malign, but much more envy seized
At sight of all this world beheld so fair.

530. *That* refers to the passage over the *Promised Land*, described in lines 531–37. It is distinct from the passage traveled by Satan and from the one *over Mount Sion*. These occasional thoroughfares are presented as avenues of divine purpose, like the stairway.

534. **eye with choice regard:** "His eye also passed, with preferential attention." Angels are later identified as God's eyes (ll. 650–53).

535. **Paneas:** mountain spring at the northern border of Israel, a chief source of the Jordan River (*flood*); also, Greek name for Dan, the city associated with this *fount*. Cp. the scriptural idiom "from Dan even to Beersheba" (e.g., 1 Sam. 3.20).

536. **Beërsaba:** Vulgate form of Beersheba, city on Israel's southern border.

538–39. The opening to the passageway occurs at the boundary separating light from the darkness of chaos.

543. **world:** cosmos, universe.

547. **discovers:** reveals.

552. **though after Heaven seen:** "Though previously he had witnessed the splendors of Heaven."

555 Round he surveys, and well might, where he stood
So high above the circling canopy
Of night's extended shade; from eastern point
Of Libra to the fleecy star that bears
Andromeda far off Atlantic seas
560 Beyond th' horizon; then from pole to pole
He views in breadth, and without longer pause
Down right into the world's first region throws
His flight precipitant, and winds with ease
Through the pure marble air his oblique way
565 Amongst innumerable stars, that shone
Stars distant, but nigh hand seemed other worlds,
Or other worlds they seemed, or happy isles,
Like those Hesperian gardens famed of old,
Fortunate fields, and groves and flow'ry vales,
570 Thrice happy isles, but who dwelt happy there
He stayed not to inquire: above them all
The golden sun in splendor likest Heaven

556–61. **circling ... breadth:** Satan views the interior of the cosmos from an opening in the *primum mobile* at its most eastern point (corresponding to *Libra*, the scales). Peering down (westward), Satan sees the dark side of the Earth and its rotating, *canopy*-like shadow (the shadow's rotation would be annual in a Copernican cosmos; diurnal in a Ptolemaic). At the western extreme from Satan, behind the Earth and sun, lies Aries, *the fleecy star* (astrologically, the ram). Its position in the sky is below that of *Andromeda* (mythological princess threatened by a sea monster). From Satan's perspective, the ram thus appears to bear the princess past the horizon of the western ocean (*Atlantic seas*). Finally, to observe the breadth of the cosmos before him, Satan looks north and south, *from pole to pole*.

562. **world's first region:** uppermost portion of the universe, above the sphere of the moon.

563–64. Satan dives straight down (*flight pre-cipitant*) through the sparkling (*marble*) air. Once among the stars, however, he follows a characteristically indirect and slanted course (*winds ... his oblique way*).

565–66. **shone/Stars distant:** "From a distance appeared to be stars" (Greek idiom).

567. **Or . . . or:** "either . . . or." Various seventeenth-century authors, and some ancients, speculated about other inhabited worlds. Milton is notably persistent about this possibility. Cp. line 670; 7.621–22; 8.140–58, 175–76. **happy isles:** Islands of the Blessed in Greek mythology, where a favored few abide in bliss rather than face death.

568. **Hesperian gardens:** where grew golden apples guarded by a dragon. Associated with Hesperus, the evening star, these gardens were thought to lie beyond the western ocean (where Aries bears Andromeda; see 556–61n). Cp. *Masque* 393–97, 981–83; *PR* 2.357.

571. **above:** more than.

Allured his eye: thither his course he bends
Through the calm firmament; but up or down
575 By center, or eccentric, hard to tell,
Or longitude, where the great luminary
Aloof the vulgar constellations thick,
That from his lordly eye keep distance due,
Dispenses light from far; they as they move
580 Their starry dance in numbers that compute
Days, months, and years, towards his all-cheering lamp
Turn swift their various motions, or are turned
By his magnetic beam, that gently warms
The universe, and to each inward part
585 With gentle penetration, though unseen,
Shoots invisible virtue even to the deep:
So wondrously was set his station bright.
There lands the fiend, a spot like which perhaps
Astronomer in the sun's lucent orb
590 Through his glazed optic tube yet never saw.
The place he found beyond expression bright,
Compared with aught on Earth, metal or stone;
Not all parts like, but all alike informed
With radiant light, as glowing iron with fire;

573–76. **thither . . . longitude:** Milton's noncommittal description of Satan's route sunward accommodates competing seventeenth-century astronomical models.

577. **Aloof:** apart from (preposition).

580. **numbers:** music of the spheres regarded as the measure of a dance (cp. 8.125; *Masque* 112–14). The choric role of the stars in pacing the drama of creation was a classical commonplace.

583. **magnetic beam:** attractive power of the sun; a pre-Newtonian principle of celestial dynamics, proposed by Kepler.

586. **virtue:** efficacy; **the deep:** here means the farthest reaches and most inward parts of the created universe, including underground parts. Sunlight does not penetrate the realm of Chaos, which is also known as "the deep."

587. **station:** Although it suggests a sedentary sun, as in the Copernican system, *station* could also refer to the fixed sphere or course of the sun in the Ptolemaic cosmos.

588–90. Galileo built the first telescope (*glazed optic tube*) and published his discoveries, sunspots among them, in *Siderius Nuncius* (1610). Cp. 1.288. *Tube* was a common seventeenth-century term for telescope. Cp. Marvell, "To the King": "So his bold tube man to the sun applied/And spots unknown in the bright star descried" (1–2).

592. **metal:** Editions 1 and 2 have "medal." See the repetition of *metal* and *stone* at lines 595–96.

595 If metal, part seemed gold, part silver clear;
    If stone, carbuncle most or chrysolite,
    Ruby or topaz, to the twelve that shone
    In Aaron's breastplate, and a stone besides
    Imagined rather oft than elsewhere seen,
600 That stone, or like to that which here below
    Philosophers in vain so long have sought,
    In vain, though by their powerful art they bind
    Volatile Hermes, and call up unbound
    In various shapes old Proteus from the sea,
605 Drained through a limbec to his native form.
    What wonder then if fields and regions here
    Breathe forth elixir pure, and rivers run
    Potable gold, when with one virtuous touch
    Th' arch-chemic sun so far from us remote
610 Produces with terrestrial humor mixed
    Here in the dark so many precious things
    Of color glorious and effect so rare?

---

596. **carbuncle:** precious stone, fiery red, like little glowing coals (the word's etymological origin) or like serpents' eyes (9.500). The gems referred to were all thought to be luminous, i.e., *informed/ With radiant light* (593–94). **chrysolite:** yellow-green gemstone.

597–98. **to . . . breastplate:** "the forementioned radiant stones plus the others on Aaron's breastplate, to the total of twelve." See Exod. 28.17–20 for a description of the breastplate.

598. **stone:** the philosopher's stone; the grand goal of alchemical aspiration, able to confer immortality and transmute base metal into gold.

601. **Philosophers:** alchemists.

602–5. **bind . . . form:** Alchemists considered mercury (*Hermes*) a primary basis of material being and subjected it to much experimentation. Liquid at room temperature, it was deemed *volatile*—difficult to *bind* or fix. *Proteus* is the shape-shifting sea god, symbolic of primary matter, who had to be restrained in his native form before he would speak true. *Limbec* is a corrupted form of *alembic,* a retort used by alchemists to distill and fix matter in its original condition. Note the repetitions of *stone* and *vain* in lines 598–602.

607–8. **Breathe . . . gold:** Like the fields and streams in Paradise (5.185–86), those on the sun *breathe forth* mists, but on the sun the exhaled mist is *elixir*—a vaporous manifestation of the philosopher's stone with life-extending properties, also identified as *potable gold.*

608. **virtuous:** efficacious.

609. **arch-chemic:** of supreme chemical power.

610. **terrestrial humor:** earthly fluid or moisture. Sunlight was thought to penetrate the earth's surface and produce precious gems from subterranean moisture (cp. l. 586). Cp. *Masque* 732–36. Similar processes occur in Heaven (6.475–81).

612. **effect:** appearance, efficacy.

Here matter new to gaze the Devil met
Undazzled, far and wide his eye commands,
615 For sight no obstacle found here, nor shade,
But all sunshine, as when his beams at noon
Culminate from th' equator, as they now
Shot upward still direct, whence no way round
Shadow from body opaque can fall, and the air,
620 Nowhere so clear, sharpened his visual ray
To objects distant far, whereby he soon
Saw within ken a glorious angel stand,
The same whom John saw also in the sun:
His back was turned, but not his brightness hid;
625 Of beaming sunny rays, a golden tiar
Circled his head, nor less his locks behind
Illustrious on his shoulders fledge with wings
Lay waving round; on some great charge employed
He seemed, or fixed in cogitation deep.
630 Glad was the spirit impure as now in hope
To find who might direct his wand'ring flight
To Paradise the happy seat of man,
His journey's end and our beginning woe.
But first he casts to change his proper shape,
635 Which else might work him danger or delay:
And now a stripling Cherub he appears,
Not of the prime, yet such as in his face
Youth smiled celestial, and to every limb

617. **Culminate from th' equator:** reach their zenith relative to the equator, i.e., at equatorial noon.

618–19. **whence . . . fall:** In the prelapsarian cosmos, the sun's rays are perpendicular to the surface at equatorial noon so that *no way round* shadows fall. On the always shadowless solar surface, the sun's beams always (*still*) shoot directly *upward*.

620–21. **Nowhere . . . far:** According to some classical theories widely accepted in the seventeenth century, vision depends on extromission, "a beam issuing out of the eye to the object" (Hume; cp. *SA* 163). The

eye was thus deemed a sunlike organ. Satan's eyebeam is *sharpened* in a literal sense, like one knife sharpened against another, and so made able to pierce *to objects distant far.*

622. **ken:** visual range.

623. "And I saw an angel standing in the sun" (Rev. 19.17).

625. **tiar:** crown.

627. **Illustrious:** brightly shining.

634. **casts:** contrives.

637. **prime:** first in order of existence or rank; primary.

Suitable grace diffused, so well he feigned;
640 Under a coronet his flowing hair
In curls on either cheek played, wings he wore
Of many a colored plume sprinkled with gold,
His habit fit for speed succinct, and held
Before his decent steps a silver wand.
645 He drew not nigh unheard, the angel bright,
Ere he drew nigh, his radiant visage turned,
Admonished by his ear, and straight was known
Th' Archangel Uriel, one of the sev'n
Who in God's presence, nearest to his throne
650 Stand ready at command, and are his eyes
That run through all the heav'ns, or down to th' Earth
Bear his swift errands over moist and dry,
O'er sea and land: him Satan thus accosts.
    "Uriel, for thou of those sev'n spirits that stand
655 In sight of God's high throne, gloriously bright,
The first art wont his great authentic will
Interpreter through highest Heav'n to bring,
Where all his sons thy embassy attend;
And here art likeliest by supreme decree
660 Like honor to obtain, and as his eye
To visit oft this new creation round;
Unspeakable desire to see, and know
All these his wondrous works, but chiefly man,
His chief delight and favor, him for whom
665 All these his works so wondrous he ordained,
Hath brought me from the choirs of Cherubim
Alone thus wand'ring. Brightest Seraph tell
In which of all these shining orbs hath man
His fixèd seat, or fixèd seat hath none,

---

643. **habit . . . succinct:** refers to the *wings he wore* (l. 641); literally, tucked up.
644. **decent:** becoming, proper.
648. **Uriel:** Hebrew for "light of God." The name is apocryphal (2 Esd. 4.1, 36). **the sev'n:** For the seven angels nearest God's throne, see Rev. 1.5, 8.2.

650–53. **his . . . land:** "Those seven, they are the eyes of the Lord, which run to and fro through the whole earth" (Zech. 4.10). Cp. lines 533–34.
656. **authentic:** authoritative.
658. **attend:** wait upon; cp. line 270.
664. **favor:** object of favor.

670　But all these shining orbs his choice to dwell;
　　　That I may find him, and with secret gaze,
　　　Or open admiration him behold
　　　On whom the great Creator hath bestowed
　　　Worlds, and on whom hath all these graces poured;
675　That both in him and all things, as is meet,
　　　The Universal Maker we may praise;
　　　Who justly hath driv'n out his rebel foes
　　　To deepest Hell, and to repair that loss
　　　Created this new happy race of men
680　To serve him better: wise are all his ways."
　　　　　So spake the false dissembler unperceived;
　　　For neither man nor angel can discern
　　　Hypocrisy, the only evil that walks
　　　Invisible, except to God alone,
685　By his permissive will, through Heav'n and Earth:
　　　And oft though wisdom wake, suspicion sleeps
　　　At wisdom's gate, and to simplicity
　　　Resigns her charge, while goodness thinks no ill
　　　Where no ill seems: which now for once beguiled
690　Uriel, though Regent of the Sun, and held
　　　The sharpest sighted spirit of all in Heav'n;
　　　Who to the fraudulent impostor foul
　　　In his uprightness answer thus returned.
　　　"Fair angel, thy desire which tends to know
695　The works of God, thereby to glorify
　　　The great Work-Master, leads to no excess
　　　That reaches blame, but rather merits praise
　　　The more it seems excess, that led thee hither
　　　From thy empyreal mansion thus alone,
700　To witness with thine eyes what some perhaps
　　　Contented with report hear only in Heav'n:
　　　For wonderful indeed are all his works,
　　　Pleasant to know, and worthiest to be all

670. "But instead can choose to dwell in any
　　of these shining orbs."

Had in remembrance always with delight;
705 But what created mind can comprehend
Their number, or the wisdom infinite
That brought them forth, but hid their causes deep.
I saw when at his word the formless mass,
This world's material mold, came to a heap:
710 Confusion heard his voice, and wild uproar
Stood ruled, stood vast infinitude confined;
Till at his second bidding darkness fled,
Light shone, and order from disorder sprung:
Swift to their several quarters hasted then
715 The cumbrous elements, earth, flood, air, fire,
And this ethereal quintessence of heav'n
Flew upward, spirited with various forms,
That rolled orbicular, and turned to stars
Numberless, as thou seest, and how they move;
720 Each had his place appointed, each his course,
The rest in circuit walls this universe.
Look downward on that globe whose hither side
With light from hence, though but reflected, shines;
That place is Earth the seat of man, that light
725 His day, which else as th' other hemisphere
Night would invade, but there the neighboring moon
(So call that opposite fair star) her aid
Timely interposes, and her monthly round
Still ending, still renewing, through mid-heav'n;
730 With borrowed light her countenance triform
Hence fills and empties to enlighten th' Earth,
And in her pale dominion checks the night.
That spot to which I point is Paradise,

---

709. **mold:** substance.

715–16. The four elements are unwieldy compared with celestial ether, the agile fifth element or *quintessence*, which Milton in the invocation identifies with light itself (l. 7).

717. **spirited with:** animated by. The endowment of form triggers the animation of matter; cp. 7.464–66.

718. **orbicular:** in circles. The natural motion of ether was thought to be circular; see Aristotle, *On the Heavens* 270b.

721. "The ether left after the stars were formed enspheres the universe."

730. **triform:** waning, waxing, full. Cp. Horace, *Odes* 3.22.

731. **Hence:** from here.

Adam's abode, those lofty shades his bow'r.
735 Thy way thou canst not miss, me mine requires."
        Thus said, he turned, and Satan bowing low,
    As to superior spirits is wont in Heav'n,
    Where honor due and reverence none neglects,
    Took leave, and toward the coast of Earth beneath,
740 Down from th' ecliptic, sped with hoped success,
    Throws his steep flight in many an airy wheel,
    Nor stayed, till on Niphates' top he lights.

---

740. **ecliptic:** the path of the sun.

742. **Niphates:** mountain bordering ancient Assyria (4.126).

BOOK IV

THE ARGUMENT

Satan now in prospect of Eden, and nigh the place where he must now attempt the bold enterprise which he undertook alone against God and man, falls into many doubts with himself, and many passions: fear, envy, and despair; but at length confirms himself in evil; journeys on to Paradise, whose outward prospect and situation is described; overleaps the bounds, sits in the shape of a cormorant on the Tree of Life, as highest in the Garden, to look about him. The Garden described; Satan's first sight of Adam and Eve; his wonder at their excellent form and happy state, but with resolution to work their fall; overhears their discourse, thence gathers that the Tree of Knowledge was forbidden them to eat of, under penalty of death; and thereon intends to found his temptation, by seducing them to transgress: then leaves them a while, to know further of their state by some other means. Meanwhile Uriel descending on a sunbeam warns Gabriel, who had in charge the gate of Paradise, that some evil spirit had escaped the deep, and passed at noon by his sphere in the shape of a good angel down to Paradise, discovered after by his furious gestures in the mount. Gabriel promises to find him ere morning. Night coming on, Adam and Eve discourse of going to their rest: their bower described; their evening worship. Gabriel drawing forth his bands of night-watch to walk the round of Paradise, appoints two strong angels to Adam's bower, lest the evil spirit should be there doing some harm to Adam or Eve sleeping; there they find him at the ear of Eve, tempting her in a dream, and bring him, though unwilling, to Gabriel; by whom questioned, he scornfully answers, prepares resistance, but hindered by a sign from Heaven, flies out of Paradise.

O for that warning voice, which he who saw
Th' Apocalypse, heard cry in Heav'n aloud,
Then when the Dragon, put to second rout,
Came furious down to be revenged on men,
5   "Woe to the inhabitants on Earth!" That now,
While time was, our first parents had been warned
The coming of their secret foe, and scaped
Haply so scaped his mortal snare; for now
Satan, now first inflamed with rage, came down,
10   The Tempter ere th' Accuser of mankind,
To wreck on innocent frail man his loss
Of that first battle, and his flight to Hell:
Yet not rejoicing in his speed, though bold,
Far off and fearless, nor with cause to boast,
15   Begins his dire attempt, which nigh the birth
Now rolling, boils in his tumultuous breast,
And like a devilish engine back recoils
Upon himself; horror and doubt distract
His troubled thoughts, and from the bottom stir
20   The Hell within him, for within him Hell
He brings, and round about him, nor from Hell
One step no more than from himself can fly
By change of place: now conscience wakes despair
That slumbered, wakes the bitter memory
25   Of what he was, what is, and what must be

1–12. The most dramatic book of the epic opens like Shakespeare's *Henry V*, with a wistful exclamation. Milton echoes Rev. 12.3–12, which prophesies an apocalyptic war in Heaven, defeat of Satan's forces, and a retaliatory attack on Earth. The juxtaposition of the Apocalypse (future), the War in Heaven (past), Satan's arrival in Paradise (the narrative present), and Milton's own present as creator of the poem generates a dizzying temporal displacement, registered in shifting verb tenses around the repeated *now* of lines 5–9.

3. **Then when:** Cp. line 970.

10. **Accuser:** St. John identifies Satan not as the devil (*diabolos*) but as the tempter of Adam and Eve and accuser (*kategoros*) of Christians seeking salvation (Rev. 12.10).

11. **wreck:** avenge (wreak); cp. 3.241.

16. **rolling:** heaving, surging.

17. **engine:** cannon (see 6.470–91). Satan is repeatedly associated with gunpowder and artillery (cp. ll. 814–18), which he invents in Book 6. Both *engine* and *invention* (or even *plot*) can translate the Latin *ingenium*.

20–23. **The Hell . . . place:** Cp. 1.253–55. The narrator's comment recalls *Doctor Faustus* 1.3.76; 2.1.121–22.

25. Cp. *SA* 22.

Worse; of worse deeds worse sufferings must ensue.
Sometimes towards Eden which now in his view
Lay pleasant, his grieved look he fixes sad,
Sometimes towards heav'n and the full-blazing sun,
30 Which now sat high in his meridian tow'r:
Then much revolving, thus in sighs began.
  "O thou that with surpassing glory crowned,
Look'st from thy sole dominion like the God
Of this new world; at whose sight all the stars
35 Hide their diminished heads; to thee I call,
But with no friendly voice, and add thy name
O Sun, to tell thee how I hate thy beams
That bring to my remembrance from what state
I fell, how glorious once above thy sphere;
40 Till pride and worse ambition threw me down
Warring in Heav'n against Heav'n's matchless King:
Ah wherefore! He deserved no such return
From me, whom he created what I was
In that bright eminence, and with his good
45 Upbraided none; nor was his service hard.
What could be less than to afford him praise,
The easiest recompense, and pay him thanks,
How due! Yet all his good proved ill in me,
And wrought but malice; lifted up so high
50 I 'sdained subjection, and thought one step higher

27–28. **Eden . . . pleasant:** Milton appears to have thought that *Eden* (now deemed Sumerian in origin) derived from the Hebrew for "delight."

30. **meridian:** noon or zenith. Richardson traces to Vergil the image of the midday sun as in a tower (*Culex* 41).

31. **revolving:** deliberating. Milton's word choice continues the characterization of Satan's mental processes as circular, often viciously so (*rolling, recoil*).

32–41. Edward Phillips, Milton's nephew and biographer, claims that he was shown these lines "several years before the poem was begun" and that they were "designed for the very beginning" of a tragedy on the same subject (Darbishire 72). In the Trinity College manuscript, Milton outlines such a tragedy under the title "Adam Unparadised." Satan's soliloquy draws on Prometheus' first speech in Aeschylus' *Prometheus Bound*.

45. **Upbraided:** reproached; cp. James 1.5.

50. **'sdained:** disdained, in a form reminiscent of the Italian *sdegnare* (to disdain). An attitude of romantic as well as religious import, "disdain" in Satan's usage at line 82 is given allegorical agency antagonistic to "submission"; cp. line 770.

Would set me highest, and in a moment quit
The debt immense of endless gratitude,
So burdensome still paying, still to owe;
Forgetful what from him I still received,
55   And understood not that a grateful mind
By owing owes not, but still pays, at once
Indebted and discharged; what burden then?
O had his powerful destiny ordained
Me some inferior angel, I had stood
60   Then happy; no unbounded hope had raised
Ambition. Yet why not? Some other power
As great might have aspired, and me though mean
Drawn to his part; but other powers as great
Fell not, but stand unshaken, from within
65   Or from without, to all temptations armed.
Hadst thou the same free will and power to stand?
Thou hadst: whom hast thou then or what to accuse,
But Heav'n's free love dealt equally to all?
Be then his love accursed, since love or hate,
70   To me alike, it deals eternal woe.
Nay cursed be thou; since against his thy will
Chose freely what it now so justly rues.
Me miserable! Which way shall I fly
Infinite wrath, and infinite despair?
75   Which way I fly is Hell; myself am Hell;
And in the lowest deep a lower deep
Still threat'ning to devour me opens wide,

---

51. **quit:** usually glossed as "repay," but the sense here more nearly approximates "to cease to be engaged in or occupied with" (*OED* I.5.a).

53–56. **still:** always.

56. **By owing owes not:** Acknowledgment of an obligation ("owning up") satisfies it. Cp. Cicero, *De Officiis* 2.20; *Pro Plancio* 28.68.

61. **power:** a rank in the angelic hierarchy, here and in line 63 used loosely to mean any angel.

66–72. Satan interrogates himself (*thou*), and his replies corroborate God's earlier self-justification (3.100–101).

75. **myself am Hell:** In the early 1660s, Louis XIV of France reportedly identified himself with the state—*"L'Etat c'est moi"*—a sentence long regarded as the epitome of royal absolutism. Satan dwells on the ramifications of his identification with Hell. See 20–23n.

To which the Hell I suffer seems a Heav'n.
O then at last relent: is there no place
80   Left for repentance, none for pardon left?
None left but by submission; and that word
Disdain forbids me, and my dread of shame
Among the spirits beneath, whom I seduced
With other promises and other vaunts
85   Than to submit, boasting I could subdue
Th' Omnipotent. Ay me, they little know
How dearly I abide that boast so vain,
Under what torments inwardly I groan;
While they adore me on the throne of Hell,
90   With diadem and scepter high advanced
The lower still I fall, only supreme
In misery; such joy ambition finds.
But say I could repent and could obtain
By act of grace my former state; how soon
95   Would highth recall high thoughts, how soon unsay
What feigned submission swore: ease would recant
Vows made in pain, as violent and void.
For never can true reconcilement grow
Where wounds of deadly hate have pierced so deep:
100   Which would but lead me to a worse relapse
And heavier fall: so should I purchase dear
Short intermission bought with double smart.
This knows my punisher; therefore as far
From granting he, as I from begging peace:

79–80. **no place/Left for repentance:** Hebrews 12.17 is widely cited as the source for Satan's phrasing. The quasi-allegorical expression of a psychological condition as a physical locality is general in this poem, however. Satan is irreversibly consigned to Hell, and his former place of bliss has been irreversibly estranged from him (5.615, 7.144).

87. **abide:** endure or persevere in; but the sense "remain in a place" is also present. See the preceding note.

90. **advanced:** exalted (referring to Satan on his throne).

94. **act of grace:** suspension of a legal penalty. While the reference to divine mercy is clear, Satan's legalese recalls Charles's phrasing in *Eikon Basilike:* "Is this the reward and thanks I am to receive for those many Acts of Grace I have lately passed?" (9.53).

97. **violent and void:** forced and therefore invalid.

105 All hope excluded thus, behold instead
      Of us outcast, exiled, his new delight,
      Mankind created, and for him this world.
      So farewell hope, and with hope farewell fear,
      Farewell remorse: all good to me is lost;
110 Evil be thou my good; by thee at least
      Divided Empire with Heav'n's King I hold
      By thee, and more than half perhaps will reign;
      As man ere long, and this new world shall know."
          Thus while he spake, each passion dimmed his face
115 Thrice changed with pale, ire, envy and despair,
      Which marred his borrowed visage, and betrayed
      Him counterfeit, if any eye beheld.
      For Heav'nly minds from such distempers foul
      Are ever clear. Whereof he soon aware,
120 Each perturbation smoothed with outward calm,
      Artificer of fraud; and was the first
      That practiced falsehood under saintly show,
      Deep malice to conceal, couched with revenge:
      Yet not enough had practiced to deceive
125 Uriel once warned; whose eye pursued him down
      The way he went, and on th' Assyrian mount
      Saw him disfigured, more than could befall
      Spirit of happy sort: his gestures fierce
      He marked and mad demeanor, then alone,
130 As he supposed, all unobserved, unseen.
      So on he fares, and to the border comes,
      Of Eden, where delicious Paradise,
      Now nearer, crowns with her enclosure green,

110. **Evil be thou my good:** Satan later recognizes that the reverse also holds true (9.122–23).

115. **pale:** darkness, gloom (cp. 10.1009). The light drains from Satan's disguised face three times (cp. 1.594–98). (Note that the Argument identifies *fear,* not ire, as the first of the three passions affecting him.) His *disfiguration* (l. 127) reverses scriptural accounts of Christ's transfiguration, in which the mountaintop illumination of Jesus—his "face shone like the sun"—manifests his heavenly nature (Matt. 17.2).

123. **couched:** lying in ambush, lurking; cp. 405–6.

126. **Assyrian mount:** Niphates (3.742).

132–45. **Eden . . . round:** Milton describes Paradise as a walled garden situated on the level summit (*champaign head*) of a hill (*steep wilderness*) on the eastern border of

As with a rural mound the champaign head
135   Of a steep wilderness, whose hairy sides
With thicket overgrown, grotesque and wild,
Access denied; and overhead up grew
Insuperable highth of loftiest shade,
Cedar, and pine, and fir, and branching palm,
140   A sylvan scene, and as the ranks ascend
Shade above shade, a woody theater
Of stateliest view. Yet higher than their tops
The verdurous wall of Paradise up sprung:
Which to our general sire gave prospect large
145   Into his nether empire neighboring round.
And higher than that wall a circling row
Of goodliest trees loaden with fairest fruit,
Blossoms and fruits at once of golden hue
Appeared, with gay enameled colors mixed:
150   On which the sun more glad impressed his beams
Than in fair evening cloud, or humid bow,
When God hath show'red the earth; so lovely seemed
That lantskip: and of pure now purer air
Meets his approach, and to the heart inspires
155   Vernal delight and joy, able to drive
All sadness but despair: now gentle gales
Fanning their odoriferous wings dispense

Eden. The trees on the densely wooded hillside resemble ascending rows of seats in a theater.

136. **grotesque:** according to the *OED*, which cites this as the first such usage in English, "of a landscape: Romantic, picturesquely irregular" (B 2.b). The implied Miltonic innovation is dubious. The word had only recently entered English from the Italian *grotesca*. It referred to the style of painting and sculpture found in excavated Roman grottoes, which featured partial human and animal forms and interwoven foliage. It was an aesthetic term applied to antic, rugged, extravagant, or fanciful produc-tions. The suggestiveness of Milton's description of the "hairy" hillside wildly overgrown with tangled thicket, its imaginative amalgamations of human and vegetable, qualify this usage as an instance of the original meaning (cp. 5.294–97).

140. **sylvan scene:** forest backdrop; translates Vergil's *sylvis scaena* (*Aen.* 1.164).

149. **enameled:** glossy, brilliant, as in coloring fixed by fire (cp. 9.525).

151. **humid bow:** rainbow (cp. *Masque* 992).

153. **lantskip:** landscape.

156. **gales:** breezes.

Native perfumes, and whisper whence they stole
Those balmy spoils. As when to them who sail
160 Beyond the Cape of Hope, and now are past
Mozambique, off at sea northeast winds blow
Sabean odors from the spicy shore
Of Araby the Blest, with such delay
Well pleased they slack their course, and many a league
165 Cheered with the grateful smell old Ocean smiles.
So entertained those odorous sweets the fiend
Who came their bane, though with them better pleased
Than Asmodeus with the fishy fume,
That drove him, though enamored, from the spouse
170 Of Tobit's son, and with a vengeance sent
From Media post to Egypt, there fast bound.
     Now to th' ascent of that steep savage hill
Satan had journeyed on, pensive and slow;
But further way found none, so thick entwined,
175 As one continued brake, the undergrowth
Of shrubs and tangling bushes had perplexed
All path of man or beast that passed that way:
One gate there only was, and that looked east
On th' other side: which when th' arch-felon saw
180 Due entrance he disdained, and in contempt,

160–65. **Cape of Hope . . . smiles:** After rounding the southern tip of Africa (*Cape of Hope*), European trade ships bore *northeast* from *Mozambique*. Diodorus Siculus (3.46), on whom Milton appears to draw here and at lines 275–79, notes that the prevailing winds of spring carry fragrance from Saba (Sheba), a region in Arabia Felix (*Araby the Blest;* modern Yemen) renowned for the *grateful* (pleasing) smell of myrrh and frankincense. The phenomenon of the aromatic Arabian breeze scenting the ocean was by Milton's time a commonplace expressive of remote knowledge: "So we the Arabian coast do know, / At distance, when the spices blow" (Waller, *Night-piece* 39–40; cp.

Herbert, *Prayer* 13–14). A related olfactory phenomenon occurs in Heaven (3.135–37).
168–71. **Asmodeus . . . bound:** In *Media* (now northwestern Iran), according to the apocryphal Book of Tobit, the demon *Asmodeus* (cp. Asmadai, 6.365 and *PR* 2.151) kills seven husbands of Sarah. Tobias, son of the blind *Tobit,* becomes her eighth husband. On the advice of the angel Raphael, Tobias repels the jealous demon by burning the heart and liver of a fish (whence the *fishy fume*). Fleeing hastily (*post*) to Egypt to escape the smell, Asmodeus is captured by the angel and bound (cp. 5.221–23).
172. **savage:** wooded, wild.
176. **had perplexed:** would have perplexed.

At one slight bound high over leaped all bound
Of hill or highest wall, and sheer within
Lights on his feet. As when a prowling wolf,
Whom hunger drives to seek new haunt for prey,
185 Watching where shepherds pen their flocks at eve
In hurdled cotes amid the field secure,
Leaps o'er the fence with ease into the fold:
Or as a thief bent to unhoard the cash
Of some rich burgher, whose substantial doors,
190 Cross-barred and bolted fast, fear no assault,
In at the window climbs, or o'er the tiles;
So clomb this first grand thief into God's fold:
So since into his Church lewd hirelings climb.
Thence up he flew, and on the Tree of Life,
195 The middle tree and highest there that grew,
Sat like a cormorant; yet not true life
Thereby regained, but sat devising death
To them who lived; nor on the virtue thought
Of that life-giving plant, but only used
200 For prospect, what well used had been the pledge
Of immortality. So little knows

---

181. **bound . . . bound:** another instance of paronomasia, jingling wordplay common in late Latin and Italian writers and characteristic of Hebrew Scripture. Cp. 1.642n.

183–87. **wolf . . . fold:** Cp. John 10.1–10, where Christ identifies himself as the proper entrance to the flock and calls those who circumvent him thieves and robbers. See 193n.

186. **hurdled cotes:** fenced shelters made of poles and intertwined branches.

188. **unhoard the cash:** undo a hidden reserve of money by removing its contents, in this case *cash* with a play on *cache.*

192. **clomb:** archaic past tense of *climb.*

193. **lewd:** base (with an ironic glance at the original meaning, "not of the clergy, lay"). In the Geneva Bible and *AV, lewd* can translate *poneron,* Greek for evil in general

(e.g., Acts 17.5; cp. 1.490, 6.182). Christ scorns the "hireling," who when a wolf attacks, "fleeth, because he is an hireling, and careth not for the sheep" (John 10.13). Milton's frequent criticisms of corrupt clergy allude to this parable and tend to merge the hireling and the wolf. Cp. 12.507–11, *Lyc* 114–29, *Sonnet 16* 14.

194. **Tree of Life:** Gen. 2.9; Rev. 2.7.

196. **cormorant:** large, voracious seabird; figuratively, someone insatiably greedy, rapacious.

200. **pledge:** "anything . . . put in the possession of another . . . as a guarantee of good faith" (*OED* 2.a). The tree of prohibition is a corresponding pledge—of humanity's obedience and faith (8.325; cp. *CD* in Yale 6:352). Satan though immortal has lost "true life" (l. 196) and now subsists in Hell, where death lives (2.624).

Any, but God alone, to value right
The good before him, but perverts best things
To worst abuse, or to their meanest use.

205 Beneath him with new wonder now he views
To all delight of human sense exposed
In narrow room Nature's whole wealth, yea more,
A Heav'n on Earth, for blissful Paradise
Of God the Garden was, by him in the east

210 Of Eden planted; Eden stretched her line
From Auran Eastward to the royal tow'rs
Of great Seleucia, built by Grecian kings,
Or where the sons of Eden long before
Dwelt in Telassar: in this pleasant soil

215 His far more pleasant Garden God ordained;
Out of the fertile ground he caused to grow
All trees of noblest kind for sight, smell, taste;
And all amid them stood the Tree of Life,
High eminent, blooming ambrosial fruit

220 Of vegetable gold; and next to life
Our death the Tree of Knowledge grew fast by,
Knowledge of good bought dear by knowing ill.
Southward through Eden went a river large,
Nor changed his course, but through the shaggy hill

225 Passed underneath engulfed, for God had thrown
That mountain as his Garden mold high raised
Upon the rapid current, which through veins
Of porous earth with kindly thirst up drawn,

---

207. **In . . . wealth:** Cp. Barabas's delight at "infinite riches in a little room" in Marlowe's *Jew of Malta* (1.1.37).

211. **Auran:** or Hauran; region south of Damascus, on Israel's eastern border (Ezek. 47.16, 18).

212. **Seleucia:** city on the Tigris River near Baghdad, built by Seleucus, c. 300 B.C.E., one of Alexander's successors and founder of a dynasty.

214. **Telassar:** ancient city within the boundaries set forth in lines 211–12, inhabited by

"the children of Eden" but conquered by the Assyrians in the eighth century B.C.E. (2 Kings 19.12; Isa. 37.12). See line 285.

222. "That doom which Adam fell into of knowing good and evil—that is to say, of knowing good by evil" (*Areop* in *MLM* 939); "since it was tasted, not only do we know evil, but also we do not even know good except through evil" (*CD* 1.10 in *MLM* 1220).

223. **a river large:** the Tigris, named at 9.71.

228. **kindly:** natural.

Rose a fresh fountain, and with many a rill
230 Watered the Garden; thence united fell
Down the steep glade, and met the nether flood,
Which from his darksome passage now appears,
And now divided into four main streams,
Runs diverse, wand'ring many a famous realm
235 And country whereof here needs no account,
But rather to tell how, if art could tell,
How from that sapphire fount the crispèd brooks,
Rolling on orient pearl and sands of gold,
With mazy error under pendant shades
240 Ran nectar, visiting each plant, and fed
Flow'rs worthy of Paradise which not nice art
In beds and curious knots, but Nature boon
Poured forth profuse on hill and dale and plain,
Both where the morning sun first warmly smote
245 The open field, and where the unpierced shade
Embrowned the noontide bow'rs: thus was this place,
A happy rural seat of various view;
Groves whose rich trees wept odorous gums and balm,
Others whose fruit burnished with golden rind
250 Hung amiable, Hesperian fables true,
If true, here only, and of delicious taste:
Betwixt them lawns, or level downs, and flocks
Grazing the tender herb, were interposed,
Or palmy hillock, or the flow'ry lap
255 Of some irriguous valley spread her store,
Flow'rs of all hue, and without thorn the rose:

237. **crispèd:** wavy.
239. **error:** used in the primary sense of the Latin noun *error,* "a wandering."
241. **nice:** fastidious, precise.
242. **curious knots:** flower beds of painstakingly intricate design; **boon:** bounteous.
246. **Embrowned:** darkened, per French and Italian usage (*embrunir; imbrunire*).
247. **seat:** local habitation, residence.
250. **amiable:** lovely (cp. Ps. 84.1 in the *AV* versus Milton's translation, *MLM* 117); **Hesperian fables:** See 3.568n.
254. **lap:** a hollow among hills (*OED* 5.b; Milton antedates by nearly a century the *OED*'s earliest quotation of this usage).
255. **irriguous:** well watered (cp. Horace, *Satires* 2.4.16).
256. **without thorn the rose:** Thorns were commonly deemed a postlapsarian phenomenon (Gen. 3.18). "Before man's fall

305 Her unadornèd golden tresses wore
      Disheveled, but in wanton ringlets waved
      As the vine curls her tendrils, which implied
      Subjection, but required with gentle sway,
      And by her yielded, by him best receivèd,
310 Yielded with coy submission, modest pride,
      And sweet reluctant amorous delay.
      Nor those mysterious parts were then concealed,
      Then was not guilty shame, dishonest shame
      Of nature's works, honor dishonorable,
315 Sin-bred, how have ye troubled all mankind
      With shows instead, mere shows of seeming pure,
      And banished from man's life his happiest life,
      Simplicity and spotless innocence.
      So passed they naked on, nor shunned the sight
320 Of God or angel, for they thought no ill:
      So hand in hand they passed, the loveliest pair
      That ever since in love's embraces met,
      Adam the goodliest man of men since born
      His sons, the fairest of her daughters Eve.
325 Under a tuft of shade that on a green
      Stood whispering soft, by a fresh fountain side
      They sat them down, and after no more toil
      Of their sweet gard'ning labor than sufficed
      To recommend cool Zephyr, and made ease
330 More easy, wholesome thirst and appetite
      More grateful, to their supper fruits they fell,
      Nectarine fruits which the compliant boughs
      Yielded them, sidelong as they sat recline

---

306. **wanton:** abundant, luxuriant; like the "mantling vine" of line 258.

310. **coy:** not demonstrative, shy.

311. **reluctant:** "struggling" (Hume). Cp. the fire of divine wrath struggling through "dusky wreaths" of smoke at 6.58. As uncomfortable as some readers may be with the suggestion of erotic struggle, the modern sense of *reluctant* as "unwilling" was not current in the seventeenth century, according to the *OED*.

312. **mysterious:** See 741–43n.

329. **Zephyr:** west wind; "the frolic wind that breathes the spring" (*L'All* 18).

331–36. Adam and Eve's contented meal reverses the punishment of Tantalus.

332. **Nectarine:** sweet as nectar; **compliant:** yielding.

On the soft downy bank damasked with flow'rs:
335 The savory pulp they chew, and in the rind
Still as they thirsted scoop the brimming stream;
Nor gentle purpose, nor endearing smiles
Wanted, nor youthful dalliance as beseems
Fair couple, linked in happy nuptial league,
340 Alone as they. About them frisking played
All beasts of th' earth, since wild, and of all chase
In wood or wilderness, forest or den;
Sporting the lion ramped, and in his paw
Dandled the kid; bears, tigers, ounces, pards,
345 Gamboled before them, th' unwieldy elephant
To make them mirth used all his might, and wreathed
His lithe proboscis; close the serpent sly
Insinuating, wove with Gordian twine
His braided train, and of his fatal guile
350 Gave proof unheeded; others on the grass
Couched, and now filled with pasture gazing sat,
Or bedward ruminating: for the sun
Declined was hasting now with prone career
To th' ocean isles, and in th' ascending scale
355 Of heav'n the stars that usher evening rose:
When Satan still in gaze, as first he stood,
Scarce thus at length failed speech recovered sad.
  "O Hell! What do mine eyes with grief behold,
Into our room of bliss thus high advanced

---

334. **damasked:** many colored.
337. **gentle purpose:** well-bred conversation.
338. **Wanted:** were lacking.
341. **chase:** unenclosed land, game preserve; also, animals to be hunted.
343. **ramped:** reared, as if climbing.
344. **Dandled:** played with; cp. Isa. 11.6; **ounces, pards:** lynxes, leopards.
348. **Insinuating:** artfully working into company, winding; **Gordian:** like the famously complicated knot.
352. **ruminating:** chewing the cud.
353. **prone career:** downward course, as of a galloping horse.

354. **ocean isles:** identified at line 592 as the Azores; **ascending scale:** ladder, stairway (*OED* n3, I.1.b), or more likely, the rising scale of a figurative cosmic balance "weighing night and day, the one ascending as the other sinks" (Newton). In the equinoctial Garden, day and night are counterpoised. At the vernal equinox, the sun is in Aries, opposite Libra (the Scales), the constellation in which the evening stars would rise (cp. Vergil, *Georg.* 1.208).
356. **as first he stood:** since he initially saw Adam and Eve (l. 288).

360 Creatures of other mold, earth-born perhaps,
   Not spirits, yet to Heav'nly spirits bright
   Little inferior; whom my thoughts pursue
   With wonder, and could love, so lively shines
   In them divine resemblance, and such grace
365 The hand that formed them on their shape hath poured.
   Ah gentle pair, ye little think how nigh
   Your change approaches, when all these delights
   Will vanish and deliver ye to woe,
   More woe, the more your taste is now of joy;
370 Happy, but for so happy ill secured
   Long to continue, and this high seat your Heav'n
   Ill fenced for Heav'n to keep out such a foe
   As now is entered; yet no purposed foe
   To you whom I could pity thus forlorn
375 Though I unpitied: league with you I seek,
   And mutual amity so strait, so close,
   That I with you must dwell, or you with me
   Henceforth; my dwelling haply may not please
   Like this fair Paradise, your sense, yet such
380 Accept your Maker's work; he gave it me,
   Which I as freely give; Hell shall unfold,
   To entertain you two, her widest gates,
   And send forth all her kings; there will be room,
   Not like these narrow limits, to receive
385 Your numerous offspring; if no better place,
   Thank him who puts me loath to this revenge
   On you who wrong me not for him who wronged.
   And should I at your harmless innocence
   Melt, as I do, yet public reason just,

360. **mold:** shape, pattern; also, Earth as humanity's native element.

361–62. **to Heav'nly spirits bright/Little inferior:** "Scarce to be less than gods thou mad'st his lot" (Ps. 8.5, Milton's translation; cp. Heb. 2.7).

370. **for so happy:** for being as fortunate as you are; cp. "for Heav'n" (l. 372).

376. **strait:** intimate; also constricted.

380–83. **he . . . kings:** Cp. Matt. 10.8, Isa. 14.9.

382. **her widest gates:** her gates as wide as possible.

387. **for:** instead of.

389. **public reason just:** legitimate concerns of state, such as honor and empire. Cp. *SA* 865–70.

390 Honor and empire with revenge enlarged,
By conquering this new world, compels me now
To do what else though damned I should abhor."
　　So spake the fiend, and with necessity,
The tyrant's plea, excused his devilish deeds.
395 Then from his lofty stand on that high tree
Down he alights among the sportful herd
Of those four-footed kinds, himself now one,
Now other, as their shape served best his end
Nearer to view his prey, and unespied
400 To mark what of their state he more might learn
By word or action marked: about them round
A lion now he stalks with fiery glare,
Then as a tiger, who by chance hath spied
In some purlieu two gentle fawns at play,
405 Straight couches close, then rising changes oft
His couchant watch, as one who chose his ground
Whence rushing he might surest seize them both
Gripped in each paw: when Adam first of men
To first of women Eve thus moving speech,
410 Turned him all ear to hear new utterance flow.
　　"Sole partner and sole part of all these joys,
Dearer thyself than all; needs must the power
That made us, and for us this ample world
Be infinitely good, and of his good
415 As liberal and free as infinite,
That raised us from the dust and placed us here
In all this happiness, who at his hand
Have nothing merited, nor can perform
Aught whereof he hath need, he who requires
420 From us no other service than to keep
This one, this easy charge, of all the trees

---

402. **lion:** Cp. 1 Pet. 5.8; Euripides, *Bacchae* 1015.

410. **Turned him all ear:** Satan turns eagerly to hear human speech. The phrasing also suggests Raphael's account of spiritual bodily function, 6.350. Cp. *Masque* 560. "All ear" is a common expression in Italian (*tutt' orecchi*).

411. **Sole ... sole:** only ... peerless. The repetition of *sole* and *part* invites wordplay touching the origin of Eve and paradisial marriage.

In Paradise that bear delicious fruit
So various, not to taste that only Tree
Of Knowledge, planted by the Tree of Life,
425 So near grows death to life, whate'er death is,
Some dreadful thing no doubt; for well thou know'st
God hath pronounced it death to taste that Tree,
The only sign of our obedience left
Among so many signs of power and rule
430 Conferred upon us, and dominion giv'n
Over all other creatures that possess
Earth, air, and sea. Then let us not think hard
One easy prohibition, who enjoy
Free leave so large to all things else, and choice
435 Unlimited of manifold delights:
But let us ever praise him, and extol
His bounty, following our delightful task
To prune these growing plants, and tend these flow'rs,
Which were it toilsome, yet with thee were sweet."
440   To whom thus Eve replied. "O thou for whom
And from whom I was formed flesh of thy flesh,
And without whom am to no end, my guide
And head, what thou hast said is just and right.
For we to him indeed all praises owe,
445 And daily thanks, I chiefly who enjoy
So far the happier lot, enjoying thee
Preeminent by so much odds, while thou
Like consort to thyself canst nowhere find.
That day I oft remember, when from sleep
450 I first awaked, and found myself reposed
Under a shade on flow'rs, much wond'ring where
And what I was, whence thither brought, and how.
Not distant far from thence a murmuring sound

---

425. **whate'er death is:** For unfallen Adam, death has no meaning beyond *pronounced* penalty (l. 427). After the Fall, the concept of death will be gradually fleshed out, culminating in Michael's gruesome visions of mortality (11.444–47, 462–65).

447. **odds:** amount or ratio by which one thing exceeds or falls short of another; common diction in Shakespeare, where it often concerns characters in competition.

451. **on:** per the first edition; the second reads "of."

Of waters issued from a cave and spread
455 Into a liquid plain, then stood unmoved
Pure as th' expanse of heav'n; I thither went
With unexperienced thought, and laid me down
On the green bank, to look into the clear
Smooth lake, that to me seemed another sky.
460 As I bent down to look, just opposite,
A shape within the wat'ry gleam appeared
Bending to look on me, I started back,
It started back, but pleased I soon returned,
Pleased it returned as soon with answering looks
465 Of sympathy and love; there I had fixed
Mine eyes till now, and pined with vain desire,
Had not a voice thus warned me, 'What thou seest,
What there thou seest fair creature is thyself,
With thee it came and goes: but follow me,
470 And I will bring thee where no shadow stays
Thy coming, and thy soft embraces, he
Whose image thou art, him thou shall enjoy
Inseparably thine, to him shalt bear
Multitudes like thyself, and thence be called
475 Mother of human race.' What could I do,
But follow straight, invisibly thus led?
Till I espied thee, fair indeed and tall,
Under a platan, yet methought less fair,
Less winning soft, less amiably mild,

460–69. Eve's narration formally echoes and significantly varies Ovid's tale of Narcissus (*Met.* 3.415ff).

466. **pined**: from the Latin noun *poena*, meaning "penalty in satisfaction for an offense or in consequence of failure to fulfill an obligation." As an intransitive verb, *pine* means "to languish with intense desire." As a transitive verb, it means "to cause pain or anguish" or "to grieve." Cp. Satan at lines 511 and 848.

470. **stays**: awaits. This line is echoed by Satan at *PR* 3.244.

478. **platan**: plane; a favorite shade tree of the Greeks and Romans, commonly described as barren (Vergil, *Georg.* 2.70, 4.146). Plato presents Socrates as reclining beneath a spreading plane tree (*Phaedrus* 230a). Horace calls it *caelebs*, which used of men means "unmarried" and of trees "without vines" (*Odes* 2.15.4). Despite the conjugal arc of Eve's narrative, Fowler maintains that Adam's association with the plane tree owes not to its classical association with "erotic love" but to a "well-known allegory" that made it a symbol of Christ, Adam's "head."

480 Than that smooth wat'ry image; back I turned,
Thou following cried'st aloud, 'Return fair Eve,
Whom fli'st thou? Whom thou fli'st, of him thou art,
His flesh, his bone; to give thee being I lent
Out of my side to thee, nearest my heart
485 Substantial life, to have thee by my side
Henceforth an individual solace dear;
Part of my soul I seek thee, and thee claim
My other half.' With that thy gentle hand
Seized mine, I yielded, and from that time see
490 How beauty is excelled by manly grace
And wisdom, which alone is truly fair."
    So spake our general mother, and with eyes
Of conjugal attraction unreproved,
And meek surrender, half embracing leaned
495 On our first father, half her swelling breast
Naked met his under the flowing gold
Of her loose tresses hid: he in delight
Both of her beauty and submissive charms
Smiled with superior love, as Jupiter
500 On Juno smiles, when he impregns the clouds
That shed May flowers; and pressed her matron lip
With kisses pure: aside the Devil turned
For envy, yet with jealous leer malign
Eyed them askance, and to himself thus plained.
505   "Sight hateful, sight tormenting! Thus these two
Imparadised in one another's arms
The happier Eden, shall enjoy their fill

480–89. **Than ... yielded:** Eve flees Adam as
Daphne flees Apollo (*Met.* 1.502ff). As
with preceding situational references to
Tantalus (ll. 331–36) and Narcissus (ll.
460–69), another classical myth of frus-
tration is undone.
486. **individual:** inseparable, distinctive.
487–88. **Part ... half:** Cp. Horace, *Odes* 1.3.8,
2.17.5.
493. **unreproved:** not subject to rebuke.
Eve's eyes work differently at 9.1036.

499–501. **Smiled ... flowers:** The simile re-
calls Vergil's account of Aether embrac-
ing his wife and of showers quickening
seed in the earth (*Georg.* 2.325–28).
500. **impregns:** impregnates.
505–35. Satan's third soliloquy of the book.
Like Shakespeare in *Othello*, Milton insists
that his audience share the development
of his villain's strategy.

Of bliss on bliss, while I to Hell am thrust,
Where neither joy nor love, but fierce desire,
510 Among our other torments not the least,
Still unfulfilled with pain of longing pines;
Yet let me not forget what I have gained
From their own mouths; all is not theirs it seems:
One fatal Tree there stands of Knowledge called,
515 Forbidden them to taste: knowledge forbidden?
Suspicious, reasonless. Why should their Lord
Envy them that? Can it be sin to know,
Can it be death? And do they only stand
By ignorance, is that their happy state,
520 The proof of their obedience and their faith?
O fair foundation laid whereon to build
Their ruin! Hence I will excite their minds
With more desire to know, and to reject
Envious commands, invented with design
525 To keep them low whom knowledge might exalt
Equal with gods; aspiring to be such,
They taste and die: what likelier can ensue?
But first with narrow search I must walk round
This garden, and no corner leave unspied;
530 A chance but chance may lead where I may meet
Some wand'ring spirit of Heav'n, by fountain side,
Or in thick shade retired, from him to draw
What further would be learned. Live while ye may,
Yet happy pair; enjoy, till I return,
535 Short pleasures, for long woes are to succeed."
      So saying, his proud step he scornful turned,
But with sly circumspection, and began

508–11. **thrust . . . pines:** Satan's account of torment by *unfulfilled . . . longing* continues the epic's extensive correlation of the spiritual with the erotic (cp. 10.992–98).

511. **Still:** always; cp. 53–56; **pines:** torments (transitive, with Satan as the understood object); cp. 466n.

515–22. **knowledge . . . ruin:** Critics debate the sincerity of Satan's sentiments: whether his indignation is genuine (Empson 1965, 69) or a rehearsal of his rhetorical strategy (Broadbent 151). But Satan is capable neither of sincerity nor of being merely strategic.

530. **A chance but chance:** "Perhaps luck . . ."

Through wood, through waste, o'er hill, o'er dale his roam.
Meanwhile in utmost longitude, where heav'n
540 With earth and ocean meets, the setting sun
Slowly descended, and with right aspect
Against the eastern gate of Paradise
Leveled his evening rays: it was a rock
Of alabaster, piled up to the clouds,
545 Conspicuous far, winding with one ascent
Accessible from earth, one entrance high;
The rest was craggy cliff, that overhung
Still as it rose, impossible to climb.
Betwixt these rocky pillars Gabriel sat
550 Chief of th' angelic guards, awaiting night;
About him exercised heroic games
Th' unarmèd youth of Heav'n, but nigh at hand
Celestial armory, shields, helms, and spears,
Hung high with diamond flaming, and with gold.
555 Thither came Uriel, gliding through the even
On a sunbeam, swift as a shooting star
In autumn thwarts the night, when vapors fired
Impress the air, and shows the mariner

539. **utmost longitude:** farthest west.

541. **right aspect:** square attitude; the setting sun is perpendicular to the vertical gate.

548. **Still:** continually.

549. **Gabriel:** "God is my strength" (Hebr.); see lines 1006–10. Widely deemed one of the four archangels (with Uriel, Raphael, and Michael), Gabriel appears in Scripture to aid Daniel and foretell the birth of John the Baptist and Jesus (Dan. 8.16, 9.21; Luke 1.19, 26). Jewish traditions identify him as one of the three angels (with Michael and Raphael) who share a peaceful meal with Abraham (Gen. 18). He is also accounted the guardian of Paradise and the angel responsible for ripening fruit.

555. **even:** Newton was the first to explain the play on *even:* "His coming upon a sunbeam was the most direct and level course that he could take; for the sun's rays were now pointed right against the eastern gate . . . where Gabriel was sitting." Homer similarly compares Athena's descent to a shooting star, a sign portentous to mariners (*Il.* 4.74–79).

557. **thwarts:** crosses. Aristotle explains shooting stars as combustible exhalations drawn from the earth and ignited aloft either through compression and condensation or by their own quickening motion. The natural motion of fire is upward, but strong winds, thought to originate at high altitude, propel the ignited vapors downward. Their oblique (*thwart*) path results from the combination of their natural motion and the wind's downward compulsion (*Meteorology* 1.4). Cp. Vergil, *Georg.* 1.365–67.

558. **Impress:** mark by exerting pressure.

From what point of his compass to beware
560 Impetuous winds: he thus began in haste.
    "Gabriel, to thee thy course by lot hath giv'n
Charge and strict watch that to this happy place
No evil thing approach or enter in;
This day at highth of noon came to my sphere
565 A Spirit, zealous, as he seemed, to know
More of th' Almighty's works, and chiefly man
God's latest Image: I described his way
Bent all on speed, and marked his airy gait;
But in the mount that lies from Eden north,
570 Where he first lighted, soon discerned his looks
Alien from Heav'n, with passions foul obscured:
Mine eye pursued him still, but under shade
Lost sight of him; one of the banished crew
I fear, hath ventured from the deep, to raise
575 New troubles; him thy care must be to find."
    To whom the wingèd warrior thus returned:
"Uriel, no wonder if thy perfect sight,
Amid the sun's bright circle where thou sitst,
See far and wide: in at this gate none pass
580 The vigilance here placed, but such as come
Well known from Heav'n; and since meridian hour
No creature thence: if spirit of other sort,
So minded, have o'erleaped these earthy bounds
On purpose, hard thou knowst it to exclude
585 Spiritual substance with corporeal bar.
But if within the circuit of these walks,
In whatsoever shape he lurk, of whom
Thou tell'st, by morrow dawning I shall know."
    So promised he, and Uriel to his charge

---

561. The practice of establishing orders or
divisions (*courses*) by lot is common in
Scripture, especially in accounts of tem-
ple duties (1 Chron. 23.6–26; Luke 1.8).
567. **described:** observed, spied (per a
seventeenth-century confusion of *describe*
and *descry*).

568. **airy gait:** flight path as well as comport-
ment in flight (cp. 3.741).
580. **vigilance:** guard or watch; metonymy is
an apt figure for designating angels,
whose entire subjectivity is perfectly
aligned with function (cp. l. 410, 6.350–51).

590 Returned on that bright beam, whose point now raised
Bore him slope downward to the sun now fall'n
Beneath th' Azores; whether the prime orb,
Incredible how swift, had thither rolled
Diurnal, or this less voluble Earth
595 By shorter flight to th' east, had left him there
Arraying with reflected purple and gold
The clouds that on his western throne attend:
Now came still evening on, and twilight gray
Had in her sober livery all things clad;
600 Silence accompanied, for beast and bird,
They to their grassy couch, these to their nests
Were slunk, all but the wakeful nightingale;
She all night long her amorous descant sung;
Silence was pleased: now glowed the firmament
605 With living sapphires: Hesperus that led
The starry host, rode brightest, till the moon
Rising in clouded majesty, at length
Apparent Queen unveiled her peerless light,
And o'er the dark her silver mantle threw.
610   When Adam thus to Eve: "Fair consort, th' hour
Of night, and all things now retired to rest
Mind us of like repose, since God hath set
Labor and rest, as day and night to men
Successive, and the timely dew of sleep
615 Now falling with soft slumbrous weight inclines
Our eyelids; other creatures all day long

---

591. **slope downward:** Because the sun has continued to sink, Uriel no longer follows a flat trajectory. The moment thus occurs just after the balance point of equinoctial day and night.

592–97. **whether ... attend:** Milton will not choose between the Copernican cosmos and the Ptolemaic, which requires the sun to revolve around the earth at unbelievable velocity.

592. **whether:** First and second editions have "whither."

594. **Diurnal:** daily; **voluble:** rolling (Lat. *volúbilis*).

603. **descant:** counterpointed song.

605. **Hesperus:** the evening star, Venus.

606–9. Milton plays on clothing as a vehicle for light, here culminating in the moon's paradoxical disrobing (cp. *L'All* 60–62, *Il Pens* 122–25, *Masque* 188–89).

608. **Apparent:** "readily seen," but also "heir" (to Hesperus, the brightest light in the night sky until the moon's appearance).

Rove idle unemployed, and less need rest;
Man hath his daily work of body or mind
Appointed, which declares his dignity,
620 And the regard of Heav'n on all his ways;
While other animals unactive range,
And of their doings God takes no account.
To morrow ere fresh morning streak the east
With first approach of light, we must be ris'n,
625 And at our pleasant labor, to reform
Yon flow'ry arbors, yonder allies green,
Our walk at noon, with branches overgrown,
That mock our scant manuring, and require
More hands than ours to lop their wanton growth:
630 Those blossoms also, and those dropping gums,
That lie bestrown unsightly and unsmooth,
Ask riddance, if we mean to tread with ease;
Meanwhile, as nature wills, night bids us rest."
    To whom thus Eve with perfect beauty adorned.
635 "My author and disposer, what thou bidd'st
Unargued I obey; so God ordains,
God is thy Law, thou mine: to know no more
Is woman's happiest knowledge and her praise.
With thee conversing I forget all time,
640 All seasons and their change, all please alike.
Sweet is the breath of morn, her rising sweet,
With charm of earliest birds; pleasant the sun
When first on this delightful land he spreads
His orient beams, on herb, tree, fruit, and flow'r,
645 Glist'ring with dew; fragrant the fertile earth
After soft showers; and sweet the coming on
Of grateful evening mild, then silent night
With this her solemn bird and this fair moon,
And these the gems of heav'n, her starry train:
650 But neither breath of morn when she ascends

---

628. **manuring:** cultivation by hand (Lat. *manus:* hand).
635. **author and disposer:** source and ruler.
640. **seasons:** periods of time, occasions.
642. **charm:** delightful harmony.
648. **solemn bird:** nightingale; cp. 7.435.

With charm of earliest birds, nor rising sun
On this delightful land, nor herb, fruit, flow'r,
Glist'ring with dew, nor fragrance after showers,
Nor grateful evening mild, nor silent night
655 With this her solemn bird, nor walk by moon,
Or glittering starlight without thee is sweet.
But wherefore all night long shine these, for whom
This glorious sight, when sleep hath shut all eyes?"
     To whom our general ancestor replied.
660 "Daughter of God and man, accomplished Eve,
These have their course to finish, round the Earth,
By morrow evening, and from land to land
In order, though to nations yet unborn,
Minist'ring light prepared, they set and rise;
665 Lest total darkness should by night regain
Her old possession, and extinguish life
In nature and all things, which these soft fires
Not only enlighten, but with kindly heat
Of various influence foment and warm,
670 Temper or nourish, or in part shed down
Their stellar virtue on all kinds that grow
On earth, made hereby apter to receive
Perfection from the sun's more potent ray.
These then, though unbeheld in deep of night,
675 Shine not in vain, nor think, though men were none,
That heav'n would want spectators, God want praise;
Millions of spiritual creatures walk the earth
Unseen, both when we wake, and when we sleep:

661. **These:** Early editions have "Those." Citing lines 657 and 674, Newton substituted "These."

665–67. **Lest . . . things:** Previously, Satan persuaded Chaos and Night of his inten- tion to return the newly created world "to her original darkness" and the *possession* of Night (2.982–86; cp. 10.415–18). It is ax- iomatic in this epic that, without light, chaos would come again.

667–75. Neoplatonic astrology classified an-imals, vegetables, and minerals according to the predominant *stellar virtue*, or astral power, that *tempers* (strengthens, attunes) them. Such *influence* was supposedly me- diated by streaming ether. After the Fall, the cosmos is adjusted so that the stars' influence is not always *kindly*, or naturally favorable (cp. 10.651ff). Their postlapsar- ian fire can be *soft* (gentle) as here, or se- vere (cp. 2.276).

All these with ceaseless praise his works behold
680 Both day and night: how often from the steep
Of echoing hill or thicket have we heard
Celestial voices to the midnight air,
Sole, or responsive each to other's note
Singing their great Creator: oft in bands
685 While they keep watch, or nightly rounding walk
With Heav'nly touch of instrumental sounds
In full harmonic number joined, their songs
Divide the night, and lift our thoughts to Heaven."
    Thus talking hand in hand alone they passed
690 On to their blissful bower; it was a place
Chos'n by the sov'reign planter, when he framed
All things to man's delightful use; the roof
Of thickest covert was inwoven shade
Laurel and myrtle, and what higher grew
695 Of firm and fragrant leaf; on either side
Acanthus, and each odorous bushy shrub
Fenced up the verdant wall; each beauteous flow'r,
Iris all hues, roses, and jessamine
Reared high their flourished heads between, and wrought
700 Mosaic; underfoot the violet,
Crocus, and hyacinth with rich inlay
Broidered the ground, more colored than with stone
Of costliest emblem: other creature here
Beast, bird, insect, or worm durst enter none;
705 Such was their awe of man. In shady bower
More sacred and sequestered, though but feigned,

---

685. **rounding:** making the rounds (literally, since the Garden is circular).

688. **Divide the night:** into watches. Roman armies sounded a trumpet when changing the watch; angelic guards do it to multipart music (*full harmonic number*).

690. **blissfull bower:** Cp. Spenser's account of the bower within the Garden of Adonis where Venus sequesters the mortally wounded Adonis from "stygian gods" (*FQ* 3.6.43–49).

694. **Laurel and myrtle:** plants sacred to Apollo and Venus, respectively. Cp. Vergil, *Ec.* 2.54–55.

701. **Crocus, and hyacinth:** Atop Mount Ida, the hoodwinked Zeus beds the scheming Hera on these freshly risen flowers (*Il.* 14.348).

703. **emblem:** in the classical sense of a surface with inlaid ornamentation, a mosaic.

705. **shady:** The first edition has "shadier," preferred by some editors.

Pan or Silvanus never slept, nor nymph,
Nor Faunus haunted. Here in close recess
With flowers, garlands, and sweet-smelling herbs
710 Espousèd Eve decked first her nuptial bed,
And Heav'nly choirs the hymenaean sung,
What day the genial angel to our sire
Brought her in naked beauty more adorned,
More lovely than Pandora, whom the Gods
715 Endowed with all their gifts, and O too like
In sad event, when to the unwiser son
Of Japhet brought by Hermes, she ensnared
Mankind with her fair looks, to be avenged
On him who had stole Jove's authentic fire.

720   Thus at their shady lodge arrived, both stood
Both turned, and under open sky adored
The God that made both sky, air, Earth and heav'n
Which they beheld, the moon's resplendent globe
And starry pole: "Thou also mad'st the night,
725 Maker omnipotent, and thou the day,
Which we in our appointed work employed
Have finished happy in our mutual help
And mutual love, the crown of all our bliss

707–8. **Pan or Silvanus . . . Faunus:** pastoral hybrids, half man and half goat, associated with secret retreats and fecundity. For Pan as a nature god, see 266n.

708. **close:** secluded, exclusive.

709. **flowers:** a rare instance where the two-syllable pronunciation is intended.

711. **hymenaean:** wedding song (after the classical marriage god, Hymen). Cp. *L'All* 125–28; *Elegy 5* 105–8.

712. **genial:** of or relating to marriage; nuptial. In Adam's version, the voice of Eve's "Heav'nly Maker" guides her to Adam (8.484–86).

714–19. **Pandora:** "all gifts" (Gk.); her story was frequently deemed an analogue of the Fall. After Prometheus ("Forethinker") steals heaven's fire for humanity's sake, Pandora is divinely contrived to bring misery upon the world. Bearing a sealed jar containing the world's ills, she is conducted by Hermes to Prometheus' brother, Epimetheus ("Afterthought")— "the unwiser son." After Epimetheus marries her, the evils are released from her jar (*Theog.* 570–612; *Works and Days* 54–105).

717. **Japhet:** Christian mythographers identified Iapetus, the Titan father of Prometheus and Epimetheus, as Noah's son Iaphet (Gen. 9.18–10.2).

719. **authentic:** possessing in itself the basis of its existence; genuine, original. Cp. 3.656.

724–35. **Thou . . . sleep:** Cp. Ps. 74.16–17. Milton shifts seamlessly from describing the prayer to quoting it.

724. **pole:** sky.

Ordained by thee, and this delicious place
730　For us too large, where thy abundance wants
Partakers, and uncropped falls to the ground.
But thou hast promised from us two a race
To fill the Earth, who shall with us extol
Thy goodness infinite, both when we wake,
735　And when we seek, as now, thy gift of sleep."
　　　This said unanimous, and other rites
Observing none, but adoration pure
Which God likes best, into their inmost bow'r
Handed they went; and eased the putting off
740　These troublesome disguises which we wear,
Straight side by side were laid, nor turned I ween
Adam from his fair spouse, nor Eve the rites
Mysterious of connubial love refused:
Whatever hypocrites austerely talk
745　Of purity and place and innocence,
Defaming as impure what God declares

---

733. **fill the Earth:** Cp. Gen. 1.28.

735. **gift of sleep:** Cp. Homer, *Il.* 9.713; Vergil, *Aen.* 2.269; Ps. 127.2.

736–38. **This . . . best:** For early readers, the Puritan edge of this prescription for piety would have been keen; cp. 12.534–35.

736. **unanimous:** literally, one-souled.

739. **Handed:** hand in hand, as at line 689.

741–43. **nor . . . refused:** The use of *rites* to mean marital sex was a commonplace warranted by St. Paul's account (Eph. 5.32) of the bodily union of husband and wife as a "mystery" symbolizing Christ's union with the Church (cp. 8.487; Shakespeare, *ADO* 2.1.373, *OTH* 1.3.258; Jonson, *Hymenaei* 137). The reverence expressed here for conjugal coition is ordinarily reserved for sacraments. In related passages, it extends to human genitalia ("mysterious parts") and the "genial bed" (l. 312, 8.598). Insistence that Adam and Eve participate mutually, neither turning away nor refusing, suggests another scriptural source for this passage. *Rite* was often spelled *right* (cp.

CMS, Masque 125) and included a strong sense of moral obligation. St. Paul deemed refusal of spousal "due benevolence" fraudulent (1 Cor. 7.3–5). Cp. "the starved lover . . . best quitted with disdain" (ll. 769–70).

741. **I ween:** I believe; "used parenthetically rather than as governing the sentence; in verse often a mere tag" (*OED* 1.h). Seventeenth-century retellings of Book 4 suggest that Milton's conviction found a sympathetic audience. Dryden's Satan thus imagines Eve as Semele to his Jove: "Have not I, like these, a body too, / Form'd for the same delights which they pursue? / I could (so variously my passions move) / Enjoy, and blast her in the act of Love" (*State of Innocence* 3.1; cp. Hopkins, *Primitive Loves* 135–235).

744–49. **hypocrites . . . man:** These lines concentrate allusions to various scriptural passages on marriage: 1 Tim. 4.1–3 (*hypocrites*), 1 Cor. 7.1 (*commands to some*), Gen. 1.28 (*Our Maker bids increase*).

Pure, and commands to some, leaves free to all.
Our Maker bids increase, who bids abstain
But our destroyer, foe to God and man?
750   Hail wedded love, mysterious law, true source
Of human offspring, sole propriety,
In Paradise of all things common else.
By thee adulterous lust was driv'n from men
Among the bestial herds to range, by thee
755   Founded in reason, loyal, just, and pure,
Relations dear, and all the charities
Of father, son, and brother first were known.
Far be it, that I should write thee sin or blame,
Or think thee unbefitting holiest place,
760   Perpetual fountain of domestic sweets,
Whose bed is undefiled and chaste pronounced,
Present, or past, as saints and patriarchs used.
Here love his golden shafts employs, here lights
His constant lamp, and waves his purple wings,
765   Reigns here and revels; not in the bought smile
Of harlots, loveless, joyless, unendeared,
Casual fruition, nor in court amours
Mixed dance, or wanton masque, or midnight ball,
Or serenade, which the starved lover sings
770   To his proud fair, best quitted with disdain.
These lulled by nightingales embracing slept,

---

751. **propriety:** exclusive possession or right of use; ownership. Wedlock is a prelapsarian institution, unlike private property (with the exception of the nuptial bower).

756. **all the charities:** affections; "comprehends all the relations, all the endearments of consanguinity and affinity" (Newton).

760–65. **Perpetual fountain . . . revels:** The references and diction—*fountain, golden shafts, lamp, purple wings*—are erotically charged and culturally diffuse; cp. 8.511–20. *Reigns here and revels* translates a description of love by Marino (*L'Adone* 2.114), a sensuous Italian poet noteworthy to Milton on account of his patron, Manso, whose acquaintance Milton prized. See *Manso, Damon* 181–97.

761. **bed is undefiled:** Cp. Heb. 13.4.

763. **love:** Cupid, whose golden arrows (*shafts*) infuse love.

768. **Mixed dance:** men and women dancing together, a practice frowned upon by Puritans, including Milton; cp. *Of Ref* (Yale 1:589). **masque:** masquerade ball.

769. **starved:** deprived of love, but also of warmth; cp. 2.600.

770. **quitted:** repaid; cp. line 51.

And on their naked limbs the flow'ry roof
Show'red roses, which the morn repaired. Sleep on
Blest pair; and O yet happiest if ye seek
775 No happier state, and know to know no more.
    Now had night measured with her shadowy cone
Half way up hill this vast sublunar vault,
And from their ivory port the Cherubim
Forth issuing at th' accustomed hour stood armed
780 To their night watches in warlike parade,
When Gabriel to his next in power thus spake.
    "Uzziel, half these draw off, and coast the south
With strictest watch; these other wheel the north,
Our circuit meets full west." As flame they part
785 Half wheeling to the shield, half to the spear.
From these, two strong and subtle spirits he called
That near him stood, and gave them thus in charge.
    "Ithuriel and Zephon, with winged speed
Search through this garden, leave unsearched no nook,
790 But chiefly where those two fair creatures lodge,

773. **repaired:** restored.

774. **Blest pair:** translates Vergil's celebration of Nisus and Euryalus (*Fortunati ambo!*), intimate friends slain by the enemy at rest in each other's arms (*Aen.* 9.446).

775. Note the repetition of *no* and *know*.

776–77. **shadowy . . . vault:** The earth's globe casts a conical shadow into the night sky, which, reaching from horizon to horizon, is portrayed as an arch (*vault*). At this moment, the *shadowy cone,* moving in diametrical opposition to the sun, has ascended halfway from the eastern horizon toward its midnight zenith. It is therefore nine o'clock, equinoctial time, the start of the second watch (ll. 779–80). Line 777 occurs halfway between line 539, where "the sun *in utmost longitude* begins its descent beneath the horizon, and 1015, the last line of Book 4," which occurs at midnight (Fowler).

778. **ivory port:** Recent editors identify this phrase as an allusion to the ivory gate of the realm of sleep, from which false dreams proceed according to Homer and Vergil (*Od.* 19.562–67; *Aen.* 6.893–96). A significant connection with the guards' imminent interruption of Eve's dream is then proposed. Such a connection is strained. Guards, not personified dreams, issue from this ivory port, which is the gate not of sleep but of Paradise (made of the white stone *alabaster* [l. 544] and thus like ivory in color).

782–85. **Uzziel:** "power of God" (Hebr.). Standing at the eastern gate, Gabriel splits the guard to check the northern and southern perimeters of the Garden until they meet again *full west. Shield* and *spear* translate a Greek idiom designating left and right.

788. **Ithuriel and Zephon:** "Discovery of God" and "Lookout" (Hebr.). Their names denote their roles as they search the interior of the Garden.

Now laid perhaps asleep secure of harm.
This evening from the sun's decline arrived
Who tells of some infernal spirit seen
Hitherward bent (who could have thought?) escaped
795 The bars of Hell, on errand bad no doubt:
Such where ye find, seize fast, and hither bring."
 So saying, on he led his radiant files,
Dazzling the Moon; these to the bower direct
In search of whom they sought: him there they found
800 Squat like a toad, close at the ear of Eve;
Assaying by his devilish art to reach
The organs of her fancy, and with them forge
Illusions as he list, phantasms and dreams,
Or if, inspiring venom, he might taint
805 Th' animal spirits that from pure blood arise
Like gentle breaths from rivers pure, thence raise
At least distempered, discontented thoughts,
Vain hopes, vain aims, inordinate desires
Blown up with high conceits engend'ring pride.
810 Him thus intent Ithuriel with his spear
Touched lightly; for no falsehood can endure
Touch of celestial temper, but returns
Of force to its own likeness: up he starts
Discovered and surprised. As when a spark

791. **secure:** unsuspecting.

793. **Who:** one who; that is, Uriel (see l. 555).

798. **these:** Ithuriel and Zephon.

802. **organs of her fancy:** Satan delves into Eve's psyche to manipulate her *fancy* or imagination, the faculty that produces mental images (*phantasms*). Cp. "raise up the organs of her fantasy" in *WIV* 5.5.55. *Organs* retains its Greek sense of "instruments"; it may also include the specific sense of "musical instrument." In Milton's time, the plural *organs* could mean "pipe organ." In effect, Satan plays upon Eve's mental apparatus as if it were a set of pipes, attempting to forge illusions in a

manner reminiscent of the erection of Pandaemonium (1.708ff). Cp. *PR* 4.407–9.

804–9. **inspiring . . . pride:** If unable to play directly on Eve's imagination, Satan hopes to unsettle the perfect humoral balance (*temper*) of her *animal spirits*. These spirits were thought to originate from the blood and carry sensory data to the brain. Breathing venom into (*inspiring*) her ear, he aims to provoke *distempered* impulses and grandiose designs (*high conceits*).

812. **celestial temper:** The spear, like incisive Ithuriel, was produced (*tempered*) in Heaven.

815   Lights on a heap of nitrous powder, laid
        Fit for the tun some magazine to store
        Against a rumored war, the smutty grain
        With sudden blaze diffused, inflames the air:
        So started up in his own shape the fiend.
820   Back stepped those two fair angels half amazed
        So sudden to behold the grisly king;
        Yet thus, unmoved with fear, accost him soon.
           "Which of those rebel spirits adjudged to Hell
        Com'st thou, escaped thy prison, and transformed,
825   Why sat'st thou like an enemy in wait
        Here watching at the head of these that sleep?"
           "Know ye not then," said Satan, filled with scorn,
        "Know ye not me? Ye knew me once no mate
        For you, there sitting where ye durst not soar;
830   Not to know me argues yourselves unknown,
        The lowest of your throng; or if ye know,
        Why ask ye, and superfluous begin
        Your message, like to end as much in vain?"
        To whom thus Zephon, answering scorn with scorn.
835   "Think not, revolted Spirit, thy shape the same,
        Or undiminished brightness, to be known
        As when thou stood'st in Heav'n upright and pure;
        That glory then, when thou no more wast good,
        Departed from thee, and thou resemblest now
840   Thy sin and place of doom obscure and foul.
        But come, for thou, be sure, shalt give account
        To him who sent us, whose charge is to keep
        This place inviolable, and these from harm."

---

815. **Lights:** lands on and ignites; **nitrous powder:** gunpowder.

816–17. ready for a barrel (*tun*) and storage in an arsenal (*magazine*) as preparation for (*against*) war; **smutty grain:** cereal grain blackened by a parasitic fungus.

821. **grisly:** gruesomely horrible; applied to Death (2.704) and Moloch (*Nat Ode* 209), both of whom are also described as kingly.

830. **argues:** is reason to think.

835–43. Zephon's retorted scorn makes pointed and repeated use of the second person singular (form of address used with inferiors).

836. Bentley would transpose *undiminished brightness*, for reasons grammatical.

So spake the Cherub, and his grave rebuke
845   Severe in youthful beauty, added grace
Invincible: abashed the Devil stood,
And felt how awful goodness is, and saw
Virtue in her shape how lovely, saw, and pined
His loss; but chiefly to find here observed
850   His luster visibly impaired; yet seemed
Undaunted. "If I must contend," said he,
"Best with the best, the sender not the sent,
Or all at once; more glory will be won,
Or less be lost." "Thy fear," said Zephon bold,
855   "Will save us trial what the least can do
Single against thee wicked, and thence weak."
     The fiend replied not, overcome with rage;
But like a proud steed reined, went haughty on,
Champing his iron curb: to strive or fly
860   He held it vain; awe from above had quelled
His heart, not else dismayed. Now drew they nigh
The western point, where those half-rounding guards
Just met, and closing stood in squadron joined
Awaiting next command. To whom their chief
865   Gabriel from the front thus called aloud.
     "O friends, I hear the tread of nimble feet
Hasting this way, and now by glimpse discern
Ithuriel and Zephon through the shade,
And with them comes a third of regal port,
870   But faded splendor wan; who by his gait
And fierce demeanor seems the Prince of Hell,

845–47. **Severe . . . is:** Satan reacts similarly to the sight of Eve (9.459–62). Cp. Vergil's description of the grave rebuke delivered by the youthful and beautiful Euryalus (*Aen.* 5.344) and Dryden's distillation in *Hind and Panther:* "For vice, though front- less and of hardened face / Is daunted at the sight of awful grace" (3.1040–41).

848. **Virtue . . . lovely:** It is a commonplace of Platonically inspired philosophy and poetry that beauty is the aesthetic expres-

sion of virtue or goodness. **pined:** grieved; see 466n.

858–59. **like . . . curb:** The simile echoes Hermes' account of Prometheus (Aeschy- lus, *Prom.* 1008).

862. **half-rounding:** See 782–85n.

868. **shade:** trees.

870–71. Verity and Fowler take Gabriel's easy recognition of Satan as validation of his aristocratic slap at Zephon (l. 830), but Gabriel goes by gait, bearing (*port*), and

Not likely to part hence without contest;
Stand firm, for in his look defiance lours."
　　　He scarce had ended, when those two approached
875　And brief related whom they brought, where found,
How busied, in what form and posture couched.
To whom with stern regard thus Gabriel spake.
　　　"Why hast thou, Satan, broke the bounds prescribed
To thy transgressions, and disturbed the charge
880　Of others, who approve not to transgress
By thy example, but have power and right
To question thy bold entrance on this place;
Employed it seems to violate sleep, and those
Whose dwelling God hath planted here in bliss?
885　　　To whom thus Satan, with contemptuous brow.
"Gabriel, thou hadst in Heav'n th' esteem of wise,
And such I held thee; but this question asked
Puts me in doubt. Lives there who loves his pain?
Who would not, finding way, break loose from Hell,
890　Though thither doomed? Thou wouldst thyself, no doubt,
And boldly venture to whatever place
Farthest from pain, where thou mightst hope to change
Torment with ease, and soonest recompense
Dole with delight, which in this place I sought;
895　To thee no reason; who know'st only good,
But evil hast not tried: and wilt object
His will who bound us? Let him surer bar
His iron gates, if he intends our stay
In that dark durance: thus much what was asked.
900　The rest is true, they found me where they say;

---

demeanor, which Zephon had little
chance to observe before Satan identified
himself.
879. **transgressions**: both "sins" (as in l. 880)
and "boundary crossings"; though sen-
tenced to Hell for his crimes, Satan now
trespasses in Paradise (see l. 909). **charge**:
responsibility; child or member of a min-
ister's congregation under protection.

880. **approve**: agree; try or test (see Satan's
rejoinder, l. 896).
886. **esteem of wise**: reputation for good
sense.
893–94. **recompense . . . delight**: exchange
pain for pleasure.
896. **object**: raise as an objection.
899. **durance**: forced confinement; **thus
much what**: so much (in reply to) what.

But that implies not violence or harm."
　　Thus he in scorn. The warlike angel moved,
Disdainfully half smiling thus replied.
"O loss of one in Heav'n to judge of wise,
905　Since Satan fell, whom folly overthrew,
And now returns him from his prison scaped,
Gravely in doubt whether to hold them wise
Or not, who ask what boldness brought him hither
Unlicensed from his bounds in Hell prescribed;
910　So wise he judges it to fly from pain
However, and to scape his punishment.
So judge thou still, presumptuous, till the wrath,
Which thou incurr'st by flying, meet thy flight
Sevenfold, and scourge that wisdom back to Hell,
915　Which taught thee yet no better, that no pain
Can equal anger infinite provoked.
But wherefore thou alone? Wherefore with thee
Came not all Hell broke loose? Is pain to them
Less pain, less to be fled, or thou than they
920　Less hardy to endure? Courageous chief,
The first in flight from pain, hadst thou alleged
To thy deserted host this cause of flight,
Thou surely hadst not come sole fugitive."
　　To which the fiend thus answered frowning stern.
925　"Not that I less endure, or shrink from pain,
Insulting angel, well thou know'st I stood
Thy fiercest, when in battle to thy aid
The blasting volleyed thunder made all speed
And seconded thy else not dreaded spear.
930　But still thy words at random, as before,
Argue thy inexperience what behooves

---

904. Gabriel ironically laments the loss of Satan as an arbiter of wisdom; see line 886.
906. **returns:** can take either *Satan* (archaic usage, reflexive) or *folly* as its subject.
911. **However:** by any means.
926. **stood:** withstood.

928. **The:** per first edition; second edition has "Thy."
930–33. **But . . . Leader:** Gabriel's remarks, says Satan, reveal his ignorance about how a dedicated leader ought to proceed after arduous undertakings and failures.
930. **at random:** without discrimination.

From hard assays and ill successes past
A faithful Leader, not to hazard all
Through ways of danger by himself untried.
935 I therefore, I alone first undertook
To wing the desolate abyss, and spy
This new created world, whereof in Hell
Fame is not silent, here in hope to find
Better abode, and my afflicted powers
940 To settle here on Earth, or in mid-air;
Though for possession put to try once more
What thou and thy gay legions dare against;
Whose easier business were to serve their Lord
High up in Heav'n, with songs to hymn his throne,
945 And practiced distances to cringe, not fight."
 To whom the warrior angel, soon replied.
"To say and straight unsay, pretending first
Wise to fly pain, professing next the spy,
Argues no leader but a liar traced,
950 Satan, and couldst thou faithful add? O name,
O sacred name of faithfulness profaned!
Faithful to whom? To thy rebellious crew?
Army of fiends, fit body to fit head;
Was this your discipline and faith engaged,
955 Your military obedience, to dissolve
Allegiance to th' acknowledged power supreme?
And thou sly hypocrite, who now wouldst seem
Patron of liberty, who more than thou
Once fawned, and cringed, and servilely adored

---

939. **afflicted:** struck down (cp. 1.186).
940. **mid-air:** After the Fall, Satan rules the middle region of the air, which extends as high as the mountaintops (1.516–17). See *PR* 1.39–47, 2.117; Eph. 2.2, 6.12.
942. **gay:** ebullient, showy, self-indulgent; a pointed retort to Zephon (ll. 838–40).
945. **practiced distances:** applies both to courtly protocol (*cringe*) and martial training, especially swordplay (*fight*).

949. Replying to Satan at lines 930–34.
958–60. Gabriel's reply allows that Heaven is a realm of groveling toadies (Empson 1965, 111). Fowler counters that the response simply conforms to Satan's insulting tenor (ll. 942–45). Cp. Prometheus' scornful words to Zeus's followers: "Worship, adore, and fawn upon . . . thy lord" (Aeschylus, *Prom.* 937).

960 Heav'n's awful Monarch? Wherefore but in hope
To dispossess him, and thyself to reign?
But mark what I aread thee now, avaunt;
Fly thither whence thou fledd'st: if from this hour
Within these hallowed limits thou appear,
965 Back to th' infernal pit I drag thee chained,
And seal thee so, as henceforth not to scorn
The facile gates of Hell too slightly barred."
    So threat'ned he, but Satan to no threats
Gave heed, but waxing more in rage replied.
970   "Then when I am thy captive talk of chains,
Proud limitary Cherub, but ere then
Far heavier load thy self expect to feel
From my prevailing arm, though Heaven's King
Ride on thy wings, and thou with thy compeers,
975 Used to the yoke, draw'st his triumphant wheels
In progress through the road of Heav'n star-paved."
        While thus he spake, th' angelic squadron bright
Turned fiery red, sharp'ning in moonèd horns
Their phalanx, and began to hem him round
980 With ported spears, as thick as when a field

---

962. **aread:** advise, order; **avaunt:** begone; diction used especially for expulsion of evil spirits.

965–67. With Gabriel's threat to *drag* a *chained* Satan to the pit and *seal* him there (note the emphatic present tense), Milton returns to the apocalyptic context evoked at lines 1–12 (Rev. 20.1–3).

967. **facile:** easily negotiated; the diction implies negligence, as does *too slightly barred,* though again Gabriel may only be responding in Satan's scornful terms (ll. 898–99).

971. **limitary:** stationed at a border or boundary; of limited authority (in reply to l. 964).

974. **Ride on thy wings:** "He rode upon a Cherub and did fly" (Ps. 18.10).

975–76. Satan refers to God's chariot (6.750ff); cp. Ezek. 1, 10, 11.22.

976. **progress:** royal tour.

978–80. **sharp'ning . . . spears:** Taken in their most specific military senses, *phalanx* and *ported* are inconsistent. Troops in a classical Greek *phalanx* interlock shields in a square formation and carry their spears projecting forward. *Ported spears* are held diagonally, across the body, spearhead at the left shoulder. The movement into a crescent shape (*sharp'ning in moonèd horns*) suggests that *phalanx* here is used in its more general sense of a group moving closely together.

980–83. **With . . . them:** The comparison of a group of warriors to a windswept field of grain is common in epic, beginning with Homer (*Il.* 2.147–50). Leonard argues that the simile, commonly used of demoralized troops (like a field of grain flattened by wind), implies the good

Of Ceres ripe for harvest waving bends
Her bearded grove of ears, which way the wind
Sways them; the careful plowman doubting stands
Lest on the threshing floor his hopeful sheaves
985 Prove chaff. On th' other side Satan alarmed
Collecting all his might dilated stood,
Like Teneriffe or Atlas unremoved:
His stature reached the sky, and on his crest
Sat Horror plumed; nor wanted in his grasp
990 What seemed both spear and shield: now dreadful deeds
Might have ensued, nor only Paradise
In this commotion, but the starry cope
Of Heav'n perhaps, or all the elements
At least had gone to wrack, disturbed and torn

---

angels' weakness. Milton's simile departs from its precedents, however. Gabriel's troops, spears ported, form a thick semicircle around Satan. Viewed together, the shafts of their spears would appear to slant in several directions, like stalks in a field of grain *waving* in the uncertain wind that precedes a storm.

981. **Ceres:** goddess of grain, mother of Proserpine (cp. 268–72n).

983–85. **the careful plowman ... chaff:** The subject conveyed by *the careful plowman* is not clear. Satan seems an unlikely candidate in light of line 985. The identification of God as the plowman is more likely in light of literary precedent, the designation of God in this book as the planter of the Garden, and the scriptural imagery of sheaves and chaff, which fits the apocalyptic role of God. The choice attributed to the plowman is also consistent with subsequent imagery of God's scales.

986. **dilated:** enlarged, owing to spirits' ability to shrink or swell at will (cp. 1.428–29).

987. **Teneriffe or Atlas unremoved:** The summit of Mount *Teneriffe* (two miles high, in the Canary Islands) was in Milton's century estimated at "fifteen miles"

(Hume). **Atlas:** cloud-capped mountain in Libya on which the sky was imagined to rest, per the myth of Atlas. **unremoved:** Latinate past participle meaning immovable (cp. l. 493). The usage is likely ironic. Faith can move mountains (1 Cor. 13.2), as angels provoked by Satan amply demonstrate (6.645–49).

988. **His stature reached the sky:** Homer's description of Discord and Vergil's of Rumor are usually adduced (*Il.* 4.443; *Aen.* 4.177), but the rendition of Passover night in the apocryphal Wisdom of Solomon is a more apt precedent for the configuration of the scene: "Night in her swift course was half spent, when thy almighty Word leapt from thy royal throne in heaven into the midst of that doomed land like a relentless warrior ... and stood and filled it all with death, his head touching the heavens, his feet on earth" (14–16).

992. **cope:** vault; see 776–77n. The threat seems overstated given God's authority over creatures: he curbs angelic muscle to preserve the landscape during the War in Heaven (6.225–29), and Gabriel will soon claim that his strength has been doubled (ll. 1006–10).

995   With violence of this conflict, had not soon
      Th' Eternal to prevent such horrid fray
      Hung forth in Heav'n his golden scales, yet seen
      Betwixt Astrea and the Scorpion sign,
      Wherein all things created first he weighed,
1000 The pendulous round Earth with balanced air
      In counterpoise, now ponders all events,
      Battles and realms: in these he put two weights
      The sequel each of parting and of fight;
      The latter quick up flew, and kicked the beam;
1005 Which Gabriel spying, thus bespake the fiend.
         "Satan, I know thy strength, and thou know'st mine,
      Neither our own but giv'n; what folly then
      To boast what arms can do, since thine no more
      Than Heav'n permits, nor mine, though doubled now
1010 To trample thee as mire: for proof look up,
      And read thy lot in yon celestial sign
      Where thou art weigh'd, and shown how light, how weak,
      If thou resist." The fiend looked up and knew
      His mounted scale aloft: nor more; but fled
1015 Murmuring, and with him fled the shades of night.

997. **golden scales:** translates Homer's phrase for the balance in which Zeus weighs destinies of opposed armies or warriors (*Il.* 8.69, 22.209). Here it refers to the constellation Libra (the *scales*) between *Astrea and the Scorpion sign.*

998. **Astrea:** the constellation of Virgo (the Virgin). *Astrea,* goddess of justice, resided on earth during the Golden Age, but human iniquity drove her up to heaven, where she became this constellation (Ovid, *Met.* 1.149ff).

999–1001. **Wherein . . . counterpoise:** Weight is a crucial quality in Scripture, where God as creator and judge is repeatedly depicted as using a scale (Job 28.24ff, Isa. 40.12, 1 Sam. 2.3).

1001. **ponders:** weighs, deliberates.

1012. In Homer and Vergil, the loser's balance sinks; the victor's ascends. But Milton follows scriptural precedent: "Thou art weighed in the balances and art found wanting" (Dan. 5.27). Gabriel's reading seems inconsistent with the claim that God weighs *the sequel each of parting and of fight* (l. 1003). The outcome is nevertheless consistent with Gabriel's threat to apprehend Satan only if he refused to depart (ll. 965–67).

1014. **nor more:** nor (said) more.

1015. Cp. the final lines of Vergil's *Aen.*

BOOK V

THE ARGUMENT

Morning approached, Eve relates to Adam her troublesome dream; he likes it not, yet comforts her. They come forth to their day labors. Their morning hymn at the door of their bower. God to render man inexcusable sends Raphael to admonish him of his obedience, of his free estate, of his enemy near at hand; who he is, and why his enemy, and whatever else may avail Adam to know. Raphael comes down to Paradise, his appearance described, his coming discerned by Adam afar off sitting at the door of his bower. He goes out to meet him, brings him to his lodge, entertains him with the choicest fruits of Paradise got together by Eve; their discourse at table. Raphael performs his message, minds Adam of his state and of his enemy; relates at Adam's request who that enemy is, and how he came to be so, beginning from his first revolt in Heaven, and the occasion thereof; how he drew his legions after him to the parts of the north, and there incited them to rebel with him, persuading all but only Abdiel, a Seraph, who in argument dissuades and opposes him, then forsakes him.

> Now Morn her rosy steps in th' eastern clime
> Advancing, sowed the earth with orient pearl,
> When Adam waked, so customed, for his sleep
> Was airy light, from pure digestion bred,
> 5   And temperate vapors bland, which th' only sound
> Of leaves and fuming rills, Aurora's fan,

---

5. **temperate vapors bland:** soothing and perfectly proportioned vapors. Sleep, it was believed, was caused by vapors arising in the stomach. Adam's benign internal system is here perfectly blended with the external breezes and streams of Eden. **th' only sound:** the sound only.

6. **fuming rills:** foaming brooks; some editors gloss fuming as "misting," but the exhalations of lines 185–6 are not said to rise

Lightly dispersed, and the shrill matin song
Of birds on every bough; so much the more
His wonder was to find unwakened Eve
10 With tresses discomposed, and glowing cheek,
As through unquiet rest: he on his side
Leaning half-raised, with looks of cordial love
Hung over her enamored, and beheld
Beauty, which whether waking or asleep,
15 Shot forth peculiar graces; then with voice
Mild, as when Zephyrus on Flora breathes,
Her hand soft touching, whispered thus. "Awake
My fairest, my espoused, my latest found,
Heav'n's last best gift, my ever new delight,
20 Awake, the morning shines, and the fresh field
Calls us; we lose the prime, to mark how spring
Our tended plants, how blows the citron grove,
What drops the myrrh, and what the balmy reed,
How nature paints her colors, how the bee
25 Sits on the bloom extracting liquid sweet."
    Such whispering waked her, but with startled eye
On Adam, whom embracing, thus she spoke.
    "O sole in whom my thoughts find all repose,
My glory, my perfection, glad I see
30 Thy face, and morn returned, for I this night,
Such night till this I never passed, have dreamed,
If dreamed, not as I oft am wont, of thee,
Works of day past, or morrow's next design,
But of offense and trouble, which my mind
35 Knew never till this irksome night; methought
Close at mine ear one called me forth to walk

---

from streams. **Aurora:** goddess of the dawn.

15. **peculiar:** its (beauty's) own, from the Latin *peculium*, "private property."

16. **Zephyrus on Flora breathes:** The west wind (*Zephyrus*) blows gently (*breathes*) on the flowers (*Flora*, goddess of flowers).

17–25. **Awake . . . liquid sweet:** The language of Adam's aubade is drawn from Song of Solomon 2.10–13, 7.12.

21. **prime:** sunrise, or the first hour of the day, which in Paradise is always six o'clock.

22. **blows:** blooms.

23. **balmy reed:** balsam.

With gentle voice, I thought it thine; it said,
'Why sleep'st thou Eve? Now is the pleasant time,
The cool, the silent, save where silence yields
40 To the night-warbling bird, that now awake
Tunes sweetest his love-labored song; now reigns
Full orbed the moon, and with more pleasing light
Shadowy sets off the face of things; in vain,
If none regard; heav'n wakes with all his eyes,
45 Whom to behold but thee, nature's desire,
In whose sight all things joy, with ravishment
Attracted by thy beauty still to gaze.'
I rose as at thy call, but found thee not;
To find thee I directed then my walk;
50 And on, methought, alone I passed through ways
That brought me on a sudden to the tree
Of interdicted knowledge: fair it seemed,
Much fairer to my fancy than by day:
And as I wond'ring looked, beside it stood
55 One shaped and winged like one of those from Heav'n
By us oft seen; his dewy locks distilled
Ambrosia; on that tree he also gazed;
And 'O fair plant,' said he, 'with fruit surcharged,
Deigns none to ease thy load and taste thy sweet,
60 Nor god, nor man; is knowledge so despised?
Or envy, or what reserve forbids to taste?
Forbid who will, none shall from me withhold
Longer thy offered good, why else set here?'
This said he paused not, but with vent'rous arm
65 He plucked, he tasted; me damp horror chilled
At such bold words vouched with a deed so bold:
But he thus overjoyed, 'O fruit divine,
Sweet of thyself, but much more sweet thus cropped,

---

38. **Why sleep'st thou Eve?:** Satan used much the same formula, as we will soon learn (l. 673), to awaken Beëlzebub, his first co-conspirator.
44. **his eyes:** the stars.
47. **still:** always.

60. **god:** angel. See *CD* 1.5.
61. **reserve:** referring to both God's restriction on the fruit and man's self-restraint.
65. **horror chilled:** Cp. 9.890.
66. **vouched with:** affirmed by.

Forbidden here, it seems, as only fit
70 For gods, yet able to make gods of men:
And why not gods of men, since good, the more
Communicated, more abundant grows,
The author not impaired, but honored more?
Here, happy creature, fair angelic Eve,
75 Partake thou also; happy though thou art,
Happier thou may'st be, worthier canst not be:
Taste this, and be henceforth among the gods
Thyself a goddess, not to Earth confined,
But sometimes in the air, as we, sometimes
80 Ascend to Heav'n, by merit thine, and see
What life the gods live there, and such live thou.'
So saying, he drew nigh, and to me held,
Even to my mouth of that same fruit held part
Which he had plucked; the pleasant savory smell
85 So quickened appetite, that I, methought,
Could not but taste. Forthwith up to the clouds
With him I flew, and underneath beheld
The Earth outstretched immense, a prospect wide
And various: wond'ring at my flight and change
90 To this high exaltation; suddenly
My guide was gone, and I, methought, sunk down,
And fell asleep; but O how glad I waked
To find this but a dream!" Thus Eve her night
Related, and thus Adam answered sad.
95   "Best image of myself and dearer half,
The trouble of thy thoughts this night in sleep
Affects me equally; nor can I like
This uncouth dream, of evil sprung I fear;
Yet evil whence? In thee can harbor none,
100 Created pure. But know that in the soul
Are many lesser faculties that serve

---

79. "The words *as we* are so placed between
the two sentences, as equally to relate to
both" (Todd).
94. **sad:** grave, serious.

98. **uncouth:** strange, unpleasant.
100–13. **But . . . late:** The main outlines of
this conventional account of the role of
"Fancy" (sometimes called "Phantasy") in

Reason as chief; among these Fancy next
Her office holds; of all external things,
Which the five watchful senses represent,
105　She forms imaginations, airy shapes,
Which reason joining or disjoining, frames
All what we affirm or what deny, and call
Our knowledge or opinion; then retires
Into her private cell when nature rests,
110　Oft in her absence mimic Fancy wakes
To imitate her; but misjoining shapes,
Wild work produces oft, and most in dreams,
Ill matching words and deeds long past or late.
Some such resemblances methinks I find
115　Of our last evening's talk, in this thy dream,
But with addition strange; yet be not sad.
Evil into the mind of god or man
May come or go, so unapproved, and leave
No spot or blame behind: Which gives me hope
120　That what in sleep thou didst abhor to dream,
Waking thou never wilt consent to do.
Be not disheartened then, nor cloud those looks
That wont to be more cheerful and serene
Than when fair morning first smiles on the world,
125　And let us to our fresh employments rise
Among the groves, the fountains, and the flow'rs
That open now their choicest bosomed smells
Reserved from night, and kept for thee in store."
　　So cheered he his fair spouse, and she was cheered,
130　But silently a gentle tear let fall
From either eye, and wiped them with her hair;

---

dreaming can be found in Renaissance en-
cyclopedias (Svendsen 1969, 36–38); Sir John
Davies, *Nosce Teipsum*, 46–47; and Robert
Burton, *The Anatomy of Melancholy*, 139–40.
109. **cell:** ventricle of the brain.
115. **our last evening's talk:** Yesterday they
spoke in general of the prohibition on
the Tree of Knowledge (4.419–28) and,

prompted by Eve's question, about why
the stars shine at night (4.657–88). Both
concerns reappear in Eve's dream. Yet
only the second conversation took place
at evening.
118. **so:** provided that it remains; **unap-
proved:** unchosen.
123. **wont to be:** are accustomed to being.

Two other precious drops that ready stood,
Each in their crystal sluice, he ere they fell
Kissed as the gracious signs of sweet remorse
135 And pious awe, that feared to have offended.
　　　So all was cleared, and to the field they haste.
But first from under shady arborous roof,
Soon as they forth were come to open sight
Of day-spring, and the sun, who scarce up risen
140 With wheels yet hov'ring o'er the ocean brim,
Shot parallel to the Earth his dewy ray,
Discovering in wide landscape all the east
Of Paradise and Eden's happy plains,
Lowly they bowed adoring, and began
145 Their orisons, each morning duly paid
In various style, for neither various style
Nor holy rapture wanted they to praise
Their Maker, in fit strains pronounced or sung
Unmeditated, such prompt eloquence
150 Flowed from their lips, in prose or numerous verse,
More tuneable than needed lute or harp
To add more sweetness, and they thus began.
　　　"These are thy glorious works, parent of good,
Almighty, thine this universal frame,
155 Thus wondrous fair; thyself how wondrous then!
Unspeakable, who sit'st above these heavens
To us invisible or dimly seen
In these thy lowest works, yet these declare
Thy goodness beyond thought, and power divine:

133–34. **he ere they fell/Kissed:** Adam's tender gesture enacts the words *be not sad* (l. 116) and *Be not disheartened then, nor cloud those looks* (l. 122) from his just-concluded speech.

146–50. Their morning prayers unite the fallen alternatives of deliberate artistic elaboration (*various style*), favored by Anglicans in Milton's day, and spontaneous inspiration (*holy rapture, Unmeditated*), favored by Puritans.

147. **wanted:** lacked.

150. **numerous:** subject to numbers, therefore measured, rhythmic, musical.

153–208. Giving voice to Creation, the orisons evoke Psalm 148 primarily, with touches drawn from the "Song of the Three Children," prescribed for morning prayers as the canticle "Benedicite omnia opera Domini" in the Book of Common Prayer.

160   Speak ye who best can tell, ye sons of light,
       Angels, for ye behold him, and with songs
       And choral symphonies, day without night,
       Circle his throne rejoicing, ye in Heav'n,
       On Earth join all ye creatures to extol
165   Him first, him last, him midst, and without end.
       Fairest of stars, last in the train of night,
       If better thou belong not to the dawn,
       Sure pledge of day, that crown'st the smiling morn
       With thy bright circlet, praise him in thy sphere
170   While day arises, that sweet hour of prime.
       Thou sun, of this great world both eye and soul,
       Acknowledge him thy greater, sound his praise
       In thy eternal course, both when thou climb'st,
       And when high noon hast gained, and when thou fall'st.
175   Moon, that now meet'st the orient sun, now fli'st
       With the fixed stars, fixed in their orb that flies,
       And ye five other wand'ring fires that move
       In mystic dance not without song, resound
       His praise, who out of darkness called up light.
180   Air, and ye elements the eldest birth
       Of nature's womb, that in quaternion run
       Perpetual circle, multiform, and mix
       And nourish all things, let your ceaseless change
       Vary to our great Maker still new praise.
185   Ye mists and exhalations that now rise
       From hill or steaming lake, dusky or gray,
       Till the sun paint your fleecy skirts with gold,
       In honor to the world's great author rise;
       Whether to deck with clouds the uncolored sky,
190   Or wet the thirsty earth with falling showers,

---

165. Cp. Rev. 22.13 ("I am the Alpha and the Omega, the first and the last"), and Ben Jonson, "To Heaven," l. 10.

166–67. **Fairest of stars:** Venus or Lucifer; **last . . . dawn:** Venus, the last star of morning, is also, as Hesperus, the first star of evening.

178. **not without song:** the music of the spheres, inaudible on Earth after the Fall; see *Nat Ode* 125–29, *Arcades* 63–73.

181. **in quaternion:** in a group of four (earth, air, fire, and water).

Rising or falling still advance his praise.
His praise ye winds, that from four quarters blow,
Breathe soft or loud; and wave your tops, ye pines,
With every plant, in sign of worship wave.
195 Fountains and ye that warble as ye flow
Melodious murmurs, warbling tune his praise.
Join voices all ye living souls, ye birds,
That singing up to heaven gate ascend,
Bear on your wings and in your notes his praise;
200 Ye that in waters glide, and ye that walk
The earth, and stately tread, or lowly creep;
Witness if I be silent, morn or even,
To hill, or valley, fountain, or fresh shade
Made vocal by my song, and taught his praise.
205 Hail universal Lord, be bounteous still
To give us only good; and if the night
Have gathered aught of evil or concealed,
Disperse it, as now light dispels the dark."
     So prayed they innocent, and to their thoughts
210 Firm peace recovered soon and wonted calm.
On to their morning's rural work they haste
Among sweet dews and flow'rs; where any row
Of fruit trees over-woody reached too far
Their pampered boughs, and needed hands to check
215 Fruitless embraces: or they led the vine
To wed her elm; she spoused about him twines
Her marriageable arms, and with her brings
Her dow'r th' adopted clusters, to adorn
His barren leaves. Them thus employed beheld
220 With pity Heav'n's high King, and to him called
Raphael, the sociable spirit, that deigned
To travel with Tobias, and secured

---

205. **still:** always.
214. **pampered:** overgrown.
215–19. **Fruitless embraces . . . leaves:** The feminine vine curled about the masculine elm was a traditional emblem of marriage; cp. Eve's vinelike hair at 4.307.

221–23. *Raphael,* Hebrew for "Health of God," helps Tobias claim his bride in the apocryphal Book of Tobit. Raphael is often associated with Christian medicine; see Cotton Mather, 48–54.

His marriage with the seven-times-wedded maid.
　　"Raphael," said he, "thou hear'st what stir on Earth
225　Satan from Hell scaped through the darksome gulf
Hath raised in Paradise, and how disturbed
This night the human pair, how he designs
In them at once to ruin all mankind.
Go therefore, half this day as friend with friend
230　Converse with Adam, in what bow'r or shade
Thou find'st him from the heat of noon retired,
To respite his day-labor with repast,
Or with repose; and such discourse bring on,
As may advise him of his happy state,
235　Happiness in his power left free to will,
Left to his own free will, his will though free,
Yet mutable; whence warn him to beware
He swerve not too secure: tell him withal
His danger, and from whom, what enemy
240　Late fall'n himself from Heav'n is plotting now
The fall of others from like state of bliss;
By violence, no, for that shall be withstood,
But by deceit and lies; this let him know,
Lest willfully transgressing he pretend
245　Surprisal, unadmonished, unforewarned."
　　So spake th' eternal Father, and fulfilled
All justice: nor delayed the wingèd saint
After his charge received, but from among
Thousand celestial ardors, where he stood
250　Veiled with his gorgeous wings, up springing light
Flew through the midst of Heav'n; th' angelic choirs
On each hand parting, to his speed gave way
Through all th' empyreal road; till at the gate
Of Heav'n arrived, the gate self-opened wide

238. **swerve:** err; **secure:** overconfident.

244–45. **pretend/Surprisal:** claim to have been the victim of a surprise attack.

249. **ardors:** angels, ardent (burning) with the love of God.

250. **Veiled:** Cp. 3.382.

253. **empyreal:** belonging to the empyrean realm beyond the outermost sphere of Creation.

254. **self-opened:** Cp. the grating gates of Hell at 2.881–82.

255   On golden hinges turning, as by work
      Divine the sov'reign architect had framed.
      From hence, no cloud, or, to obstruct his sight,
      Star interposed, however small he sees,
      Not unconform to other shining globes,
260   Earth and the gard'n of God, with cedars crowned
      Above all hills. As when by night the glass
      Of Galileo, less assured, observes
      Imagined lands and regions in the moon:
      Or pilot from amidst the Cyclades
265   Delos or Samos first appearing kens
      A cloudy spot. Down thither prone in flight
      He speeds, and through the vast ethereal sky
      Sails between worlds and worlds, with steady wing
      Now on the polar winds, then with quick fan
270   Winnows the buxom air; till within soar
      Of tow'ring eagles, to all the fowls he seems
      A phoenix, gazed by all, as that sole bird
      When to enshrine his relics in the sun's
      Bright temple, to Egyptian Thebes he flies.
275   At once on th' eastern cliff of Paradise
      He lights, and to his proper shape returns
      A Seraph winged; six wings he wore, to shade
      His lineaments divine; the pair that clad

257–59. No cloud or star interposed itself between Raphael and the sight of Earth, which appeared as small as the other stars.

259. **Not unconform to:** like to.

263. **Imagined:** conjectured. Galileo's conjectures about lunar topography are not rejected at 1.288–91; Raphael seems to sanction their rejection at 5.419–20, but leaves the question open at 8.144–45.

264–65. **Cyclades . . . Samos:** islands in the Aegean, including the supposedly floating island of *Delos; Samos,* an island off the coast of Asia Minor, did not belong to the Cyclades.

265. **kens:** discerns.

266. **prone:** bent forward and downward.

270. **Winnows the buxom air:** parts the yielding air. On *buxom* see 2.842n and *L'All* 24n.

271. **tow'ring eagles:** Descending Raphael has just reached the apex of ascending eagles.

271–74. **to all . . . flies:** To earthly birds, the bright and unique Raphael seems a phoenix. This mythical bird, of which there was only one, regenerated every five hundred or one thousand years by immolating itself, then depositing its own ashes (*relics*) at the temple of the sun in the Egyptian city of Heliopolis.

277. **six wings:** like the angels in Isa. 6.2.

Each shoulder broad, came mantling o'er his breast
280 With regal ornament; the middle pair
Girt like a starry zone his waist, and round
Skirted his loins and thighs with downy gold
And colors dipped in Heav'n; the third his feet
Shadowed from either heel with feathered mail
285 Sky-tinctured grain. Like Maia's son he stood,
And shook his plumes, that Heav'nly fragrance filled
The circuit wide. Straight knew him all the bands
Of Angels under watch; and to his state,
And to his message high in honor rise;
290 For on some message high they guessed him bound.
Their glittering tents he passed, and now is come
Into the blissful field, through groves of myrrh,
And flow'ring odors, cassia, nard, and balm;
A wilderness of sweets; for nature here
295 Wantoned as in her prime, and played at will
Her virgin fancies, pouring forth more sweet,
Wild above rule or art; enormous bliss.
Him through the spicy forest onward come
Adam discerned, as in the door he sat
300 Of his cool bow'r, while now the mounted sun
Shot down direct his fervid rays to warm
Earth's inmost womb, more warmth than Adam needs;
And Eve within, due at her hour prepared
For dinner savory fruits, of taste to please
305 True appetite, and not disrelish thirst

279. **mantling:** covering him, as with a mantle.
281. **starry zone:** belt of stars (cp. ii.247).
284. **feathered mail:** The feathers lie in overlapping rows suggestive of the metal plates in mail armor.
285. **Sky-tinctured:** blue, a sacred color among the Israelites, as Fowler notes, citing Cowley's *Davideis*, bk. i, n. 60; **grain:** dye; **Maia's son:** Mercury, messenger of the gods.
288. **state:** status.
293. **cassia, nard, and balm:** aromatic spices.

296. **more sweet:** Nature's splurging sweetness recalls Eve at 4.439, 641–56. She translates this aspect of Eden into the spiritual Paradise of their marriage.
297. **Wild above rule or art:** The organic at its height is superior to artifice at its height, as we have just seen in the "clothing" of Raphael; **enormous:** beyond the norm, immense.
300. **while now:** Raphael arrives precisely at noon.
305. **disrelish:** destroy the relish for.

Of nectarous draughts between, from milky stream,
Berry or grape: to whom thus Adam called.
    "Haste hither Eve, and worth thy sight behold
Eastward among those trees, what glorious shape

310 Comes this way moving; seems another morn
Ris'n on mid-noon; some great behest from Heav'n
To us perhaps he brings, and will vouchsafe
This day to be our guest. But go with speed,
And what thy stores contain, bring forth and pour

315 Abundance, fit to honor and receive
Our Heav'nly stranger; well we may afford
Our givers their own gifts, and large bestow
From large bestowed, where nature multiplies
Her fertile growth, and by disburd'ning grows

320 More fruitful, which instructs us not to spare."
    To whom thus Eve. "Adam, earth's hallowed mold
Of God inspired, small store will serve, where store,
All seasons, ripe for use hangs on the stalk;
Save what by frugal storing firmness gains

325 To nourish, and superfluous moist consumes:
But I will haste and from each bough and brake,
Each plant and juiciest gourd will pluck such choice
To entertain our angel guest, as he
Beholding shall confess that here on Earth

330 God hath dispensed his bounties as in Heav'n."
    So saying, with dispatchful looks in haste
She turns, on hospitable thoughts intent
What choice to choose for delicacy best,
What order, so contrived as not to mix

335 Tastes, not well joined, inelegant, but bring
Taste after taste upheld with kindliest change,

---

306. **nectarous:** as sweet as nectar; **milky:** sweet (not salty).

319. **disburd'ning:** harvesting.

321. **earth's hallowed mold:** *Adam* is sometimes said to derive from the Hebrew for "red," alluding to the red earth from which he was formed.

324. **frugal:** careful in the use of food (from Lat. *frux*, "fruit"). Thriftiness is not implied.

333–36. "Eve's composing of food" is "a trope for poetry" (D. McColley 1993, 133), the culinary equivalent of Milton's "the sense variously drawn out from one verse into another" (see his note on *The Verse,* p. 9).

"Eastward among those trees, what glorious shape /
Comes this way moving" (5.309–10).

Bestirs her then, and from each tender stalk
Whatever Earth all-bearing mother yields
In India east or west, or middle shore
340 In Pontus or the Punic Coast, or where
Alcinous reigned, fruit of all kinds, in coat,
Rough, or smooth rined, or bearded husk, or shell
She gathers, tribute large, and on the board
Heaps with unsparing hand; for drink the grape
345 She crushes, inoffensive must, and meathes
From many a berry, and from sweet kernels pressed
She tempers dulcet creams, nor these to hold
Wants her fit vessels pure, then strews the ground
With rose and odors from the shrub unfumed.
350 Meanwhile our primitive great sire, to meet
His godlike guest, walks forth, without more train
Accompanied than with his own complete
Perfections, in himself was all his state,
More solemn than the tedious pomp that waits
355 On princes, when their rich retinue long
Of horses led, and grooms besmeared with gold
Dazzles the crowd, and sets them all agape.
Nearer his presence Adam though not awed,
Yet with submiss approach and reverence meek,
360 As to a superior nature, bowing low,
    Thus said. "Native of Heav'n, for other place
None can than Heav'n such glorious shape contain;
Since by descending from the thrones above,
Those happy places thou hast deigned a while
365 To want, and honor these, vouchsafe with us
Two only, who yet by sov'reign gift possess

---

339. **India:** Indies; **middle shore:** lands to the north (*Pontus,* the shore of the Black Sea) and the south (*Punic,* the shore of North Africa) of the Mediterranean Sea.

341. **Alcinous:** Homer's King of the Phaeacians, whose garden bore fruit in every season (*Od.* 7.112–32).

345. **meathes:** sweet drinks; obsolete spelling of *meads.*

346. Metrically, the double anapests make for an unusual line.

349. **unfumed:** unburned (unlike incense in the fallen world).

350. **primitive:** primary, original.

353. **state:** ceremonial display.

356. **besmeared with gold:** See Horace, *Odes* 4.9.14f.

This spacious ground, in yonder shady bow'r
To rest, and what the garden choicest bears
To sit and taste, till this meridian heat
370 Be over, and the sun more cool decline."
    Whom thus the angelic Virtue answered mild.
"Adam, I therefore came, nor art thou such
Created, or such place hast here to dwell,
As may not oft invite, though spirits of Heav'n
375 To visit thee; lead on then where thy bow'r
O'ershades; for these mid-hours, till evening rise
I have at will." So to the sylvan lodge
They came, that like Pomona's arbor smiled
With flow'rets decked and fragrant smells; but Eve
380 Undecked, save with herself more lovely fair
Than wood-nymph, or the fairest goddess feigned
Of three that in Mount Ida naked strove,
Stood to entertain her guest from Heav'n; no veil
She needed, virtue-proof, no thought infirm
385 Altered her cheek. On whom the angel "Hail"
Bestowed, the holy salutation used
Long after to blest Mary, second Eve.
    "Hail mother of mankind, whose fruitful womb
Shall fill the world more numerous with thy sons
390 Than with these various fruits the trees of God
Have heaped this table." Raised of grassy turf
Their table was, and mossy seats had round,
And on her ample square from side to side
All autumn piled, though spring and autumn here

371. **Virtue:** one of the lower angelic orders. Milton uses these hierarchical titles interchangeably, since Raphael is also termed a Seraph (5.277) and an Archangel (7.41).

378. **Pomona's arbor:** the lodging of the goddess of fruit trees, to whom Eve is compared at 9.393.

381. **fairest goddess:** Aphrodite, whom Paris chose over Athena and Juno. Since his reward was Helen, his choice was the mythical origin of the Trojan War. The episode was popular in Renaissance painting and literature.

384. **virtue-proof:** armored by, and therefore protected by, virtue.

385–87. **"Hail" . . . second Eve:** The passage alludes to Luke 1.28, where the angel Gabriel greets Mary: "Hail, thou that art highly favored, the Lord is with thee: blessed art thou among women." On Mary as second Eve, see 10.183n.

395   Danced hand in hand. A while discourse they hold;
        No fear lest dinner cool; when thus began
        Our author. "Heav'nly stranger, please to taste
        These bounties which our Nourisher, from whom
        All perfect good unmeasured out descends,
400   To us for food and for delight hath caused
        The earth to yield; unsavory food perhaps
        To spiritual natures; only this I know,
        That one celestial father gives to all."
           To whom the angel. "Therefore what he gives
405   (Whose praise be ever sung) to man in part
        Spiritual, may of purest spirits be found
        No ingrateful food; and food alike those pure
        Intelligential substances require
        As doth your rational; and both contain
410   Within them every lower faculty
        Of sense, whereby they hear, see, smell, touch, taste,
        Tasting concoct, digest, assimilate,
        And corporeal to incorporeal turn.
        For know, whatever was created, needs
415   To be sustained and fed; of elements
        The grosser feeds the purer, earth the sea,
        Earth and the sea feed air, the air those fires
        Ethereal, and as lowest first the moon;
        Whence in her visage round those spots, unpurged
420   Vapors not yet into her substance turned.
        Nor doth the moon no nourishment exhale
        From her moist continent to higher orbs.
        The Sun that light imparts to all, receives
        From all his alimental recompense

---

397. **author:** progenitor.

408. **Intelligential substances:** angels. The word *substance,* used variously in metaphysics, here declares that the angels inhabit a *degree* of matter (see ll. 473–74) in which intelligence is pervasive: smart stuff, as it were.

412. **concoct, digest, assimilate:** Three stages in the physiology of nourishment: in concoction, food is broken down into a milky fluid called "chyle"; it is then digested, or dispersed by means of blood to the various parts of the body; finally it is assimilated, transformed into the nourished being.

419–20. See 263n.

425　In humid exhalations, and at even
　　　　Sups with the ocean: though in Heav'n the trees
　　　　Of life ambrosial fruitage bear, and vines
　　　　Yield nectar, though from off the boughs each morn
　　　　We brush mellifluous dews, and find the ground
430　Covered with pearly grain: yet God hath here
　　　　Varied his bounty so with new delights,
　　　　As may compare with Heaven; and to taste
　　　　Think not I shall be nice." So down they sat,
　　　　And to their viands fell, nor seemingly
435　The angel, nor in mist, the common gloss
　　　　Of theologians, but with keen dispatch
　　　　Of real hunger, and concoctive heat
　　　　To transubstantiate; what redounds, transpires
　　　　Through spirits with ease; nor wonder; if by fire
440　Of sooty coal the empiric alchemist
　　　　Can turn, or holds it possible to turn

---

429. **mellifluous:** fluid, sweet.

430. **pearly grain:** dew, but also evoking the manna or angel's food of Exod. 16.14 and Ps. 78.

433. **nice:** fastidious, hard to please.

434. **nor seemingly:** not just apparently (as opposed to really).

435. **nor in mist:** nor in vapor, as when a visiting angel takes on an airy body; **common gloss:** This part of the poem, we are given to know, is *not* conventional. That angels are corporeal, and therefore eat, is entailed by the spiritual materialism set forth in Milton's *CD* 1.7: all Creation is material, even the human soul (*MLM* 1205–06).

437. **real hunger, and concoctive heat:** Raphael's body has the same heat that was thought to fuel the digestive process in the human body.

438. **transubstantiate:** to transform one substance (earthly fruit) into another (the angelic body).

438–39. **what . . . ease:** Unassimilated food (*what redounds*) escapes vaporously through the pores of angels, reminding fallen readers of the more trying evacuations they know so well. "This artfully avoids the indecent idea, which would else have been apt to have arisen on the Angel's feeding, and withal gives a delicacy to these spirits, which finely distinguishes them from us in one of the most humbling circumstances relating to our bodies" (Richardson).

439–43. **nor wonder . . . mine:** The upward transformations claimed in alchemy are intended to make the idea of an angel assimilating earthly food seem plausible rather than an inexplicable *wonder*. At least one physician in the Paracelsan tradition, Jean-Baptiste van Helmont, developed the idea of digestion as an "inner alchemist" (see Multhauf; Pagel 1955 and 1956).

440. **empiric:** experimental. The word is sometimes pejorative, and means "quack." Milton may be contrasting the *empiric alchemist*, concentrating on the refinement of metals, with adepts of a more philosophical and spiritual outlook.

Metals of drossiest ore to perfect gold
As from the mine. Meanwhile at table Eve
Ministered naked, and their flowing cups
445 With pleasant liquors crowned: O innocence
Deserving Paradise! if ever, then,
Then had the sons of God excuse to have been
Enamored at that sight; but in those hearts
Love unlibidinous reigned, nor jealousy
450 Was understood, the injured lover's hell.
    Thus when with meats and drinks they had sufficed,
Not burdened nature, sudden mind arose
In Adam, not to let th' occasion pass
Given him by this great conference to know
455 Of things above his world, and of their being
Who dwell in Heav'n, whose excellence he saw
Transcend his own so far, whose radiant forms
Divine effulgence, whose high power so far
Exceeded human, and his wary speech
460 Thus to th' empyreal minister he framed.
    "Inhabitant with God, now know I well
Thy favor, in this honor done to man,
Under whose lowly roof thou hast vouchsafed
To enter, and these earthly fruits to taste,
465 Food not of angels, yet accepted so,
As that more willingly thou couldst not seem
As Heav'n's high feasts to have fed: yet what compare?"
    To whom the wingèd hierarch replied.

---

445. **crowned:** filled to the top.
446–48. **if ever ... sight:** Milton alludes to Gen. 6.2: "The sons of God saw the daughters of men that they were fair; and they took them wives." Most exegetes took "sons of God" to refer to men, but some thought them to be fallen angels. Milton is saying that if angels ever were attracted to earthly women, the desire would in this instance have been excusable, since it would have arisen in re-

sponse to Eve's innocence, not her sexual wiles.
449–50. All three, in other words, loved without sexual desire, and Adam did not feel jealous.
467. **yet what compare?:** "Yet what comparison can there possibly be between heavenly and earthly feasts?" Adam asks for a comparison, a metaphor, joining Earth and Heaven, and in reply will be given the literal basis for all such metaphors: matter.

"O Adam, one Almighty is, from whom
470　All things proceed, and up to him return,
　　If not depraved from good, created all
　　Such to perfection, one first matter all,
　　Endued with various forms, various degrees
　　Of substance, and in things that live, of life;
475　But more refined, more spiritous, and pure,
　　As nearer to him placed or nearer tending
　　Each in their several active spheres assigned,
　　Till body up to spirit work, in bounds
　　Proportioned to each kind. So from the root
480　Springs lighter the green stalk, from thence the leaves
　　More airy, last the bright consummate flow'r
　　Spirits odorous breathes: flow'rs and their fruit
　　Man's nourishment, by gradual scale sublimed
　　To vital spirits aspire, to animal,
485　To intellectual, give both life and sense,
　　Fancy and understanding, whence the soul
　　Reason receives, and reason is her being,
　　Discursive, or intuitive; discourse
　　Is oftest yours, the latter most is ours,
490　Differing but in degree, of kind the same.
　　Wonder not then, what God for you saw good

469. **O:** A speech about the circular journey of matter begins appropriately with a typographical circle.

472. **one first matter all:** A remarkable conjunction of major philosophical words. In *CD* 1.7, Milton argues that the world was created not out of nothing but rather out of preexistent matter, the realm of Chaos visited by Satan in 2.951–1022.

478. **bounds:** both "limits" and "leaps" (Leonard).

483–85. Raphael adopts the language of Galenic physiology, in which food is elevated or *sublimed* into *vital spirits,* which reside in the heart and are the vehicles of passion, and *animal* spirits, which reside in the brain and are the vehicles of rational thought. No source has ever been adduced for *intellectual* spirits, which Milton postulates, it would seem, in order to supply a material basis for the intuitive capacities of men and angels.

490. The epic's definitive statement on the ontological relationship of man to angel, Earth to Heaven, matter to spirit; that the phrase was in common use can be inferred from its appearance in the verse of Katherine Philips: "The same in kind, though diff'ring in degree" ("On Controversies in Religion"). She died in 1664, three years before the publication of Milton's epic, and was not likely to have seen it in manuscript.

If I refuse not, but convert, as you,
To proper substance; time may come when men
With angels may participate, and find
495 No inconvenient diet, nor too light fare:
And from these corporal nutriments perhaps
Your bodies may at last turn all to spirit,
Improved by tract of time, and winged ascend
Ethereal, as we, or may at choice
500 Here or in Heav'nly paradises dwell;
If ye be found obedient, and retain
Unalterably firm his love entire
Whose progeny you are. Meanwhile enjoy
Your fill what happiness this happy state
505 Can comprehend, incapable of more."
　　　To whom the patriarch of mankind replied.
"O favorable spirit, propitious guest,
Well hast thou taught the way that might direct
Our knowledge, and the scale of nature set
510 From center to circumference, whereon
In contemplation of created things
By steps we may ascend to God. But say,
What meant that caution joined, 'If ye be found
Obedient'? Can we want obedience then
515 To him, or possibly his love desert
Who formed us from the dust, and placed us here
Full to the utmost measure of what bliss
Human desires can seek or apprehend?"
　　　To whom the Angel. "Son of Heav'n and Earth,
520 Attend: that thou are happy, owe to God;
That thou continu'st such, owe to thyself,

497. Cp. *Masque,* 558–61.
498. **tract:** a stretch or lapse.
499–500. Utopias are often criticized for their stasis. Here Raphael introduces the possibility of dynamic improvement into Edenic life.
505. **incapable:** unable to contain.
509. **scale of nature:** The *scale* or ladder of Nature, by which the mind may ascend from particularity to unity or Earth to Heaven, is a commonplace image in philosophy and theology. It was often linked with Jacob's vision in Gen. 28.12 and with the golden chain connecting heaven and earth in Homer's *Il.* 8.19 (Macrobius, *Commentary on the Dream of Scipio,* 1.14.15).

That is, to thy obedience; therein stand.
This was that caution giv'n thee; be advised.
God made thee perfect, not immutable;
525 And good he made thee, but to persevere
He left it in thy power, ordained thy will
By nature free, not overruled by fate
Inextricable, or strict necessity;
Our voluntary service he requires,
530 Not our necessitated, such with him
Finds no acceptance, nor can find, for how
Can hearts, not free, be tried whether they serve
Willing or no, who will but what they must
By destiny, and can no other choose?
535 Myself and all th' angelic host that stand
In sight of God enthroned, our happy state
Hold, as you yours, while our obedience holds;
On other surety none; freely we serve,
Because we freely love, as in our will
540 To love or not; in this we stand or fall:
And some are fall'n, to disobedience fall'n,
And so from Heav'n to deepest Hell; O fall
From what high state of bliss into what woe!"
  To whom our great progenitor. "Thy words
545 Attentive, and with more delighted ear,
Divine instructor, I have heard, than when
Cherubic songs by night from neighboring hills
Aerial music send: nor knew I not
To be both will and deed created free;
550 Yet that we never shall forget to love
Our Maker, and obey him whose command
Single, is yet so just, my constant thoughts
Assured me, and still assure: though what thou tell'st
Hath passed in Heav'n, some doubt within me move,
555 But more desire to hear, if thou consent,
The full relation, which must needs be strange,

---

538. **surety**: ground of certainty, guarantee   547. **Cherubic songs**: See 4.680–88.
of secure possession.   552. **yet**: also.

Worthy of sacred silence to be heard;
And we have yet large day, for scarce the sun
Hath finished half his journey, and scarce begins
560   His other half in the great zone of heav'n."
        Thus Adam made request, and Raphael
After short pause assenting, thus began.
        "High matter thou enjoin'st me, O prime of men,
Sad task and hard, for how shall I relate
565   To human sense th' invisible exploits
Of warring spirits; how without remorse
The ruin of so many glorious once
And perfect while they stood; how last unfold
The secrets of another world, perhaps
570   Not lawful to reveal? Yet for thy good
This is dispensed, and what surmounts the reach
Of human sense, I shall delineate so,
By lik'ning spiritual to corporal forms,
As may express them best, though what if Earth
575   Be but the shadow of Heav'n, and things therein
Each to other like, more than on Earth is thought?
        "As yet this world was not, and Chaos wild
Reigned where these heav'ns now roll, where Earth now rests
Upon her center poised, when on a day
580   (For time, though in eternity, applied
To motion, measures all things durable
By present, past, and future) on such day

557. **sacred silence:** echoing Horace, *Odes* 2.13.29–32.

566. **remorse:** pity.

571. **dispensed:** made lawful.

573. **lik'ning spiritual to corporal forms:** But as we know from the discussion that arose over Raphael's eating, spiritual and corporal forms differ only in degree; metaphor has ontological sanction.

575–76. The idea of Earth being the shadow of Heaven is sometimes meant to stress the difference, but Milton clearly thinks of them as being alike, analogical.

576. **more than on Earth is thought:** The only time that an earthling thought heavenly things too little like earthly things was when Adam assumed that Raphael could not eat earthly food. The error will be multiplied in the future: not everyone is a spiritual materialist, and even Adam took some convincing.

580–82. **For time ... future:** On the unconventional idea that time precedes the Creation, see Milton's *CD* 1.7 (*MLM* 1204). On the idea that time is the measure of motion, see Aristotle, *Physics* 4.2.219, and lines 7–8 of Milton's second epitaph on Hobson.

As Heav'n's great year brings forth, th' empyreal host
Of angels by imperial summons called,
585 Innumerable before th' Almighty's throne
Forthwith from all the ends of Heav'n appeared
Under their hierarchs in orders bright;
Ten thousand thousand ensigns high advanced,
Standards, and gonfalons twixt van and rear
590 Stream in the air, and for distinction serve
Of hierarchies, of orders, and degrees;
Or in their glittering tissues bear emblazed
Holy memorials, acts of zeal and love
Recorded eminent. Thus when in orbs
595 Of circuit inexpressible they stood,
Orb within orb, the Father infinite,
By whom in bliss embosomed sat the Son,
Amidst as from a flaming mount, whose top
Brightness had made invisible, thus spake.
600   "'Hear all ye angels, progeny of light,
Thrones, Dominations, Princedoms, Virtues, Powers,
Hear my decree, which unrevoked shall stand.
This day I have begot whom I declare
My only Son, and on this holy hill
605 Him have anointed, whom ye now behold
At my right hand; your head I him appoint;
And by myself have sworn to him shall bow
All knees in Heav'n, and shall confess him Lord:

---

583. **Heav'n's great year:** On Earth a *great
year* is the time required for the fixed stars
to complete a full revolution, computed
by Plato at 36,000 years (*Timaeus* 39D); we
are left to imagine what Heaven's ana-
logue of this cycle would be.

589. **gonfalons:** banners hung from cross-
pieces affixed to standards, as to this day
in religious ceremonies.

601. The line names five of the traditional
nine orders of angels. Satan, obviously
impressed by this aspect of divine rhetoric,
repeats the sonorous roll call of titles
throughout his career (1.315–16, 2.11, 2.430,

5.772; *PR* 2.121). He thinks they signify the
inalienable right to rule Heaven (ll.
800–802).

603. **This day I have begot:** Considering
Gen. 22.16, Ps. 2.6–7, and Heb. 1.5, Milton
argued in *CD* 1.5 that the begetting of the
Son was a metaphor for his exaltation
above the angels. The passage dramatizes
that interpretation.

607. **by myself have sworn:** the formula of
God's vowing found in Gen. 22.16, Isa.
45.23, Heb. 6.13–19; see Donne, "A Hymn
to God the Father," l. 15.

Under his great vicegerent reign abide
610 United as one individual soul
Forever happy: him who disobeys
Me disobeys, breaks union, and that day
Cast out from God and blessed vision, falls
Into utter darkness, deep engulfed, his place
615 Ordained without redemption, without end.'
     "So spake th' Omnipotent, and with his words
All seemed well pleased, all seemed, but were not all.
That day, as other solemn days, they spent
In song and dance about the sacred hill,
620 Mystical dance, which yonder starry sphere
Of planets and of fixed in all her wheels
Resembles nearest, mazes intricate,
Eccentric, intervolved, yet regular
Then most, when most irregular they seem,
625 And in their motions harmony divine
So smooths her charming tones, that God's own ear
Listens delighted. Evening now approached
(For we have also our evening and our morn,
We ours for change delectable, not need)
630 Forthwith from dance to sweet repast they turn
Desirous; all in circles as they stood,
Tables are set, and on a sudden piled
With angel's food, and rubied nectar flows
In pearl, in diamond, and massy gold
635 Fruit of delicious vines, the growth of Heav'n.
On flow'rs reposed, and with fresh flow'rets crowned,

---

609. **vicegerent:** the representative of a ruler.
610. **individual:** indivisible.
611. **him who disobeys:** whoever disobeys him.
618. **solemn days:** days set aside for religious ceremonies.
621. **fixed:** fixed stars.
623. **Eccentric:** In the Ptolemaic system, an eccentric is a planetary orbit of which the Earth is not the center; these eccentric centers revolve about the earth. **intervolved:** interlocked, like the two centers of an eccentric orbit.
627. **now:** added in 1674.
636–40. These lines revise and expand Editon 1, which reads, "They eat, they drink, and with refection sweet/Are filled, before th' all bounteous King, who show'red."

They eat, they drink, and in communion sweet
Quaff immortality and joy, secure
Of surfeit where full measure only bounds
640 Excess, before th' all bounteous King, who show'red
With copious hand, rejoicing in their joy.
Now when ambrosial night with clouds exhaled
From that high mount of God, whence light and shade
Spring both, the face of brightest Heav'n had changed
645 To grateful twilight (for night comes not there
In darker veil) and roseate dews disposed
All but the unsleeping eyes of God to rest,
Wide over all the plain, and wider far
Than all this globous earth in plain outspread,
650 (Such are the courts of God) th' angelic throng
Dispersed in bands and files their camp extend
By living streams among the trees of life,
Pavilions numberless, and sudden reared,
Celestial tabernacles, where they slept
655 Fanned with cool winds, save those who in their course
Melodious hymns about the sov'reign throne
Alternate all night long: but not so waked
Satan, so call him now, his former name
Is heard no more in Heav'n; he of the first,
660 If not the first Archangel, great in power,
In favor and in pre-eminence, yet fraught
With envy against the Son of God, that day
Honored by his great Father, and proclaimed
Messiah King anointed, could not bear
665 Through pride that sight, and thought himself impaired.
Deep malice thence conceiving and disdain,
Soon as midnight brought on the dusky hour
Friendliest to sleep and silence, he resolved

---

637. **communion:** fellowship.

652. **streams among the trees of life:** See Rev. 22.2.

658. **former name:** his original, prerebellion name, now blotted out from the heavenly records (1.362–63). One tradition, derived from Isa. 14.12, took the former name to be Lucifer, but Raphael does not confirm this directly until 5.760.

664. **Messiah:** Hebrew, meaning "anointed."

With all his legions to dislodge, and leave
670 Unworshipped, unobeyed the throne supreme
Contemptuous, and his next subordinate
Awak'ning, thus to him in secret spake.

"'Sleep'st thou companion dear, what sleep can close
Thy eyelids? And remember'st what decree
675 Of yesterday, so late hath passed the lips
Of Heav'n's Almighty? Thou to me thy thoughts
Wast wont, I mine to thee was wont to impart;
Both waking we were one; how then can now
Thy sleep dissent? New laws thou seest imposed;
680 New laws from him who reigns, new minds may raise
In us who serve, new counsels, to debate
What doubtful may ensue, more in this place
To utter is not safe. Assemble thou
Of all those myriads which we lead the chief;
685 Tell them that by command, ere yet dim night
Her shadowy cloud withdraws, I am to haste,
And all who under me their banners wave,
Homeward with flying march where we possess
The quarters of the north, there to prepare
690 Fit entertainment to receive our King
The great Messiah, and his new commands,
Who speedily through all the hierarchies
Intends to pass triumphant, and give laws.'

"So spake the false Archangel, and infused
695 Bad influence into th' unwary breast
Of his associate; he together calls,
Or several one by one, the regent powers,
Under him regent, tells, as he was taught,
That the most high commanding, now ere night,

---

669. **dislodge:** break camp.
671. **subordinate:** His fallen name is Beëlzebub (1.81).
673. **Sleep'st thou:** An epic formula for awakening someone, found in Homer (*Il.* 2.560), Vergil (*Aen.* 4.560, 7.421), and Milton's *On the Fifth of November*, 92.

680. **minds:** purposes.
685. **by command:** a lie, since God has not commanded their departure.
689. **north:** where Satan's throne was traditionally located (Isa. 14.13).
695. **Bad influence:** perhaps with an astrological undertone.

700 Now ere dim night had disencumbered Heav'n,
The great hierarchal standard was to move;
Tells the suggested cause, and cast between
Ambiguous words and jealousies, to sound
Or taint integrity; but all obeyed
705 The wonted signal, and superior voice
Of their great potentate; for great indeed
His name, and high was his degree in Heav'n;
His count'nance, as the morning star that guides
The starry flock, allured them, and with lies
710 Drew after him the third part of Heav'n's host:
Meanwhile th' eternal eye, whose sight discerns
Abstrusest thoughts, from forth his holy mount
And from within the golden lamps that burn
Nightly before him, saw without their light
715 Rebellion rising, saw in whom, how spread
Among the sons of morn, what multitudes
Were banded to oppose his high decree;
And smiling to his only Son thus said.

  " 'Son, thou in whom my glory I behold
720 In full resplendence, heir of all my might,
Nearly it now concerns us to be sure
Of our omnipotence, and with what arms
We mean to hold what anciently we claim
Of deity or empire, such a foe
725 Is rising, who intends to erect his throne
Equal to ours, throughout the spacious north;
Nor so content, hath in his thought to try
In battle, what our power is, or our right.
Let us advise, and to this hazard draw
730 With speed what force is left, and all employ

---

700. Night's removal of darkness and the stars is made to seem an echo of Satan moving his troops.

710. **the third part:** See Rev. 12.4.

712. **Abstrusest:** most secret.

718. **smiling:** alerting us to the mocking tone of the forthcoming speech, where the omnipotent Father speaks as a Shakespearean monarch alarmed by the threat of rebellion.

721. **Nearly:** "closely," "intimately," as in Shakespeare's "something nearly that concerns yourselves" (*MND* I.I.126).

725–26. Cp. Isa. 14.12–13.

In our defense, lest unawares we lose
This our high place, our sanctuary, our hill.'
    "To whom the Son with calm aspect and clear
Lightning divine, ineffable, serene,
735 Made answer. 'Mighty Father, thou thy foes
Justly hast in derision, and secure
Laugh'st at their vain designs and tumults vain,
Matter to me of glory, whom their hate
Illustrates, when they see all regal power
740 Giv'n me to quell their pride, and in event
Know whether I be dextrous to subdue
Thy rebels, or be found the worst in Heav'n.'
    "So spake the Son, but Satan with his powers
Far was advanced on wingèd speed, an host
745 Innumerable as the stars of night,
Or stars of morning, dewdrops, which the sun
Impearls on every leaf and every flower.
Regions they passed, the mighty regencies
Of Seraphim and Potentates and Thrones
750 In their triple degrees, regions to which
All thy dominion, Adam, is no more
Than what this garden is to all the earth,
And all the sea, from one entire globose
Stretched into longitude; which having passed
755 At length into the limits of the north
They came, and Satan to his royal seat
High on a hill, far blazing, as a mount

---

736. **Justly hast in derision:** Ps. 2.4: "He that sitteth in the heavens shall laugh: The Lord shall have them in derision."

739. **Illustrates:** makes illustrious (by defeating them in battle).

740. **in event:** by the outcome.

741. **dextrous:** both "skillful" and "right-handed" (the Son sits on God's right hand [l. 606], and is, so to speak, his right-hand man).

746. **Or stars of morning, dewdrops:** The sudden shift of magnitude from stars to dewdrops recalls the similes of Book 1.

748. **regencies:** dominions.

750. **triple degrees:** The nine orders of angels were often arranged in three groups of three; see Spenser's "trinal triplicities" in *FQ* 1.39.

750–54. **regions . . . longitude:** Again the issue is magnitude: the planet Earth, spread on a flat plane, is to the regions traversed by the rebel angels as Eden is to the entire earth.

Raised on a mount, with pyramids and tow'rs
From diamond quarries hewn, and rocks of gold,
760 The palace of great Lucifer, (so call
That structure in the dialect of men
Interpreted) which not long after, he
Affecting all equality with God,
In imitation of that mount whereon
765 Messiah was declared in sight of Heav'n,
The Mountain of the Congregation called;
For thither he assembled all his train,
Pretending so commanded to consult
About the great reception of their King,
770 Thither to come, and with calumnious art
Of counterfeited truth thus held their ears.
    " 'Thrones, Dominations, Princedoms, Virtues, Powers,
If these magnific titles yet remain
Not merely titular, since by decree
775 Another now hath to himself engrossed
All power, and us eclipsed under the name
Of King anointed, for whom all this haste
Of midnight march, and hurried meeting here,
This only to consult how we may best
780 With what may be devised of honors new
Receive him coming to receive from us
Knee-tribute yet unpaid, prostration vile,
Too much to one, but double how endured,
To one and to his image now proclaimed?
785 But what if better counsels might erect
Our minds and teach us to cast off this yoke?
Will ye submit your necks, and choose to bend
The supple knee? Ye will not, if I trust

---

758. **pyramids:** Milton's association of pyramids with pomp and immortal longings can be discerned as early as *On Shakespeare*. See also *RCG* (Yale 1:790).

763. **Affecting:** aspiring to, making an ostentatious display of.

764. **that mount:** referring to the mount of line 598.

766. **Mountain of the Congregation:** See Isa. 14.13.

775. **engrossed:** monopolized.

786. **this yoke:** Christ maintains that his yoke is "easy" in Matt. 11.29–30.

To know ye right, or if ye know yourselves
790   Natives and sons of Heav'n possessed before
By none, and if not equal all, yet free,
Equally free; for orders and degrees
Jar not with liberty, but well consist.
Who can in reason then or right assume
795   Monarchy over such as live by right
His equals, if in power and splendor less,
In freedom equal? Or can introduce
Law and edict on us, who without law
Err not, much less for this to be our Lord,
800   And look for adoration to th' abuse
Of those imperial titles which assert
Our being ordained to govern, not to serve?'
     "Thus far his bold discourse without control
Had audience, when among the Seraphim
805   Abdiel, than whom none with more zeal adored
The deity, and divine commands obeyed,
Stood up, and in a flame of zeal severe
The current of his fury thus opposed.
     "'O argument blasphemous, false and proud!
810   Words which no ear ever to hear in Heav'n
Expected, least of all from thee, ingrate,
In place thyself so high above thy peers.
Canst thou with impious obloquy condemn
The just decree of God, pronounced and sworn,
815   That to his only Son by right endued
With regal scepter, every soul in Heav'n
Shall bend the knee, and in that honor due
Confess him rightful King? Unjust thou say'st,
Flatly unjust, to bind with laws the free,

---

799. **this:** this entity placed over us only by improper law and edict.

805. **Abdiel:** Hebrew meaning "Servant of God." Milton's most important addition to the traditional cast of Judeo-Christian angels; see West 154 on the origins of the name. **zeal:** a trait admired by Protestants and by Milton, who defined it as "an eager desire to sanctify the divine name, together with a feeling of indignation against things which tend to the violation or contempt of religion" (*CD* 2.6 in *MLM* 1146; see also *Apology* in Yale 1:900–901).

820   And equal over equals to let reign,
      One over all with unsucceeded power.
      Shalt thou give law to God, shalt thou dispute
      With him the points of liberty, who made
      Thee what thou art, and formed the pow'rs of Heav'n
825   Such as he pleased, and circumscribed their being?
      Yet by experience taught we know how good,
      And of our good, and of our dignity
      How provident he is, how far from thought
      To make us less, bent rather to exalt
830   Our happy state under one head more near
      United. But to grant it thee unjust,
      That equal over equals monarch reign:
      Thyself though great and glorious dost thou count,
      Or all angelic nature joined in one,
835   Equal to him begotten Son, by whom
      As by his Word the mighty Father made
      All things, ev'n thee, and all the spirits of Heav'n
      By him created in their bright degrees,
      Crowned them with glory, and to their glory named
840   Thrones, Dominations, Princedoms, Virtues, Powers,
      Essential powers, nor by his reign obscured,
      But more illustrious made, since he the head
      One of our number thus reduced becomes,
      His laws our laws, all honor to him done
845   Returns our own. Cease then this impious rage,
      And tempt not these; but hasten to appease
      Th' incensèd Father, and th' incensèd Son,
      While pardon may be found in time besought.'
        "So spake the fervent Angel, but his zeal
850   None seconded, as out of season judged,

---

821. **unsucceeded:** without successor, unending.

835–40. Based on Col. 1.16–17: "By him were all things created, . . . whether they be thrones, or dominions, or principalities, or powers: all things were created by him, and for him."

842–45. **But . . . own:** "The argument seems to be that Christ, by becoming the head of the angels, became in a measure one of them, and so ennobled their nature" (Verity). Such, of course, is precisely the effect of his Incarnation on humankind.

Or singular and rash, whereat rejoiced
Th' Apostate, and more haughty thus replied.
'That we were formed then say'st thou? And the work
Of secondary hands, by task transferred
855   From Father to his Son? Strange point and new!
Doctrine which we would know whence learnt: who saw
When this creation was? Remember'st thou
Thy making, while the Maker gave thee being?
We know no time when we were not as now;
860   Know none before us, self-begot, self-raised
By our own quick'ning power, when fatal course
Had circled his full orb, the birth mature
Of this our native Heav'n, ethereal sons.
Our puissance is our own, our own right hand
865   Shall teach us highest deeds, by proof to try
Who is our equal: then thou shalt behold
Whether by supplication we intend
Address, and to begirt th' Almighty throne
Beseeching or besieging. This report,
870   These tidings carry to th' anointed King;
And fly, ere evil intercept thy flight.'
     "He said, and as the sound of waters deep
Hoarse murmur echoed to his words applause
Through the infinite host, nor less for that
875   The flaming seraph fearless, though alone
Encompassed round with foes, thus answered bold.
     " 'O alienate from God, O spirit accursed,
Forsaken of all good; I see thy fall

856–58. See Augustine's *Confessions* 1.6 on how we do not remember our beginnings but cannot suppose that we fabricated ourselves, and therefore honor our Maker. Adam at his awakening follows this line of thought (8.270–82). Milton might have derived the idea of the rebel angels denying their creation from Dante, *Par.* 29.58–60.

860. **self-begot, self-raised:** The sudden eruption of the word *self* recalls Shakespeare's *R3,* 5.3.183–204, and glances at the despairing hell of selfhood at 4.73–113.

864. **own right hand:** as opposed to God's (see 741n). Cp. Ps. 45.4.

868. **Address:** dutiful approach, with also a military sense of skillful engagement.

869. **Beseeching or besieging:** Out of supplication comes, treacherously, a new way of approaching the throne of God; *besieging* only sounds like *beseeching.* Cp. 1.642n.

Determined, and thy hapless crew involved
880 In this perfidious fraud, contagion spread
Both of thy crime and punishment: henceforth
Not more be troubled how to quit the yoke
Of God's Messiah; those indulgent laws
Will not be now vouchsafed, other decrees
885 Against thee are gone forth without recall;
That golden scepter which thou didst reject
Is now an iron rod to bruise and break
Thy disobedience. Well thou didst advise,
Yet not for thy advice or threats I fly
890 These wicked tents devoted, lest the wrath
Impendent, raging into sudden flame,
Distinguish not: for soon expect to feel
His thunder on thy head, devouring fire.
Then who created thee lamenting learn,
895 When who can uncreate thee thou shalt know.'
    "So spake the Seraph Abdiel faithful found,
Among the faithless, faithful only he;
Among innumerable false, unmoved,
Unshaken, unseduced, unterrified,
900 His loyalty he kept, his love, his zeal;
Nor number, nor example with him wrought
To swerve from truth, or change his constant mind
Though single. From amidst them forth he passed,
Long way through hostile scorn, which he sustained
905 Superior, nor of violence feared aught;
And with retorted scorn his back he turned
On those proud tow'rs to swift destruction doomed."

---

883. **those indulgent laws:** alluding to the
  laws of line 693.
890. **devoted:** doomed.
899. Similar effects with the prefix *un-* occur
  at 2.185, 3.231. In describing Abdiel's soli-
  tary steadfastness, Milton may also have

had in mind his own position at the
Restoration.
906. **retorted scorn:** Abdiel's physical ges-
  ture of scornfully turning his back on the
  scornful rebel angels enacts the etymology
  of *retorted*, from the Latin *retortus,* "turned
  back."

Book VI

The Argument

Raphael continues to relate how Michael and Gabriel were sent forth to battle against Satan and his angels. The first fight described: Satan and his powers retire under night: he calls a council, invents devilish engines, which in the second day's fight put Michael and his angels to some disorder; but they at length pulling up mountains overwhelmed both the forces and machines of Satan. Yet the tumult not so ending, God on the third day sends Messiah his Son, for whom he had reserved the glory of that victory. He in the power of his Father coming to the place, and causing all his legions to stand still on either side, with his chariot and thunder driving into the midst of his enemies, pursues them unable to resist towards the wall of Heaven, which opening, they leap down with horror and confusion into the place of punishment prepared for them in the deep. Messiah returns with triumph to his Father.

> "All night the dreadless angel unpursued
> Through Heav'n's wide champaign held his way, till Morn,
> Waked by the circling Hours, with rosy hand
> Unbarr'd the gates of light. There is a cave
> 5   Within the Mount of God, fast by his throne,

1. **dreadless angel:** Abdiel, fearless and without a doubt (see 5.899–905).
2. **champaign:** (1) wide expanse of open countryside; (2) common land ("The least turf of hallowed glebe is with God himself of more value than all the champaign of common possession," Jeremy Taylor, 2.34); (3) a plain as a battlefield (see l. 15).
2–11. **Morn . . . Heav'n:** Like Book 5, Book 6

begins with an allusion to the best-known Homeric personification, rosy-fingered Dawn. Milton's Dawn is distinctively awakened by the *Hours* in the *circling* configuration of a clock (cp. 4.267). Unlike Hesiod, who puts the abode of alternating day and night in the abyss (*Theog.* 744–54), Milton elevates their *perpetual round* to Heaven's most sacred site, *fast by*

Where light and darkness in perpetual round
Lodge and dislodge by turns, which makes through Heav'n
Grateful vicissitude, like day and night;
Light issues forth, and at the other door
10   Obsequious darkness enters, till her hour
To veil the Heav'n, though darkness there might well
Seem twilight here; and now went forth the Morn
Such as in highest Heav'n, arrayed in gold
Empyreal, from before her vanished night,
15   Shot through with orient beams: when all the plain
Covered with thick embattled squadrons bright,
Chariots and flaming arms, and fiery steeds
Reflecting blaze on blaze, first met his view:
War he perceived, war in procinct, and found
20   Already known what he for news had thought
To have reported: gladly then he mixed
Among those friendly powers who him received
With joy and acclamations loud, that one
That of so many myriads fall'n, yet one
25   Returned not lost: on to the sacred hill
They led him high applauded, and present
Before the seat supreme; from whence a voice
From midst a golden cloud thus mild was heard.
     "'Servant of God, well done, well hast thou fought
30   The better fight, who single hast maintained
Against revolted multitudes the cause
Of truth, in word mightier than they in arms;
And for the testimony of truth hast borne
Universal reproach, far worse to bear
35   Than violence: for this was all thy care

(near) God's *throne*. Milton grew up in a household with its own clock, at a time when it first became possible for wealthier citizens to own one.

10. **Obsequious**: obedient, sequent; like one observing rites of mourning (cp. *Lyc* headnote; *SA* 1732).

19. **in procinct**: from the Latin *in procinctu*, "girded up, prepared for battle."

29–30. "Well done, thou good and faithful servant"(Matt. 25.21); "fight the good fight" (1 Tim. 6.12).

33–35. **for the testimony . . . violence**: "For thy sake I have borne reproach" (Ps. 69.7). Cp. Spenser: "Evil deeds may better than bad words be bore" (*FQ* 4.4.4).

To stand approved in sight of God, though worlds
Judged thee perverse: the easier conquest now
Remains thee, aided by this host of friends,
Back on thy foes more glorious to return
40 Than scorned thou didst depart, and to subdue
By force, who reason for their law refuse,
Right reason for their law, and for their King
Messiah, who by right of merit reigns.
Go Michael of celestial armies prince,
45 And thou in military prowess next
Gabriel, lead forth to battle these my sons
Invincible, lead forth my armèd Saints
By thousands and by millions ranged for fight;
Equal in number to that godless crew
50 Rebellious, them with fire and hostile arms
Fearless assault, and to the brow of Heav'n
Pursuing drive them out from God and bliss,
Into their place of punishment, the gulf
Of Tartarus, which ready opens wide
55 His fiery chaos to receive their fall.'
    "So spake the sov'reign voice, and clouds began
To darken all the hill, and smoke to roll

---

42. **Right reason:** Scholastic theologians adapted the concept of an *a priori* faculty of moral judgment from the *recta ratio* of Stoic philosophy. Milton cites Cicero (*Philippics* 11.12.28): "Right reason [is] derived from divine will which commands what is right and forbids what is wrong" (*1Def*, Yale 4:1.383; cp. *Brief Notes*, Yale 7:479). See Hoopes.

44. **Michael:** "Who is like God?" (Hebr.). He is named as Satan's opponent in Revelation, Milton's main source for the War in Heaven (12.7). Milton transfers to Christ many of the distinctions traditionally accorded Michael, including credit for vanquishing Satan.

46. **Gabriel:** "man of God" (Hebr.). See 4.549n.

49. **Equal:** Equality is a slippery concept in the epic. As Satan later acknowledges, "most" (two-thirds) of the angels remain loyal to God (l. 166; cp. l. 156, 2.692, 5.710).

54. **Tartarus:** Hell; see 2.69n.

55. **chaos:** Fowler glosses this usage as indicating the uncreated realm of primordial matter, but God uses the term in its primitive sense of "yawning gulf, chasm" (*OED* 1; cp. ll. 871–75).

56–60. Editors note that smoke, fire, and trumpet signal God's presence when he gives Moses the Ten Commandments (Exod. 19.18–19). The typological structure of the narrative suggests that Milton alludes primarily to Hebrews 12, however, in which St. Paul localizes the Exodus account to insist on the apocalyptic transcendence and universality of Christ's kingdom: "For ye are not come unto the

In dusky wreaths, reluctant flames, the sign
Of wrath awaked: nor with less dread the loud
60   Ethereal trumpet from on high gan blow:
At which command the powers militant,
That stood for Heav'n, in mighty quadrate joined
Of union irresistible, moved on
In silence their bright legions, to the sound
65   Of instrumental harmony that breathed
Heroic ardor to advent'rous deeds
Under their godlike leaders, in the cause
Of God and his Messiah. On they move
Indissolubly firm; nor obvious hill,
70   Nor strait'ning vale, nor wood, nor stream divides
Their perfect ranks; for high above the ground
Their march was, and the passive air upbore
Their nimble tread, as when the total kind
Of birds in orderly array on wing
75   Came summoned over Eden to receive
Their names of thee; so over many a tract
Of Heav'n they marched, and many a province wide
Tenfold the length of this terrene: at last
Far in th' horizon to the north appeared
80   From skirt to skirt a fiery region, stretched
In battailous aspect, and nearer view

---

mount that might be touched, and that burned with fire, nor unto blackness, and darkness, and tempest, and the sound of a trumpet. . . . But ye are come unto mount Sion, and unto the city of the living God, the heavenly Jerusalem, and to an innumerable company of angels" (18–22). Cp. 833–34n.

58. **reluctant:** struggling (of the fire working through smoke); cp. 4.311. The *OED* does not cite an example of the modern sense before the eighteenth century.

60. **gan:** began to.

62. **stood for Heav'n:** maintained loyalty to God (in contrast to the *Apostate;* cp. l. 100).

63–65. **Of union irresistible . . . harmony:**

Cp. the quiet calm of the fallen angels, marching in squared formation to the sound of flutes playing Dorian music (1.549–61). "Homer thus marches his Grecians silent and sedate" (Todd; *Il.* 3.8).

69. **obvious:** standing in the way.

73–76. **Their nimble tread . . . thee:** Cp. Gen. 2.20.

78. **terrene:** earthly (referring back to *province*).

79–83. **horizon . . . shields:** The full extent of the northern horizon is filled with Satan's troops, whose armor shines with fiery light. For Satan's association with the north, see 5.689.

Bristled with upright beams innumerable
Of rigid spears, and helmets thronged, and shields
Various, with boastful argument portrayed,
85 The banded powers of Satan hasting on
With furious expedition; for they weened
That selfsame day by fight, or by surprise
To win the Mount of God, and on his throne
To set the envier of his state, the proud
90 Aspirer, but their thoughts proved fond and vain
In the mid way: though strange to us it seemed
At first, that angel should with angel war,
And in fierce hosting meet, who wont to meet
So oft in festivals of joy and love
95 Unanimous, as sons of one great Sire
Hymning th' Eternal Father: but the shout
Of battle now began, and rushing sound
Of onset ended soon each milder thought.
High in the midst exalted as a god
100 Th' Apostate in his sun-bright chariot sat
Idol of majesty divine, enclosed
With flaming Cherubim, and golden shields;
Then lighted from his gorgeous throne, for now
'Twixt host and host but narrow space was left,
105 A dreadful interval, and front to front
Presented stood in terrible array
Of hideous length: before the cloudy van,

---

84. **argument:** design, subject (cp. 1.24, 9.13, *Damon* 189).
86. **expedition:** speed, aggressiveness; **weened:** thought, expected.
90. **fond:** foolish, conceited.
91. **In the mid way:** little-used idiom, meaning "halfway through," e.g., one's life (11.631; cp. Mary Herbert's translation of Ps. 102.24). In other words, Satan and his army fall well short of their intended goal. Fowler suspects numerological resonance because the Son ascends the char-

iot to defeat the rebels halfway through the epic (l. 762). Cp. 129n.
93. **hosting:** battle, from the noun *host*, "army" (see l. 104), but with a play on "entertain hospitably"; **wont:** were used.
100. **Apostate:** Greek *apo* (from, off), *stat* (stand).
107. **cloudy van:** the front line (*van*) of an army massed for battle and thus resembling a threatening cloud, as Milton's simile at 2.533–38 indicates. On Satan's proclivity for the front line or *edge* of battle, see 1.276–77.

On the rough edge of battle ere it joined,
Satan with vast and haughty strides advanced,
110 Came tow'ring, armed in adamant and gold;
Abdiel that sight endured not, where he stood
Among the mightiest, bent on highest deeds,
And thus his own undaunted heart explores.

    " 'O Heav'n! That such resemblance of the Highest
115 Should yet remain, where faith and realty
Remain not; wherefore should not strength and might
There fail where virtue fails, or weakest prove
Where boldest; though to sight unconquerable?
His puissance, trusting in th' Almighty's aid,
120 I mean to try, whose reason I have tried
Unsound and false; nor is it aught but just,
That he who in debate of truth hath won,
Should win in arms, in both disputes alike
Victor; though brutish that contest and foul,
125 When reason hath to deal with force, yet so
Most reason is that reason overcome.'

    "So pondering, and from his armèd peers
Forth stepping opposite, half way he met
His daring foe, at this prevention more
130 Incensed, and thus securely him defied.

    " 'Proud, art thou met? Thy hope was to have reached
The highth of thy aspiring unopposed,
The throne of God unguarded, and his side
Abandoned at the terror of thy power
135 Or potent tongue; fool, not to think how vain
Against th' Omnipotent to rise in arms;
Who out of smallest things could without end

---

115. **realty:** reality, sincerity.
118. **boldest:** most insolent, presumptuous.
120. **tried:** proved, judged after trial.
125–26. **reason . . . reason:** playing on the distinction between the principle or faculty of *reason* (capitalized in early editions) and *reason* as the rationale or explanation for an outcome (lowercase).
129. **prevention:** obstruction, in the literal sense of "coming before." Abdiel stops Satan "in the mid way" (cp. l. 91).
130. **securely:** confidently.
131. **Proud:** continuing the evasion of Satan's previous name, Abdiel names him according to his dominant trait.
137–39. **Who . . . folly:** "God hath chosen the weak things of the world to confound the things which are mighty; and base things

Have raised incessant armies to defeat
Thy folly; or with solitary hand
140 Reaching beyond all limit at one blow
Unaided could have finished thee, and whelmed
Thy legions under darkness; but thou seest
All are not of thy train; there be who faith
Prefer, and piety to God, though then
145 To thee not visible, when I alone
Seemed in thy world erroneous to dissent
From all: my sect thou seest, now learn too late
How few sometimes may know, when thousands err.'
    "Whom the grand foe with scornful eye askance
150 Thus answered. 'Ill for thee, but in wished hour
Of my revenge, first sought for thou return'st
From flight, seditious angel, to receive
Thy merited reward, the first assay
Of this right hand provoked, since first that tongue
155 Inspired with contradiction durst oppose
A third part of the gods, in synod met
Their deities to assert, who while they feel
Vigor divine within them, can allow
Omnipotence to none. But well thou com'st
160 Before thy fellows, ambitious to win
From me some plume, that thy success may show
Destruction to the rest: this pause between

of the world, and things which are de-
spised, hath God chosen, yea, and things
which are not, to bring to nought things
which are: that no flesh should glory in
his presence" (1 Cor. 1.27–29).
147. **sect:** body of followers or adherents; a
term applied by contemptuous episcopal
loyalists to all dissenters ("sectaries"),
Milton among them. Cp. *Eikon:* "I never
knew that time in England when men of
truest religion were not counted sec-
taries" (*MLM* 1066).
149. **askance:** a facial tic that becomes char-
acteristic of Satan (cp. 4.504).

153. **assay:** endeavor, trial.
156. **synod:** assembly; during the seven-
teenth century, often used of ecclesiasti-
cal assemblies (especially Presbyterian)
and astrological conjunctions (see 10.661).
Shakespeare in his later plays also applies
synod to meetings of gods, presumably be-
cause of the mythological identification
of gods and heavenly bodies (see, e.g.,
ANT 3.10.4, *COR* 5.2.68–69). Cp. 2.391.
161. **success:** what follows; as elsewhere, in
ironic play with its more usual positive
sense (see 2.9).

(Unanswered lest thou boast) to let thee know;
At first I thought that liberty and Heav'n
165 To Heav'nly souls had been all one; but now
I see that most through sloth had rather serve,
Minist'ring spirits, trained up in feast and song;
Such hast thou armed, the minstrelsy of Heav'n,
Servility with freedom to contend,
170 As both their deeds compared this day shall prove.'
    "To whom in brief thus Abdiel stern replied.
'Apostate, still thou err'st, nor end wilt find
Of erring, from the path of truth remote:
Unjustly thou deprav'st it with the name
175 Of servitude to serve whom God ordains,
Or Nature; God and Nature bid the same,
When he who rules is worthiest, and excels
Them whom he governs. This is servitude,
To serve th' unwise, or him who hath rebelled
180 Against his worthier, as thine now serve thee,
Thyself not free, but to thyself enthralled;
Yet lewdly dar'st our minist'ring upbraid.
Reign thou in Hell thy kingdom, let me serve
In Heav'n God ever blest, and his divine
185 Behests obey, worthiest to be obeyed,
Yet chains in Hell, not realms expect: meanwhile

---

163. **Unanswered . . . boast:** i.e., lest Abdiel boast that Satan had no reply. How Abdiel will boast after the destruction threatened him is not addressed.

166–68. Scripturally, angels are deemed "ministers" and carry out executive duties as God's agents or representatives (Matt. 4.11, Heb. 1.14). Raphael on his mission to Paradise is thus called "empyreal minister" (5.640). Satan exploits the shared Latin root with *minstrel* to deride the obedient angels as servile entertainers, a theme he revisits at 4.941–45. Cp. Lear's condemnation of the thundering elements as "servile ministers" (*LR* 3.2.21), and Nashe's anticipation of the wordplay: "What a stir he keeps against dumb min-

isters, and never writes nor talks of them, but he calleth them minstrels" (8).

169. **Servility with freedom:** slaves with free angels (abstract for concrete).

174. **deprav'st:** disparage.

176–78. **God . . . governs:** "God being the author of nature, her voice is but his instrument" (Hooker 1.3). The same assumption of agreement between divine and natural law underlies Milton's concession in *Tetrachordon* that a wife would properly govern her husband if superior to him in reason (see *MLM* 993).

182. **lewdly:** wickedly, basely; cp. 4.193.

183–84. **Reign . . . blest:** Satan voices his contrary preference at 1.263 (see n).

From me returned, as erst thou saidst, from flight,
This greeting on thy impious crest receive.'
   "So saying, a noble stroke he lifted high,
190 Which hung not, but so swift with tempest fell
On the proud crest of Satan, that no sight,
Nor motion of swift thought, less could his shield
Such ruin intercept: ten paces huge
He back recoiled; the tenth on bended knee
195 His massy spear upstayed; as if on Earth
Winds under ground or waters forcing way
Sidelong, had pushed a mountain from his seat
Half sunk with all his pines. Amazement seized
The rebel Thrones, but greater rage to see
200 Thus foiled their mightiest, ours joy filled, and shout,
Presage of victory and fierce desire
Of battle: whereat Michael bid sound
Th' archangel trumpet; through the vast of Heaven
It sounded, and the faithful armies rung
205 Hosanna to the Highest: nor stood at gaze
The adverse legions, nor less hideous joined
The horrid shock: now storming fury rose,
And clamor such as heard in Heav'n till now
Was never, arms on armor clashing brayed
210 Horrible discord, and the madding wheels
Of brazen chariots raged; dire was the noise
Of conflict; overhead the dismal hiss
Of fiery darts in flaming volleys flew,
And flying vaulted either host with fire.

---

194. **bended knee:** Cp. the knee-tribute previously disdained (5.782, 787–88).

195–98. **as if . . . pines:** Raphael's simile recalls the narrator's resort to seismic pressures to convey the phenomena of Hell (see, e.g., 1.230–37). Mountains appear immovable, but Milton deems faith sufficient to move them, as 1 Cor. 13.2 implies (see ll. 649–50; cp. 4.987, *SA* 1647–48).

199. **rebel Thrones:** A single angelic order stands for all (synecdoche). Leonard remarks that the choice of *Thrones* is "politically suggestive" (see 12.36).

210. **madding:** manic. The diction is odd, but the general point is clear; the jarring sounds and sights of war produce insane frenzy.

213–14. The local conditions anticipate the environment of Hell, complete with a dome of fire produced by thick volleys of flaming arrows and the prophetic sound of their *dismal hiss* (cp. 1.298, 10.508).

215 So under fiery cope together rushed
    Both battles main, with ruinous assault
    And inextinguishable rage; all Heav'n
    Resounded, and had Earth been then, all Earth
    Had to her center shook. What wonder? When
220 Millions of fierce encount'ring angels fought
    On either side, the least of whom could wield
    These elements, and arm him with the force
    Of all their regions: how much more of power
    Army against army numberless to raise
225 Dreadful combustion warring, and disturb,
    Though not destroy, their happy native seat;
    Had not th' Eternal King omnipotent
    From his stronghold of Heav'n high overruled
    And limited their might; though numbered such
230 As each divided legion might have seemed
    A numerous host, in strength each armèd hand
    A legion; led in fight, yet leader seemed
    Each warrior single as in chief, expert
    When to advance, or stand, or turn the sway
235 Of battle, open when, and when to close
    The ridges of grim war; no thought of flight,
    None of retreat, no unbecoming deed
    That argued fear; each on himself relied,
    As only in his arm the moment lay
240 Of victory; deeds of eternal fame
    Were done, but infinite: for wide was spread

216. **battles main:** central bodies of the armies.

222–23. **These elements . . . regions:** Raphael refers to the four *elements* that constitute Adam's world—earth, air, fire, and water—each predominating in its *region*.

225. **combustion:** tumult, wild commotion.

229–36. **though numbered . . . war:** "Each legion was in number like an army, each single warrior was in strength like a le-gion, and, though led in fight, was as expert as a commander-in-chief. So that the angels are celebrated first for their *number*, then for their *strength*, and lastly for their *expertness* in war" (Newton).

236. **ridges:** ranks (per *close* in l. 235); the reference is probably agricultural (furrows), despite Lewis's objection (135).

239. **moment:** determining influence, that which tips the balance.

That war and various; sometimes on firm ground
A standing fight, then soaring on main wing
Tormented all the air; all air seemed then
245   Conflicting fire: long time in even scale
The battle hung; till Satan, who that day
Prodigious power had shown, and met in arms
No equal, ranging through the dire attack
Of fighting Seraphim confused, at length
250   Saw where the sword of Michael smote, and felled
Squadrons at once; with huge two-handed sway
Brandished aloft the horrid edge came down
Wide-wasting; such destruction to withstand
He hasted, and opposed the rocky orb
255   Of tenfold adamant, his ample shield
A vast circumference: at his approach
The great archangel from his warlike toil
Surceased, and glad as hoping here to end
Intestine war in Heav'n, the arch-foe subdued
260   Or captive dragged in chains, with hostile frown
And visage all enflamed first thus began.

243. **main:** powerful.

244. **Tormented:** disturbed, stirred.

248. **No equal:** The phrase has long stirred critical controversy because it seems to contradict the scene in which Satan is *foiled* by Abdiel (l. 200). Newton explains that Abdiel's moment of triumph was accidental and that if the combat had continued, Satan would have "prov'd an overmatch for Abdiel." A. H. Gilbert cites the inconsistency as evidence that the combat with Abdiel is a late insertion to a battle narrative that originally adhered more closely to a Homeric model, "in which the leaders of the hosts fight" (1947, 5). For Fish, the apparent inconsistency is a didactic trap set by the narrator to undermine Abdiel's "sense of justice" and "military pretensions" (1967, 187). Those "pretensions" seem justified at lines 369–71, however, and the present editors take *no*

equal to imply only that Abdiel is inferior to Satan in rank or hierarchical position. The primary sense of the noun *equal* signifies "one that is very similar to another in rank or position." The significance and dramatic impact of Abdiel's *noble stroke* is, if anything, underscored by his social inferiority.

250. **sword of Michael:** The Archangel's grand weapon is a telling point of reference in Milton's depiction of Satan (2.294–95, 11.247–48), though it has no basis in Scripture. Some regard it as the "two-handed engine" of *Lycidas*.

254–56. **rocky orb . . . circumference:** Satan's shield, vast as the moon's orb (1.287), is made of a mythical, impenetrable stone (*adamant*) ten layers thick.

259. **Intestine war:** civil war, but *intestine* also applies literally (e.g., ll. 587–88).

" 'Author of evil, unknown till thy revolt,
Unnamed in Heav'n, now plenteous, as thou seest
These acts of hateful strife, hateful to all,
265   Though heaviest by just measure on thyself
And thy adherents: how hast thou disturbed
Heav'n's blessèd peace, and into nature brought
Misery, uncreated till the crime
Of thy rebellion? How hast thou instilled
270   Thy malice into thousands, once upright
And faithful, now proved false? But think not here
To trouble holy rest; Heav'n casts thee out
From all her confines. Heav'n the seat of bliss
Brooks not the works of violence and war.
275   Hence then, and evil go with thee along
Thy offspring, to the place of evil, Hell,
Thou and thy wicked crew; there mingle broils,
Ere this avenging sword begin thy doom,
Or some more sudden vengeance winged from God
280   Precipitate thee with augmented pain.'
     "So spake the prince of angels; to whom thus
The Adversary. 'Nor think thou with wind
Of airy threats to awe whom yet with deeds
Thou canst not. Hast thou turned the least of these
285   To flight, or if to fall, but that they rise
Unvanquished, easier to transact with me
That thou shouldst hope, imperious, and with threats
To chase me hence? Err not that so shall end
The strife which thou call'st evil, but we style

262–71. **Author . . . false:** Michael's rage and wonder seem genuine, not merely rhetorical. In light of his princely status and angel's characteristic imperturbability, this reaction is a striking measure of what Satan has wrought by his rebellion.

276. **Thy offspring:** perhaps an allusion to Sin (see 2.743–60).

282. **Adversary:** translates "Satan."

284–88. **Hast thou . . . hence?:** i.e., "Have you turned the weakest in my army to flight, or have any fallen failed to rise again undefeated, that you should hope to deal (*transact*) so easily with me as to chase me away with imperious threats?" Satan's speeches here and before his clash with Abdiel are incoherent.

288. **Err not that:** "don't erroneously suppose."

290 The strife of glory: which we mean to win,
     Or turn this Heav'n itself into the Hell
     Thou fablest, here however to dwell free,
     If not to reign: meanwhile thy utmost force,
     And join him named Almighty to thy aid,
295 I fly not, but have sought thee far and nigh.'
         "They ended parle, and both addressed for fight
     Unspeakable; for who, though with the tongue
     Of angels, can relate, or to what things
     Liken on Earth conspicuous, that may lift
300 Human imagination to such highth
     Of godlike power: for likest gods they seemed,
     Stood they or moved, in stature, motion, arms
     Fit to decide the empire of great Heav'n.
     Now waved their fiery swords, and in the air
305 Made horrid circles; two broad suns their shields
     Blazed opposite, while expectation stood
     In horror; from each hand with speed retired
     Where erst was thickest fight, th' angelic throng,
     And left large field, unsafe within the wind
310 Of such commotion, such as to set forth
     Great things by small, if nature's concord broke,
     Among the constellations war were sprung,
     Two planets rushing from aspect malign

290. **The strife of glory:** Cp. the Son's interpretation of the conflict (5.738–39).
296. **parle:** parley; **addressed:** prepared, but in play with *parle* and *unspeakable*.
297–98. **tongue/Of angels:** recalls St. Paul's insistence on the emptiness of oratory without charity (1 Cor. 13.1), a fitting transition from talking to fighting.
299. **conspicuous:** "perceivable," modifies *things.* In asking what could *lift / Human imagination to such highth / Of godlike power,* Raphael seeks an aesthetic of the sublime.
303. **empire:** command, control.
306–7. **while expectation stood/In horror:** The personification of *expectation* conveys the angels' alarm; cp. Shakespeare, *ANT*

3.6.47, where expectation is "faint" from lack of satisfaction, and *H5* 2.Prol.8: "Now sits Expectation in the air."
310–15. Fowler notes the passage's ironic anticipation of the fallen world, when celestial order is deliberately altered so that malignant opposition between planets becomes a regular astrological occurrence (10.657–61). Here, however, cosmic *concord* is imagined not simply as altered for the worse but as broken, and the planets not merely in *aspect malign* but rushing toward each other "in mere oppugnancy," as Shakespeare's Ulysses says in a precedent passage (*TRO* 2.III). The sublimely horrifying prospect of Michael

Of fiercest opposition in mid sky,
315 Should combat, and their jarring spheres confound.
Together both with next to almighty arm,
Uplifted imminent one stroke they aimed
That might determine, and not need repeat,
As not of power, at once; nor odds appeared
320 In might or swift prevention; but the sword
Of Michael from the armory of God
Was giv'n him tempered so, that neither keen
Nor solid might resist that edge: it met
The sword of Satan with steep force to smite
325 Descending, and in half cut sheer, nor stayed,
But with swift wheel reverse, deep ent'ring shared
All his right side; then Satan first knew pain,
And writhed him to and fro convolved; so sore
The griding sword with discontinuous wound
330 Passed through him, but th' ethereal substance closed
Not long divisible, and from the gash
A stream of nectarous humor issuing flowed
Sanguine, such as celestial spirits may bleed,
And all his armor stained erewhile so bright.

---

and Satan's imminent combat dwarfs (*great things by small*) that of planets hurtling toward each other on a collision course.

318–19. **determine . . . once:** decide the outcome and not need to be repeated because it lacked the necessary power to finish the fight in itself (*at once*). The common gloss of *as not of power*—"because so powerful a blow could not be repeated"—is unconvincing.

320. **prevention:** anticipation.

321. **armory of God:** mentioned in Jer. 50.25. Cp. the irresistible sword given Arthegall by Astraea, goddess of justice: "Wheresoever it did light, it thoroughly sheared" (*FQ* 5.1.10).

323–27. **Nor solid might . . . side:** Though hardly Homeric in his dissection of battle, Raphael is careful to relate how Satan's wound occurs. Michael's sword *descending* cuts Satan's sword sheer in two; then Michael executes a *swift wheel reverse* (a backhand upstroke) that cuts off (*shared*) Satan's entire *right side*. Satan's left (Lat. *sinister*) side remains.

328. **convolved:** rolled together; coiled up. Satan's reaction to the pain prefigures his metamorphosis into a serpent (10.511ff).

329. **griding:** slashing, piercing; **discontinuous:** gaping; "in allusion to the old definition of a wound that it separates the continuity of the parts" (Newton).

332–33. **nectarous . . . bleed:** *Celestial spirits* bleed a bodily fluid, or *humor,* whose *sanguine* color owes to the "rubied nectar" they drink (5.633); cp. Homer's similar treatment of divine bleeding, *Il.* 5.339–42.

335 Forthwith on all sides to his aid was run
By angels many and strong, who interposed
Defense, while others bore him on their shields
Back to his chariot, where it stood retired
From off the files of war; there they him laid
340 Gnashing for anguish and despite and shame
To find himself not matchless, and his pride
Humbled by such rebuke, so far beneath
His confidence to equal God in power.
Yet soon he healed; for spirits that live throughout
345 Vital in every part, not as frail man
In entrails, heart or head, liver or reins,
Cannot but by annihilating die;
Nor in their liquid texture mortal wound
Receive, no more than can the fluid air:
350 All heart they live, all head, all eye, all ear,
All intellect, all sense, and as they please,
They limb themselves, and color, shape or size
Assume, as likes them best, condense or rare.
    "Meanwhile in other parts like deeds deserved
355 Memorial, where the might of Gabriel fought,
And with fierce ensigns pierced the deep array
Of Moloch furious king, who him defied,
And at his chariot wheels to drag him bound

335–36. **was run/By angels:** Latinate syntax (*cursum est*) indicating that his troops ran to aid him. Such scenes occur frequently in Homer (e.g., *Il.* 14.428–32).

345–53. On the versatile homogeneity of angels, see 1.425n. Kerrigan notes how enviable such a physiology would be for a man with defective eyes (1983, 215–16, 227–28, 257–62; cp. *SA* 93–97).

346. **reins:** kidneys.

347. **annihilating:** Whether or not existence is escapable for angels is an open question; see 2.92–93, 151–54. In Milton's monist theory of creation *ex deo,* certainly no created being can, in the literal sense of annihilation, become "nothing." The

closest to annihiliation a creature can come is dissolution into constituent atoms, or as Belial puts it, "swallowed up and lost/In the wide womb of uncreated Night" (2.149–50).

353. **likes:** pleases; an instance of the ethical dative; **condense or rare:** thick or thin in density.

356. **ensigns:** standards or banners of military units, here also the units themselves.

357. **Moloch:** "The name is not supposed to exist until after man's Fall (see 1.364–65). Raphael might foreknow the names of future devils (cp. 12.140), but to name them here implies the failure of his mission. He had withheld 'Beëlzebub' from

Threatened, nor from the Holy One of Heav'n
360 Refrained his tongue blasphemous; but anon
Down clov'n to the waste, with shattered arms
And uncouth pain fled bellowing. On each wing
Uriel and Raphael his vaunting foe,
Though huge, and in a rock of diamond armed,
365 Vanquished Adramelec, and Asmadai,
Two potent Thrones, that to be less than gods
Disdained, but meaner thoughts learned in their flight,
Mangled with ghastly wounds through plate and mail.
Nor stood unmindful Abdiel to annoy
370 The atheist crew, but with redoubled blow
Ariel and Arioch, and the violence
Of Ramiel scorched and blasted overthrew.
I might relate of thousands, and their names
Eternize here on Earth; but those elect

Bk. 5 . . . but now allows many devils' names to infiltrate Bk. 6" (Leonard). Like the narrator in Books 1 and 2, however, Raphael does not have many options. The original names of the fallen angels have been erased, and fallen humanity has not yet supplied them with new ones.

359–60. **nor . . . blasphemous:** "Whom hast thou reproached and blasphemed? . . . the Holy One of Israel" (2 Kings 19.22).

362. **uncouth:** unfamiliar.

363. *Raphael* refers to himself in the third person, which may owe to the historian's objectivity or indicate that Adam and Eve do not know the name of their guest.

364. **in a rock of diamond:** Cp. *Sonnet 6*, 7–8.

365. **Adramelec and Asmadai:** *Adramelec* was idolized by the Sepharvites in Samaria under Assyrian dominion (2 Kings 17.31). Worshiped as a sun god, he is defeated by Uriel, "regent of that orb" (3, Argument). *Asmadai* (Asmodeus) is vanquished by Raphael, his captor in the apocryphal Book of Tobit (see 4.168–71n).

371–72. **Ariel and Arioch . . . Ramiel:** The meaning of *Ariel* is uncertain, though it is often glossed as "lion of God." It is the

proper name of a man as well as a poetic name for Jerusalem (e.g., Isa. 29.1–2). Milton would also have remembered Shakespeare's character (*TMP*). *Arioch* (lion-like) is the scriptural name of two kings and a captain (Gen. 14.1, 9; Judg. 1.6; Dan. 2.14). More pertinently, Rabbinical sources identify the king from Genesis with Antiochus Epiphanes (176–64 B.C.E.), King of Syria and perpetrator of "the Abomination of Desolation," in which a statue of Zeus was erected in the temple and Jews forced to worship it (1 Macc. 1.11–6.16). *Ramiel*, the most obscure reference, means "thunder of God"; Milton may have known the name from an extant fragment of the apocryphal Book of Baruch, which centers on the destruction of Jerusalem. If so, the three angels defeated by Abdiel are associated with apostasy and destruction in the holy city.

373–85. Content with God's praise, good angels *seek not the praise of men* (cp. *Lyc* 78–84). The rebels, their names *cancelled* from God's book, cannot win praise in Heaven, though they as creatures desire it instinctively. That they will seek the consolation

375 Angels contented with their fame in Heav'n
Seek not the praise of men: the other sort
In might though wondrous and in acts of war,
Nor of renown less eager, yet by doom
Cancelled from Heav'n and sacred memory,
380 Nameless in dark oblivion let them dwell.
For strength from truth divided and from just,
Illaudable, naught merits but dispraise
And ignominy, yet to glory aspires
Vainglorious, and through infamy seeks fame:
385 Therefore eternal silence be their doom.
    "And now their mightiest quelled, the battle swerved,
With many an inroad gored; deformèd rout
Entered, and foul disorder; all the ground
With shivered armor strown, and on a heap
390 Chariot and charioteer lay overturned
And fiery foaming steeds; what stood, recoiled
O'erwearied, through the faint Satanic host
Defensive scarce, or with pale fear surprised,
Then first with fear surprised and sense of pain
395 Fled ignominious, to such evil brought
By sin of disobedience, till that hour
Not liable to fear or flight or pain.
Far otherwise th' inviolable saints
In cubic phalanx firm advanced entire,
400 Invulnerable, impenetrably armed:
Such high advantages their innocence
Gave them above their foes, not to have sinned,
Not to have disobeyed; in fight they stood
Unwearied, unobnoxious to be pained

---

of humanity's praise is left implicit. That they will succeed in their quest is presumed by the appearance of their earthly names in Raphael's narrative (see 357n).

382. Illaudable: unworthy of praise.
386. the battle: the [rebel] army.
391. what: those who.
393. Defensive scarce: scarcely defending themselves.

399. cubic phalanx: Angels aloft, unlike human armies, can assume a cubic formation, both geometrically foursquare and, in the figurative sense, firm and unwavering. Cp. the hollow cube deployed by the rebels (l. 552).
404. unobnoxious: not liable (cp. l. 397).

405 By wound, though from their place by violence moved.
    "Now night her course began, and over Heav'n
Inducing darkness, grateful truce imposed,
And silence on the odious din of war:
Under her cloudy covert both retired,
410 Victor and Vanquished: on the foughten field
Michael and his angels prevalent
Encamping, placed in guard their watches round,
Cherubic waving fires: on th' other part
Satan with his rebellious disappeared,
415 Far in the dark dislodged, and void of rest,
His potentates to council called by night;
And in the midst thus undismayed began.
    " 'O now in danger tried, now known in arms
Not to be overpowered, companions dear,
420 Found worthy not of liberty alone,
Too mean pretense, but what we more affect,
Honor, dominion, glory, and renown,
Who have sustained one day in doubtful fight,
(And if one day, why not eternal days?)
425 What Heaven's Lord had powerfullest to send
Against us from about his throne, and judged
Sufficient to subdue us to his will,
But proves not so: then fallible, it seems,
Of future we may deem him, though till now
430 Omniscient thought. True is, less firmly armed,

---

410. **foughten field:** battlefield (cp. Shakespeare, *H5* 4.6.18).

411. **prevalent:** prevailing.

413. **Cherubic waving fires:** "flaming Cherubim" (l. 102), regularly assigned guard duty (e.g., 4.778–85).

415. **dislodged:** shifted position (5.669), or was forced to shift position. The active-passive ambiguity seems especially apt because the site of Satan's relocation is *far in the dark* (5.614).

416. Tactical councils on the night of a battlefield setback occur in Homer (*Il.* 9) and Vergil (*Aen.* 9.224–313).

421. **mean pretense:** "low aim," ironically accompanied by "base deception"; **affect:** "strive after," ironically accompanied by "pretend."

423. **doubtful fight:** indecisive conflict; cp. "dubious battle" (1.104).

429. **Of future:** Editors generally gloss "in future," after the idiom "of old." But Hume's reading of the phrase as a supposed limit on divine knowledge ("of future events") is also possible.

430. **Omniscient thought:** Yet Satan called a secret meeting (5.683ff).

Some disadvantage we endured and pain,
Till now not known, but known as soon contemned,
Since now we find this our empyreal form
Incapable of mortal injury
435 Imperishable, and though pierced with wound,
Soon closing, and by native vigor healed.
Of evil then so small as easy think
The remedy; perhaps more valid arms,
Weapons more violent, when next we meet,
440 May serve to better us, and worse our foes,
Or equal what between us made the odds,
In nature none: if other hidden cause
Left them superior, while we can preserve
Unhurt our minds, and understanding sound,
445 Due search and consultation will disclose.'
    "He sat; and in th' assembly next upstood
Nisroch, of Principalities the prime;
As one he stood escaped from cruel fight,
Sore toiled, his riven arms to havoc hewn,
450 And cloudy in aspect thus answering spake.
'Deliverer from new lords, leader to free
Enjoyment of our right as gods; yet hard
For gods, and too unequal work we find
Against unequal arms to fight in pain,
455 Against unpained, impassive; from which evil
Ruin must needs ensue; for what avails
Valor or strength, though matchless, quelled with pain
Which all subdues, and makes remiss the hands
Of mightiest. Sense of pleasure we may well
460 Spare out of life perhaps, and not repine,
But live content, which is the calmest life:
But pain is perfect misery, the worst

---

432. **known as soon contemned:** no sooner
felt than scorned.
440. **worse:** harm.
447. **Nisroch:** Assyrian deity; while wor-
shiping at Nisroch's temple after a dis-
astrous campaign against Israel, the As-
syrian ruler Sennacherib was slain by his
own sons (2 Kings 19.37, Isa. 37.38).
449. **to havoc hewn:** cut to pieces.
455. **impassive:** invulnerable to pain.
458. **remiss:** slack.

Of evils, and excessive, overturns
All patience. He who therefore can invent
465 With what more forcible we may offend
Our yet unwounded enemies, or arm
Ourselves with like defense, to me deserves
No less than for deliverance what we owe.'
     "Whereto with look composed Satan replied.
470 'Not uninvented that, which thou aright
Believ'st so main to our success, I bring;
Which of us who beholds the bright surface
Of this ethereous mold whereon we stand,
This continent of spacious Heav'n, adorned
475 With plant, fruit, flow'r ambrosial, gems and gold,
Whose eye so superficially surveys
These things, as not to mind from whence they grow
Deep under ground, materials dark and crude,
Of spiritous and fiery spume, till touched
480 With Heav'n's ray, and tempered they shoot forth
So beauteous, op'ning to the ambient light.
These in their dark nativity the deep
Shall yield us pregnant with infernal flame,
Which into hollow engines long and round

---

464. **He who:** What follows is an implicit, conditional threat to Satan's sole leadership.

465. **offend:** hit, hurt.

467–68. **to me ... owe:** "in my view deserves no less than what we owe [Satan] for our deliverance."

471. **main:** key.

472–81. For related accounts of light's productive interaction with potent subterranean matter, see 3.608–12, 8.91–97; cp. *Masque* 732–36.

473. **ethereous:** Milton substitutes the Greco-Latin form of the adjective rather than make the tongue-twisting combination *ethereal mold.*

478. **materials dark and crude:** Chaos substantiates Heaven too (MacCaffrey 162–64); cp. ll. 482–83, 510–12, 2.941.

479–80. The action of light touching potent sulfurous material and causing it to *shoot forth* appears to have suggested Satan's invention. It is the archetypal instance of Satan's bent for violating generative processes to accomplish his ends.

479. **spiritous:** highly refined, pure; **spume:** "of the Lat. *spuma,* froth, foam, a word expressing well the crude consistence of sulfur and other subterranean materials, the efficients of fertility" (Hume).

483. **infernal:** Satan uses the word in its classical sense of "underground," though the ironic association with Hell is unavoidable for Milton's readers.

484. **engines:** war machines; cp. 4.17–18. Milton was widely anticipated in laying the invention of artillery at the Devil's door; see, e.g., Spenser, *FQ* 1.7.13.

485 Thick-rammed, at th' other bore with touch of fire
Dilated and infuriate shall send forth
From far with thund'ring noise among our foes
Such implements of mischief as shall dash
To pieces, and o'erwhelm whatever stands
490 Adverse, that they shall fear we have disarmed
The thunderer of his only dreaded bolt.
Nor long shall be our labor, yet ere dawn,
Effect shall end our wish. Meanwhile revive;
Abandon fear; to strength and counsel joined
495 Think nothing hard, much less to be despaired.'
He ended, and his words their drooping cheer
Enlightened, and their languished hope revived.
Th' invention all admired, and each, how he
To be th' inventor missed, so easy it seemed
500 Once found, which yet unfound most would have thought
Impossible: yet haply of thy race
In future days, if malice should abound,
Some one intent on mischief, or inspired
With dev'lish machination might devise
505 Like instrument to plague the sons of men
For sin, on war and mutual slaughter bent.
Forthwith from council to the work they flew,
None arguing stood, innumerable hands
Were ready, in a moment up they turned
510 Wide the celestial soil, and saw beneath
Th' originals of nature in their crude
Conception; sulfurous and nitrous foam
They found, they mingled, and with subtle art,

---

485. **bore:** hole bored into the cannon's barrel and filled with powder (called *touch*) that fired the cannon when lit.
494. **counsel:** judgment, wisdom. Physical prowess and strategic intelligence are classically the two main martial virtues, exemplified by Achilles and Odysseus.
496. **cheer:** mood, spirits.
498. **admired:** wondered at.

507–9. The abrupt style conveys haste.
510–20. The rebels' procedure here bears comparison with the construction of Pandaemonium (1.686ff).
512. **nitrous foam:** potassium nitrate or saltpeter; material of *spiritous and fiery spume* mentioned at line 479 and a basic ingredient of gunpowder.

Concocted and adusted they reduced
515 To blackest grain, and into store conveyed:
Part hidden veins digged up (nor hath this Earth
Entrails unlike) of mineral and stone,
Whereof to found their engines and their balls
Of missive ruin; part incentive reed
520 Provide, pernicious with one touch to fire.
So all ere day-spring, under conscious night
Secret they finished, and in order set,
With silent circumspection unespied.
Now when fair morn orient in Heav'n appeared
525 Up rose the victor angels, and to arms
The matin trumpet sung: in arms they stood
Of golden panoply, refulgent host,
Soon banded; others from the dawning hills
Looked round, and scouts each coast light-armèd scour,
530 Each quarter, to descry the distant foe,
Where lodged, or whither fled, or if for fight,
In motion or in halt: him soon they met
Under spread ensigns moving nigh, in slow
But firm battalion; back with speediest sail
535 Zophiel, of Cherubim the swiftest wing,
Came flying, and in mid-air aloud thus cried.
    "'Arm, warriors, arm for fight, the foe at hand,
Whom fled we thought, will save us long pursuit
This day, fear not his flight; so thick a cloud
540 He comes, and settled in his face I see
Sad resolution and secure: let each

514. **concocted and adusted:** combined and dried.

515. **blackest grain:** Satan in Book 4 is identified with the *smutty grain* of his invention (816–17 and n).

518. **found:** cast as in a foundry; cp. 1.703; **engines:** cannons.

519. **missive:** sent, delivered from a distance; **incentive reed:** match.

520. **pernicious:** deadly; sudden (meanings with distinct Latin roots).

521. **conscious:** privy to; translates Ovid's *nox conscia* and to a similar end (*Met.* 13.15). The common observation that Raphael here personifies night as a guiltily aware accomplice is unjustified.

535. **Zophiel:** "spy of God"; one of Michael's chieftains, according to the Zohar (Soncino Zohar, Bemidbar, sec. 3, p. 154a).

541. **Sad:** serious, grim; **secure:** confident.

His adamantine coat gird well, and each
Fit well his helm, grip fast his orbèd shield,
Borne ev'n or high, for this day will pour down,
545 If I conjecture aught, no drizzling shower,
But rattling storm of arrows barbed with fire.'
So warned he them aware themselves, and soon
In order, quit of all impediment;
Instant without disturb they took alarm,
550 And onward move embattled; when behold
Not distant far with heavy pace the foe
Approaching gross and huge; in hollow cube
Training his devilish enginery, impaled
On every side with shadowing squadrons deep,
555 To hide the fraud. At interview both stood
A while, but suddenly at head appeared
Satan: and thus was heard commanding loud.
  " 'Vanguard, to right and left the front unfold;
That all may see who hate us, how we seek
560 Peace and composure, and with open breast
Stand ready to receive them, if they like
Our overture, and turn not back perverse;
But that I doubt, however witness Heaven,
Heav'n witness thou anon, while we discharge
565 Freely our part; ye who appointed stand
Do as you have in charge, and briefly touch

---

544. **ev'n or high:** in front of the body or overhead (to ward off flaming arrows).

547. **aware themselves:** already wary.

548. **impediment:** carriage and baggage of an army.

549. "Instantaneous, without disorder, they sprang to arms." Here as elsewhere, Milton indicates angels in action with substantive adjectives, rather than by using an adverb to describe how they act; see, e.g., "union of pure, with pure/Desiring" (8.627–28). The angels are *instant* in this case, with the result that they respond instantly.

550. **embattled:** in battle formation.

553. **Training:** dragging; **enginery:** artillery; **impaled:** hedged, enclosed.

555. **At interview:** in mutual view.

560. **composure:** agreement, settlement; **breast:** heart, front lines; initiates the series of puns that infects the following lines.

562–67. **overture:** opening of negotiations; opening of a cannon's muzzle (from Lat. *apertura*, hole). The more obvious puns in the following lines include *discharge*, *charge*, *touch*, and *loud* as Satan orders his troops to fire under the linguistic cover of a peace initiative. Editors and critics have long groaned over these puns, but Satan

What we propound, and loud that all may hear.'
  "So scoffing in ambiguous words, he scarce
Had ended when to right and left the front
570 Divided, and to either flank retired.
Which to our eyes discovered new and strange,
A triple-mounted row of pillars laid
On wheels (for like to pillars most they seemed
Or hollowed bodies made of oak or fir
575 With branches lopped, in wood or mountain felled)
Brass, iron, stony mold, had not their mouths
With hideous orifice gaped on us wide,
Portending hollow truce; at each behind
A Seraph stood, and in his hand a reed
580 Stood waving tipped with fire; while we suspense,
Collected stood within our thoughts amused,
Not long, for sudden all at once their reeds
Put forth, and to a narrow vent applied
With nicest touch. Immediate in a flame,
585 But soon obscured with smoke, all Heav'n appeared,
From those deep-throated engines belched, whose roar
Emboweled with outrageous noise the air,
And all her entrails tore, disgorging foul
Their devilish glut, chained thunderbolts and hail
590 Of iron globes, which on the victor host
Leveled, with such impetuous fury smote,

---

and the rebels are at last enjoying themselves.

572. **triple-mounted:** mounted threefold in a row (see ll. 604–5, 650), perhaps in anticipation of the Son's *three-bolted thunder* (l. 764).

576. **mold:** substance. Raphael says that the cannons look like pillars or hollowed-out tree trunks on wheels, except that they are made of metal or stone.

580. **suspense:** undecided, with a play on "dangling in air." The angels are literally and figuratively "hanging fire."

581. **amused:** preoccupied; deceived.

585. As the cannons fire, the angels see *all*

Heav'n first in a flame and then obscured in smoke.

586–89. **From those . . . glut:** Note the alimental imagery, predominantly of inversion and spasm: *deep-throated, belched, emboweled* (filled to bursting), *entrails tore, disgorging, glut.* Shared imagery ties Satan's perverse engines of destruction to his generative history with Sin and Death (cp. 2.755–802). See also God's description of the impact of Sin and Death on the world, 10.630–37.

589–94. **chained thunderbolts . . . rolled:** S. Fallon argues that Milton associates the Devil with Hobbes, who believed that

That whom they hit, none on their feet might stand,
Though standing else as rocks, but down they fell
By thousands, angel on archangel rolled;
595 The sooner for their arms, unarmed they might
Have easily as spirits evaded swift
By quick contraction or remove; but now
Foul dissipation followed and forced rout;
Nor served it to relax their serried files.
600 What should they do? If on they rushed, repulse
Repeated, and indecent overthrow
Doubled, would render them yet more despised,
And to their foes a laughter; for in view
Stood ranked of Seraphim another row
605 In posture to displode their second tire
Of thunder: back defeated to return
They worse abhorred. Satan beheld their plight,
And to his mates thus in derision called.
     "'O friends, why come not on these victors proud?
610 Erewhile they fierce were coming, and when we,
To entertain them fair with open front
And breast, (what could we more?) propounded terms
Of composition, straight they changed their minds,
Flew off, and into strange vagaries fell,

---

everything that exists is matter in motion. With the moving of the angels, Milton gives the Devil (and Hobbes) his due (1991, 228–29).

595–97. **The sooner ... remove:** On spirits' ability to reduce or expand their bodies, see, e.g., ll. 351–53, 1.789–90.

595. **The sooner for their arms:** Fish sees this as a mock-heroic moment because the armor of the good angels confers vulnerability (1967, 179). As many have suggested, however, their armor signifies the armor of faith, complete with shields "able to quench all the fiery darts of the wicked" (Eph. 6.16). Though their faith protects them from direct assault by evil, their vulnerability to deceit is consider-

able (see the deception of Uriel, 3.686–89).

598. **dissipation:** dispersion.

599. "Nor did it help any to open up their close ranks."

601. **indecent:** unseemly.

603. **laughter:** "a sudden glory arising from some sudden conception of some eminency in ourselves, by comparison with the infirmity of others, or with our own formerly" (Hobbes 55).

605. **displode:** fire; **tire:** volley.

611–12. **open front:** both "honest face" and "divided front line"; for *breast*, see 560n.

614–27. Satan continues scoffing at his opponents, describing their violent dispersal by artillery as if it were a response to a

615   As they would dance, yet for a dance they seemed
        Somewhat extravagant and wild, perhaps
        For joy of offered peace: but I suppose
        If our proposals once again were heard
        We should compel them to a quick result.'
620   "To whom thus Belial in like gamesome mood.
        'Leader, the terms we sent were terms of weight,
        Of hard contents, and full of force urged home,
        Such as we might perceive amused them all,
        And stumbled many: who receives them right,
625   Had need from head to foot well understand;
        Not understood, this gift they have besides,
        They show us when our foes walk not upright.'
            "So they among themselves in pleasant vein
        Stood scoffing, heightened in their thoughts beyond
630   All doubt of victory, eternal might
        To match with their inventions they presumed
        So easy, and of his thunder made a scorn,
        And all his host derided, while they stood
        A while in trouble; but they stood not long,
635   Rage prompted them at length, and found them arms
        Against such hellish mischief fit to oppose.
        Forthwith (behold the excellence, the power
        Which God hath in his mighty angels placed)
        Their arms away they threw, and to the hills
640   (For Earth hath this variety from Heav'n
        Of pleasure situate in hill and dale)
        Light as the lightning glimpse they ran, they flew,

---

peace negotiation. Hence his plays on *re-sult* (outcome, jump back), *stumble* (perplex, trip), *understand* (comprehend, prop up). In wondering whether they are dancing, he again taunts them with behaving like minstrels (166–68n; cp. Aeneas's similar scorn (Homer, *Il.* 16.617). It is ritual taunting revived in Westerns; tough guys don't dance.

623. **amused:** held their attention, diverted them.

635. Expanding Vergil's *furor arma ministrat* (*Aen.* 1.150). Instead of peasants throwing rocks, we witness angels heaving mountains.

639–46. Removal of hills and mountains features prominently in the epic's geological and geographical similes as well as its mythological and scriptural allusions, almost always with apocalyptic resonance (see 195–98n, 1.230–35n, 4.987n). In this instance, which has the distinction of being

From their foundations loos'ning to and fro
They plucked the seated hills with all their load,
645   Rocks, waters, woods, and by the shaggy tops
Uplifting bore them in their hands: amaze,
Be sure, and terror seized the rebel host,
When coming towards them so dread they saw
The bottom of the mountains upward turned,
650   Till on those cursèd engines' triple-row
They saw them whelmed, and all their confidence
Under the weight of mountains buried deep,
Themselves invaded next, and on their heads
Main promontories flung, which in the air
655   Came shadowing, and oppressed whole legions armed,
Their armor helped their harm, crushed in and bruised
Into their substance pent, which wrought them pain
Implacable, and many a dolorous groan,
Long struggling underneath, ere they could wind
660   Out of such prison, though spirits of purest light,
Purest at first, now gross by sinning grown.
The rest in imitation to like arms
Betook them, and the neighboring hills uptore;
So hills amid the air encountered hills
665   Hurled to and fro with jaculation dire
That underground they fought in dismal shade;
Infernal noise; war seemed a civil game

---

an actual narrative event, Milton alludes to the tribulation before the Second Coming. Here, however, furious angels "flee into the mountains" to tear them up by the roots and fling them, nearly destroying Heaven (Matt. 24.16–22). The final instance of mountain moving in the poem occurs as part of a divine judgment, when the Flood pushes the mount of Paradise from its place (11.829–38).

646. **amaze:** amazement, dread, with ironic allusion to Ps. 121.1: "I will lift up mine eyes unto the hills, whence cometh my help."

650. **triple-row:** Cp. 572n.

653. **invaded:** attacked.

654. **Main:** massive, entire.

655. **oppressed:** crushed.

657. **pent:** closely confined; cp. Shakespeare: "a liquid prisoner pent in walls of glass" (*Sonnet 5*, l. 10).

665–66. **jaculation . . . dismal shade:** Cp. the *dismal hiss* of the *fiery darts* on the first day of the war and the hellish canopy of flame they form above the battlefield (ll. 212–13). *Jaculum* is Latin for "dart"; *jaculation* means "throw." The verb for throwing darts seems overtly out of scale when applied to hills or mountains. The war has escalated dramatically from the first day.

To this uproar; horrid confusion heaped
Upon confusion rose: and now all Heav'n
670 Had gone to wrack, with ruin overspread,
Had not th' almighty Father where he sits
Shrined in his sanctuary of Heav'n secure,
Consulting on the sum of things, foreseen
This tumult, and permitted all, advised:
675 That his great purpose he might so fulfill,
To honor his anointed Son avenged
Upon his enemies, and to declare
All power on him transferred: whence to his Son
Th' assessor of his throne he thus began.

680   " 'Effulgence of my glory, Son beloved,
Son in whose face invisible is beheld
Visibly, what by deity I am,
And in whose hand what by decree I do,
Second omnipotence, two days are passed,
685 Two days, as we compute the days of Heav'n,
Since Michael and his powers went forth to tame
These disobedient; sore hath been their fight,
As likeliest was, when two such foes met armed;
For to themselves I left them, and thou know'st,
690 Equal in their creation they were formed,
Save what sin hath impaired, which yet hath wrought
Insensibly, for I suspend their doom;
Whence in perpetual fight they needs must last
Endless, and no solution will be found:
695 War wearied hath performed what war can do,
And to disordered rage let loose the reins,

673. **sum of things:** Milton's literal translation of *summa rerum,* or the established order of existence (Lucretius 1.333, 756, 1008). Ovid uses a similar phrase to mean "the highest public interest" as he relates the myth of Phaeton, ironically pertinent here inasmuch as Apollo's inept son is blasted from his father's chariot to preserve universal order (*Met.* 5.379–391).

679. **assessor:** sharer; literally, "one who sits by."

681–82. **invisible is beheld/Visibly:** "the image of the invisible God" (Col. 1.15). The oxymoronic effect owes to the use of *invisible* as a noun, i.e., "one who is invisible."

684. **Second omnipotence:** indicates the derivative or secondary nature of the Son's power (ll. 703–5; cp. John 5.19).

With mountains as with weapons armed, which makes
Wild work in Heav'n, and dangerous to the main.
Two days are therefore passed, the third is thine;
700   For thee I have ordained it, and thus far
Have suffered, that the glory may be thine
Of ending this great war, since none but thou
Can end it. Into thee such virtue and grace
Immense I have transfused, that all may know
705   In Heav'n and Hell thy power above compare,
And this perverse commotion governed thus,
To manifest thee worthiest to be heir
Of all things, to be heir and to be King
By sacred unction, thy deservèd right.
710   Go then thou mightiest in thy Father's might,
Ascend my chariot, guide the rapid wheels
That shake Heav'n's basis, bring forth all my war,
My bow and thunder, my almighty arms
Gird on, and sword upon thy puissant thigh;
715   Pursue these sons of darkness, drive them out
From all Heav'n's bounds into the utter deep:
There let them learn, as likes them, to despise
God and Messiah his anointed King.'
    "He said, and on his Son with rays direct
720   Shone full, he all his Father full expressed
Ineffably into his face received,
And thus the filial Godhead answering spake:

---

698. **main:** continent of Heaven.

699. **the third is thine:** "Milton, by continuing the war for three days, and reserving the victory upon the third for the Messiah alone, plainly alludes to the circumstances of his death and resurrection" (Newton).

701. **suffered:** permitted.

707–8. **heir/Of all things:** quotation of Heb. 1.2.

712. **war:** synecdoche for instruments of war.

716. **utter:** outer.

720–21. "For God, who commanded the light to shine out of darkness, hath shined in our hearts, to give the light of the knowledge of the glory of God in the face of Jesus Christ" (2 Cor. 4.6). Cp. 10.63–67. **expressed/Ineffably:** another seeming oxymoron (see ll. 681–82, 684), here describing the *full* expression of the Father into his Son's face. It is after this silent communication that the Son is called *the filial Godhead* (l. 722). His subsequent reply (ll. 723–41) is woven from scriptures detailing relations between Father and Son.

" 'O Father, O supreme of Heav'nly thrones,
First, highest, holiest, best, thou always seek'st
725 To glorify thy Son, I always thee,
As is most just; this I my glory account,
My exaltation, and my whole delight,
That thou in me well pleased, declar'st thy will
Fulfilled, which to fulfill is all my bliss.
730 Scepter and power, thy giving, I assume,
And gladlier shall resign, when in the end
Thou shalt be all in all, and I in thee
Forever, and in me all whom thou lov'st:
But whom thou hat'st, I hate, and can put on
735 Thy terrors, as I put thy mildness on,
Image of thee in all things; and shall soon,
Armed with thy might, rid Heav'n of these rebelled,
To their prepared ill mansion driven down
To chains of darkness, and th' undying worm,
740 That from thy just obedience could revolt,
Whom to obey is happiness entire.
Then shall thy saints unmixed, and from th' impure
Far separate, circling thy holy mount
Unfeignèd hallelujahs to thee sing,
745 Hymns of high praise, and I among them chief.'
So said, he o'er his scepter bowing, rose
From the right hand of glory where he sat,
And the third sacred morn began to shine

---

725. "Glorify thy Son, that thy Son also may glorify thee" (John 17.1).

728. **That thou in me well pleased:** "This is my beloved Son, in whom I am well pleased" (Matt. 3.17).

731–32. **gladlier . . . all:** "When all things shall be subdued unto him, then shall the Son also himself be subject unto him that put all things under him, that God may be all in all" (1 Cor. 15.28).

734. **But whom thou hat'st, I hate:** "Do I not hate them, O Lord, that hate thee? And am I not grieved with those that rise up against thee?" (Ps. 139.21).

738. **prepared ill mansion:** Hell. The grim counterpoint to John 14.2: "In my father's house are many mansions. . . . I go to prepare a place for you."

739. "God delivered them into chains of darkness" (2 Pet. 2.4); "where their worm dieth not" (Mark 9.44). Cp. Isa. 66.24, Jude 6.

744. **Unfeignèd hallelujahs:** Contrast Mammon's disdain for *forced hallelujahs* (2.243).

Dawning through Heav'n: forth rushed with whirlwind sound
750 The chariot of paternal deity,
Flashing thick flames, wheel within wheel undrawn,
Itself instinct with spirit, but convoyed
By four cherubic shapes, four faces each
Had wondrous, as with stars their bodies all
755 And wings were set with eyes, with eyes the wheels
Of beryl, and careering fires between;
Over their heads a crystal firmament,
Whereon a sapphire throne, inlaid with pure
Amber, and colors of the show'ry arch.
760 He in celestial panoply all armed
Of radiant urim, work divinely wrought,
Ascended, at his right hand Victory
Sat eagle-winged, beside him hung his bow
And quiver with three-bolted thunder stored,
765 And from about him fierce effusion rolled
Of smoke and bickering flame, and sparkles dire;
Attended with ten thousand thousand saints,
He onward came, far off his coming shone,
And twenty thousand (I their number heard)

749–59. **forth rushed . . . arch:** Milton's description of the throne-chariot of the deity and its four-faced cherubic transmission is built from details in Ezekiel 1 and 10. Noting the contrast between this animate chariot and the merely material weapons of the devils, S. Fallon argues that the War in Heaven pits Milton's animist materialism against Satan's (and Hobbes's) mechanist materialism (1991, 226–31, 237–41).

752. **instinct with:** impelled by.

756. **beryl:** transparent mineral; **careering:** darting, flashing.

759. **show'ry arch:** rainbow.

761. **radiant urim:** Milton thought *urim* among twelve gemstones mounted on the "breastplate of judgment," worn by the high priest and used as a divine oracle (Exod. 28.30): "Urim and Thummim, those oraculous gems/On Aaron's breast"

(*PR* 3.14–15). Fowler cites hermetic writers' identification of urim with the philosopher's stone, but Milton more likely had Josephus's account in mind: "God declared beforehand, by those twelve stones . . . when they should be victorious in battle; for so great a splendor shone forth from them before the army began to march, that all the people were sensible of God's being present for their assistance." (*Antiq.* 3.8.9).

762–64. *Victory* is a winged goddess who aids Zeus in his thundering defeat of the Titans and the Giants. The eagle is his bird. Milton may have in mind Pausanias' description of the statue of Zeus at Olympia: "in his right hand a figure of Victory" (5.11.1).

766. **bickering:** quivering, flashing.

767–70. The numbers are scripturally based; see Rev. 5.11, Jude 14, Ps. 68.17.

770 Chariots of God, half on each hand were seen:
He on the wings of Cherub rode sublime
On the crystalline sky, in sapphire throned.
Illustrious far and wide, but by his own
First seen, them unexpected joy surprised,

775 When the great ensign of Messiah blazed
Aloft by angels borne, his sign in Heav'n:
Under whose conduct Michael soon reduced
His army, circumfused on either wing,
Under their head embodied all in one.

780 Before him power divine his way prepared;
At his command the uprooted hills retired
Each to his place, they heard his voice and went
Obsequious, Heav'n his wonted face renewed,
And with fresh flow'rets hill and valley smiled.

785 This saw his hapless foes but stood obdured,
And to rebellious fight rallied their powers
Insensate, hope conceiving from despair.
In Heav'nly spirits could such perverseness dwell?
But to convince the proud what signs avail,

790 Or wonders move th' obdurate to relent?
They hardened more by what might most reclaim,
Grieving to see his glory, at the sight
Took envy, and aspiring to his highth,
Stood re-embattled fierce, by force or fraud

795 Weening to prosper, and at length prevail
Against God and Messiah, or to fall
In universal ruin last, and now

---

771. "And he rode upon a cherub, and did fly"
(2 Sam. 22.11, Ps. 18.10). **sublime:** lifted up,
on the chariot's *crystal firmament* and *sapphire throne* (ll. 757–58).

773. **Illustrious:** shining brightly; see
5.738–39.

776. **his sign:** "And then shall appear the sign
of the Son of man in heaven" (Matt.
24.30).

777. **reduced:** "led back," with a secondary
sense of "diminished." See next note.

779. **their head:** See 5.606 and cp. Abdiel's
interpretation of the Son's exaltation: "he
the head/One of our number thus reduced becomes" (5.842–43).

785. **obdured:** hardened; cp. 3.200.

791. **hardened more:** like Pharaoh (see *CD*
1.4).

797. **last:** Bentley would change to "lost," not
unreasonably.

To final battle drew, disdaining flight,
Or faint retreat; when the great Son of God
800   To all his host on either hand thus spake.
        " 'Stand still in bright array ye saints, here stand
Ye angels armed, this day from battle rest;
Faithful hath been your warfare, and of God
Accepted, fearless in his righteous cause,
805   And as ye have received, so have ye done
Invincibly; but of this cursèd crew
The punishment to other hand belongs,
Vengeance is his, or whose he sole appoints;
Number to this day's work is not ordained
810   Nor multitude, stand only and behold
God's indignation on these godless poured
By me, not you but me they have despised,
Yet envied; against me is all their rage,
Because the Father, t' whom in Heav'n supreme
815   Kingdom and power and glory appertains,
Hath honored me according to his will.
Therefore to me their doom he hath assigned;
That they may have their wish, to try with me
In battle which the stronger proves, they all,
820   Or I alone against them, since by strength
They measure all, of other excellence
Not emulous, nor care who them excels;
Nor other strife with them do I vouchsafe.'
        "So spake the Son, and into terror changed
825   His count'nance too severe to be beheld
And full of wrath bent on his enemies.
        At once the Four spread out their starry wings

---

801. **Stand still . . . saints:** Moses similarly orders the Hebrews to stand and witness the destruction of Pharaoh's army (Exod. 14.13).

808. "Vengeance is mine; I will repay, saith the Lord" (Rom. 12.19; cp. Deut. 32.35).

815. "For thine is the kingdom, and the power, and the glory" (Matt. 6.13).

827. **the Four:** the chariot's *four cherubic shapes* (l. 753); **starry wings:** The wings were previously described as *set with eyes* (l. 755; cp. Ezek. 10.12); the poetic equation of eyes and stars is, however, commonplace.

With dreadful shade contiguous, and the orbs
Of his fierce chariot rolled, as with the sound
830 Of torrent floods, or of a numerous host.
He on his impious foes right onward drove,
Gloomy as night; under his burning wheels
The steadfast empyrean shook throughout,
All but the throne itself of God. Full soon
835 Among them he arrived; in his right hand
Grasping ten thousand thunders, which he sent
Before him, such as in their souls infixed
Plagues; they astonished all resistance lost,
All courage; down their idle weapons dropped;
840 O'er shields and helms, and helmèd heads he rode
Of Thrones and mighty Seraphim prostrate,
That wished the mountains now might be again
Thrown on them as a shelter from his ire.
Nor less on either side tempestuous fell
845 His arrows, from the fourfold-visaged Four,
Distinct with eyes, and from the living wheels
Distinct alike with multitude of eyes;

---

828. **contiguous:** "Their wings were joined one to another" (Ezek. 1.9).

831. **right onward:** Milton thought of himself as proceeding in the same way; cp. *Sonnet 22* 8–9.

833–34. **The steadfast empyrean . . . God:** In the first speech of the epic, Satan claims that the battle did shake God's throne (1.105). Editors cite as Heaven-shaking precedents Hesiod's account of Zeus's battle with Typhoeus (*Theog.* 842–43) and various scriptures, including Isa. 13.12–13, and 2 Sam. 22.8. Overlooked is Heb. 12.26, the key verse for *Lycidas* (Tayler 1979, 234–36) and one fundamental to the typological structure and range of the War in Heaven, from Moses receiving the Law to Christ's Second Coming (cp. 56–60n): "[His] voice then shook the earth: but now he hath promised, saying, 'Yet once more I shake not the earth only, but also heaven.'"

838. **Plagues:** afflictions, strokes of divine retribution. Editors cite the plagues of Egypt under Pharaoh, who is contextually present. In prophecy of the apocalypse, plagues, thunder, lightning, and earthquake are grouped together (see, e.g., Rev. 17).

840–41. In *Apology*, Milton personifies "the invincible warrior Zeal," riding a chariot like the one described in Ezekiel and driving "over the heads of scarlet prelates, and such as are insolent to maintain traditions, bruising their stiff necks under his flaming wheels" (Yale 1:900).

842–43. "And [they] said to the mountains and rocks, 'fall on us, and hide us from the . . . wrath of the Lamb'" (Rev. 6.16; cp. Luke 23.30, Hosea 10.8).

846. **Distinct:** adorned.

One spirit in them ruled, and every eye
Glared lightning, and shot forth pernicious fire
850   Among th' accursed, that withered all their strength,
And of their wonted vigor left them drained,
Exhausted, spiritless, afflicted, fall'n.
Yet half his strength he put not forth, but checked
His thunder in mid-volley, for he meant
855   Not to destroy, but root them out of Heav'n:
The overthrown he raised, and as a herd
Of goats or timorous flock together thronged
Drove them before him thunderstruck, pursued
With terrors and with furies to the bounds
860   And crystal wall of Heav'n, which op'ning wide,
Rolled inward, and a spacious gap disclosed
Into the wasteful deep; the monstrous sight
Strook them with horror backward, but far worse
Urged them behind; headlong themselves they threw
865   Down from the verge of Heav'n; eternal wrath
Burnt after them to the bottomless pit.
    "Hell heard th' unsufferable noise, Hell saw
Heav'n ruining from Heav'n and would have fled
Affrighted; but strict fate had cast too deep
870   Her dark foundations, and too fast had bound.
Nine days they fell; confounded Chaos roared,
And felt tenfold confusion in their fall
Through his wild anarchy, so huge a rout

---

849. **pernicious:** deadly, sudden; cp. l. 520.

857. **goats:** In Scripture the damned are compared to goats, whom at the Last Judgment Christ will gather in his left hand before passing sentence: "Depart from me, ye cursed, into everlasting fire, prepared for the devil and his angels" (Matt. 25.41).

861. **Rolled inward:** rolled up or together; cp. Rev. 6.14: "And the heaven departed [was removed] as a scroll when it is rolled together." **disclosed:** bared, opened.

862. **wasteful:** full of emptiness (Elledge).

868. **ruining:** falling.

869. **fate:** God's curse (2.622–23). "Fate or *fatum* is only what is *fatum*, spoken, by some almighty power" (*CD* 1.2 in *MLM* 1146).

871. **Nine days they fell:** After falling for nine days, they lie stunned for another nine on the lake in Hell (1.50–53). In Hesiod, the rebellious Titans fall for nine days from Heaven to Earth and nine more from earth to Tartarus (*Theog.* 720–25).

873. **rout:** mob, those defeated.

"headlong themselves they threw /
Down from the verge of Heav'n" (6.864–65).

Encumbered him with ruin: Hell at last
875 Yawning received them whole, and on them closed,
Hell their fit habitation fraught with fire
Unquenchable, the house of woe and pain.
Disburdened Heav'n rejoiced, and soon repaired
Her mural breach, returning whence it rolled.
880 Sole victor from th' expulsion of his foes
Messiah his triumphal chariot turned:
To meet him all his saints, who silent stood
Eye-witnesses of his almighty acts,
With jubilee advanced; and as they went,
885 Shaded with branching palm, each order bright
Sung triumph, and him sung victorious King,
Son, Heir, and Lord, to him dominion giv'n,
Worthiest to reign: he celebrated rode
Triumphant through mid-Heav'n, into the courts
890 And temple of his mighty Father throned
On high: who into glory him received,
Where now he sits at the right hand of bliss.
    "Thus measuring things in Heav'n by things on Earth
At thy request, and that thou may'st beware
895 By what is past, to thee I have revealed
What might have else to human race been hid;
The discord which befell, and war in Heav'n
Among th' angelic powers, and the deep fall
Of those too high aspiring, who rebelled
900 With Satan, he who envies now thy state,
Who now is plotting how he may seduce

874–75. **Hell ... closed:** "Therefore hell hath enlarged herself, and opened her mouth without measure" (Isa. 5.14).

884. **jubilee:** joyful shouting.

885. **palm:** symbolic of triumph, as at *SA* 1735. "[The people] took branches of palm trees, and went forth to meet him, and cried, Hosanna: Blessed is the King of Israel that cometh in the name of the Lord" (John 22.12–13; cp. Rev. 7.9).

892. **right hand:** St. Paul describes Christ after his ascension into Heaven as sitting "on the right hand of the Majesty on high" (Heb. 1.3).

900–907. Raphael's most explicit and specific warning of Satan's plot against humanity and its motive. He does not mention the apprehension of Satan at Eve's ear during the previous night.

Thee also from obedience, that with him
Bereaved of happiness thou may'st partake
His punishment, eternal misery;
905 Which would be all his solace and revenge,
As a despite done against the Most High,
Thee once to gain companion of his woe.
But listen not to his temptations, warn
Thy weaker; let it profit thee to have heard
910 By terrible example the reward
Of disobedience; firm they might have stood,
Yet fell; remember, and fear to transgress."

909. **Thy weaker:** Eve, the "weaker vessel"
(1 Pet. 3.7). She is present for Raphael's
narration and at this moment.

BOOK VII

THE ARGUMENT

Raphael at the request of Adam relates how and wherefore this world
was first created: that God, after the expelling of Satan and his angels
out of Heaven, declared his pleasure to create another world and
other creatures to dwell therein; sends his Son with glory and atten-
dance of angels to perform the work of Creation in six days; the angels
celebrate with hymns the performance thereof, and his reascension
into Heaven.

> Descend from Heav'n Urania, by that name
> If rightly thou art called, whose voice divine
> Following, above th' Olympian hill I soar,
> Above the flight of Pegasean wing.
> 5   The meaning, not the name I call: for thou
> Nor of the Muses nine, nor on the top
> Of old Olympus dwell'st, but Heav'nly born,
> Before the hills appeared, or fountain flowed,
> Thou with eternal Wisdom didst converse,

1. **Descend from Heav'n:** evoking Horace's *descende caelo . . . Calliope* (*Odes* 4.1.2); **Urania:** the Muse of astronomy in Roman times, but transformed into the Muse of Christian poetry by du Bartas in *La Muse Chrestiene* (1574).

3. **above th' Olympian hill:** Cp. 1.15.

4. **Pegasean wing:** The winged horse Pegasus ascended to the heavens of Greek mythology, but Milton has risen incomparably higher, to the Heaven of the Christian God.

5. **The meaning, not the name:** *Urania* means "heavenly one" in Latin, but Milton calls upon a power found in the Christian Heaven.

9. **Wisdom:** Wisdom was born "before the hills," before all Creation, in Prov. 8.24–31. Milton identified her as a personification of the Father's wisdom (*CD* 1.7 in *MLM* 1199). **converse:** live in company with (Lat. *conversari*).

10   Wisdom thy sister, and with her didst play
     In presence of th' Almighty Father, pleased
     With thy celestial song. Up led by thee
     Into the Heav'n of Heav'ns I have presumed,
     An earthly guest, and drawn empyreal air,
15   Thy temp'ring; with like safety guided down
     Return me to my native element:
     Lest from this flying steed unreined, (as once
     Bellerophon, though from a lower clime)
     Dismounted, on th' Aleian field I fall
20   Erroneous there to wander and forlorn.
     Half yet remains unsung, but narrower bound
     Within the visible diurnal sphere;
     Standing on earth, not rapt above the pole,
     More safe I sing with mortal voice, unchanged
25   To hoarse or mute, though fall'n on evil days,
     On evil days though fall'n, and evil tongues;
     In darkness, and with dangers compassed round,

---

13. **Heav'n of Heav'ns**: the supreme Heaven (an English version of the Hebrew superlative).

15. **Thy temp'ring**: "made suitable by thee for an earthly guest."

17–20. Milton defines his hapless condition without the Muse's aid by reference to the fate of *Bellerophon*, who tried unsuccessfully to ride Pegasus (see l. 4) to heaven and fell upon the *Aleian field* (land of wandering), where he died *erroneous* (i.e., in a state of distraction). According to some, his fall blinded him (Conti, *Mythologiae* 9.4).

18. **clime**: region.

21–22. Save for episodes in Books 10 and 11, the remaining action of the poem takes place on Earth.

22. **visible diurnal sphere**: the visible universe, which appears to rotate around the Earth on a daily basis.

23. **rapt**: transported; **pole**: the highest spot in the universe, at which it is chained to Heaven (2.1051–52). Milton went *above the pole* when representing the divine council at the opening of Book 3.

25. **hoarse**: In *RCG*, Milton ruefully noted that pamphlets were "a troubled sea of noises and hoarse disputes" (*MLM.* 843). **mute**: probably alludes to the silencing of many Puritan authors during the Restoration. Milton's point is that his poem has suffered neither of the common fates (becoming *hoarse or mute*) of Puritan pamphleteers. **evil days**: After the restoration of the English monarchy in May 1660, an order was issued for Milton's arrest. He was in fact arrested after hiding out for some weeks, and released in December. During this time some of his books were burned.

26. **evil tongues**: Among the many authors who reviled Milton during the Restoration were Roger L'Estrange, George Starkey, David Lloyd, Thomas Ford, Robert South, and Samuel Parker.

27. **darkness**: blindness, from which Milton had suffered since 1652.

And solitude; yet not alone, while thou
Visit'st my slumbers nightly, or when morn
30   Purples the east: still govern thou my song,
Urania, and fit audience find, though few.
But drive far off the barbarous dissonance
Of Bacchus and his revellers, the race
Of that wild rout that tore the Thracian bard
35   In Rhodope, where woods and rocks had ears
To rapture, till the savage clamor drowned
Both harp and voice; nor could the Muse defend
Her son. So fail not thou, who thee implores:
For thou art Heav'nly, she an empty dream.
40   Say Goddess, what ensued when Raphael,
The affable archangel, had forewarned
Adam by dire example to beware
Apostasy, by what befell in Heaven
To those apostates, lest the like befall
45   In Paradise to Adam or his race,
Charged not to touch the interdicted tree,
If they transgress, and slight that sole command,
So easily obeyed amid the choice
Of all tastes else to please their appetite,
50   Though wand'ring. He with his consorted Eve
The story heard attentive, and was filled
With admiration, and deep muse to hear
Of things so high and strange, things to their thought

28–30. **while thou . . . east:** Biographers report that Milton composed either at night or early in the morning (Darbishire 33, 291). Cp. 3.29–32; 9.21–24.

32. **barbarous dissonance:** The phrase also appears in *Masque* (l. 550).

33–37. **the race . . . voice:** The poet Orpheus was torn to pieces by the Maenads, female followers of Bacchus, after he rejected the love of women. His mother, the epic Muse Calliope, could not save him, as Milton also stresses in *Lyc* 58–63. But Urania, a higher Muse, can protect her inspired poet.

46. **touch:** "Ye shall not eat of it, neither shall ye touch it, lest ye die" (Gen. 3.3); cp. 9.651.

47. **sole command:** The singularity of the commandment has already been stressed (1.32; 4.421, 423–24, 428).

50. **wand'ring:** innocently curious wandering at this point, but the word does have the fallen sense of "going astray, losing one's moral bearings," as perhaps in line 20. **consorted:** espoused.

52. **admiration:** wonder; **muse:** meditation.

So unimaginable as hate in Heav'n,
55 And war so near the peace of God in bliss
With such confusion: but the evil soon
Driv'n back redounded as a flood on those
From whom it sprung, impossible to mix
With blessedness. Whence Adam soon repealed
60 The doubts that in his heart arose: and now
Led on, yet sinless, with desire to know
What nearer might concern him, how this world
Of heav'n and earth conspicuous first began,
When, and whereof created, for what cause,
65 What within Eden or without was done
Before his memory, as one whose drouth
Yet scarce allayed still eyes the current stream,
Whose liquid murmur heard new thirst excites,
Proceeded thus to ask his Heav'nly guest.
70   "Great things, and full of wonder in our ears,
Far differing from this world, thou hast revealed
Divine interpreter, by favor sent
Down from the Empyrean to forewarn
Us timely of what might else have been our loss,
75 Unknown, which human knowledge could not reach:
For which to the infinitely Good we owe
Immortal thanks, and his admonishment
Receive with solemn purpose to observe
Immutably his sov'reign will, the end
80 Of what we are. But since thou hast vouchsafed
Gently for our instruction to impart
Things above earthly thought, which yet concerned
Our knowing, as to highest wisdom seemed,
Deign to descend now lower, and relate
85 What may no less perhaps avail us known,

---

57. **redounded:** recoiled.
59. **repealed:** recalled.
63. **conspicuous:** visible.
72. **Divine interpreter:** "Mercury, who is the president of language, is called *deorum hominumque interpres*" (Jonson, *Discoveries*, in Herford et al. 8:621). Raphael is the Christian Mercury. See also 3.656–57.
79. **end:** purpose.
83. **seemed:** seemed good.
85. **avail us known:** prove valuable to us when known.

How first began this heav'n which we behold
Distant so high, with moving fires adorned
Innumerable, and this which yields or fills
All space, the ambient air wide interfused
90 Embracing round this florid Earth; what cause
Moved the Creator in his holy rest
Through all eternity so late to build
In Chaos, and the work begun, how soon
Absolved, if unforbid thou may'st unfold
95 What we, not to explore the secrets ask
Of his eternal empire, but the more
To magnify his works, the more we know.
And the great light of day yet wants to run
Much of his race though steep, suspense in heav'n
100 Held by thy voice, thy potent voice he hears,
And longer will delay to hear thee tell
His generation, and the rising birth
Of nature from the unapparent deep:
Or if the star of ev'ning and the moon
105 Haste to thy audience, Night with her will bring
Silence, and Sleep list'ning to thee will watch,
Or we can bid his absence, till thy song
End, and dismiss thee ere the morning shine."
      Thus Adam his illustrious guest besought:
110 And thus the godlike angel answered mild.
"This also thy request with caution asked
Obtain: though to recount almighty works
What words or tongue of Seraph can suffice,
Or heart of man suffice to comprehend?
115 Yet what thou canst attain, which best may serve

88. **yields or fills:** Air "yields space to all bodies, and . . . fills up the deserted space [when the bodies move]" (Richardson).

94. **Absolved:** finished; **unforbid:** unforbidden.

97. **magnify:** glorify. "Remember that thou magnify his work, which men behold" (Job 36.24).

98. **yet wants:** still has to.

99. **suspense:** attentive, hanging.

100. **he hears:** The sun or *great light of day* in line 98 is here personified.

103. **unapparent deep:** no longer perceptible Chaos.

106. **will watch:** will stay awake. Sleep (personified) is the subject of this verb.

107. **his:** Sleep's.

To glorify the Maker, and infer
Thee also happier, shall not be withheld
Thy hearing, such commission from above
I have received, to answer thy desire
120   Of knowledge within bounds; beyond abstain
To ask, nor let thine own inventions hope
Things not revealed, which th' invisible King,
Only omniscient, hath suppressed in night,
To none communicable in Earth or Heaven:
125   Enough is left besides to search and know.
But knowledge is as food, and needs no less
Her temperance over appetite, to know
In measure what the mind may well contain,
Oppresses else with surfeit, and soon turns
130   Wisdom to folly, as nourishment to wind.
      "Know then, that after Lucifer from Heav'n
(So call him, brighter once amidst the host
Of angels, than that star the stars among)
Fell with his flaming legions through the deep
135   Into his place, and the great Son returned
Victorious with his saints, th' omnipotent
Eternal Father from his throne beheld
Their multitude, and to his Son thus spake.
      "'At least our envious foe hath failed, who thought
140   All like himself rebellious, by whose aid
This inaccessible high strength, the seat
Of Deity supreme, us dispossessed,
He trusted to have seized, and into fraud

---

116. **infer:** render.
120. **Of knowledge within bounds:** On this
    theme, cp. 8.173–97.
121. **inventions:** speculations; **hope:** hope for.
124. **in Earth or Heaven:** The passage has
    apparently been calling attention to the
    bounds on human knowledge, but now
    we learn that the bounds in question limit
    angelic knowledge as well.
132. **So call him:** In classical Latin, Lucifer
    (from Gk. for "light-bringer") refers to

Venus, the morning star. The Christian
Fathers called Satan by the name of Lu-
cifer, perhaps in reference to his original
brightness. In Milton's four drafts for a
tragedy on the fall of man in the *CMS*, the
character is referred to as Lucifer, not
Satan. Cp. 5.760, 10.425.
136. **saints:** angels.
143. **fraud:** The word has its usual meaning
    of dishonesty and deception, but also the
    sense of Latin *fraus* (crime, injury). Satan

Drew many, whom their place knows here no more;
145 Yet far the greater part have kept, I see,
Their station, Heav'n yet populous retains
Number sufficient to possess her realms
Though wide, and this high temple to frequent
With ministeries due and solemn rites:
150 But lest his heart exalt him in the harm
Already done, to have dispeopled Heav'n,
My damage fondly deemed, I can repair
That detriment, if such it be to lose
Self-lost, and in a moment will create
155 Another world, out of one man a race
Of men innumerable, there to dwell,
Not here, till by degrees of merit raised
They open to themselves at length the way
Up hither, under long obedience tried,
160 And Earth be chang'd to Heav'n, and Heav'n to Earth,
One kingdom, joy and union without end.
Meanwhile inhabit lax, ye powers of Heav'n,
And thou my Word, begotten Son, by thee
This I perform, speak thou, and be it done:
165 My overshadowing Spirit and might with thee
I send along, ride forth, and bid the deep
Within appointed bounds be heav'n and earth;

---

not only drew his followers into deceit; he
ruined them.
144. **their place knows here no more:** a
scriptural idiom (Ps. 101.16, Job 7.10); cp.
11.50–57.
145. **the greater part:** Cp. 2.692n.
146. **station:** post, duty.
150–55. Empson concludes that God creates
us "to spite the devils." The passage says
as much; but God also stresses that the
Creation was not necessitated by the de-
fection of the rebel angels.
152. **fondly:** foolishly.
156. **men innumerable:** A finite number of
angels were created; they do not repro-

duce. The breeding race of men, by con-
trast, is *innumerable* (unnumbered). See
Augustine, *City of God* 22.1. Thomas
Browne wrote of "the fertility of Adam,
and the magic of that sperm that hath di-
lated into so many millions" (*Religio
Medici* 1.48).
162. **inhabit lax:** "dwell at ease" (having van-
quished the rebels) and "dwell at large"
(having more of Heaven to yourselves).
165. The Son creates the world, but using the
Spirit and *might* of the Father. This combi-
nation of agency and service is typical of
Milton's Arian Christology (see 3.169–72,
384–96; 6.680–83).

Boundless the deep, because I am who fill
Infinitude, nor vacuous the space.
170 Though I uncircumscribed myself retire,
And put not forth my goodness, which is free
To act or not, necessity and chance
Approach not me, and what I will is fate.'
    "So spake th' Almighty, and to what he spake
175 His Word, the filial Godhead, gave effect.
Immediate are the acts of God, more swift
Than time or motion, but to human ears
Cannot without process of speech be told,
So told as earthly notion can receive.
180 Great triumph and rejoicing was in Heav'n
When such was heard declared th' Almighty's will;
Glory they sung to the most high, good will
To future men, and in their dwellings peace:
Glory to him whose just avenging ire
185 Had driven out th' ungodly from his sight
And th' habitations of the just; to him
Glory and praise, whose wisdom had ordained

168–71. **Boundless . . . goodness:** The passage is highly compressed. The *deep* (uncreated Chaos) will not be any less *boundless* because of Creation. It is infinite because filled by an infinite God, who can nonetheless, and also with no loss of infinity, *retire* from it.

171. **free:** "In God a certain immutable internal necessity to do good, independent of all outside influence, can be consistent with absolute freedom of action" (*CD* 1.3 in *MLM* 1155). It is crucial to Milton that God be free to put forth his goodness in Creation, or *not*.

172. **necessity and chance:** a philosophical binary that the Christian God was often said to transcend (Augustine, *City of God* 5.1.8–10, on necessity; Boethius, *The Consolation of Philosophy* 4.1–2, on chance). In Milton, Chance rules only embryonic atoms (2.907), and necessity is "the tyrant's plea" (4.394).

173. **what I will is fate:** "Fate or *fatum* is only what is *fatum*, spoken, by some almighty power" (*CD* 1.2 in *MLM* 1146). Paradoxes would seem to be on the horizon: if God wills our will to be free, then freedom is fate. But Milton tried to keep divine and human freedom at a distance from such dialectical cleverness. Theologically, politically, and aesthetically, liberty was his most cherished concept.

175. **the filial Godhead:** the Son.

176. **Immediate are the acts of God:** Augustine maintained that the six days of Creation in Genesis symbolize one instantaneous act (*De Genesi* 1.1–3).

178. **process of speech:** the successive acts that constitute speech.

179. **earthly notion:** human understanding.

180–83. The passage is based on Job 38.7 and Luke 2.14.

Good out of evil to create, instead
Of spirits malign a better race to bring
190 Into their vacant room, and thence diffuse
His good to worlds and ages infinite.
So sang the hierarchies: meanwhile the Son
On his great expedition now appeared,
Girt with omnipotence, with radiance crowned
195 Of majesty divine, sapience and love
Immense, and all his Father in him shone.
About his chariot numberless were poured
Cherub and Seraph, Potentates and Thrones,
And Virtues, wingèd spirits, and chariots winged,
200 From the armory of God, where stand of old
Myriads between two brazen mountains lodged
Against a solemn day, harnessed at hand,
Celestial equipage; and now came forth
Spontaneous, for within them spirit lived,
205 Attendant on their Lord: Heav'n opened wide
Her ever-during gates, harmonious sound
On golden hinges moving, to let forth
The King of Glory in his powerful Word
And Spirit coming to create new worlds.
210 On Heav'nly ground they stood, and from the shore
They viewed the vast immeasurable abyss
Outrageous as a sea, dark, wasteful, wild,
Up from the bottom turned by furious winds
And surging waves, as mountains to assault
215 Heav'n's highth, and with the center mix the pole.
      " 'Silence, ye troubled waves, and thou deep, peace,'

---

188. **Good out of evil:** remembering 1.162–63 and anticipating 7.613–16 and 12.469–78.

194. **Girt:** armed.

197. **poured:** crowded together; not arranged in an orderly fashion.

200. **armory of God:** "The Lord hath opened his armory" (Jer. 50.25). See 6.321.

201. Four chariots are seen between two mountains in Zech. 6.1.

202. **Against:** in readiness for.

203–5. **now . . . Lord:** See the animated chariot of 6.845–50.

205. **opened wide:** Cp. the self-opening gate of 5.254–55, derived from Ps. 24.7.

206. **ever-during:** everlasting.

212. **Outrageous:** immense, unrestrained; **wasteful:** desolate.

Said then th' omnific Word, 'your discord end.'
   "Nor stayed, but on the wings of Cherubim
Uplifted, in paternal glory rode
220 Far into Chaos, and the world unborn;
For Chaos heard his voice: him all his train
Followed in bright procession to behold
Creation, and the wonders of his might.
Then stayed the fervid wheels, and in his hand
225 He took the golden compasses, prepared
In God's eternal store, to circumscribe
This universe, and all created things:
One foot he centered, and the other turned
Round through the vast profundity obscure,
230 And said, 'Thus far extend, thus far thy bounds,
This be thy just circumference, O world.'
Thus God the heav'n created, thus the earth,
Matter unformed and void: darkness profound
Covered th' abyss: but on the wat'ry calm
235 His brooding wings the Spirit of God outspread,
And vital virtue infused, and vital warmth
Throughout the fluid mass, but downward purged
The black tartareous cold infernal dregs
Adverse to life: then founded, then conglobed
240 Like things to like, the rest to several place
Disparted, and between spun out the air,
And Earth self-balanced on her center hung.

217. **omnific:** all-creating. We have replaced the colon at the end of this line in 1667 with a period and sacrificed an effect: as the colon would have suggested, *omnific Word* is the subject of the next syntactical unit's verbs (*stayed, uplifted, rode*).

224. **fervid:** glowing (from motion).

225. **compasses:** Wisdom declares in Prov. 8:27, "I was there: then he set a compass upon the face of the depth." Cp. Dante, *Par.* 19.40–42.

226. **circumscribe:** mark out the limits of.

231. **just:** exact.

233. **Matter unformed and void:** "The earth was without form, and void" (Gen. 1.2).

235. **brooding wings:** See 1.20–22.

236. **vital virtue:** the stuff of life.

238. **tartareous:** hellish.

239. **founded:** usually glossed as "laid the foundation," but Leonard's "attached" fits the context perfectly. The word has biblical precedent (Ps. 89.11; Prov. 3.19). **conglobed:** gathered into separate spheres.

241. **Disparted:** separated in different directions.

242. **self-balanced:** Cp. *Nat Ode* 117–24; **her center:** See 4.1000–1001; 5.578–79.

" 'Let there be light,' said God, and forthwith light
Ethereal, first of things, quintessence pure
245   Sprung from the deep, and from her native east
To journey through the airy gloom began,
Sphered in a radiant cloud, for yet the sun
Was not; she in a cloudy tabernacle
Sojourned the while. God saw the light was good;
250   And light from darkness by the hemisphere
Divided: light the day, and darkness night
He named. Thus was the first day ev'n and morn:
Nor passed uncelebrated, nor unsung
By the celestial choirs, when orient light
255   Exhaling first from darkness they beheld;
Birthday of heav'n and Earth; with joy and shout
The hollow universal orb they filled,
And touched their golden harps, and hymning praised
God and his works; Creator him they sung,
260   Both when first ev'ning was, and when first morn.
    "Again, God said, 'Let there be firmament
Amid the waters, and let it divide
The waters from the waters': and God made
The firmament, expanse of liquid, pure,
265   Transparent, elemental air, diffused

243–52. Milton's version of Gen. 1.3–5.

244. Since the sun and other heavenly bodies are not created until the fourth day, commentators had somehow to distinguish ordinary celestial light from the light of Gen. 1.3. Milton identifies the primal light with ether, a fifth element (*quintessence*) thought to be ubiquitous above the sphere of the moon.

248. **tabernacle:** dwelling. "He set a tabernacle for the sun" (Ps. 19.4).

252. **ev'n and morn:** The Hebrew day was measured from evening to evening, though the meaning of *evening* was disputed. According to Fowler, "Milton clearly followed Jerome in reckoning from sunset" (Introduction, 30). *Ev'n* here must therefore mean "sunset."

254. **orient:** bright, eastern.

255. **Exhaling:** rising as a vapor. The earth was thought to emit vaporous clouds (exhalations) that rose toward the heavens and often combusted. Milton implicitly compares the separation of light from darkness to this phenomenon.

261–74. Milton's version of Gen. 1.6–8. The waters above the firmament are identified with the space between the earth and the crystalline sphere at the rim of the universe; the lower waters are the earth's oceans.

264. **expanse:** a correct translation of the Hebrew word rendered "firmament" in the *AV*.

In circuit to the uttermost convex
Of this great round: partition firm and sure,
The waters underneath from those above
Dividing: for as Earth, so he the world

270 Built on circumfluous waters calm, in wide
Crystalline ocean, and the loud misrule
Of Chaos far removed, lest fierce extremes
Contiguous might distemper the whole frame:
And heav'n he named the firmament: so ev'n

275 And morning chorus sung the second day.
   "The Earth was formed, but in the womb as yet
Of waters, embryon immature involved,
Appeared not: over all the face of Earth
Main ocean flowed, not idle, but with warm

280 Prolific humor soft'ning all her globe,
Fermented the great mother to conceive,
Satiate with genial moisture, when God said,
'Be gathered now ye waters under heav'n
Into one place, and let dry land appear.'

285 Immediately the mountains huge appear
Emergent, and their broad bare backs upheave
Into the clouds, their tops ascend the sky:
So high as heaved the tumid hills, so low
Down sunk a hollow bottom broad and deep,

290 Capacious bed of waters: thither they
Hasted with glad precipitance, uprolled
As drops on dust conglobing from the dry;
Part rise in crystal wall, or ridge direct,
For haste; such flight the great command impressed

295 On the swift floods: as armies at the call

267. **this great round:** the universe.
269. **the world:** the universe.
273. **distemper the whole frame:** disturb the order of the elements, making the universe too hot or too cold.
277. **embryon immature involved:** wrapped (by waters) in an immature embryonic state.

281. **great mother:** Earth, who is both the mother and her child.
282. **genial:** fertilizing.
288. **tumid:** swollen.
291. **precipitance:** flowing, falling.
292. **conglobing:** assembling into spheres.
293. **crystal wall:** See the description of the parting of the Red Sea at 12.196–97. **ridge direct:** move forward like waves.

Of trumpet (for of armies thou hast heard)
Troop to their standard, so the wat'ry throng,
Wave rolling after wave, where way they found,
If steep, with torrent rapture, if through plain,
300   Soft-ebbing; nor withstood them rock or hill,
But they, or under ground, or circuit wide
With serpent error wand'ring, found their way,
And on the washy ooze deep channels wore;
Easy, ere God had bid the ground be dry,
305   All but within those banks, where rivers now
Stream, and perpetual draw their humid train.
The dry land, earth, and the great receptacle
Of congregated waters he called seas:
And saw that it was good, and said, 'Let th' earth
310   Put forth the verdant grass, herb yielding seed,
And fruit tree yielding fruit after her kind;
Whose seed is in herself upon the earth.'
He scarce had said, when the bare earth, till then
Desert and bare, unsightly, unadorned,
315   Brought forth the tender grass, whose verdure clad
Her universal face with pleasant green,
Then herbs of every leaf, that sudden flow'red
Op'ning their various colors, and made gay
Her bosom smelling sweet: and these scarce blown,
320   Forth flourished thick the clust'ring vine, forth crept
The swelling gourd, up stood the corny reed

299. **with torrent rapture:** with torrential force, with rapturous obedience.

302. **serpent error wand'ring:** a crucial text for critics who argue for the presence of unfallen and fallen languages in the poem, since all three words have a sinful signification, but also an "innocent" one: *serpent* could mean "serpentine"; *error* mean "winding course"; and *wand'ring* mean "moving now this way, now that way." See Ricks 1963, 110; Fish 1967, 130–41.

308. **congregated waters:** For Gen. 1.10 the Vulgate reads *congregationesque aquarum*.

309–33. Milton's version of Gen. 1.11–13.

313–19. **the bare earth . . . sweet:** Here, as throughout the account of Creation, Milton describes the shaping activity of *logoi spermatikoi* (seminal seeds) embedded in matter. Augustine had adapted from Stoic cosmology the notion of these seeds or *rationes seminales* informed with the Creator's ideas of all things (*De Trinitate* 3.8.3). The Son speaks, the *logoi spermatikoi* obediently unfold. For more on this tradition, see Curry 1937, 29–49.

321. **swelling:** Both 1667 and 1674 read "smelling."

Embattled in her field: add the humble shrub,
And bush with frizzled hair implicit: last
Rose as in dance the stately trees, and spread
325 Their branches hung with copious fruit; or gemmed
Their blossoms: with high woods the hills were crowned,
With tufts the valleys and each fountain side,
With borders long the rivers. That Earth now
Seemed like to Heav'n, a seat where gods might dwell,
330 Or wander with delight, and love to haunt
Her sacred shades: though God had yet not rained
Upon the earth, and man to till the ground
None was, but from the earth a dewy mist
Went up and watered all the ground, and each
335 Plant of the field, which ere it was in the earth
God made, and every herb, before it grew
On the green stem; God saw that it was good:
So ev'n and morn recorded the third day.
      "Again th' Almighty spake: 'Let there be lights
340 High in th' expanse of heaven to divide
The day from night; and let them be for signs,
For seasons, and for days, and circling years,
And let them be for lights as I ordain
Their office in the firmament of heav'n
345 To give light on the Earth'; and it was so.
And God made two great lights, great for their use
To man, the greater to have rule by day,
The less by night altern: and made the stars,
And set them in the firmament of heav'n
350 To illuminate the Earth, and rule the day
In their vicissitude, and rule the night,
And light from darkness to divide. God saw,
Surveying his great work, that it was good:
For of celestial bodies first the sun

---

322. **Embattled:** See the cornlike spears of
4.980–82; **add:** moreover.
323. **hair:** leaves and branches; **implicit:** en-
tangled.
325. **gemmed:** budded (from Lat. *gemmare*).

332. **man to till the ground:** See Gen. 2.5.
338. **recorded:** bore witness to.
339–86. Milton's version of Gen. 1.14–19.
348. **altern:** by turns.
351. **vicissitude:** alternation.

355 A mighty sphere he framed, unlightsome first,
　　Though of ethereal mold: then formed the moon
　　Globose, and every magnitude of stars,
　　And sowed with stars the heav'n thick as a field:
　　Of light by far the greater part he took,
360 Transplanted from her cloudy shrine, and placed
　　In the sun's orb, made porous to receive
　　And drink the liquid light, firm to retain
　　Her gathered beams, great palace now of light.
　　Hither as to their fountain other stars
365 Repairing, in their golden urns draw light,
　　And hence the morning planet gilds her horns;
　　By tincture or reflection they augment
　　Their small peculiar, though from human sight
　　So far remote, with diminution seen.
370 First in his east the glorious lamp was seen,
　　Regent of day, and all th' horizon round
　　Invested with bright rays, jocund to run
　　His longitude through heav'n's high road: the gray
　　Dawn, and the Pleiades before him danced
375 Shedding sweet influence: less bright the moon,
　　But opposite in leveled west was set
　　His mirror, with full face borrowing her light
　　From him, for other light she needed none
　　In that aspect, and still that distance keeps
380 Till night, then in the east her turn she shines,
　　Revolved on heav'n's great axle, and her reign

356. **of ethereal mold:** made from quintessential matter (see 244n).

357. **every magnitude of stars:** stars of every degree of brightness.

366. **morning planet:** Venus or Lucifer; **her:** So 1667; 1674 has "his." Venus would fit *her*, Lucifer *his*, but *morning planet* could be either, and there is no strong reason for preferring one reading to the other.

367. **tincture or reflection:** absorbing or reflecting the sun's light.

368. **Their small peculiar:** their own small light.

372. **Invested:** clothed, arrayed; **jocund to run:** See Ps. 19.4–5.

373. **longitude:** course from east to west.

374–75. **Pleiades . . . influence:** Job 38.31: "Canst thou bind the sweet influences to the Pleiades?"

376. **leveled west:** due west (directly opposite).

377. **His mirror:** in the sense that the moon reflects the sun's light.

379. **In that aspect:** in that position (when the moon is full).

381. **axle:** axis.

With thousand lesser lights dividual holds,
With thousand thousand stars, that then appeared
Spangling the hemisphere: then first adorned
385 With their bright luminaries that set and rose,
Glad ev'ning and glad morn crowned the fourth day.
    "And God said, 'Let the waters generate
Reptile with spawn abundant, living soul:
And let fowl fly above the earth, with wings
390 Displayed on the op'n firmament of heav'n.'
And God created the great whales, and each
Soul living, each that crept, which plenteously
The waters generated by their kinds,
And every bird of wing after his kind;
395 And saw that it was good, and blessed them, saying,
'Be fruitful, multiply, and in the seas
And lakes and running streams the waters fill;
And let the fowl be multiplied on the earth.'
Forthwith the sounds and seas, each creek and bay
400 With fry innumerable swarm, and shoals
Of fish that with their fins and shining scales
Glide under the green wave, in schools that oft
Bank the mid sea: part single or with mate
Graze the seaweed their pasture, and through groves
405 Of coral stray, or sporting with quick glance
Show to the sun their waved coats dropped with gold,
Or in their pearly shells at ease, attend
Moist nutriment, or under rocks their food
In jointed armor watch: on smooth the seal,
410 And bended dolphins play: part huge of bulk
Wallowing unwieldy, enormous in their gait
Tempest the ocean: there leviathan

---

382. **dividual:** divided.
387–448. Milton's version of Gen. 1.20–23.
388. **Reptile:** creeping things, including fish.
390. **Displayed:** spread out.
393. **by their kinds:** according to their species.

403. **Bank the mid sea:** form living banks or shelves.
409. **smooth:** smooth or calm water.
410. **bended:** arching themselves.
412. **leviathan:** the whale; an animal as opposed to the satanic emblem of 1.200–208.

    Hugest of living creatures, on the deep
    Stretched like a promontory sleeps or swims,
415 And seems a moving land, and at his gills
    Draws in, and at his trunk spouts out a sea.
    Meanwhile the tepid caves, and fens and shores
    Their brood as numerous hatch, from the egg that soon
    Bursting with kindly rupture forth disclosed
420 Their callow young, but feathered soon and fledge
    They summed their pens, and soaring th' air sublime
    With clang despised the ground, under a cloud
    In prospect; there the eagle and the stork
    On cliffs and cedar tops their eyries build:
425 Part loosely wing the region, part more wise
    In common, ranged in figure wedge their way,
    Intelligent of seasons, and set forth
    Their airy caravan high over seas
    Flying, and over lands with mutual wing
430 Easing their flight; so steers the prudent crane
    Her annual voyage, borne on winds; the air
    Floats, as they pass, fanned with unnumbered plumes:
    From branch to branch the smaller birds with song
    Solaced the woods, and spread their painted wings
435 Till ev'n, nor then the solemn nightingale
    Ceased warbling, but all night tuned her soft lays:
    Others on silver lakes and rivers bathed
    Their downy breast; the swan with archèd neck

415–16. **gills . . . trunk:** perhaps a residue of the medieval correspondence between whales and elephants, though words like *gills* and *trunk* had a considerable range of reference (see Edwards 110–13).

419. **kindly:** natural.

420. **callow:** unfeathered; **fledge:** fledged.

421. **summed their pens:** gained their full complement of feathers.

422. **clang:** harsh cry; **despised:** looked down upon.

422–23. **under a cloud/In prospect:** There was such a mass of birds that the ground seemed to be under a cloud.

425. **loosely:** singly.

427. **Intelligent:** cognizant. There are no seasons until the celestial adjustments of 10.651–707. No adjustments will have to be made in the birds themselves. They are hardwired from day one with the inclination to migrate.

429–30. **Flying . . . flight:** Some migrating birds were supposed to take turns resting on one another (Svendsen 1969, 158).

432. **Floats:** undulates.

434. **Solaced:** cheered; **painted:** imitated from Vergil, *Aen.* 4.525.

Between her white wings mantling proudly, rows
440 Her state with oary feet: yet oft they quit
The dank, and rising on stiff pennons, tower
The mid-aerial sky: others on ground
Walked firm; the crested cock whose clarion sounds
The silent hours, and th' other whose gay train
445 Adorns him, colored with the florid hue
Of rainbows and starry eyes. The waters thus
With fish replenished, and the air with fowl,
Ev'ning and morn solemnized the fifth day.
    "The sixth and of creation last arose
450 With ev'ning harps and matin, when God said,
'Let th' earth bring forth soul living in her kind,
Cattle and creeping things, and beast of the earth,
Each in their kind.' The earth obeyed, and straight
Op'ning her fertile womb teemed at a birth
455 Innumerous living creatures, perfect forms,
Limbed and full-grown: out of the ground uprose
As from his lair the wild beast where he wons
In forest wild, in thicket, brake, or den;
Among the trees in pairs they rose, they walked:
460 The cattle in the fields and meadows green:
Those rare and solitary, these in flocks
Pasturing at once, and in broad herds upsprung.
The grassy clods now calved, now half appeared
The tawny lion, pawing to get free
465 His hinder parts, then springs as broke from bonds,

---

439. **mantling:** forming a mantle (by raising their wings).
440. **Her state:** her stature or rank.
441. **dank:** pool; **pennons:** pinions; **tower:** rise into.
442. **mid-aerial sky:** the midair, a cold region where clouds are found.
444. **th' other:** the other cock (i.e., the peacock).
446. **eyes:** the eye-shaped configurations on the plumage of peacocks.
450–98. Milton's version of Gen. 1.24–25.

451. **soul:** Both early editions read "foul" (fowl), which have already been created.
454. **teemed:** brought forth.
457. **wons:** dwells.
461. **rare:** here and there.
464. **lion:** the first land animal to be named, which seems to defer to the old bestiaries that accounted him "king of beasts." Milton's lion is *rampant* (rearing up), as in heraldry, but *calved* and *brinded* associate the lion with humbler beasts (Edwards 126).

And rampant shakes his brinded main; the ounce,
The libbard, and the tiger, as the mole
Rising, the crumbled earth above them threw
In hillocks; the swift stag from under ground
470 Bore up his branching head: scarce from his mold
Behemoth biggest born of earth upheaved
His vastness: fleeced the flocks and bleating rose,
As plants: ambiguous between sea and land
The river horse and scaly crocodile.
475 At once came forth whatever creeps the ground,
Insect or worm; those waved their limber fans
For wings, and smallest lineaments exact
In all the liveries decked of summer's pride
With spots of gold and purple, azure and green:
480 These as a line their long dimension drew,
Streaking the ground with sinuous trace; not all
Minims of nature; some of serpent kind
Wondrous in length and corpulence involved
Their snaky folds, and added wings. First crept
485 The parsimonious emmet, provident
Of future, in small room large heart enclosed,
Pattern of just equality perhaps
Hereafter, joined in her popular tribes
Of commonalty: swarming next appeared
490 The female bee that feeds her husband drone

471. **Behemoth:** the elephant.
474. **river horse:** translates "hippopotamus";
   scaly crocodile: In the tradition of European natural history, the crocodile was the epitome of strangeness; see Shakespeare, *ANT* 2.7.41–51. It was famous for its false tears, its cruelty, its odd relationship to a bird that supposedly gnawed its entrails. In this respect, Milton's *scaly crocodile*, "stripped of lore and lessons," provides another example of his interest in "freeing animals from their symbolic places" (Edwards 120, 127).
476. **worm:** a designation for serpents as well as insects (which *creep the ground*).

482. **Minims:** smallest creatures.
483. **involved:** coiled.
485. **parsimonious emmet:** thrifty ant.
486. **large heart:** capacious intellect.
487–89. **Pattern ... commonalty:** Ants were often praised for their prudence and democratic commonality; Aristotle had remarked that they knew no king (Svendsen 1969, 150–52).
490. **The female bee:** In Milton's day it was believed that worker bees were sterile females and drones male. Bees were traditionally monarchical (Shakespeare, *H5* 1.2.183–204), but Milton disputed that belief in *1Def.* (Yale 4:348–50).

Deliciously, and builds her waxen cells
With honey stored: the rest are numberless,
And thou their natures know'st, and gav'st them names,
Needless to thee repeated; nor unknown
495   The serpent subtlest beast of all the field,
Of huge extent sometimes, with brazen eyes
And hairy main terrific, though to thee
Not noxious, but obedient at thy call.
Now heav'n in all her glory shone, and rolled
500   Her motions, as the great First Mover's hand
First wheeled their course; Earth in her rich attire
Consummate lovely smiled; air, water, earth,
By fowl, fish, beast, was flown, was swum, was walked
Frequent; and of the sixth day yet remained;
505   There wanted yet the master work, the end
Of all yet done; a creature who not prone
And brute as other creatures, but endued
With sanctity of reason, might erect
His stature, and upright with front serene
510   Govern the rest, self-knowing, and from thence
Magnanimous to correspond with Heav'n,
But grateful to acknowledge whence his good
Descends, thither with heart and voice and eyes
Directed in devotion, to adore
515   And worship God supreme, who made him chief
Of all his works: therefore th' omnipotent

493. **gav'st them names:** See 8.342–54.
497. **hairy main:** Vergil described the serpents that strangled Laocoön as having bloodred manes (*Aen.* 2.203–7); **terrific:** terrifying.
498. **Not noxious:** not evil or harmful.
504. **Frequent:** in throngs.
505. **the end:** the completion of Creation and the being for whom all the rest had been done.
508–10. **might . . . self-knowing:** Man's uprightness was noted by Ovid, *Met.* 1.76–86, and was commonly treated by Christian

writers as a sign of moral and spiritual dignity.
509. **front:** forehead.
510. **self-knowing:** knowing himself as created in the image and likeness of God; Shakespeare's Isabella memorably declares that this knowledge is sadly curtailed among fallen men (*MM* 2.2.120–24). **from thence:** as a result of these qualities.
511. **Magnanimous:** great-souled, high-minded; **to correspond with:** to be an image of, to be in contact with.

Eternal Father (for where is not he
Present) thus to his Son audibly spake.
    " 'Let us make now man in our image, man
520 In our similitude, and let them rule
Over the fish and fowl of sea and air,
Beast of the field, and over all the earth,
And every creeping thing that creeps the ground.'
This said, he formed thee, Adam, thee O man
525 Dust of the ground, and in thy nostrils breathed
The breath of life; in his own image he
Created thee, in the image of God
Express, and thou becam'st a living soul.
Male he created thee, but thy consort
530 Female for race; then blessed mankind, and said,
'Be fruitful, multiply, and fill the Earth,
Subdue it, and throughout dominion hold
Over fish of the sea, and fowl of the air,
And every living thing that moves on the Earth.'
535 Wherever thus created, for no place
Is yet distinct by name, thence, as thou know'st
He brought thee into this delicious grove,
This garden, planted with the trees of God,
Delectable both to behold and taste;
540 And freely all their pleasant fruit for food
Gave thee, all sorts are here that all th' Earth yields,
Variety without end; but of the tree
Which tasted works knowledge of good and evil,
Thou may'st not; in the day thou eat'st, thou di'st;
545 Death is the penalty imposed, beware,
And govern well thy appetite, lest Sin
Surprise thee, and her black attendant Death.
Here finished he, and all that he had made
Viewed, and behold all was entirely good;
550 So ev'n and morn accomplished the sixth day:
Yet not till the Creator from his work

519–34. Milton's version of Gen. 1.26–31.
528. **Express:** exactly depicted.

530–34. **blessed ... Earth:** See Gen. 1.28.
537. **delicious:** delightful.

Desisting, though unwearied, up returned
Up to the Heav'n of Heav'ns his high abode,
Thence to behold this new created world
555 Th' addition of his empire, how it showed
In prospect from his throne, how good, how fair,
Answering his great idea. Up he rode
Followed with acclamation and the sound
Symphonious of ten thousand harps that tuned
560 Angelic harmonies: the Earth, the air
Resounded, (thou remember'st, for thou heard'st)
The heav'ns and all the constellations rung,
The planets in their stations list'ning stood,
While the bright pomp ascended jubilant.
565 'Open, ye everlasting gates,' they sung,
'Open, ye Heav'ns, your living doors; let in
The great Creator from his work returned
Magnificent, his six days' work, a world;
Open, and henceforth oft; for God will deign
570 To visit oft the dwellings of just men
Delighted, and with frequent intercourse
Thither will send his wingèd messengers
On errands of supernal grace.' So sung
The glorious train ascending: he through Heav'n,
575 That opened wide her blazing portals, led
To God's eternal house direct the way,
A broad and ample road, whose dust is gold
And pavement stars, as stars to thee appear,
Seen in the galaxy, that Milky Way

---

552. **unwearied:** The Son did not "rest" on the seventh day because his strength was in any sense depleted.

557. **idea:** the only occurrence of the word *idea* in Milton's English poetry. It bears the Platonic-Augustinian sense of "ideal form, pattern." Thus Simon Goulart: "The idea, the form and pattern of them [all things] was in the science and intelligence of God . . . as Saint Augustine and others have expounded" (1621, 8–9).

559. **Symphonius:** harmonious; **tuned:** played.

564. **pomp:** procession; **jubilant:** shouting with joy.

565–67. Based on Ps. 23.7.

569–73. **for . . . grace:** *CD* 1.9 discusses the earthly missions of angels.

579. **Milky Way:** The road to Heaven is like the Milky Way but not the Milky Way itself, as it is in Ovid, *Met.* 1.168–71.

580 Which nightly as a circling zone thou seest
    Powdered with stars. And now on Earth the seventh
    Ev'ning arose in Eden, for the sun
    Was set, and twilight from the east came on,
    Forerunning night; when at the holy mount
585 Of Heav'n's high-seated top, th' imperial throne
    Of Godhead, fixed forever firm and sure,
    The Filial Power arrived, and sat him down
    With his great Father, for he also went
    Invisible, yet stayed (such privilege
590 Hath omnipresence) and the work ordained,
    Author and end of all things, and from work
    Now resting, blessed and hallowed the sev'nth day,
    As resting on that day from all his work,
    But not in silence holy kept; the harp
595 Had work and rested not, the solemn pipe,
    And dulcimer, all organs of sweet stop,
    All sounds on fret by string or golden wire
    Tempered soft tunings, intermixed with voice
    Choral or unison: of incense clouds
600 Fuming from golden censers hid the mount.
    Creation and the six days' acts they sung,
    'Great are thy works, Jehovah, infinite
    Thy power; what thought can measure thee or tongue
    Relate thee; greater now in thy return
605 Than from the giant angels; thee that day
    Thy thunders magnified; but to create

588–90. The editions of 1667 and 1674 punctuate confusingly: "With his great Father (for he also went/Invisible, yet stayed (such privilege/Hath omnipresence)."

594. **not in silence holy kept:** The prominence of music at the first Sabbath indicates Milton's disagreement with the stricter versions of Puritan Sabbatarianism (Berry 61–101).

596. **dulcimer:** a stringed instrument played with small hammers; **stop:** the register of an organ.

597. **fret:** a ridge on the fingerboard of a stringed instrument.

599. **Choral or unison:** in parts or in unison.

605. **giant angels:** referring to the defeat of the rebel angels but alluding to Jove's defeat of the giants. Cp. 1.50–52, 199–200, 230–37; 6.643–66.

606–7. **but . . . destroy:** Satan seeks glory from the lesser course of destroying the work of Creation (9.129–38).

Is greater than created to destroy.
Who can impair thee, mighty king, or bound
Thy empire? Easily the proud attempt
610   Of spirits apostate and their counsels vain
Thou hast repelled, while impiously they thought
Thee to diminish, and from thee withdraw
The number of thy worshippers. Who seeks
To lessen thee, against his purpose serves
615   To manifest the more thy might: his evil
Thou usest, and from thence creat'st more good.
Witness this new-made world, another Heav'n
From Heaven gate not far, founded in view
On the clear hyaline, the glassy sea;
620   Of amplitude almost immense, with stars
Numerous, and every star perhaps a world
Of destined habitation; but thou know'st
Their seasons: among these the seat of men,
Earth with her nether ocean circumfused,
625   Their pleasant dwelling place. Thrice happy men,
And sons of men, whom God hath thus advanced,
Created in his image, there to dwell
And worship him, and in reward to rule
Over his works, on earth, in sea, or air,
630   And multiply a race of worshippers
Holy and just: thrice happy if they know
Their happiness, and persevere upright.'
        "So sung they, and the empyrean rung,

---

619. **hyaline:** the transliterated Greek word for the "sea of glass" before God's throne in Rev. 4.6.

621–22. **every . . . habitation:** On the possibility of other worlds being inhabited, see 3.566–71, 8.152–58. On the possibility that man might colonize other worlds, see 3.667–70 and 5.500.

622–23. **thou know'st/Their seasons:** "It is not for you to know the times or the seasons, which the Father hath put in his own power" (Acts 1.7).

624. **nether ocean:** the earth's seas, the waters below the firmament.

628–29. **to rule/Over his works:** "Thou madest him to have dominion over the works of thy hands" (Ps. 8.6).

631–32. **thrice . . . happiness:** an adaptation of Vergil's *Georg.* 2.458, and one of a number of statements in the poem about the close relationship between Adam and Eve's happiness and their knowledge of that happiness. See 4.774–75 especially.

632. **persevere:** continue in a state of grace.

With hallelujahs: thus was Sabbath kept.
635 And thy request think now fulfilled, that asked
How first this world and face of things began,
And what before thy memory was done
From the beginning, that posterity
Informed by thee might know; if else thou seek'st
640 Aught, not surpassing human measure, say."

636. **face of things:** the visible world sur-
rounding us.

BOOK VIII

THE ARGUMENT

Adam inquires concerning celestial motions, is doubtfully answered, and exhorted to search rather things more worthy of knowledge. Adam assents, and still desirous to detain Raphael, relates to him what he remembered since his own creation, his placing in Paradise, his talk with God concerning solitude and fit society, his first meeting and nuptials with Eve. His discourse with the angel thereupon, who after admonitions repeated departs.

The angel ended, and in Adam's ear
So charming left his voice, that he a while
Thought him still speaking, still stood fixed to hear;
Then as new waked thus gratefully replied.
5   "What thanks sufficient, or what recompense
Equal have I to render thee, divine
Historian, who thus largely hast allayed
The thirst I had of knowledge, and vouchsafed
This friendly condescension to relate
10   Things else by me unsearchable, now heard
With wonder, but delight, and, as is due,
With glory attributed to the high
Creator; something yet of doubt remains,
Which only thy solution can resolve.

1–4. The first three and half lines were added to the second edition of 1674. In the long Book 7 of 1667, the pause after Raphael's narration was marked by a sin-

gle line: "To whom thus Adam gratefully replied."
9. **condescension:** courteous disregard of rank.

15   When I behold this goodly frame, this world
       Of heav'n and Earth consisting, and compute
       Their magnitudes, this Earth a spot, a grain,
       An atom, with the firmament compared
       And all her numbered stars, that seem to roll
20   Spaces incomprehensible (for such
       Their distance argues and their swift return
       Diurnal) merely to officiate light
       Round this opacous Earth, this punctual spot,
       One day and night; in all their vast survey
25   Useless besides, reasoning I oft admire,
       How nature wise and frugal could commit
       Such disproportions, with superfluous hand
       So many nobler bodies to create,
       Greater so manifold to this one use,
30   For aught appears, and on their orbs impose
       Such restless revolution day by day
       Repeated, while the sedentary Earth,
       That better might with far less compass move,
       Served by more noble than herself, attains
35   Her end without least motion, and receives,
       As tribute such a sumless journey brought
       Of incorporeal speed, her warmth and light;
       Speed, to describe whose swiftness number fails."
         So spake our sire, and by his count'nance seemed
40   Ent'ring on studious thoughts abstruse, which Eve

15–38. Eve was the first to wonder about the curious abundance of the nighttime sky (4.657–58). Adam tried to answer her query (4.660–88), as did Satan in the dream he created for Eve (5.41–47). Adam now broadens her question to include other celestial instances of apparent wastefulness and favoritism toward earth. Cp. *Prolusion 7* (*MLM* 795–96).

15. **this goodly frame:** a phrase used by Hamlet (2.2.316).

17–18. **a spot, a grain,/An atom:** The tininess of the earth was apparent to ancient astronomers.

19. **numbered:** numerous, as in 7.621.

22. **officiate:** supply, minister.

23. **opacous:** dark; **punctual spot:** spot the size of a point (Lat. *punctum*) in relation to the spaces of the firmament, but also in the sense of "subject to exact timing."

25. **admire:** wonder, but with a sense of perplexity (the *something yet of doubt* in l. 13).

30. **For aught appears:** for all that can be seen.

32. **sedentary:** motionless.

36. **sumless:** immeasurable (see l. 38).

Perceiving where she sat retired in sight,
With lowliness majestic from her seat,
And grace that won who saw to wish her stay,
Rose, and went forth among her fruits and flow'rs,
45   To visit how they prospered, bud and bloom,
Her nursery; they at her coming sprung
And touched by her fair tendance gladlier grew.
Yet went she not, as not with such discourse
Delighted, or not capable her ear
50   Of what was high: such pleasure she reserved,
Adam relating, she sole auditress;
Her husband the relater she preferred
Before the angel, and of him to ask
Chose rather; he, she knew, would intermix
55   Grateful digressions, and solve high dispute
With conjugal caresses; from his lip
Not words alone pleased her. O when meet now
Such pairs, in love and mutual honor joined?
With goddesslike demeanor forth she went;
60   Not unattended, for on her as queen
A pomp of winning Graces waited still,
And from about her shot darts of desire
Into all eyes to wish her still in sight.
And Raphael now to Adam's doubt proposed
65   Benevolent and facile thus replied.
     "To ask or search I blame thee not, for heav'n
Is as the book of God before thee set,
Wherein to read his wondrous works, and learn
His seasons, hours, or days, or months, or years:
70   This to attain, whether heav'n move or Earth,
Imports not, if thou reckon right; the rest
From man or angel the great Architect

62. **darts of desire:** not sexual desire, as in love poetry, but desire that she remain *still in sight* (l. 63).

65. **facile:** affable. Raphael does not deem Adam's doubt about the wisdom of the celestial design malignant or accusatory.

67. **Is as the book of God:** Cp. 3.47.

70. **whether heav'n move or Earth:** a difference between the Ptolemaic and Copernican systems; but there were many compromise positions between the two (see G. McColley 217–44; Babb 78–94).

Did wisely to conceal, and not divulge
His secrets to be scanned by them who ought
75   Rather admire; or if they list to try
Conjecture, he his fabric of the heav'ns
Hath left to their disputes, perhaps to move
His laughter at their quaint opinions wide
Hereafter, when they come to model heav'n
80   And calculate the stars, how they will wield
The mighty frame, how build, unbuild, contrive
To save appearances, how gird the sphere
With centric and eccentric scribbled o'er,
Cycle and epicycle, orb in orb:
85   Already by thy reasoning this I guess,
Who art to lead thy offspring, and supposest
That bodies bright and greater should not serve
The less not bright, nor heav'n such journeys run,
Earth sitting still, when she alone receives
90   The benefit: consider first, that great

75. **admire:** behold with wonder.

78. **His laughter:** Psalm 2.4: "He that sitteth in the heavens shall laugh." A. O. Lovejoy considered Milton's God a "singularly detestable being" for devising cosmic riddles so that he could laugh at the false solutions (1962, 140). However, God will laugh not primarily at the falseness of astronomical theories but at the way astronomers play God in modeling the heavens. **quaint:** ingenious; **wide:** wide of the truth.

80. **calculate:** predict the motions of; **wield:** direct, guide.

82. **save appearances:** a scholastic term for fitting hypothesis to observation, a process particularly evident in the history of astronomy, where theories were modified repeatedly to account for local observations inconsistent with general assumptions.

83. **centric and eccentric:** spheres centered on, and not centered on, the earth. Kepler's teacher, Tycho Brahe, proposed that the sun was the center of the planetary

orbits, while the fixed stars were centered on the earth. **scribbled o'er:** Raphael is making fun of complex astrological diagrams; cp. Donne, "An Anatomy of the World": "Man hath weaved out a net, and this net thrown / Upon the heavens, and now they are his own" (279–80).

84. In the Ptolemaic system planets traverse a circular *orb,* or orbit, but turn smaller circles (*epicycles*) within this larger cycle. Meant to account for observed differences of orbital velocity among the planets, the theory of epicycles is a notable example of "saving the appearances" (see 82n).

85–90. **Already . . . benefit:** Raphael maintains that he has been able to guess from Adam's thinking some of the forthcoming perplexity in the astronomy to be developed by his offspring. In particular, Adam mistakes brightness for excellence and on that ground supposes that the *opacous* earth (l. 23) should not be served by more resplendent heavenly bodies, such as the sun.

Or bright infers not excellence: the Earth
Though, in comparison of heav'n, so small,
Nor glistering, may of solid good contain
More plenty than the sun that barren shines
95   Whose virtue on itself works no effect,
But in the fruitful Earth; there first received
His beams, unactive else, their vigor find.
Yet not to Earth are those bright luminaries
Officious, but to thee Earth's habitant.
100   And for the heav'n's wide circuit, let it speak
The Maker's high magnificence, who built
So spacious, and his line stretched out so far;
That man may know he dwells not in his own;
An edifice too large for him to fill,
105   Lodged in a small partition, and the rest
Ordained for uses to his Lord best known.
The swiftness of those circles attribute,
Though numberless, to his omnipotence,
That to corporeal substances could add
110   Speed almost spiritual; me thou think'st not slow,
Who since the morning hour set out from Heav'n
Where God resides, and ere mid-day arrived
In Eden, distance inexpressible
By numbers that have name. But this I urge,
115   Admitting motion in the heav'ns, to show
Invalid that which thee to doubt it moved;
Not that I so affirm, though so it seem
To thee who hast thy dwelling here on Earth.
God to remove his ways from human sense,
120   Placed heav'n from Earth so far, that earthly sight,
If it presume, might err in things too high,
And no advantage gain. What if the sun

---

99. **Officious:** attentive, dutiful.

109–10. **That . . . spiritual:** The corporeal planets are almost as swift as spiritual angels, which is a sign of God's omnipotence in molding matter.

117. **Not that I so affirm:** Raphael makes it clear that he is not delivering true, once-and-for-all knowledge of the heavens but confounding Adam's assumption that he had, or could in principle attain, such knowledge.

Be center to the world, and other stars
By his attractive virtue and their own
125   Incited, dance about him various rounds?
Their wand'ring course now high, now low, then hid,
Progressive, retrograde, or standing still,
In six thou seest, and what if sev'nth to these
The planet Earth, so steadfast though she seem,
130   Insensibly three different motions move?
Which else to several spheres thou must ascribe,
Moved contrary with thwart obliquities,
Or save the sun his labor, and that swift
Nocturnal and diurnal rhomb supposed,
135   Invisible else above all stars, the wheel
Of day and night; which needs not thy belief,
If Earth industrious of herself fetch day
Traveling east, and with her part averse
From the sun's beam meet night, her other part
140   Still luminous by his ray. What if that light
Sent from her through the wide transpicuous air,
To the terrestrial moon be as a star
Enlight'ning her by day, as she by night
This Earth? Reciprocal, if land be there,
145   Fields and inhabitants: her spots thou seest
As clouds, and clouds may rain, and rain produce

---

124. **attractive virtue:** Kepler supposed that the planets were held in their orbits by the sun's magnetism.

128. The *six* are the moon, Mercury, Venus, Mars, Jupiter, and Saturn.

129. **The planet Earth:** The most striking result of the Copernican theory was the idea that the earth was simply another planet (the seventh).

130. **three different motions:** "The three different motions, which the Copernicans attribute to the earth, are the *diural* round her own axis, the *annual* round the sun, and the *motion of libration* as it is called, whereby the earth so proceeds in her orbit, as that her axis is constantly paral-

lel to the axis of the world [universe]" (Newton).

131–32. "Even if you do not posit a moving earth, you will have to posit spheres moving in contrary and awkward directions."

133–40. **Or save ... ray:** Copernicus was able to make the sun responsible for astronomical effects earlier attributed to the *swift . . . rhomb,* or *primum mobile,* the great wheel turning rapidly beyond the fixed stars and imparting orbital motions to the planets. But this earlier picture of things *needs not thy belief,* need not be believed by Adam, if he assumes that the earth of its own power revolves on a daily basis, thus creating the alternation of day and night.

145. **inhabitants:** Cp. 3.460–62.

Fruits in her softened soil, for some to eat
Allotted there; and other suns perhaps
With their attendant moons thou wilt descry
150 Communicating male and female light,
Which two great sexes animate the world,
Stored in each orb perhaps with some that live.
For such vast room in nature unpossessed
By living soul, desert and desolate,
155 Only to shine, yet scarce to contribute
Each orb a glimpse of light, conveyed so far
Down to this habitable, which returns
Light back to them, is obvious to dispute.
But whether thus these things, or whether not,
160 Whether the sun predominant in heav'n
Rise on the Earth, or Earth rise on the sun,
He from the east his flaming road begin,
Or she from west her silent course advance
With inoffensive pace that spinning sleeps
165 On her soft axle, while she paces ev'n,
And bears thee soft with the smooth air along,
Solicit not thy thoughts with matters hid,
Leave them to God above, him serve and fear;
Of other creatures, as him pleases best,
170 Wherever placed, let him dispose: joy thou
In what he gives to thee, this Paradise
And thy fair Eve; heav'n is for thee too high
To know what passes there; be lowly wise:
Think only what concerns thee and thy being;

148–49. **other suns . . . moons:** Advocates of an infinite universe, such as Giordano Bruno and Henry More, believed that the so-called fixed stars were suns with their own planetary systems; Galileo observed the *attendant moons* of Jupiter and Saturn. Cp. 1.650, 3.566–71, 7.621–22; also Spenser, *FQ* 2.1.3.

150. **male and female light:** original and reflected light.

151. No one has found a convincing source for this striking line, with its absolute confidence in the universality of gender and the conjunction of gender and life.

162. **He:** the sun.

163–66. These fine lines are sufficient to dispel the old idea that Milton found the Ptolemaic system inherently more poetic than the Copernican one.

163. **she:** the earth.

167. **Solicit not:** trouble not.

175 Dream not of other worlds, what creatures there
Live, in what state, condition or degree,
Contented that thus far hath been revealed
Not of Earth only but of highest Heav'n."
        To whom thus Adam cleared of doubt, replied.
180 "How fully hast thou satisfied me, pure
Intelligence of Heav'n, angel serene,
And freed from intricacies, taught to live,
The easiest way, nor with perplexing thoughts
To interrupt the sweet of life, from which
185 God hath bid dwell far off all anxious cares,
And not molest us, unless we ourselves
Seek them with wand'ring thoughts, and notions vain.
But apt the mind or fancy is to rove
Unchecked, and of her roving is no end;
190 Till warned, or by experience taught, she learn,
That not to know at large of things remote
From use, obscure and subtle, but to know
That which before us lies in daily life,
Is the prime wisdom; what is more, is fume,
195 Or emptiness, or fond impertinence,
And renders us in things that most concern
Unpracticed, unprepared, and still to seek.
Therefore from this high pitch let us descend
A lower flight, and speak of things at hand
200 Useful, whence haply mention may arise
Of something not unseasonable to ask
By sufferance, and thy wonted favor deigned.
Thee I have heard relating what was done

175. **what creatures:** That other planets might harbor life was a common speculation in Milton's day.

183. **easiest way:** Milton entitled a prose work *The Ready and Easy Way* (1660). *Way,* which here means "course of action" (*OED* 12), is a key word in the poem. *Paradise Lost* intends to "justify the ways of God" (1.26) and ends with "way" (12.649). It should be borne in mind that in Acts 9.2, 19.9, 24.14, 24.22, et cetera, *way* signifies Christianity.

194. **fume:** literally "vapor" or "smoke," figuratively "something unsubstantial, transient, imaginary"; see *Apology* (Yale 1:193): "the pride of a metaphysical fume."

195. **fond:** foolish.

197. **still to seek:** without a clue.

202. **sufferance:** permission; **wonted:** customary.

Ere my remembrance: now hear me relate
205 My story, which perhaps thou hast not heard;
And day is yet not spent; till then thou seest
How subtly to detain thee I devise,
Inviting thee to hear while I relate,
Fond, were it not in hope of thy reply:
210 For while I sit with thee, I seem in Heav'n,
And sweeter thy discourse is to my ear
Than fruits of palm-tree pleasantest to thirst
And hunger both, from labor, at the hour
Of sweet repast; they satiate, and soon fill,
215 Though pleasant, but thy words with grace divine
Imbued, bring to their sweetness no satiety."
　　　To whom thus Raphael answered Heav'nly meek.
"Nor are thy lips ungraceful, sire of men,
Nor tongue ineloquent; for God on thee
220 Abundantly his gifts hath also poured
Inward and outward both, his image fair:
Speaking or mute all comeliness and grace
Attends thee, and each word, each motion forms.
Nor less think we in Heav'n of thee on Earth
225 Than of our fellow servant, and inquire
Gladly into the ways of God with man:
For God we see hath honored thee, and set
On man his equal love: say therefore on;
For I that day was absent, as befell,
230 Bound on a voyage uncouth and obscure,
Far on excursion toward the gates of Hell;
Squared in full legion (such command we had)
To see that none thence issued forth a spy,
Or enemy, while God was in his work,
235 Lest he incensed at such eruption bold,
Destruction with creation might have mixed.

209. **Fond:** foolish.

225. **fellow servant:** As the angel told a worshipful St. John, "I am thy fellow servant" (Rev. 22.9).

226. **ways of God with man:** See 183n, 1.26n.

229. **that day:** the sixth day of Creation? Presumably Raphael witnessed the other days, whose events he has just narrated.

230. **uncouth:** strange, desolate.

Not that they durst without his leave attempt,
But us he sends upon his high behests
For state, as sov'reign King, and to inure
240   Our prompt obedience. Fast we found, fast shut
The dismal gates, and barricadoed strong;
But long ere our approaching heard within
Noise, other than the sound of dance or song,
Torment, and loud lament, and furious rage.
245   Glad we returned up to the coasts of light
Ere Sabbath evening: so we had in charge.
But thy relation now; for I attend,
Pleased with thy words no less than thou with mine."
     So spake the godlike power, and thus our sire.
250   "For man to tell how human life began
Is hard; for who himself beginning knew?
Desire with thee still longer to converse
Induced me. As new waked from soundest sleep
Soft on the flow'ry herb I found me laid
255   In balmy sweat, which with his beams the sun
Soon dried, and on the reeking moisture fed.
Straight toward heav'n my wond'ring eyes I turned,
And gazed a while the ample sky, till raised
By quick instinctive motion up I sprung,
260   As thitherward endeavoring, and upright
Stood on my feet; about me round I saw
Hill, dale, and shady woods, and sunny plains,
And liquid lapse of murmuring streams; by these,

---

239. **state:** ceremony.

243–44. Cp. Aeneas hearing the groans and cries behind the gate to Tartarus (Vergil, *Aen.* 6.557–59), Astolfo listening at the gates of Hell (Ariosto, *OF* 34.4), and Dante greeted by wailings and lamentations upon entering Hell (*Inf.* 3.22–29).

246. **Sabbath evening:** the beginning of the seventh day of Creation. Milton here adopts the Hebrew custom of measuring the day from sunset to sunset.

255. **balmy sweat:** In one of the first post-modern essays on *Paradise Lost,* Hartman declares that balmy sweat mingles "the balm of fruitfulness and the sweat of the curse, the labor to come and the regeneration to come from that" (147). But Edwards suggests that this reading spoils Paradise with the consequences of the Fall: "Adam's balmy sweat is, simply, sweet-scented sweat" (197).

256. **reeking:** steaming.

263. **lapse:** flow.

Creatures that lived, and moved, and walked, or flew,
265 Birds on the branches warbling; all things smiled,
With fragrance and with joy my heart o'erflowed.
Myself I then perused, and limb by limb
Surveyed, and sometimes went, and sometimes ran
With supple joints, as lively vigor led:
270 But who I was, or where, or from what cause,
Knew not; to speak I tried, and forthwith spake,
My tongue obeyed and readily could name
Whate'er I saw. 'Thou sun,' said I, 'fair light,
And thou enlightened earth, so fresh and gay,
275 Ye hills and dales, ye rivers, woods, and plains,
And ye that live and move, fair creatures, tell,
Tell, if ye saw, how came I thus, how here?
Not of myself; by some great Maker then,
In goodness and in power pre-eminent;
280 Tell me, how may I know him, how adore,
From whom I have that thus I move and live,
And feel that I am happier than I know.'
While thus I called, and strayed I knew not whither,
From where I first drew air, and first beheld
285 This happy light, when answer none returned,
On a green shady bank profuse of flow'rs
Pensive I sat me down; there gentle sleep
First found me, and with soft oppression seized
My drowsèd sense, untroubled, though I thought
290 I then was passing to my former state
Insensible, and forthwith to dissolve:
When suddenly stood at my head a dream,
Whose inward apparition gently moved

273–74. **Thou sun . . . earth:** In his very first
words, Adam articulates in nascent form
the ideas that lead to his puzzlement
about the heavens (see 85–90n).

281. Acts 17.28: "For in him we live, and move,
and have our being."

282. **happier than I know:** Cp. 4.774–75.

287. **Pensive:** The combination of happiness
and pensiveness in this passage suggests

that Milton, returning imaginatively to
the themes of his youthful poetry, is
blending elements of *L'Allegro* and *Il
Penseroso*. The pensive man also goes to
sleep during the daytime, and dreams
(142–50), and the happy man speaks of
"Such sights as youthful poets dream/On
summer eves by haunted stream" (129–30).

288. **oppression:** weighing down.

My fancy to believe I yet had being,
295 And lived: one came, methought, of shape divine,
And said, 'Thy mansion wants thee, Adam, rise,
First man, of men innumerable ordained
First father, called by thee I come thy guide
To the garden of bliss, thy seat prepared.'
300 So saying, by the hand he took me raised,
And over fields and waters, as in air
Smooth sliding without step, last led me up
A woody mountain, whose high top was plain,
A circuit wide, enclosed, with goodliest trees
305 Planted, with walks, and bowers, that what I saw
Of Earth before scarce pleasant seemed. Each tree
Loaden with fairest fruit, that hung to the eye
Tempting, stirred in me sudden appetite
To pluck and eat; whereat I waked, and found
310 Before mine eyes all real, as the dream
Had lively shadowed: here had new begun
My wand'ring, had not he who was my guide
Up hither, from among the trees appeared
Presence divine. Rejoicing, but with awe
315 In adoration at his feet I fell
Submiss: he reared me, and 'Whom thou sought'st I am,'
Said mildly, 'Author of all this thou seest
Above, or round about thee or beneath.
This Paradise I give thee, count it thine
320 To till and keep, and of the fruit to eat:
Of every tree that in the garden grows
Eat freely with glad heart; fear here no dearth:
But of the tree whose operation brings
Knowledge of good and ill, which I have set
325 The pledge of thy obedience and thy faith,
Amid the garden by the Tree of Life,
Remember what I warn thee, shun to taste,
And shun the bitter consequence: for know,

302. **Smooth . . . led:** The *l-* sounds slide
smoothly through the *s-* sounds.

The day thou eat'st thereof, my sole command
330   Transgressed, inevitably thou shalt die;
      From that day mortal, and this happy state
      Shalt lose, expelled from hence into a world
      Of woe and sorrow.' Sternly he pronounced
      The rigid interdiction, which resounds
335   Yet dreadful in mine ear, though in my choice
      Not to incur; but soon his clear aspect
      Returned and gracious purpose thus renewed.
      'Not only these fair bounds, but all the Earth
      To thee and to thy race I give; as lords
340   Possess it, and all things that therein live,
      Or live in sea, or air, beast, fish, and fowl.
      In sign whereof each bird and beast behold
      After their kinds; I bring them to receive
      From thee their names, and pay thee fealty
345   With low subjection; understand the same
      Of fish within their wat'ry residence,
      Not hither summoned, since they cannot change
      Their element to draw the thinner air.'
      As thus he spake, each bird and beast behold
350   Approaching two and two, these cow'ring low
      With blandishment, each bird stooped on his wing.
      I named them, as they passed, and understood
      Their nature, with such knowledge God endued
      My sudden apprehension: but in these
355   I found not what methought I wanted still;
      And to the Heav'nly vision thus presumed.
          " 'O by what name, for thou above all these,
      Above mankind, or aught than mankind higher,
      Surpassest far my naming, how may I
360   Adore thee, Author of this universe,
      And all this good to man, for whose well-being

---

331. **From that day mortal:** the usual inter-
    pretation of Gen. 2.17: "For in the day you
    eat of it you shall die."
350. **two and two:** There is no indication in
    Gen. 2.19–20 that the animals parade by

Adam in pairs, as they will again when
entering Noah's ark "two and two" (Gen.
7.9). Milton's Adam seems intended to
think about companionship, which he
does (Gallagher 1990, 36).

So amply, and with hands so liberal
Thou hast provided all things: but with me
I see not who partakes. In solitude
365 What happiness, who can enjoy alone,
Or all enjoying, what contentment find?'
Thus I presumptuous; and the vision bright,
As with a smile more brightened, thus replied.
 " 'What call'st thou solitude, is not the Earth
370 With various living creatures, and the air
Replenished, and all these at thy command
To come and play before thee? Know'st thou not
Their language and their ways? They also know,
And reason not contemptibly; with these
375 Find pastime, and bear rule; thy realm is large.'
So spake the Universal Lord, and seemed
So ordering. I with leave of speech implored,
And humble deprecation thus replied.
 " 'Let not my words offend thee, Heav'nly power,
380 My Maker, be propitious while I speak.
Hast thou not made me here thy substitute,
And these inferior far beneath me set?
Among unequals what society
Can sort, what harmony or true delight?
385 Which must be mutual, in proportion due
Giv'n and received; but in disparity
The one intense, the other still remiss
Cannot well suit with either, but soon prove
Tedious alike: of fellowship I speak
390 Such as I seek, fit to participate
All rational delight, wherein the brute
Cannot be human consort; they rejoice
Each with their kind, lion with lioness;

---

373. **Their language:** Since animals do not speak (9.557), Leonard must be right in asserting that *language* here means "inarticulate sounds used by the lower animals" (*OED* 1c).

379. See Abraham's similar preface when negotiating with God (Gen. 18.30).
383. **unequals:** Adam is here referring to the gap between himself and animals.
384. **sort:** fit.
387. **intense:** taut; **remiss:** slack.

So fitly them in pairs thou hast combined;
395 Much less can bird with beast, or fish with fowl
So well converse, nor with the ox the ape;
Worse then can man with beast, and least of all.'
    "Whereto th' Almighty answered, not displeased.
'A nice and subtle happiness I see
400 Thou to thyself proposest, in the choice
Of thy associates, Adam, and wilt taste
No pleasure, though in pleasure, solitary.
What think'st thou then of me, and this my state,
Seem I to thee sufficiently possessed
405 Of happiness, or not? Who am alone
From all eternity, for none I know
Second to me or like, equal much less.
How have I then with whom to hold converse
Save with the creatures which I made, and those
410 To me inferior, infinite descents
Beneath what other creatures are to thee?'
    "He ceased, I lowly answered. 'To attain
The highth and depth of thy eternal ways
All human thoughts come short, supreme of things;
415 Thou in thyself art perfect, and in thee
Is no deficience found; not so is man,
But in degree, the cause of his desire
By conversation with his like to help,
Or solace his defects. No need that thou
420 Shouldst propagate, already infinite,
And through all numbers absolute, though one;

---

399. **nice:** refined, difficult to please (*OED* 7, the "good sense").

405–7. **Who . . . less:** These lines are central to a debate over the identity of the divine presence speaking to Adam. Since Milton's Son is not coeternal with the Father, the claim to be *alone/From all eternity* suggests that the Father speaks.

417. **But in degree:** Man is perfect only in his station (which is of a kind to require a partner).

419. **solace:** alleviate.

419–21. **No need . . . one:** Adam, who began his religious life with the intuition of a Maker (ll. 278–79), here takes a leap forward in sophistication. *Through all numbers absolute* Englishes the Latin *omnibus numeris absolutus*, meaning "complete in every part," as in a well-written book (Pliny the Younger, *Letters* 9.38). Yet God is *infinite*—hence the completeness of his parts must be an innate idea, not an

But man by number is to manifest
His single imperfection, and beget
Like of his like, his image multiplied,
425 In unity defective, which requires
Collateral love, and dearest amity.
Thou in thy secrecy although alone,
Best with thyself accompanied, seek'st not
Social communication, yet so pleased,
430 Canst raise thy creature to what highth thou wilt
Of union or communion, deified;
I by conversing cannot these erect
From prone, nor in their ways complacence find.'
Thus I emboldened spake, and freedom used
435 Permissive, and acceptance found, which gained
This answer from the gracious voice divine.
  " 'Thus far to try thee, Adam, I was pleased,
And find thee knowing not of beasts alone,
Which thou hast rightly named, but of thyself,
440 Expressing well the spirit within thee free,
My image, not imparted to the brute,
Whose fellowship therefore unmeet for thee
Good reason was thou freely shouldst dislike,
And be so minded still; I, ere thou spak'st,
445 Knew it not good for man to be alone,
And no such company as then thou saw'st
Intended thee, for trial only brought,
To see how thou could'st judge of fit and meet:
What next I bring shall please thee, be assured,
450 Thy likeness, thy fit help, thy other self,

---

empirical observation. And God, despite his complete and infinite parts, is paradoxically *one*.

422–26. Man has a *single imperfection,* his *unity* is *defective,* because unlike God he requires another being to multiply his image.

426. **Collateral:** etymologically "side by side," accompanying.

435. **Permissive:** allowed.

445. From Gen. 2.18: "God said, 'It is not good that man should be alone.' "

450. **thy other self:** an addition to Gen. 2.18 that Milton thought intended in the Hebrew (*MLM* 1000–1001). The Latin *alter ego* means "friend," which suggests that Milton is giving biblical sanction to the seventeenth-century ideal of "companionate marriage" (see Stone 361–74).

Thy wish exactly to thy heart's desire.'
  "He ended, or I heard no more, for now
My Earthly by his Heav'nly overpowered,
Which it had long stood under, strained to the highth
455 In that celestial colloquy sublime,
As with an object that excels the sense,
Dazzled and spent, sunk down, and sought repair
Of sleep, which instantly fell on me, called
By nature as in aid, and closed mine eyes.
460 Mine eyes he closed, but open left the cell
Of fancy my internal sight, by which
Abstract as in a trance methought I saw,
Though sleeping, where I lay, and saw the shape
Still glorious before whom awake I stood,
465 Who stooping opened my left side, and took
From thence a rib, with cordial spirits warm,
And life-blood streaming fresh; wide was the wound,
But suddenly with flesh filled up and healed:
The rib he formed and fashioned with his hands;
470 Under his forming hands a creature grew,
Manlike, but different sex, so lovely fair,
That what seemed fair in all the world, seemed now
Mean, or in her summed up, in her contained
And in her looks, which from that time infused
475 Sweetness into my heart, unfelt before,
And into all things from her air inspired
The spirit of love and amorous delight.
She disappeared, and left me dark. I waked
To find her, or forever to deplore
480 Her loss, and other pleasures all abjure:
When out of hope, behold her, not far off,
Such as I saw her in my dream, adorned

---

453. **Earthly:** earthly nature.
454. **stood under:** been exposed to.
462–82. Cp. *Sonnet 23*.
465–67. **left side . . . fresh:** The Bible does not specify from which side the rib came, but tradition overwhelmingly chose the left, in part because of nearness to the heart (see l. 484; A. Williams 90–91).
466. **cordial spirits:** vital spirits residing in the heart's blood.
481. **When out of hope:** when I had ceased to hope.

With what all Earth or Heaven could bestow
To make her amiable: on she came,
485 Led by her Heav'nly Maker, though unseen,
And guided by his voice, nor uninformed
Of nuptial sanctity and marriage rites:
Grace was in all her steps, heav'n in her eye,
In every gesture dignity and love.
490 I overjoyed could not forbear aloud.
    " 'This turn hath made amends; thou hast fulfilled
Thy words, Creator bounteous and benign,
Giver of all things fair, but fairest this
Of all thy gifts, nor enviest. I now see
495 Bone of my bone, flesh of my flesh, my self
Before me; woman is her name, of man
Extracted; for this cause he shall forgo
Father and mother, and to his wife adhere;
And they shall be one flesh, one heart, one soul.'
500   "She heard me thus, and though divinely brought,
Yet innocence and virgin modesty,
Her virtue and the conscience of her worth,
That would be wooed, and not unsought be won,
Not obvious, not obtrusive, but retired,
505 The more desirable, or to say all,
Nature herself, though pure of sinful thought,
Wrought in her so, that seeing me, she turned;
I followed her, she what was honor knew,
And with obsequious majesty approved
510 My pleaded reason. To the nuptial bow'r
I led her blushing like the morn: all heav'n,
And happy constellations on that hour

---

494. **nor enviest:** nor given reluctantly, begrudgingly.
499. **one heart, one soul:** an addition to Gen. 2.23–24, again suggesting companionate marriage (see 450n).
502. **conscience:** internal awareness. Cp. Eve's account of her initial turning away at 4.477–80.

509. **obsequious:** acquiescent (not servile).
511. **blushing:** Most blushes in the fallen world indicate shame. But there are innocent blushes, too, compounded of shyness and a sense of awe at participating in a great thing. The syntax leaves open the possibility that Adam is also blushing.

Shed their selectest influence; the earth
Gave sign of gratulation, and each hill;
515 Joyous the birds; fresh gales and gentle airs
Whispered it to the woods, and from their wings
Flung rose, flung odors from the spicy shrub,
Disporting, till the amorous bird of night
Sung spousal, and bid haste the ev'ning star
520 On his hill top, to light the bridal lamp.
Thus I have told thee all my state, and brought
My story to the sum of earthly bliss
Which I enjoy, and must confess to find
In all things else delight indeed, but such
525 As used or not, works in the mind no change,
Nor vehement desire, these delicacies
I mean of taste, sight, smell, herbs, fruits, and flow'rs,
Walks, and the melody of birds; but here
Far otherwise, transported I behold,
530 Transported touch; here passion first I felt,
Commotion strange, in all enjoyments else
Superior and unmoved, here only weak
Against the charm of beauty's powerful glance.
Or nature failed in me, and left some part
535 Not proof enough such object to sustain,
Or from my side subducting, took perhaps
More than enough; at least on her bestowed
Too much of ornament, in outward show
Elaborate, of inward less exact.
540 For well I understand in the prime end
Of nature her th' inferior, in the mind
And inward faculties, which most excel,
In outward also her resembling less

---

513. **influence:** emanation from the heavens, here entirely favorable; cp. 10.661–64.

519. **ev'ning star:** Hesperus or Venus, whose appearance in the sky is a signal in the epithalamium tradition to light the bridal lamps and torches and bring the bride to the bride-groom. See Spenser, *Epithalamion* 286–95; *DDD* in *MLM* 873–74.

532–33. Cp. *SA* 1003–1007.

536. **subducting:** subtracting.

537–39. Cp. *SA* 1025–30.

His image who made both, and less expressing
545 The character of that dominion giv'n
O'er other creatures; yet when I approach
Her loveliness, so absolute she seems
And in herself complete, so well to know
Her own, that what she wills to do or say,
550 Seems wisest, virtuousest, discreetest, best;
All higher knowledge in her presence falls
Degraded, wisdom in discourse with her
Looses discount'nanced, and like folly shows;
Authority and reason on her wait,
555 As one intended first, not after made
Occasionally; and to consummate all,
Greatness of mind and nobleness their seat
Build in her loveliest, and create an awe
About her, as a guard angelic placed."
560 To whom the Angel with contracted brow.
        "Accuse not nature, she hath done her part;
Do thou but thine, and be not diffident
Of Wisdom; she deserts thee not, if thou
Dismiss not her when most thou need'st her nigh,
565 By attributing overmuch to things
Less excellent, as thou thyself perceiv'st.
For what admir'st thou, what transports thee so,
An outside? Fair no doubt, and worthy well
Thy cherishing, thy honoring, and thy love,
570 Not thy subjection: weigh with her thyself;
Then value: ofttimes nothing profits more
Than self-esteem, grounded on just and right
Well managed; of that skill the more thou know'st,

---

547. **absolute:** complete, perfect; Adam ear-
lier used the word of God (ll. 419–21n).
553. **Looses:** goes to pieces.
555. **As one intended first:** Adam sees Eve
as himself.
559. **guard angelic placed:** "Adam has just
used, by ironic anticipation, the image of
Paradise after he has been excluded from

it," Frye wrote (1965, 64), thinking of
12.641–44.
556. **Occasionally:** on the occasion of
Adam's request.
562. **diffident:** mistrustful.
572. **self-esteem:** Milton may well have
coined the term in *Apology;* see *MLM* 850
(Leonard).

The more she will acknowledge thee her head,
575 And to realities yield all her shows:
Made so adorn for thy delight the more,
So awful, that with honor thou may'st love
Thy mate, who sees when thou art seen least wise.
But if the sense of touch whereby mankind
580 Is propagated seem such dear delight
Beyond all other, think the same vouchsafed
To cattle and each beast; which would not be
To them made common and divulged, if aught
Therein enjoyed were worthy to subdue
585 The soul of man, or passion in him move.
What higher in her society thou find'st
Attractive, human, rational, love still;
In loving thou dost well, in passion not,
Wherein true love consists not; love refines
590 The thoughts, and heart enlarges, hath his seat
In reason, and is judicious, is the scale
By which to Heav'nly love thou may'st ascend,
Not sunk in carnal pleasure, for which cause
Among the beasts no mate for thee was found."
595   To whom thus half abashed Adam replied.
"Neither her outside formed so fair, nor aught
In procreation common to all kinds
(Though higher of the genial bed by far,
And with mysterious reverence I deem)
600 So much delights me as those graceful acts,

---

574. **head:** "The head of the woman is the man" (1 Cor. 11.3).

575. **shows:** appearances. Turner finds the passage "particularly appalling" (280) because he takes *shows* to mean "pretenses, wiles," as if Eve were deliberately nurturing her husband's uxoriousness.

576. **adorn:** adorned.

577. **awful:** awe-inspiring.

583. **divulged:** done openly.

591–92. **the scale . . . ascend:** Earthly love as the *scale* or ladder by which we may as-

cend to *Heav'nly love* is a central feature of Neoplatonic works such as Marsilio Ficino's *Commentary on Plato's Symposium* and Spenser's *Four Hymns.*

598. **genial:** nuptial. As before he demonstrated his freedom in disputing with God (ll. 379–97, 412–33), so here Adam rejects Raphael's insistence that marital sexuality is no more than what animals do. He rather values it with the *reverence* appropriate to religious mysteries. Cp. *Tetrachordon* (*MLM* 1004).

Those thousand decencies that daily flow
From all her words and actions mixed with love
And sweet compliance, which declare unfeigned
Union of mind, or in us both one soul;
605 Harmony to behold in wedded pair
More grateful than harmonious sound to the ear.
Yet these subject not; I to thee disclose
What inward thence I feel, not therefore foiled,
Who meet with various objects, from the sense
610 Variously representing; yet still free
Approve the best, and follow what I approve.
To love thou blam'st me not, for love thou say'st
Leads up to Heav'n, is both the way and guide;
Bear with me then, if lawful what I ask;
615 Love not the Heav'nly spirits, and how their love
Express they, by looks only, or do they mix
Irradiance, virtual or immediate touch?"
    To whom the angel with a smile that glowed
Celestial rosy red, love's proper hue,
620 Answered. "Let it suffice thee that thou know'st
Us happy, and without love no happiness.
Whatever pure thou in the body enjoy'st
(And pure thou wert created) we enjoy
In eminence, and obstacle find none
625 Of membrane, joint, or limb, exclusive bars:
Easier than air with air, if spirits embrace,
Total they mix, union of pure with pure

608. **foiled:** overcome.

617. **virtual:** in effect, not actually (modifies *touch*). Adam imagines three ways in which angels might express love (if they do): by looks, by mingling their radiance, or by actual (*immediate*) touch. Cp. his earlier interest in whether angels eat what humans eat (5.401–403, 466–67).

618–19. Todd: "Does not Milton here mean that the Angel both smiled and blushed at Adam's curiosity?" He does, and goes on to say that a red blush is love's *proper*, correct or natural, *hue.* Cp. 5.111.

624–25. The passage has in mind the criticism of sexual intercourse voiced at the opening of Book 4 of Lucretius' *On the Nature of Things.* Human lovers desire full union, such as that enjoyed by Milton's angels, but are repeatedly frustrated in having to make do with the friction of surfaces: "Again they in each other would be lost,/But still by adamantine bars are crossed" (trans. John Dryden).

624. **In eminence:** in an elevated manner.

625. **exclusive:** excluding.

Desiring; nor restrained conveyance need
As flesh to mix with flesh, or soul with soul.
630 But I can now no more; the parting sun
Beyond the Earth's green cape and verdant isles
Hesperean sets, my signal to depart.
Be strong, live happy, and love, but first of all
Him whom to love is to obey, and keep
635 His great command; take heed lest passion sway
Thy judgment to do aught, which else free will
Would not admit; thine and of all thy sons
The weal or woe in thee is placed; beware.
I in thy persevering shall rejoice,
640 And all the blest: stand fast; to stand or fall
Free in thine own arbitrament it lies.
Perfect within, no outward aid require;
And all temptation to transgress repel."
    So saying, he arose; whom Adam thus
645 Followed with benediction. "Since to part,
Go Heav'nly guest, ethereal messenger,
Sent from whose sov'reign goodness I adore.
Gentle to me and affable hath been
Thy condescension, and shall be honored ever
650 With grateful memory: thou to mankind
Be good and friendly still, and oft return."
    So parted they, the angel up to Heav'n
From the thick shade, and Adam to his bow'r.

---

628. **restrained conveyance:** restraining transportation (such as the human body). Angels can apparently mix at a distance, uniting what Adam considered a disjunctive choice between *virtual* and *immediate touch* (l. 617).

631. **green cape:** Cape Verde; **verdant isles:** the Cape Verde Islands off the west (*Hesperean*) coast of Africa.
645. **Since to part:** since we must part.

Book IX

The Argument

Satan having compassed the Earth, with meditated guile returns as a mist by night into Paradise, enters into the serpent sleeping. Adam and Eve in the morning go forth to their labors, which Eve proposes to divide in several places, each laboring apart. Adam consents not, alleging the danger, lest that enemy, of whom they were forewarned, should attempt her found alone. Eve, loath to be thought not circumspect or firm enough, urges her going apart, the rather desirous to make trial of her strength. Adam at last yields: the serpent finds her alone; his subtle approach, first gazing, then speaking, with much flattery extolling Eve above all other creatures. Eve, wondering to hear the serpent speak, asks how he attained to human speech and such understanding not till now. The serpent answers, that by tasting of a certain tree in the garden he attained both to speech and reason, till then void of both. Eve requires him to bring her to that tree, and finds it to be the Tree of Knowledge forbidden. The serpent now grown bolder, with many wiles and arguments induces her at length to eat. She, pleased with the taste, deliberates a while whether to impart thereof to Adam or not, at last brings him of the fruit, relates what persuaded her to eat thereof. Adam at first amazed, but perceiving her lost, resolves through vehemence of love to perish with her, and extenuating the trespass eats also of the fruit. The effects thereof in them both: they seek to cover their nakedness; then fall to variance and accusation of one another.

No more of talk where God or angel guest
With man, as with his friend, familiar used
To sit indulgent, and with him partake
Rural repast, permitting him the while
5   Venial discourse unblamed: I now must change
Those notes to tragic; foul distrust, and breach
Disloyal on the part of man, revolt,
And disobedience; on the part of Heav'n,
Now alienated, distance and distaste,
10   Anger and just rebuke, and judgment giv'n,
That brought into this world a world of woe,
Sin and her shadow Death, and Misery,
Death's harbinger: sad task, yet argument
Not less but more heroic than the wrath
15   Of stern Achilles on his foe pursued
Thrice fugitive about Troy wall; or rage
Of Turnus for Lavinia disespoused,
Or Neptune's ire or Juno's, that so long
Perplexed the Greek and Cytherea's son;
20   If answerable style I can obtain
Of my celestial patroness, who deigns
Her nightly visitation unimplored,
And dictates to me slumb'ring, or inspires

---

1. **No more:** *No/know* and *more* have earlier appeared in memorable formulations about the limits of knowledge that Adam and Eve must observe (4.637, 775; 8.194); now, at the beginning of the book in which those limits will be violated, Milton reconfigures these words to announce a fundamental break with unfallen existence. **God or angel:** Adam spoke with God (8.295–451), and Books 5–8 have chronicled the friendly visit of Raphael to Paradise.
2. **familiar:** in a familial manner, intimate.
5. **Venial:** innocent; **unblamed:** unblamable.
13. **sad task:** Raphael used the same phrase (5.564) in introducing his narrative of the fall of the rebel angels.

13–19. **yet . . . son:** Milton compares his *argument* or subject matter to earlier accounts of wrath in the epic tradition, Homer on Achilles' defeat of Hector (*Il.* 22), Vergil on the bellicose rage of Turnus (*Aen.* 7), Homer on Neptune's grudge against Odysseus, and Vergil on Juno's grudge against Aeneas, *Cytherea's* (Venus') *son.* The point is that the wrath in Milton's story, the wrath of the Christian God against human sin, is just, not capricious.
19. **Perplexed:** tormented.
20. **answerable:** commensurate (with his *more heroic* subject).
22. **unimplored:** Oddly, Milton in fact "implores" his muse at 7.38.

Easy my unpremeditated verse:
25 Since first this subject for heroic song
Pleased me long choosing, and beginning late;
Not sedulous by nature to indite
Wars, hitherto the only argument
Heroic deemed, chief mast'ry to dissect
30 With long and tedious havoc fabled knights
In battles feigned; the better fortitude
Of patience and heroic martyrdom
Unsung; or to describe races and games,
Or tilting furniture, emblazoned shields,
35 Impresses quaint, caparisons and steeds;
Bases and tinsel trappings, gorgeous knights
At joust and tournament; then marshalled feast
Served up in hall with sewers and seneschals;
The skill of artifice or office mean,
40 Not that which justly gives heroic name
To person or to poem. Me of these
Nor skilled nor studious, higher argument
Remains, sufficient of itself to raise
That name, unless an age too late, or cold

---

24. **unpremeditated:** Cp. the morning prayers of 5.149; in *Eikonoklastes,* Milton argues that prayers should not be imprisoned "in a pinfold of set words" (Yale 3:505).

27. **indite:** compose.

34. **tilting furniture:** jousting equipment, which Milton proceeds to list: shields emblazoned with *impresses quaint* (clever emblems), *caparisons* and *bases* (equestrian trappings).

37–38. **then marshalled feast . . . seneschals:** The feast is *marshalled,* full of elaborate arrangements and displays. *Sewers,* supervised by their chief, the *seneschal,* seated the guests and served the meal. Milton's disdain for the ritual civility of the feast may in part be motivated by the primal bad feast he is soon to narrate.

39. **office:** position, duty. Romance is rejected as a poetry devoted to the superficial artifice of noble manners and amusements.

44. **That name:** the *heroic name* of line 40; **an age too late:** sometimes explained as universal decay, a theory Milton opposed in *Naturam non pati senium.* He might have felt that England, after the Restoration, had proved itself unworthy of a divinely inspired epic. He stated in *RCG* that the creation of ambitious Christian art might depend on the "fate of this age" (*MLM* 841).

44–45. **unless . . . wing:** Milton feared that Aristotle was right in declaring that a cold climate such as England's (at least in comparison with the Mediterranean climates that spawned Homer and Vergil) might leave the mind unripe. See Fink.

45 Climate, or years damp my intended wing
Depressed, and much they may, if all be mine,
Not hers who brings it nightly to my ear.
         The sun was sunk, and after him the star
Of Hesperus, whose office is to bring
50 Twilight upon the Earth, short arbiter
'Twixt day and night, and now from end to end
Night's hemisphere had veiled the horizon round:
When Satan who late fled before the threats
Of Gabriel out of Eden, now improved
55 In meditated fraud and malice, bent
On man's destruction, maugre what might hap
Of heavier on himself, fearless returned.
By night he fled, and at midnight returned
From compassing the Earth, cautious of day,
60 Since Uriel, Regent of the Sun, descried
His entrance, and forewarned the Cherubim
That kept their watch; thence full of anguish driv'n,
The space of seven continued nights he rode
With darkness, thrice the equinoctial line
65 He circled, four times crossed the car of night
From pole to pole, traversing each colure;
On the eighth returned, and on the coast averse
From entrance or Cherubic watch, by stealth
Found unsuspected way. There was a place,
70 Now not, though sin, not time, first wrought the change,

45. **or years:** Milton was almost sixty when his epic was published; George Herbert's "The Forerunners," written in his thirties, anticipates senility. **damp:** discourage (*OED* 3).

46. **Depressed:** brought down. Psychological failure is here expressed in the metaphor of failed flight, lower than what Milton intends. Cp. the metaphor of winged flight at 3.13 and 7.4.

49. **Hesperus:** Venus, the evening star.

56. **maugre:** despite.

58–69. **By night . . . way:** Satan keeps to the darkness for an entire week to evade de-
tection by Uriel. For three days he remains on the equator, flying ahead of the advance of sunlight. He spends the other four days *compassing the Earth* from north to south, *traversing each colure*—a reference to two great circles that intersect at right angles on the earth's poles. "He crosses the world, but not in benediction" (Evans in Broadbent edition).

67. **coast averse:** the north side of Eden, which is *averse* (turned away from) the eastern entrance, where cherubim keep watch.

Where Tigris at the foot of Paradise
Into a gulf shot underground, till part
Rose up a fountain by the Tree of Life;
In with the river sunk, and with it rose
75   Satan involved in rising mist, then sought
Where to lie hid; sea he had searched and land
From Eden over Pontus, and the pool
Maeotis, up beyond the river Ob;
Downward as far Antarctic; and in length
80   West from Orontes to the ocean barred
At Darien, thence to the land where flows
Ganges and Indus: thus the orb he roamed
With narrow search; and with inspection deep
Considered every creature, which of all
85   Most opportune might serve his wiles, and found
The serpent subtlest beast of all the field.
Him after long debate, irresolute
Of thoughts revolved, his final sentence chose
Fit vessel, fittest imp of fraud, in whom
90   To enter, and his dark suggestions hide
From sharpest sight: for in the wily snake,
Whatever sleights none would suspicious mark,
As from his wit and native subtlety
Proceeding, which in other beasts observed
95   Doubt might beget of diabolic pow'r
Active within beyond the sense of brute.
Thus he resolved, but first from inward grief
His bursting passion into plaints thus poured:
        "O Earth, how like to Heav'n, if not preferred
100   More justly, seat worthier of gods, as built
With second thoughts, reforming what was old!

77–82. **From Eden ... Indus:** Satan spans the globe in search of his *fit vessel* (l. 89) in the animal kingdom. He journeys north from Paradise, to the *Pontus* (Black Sea), the *pool Maeotis* (Sea of Azov), and the *Ob* (a river in Siberia), then down the other side of the earth to Antarctica, and west to the *Orontes* (a river in Syria), to *Darien* (Panama), to the *Ganges* in India, and finally to the *Indus,* a river near Eden.

89. **fittest imp:** An *imp* is a graft or shoot; Satan's graft of fraud will be *fittest,* most likely to thrive, on the snake.

93. **native subtlety:** See Gen. 3.1.

For what god after better worse would build?
Terrestrial Heav'n, danced round by other heav'ns
That shine, yet bear their bright officious lamps,
105 Light above light, for thee alone, as seems,
In thee concent'ring all their precious beams
Of sacred influence: as God in Heav'n
Is center, yet extends to all, so thou
Cent'ring receiv'st from all those orbs; in thee,
110 Not in themselves, all their known virtue appears
Productive in herb, plant, and nobler birth
Of creatures animate with gradual life
Of growth, sense, reason, all summed up in man.
With what delight could I have walked thee round,
115 If I could joy in aught, sweet interchange
Of hill and valley, rivers, woods and plains,
Now land, now sea, and shores with forest crowned,
Rocks, dens, and caves; but I in none of these
Find place or refuge; and the more I see
120 Pleasures about me, so much more I feel
Torment within me, as from the hateful siege
Of contraries; all good to me becomes
Bane, and in Heav'n much worse would be my state.
But neither here seek I, no nor in Heav'n
125 To dwell, unless by mast'ring Heav'n's Supreme;
Nor hope to be myself less miserable
By what I seek, but others to make such
As I, though thereby worse to me redound:
For only in destroying I find ease
130 To my relentless thoughts; and him destroyed,
Or won to what may work his utter loss,
For whom all this was made, all this will soon
Follow, as to him linked in weal or woe;

103–105. Adam suffered from the same mis-apprehension about the heavens (8.273–74n) and was corrected by Raphael (8.85–90n).

113. **growth, sense, reason:** progressing from vegetable (*growth*) to animal (*sense*) to rational (*reason*).

121–22. **hateful siege/Of contraries:** Here as elsewhere, Satan recoils from the beautiful, the pleasing, and the good. Cp. the "grateful vicissitude" of 6.8.

In woe then, that destruction wide may range:
135 To me shall be the glory sole among
The infernal Powers, in one day to have marred
What he Almighty styled, six nights and days
Continued making, and who knows how long
Before had been contriving, though perhaps
140 Not longer than since I in one night freed
From servitude inglorious well nigh half
Th' angelic name, and thinner left the throng
Of his adorers: he to be avenged,
And to repair his numbers thus impaired,
145 Whether such virtue spent of old now failed
More angels to create, if they at least
Are his created, or to spite us more,
Determined to advance into our room
A creature formed of earth, and him endow,
150 Exalted from so base original,
With Heav'nly spoils, our spoils: what he decreed
He effected; man he made, and for him built
Magnificent this world, and Earth his seat,
Him lord pronounced, and, O indignity!
155 Subjected to his service angel wings,
And flaming ministers to watch and tend
Their earthy charge: of these the vigilance
I dread, and to elude, thus wrapped in mist
Of midnight vapor glide obscure, and pry
160 In every bush and brake, where hap may find
The serpent sleeping, in whose mazy folds
To hide me, and the dark intent I bring.
O foul descent! That I who erst contended
With gods to sit the highest, am now constrained
165 Into a beast, and mixed with bestial slime,
This essence to incarnate and imbrute,

142. **name:** race, stock.
144. **to repair his numbers:** not, according to 3.289, God's original motive for the Creation, but a motive (7.152–53).
166. **This essence:** Satan's angelic matter, ear-

lier said to be uncompounded or undifferentiated with regard to human fixities such as body parts (1.423–31). **incarnate:** Satan's parody of the Incarnation is undertaken with high-minded disdain, not love.

That to the highth of deity aspired;
But what will not ambition and revenge
Descend to? Who aspires must down as low
170 As high he soared, obnoxious first or last
To basest things. Revenge, at first though sweet,
Bitter ere long back on itself recoils;
Let it; I reck not, so it light well aimed,
Since higher I fall short, on him who next
175 Provokes my envy, this new favorite
Of Heav'n, this man of clay, son of despite,
Whom us the more to spite his Maker raised
From dust: spite then with spite is best repaid."
    So saying, through each thicket dank or dry,
180 Like a black mist low creeping, he held on
His midnight search, where soonest he might find
The serpent: him fast sleeping soon he found
In labyrinth of many a round self-rolled,
His head the midst, well stored with subtle wiles:
185 Not yet in horrid shade or dismal den,
Nor nocent yet, but on the grassy herb
Fearless unfeared he slept: in at his mouth
The Devil entered, and his brutal sense,
In heart or head, possessing soon inspired
190 With act intelligential, but his sleep
Disturbed not, waiting close th' approach of morn.
Now whenas sacred light began to dawn
In Eden on the humid flow'rs, that breathed
Their morning incense, when all things that breathe,
195 From th' Earth's great altar send up silent praise
To the Creator, and his nostrils fill

---

170. **obnoxious:** exposed.
171. **Revenge, at first though sweet:** repudiating the proverb "Revenge is sweet" (Tilley R90).
172. **on itself recoils:** The metaphor of cannon, Satan's self-defining invention (cp. 4.17), continues in the gunnery language of lines 173–74.

174. **higher:** when aiming higher.
176. **son of despite:** son of scorn, with the added suggestion that man was created to spite Satan; on Satan's spite, see 2.384–85.
186. **Nor nocent:** not harmful. Milton's unusual phrase signifies "innocence" but suggests its opposite.
191. **close:** in hiding.

With grateful smell, forth came the human pair
And joined their vocal worship to the choir
Of creatures wanting voice; that done, partake
200 The season, prime for sweetest scents and airs;
Then commune how that day they best may ply
Their growing work: for much their work outgrew
The hands' dispatch of two gard'ning so wide.
And Eve first to her husband thus began.
205   "Adam, well may we labor still to dress
This garden, still to tend plant, herb and flow'r,
Our pleasant task enjoined, but till more hands
Aid us, the work under our labor grows,
Luxurious by restraint; what we by day
210 Lop overgrown, or prune, or prop, or bind,
One night or two with wanton growth derides
Tending to wild. Thou therefore now advise
Or hear what to my mind first thoughts present;
Let us divide our labors, thou where choice
215 Leads thee, or where most needs, whether to wind
The woodbine round this arbor, or direct
The clasping ivy where to climb, while I
In yonder spring of roses intermixed
With myrtle, find what to redress till noon:
220 For while so near each other thus all day
Our task we choose, what wonder if so near
Looks intervene and smiles, or object new
Casual discourse draw on, which intermits
Our day's work brought to little, though begun
225 Early, and th' hour of supper comes unearned."
          To whom mild answer Adam thus returned.
"Sole Eve, associate sole, to me beyond
Compare above all living creatures dear,
Well hast thou motioned, well thy thoughts employed

205. **still:** continually. For the first time, Eve
  initiates a conversation.
213. **hear:** 1667; 1674 reads "bear."
215–17. **to wind . . . to climb:** Both ivy and

woodbine are in need of a prop, as Eve
  soon will be (ll. 431–33).
218. **spring:** thicket.
219. **redress:** put upright.

230 How we might best fulfill the work which here
God hath assigned us, nor of me shalt pass
Unpraised: for nothing lovelier can be found
In woman than to study household good,
And good works in her husband to promote.
235 Yet not so strictly hath our Lord imposed
Labor, as to debar us when we need
Refreshment, whether food, or talk between,
Food of the mind, or this sweet intercourse
Of looks and smiles, for smiles from reason flow,
240 To brute denied, and are of love the food,
Love not the lowest end of human life.
For not to irksome toil, but to delight
He made us, and delight to reason joined.
These paths and bowers doubt not but our joint hands
245 Will keep from wilderness with ease, as wide
As we need walk, till younger hands ere long
Assist us: but if much converse perhaps
Thee satiate, to short absence I could yield.
For solitude sometimes is best society,
250 And short retirement urges sweet return.
But other doubt possesses me, lest harm
Befall thee severed from me; for thou know'st
What hath been warned us, what malicious foe
Envying our happiness, and of his own
255 Despairing, seeks to work us woe and shame
By sly assault; and somewhere nigh at hand
Watches, no doubt, with greedy hope to find
His wish and best advantage, us asunder,
Hopeless to circumvent us joined, where each
260 To other speedy aid might lend at need;
Whether his first design be to withdraw

240. **of love the food:** For Ovid hope is the food of love (*Met.* 9.749); for Shakespeare's Orsino music is the food of love (*TN* I.I.I); for Adam smiles are the food of love—and smiles, we know, lead to kisses (4.499–502).

247–48. **but . . . yield:** Having dismissed the idea that Eden cannot be sufficiently tamed through their current work habits, Adam speculates that Eve has had enough *converse* (conversation).

249. Cp. *Masque* 375–80.

Our fealty from God, or to disturb
Conjugal love, than which perhaps no bliss
Enjoyed by us excites his envy more;
265 Or this, or worse, leave not the faithful side
That gave thee being, still shades thee and protects.
The wife, where danger or dishonor lurks,
Safest and seemliest by her husband stays,
Who guards her, or with her the worst endures."
270   To whom the virgin majesty of Eve,
As one who loves, and some unkindness meets,
With sweet austere composure thus replied.
     "Offspring of Heav'n and Earth, and all Earth's lord,
That such an enemy we have, who seeks
275 Our ruin, both by thee informed I learn,
And from the parting angel overheard
As in a shady nook I stood behind,
Just then returned at shut of evening flow'rs.
But that thou shouldst my firmness therefore doubt
280 To God or thee, because we have a foe
May tempt it, I expected not to hear.
His violence thou fear'st not, being such,
As we, not capable of death or pain,
Can either not receive, or can repel.
285 His fraud is then thy fear, which plain infers
Thy equal fear that my firm faith and love
Can by his fraud be shaken or seduced;
Thoughts, which how found they harbor in thy breast
Adam, misthought of her to thee so dear?"
290   To whom with healing words Adam replied.
     "Daughter of God and man, immortal Eve,

---

265. **Or:** whether.
270. **virgin majesty:** Technically, Eve is not
    a virgin. But *virgo* in Latin and *virginale* in
    Italian can sometimes denote "beauty,"
    "freshness," "sweetness," "modesty"
    (Todd), or simply "woman" (Hume). In
    English, *virgin* can mean "chaste" (*OED* 1)

and hence be applied to married women,
as Puritans especially stressed.
272. **sweet austere composure:** The adjec-
    tives verge on oxymoron.
276. **parting angel overheard:** It is likely
    that Eve overheard 8.630–43, which begins
    with Raphael taking the "parting sun" to
    be his signal to "depart."

For such thou art, from sin and blame entire:
Not diffident of thee do I dissuade
Thy absence from my sight, but to avoid
295 Th' attempt itself, intended by our foe.
For he who tempts, though in vain, at least asperses
The tempted with dishonor foul, supposed
Not incorruptible of faith, not proof
Against temptation: thou thyself with scorn
300 And anger wouldst resent the offered wrong,
Though ineffectual found: misdeem not then,
If such affront I labor to avert
From thee alone, which on us both at once
The enemy, though bold, will hardly dare,
305 Or daring, first on me th' assault shall light.
Nor thou his malice and false guile contemn;
Subtle he needs must be, who could seduce
Angels, nor think superfluous others' aid.
I from the influence of thy looks receive
310 Access in every virtue, in thy sight
More wise, more watchful, stronger, if need were
Of outward strength; while shame, thou looking on,
Shame to be overcome or overreached
Would utmost vigor raise, and raised unite.
315 Why shouldst not thou like sense within thee feel
When I am present, and thy trial choose
With me, best witness of thy virtue tried."
    So spake domestic Adam in his care
And matrimonial love; but Eve, who thought
320 Less attributed to her faith sincere,
Thus her reply with accent sweet renewed.
    "If this be our condition, thus to dwell
In narrow circuit straitened by a foe,

---

292. **entire:** unblemished.
293. **diffident:** mistrustful.
296–301. **For he . . . found:** Adam seems to be falsely denying that he had entertained the thought (at ll. 265–69) that Eve, if apart from him, might fall. He temporar-

ily projects that thought onto Satan, who does indeed have it.
310. **Access:** increase.
314. **raised unite:** unite all his strengths in a state of generally heightened vigor.
320. **Less:** too little.

Subtle or violent, we not endued
325 Single with like defense, wherever met,
How are we happy, still in fear of harm?
But harm precedes not sin: only our Foe
Tempting affronts us with his foul esteem
Of our integrity: his foul esteem
330 Sticks no dishonor on our front, but turns
Foul on himself; then wherefore shunned or feared
By us? Who rather double honor gain
From his surmise proved false, find peace within,
Favor from Heav'n, our witness from th' event.
335 And what is faith, love, virtue unassayed
Alone, without exterior help sustained?
Let us not then suspect our happy state
Left so imperfect by the Maker wise,
As not secure to single or combined.
340 Frail is our happiness, if this be so,
And Eden were no Eden thus exposed."
     To whom thus Adam fervently replied.
"O woman, best are all things as the will
Of God ordained them, his creating hand
345 Nothing imperfect or deficient left
Of all that he created, much less man,
Or aught that might his happy state secure,
Secure from outward force; within himself
The danger lies, yet lies within his power:
350 Against his will he can receive no harm.
But God left free the will, for what obeys
Reason, is free, and reason he made right,
But bid her well beware, and still erect,
Least by some fair appearing good surprised
355 She dictate false, and misinform the will
To do what God expressly hath forbid.
Not then mistrust, but tender love enjoins,
That I should mind thee oft, and mind thou me.

326. **still:** always.
335–36. Cp. *Areop* (*MLM* 939, 944).

341. **Eden were no Eden:** See 4.27–28n.
353. **still:** always.

Firm we subsist, yet possible to swerve,
360 Since reason not impossibly may meet
Some specious object by the foe suborned,
And fall into deception unaware,
Not keeping strictest watch, as she was warned.
Seek not temptation then, which to avoid
365 Were better, and most likely if from me
Thou sever not: trial will come unsought.
Wouldst thou approve thy constancy, approve
First thy obedience; th' other who can know,
Not seeing thee attempted, who attest?
370 But if thou think, trial unsought may find
Us both securer than thus warned thou seem'st,
Go; for thy stay, not free, absents thee more;
Go in thy native innocence, rely
On what thou hast of virtue, summon all,
375 For God towards thee hath done his part, do thine."
So spake the patriarch of mankind, but Eve
Persisted, yet submiss, though last, replied.

"With thy permission then, and thus forewarned
Chiefly by what thy own last reasoning words
380 Touched only, that our trial, when least sought,
May find us both perhaps far less prepared,
The willinger I go, nor much expect
A foe so proud will first the weaker seek;
So bent, the more shall shame him his repulse."
385 Thus saying, from her husband's hand her hand
Soft she withdrew, and like a wood-nymph light
Oread or Dryad, or of Delia's train,
Betook her to the groves, but Delia's self
In gait surpassed and goddesslike deport,

---

363. **she:** reason.
367. **approve:** prove.
371. **securer:** more careless.
372. **Go; for thy stay:** The conjunction of *go* and *stay* prepares, well over 3,000 lines in advance, for a major poetic effect at the end of the poem (12.615–20n, 648–49n).

386. **light:** light-footed.
387. **Oread:** mountain nymph; **Dryad:** wood nymph; **Delia's train:** the attendants of Diana, goddess of the moon, the hunt, and chastity.

390 Though not as she with bow and quiver armed,
But with such gard'ning tools as art yet rude,
Guiltless of fire had formed, or angels brought.
To Pales, or Pomona thus adorned,
Likeliest she seemed, Pomona when she fled
395 Vertumnus, or to Ceres in her prime,
Yet virgin of Proserpina from Jove.
Her long with ardent look his eye pursued
Delighted, but desiring more her stay.
Oft he to her his charge of quick return
400 Repeated, she to him as oft engaged
To be returned by noon amid the bow'r,
And all things in best order to invite
Noontide repast, or afternoon's repose.
O much deceived, much failing, hapless Eve,
405 Of thy presumed return! Event perverse!
Thou never from that hour in Paradise
Found'st either sweet repast, or sound repose;
Such ambush hid among sweet flow'rs and shades
Waited with hellish rancor imminent
410 To intercept thy way, or send thee back
Despoiled of innocence, of faith, of bliss.
For now, and since first break of dawn the fiend,
Mere serpent in appearance, forth was come,
And on his quest, where likeliest he might find
415 The only two of mankind, but in them
The whole included race, his purposed prey.
In bow'r and field he sought, where any tuft

---

393. **Pales:** the Roman goddess of flocks; **Pomona:** the goddess of fruit trees.

395. **Vertumnus:** a garden god who pursued Pomona.

396. **Yet virgin of Proserpina:** before she bore Proserpina, whose rape by Pluto anticipates Eve's fall. See 4.268–72n.

404–11. A rich apostrophe. The "Eve" in *deceived* and *event,* puns hitherto muted, erupts into full clarity. We first take *deceived* and *failing* in a general sense, an-

nouncing the whole process of her fall, but in the next lines must localize their reference to her failing, deceived presumption about her return. In this one mistake, however, lie all mistakes (Ricks 97). The loss of sound sleep and sweet repast recalls Shakespeare's conscience-stricken Macbeth.

405. **Event perverse:** unforeseen outcome.

413. **Mere:** pure, unmixed.

Of grove or garden-plot more pleasant lay,
Their tendance or plantation for delight,
420   By fountain or by shady rivulet
He sought them both, but wished his hap might find
Eve separate; he wished, but not with hope
Of what so seldom chanced, when to his wish,
Beyond his hope, Eve separate he spies,
425   Veiled in a cloud of fragrance, where she stood,
Half spied, so thick the roses bushing round
About her glowed, oft stooping to support
Each flow'r of slender stalk, whose head though gay
Carnation, purple, azure, or specked with gold,
430   Hung drooping unsustained; them she upstays
Gently with myrtle band, mindless the while,
Herself, though fairest unsupported flow'r,
From her best prop so far, and storm so nigh.
Nearer he drew, and many a walk traversed
435   Of stateliest covert, cedar, pine, or palm,
Then voluble and bold, now hid, now seen
Among thick-woven arborets and flow'rs
Imbordered on each bank, the hand of Eve:
Spot more delicious than those gardens feigned
440   Or of revived Adonis, or renowned
Alcinous, host of old Laertes' son,
Or that, not mystic, where the sapient king
Held dalliance with his fair Egyptian spouse.
Much he the place admired, the person more.
445   As one who long in populous city pent,
Where houses thick and sewers annoy the air,

---

431. **mindless:** heedless.
432. See 4.269–71.
436. **voluble:** from the Latin *volubilis,* rolling.
438. **Imbordered:** planted as borders; **hand:** handiwork.

439–44. The catalog of gardens less delicious than Eden begins with those of Adonis, which Spenser represented as a paradise (*FQ* 3.6.39–42), and Alcinous, whose garden is visited by Odysseus (Homer, *Od.* 7.112–35). The last, *not mystic* (allegorical), is the garden where *sapient* Solomon entertained his wife, Pharaoh's daughter (Song of Solomon 6.2).

446. **sewers annoy the air:** as they certainly annoyed the air of London; see John Evelyn, *Fumifugium: or, the Inconveniencie of the Aer and Smoak of London Dissipated* (1661),

Forth issuing on a summer's morn to breathe
Among the pleasant villages and farms
Adjoined, from each thing met conceives delight,
450 The smell of grain, or tedded grass, or kine,
Or dairy, each rural sight, each rural sound;
If chance with nymphlike step fair virgin pass,
What pleasing seemed, for her now pleases more,
She most, and in her look sums all delight.
455 Such pleasure took the serpent to behold
This flow'ry plat, the sweet recess of Eve
Thus early, thus alone; her Heav'nly form
Angelic, but more soft, and feminine,
Her graceful innocence, her every air
460 Of gesture or least action overawed
His malice, and with rapine sweet bereaved
His fierceness of the fierce intent it brought:
That space the evil one abstracted stood
From his own evil, and for the time remained
465 Stupidly good, of enmity disarmed,
Of guile, of hate, of envy, of revenge;
But the hot Hell that always in him burns,
Though in mid-Heav'n, soon ended his delight,
And tortures him now more, the more he sees
470 Of pleasure not for him ordained: then soon
Fierce hate he recollects, and all his thoughts
Of mischief, gratulating, thus excites.
　　"Thoughts, whither have ye led me, with what sweet
Compulsion thus transported to forget
475 What hither brought us, hate, not love, nor hope
Of Paradise for Hell, hope here to taste

---

who argued that smoke and odors had made the city into "the suburbs of Hell" (6).
450. **tedded:** mown and spread out to dry; **kine:** archaic plural of *cow.*
453. **for:** because of.
456. **plat:** plot of ground.
458. **more soft:** Cp. 4.479.

463. **That space:** for that space of time.
467. Confirming lines 254–55, but ironically (the mind cannot make a Heaven of Hell).
472. **gratulating:** greeting; **excites:** stirs up (his thoughts, by addressing or greeting them).

Of pleasure, but all pleasure to destroy,
Save what is in destroying; other joy
To me is lost. Then let me not let pass
480 Occasion which now smiles; behold alone
The woman, opportune to all attempts,
Her husband, for I view far round, not nigh,
Whose higher intellectual more I shun,
And strength, of courage haughty, and of limb
485 Heroic built, though of terrestrial mold,
Foe not informidable, exempt from wound,
I not; so much hath Hell debased, and pain
Enfeebled me, to what I was in Heav'n.
She fair, divinely fair, fit love for gods,
490 Not terrible, though terror be in love
And beauty, not approached by stronger hate,
Hate stronger, under show of love well feigned,
The way which to her ruin now I tend."
　　So spake the enemy of mankind, enclosed
495 In serpent, inmate bad, and toward Eve
Addressed his way, not with indented wave,
Prone on the ground, as since, but on his rear,
Circular base of rising folds, that tow'red
Fold above fold a surging maze, his head
500 Crested aloft, and carbuncle his eyes;
With burnished neck of verdant gold, erect
Amidst his circling spires, that on the grass
Floated redundant: pleasing was his shape,
And lovely, never since of serpent kind
505 Lovelier, not those that in Illyria changed
Hermione and Cadmus, or the god
In Epidaurus; nor to which transformed

---

480. **Occasion:** opportunity or falling together, from the Latin root *cadere,* "to fall."
485. **mold:** material.
490–92. "Beauty and love inspire awe, unless counteracted by a stronger hatred." The spondee in the chiasmic *Hate strong* makes the point metrically.

496. **indented:** sliding back and forth, zigzagging.
500. **carbuncle:** red gem.
505–10. **Lovelier . . . Rome:** Satan is compared to serpents in classical literature into which men and gods were transformed. *Cadmus,* founder of Thebes, was

Ammonian Jove, or Capitoline was seen,
He with Olympias, this with her who bore
510 Scipio the highth of Rome. With tract oblique
At first, as one who sought access, but feared
To interrupt, sidelong he works his way.
As when a ship by skillful steersman wrought
Nigh river's mouth or foreland, where the wind
515 Veers oft, as oft so steers, and shifts her sail;
So varied he, and of his tortuous train
Curled many a wanton wreath in sight of Eve,
To lure her eye; she busied heard the sound
Of rustling leaves, but minded not, as used
520 To such disport before her through the field,
From every beast, more duteous at her call,
Than at Circean call the herd disguised.
He bolder now, uncalled before her stood;
But as in gaze admiring: oft he bowed
525 His turret crest, and sleek enamelled neck,
Fawning, and licked the ground whereon she trod.
His gentle dumb expression turned at length
The eye of Eve to mark his play; he glad
Of her attention gained, with serpent tongue
530 Organic, or impulse of vocal air,
His fraudulent temptation thus began.

---

changed into a snake, as was his wife, *Hermione,* when she embraced his serpentine form. The god of healing, Asclepius, journeyed as a serpent from his shrine in *Epidaurus* to Rome in order to stop a plague. In Plutarch's *Life of Alexander,* we learn that Philip of Macedonia saw his wife in bed with a snake. The oracle identified the serpent as Jupiter-Ammon. He was thus the divine father of Alexander the Great, foreshadowing Jupiter Capitolinus, who would assume a serpent body in siring *Scipio* Africanus.

510–14. Klemp (1977) noticed that the first letters of these lines spell *Satan.*

522. The sorceress Circe transformed men into obedient animals (*Od.* 10.212–19).

525. **turret:** towering; **enamelled:** smooth and variegated in color like enamel.

526. Here Satan, who balked at "prostration vile" in Heaven (5.782), invents *proskynesis,* the prostrate devotion paid to tyrants; Alexander the Great tried unsuccessfully to introduce this Persian custom into his court (Kerrigan 1998, 130).

529–30. with . . . air: Satan caused the serpent to speak either by using its tongue as an instrument or by impressing his words on the nearby air (A. Williams 116–117).

"He bolder now, uncalled before her stood" (9.523).

     "Wonder not, sovereign mistress, if perhaps
     Thou canst, who art sole wonder, much less arm
     Thy looks, the heav'n of mildness, with disdain,
535 Displeased that I approach thee thus, and gaze
     Insatiate, I thus single, nor have feared
     Thy awful brow, more awful thus retired.
     Fairest resemblance of thy Maker fair,
     Thee all things living gaze on, all things thine
540 By gift, and thy celestial beauty adore
     With ravishment beheld, there best beheld
     Where universally admired; but here
     In this enclosure wild, these beasts among,
     Beholders rude, and shallow to discern
545 Half what in thee is fair, one man except,
     Who sees thee? (and what is one?) who shouldst be seen
     A goddess among gods, adored and served
     By angels numberless, thy daily train."
        So glozed the Tempter, and his proem tuned;
550 Into the heart of Eve his words made way,
     Though at the voice much marveling; at length
     Not unamazed she thus in answer spake.
     "What may this mean? Language of man pronounced
     By tongue of brute, and human sense expressed?
555 The first at least of these I thought denied
     To beasts, whom God on their creation-day
     Created mute to all articulate sound;
     The latter I demur, for in their looks
     Much reason, and in their actions oft appears.
560 Thee, serpent, subtlest beast of all the field
     I knew, but not with human voice endued;
     Redouble then this miracle, and say,
     How cam'st thou speakable of mute, and how
     To me so friendly grown above the rest

---

532. **Wonder not:** punningly announcing the theme of one, oneness, and singularity that winds through the speech.
544. **shallow to discern:** without the intelligence to discern.

549. **glozed:** spoke flatteringly; **proem:** prelude.
558. **demur:** hesitate over.
563. **speakable:** able to speak.

565   Of brutal kind, that daily are in sight?
       Say, for such wonder claims attention due."
         To whom the guileful Tempter thus replied.
       "Empress of this fair world, resplendent Eve,
       Easy to me it is to tell thee all
570   What thou command'st, and right thou shouldst be obeyed:
       I was at first as other beasts that graze
       The trodden herb, of abject thoughts and low,
       As was my food, nor aught but food discerned
       Or sex, and apprehended nothing high:
575   Till on a day roving the field, I chanced
       A goodly tree far distant to behold
       Loaden with fruit of fairest colors mixed,
       Ruddy and gold: I nearer drew to gaze;
       When from the boughs a savory odor blown,
580   Grateful to appetite, more pleased my sense
       Than smell of sweetest fennel or the teats
       Of ewe or goat dropping with milk at ev'n,
       Unsucked of lamb or kid, that tend their play.
       To satisfy the sharp desire I had
585   Of tasting those fair apples, I resolved
       Not to defer; hunger and thirst at once,
       Powerful persuaders, quickened at the scent
       Of that alluring fruit, urged me so keen.
       About the mossy trunk I wound me soon,
590   For high from ground the branches would require
       Thy utmost reach or Adam's: round the Tree
       All other beasts that saw, with like desire
       Longing and envying stood, but could not reach.
       Amid the Tree now got, where plenty hung

571–612. The fourth and final of the major autobiographies in the poem: Sin's (2.747–809), Eve's (4.449–91), Adam's (8.250–520), and now the serpent's fraudulent story.

581. **fennel:** Serpents were supposed to be fond of this herb (Pliny, *Natural History* 19.9); they were also thought to suck the teats of sheep and goats. Serpent lore aside, it is brilliant strategy to present the Tree of Knowledge as, metaphorically, an unappreciated mother.

585. **apples:** The double sense of the Latin *malum* (apple, evil) sponsored a tradition identifying the forbidden fruit as an apple.

586. **defer:** delay.

595 Tempting so nigh, to pluck and eat my fill
　　I spared not, for such pleasure till that hour
　　At feed or fountain never had I found.
　　Sated at length, ere long I might perceive
　　Strange alteration in me, to degree
600 Of reason in my inward powers, and speech
　　Wanted not long, though to this shape retained.
　　Thenceforth to speculations high or deep
　　I turned my thoughts, and with capacious mind
　　Considered all things visible in heav'n,
605 Or Earth, or middle, all things fair and good;
　　But all that fair and good in thy divine
　　Semblance, and in thy beauty's heav'nly ray
　　United I beheld; no fair to thine
　　Equivalent or second, which compelled
610 Me thus, though importune perhaps, to come
　　And gaze, and worship thee of right declared
　　Sov'reign of creatures, universal dame."
　　　　So talked the spirited sly snake; and Eve
　　Yet more amazed unwary thus replied.
615 　　"Serpent, thy overpraising leaves in doubt
　　The virtue of that fruit, in thee first proved:
　　But say, where grows the tree, from hence how far?
　　For many are the trees of God that grow
　　In Paradise, and various, yet unknown
620 To us, in such abundance lies our choice,

596–97. Adam and Eve will entertain the same high estimate of the forbidden fruit's taste (ll. 786–87, 1022–24).

598–612. Having the serpent represent his powers of speech and reasoning as the effects of eating the forbidden fruit is a masterstroke. Evans (276–77) maintains that Milton's only precedent was Joseph Beaumont's *Psyche* (1648), a long and uninspired poem whose serpent does indeed claim to have gained language and wisdom from the fruit (canto 6, ll. 1699–1710), and tempts Eve with the idea that she may gain even loftier wisdom from such a meal, since she is starting at a higher level than the brute (1711–22). But Beaumont only vaguely anticipates the crisp argument to be advanced by Milton's Satan (see 710–12n).

605. **middle:** the air.

606–608. **But . . . beheld:** Cp. 8.472–74.

613. **spirited sly snake:** a sibilant phrase, anticipating the prolonged hissing of 10.508–77.

616. **virtue:** power.

As leaves a greater store of fruit untouched,
Still hanging incorruptible, till men
Grow up to their provision, and more hands
Help to disburden nature of her birth."

625　To whom the wily adder, blithe and glad.
"Empress, the way is ready, and not long,
Beyond a row of myrtles, on a flat,
Fast by a fountain, one small thicket past
Of blowing myrrh and balm; if thou accept

630　My conduct, I can bring thee thither soon."
"Lead then," said Eve. He leading swiftly rolled
In tangles, and made intricate seem straight,
To mischief swift. Hope elevates, and joy
Brightens his crest, as when a wand'ring fire,

635　Compact of unctuous vapor, which the night
Condenses, and the cold environs round,
Kindled through agitation to a flame,
Which oft, they say, some evil spirit attends
Hovering and blazing with delusive light,

640　Misleads th' amazed night-wanderer from his way
To bogs and mires, and oft through pond or pool,
There swallowed up and lost, from succor far.
So glistered the dire snake, and into fraud
Led Eve our credulous mother, to the Tree

645　Of prohibition, root of all our woe;
Which when she saw, thus to her guide she spake.
"Serpent, we might have spared our coming hither,

---

623. **their provision:** the fruits provided for them.

629. **blowing:** blooming.

634. **wand'ring fire:** the *ignis fatuus* or "will-o'-the-wisp," as in *Masque* 433. See Winny 168–70 and Burton, *The Anatomy of Melancholy* 166.

635. **Compact of:** composed of.

640. **amazed:** both perplexed and lost, as in a labyrinth.

641. **pond or pool:** an indication that Eve is being led not just to the Tree of Knowledge but back to her initial infatuation with her own image (4.456–65).

644–45. "'Into fraud led Eve ...' overlaps magnificently with '... led Eve to the Tree,' so that what begins as a moving and ancient moral metaphor (lead us not into temptation) crystallizes with terrifying literalness" (Ricks 1963, 76).

Fruitless to me, though fruit be here to excess,
The credit of whose virtue rest with thee,
650 Wondrous indeed, if cause of such effects.
But of this Tree we may not taste nor touch;
God so commanded, and left that command
Sole daughter of his voice; the rest, we live
Law to ourselves, our reason is our law."
655 　　To whom the Tempter guilefully replied.
"Indeed? Hath God then said that of the fruit
Of all these garden trees ye shall not eat,
Yet lords declared of all in earth or air?"
　　To whom thus Eve yet sinless. "Of the fruit
660 Of each tree in the garden we may eat,
But of the fruit of this fair Tree amidst
The garden, God hath said, 'Ye shall not eat
Thereof, nor shall ye touch it, lest ye die.'"
　　She scarce had said, though brief, when now more bold
665 The Tempter, but with show of zeal and love
To man, and indignation at his wrong,
New part puts on, and as to passion moved,
Fluctuates disturbed, yet comely and in act
Raised, as of some great matter to begin.
670 As when of old some orator renowned
In Athens or free Rome, where eloquence
Flourished, since mute, to some great cause addressed,
Stood in himself collected, while each part,
Motion, each act won audience ere the tongue,
675 Sometimes in highth began, as no delay
Of preface brooking through his zeal of right.
So standing, moving, or to highth upgrown
The Tempter all impassioned thus began.
　　"O sacred, wise, and wisdom-giving plant,

---

648. **Fruitless:** pointless, but also literally fruitless, since she cannot eat this fruit; Milton anticipates the fully fallen sense of the word at line 1188.
668. **Fluctuates:** undulates.
672. **since mute:** Eloquence itself is said to be extinct, not just in Greece and Rome; judging from *PR* 4.356–60, Milton may not have regarded the loss to be altogether negative.
674. **Motion:** gesture; **audience:** attention.
679–83. This speech, a brief travesty of *Paradise*

680 Mother of science, now I feel thy power
     Within me clear, not only to discern
     Things in their causes, but to trace the ways
     Of highest agents, deemed however wise.
     Queen of this universe, do not believe

685 Those rigid threats of death; ye shall not die:
     How should ye? By the fruit? It gives you life
     To knowledge. By the threat'ner? Look on me,
     Me who have touched and tasted, yet both live,
     And life more perfect have attained than fate

690 Meant me, by vent'ring higher than my lot.
     Shall that be shut to man, which to the beast
     Is open? Or will God incense his ire
     For such a petty trespass, and not praise
     Rather your dauntless virtue, whom the pain

695 Of death denounced, whatever thing death be,
     Deterred not from achieving what might lead
     To happier life, knowledge of good and evil;
     Of good, how just? Of evil, if what is evil
     Be real, why not known, since easier shunned?

700 God therefore cannot hurt ye, and be just;
     Not just, not God; not feared then, nor obeyed:
     Your fear itself of death removes the fear.
     Why then was this forbid? Why but to awe,
     Why but to keep ye low and ignorant,

705 His worshipers; he knows that in the day
     Ye eat thereof, your eyes that seem so clear,
     Yet are but dim, shall perfectly be then
     Opened and cleared, and ye shall be as gods,
     Knowing both good and evil as they know.

Lost intending to prove the ways of God to man unjust, begins appropriately with an invocation to the *power* of the forbidden fruit inside the serpent and (so he claims) manifest in his very words. Cp. the four invocations at the beginnings of Books 1, 3, 7, and 9.

680. **science:** in the wide original sense of the Latin *scientia,* "knowledge."

698–99. **Of evil ... shunned?:** A potent bit of sophistry stemming from the double meaning of *known:* (1) known by rational apprehension; (2) known by experience. Eve knows in sense 1 that eating the fruit is evil. But if eating the fruit becomes

710 That ye should be as gods, since I as man,
Internal man, is but proportion meet,
I of brute human, ye of human gods.
So ye shall die perhaps, by putting off
Human, to put on gods, death to be wished,
715 Though threatened, which no worse than this can bring.
And what are gods that man may not become
As they, participating godlike food?
The gods are first, and that advantage use
On our belief, that all from them proceeds;
720 I question it, for this fair Earth I see,
Warmed by the sun, producing every kind,
Them nothing: if they all things, who enclosed
Knowledge of good and evil in this Tree,
That whoso eats thereof, forthwith attains
725 Wisdom without their leave? And wherein lies
Th' offense, that man should thus attain to know?
What can your knowledge hurt him, or this Tree
Impart against his will if all be his?
Or is it envy, and can envy dwell
730 In Heav'nly breasts? These, these and many more
Causes import your need of this fair fruit.
Goddess humane, reach then, and freely taste."
    He ended, and his words replete with guile
Into her heart too easy entrance won:
735 Fixed on the fruit she gazed, which to behold

---

known in sense 2, she can hardly use that
knowledge to shun evil. For in that case,
she will have done evil. It is the difference
between innocence and experience.

710–12. The power of speech becomes
Satan's most tangible argument: as eating
the fruit allowed him to change from
brute to human, rising a notch in the
chain of being, so eating the fruit will
allow Eve to change from human to
angel, a *proportion meet*. See 598–612n. The
irony is pointed. The snake has not as-
cended the scale of being; Satan has in
fact descended into the snake (ll. 163–71).

717. **participating:** partaking of.
720. **question:** Cp. 5.853–63, where Satan
doubts whether the Son or anyone else
created angels. The introduction of ques-
tioning is crucial; note the high propor-
tion of questions in lines 686–732, 747–79.
722. **if they all things:** if they author all
things.
732. **humane:** gracious, as in 2.109 and *PR*
1.221.
735–43. A passage built on the structure of the
five senses, moving from sight to sound to
smell, then to the desire *to touch or taste*,
given imperative force in Satan's last words

Might tempt alone, and in her ears the sound
Yet rung of his persuasive words, impregned
With reason, to her seeming, and with truth;
Meanwhile the hour of noon drew on, and waked
740 An eager appetite, raised by the smell
So savory of that fruit, which with desire,
Inclinable now grown to touch or taste,
Solicited her longing eye; yet first
Pausing a while, thus to herself she mused.
745   "Great are thy virtues, doubtless, best of fruits,
Though kept from man, and worthy to be admired,
Whose taste, too long forborne, at first assay
Gave elocution to the mute, and taught
The tongue not made for speech to speak thy praise:
750 Thy praise he also who forbids thy use,
Conceals not from us, naming thee the Tree
Of Knowledge, knowledge both of good and evil;
Forbids us then to taste, but his forbidding
Commends thee more, while it infers the good
755 By thee communicated, and our want:
For good unknown, sure is not had, or had
And yet unknown, is as not had at all.
In plain then, what forbids he but to know,
Forbids us good, forbids us to be wise?
760 Such prohibitions bind not. But if death
Bind us with after-bands, what profits then
Our inward freedom? In the day we eat
Of this fair fruit, our doom is, we shall die.
How dies the serpent? He hath eat'n and lives,
765 And knows, and speaks, and reasons, and discerns,
Irrational till then. For us alone
Was death invented? Or to us denied
This intellectual food, for beasts reserved?

(*reach then, and freely taste*, l. 732), and in the end circling back to *her longing eye*.

744. **to herself she mused:** the first time in the poem that Milton represents the silent inward speech of Adam or Eve.

756–57. **good unknown:** good unexperienced; **yet unknown:** good not apprehended rationally. The word-tree derived from "knowledge" has become a treacherous labyrinth. See 698–99n.

For beasts it seems: yet that one beast which first
770 Hath tasted, envies not, but brings with joy
The good befall'n him, author unsuspect,
Friendly to man, far from deceit or guile.
What fear I then, rather what know to fear
Under this ignorance of good and evil,
775 Of God or death, of law or penalty?
Here grows the cure of all, this fruit divine,
Fair to the eye, inviting to the taste,
Of virtue to make wise: what hinders then
To reach, and feed at once both body and mind?"
780　So saying, her rash hand in evil hour
Forth reaching to the fruit, she plucked, she ate:
Earth felt the wound, and Nature from her seat
Sighing through all her works gave signs of woe,
That all was lost. Back to the thicket slunk
785 The guilty serpent, and well might, for Eve
Intent now wholly on her taste, naught else
Regarded, such delight till then, as seemed,
In fruit she never tasted, whether true
Or fancied so, through expectation high
790 Of knowledge, nor was Godhead from her thought.
Greedily she engorged without restraint,
And knew not eating death: satiate at length,
And heightened as with wine, jocund and boon,
Thus to herself she pleasingly began.
795　"O sov'reign, virtuous, precious of all trees
In Paradise, of operation blessed
To sapience, hitherto obscured, infamed,

---

771. **author unsuspect:** authority above sus-
picion.
776. **cure:** Eve means "remedy," but editors
hear an unintended pun on the Latin *cura*,
"care."
780. **hand:** Is hand the subject or object of
reaching in line 781? (Evans in Broadbent);
evil hour: noon.
784. **all was lost:** The poem has arrived at
the meaning of its title.

792. **knew not eating death:** At least four
meanings are copresent: "She did not ex-
perience death while eating"; "She did
not know death, which devours"; "She
did not know she was eating death";
"She did not gain knowledge when eating
death."
797. **sapience:** knowledge, from the Latin
sapere, "to taste."

And thy fair fruit let hang, as to no end
Created; but henceforth my early care,
800 Not without song, each morning, and due praise
Shall tend thee, and the fertile burden ease
Of thy full branches offered free to all;
Till dieted by thee I grow mature
In knowledge, as the gods who all things know;
805 Though others envy what they cannot give;
For had the gift been theirs, it had not here
Thus grown. Experience, next to thee I owe,
Best guide; not following thee, I had remained
In ignorance, thou open'st wisdom's way,
810 And giv'st access, though secret she retire.
And I perhaps am secret; Heav'n is high,
High and remote to see from thence distinct
Each thing on Earth; and other care perhaps
May have diverted from continual watch
815 Our great forbidder, safe with all his spies
About him. But to Adam in what sort
Shall I appear? Shall I to him make known
As yet my change, and give him to partake
Full happiness with me, or rather not,
820 But keep the odds of knowledge in my power
Without copartner? So to add what wants
In female sex, the more to draw his love,
And render me more equal, and perhaps,
A thing not undesirable, sometime
825 Superior; for inferior who is free?
This may be well: but what if God have seen,
And death ensue? Then I shall be no more,
And Adam wedded to another Eve,
Shall live with her enjoying, I extinct;
830 A death to think. Confirmed then I resolve;

---

820. **odds:** advantage; see 4.447n.

823. **more equal:** The first words that Milton uses to define gender differences are "Not equal, as their sex not equal seemed" (4.296).

825. **for inferior who is free?:** as Satan has maintained (6.164–70).

827. **I shall be no more:** Heard at the opening of this book, *no more* is here applied to death and oblivion (see 1n).

Adam shall share with me in bliss or woe:
So dear I love him, that with him all deaths
I could endure, without him live no life."

　　So saying, from the Tree her step she turned,
835　But first low reverence done, as to the power
That dwelt within, whose presence had infused
Into the plant sciential sap, derived
From nectar, drink of gods. Adam the while
Waiting desirous her return, had wove
840　Of choicest flow'rs a garland to adorn
Her tresses, and her rural labors crown,
As reapers oft are wont their harvest queen.
Great joy he promised to his thoughts, and new
Solace in her return, so long delayed;
845　Yet oft his heart, divine of something ill,
Misgave him; he the falt'ring measure felt;
And forth to meet her went, the way she took
That morn when first they parted; by the Tree
Of Knowledge he must pass, there he her met,
850　Scarce from the tree returning; in her hand
A bough of fairest fruit that downy smiled,
New gathered, and ambrosial smell diffused.
To him she hasted, in her face Excuse
Came prologue, and Apology to prompt,
855　Which with bland words at will she thus addressed.

　　"Hast thou not wondered, Adam, at my stay?
Thee I have missed, and thought it long, deprived

835. **low reverence:** "She ... now worships a vegetable" (Lewis 122).

837. **sciential:** conferring knowledge on those who partake of it.

845. **divine of something ill:** A stricken heart often signals a bad omen or premonition, as in *HAM* 5.2.208: "How ill all's here about my heart."

846. **falt'ring measure:** The elision of the middle syllable in *faltering* keeps Adam's *measure* or heartbeat in an iambic mold; the pun on *falt/fault* (*fault'ring* was the original spelling) suggests cardiac problems to come.

851. **downy smiled:** seemed attractive covered with down.

853–54. **in her face ... prompt:** "Excuse, the pleading expression on her face, was the prologue to Apology [Justification], and continued to serve as this actor's prompter."

855. **bland:** smooth, containing blandishments.

Thy presence, agony of love till now
Not felt, nor shall be twice, for never more
860 Mean I to try, what rash untried I sought,
The pain of absence from thy sight. But strange
Hath been the cause, and wonderful to hear:
This Tree is not as we are told, a tree
Of danger tasted, nor to evil unknown
865 Op'ning the way, but of divine effect
To open eyes, and make them gods who taste;
And hath been tasted such: the serpent wise,
Or not restrained as we, or not obeying,
Hath eaten of the fruit, and is become,
870 Not dead, as we are threatened, but thenceforth
Endued with human voice and human sense,
Reasoning to admiration, and with me
Persuasively hath so prevailed, that I
Have also tasted, and have also found
875 Th' effects to correspond, opener mine eyes,
Dim erst, dilated spirits, ampler heart,
And growing up to Godhead; which for thee
Chiefly I sought, without thee can despise.
For bliss, as thou hast part, to me is bliss,
880 Tedious, unshared with thee, and odious soon.
Thou therefore also taste, that equal lot
May join us, equal joy, as equal love;
Lest thou not tasting, different degree
Disjoin us, and I then too late renounce
885 Deity for thee, when fate will not permit."
    Thus Eve with count'nance blithe her story told;
But in her cheek distemper flushing glowed.
On th' other side, Adam, soon as he heard
The fatal trespass done by Eve, amazed,
890 Astonied stood and blank, while horror chill
Ran through his veins, and all his joints relaxed;
From his slack hand the garland wreathed for Eve

---

868. **Or ... or:** either ... or.
890. **Astonied:** astonished, with pun on "as

stone"; **horror chill:** cp. Vergil's *frigidus*
horror (*Aen.* 3.29).

Down dropped, and all the faded roses shed:
Speechless he stood and pale, till thus at length
895 First to himself he inward silence broke.
 "O fairest of creation, last and best
Of all God's works, creature in whom excelled
Whatever can to sight or thought be formed,
Holy, divine, good, amiable, or sweet!
900 How art thou lost, how on a sudden lost,
Defaced, deflow'red, and now to death devote?
Rather how hast thou yielded to transgress
The strict forbiddance, how to violate
The sacred fruit forbidd'n! Some cursèd fraud
905 Of enemy hath beguiled thee, yet unknown,
And me with thee hath ruined, for with thee
Certain my resolution is to die;
How can I live without thee, how forgo
Thy sweet converse and love so dearly joined,
910 To live again in these wild woods forlorn?
Should God create another Eve, and I
Another rib afford, yet loss of thee
Would never from my heart; no no, I feel
The link of nature draw me: flesh of flesh,
915 Bone of my bone thou art, and from thy state
Mine never shall be parted, bliss or woe."
So having said, as one from sad dismay
Recomforted, and after thoughts disturbed
Submitting to what seemed remediless,

893. **faded roses**: A first instance of decay in Eden (Fowler). Evans thinks the faded roses symbolize Eve's mortality. But since fallen roses will acquire thorns (4.256), and since these woven flowers were intended to crown (l. 841), the decayed garland may also be meant to evoke Christ's crown of thorns.

895. **he inward silence broke**: as Eve also did before her fall (744n).

896. **last and best**: last but not best, Raphael warned (8.565–66).

901. **deflow'red**: Accounts of the Fall sometimes made use of sexual metaphors such as ravishment, seduction, and infidelity (A. Williams 120, 125), and sometimes included speculations about the actual deterioration of human sexuality (Turner 124–73). **devote**: consecrated.

911. **another Eve**: Eve also rejected this idea (ll. 828–30).

916. **bliss or woe**: echoing Eve at line 831.

920 Thus in calm mood his words to Eve he turned.
    "Bold deed thou hast presumed, advent'rous Eve,
    And peril great provoked, who thus hath dared
    Had it been only coveting to eye
    That sacred fruit, sacred to abstinence,
925 Much more to taste it under ban to touch.
    But past who can recall, or done undo?
    Not God omnipotent, nor Fate, yet so
    Perhaps thou shalt not die, perhaps the fact
    Is not so heinous now, foretasted fruit,
930 Profaned first by the serpent, by him first
    Made common and unhallowed ere our taste;
    Nor yet on him found deadly; he yet lives,
    Lives, as thou saidst, and gains to live as man
    Higher degree of life, inducement strong
935 To us, as likely tasting to attain
    Proportional ascent, which cannot be
    But to be gods, or angels, demi-gods.
    Nor can I think that God, creator wise,
    Though threat'ning, will in earnest so destroy
940 Us his prime creatures, dignified so high,
    Set over all his works, which in our fall,
    For us created, needs with us must fail,
    Dependent made; so God shall uncreate,
    Be frustrate, do, undo, and labor lose,
945 Not well conceived of God, who though his power
    Creation could repeat, yet would be loath
    Us to abolish, lest the Adversary
    Triumph and say, 'Fickle their state whom God
    Most favors; who can please him long? Me first
950 He ruined, now mankind; whom will he next?'

---

924. **sacred:** set apart, unlike all other fruits (in being subject to abstinence).

926. The line contains two nearly synonymous proverbs: "Things past cannot be recalled" (Tilley T203) and "Things done cannot be undone" (Tilley T200).

928. **fact:** deed and crime.

936. **Proportional ascent:** echoing Satan at lines 710–12.

947–51. **lest . . . foe:** And indeed, Satan will not be allowed to gloat—a first intuition of the protevangelium (10.175–81n) and its enactment in Hell (10.504–77).

Matter of scorn, not to be given the foe.
However I with thee have fixed my lot,
Certain to undergo like doom; if death
Consort with thee, death is to me as life;
955 So forcible within my heart I feel
The bond of nature draw me to my own,
My own in thee, for what thou art is mine;
Our state cannot be severed, we are one,
One flesh; to lose thee were to lose myself."
960   So Adam, and thus Eve to him replied.
"O glorious trial of exceeding love,
Illustrious evidence, example high!
Engaging me to emulate, but short
Of thy perfection, how shall I attain,
965 Adam, from whose dear side I boast me sprung,
And gladly of our union hear thee speak,
One heart, one soul in both; whereof good proof
This day affords, declaring thee resolved,
Rather than death or aught than death more dread
970 Shall separate us, linked in love so dear,
To undergo with me one guilt, one crime,
If any be, of tasting this fair fruit,
Whose virtue, for of good still good proceeds,
Direct, or by occasion hath presented
975 This happy trial of thy love, which else
So eminently never had been known.
Were it I thought death menaced would ensue
This my attempt, I would sustain alone
The worst, and not persuade thee, rather die
980 Deserted, than oblige thee with a fact
Pernicious to thy peace, chiefly assured
Remarkably so late of thy so true,
So faithful love unequaled; but I feel

---

954. **death is to me as life:** Editors hear an
echo of Satan's "Evil be thou my good"
(4.110), but the resemblance is more ver-
bal than moral or psychological.

980. **oblige:** make liable to a penalty (Lat.
obligare).

Far otherwise th' event, not death, but life
985 Augmented, opened eyes, new hopes, new joys,
Taste so divine, that what of sweet before
Hath touched my sense, flat seems to this, and harsh.
On my experience, Adam, freely taste,
And fear of death deliver to the winds."
990   So saying, she embraced him, and for joy
Tenderly wept, much won that he his love
Had so ennobled, as of choice to incur
Divine displeasure for her sake, or death.
In recompense (for such compliance bad
995 Such recompense best merits) from the bough
She gave him of that fair enticing fruit
With liberal hand: he scrupled not to eat
Against his better knowledge, not deceived,
But fondly overcome with female charm.
1000 Earth trembled from her entrails, as again
In pangs, and Nature gave a second groan;
Sky loured, and muttering Thunder, some sad drops
Wept at completing of the mortal sin
Original; while Adam took no thought,
1005 Eating his fill, nor Eve to iterate
Her former trespass feared, the more to soothe
Him with her loved society, that now
As with new wine intoxicated both
They swim in mirth, and fancy that they feel
1010 Divinity within them breeding wings
Wherewith to scorn the earth: but that false fruit
Far other operation first displayed,
Carnal desire inflaming; he on Eve
Began to cast lascivious eyes, she him
1015 As wantonly repaid; in lust they burn:
Till Adam thus gan Eve to dalliance move.

988. **freely taste:** echoing Satan at line 732.
998. **not deceived:** Cp. 1 Tim. 2.14: "Adam was not deceived, but the woman being deceived was in the transgression."
999. **fondly:** foolishly.

1003–1004. **sin/Original:** The only appearance of the famous theological phrase in the poem; for Milton's understanding of it, see *CD* I.II.
1016. **dalliance:** amorous play.

"Eve, now I see thou art exact of taste,
And elegant, of sapience no small part,
Since to each meaning savor we apply,
1020 And palate call judicious; I the praise
Yield thee, so well this day thou hast purveyed.
Much pleasure we have lost, while we abstained
From this delightful fruit, nor known till now
True relish, tasting; if such pleasure be
1025 In things to us forbidden, it might be wished,
For this one tree had been forbidden ten.
But come, so well refreshed, now let us play,
As meet is, after such delicious fare;
For never did thy beauty since the day
1030 I saw thee first and wedded thee, adorned
With all perfections, so inflame my sense
With ardor to enjoy thee, fairer now
Than ever, bounty of this virtuous Tree."
     So said he, and forbore not glance or toy
1035 Of amorous intent, well understood
Of Eve, whose eye darted contagious fire.
Her hand he seized, and to a shady bank,
Thick overhead with verdant roof embow'red
He led her nothing loath; flow'rs were the couch,
1040 Pansies, and violets, and asphodel,
And hyacinth, earth's freshest softest lap.
There they their fill of love and love's disport
Took largely, of their mutual guilt the seal,

1017–20. **Eve . . . judicious:** The idea, somewhat tortuously expressed, is that we apply words like *savor* and *judicious* to both questions of taste and questions of wisdom—hence the word *sapience*, epitomizing such usages, brilliantly denotes both taste and wisdom.

1018. **elegant:** in the sense of the Latin *elegans*, "refined in taste."

1025–26. **it . . . ten:** His fond wish will be granted when God delivers the Ten Commandments to Moses.

1028. **meet:** "appropriate," the deliciousness of the meal having awakened an appetite for its delicious purveyor; also glancing at *help meet*, one of Eve's titles, and by a pun on *meat* (meaning food in general), anticipating their new carnivorous diet.

1029–32. See Homer, *Od.* 14.314–16.

1037. **Her hand he seized:** not gently, as at 4.488–89.

1043. **of their mutual guilt the seal:** A *seal* makes a document official. So the mutual act of intercourse, as it were, brazenly

The solace of their sin, till dewy sleep
1045 Oppressed them, wearied with their amorous play.
Soon as the force of that fallacious fruit,
That with exhilarating vapor bland
About their spirits had played, and inmost powers
Made err, was now exhaled, and grosser sleep
1050 Bred of unkindly fumes, with conscious dreams
Encumbered, now had left them, up they rose
As from unrest, and each the other viewing,
Soon found their eyes how opened, and their minds
How darkened; innocence, that as a veil
1055 Had shadowed them from knowing ill, was gone,
Just confidence, and native righteousness
And honor from about them, naked left
To guilty Shame: he covered, but his robe
Uncovered more. So rose the Danite strong,
1060 Herculean Samson, from the harlot-lap
Of Philistean Dalila, and waked
Shorn of his strength, they destitute and bare
Of all their virtue: silent, and in face
Confounded long they sat, as stricken mute,
1065 Till Adam, though not less than Eve abashed,
At length gave utterance to these words constrained.
    "O Eve, in evil hour thou didst give ear
To that false worm, of whomsoever taught
To counterfeit man's voice, true in our fall,
1070 False in our promised rising; since our eyes
Opened we find indeed, and find we know

---

authenticates their mutual crime: "We
have done this, we who were given sexu-
ality with the commandment to be fruit-
ful and multiply."
1048. **spirits:** a technical term in medical
physiology, denoting vaporous sub-
stances in the blood that carry out com-
munications between the soul and body.
See Thomas Wright, *The Passions of the
Minde in Generall* (1604), 59–68 and passim;
Donne, "The Extasie," 61–64.

1050. **unkindly:** unnatural; **conscious:** full of
guilty knowledge.
1058. **he:** Shame.
1059. **Danite:** Samson's father belonged to
the tribe of Dan.
1060. **Herculean:** strong like Hercules;
harlot-lap: The word *harlot* does not ap-
pear in Milton's *Samson Agonistes*, where
Dalila is the hero's wife.
1067. **Eve, in evil:** The pun is prelude to a
host of accusations.

Both good and evil, good lost, and evil got,
Bad fruit of knowledge, if this be to know,
Which leaves us naked thus, of honor void,
1075 Of innocence, of faith, of purity,
Our wonted ornaments now soiled and stained,
And in our faces evident the signs
Of foul concupiscence; whence evil store;
Even shame, the last of evils; of the first
1080 Be sure then. How shall I behold the face
Henceforth of God or angel, erst with joy
And rapture so oft beheld? Those Heav'nly shapes
Will dazzle now this Earthly, with their blaze
Insufferably bright. O might I here
1085 In solitude live savage, in some glade
Obscured, where highest woods impenetrable
To star or sunlight, spread their umbrage broad
And brown as evening: cover me ye pines,
Ye cedars, with innumerable boughs
1090 Hide me, where I may never see them more.
But let us now, as in bad plight, devise
What best may for the present serve to hide
The parts of each from other, that seem most
To shame obnoxious, and unseemliest seen,
1095 Some tree whose broad smooth leaves together sewed,
And girded on our loins, may cover round
Those middle parts, that this newcomer, Shame,
There sit not, and reproach us as unclean."
    So counseled he, and both together went
1100 Into the thickest wood; there soon they chose
The fig tree, not that kind for fruit renowned,
But such as at this day to Indians known

1078. **evil store:** evil aplenty.
1079. **Even shame, the last of evils:** Shame, because it initiates repentance, is the last manifestation of the evil that caused it (*the first*).
1083. **Earthly:** earthly nature.

1087. **umbrage:** shadow, foliage.
1094. **obnoxious:** exposed.
1101. **fig tree:** the banyan, not the common variety. For details and sources, see Svendsen 1969, 31–32, 134–36.

In Malabar or Deccan spreads her arms
Branching so broad and long, that in the ground
1105 The bended twigs take root, and daughters grow
About the mother tree, a pillared shade
High overarched, and echoing walks between;
There oft the Indian herdsman shunning heat
Shelters in cool, and tends his pasturing herds
1110 At loopholes cut through thickest shade: those leaves
They gathered, broad as Amazonian targe,
And with what skill they had, together sewed,
To gird their waist, vain covering if to hide
Their guilt and dreaded shame; O how unlike
1115 To that first naked glory. Such of late
Columbus found th' American so girt
With feathered cincture, naked else and wild
Among the trees on isles and woody shores.
Thus fenced, and as they thought, their shame in part
1120 Covered, but not at rest or ease of mind,
They sat them down to weep, nor only tears
Rained at their eyes, but high winds worse within
Began to rise, high passions, anger, hate,
Mistrust, suspicion, discord, and shook sore
1125 Their inward state of mind, calm region once
And full of peace, now tossed and turbulent:
For understanding ruled not, and the will
Heard not her lore, both in subjection now
To sensual appetite, who from beneath
1130 Usurping over sov'reign reason claimed
Superior sway: from thus distempered breast,
Adam, estranged in look and altered style,

1103. **Malabar:** southwest coast of India; **Deccan:** the peninsula of India (including Malabar).

1111. **as Amazonian targe:** as an Amazon's shield (notable for its size).

1115. **naked glory:** The paradoxical force of the phrase stems from the idea of *glory* (Heb. *kabod*) as an adornment, a radiance of being (Rumrich 1987, 20–21, 131–32).

1116. **Columbus:** one of the two near contemporaries mentioned in the poem (see 1.288–91n).

1117. **cincture:** belt.

Speech intermitted thus to Eve renewed.
   "Would thou hadst hearkened to my words, and stayed
1135 With me, as I besought thee, when that strange
Desire of wand'ring this unhappy morn.
I know not whence possessed thee; we had then
Remained still happy, not as now, despoiled
Of all our good, shamed, naked, miserable.
1140 Let none henceforth seek needless cause to approve
The faith they owe; when earnestly they seek
Such proof, conclude, they then begin to fail."
   To whom soon moved with touch of blame thus Eve.
"What words have passed thy lips, Adam severe,
1145 Imput'st thou that to my default, or will
Of wand'ring, as thou call'st it, which who knows
But might as ill have happened thou being by,
Or to thyself perhaps: hadst thou been there,
Or here th' attempt, thou couldst not have discerned
1150 Fraud in the serpent, speaking as he spake;
No ground of enmity between us known,
Why he should mean me ill, or seek to harm.
Was I to have never parted from thy side?
As good have grown there still a lifeless rib.
1155 Being as I am, why didst not thou the head
Command me absolutely not to go,
Going into such danger as thou saidst?
Too facile then thou didst not much gainsay,
Nay, didst permit, approve, and fair dismiss.
1160 Hadst thou been firm and fixed in thy dissent,
Neither had I transgressed, nor thou with me."
   To whom then first incensed Adam replied.
"Is this the love, is this the recompense
Of mine to thee, ingrateful Eve, expressed
1165 Immutable when thou wert lost, not I,
Who might have lived and joyed immortal bliss,
Yet willingly chose rather death with thee:

1133. **intermitted:** interrupted (by the quest
  for covering).

And am I now upbraided, as the cause
Of thy transgressing? Not enough severe,
1170 It seems, in thy restraint: what could I more?
I warned thee, I admonished thee, foretold
The danger, and the lurking enemy
That lay in wait; beyond this had been force,
And force upon free will hath here no place.
1175 But confidence then bore thee on, secure
Either to meet no danger, or to find
Matter of glorious trial; and perhaps
I also erred in overmuch admiring
What seemed in thee so perfect, that I thought
1180 No evil durst attempt thee, but I rue
That error now, which is become my crime,
And thou th' accuser. Thus it shall befall
Him who to worth in women overtrusting
Lets her will rule; restraint she will not brook,
1185 And left to herself, if evil thence ensue,
She first his weak indulgence will accuse."
      Thus they in mutual accusation spent
The fruitless hours, but neither self-condemning,
And of their vain contest appeared no end.

1187. **mutual accusation:** *Mutual guilt* (l. 1043) has now deteriorated into a quarreling *mutual accusation.*
1188. **fruitless hours:** See 648n.
1189. **no end:** *No more* at the beginning of the book, declaring unfallen favors at an end, is balanced against the concluding *no end,* declaring fallen ills (so it appears) interminable.

Book X

The Argument

Man's transgression known, the guardian angels forsake Paradise, and return up to Heaven to approve their vigilance, and are approved, God declaring that the entrance of Satan could not be by them prevented. He sends his Son to judge the transgressors, who descends and gives sentence accordingly; then in pity clothes them both, and reascends. Sin and Death, sitting till then at the gates of Hell, by wondrous sympathy feeling the success of Satan in this new world, and the sin by man there committed, resolve to sit no longer confined in Hell, but to follow Satan their sire up to the place of man. To make the way easier from Hell to this world to and fro, they pave a broad highway or bridge over Chaos, according to the track that Satan first made; then preparing for Earth, they meet him proud of his success returning to Hell; their mutual gratulation. Satan arrives at Pandaemonium; in full assembly relates with boasting his success against man; instead of applause is entertained with a general hiss by all his audience, transformed with himself also suddenly into serpents, according to his doom given in Paradise; then deluded with a show of the forbidden tree springing up before them, they greedily reaching to take of the fruit, chew dust and bitter ashes. The proceedings of Sin and Death; God foretells the final victory of his Son over them, and the renewing of all things, but for the present commands his angels to make several alterations in the heavens and elements. Adam more and more perceiving his fallen condition, heavily bewails, rejects the condolement of Eve. She persists and at length appeases him; then to evade the curse likely to fall on their offspring, proposes to Adam violent ways which he approves not, but conceiving better hope, puts her in mind of the late promise made them, that her seed should be revenged on the Serpent, and exhorts her with him to seek peace of the offended Deity, by repentance and supplication.

Meanwhile the heinous and despiteful act
Of Satan done in Paradise, and how
He in the serpent, had perverted Eve,
Her husband she, to taste the fatal fruit,
5 Was known in Heav'n; for what can scape the eye
Of God all-seeing, or deceive his heart
Omniscient, who in all things wise and just,
Hindered not Satan to attempt the mind
Of man, with strength entire, and free will armed,
10 Complete to have discovered and repulsed
Whatever wiles of foe or seeming friend.
For still they knew, and ought to have still remembered
The high injunction not to taste that fruit,
Whoever tempted; which they not obeying,
15 Incurred, what could they less, the penalty,
And manifold in sin, deserved to fall.
Up into Heav'n from Paradise in haste
Th' angelic guards ascended, mute and sad
For man, for of his state by this they knew,
20 Much wond'ring how the subtle fiend had stol'n
Entrance unseen. Soon as th' unwelcome news
From Earth arriv'd at Heaven Gate, displeased
All were who heard, dim sadness did not spare
That time celestial visages, yet mixed
25 With pity, violated not their bliss.
About the new-arrived, in multitudes
Th' ethereal people ran, to hear and know
How all befell: they towards the throne supreme
Accountable made haste to make appear
30 With righteous plea, their utmost vigilance,
And easily approved; when the Most High
Eternal Father from his secret cloud,
Amidst in thunder uttered thus his voice.

---

10. **Complete:** fully equipped.

12. **still:** always.

16. **manifold in sin:** various in sin. On the multiplicity of the sin of the Fall, see *CD* 1.11 (*MLM* 1235–36); A. Williams 121–22.

29–31. **Accountable . . . approved:** "The guardian angels, accountable for their actions, hastily approached the throne to plead their vigilance, which God readily confirmed: the guards were not to blame."

"Assembled angels, and ye Powers returned
35   From unsuccessful charge, be not dismayed,
Nor troubled at these tidings from the Earth,
Which your sincerest care could not prevent,
Foretold so lately what would come to pass,
When first this Tempter crossed the gulf from Hell.
40   I told ye then he should prevail and speed
On his bad errand, man should be seduced
And flattered out of all, believing lies
Against his Maker; no decree of mine
Concurring to necessitate his fall,
45   Or touch with lightest moment of impulse
His free will, to her own inclining left
In even scale. But fall'n he is, and now
What rests but that the mortal sentence pass
On his transgression, death denounced that day,
50   Which he presumes already vain and void,
Because not yet inflicted, as he feared,
By some immediate stroke; but soon shall find
Forbearance no acquittance ere day end.
Justice shall not return as bounty scorned.
55   But whom send I to judge them? Whom but thee
Vicegerent Son, to thee I have transferred
All judgment, whether in Heav'n, or Earth, or Hell.
Easy it might be seen that I intend
Mercy colleague with justice, sending thee
60   Man's friend, his Mediator, his designed
Both ransom and Redeemer voluntary,
And destined man himself to judge man fall'n."
So spake the Father, and unfolding bright
Toward the right hand his glory, on the Son

40. **speed:** be successful.
45. **moment:** the minimum weight neces-
sary to disturb the equilibrium of a bal-
ance (the *even scale* of l. 47). Cp. 6.239,
245–46.
48. **rests:** remains.
53. **Forbearance no acquittance:** A debt is

not settled just because payment has not
yet been demanded; see Tilley F584.
54. "Man will not scorn my justice [for not
being duly delivered] as he scorned my
gift of Paradise."
56–57. **to thee . . . judgment:** John 5.22.

65 Blazed forth unclouded deity; he full
Resplendent all his Father manifest
Expressed, and thus divinely answered mild.
　　"Father Eternal, thine is to decree,
Mine both in Heav'n and Earth to do thy will
70 Supreme, that thou in me thy Son beloved
May'st ever rest well pleased. I go to judge
On Earth these thy transgressors, but thou know'st,
Whoever judged, the worst on me must light,
When time shall be, for so I undertook
75 Before thee; and not repenting, this obtain
Of right, that I may mitigate their doom
On me derived, yet I shall temper so
Justice with mercy, as may illustrate most
Them fully satisfied, and thee appease.
80 Attendance none shall need, nor train, where none
Are to behold the judgment but the judged,
Those two; the third best absent is condemned,
Convict by flight, and rebel to all law;
Conviction to the serpent none belongs."
85 　　Thus saying, from his radiant seat he rose
Of high collateral glory: him Thrones and Powers,
Princedoms, and Dominations ministrant
Accompanied to Heaven gate, from whence
Eden and all the coast in prospect lay.
90 Down he descended straight; the speed of gods
Time counts not, though with swiftest minutes winged.
Now was the sun in western cadence low
From noon, and gentle airs due at their hour
To fan the earth now waked, and usher in

---

78. **illustrate most:** show above all.
79. **Them:** justice and mercy. Cp. *Nat Ode,* stanza 15.
80. **Attendance none shall need:** "I will not need a retinue."
82. **the third:** Satan.
83. **Convict:** convicted.
84. **Conviction:** both "proof of guilt" and "condition of being convinced of sin" (*OED* 8).
86. **collateral:** side by side.
90–91. **the speed . . . winged:** The implication is that time, however finely measured, contains no unit short enough to express the instantaneous speed of the Son.
92. **cadence:** falling.

95   The evening cool, when he from wrath more cool
      Came the mild Judge and Intercessor both
      To sentence man: the voice of God they heard
      Now walking in the garden, by soft winds
      Brought to their ears, while day declined; they heard,
100 And from his presence hid themselves among
      The thickest trees, both man and wife, till God
      Approaching, thus to Adam called aloud.
        "Where art thou Adam, wont with joy to meet
      My coming seen far off? I miss thee here,
105 Not pleased, thus entertained with solitude,
      Where obvious duty erewhile appeared unsought:
      Or come I less conspicuous, or what change
      Absents thee, or what chance detain? Come forth."
      He came, and with him Eve, more loath, though first
110 To offend, discount'nanced both, and discomposed;
      Love was not in their looks, either to God
      Or to each other, but apparent guilt,
      And shame, and perturbation, and despair,
      Anger, and obstinacy, and hate, and guile.
115 Whence Adam falt'ring long, thus answered brief.
        "I heard thee in the garden, and of thy voice
      Afraid, being naked, hid myself." To whom
      The gracious judge without revile replied.
        "My voice thou oft hast heard, and hast not feared,
120 But still rejoiced, how is it now become
      So dreadful to thee? That thou art naked, who
      Hath told thee? Hast thou eaten of the tree
      Whereof I gave thee charge thou shouldst not eat?"
        To whom thus Adam sore beset replied.
125 "O Heav'n! In evil strait this day I stand
      Before my Judge, either to undergo
      Myself the total crime, or to accuse
      My other self, the partner of my life;

---

106. **obvious:** The word, meaning (1) "plain"
    and (2) "coming in the way," defines both
    the obviousness of the duty and the duty
    to be obvious before a visiting deity.

118. **revile:** reviling.

120. **still:** always, ever.

128. **other self:** See 8.450n.

Whose failing, while her faith to me remains,
130 I should conceal, and not expose to blame
By my complaint; but strict necessity
Subdues me, and calamitous constraint
Lest on my head both sin and punishment,
However insupportable, be all
135 Devolved; though should I hold my peace, yet thou
Wouldst easily detect what I conceal.
This woman whom thou mad'st to be my help,
And gav'st me as thy perfect gift, so good,
So fit, so acceptable, so divine,
140 That from her hand I could suspect no ill,
And what she did, whatever in itself,
Her doing seemed to justify the deed;
She gave me of the tree, and I did eat."
        To whom the sov'reign Presence thus replied.
145 "Was she thy God, that her thou didst obey
Before his voice, or was she made thy guide,
Superior, or but equal, that to her
Thou didst resign thy manhood, and the place
Wherein God set thee above her made of thee,
150 And for thee, whose perfection far excelled
Hers in all real dignity: adorned
She was indeed, and lovely to attract
Thy love, not thy subjection, and her gifts
Were such as under government well seemed,
155 Unseemly to bear rule, which was thy part
And person, hadst thou known thyself aright."
        So having said, he thus to Eve in few:
"Say woman, what is this which thou hast done?"
        To whom sad Eve with shame nigh overwhelmed,
160 Confessing soon, yet not before her judge
Bold or loquacious, thus abashed replied.
"The Serpent me beguiled and I did eat."

---

135. **Devolved:** caused to fall upon (*OED* 3c).
137–43. Here Milton elaborates Gen. 3.12.
Contrast Eve's simple confession in lines
159–62, where he closely follows Gen. 3.13.

155–56. **part/And person:** role and charac-
ter (in a play).

> Which when the Lord God heard, without delay
> To judgment he proceeded on th' accused
165 Serpent though brute, unable to transfer
> The guilt on him who made him instrument
> Of mischief, and polluted from the end
> Of his creation; justly then accursed,
> As vitiated in nature: more to know
170 Concerned not man (since he no further knew)
> Nor altered his offense; yet God at last
> To Satan first in sin his doom applied,
> Though in mysterious terms, judged as then best:
> And on the serpent thus his curse let fall.
175 "Because thou hast done this, thou art accursed
> Above all cattle, each beast of the field;
> Upon thy belly groveling thou shalt go,
> And dust shalt eat all the days of thy life.
> Between thee and the woman I will put
180 Enmity, and between thine and her seed;
> Her seed shall bruise thy head, thou bruise his heel."
> So spake this oracle, then verified
> When Jesus son of Mary, second Eve,
> Saw Satan fall like lightning down from heav'n,
185 Prince of the Air; then rising from his grave
> Spoiled Principalities and Powers, triumphed

165–66. **unable ... instrument:** The serpent is unable to transfer the guilt to Satan, who made the serpent his instrument.

173. **mysterious:** mystical, prefiguring.

175–81. A major passage in the design of the poem, in that these *mysterious terms* are progressively opened or dilated in the remaining books until they convey the entirety of the Christian revelation. At lines 504–17 the curse on the serpent is literally transferred to Satan and the devils. The mysterious terms are then gradually explicated in lines 1030–40; 11.115–16, 154–55; 12.327–30, 376–85, 429–35, 451–55, 620–23. Genesis 3.15, on which this passage is based, is sometimes termed a "protevan-

gelium" or "first gospel." Luther thought the first gospel was intended to console Eve, since *second Eve* (l. 183) will contribute humanity to Jesus, while Calvin insisted that "seed of the woman" meant all mankind. Milton presents both views. See Hunter et al., *A Milton Encyclopedia*, "Protevangelium."

183. **second Eve:** an idea familiar in Christian "figural" interpretation of the Bible (see Auerbach 11–78), as is the corresponding notion of Jesus as second or "last" Adam (1 Cor. 15.45).

184. **Satan fall like lightning:** Luke 10.18–19.

185. **Prince of the Air:** a commonplace epithet for Satan (Eph. 2.2). Cp. *PR* 1.39–47.

In open show, and with ascension bright
Captivity led captive through the air,
The realm itself of Satan long usurped,
190 Whom he shall tread at last under our feet;
Even he who now foretold his fatal bruise,
And to the woman thus his sentence turned.
    "Thy sorrow I will greatly multiply
By thy conception; children thou shalt bring
195 In sorrow forth, and to thy husband's will
Thine shall submit, he over thee shall rule."
    On Adam last thus judgment he pronounced.
"Because thou hast hearkened to the voice of thy wife,
And eaten of the tree concerning which
200 I charged thee, saying, 'Thou shalt not eat thereof,'
Cursed is the ground for thy sake, thou in sorrow
Shalt eat thereof all the days of thy life;
Thorns also and thistles it shall bring thee forth
Unbid, and thou shalt eat th' herb of th' field,
205 In the sweat of thy face shalt thou eat bread,
Till thou return unto the ground, for thou
Out of the ground wast taken, know thy birth,
For dust thou art, and shalt to dust return."
    So judged he man, both Judge and Savior sent,
210 And th' instant stroke of death denounced that day
Removed far off; then pitying how they stood
Before him naked to the air, that now
Must suffer change, disdained not to begin
Thenceforth the form of servant to assume,
215 As when he washed his servants' feet, so now
As father of his family he clad
Their nakedness with skins of beasts, or slain,

195–96. **thy husband's . . . rule:** Milton in *CD* 1.10 (*MLM* 1222) maintains that Adam's authority over Eve is strengthened after the Fall, but there are intimations in the poem that postlapsarian Adam and Eve enjoy new equalities—equal in guilt, equal in their Christian enmity toward the serpent, equal in "one faith unanimous" (12.603).

210. **denounced:** announced as a calamity soon to occur.

215. See John 13.5.

217–18. **or . . . Or:** either . . . or. The skins of Gen. 3.21 had long been a provocation to

Or as the snake with youthful coat repaid;
And thought not much to clothe his enemies:
220 Nor he their outward only with the skins
Of beasts, but inward nakedness, much more
Opprobrious, with his robe of righteousness,
Arraying covered from his Father's sight.
To him with swift ascent he up returned,
225 Into his blissful bosom reassumed
In glory as of old, to him appeased
All, though all-knowing, what had passed with man
Recounted, mixing intercession sweet.
Meanwhile ere thus was sinned and judged on Earth,
230 Within the gates of Hell sat Sin and Death,
In counterview within the gates, that now
Stood open wide, belching outrageous flame
Far into Chaos, since the fiend passed through,
Sin opening, who thus now to Death began.
235 "O Son, why sit we here each other viewing
Idly, while Satan our great author thrives
In other worlds, and happier seat provides
For us his offspring dear? It cannot be
But that success attends him; if mishap,
240 Ere this he had returned, with fury driv'n
By his avengers, since no place like this
Can fit his punishment, or their revenge.
Methinks I feel new strength within me rise,
Wings growing, and dominion giv'n me large
245 Beyond this deep; whatever draws me on,

---

exegetes, as Hume noted: "Interpreters
torment the text . . . with their curious in-
quiries, 'Who slew the beasts? Who flay'd
'em?' "

219. **thought not much:** thought it nothing
to object to or hesitate to perform (*OED*
10d).

222. **robe of righteousness:** Isa. 61.10.

230. **Sin and Death:** Book 10 "has a greater
variety of persons in it than any other in
the whole poem. The author, upon the

winding up of his action, introduces all
those who had any concern in it, and
shows with great beauty the influence
which it had upon each of them. It is like
the last act of a well-written tragedy"
(Addison 157).

236. **author:** father.

241. **like this:** so well as this.

243–45. **Methinks . . . deep:** Since Adam and
Eve feel wings growing on them soon
after the Fall (9.1009–10), Sin's similar

Or sympathy, or some connatural force
Powerful at greatest distance to unite
With secret amity things of like kind
By secretest conveyance. Thou my shade
250 Inseparable must with me along:
For Death from Sin no power can separate.
But lest the difficulty of passing back
Stay his return perhaps over this gulf
Impassable, impervious, let us try
255 Advent'rous work, yet to thy power and mine
Not unagreeable, to found a path
Over this main from Hell to that new world
Where Satan now prevails, a monument
Of merit high to all th' infernal host,
260 Easing their passage hence, for intercourse,
Or transmigration, as their lot shall lead.
Nor can I miss the way, so strongly drawn
By this new felt attraction and instinct."
Whom thus the meager shadow answered soon.
265 "Go whither fate and inclination strong
Leads thee, I shall not lag behind, nor err
The way, thou leading, such a scent I draw
Of carnage, prey innumerable, and taste
The savor of death from all things there that live:
270 Nor shall I to the work thou enterprisest
Be wanting, but afford thee equal aid."
So saying, with delight he snuffed the smell
Of mortal change on Earth. As when a flock
Of ravenous fowl, though many a league remote,
275 Against the day of battle, to a field

---

illusion may appear at the same moment
(Fowler). Sin lays claim to the "domin-
ion" originally given to Adam and Eve
(4.430–32), and extends that rule to in-
clude Adam, Eve, and their offspring.
249. **conveyance:** communication.
254–323. Leonard notes that prodigious feats
of building are conventional in epic; Mil-
ton has already represented the raising of

Pandaemonium (1.678–730), the invention
of cannon (6.507–23), and the Creation.
257. **main:** Chaos's ocean.
261. **transmigration:** permanent migration
to Earth.
264. **meager:** emaciated.
272. **snuffed:** detected by means of its odor.
275. **Against:** in anticipation of.

Where armies lie encamped, come flying, lured
With scent of living carcasses designed
For death, the following day, in bloody fight.
So scented the grim feature, and upturned
280 His nostril wide into the murky air,
Sagacious of his quarry from so far.
Then both from out Hell gates into the waste
Wide anarchy of Chaos damp and dark
Flew diverse, and with power (their power was great)
285 Hovering upon the waters; what they met
Solid or slimy, as in raging sea
Tossed up and down, together crowded drove
From each side shoaling towards the mouth of Hell.
As when two polar winds blowing adverse
290 Upon the Cronian Sea, together drive
Mountains of ice, that stop th' imagined way
Beyond Petsora eastward, to the rich
Cathayan Coast. The aggregated soil
Death with his mace petrific, cold and dry,
295 As with a trident smote, and fixed as firm
As Delos floating once; the rest his look
Bound with Gorgonian rigor not to move,
And with asphaltic slime; broad as the gate,
Deep to the roots of Hell the gathered beach
300 They fastened, and the mole immense wrought on
Over the foaming deep high-arched, a bridge

---

277. **designed:** marked out for.
279. **feature:** shape, form.
280. **murky:** dark.
281. **Sagacious:** (1) quick of scent and (2) wise. "A fit comparison for the *chief hell-hound*" (Hume).
284. **diverse:** in different directions.
288. **shoaling:** crowding together.
290. **Cronian Sea:** Arctic Ocean (icebound).
291–93. **th' imagined way . . . Coast:** the fabled northeast passage between Siberia— where the *Pechora* (Petsora) River is found; see Milton's *Muscovia* in Yale 8:479—and China (*Cathay*) that explorers

such as Henry Hudson only *imagined*, since the waters were blocked with ice.
293–98. **The aggregated soil . . . slime:** With his petrifying mace (scepter), Death fixes the cold and dry qualities, and isolates the hot and moist, which he turns into a mortar, using both asphalt and his Gorgon-like ability to turn the objects of his gaze to stone.
296. **Delos:** Neptune secured the floating island of Delos by chains to the bottom of the Aegean Sea so that Latona could safely give birth to Apollo and Diana.
300. **mole:** great causeway or bridge.

Of length prodigious joining to the wall
Immovable of this now fenceless world
Forfeit to Death; from hence a passage broad,
305   Smooth, easy, inoffensive down to Hell.
So, if great things to small may be compared,
Xerxes, the liberty of Greece to yoke,
From Susa his Memnonian palace high
Came to the sea, and over Hellespont
310   Bridging his way, Europe with Asia joined,
And scourged with many a stroke th' indignant waves.
Now had they brought the work by wondrous art
Pontifical, a ridge of pendant rock
Over the vexed abyss, following the track
315   Of Satan, to the selfsame place where he
First lighted from his wing, and landed safe
From out of Chaos to the outside bare
Of this round world: with pins of adamant
And chains they made all fast, too fast they made
320   And durable; and now in little space
The confines met of empyrean Heav'n
And of this world, and on the left hand Hell
With long reach interposed; three sev'ral ways
In sight, to each of these three places led.
325   And now their way to Earth they had descried,
To Paradise first tending, when behold
Satan in likeness of an angel bright
Betwixt the Centaur and the Scorpion steering

---

305. **inoffensive:** free from obstacles, with a punning glance back at *fenceless* in line 303.

307–11. *Xerxes* of Persia built a bridge of ships across the *Hellespont* in order to invade Greece and ordered the sea whipped when the bridge was destroyed.

308. **Susa:** the winter palace of Persian kings, called *Memnonian* after Memnos, legendary son of Tithonus and Aurora.

311. **indignant:** both "resentful" from the Latin *indignans* and "unworthy of punishment" from the Latin *indignis* (Fowler).

312–13. **art/Pontifical:** both "bridge-building art" and "popish art." Eighteenth-century editors thought the pun in dubious taste (Todd).

314. **vexed:** storm torn.

321. **confines:** borders.

328–29. **Betwixt . . . zenith:** Satan flies between the *Centaur* (Sagittarius) and the *Scorpion* (Scorpio), where the constellation Anguis, the serpent held by Ophiucus, is located. Satan entered the universe at the head of the serpent, in Libra

His zenith, while the sun in Aries rose:
330 Disguised he came, but those his children dear
Their parent soon discerned, though in disguise.
He after Eve seduced, unminded slunk
Into the wood fast by, and changing shape
To observe the sequel, saw his guileful act
335 By Eve, though all unweeting, seconded
Upon her husband, saw their shame that sought
Vain covertures; but when he saw descend
The Son of God to judge them, terrified
He fled, not hoping to escape, but shun
340 The present, fearing guilty what his wrath
Might suddenly inflict; that past, returned
By night, and list'ning where the hapless pair
Sat in their sad discourse, and various plaint,
Thence gathered his own doom, which understood
345 Not instant, but of future time. With joy
And tidings fraught, to Hell he now returned,
And at the brink of Chaos, near the foot
Of this new wondrous pontifice, unhoped
Met who to meet him came, his offspring dear.
350 Great joy was at their meeting, and at sight
Of that stupendous bridge his joy increased.
Long he admiring stood, till Sin, his fair
Enchanting daughter, thus the silence broke.
    "O Parent, these are thy magnific deeds,
355 Thy trophies, which thou view'st as not thine own;
Thou art their author and prime architect:
For I no sooner in my heart divined,
My heart, which by a secret harmony

(3.556–61n), and now leaves it at the tail of the serpent, enacting in astrological terms his possession of the snake. See Fowler for details. His entrance and exit also participate in the root image systems of eating and digestion.

334. **sequel:** consequence.

342–45. **list'ning . . . time:** This can only refer to lines 1030–40, which imply that the entire turbulent night of lines 720–1104 takes place earlier in chronological time than the present encounter between Satan, Sin, and Death (Leonard).

344. **which understood:** which he understood.

Still moves with thine, joined in connection sweet,
360 That thou on Earth hadst prospered, which thy looks
Now also evidence, but straight I felt
Though distant from thee worlds between, yet felt
That I must after thee with this thy son;
Such fatal consequence unites us three:
365 Hell could no longer hold us in her bounds,
Nor this unvoyageable gulf obscure
Detain from following thy illustrious track.
Thou hast achieved our liberty, confined
Within Hell gates till now, thou us empow'red
370 To fortify thus far, and overlay
With this portentous bridge the dark abyss.
Thine now is all this world, thy virtue hath won
What thy hands builded not, thy wisdom gained
With odds what war hath lost, and fully avenged
375 Our foil in Heav'n; here thou shalt monarch reign,
There didst not; there let him still victor sway,
As battle hath adjudged, from this new world
Retiring, by his own doom alienated,
And henceforth monarchy with thee divide
380 Of all things parted by th' empyreal bounds,
His quadrature, from thy orbicular world,
Or try thee now more dang'rous to his throne."
　　　Whom thus the Prince of Darkness answered glad.
　　"Fair daughter, and thou son and grandchild both,
385 High proof ye now have giv'n to be the race
Of Satan (for I glory in the name,

---

364. **consequence:** of which Satan is the cause or author; evil's consequence is established in the opening lines of the epic, in the "fruit" whose taste brings Death into the world, and again when Satan as "cause" is first named at 1.34.

371. **portentous:** marvelous and ominous.

378. **doom:** judgment; **alienated:** See 9.9 for the apparent truth of Sin's claim; she does not yet understand the Incarnation, the countermovement to God's alienation.

379. Sin implies the Manichaean idea of a universe divided between God's and Satan's empires; see 4.110–12.

381. **His quadrature:** "And the city [of God] lieth four-square, and the length is as large as the breadth" (Rev. 21.16). The bounds of Heaven are left undetermined at 2.1048.

386–87. The name Satan is Hebrew for "adversary."

Antagonist of Heav'n's Almighty King)
Amply have merited of me, of all
Th' infernal empire, that so near Heav'n's door
390　Triumphal with triumphal act have met,
Mine with this glorious work, and made one realm
Hell and this world, one realm, one continent
Of easy thoroughfare. Therefore while I
Descend through darkness, on your road with ease
395　To my associate powers, them to acquaint
With these successes, and with them rejoice,
You two this way, among these numerous orbs
All yours, right down to Paradise descend;
There dwell and reign in bliss, thence on the Earth
400　Dominion exercise and in the air,
Chiefly on man, sole lord of all declared,
Him first make sure your thrall, and lastly kill.
My substitutes I send ye, and create
Plenipotent on Earth, of matchless might
405　Issuing from me: on your joint vigor now
My hold of this new kingdom all depends,
Through Sin to Death exposed by my exploit.
If your joint power prevails, th' affairs of Hell
No detriment need fear. Go and be strong."
410　　So saying he dismissed them, they with speed
Their course through thickest constellations held
Spreading their bane; the blasted stars looked wan,
And planets, planet-struck, real eclipse
Then suffered. Th' other way Satan went down

---

390. The triumphal arch of the bridge memorializes Satan's triumph on Earth.
400. Here Satan parodies God, who gave "dominion" over Creation to Adam and Eve. See lines 243–45n.
404. **Plenipotent:** fully powerful.
408. **prevails:** 1674; the 1667 edition reads "prevail."
409. **No detriment need fear:** alluding to the formula (*Providere nequid respublica*

detrimenti accipiat) by which the Roman Senate conferred special powers on consuls (Newton); **detriment:** injury.
412. **blasted:** withered; an effect usually ascribed to ill wind or malignant astral influence.
413. **planet-struck:** struck by a malignant planet; **real eclipse:** not just apparently darkened, as in an eclipse beheld on earth, but really darkened.

415 The causey to Hell gate; on either side
     Disparted Chaos overbuilt exclaimed,
     And with rebounding surge the bars assailed,
     That scorned his indignation: through the gate,
     Wide open and unguarded, Satan passed,
420 And all about found desolate; for those
     Appointed to sit there, had left their charge,
     Flown to the upper world; the rest were all
     Far to the inland retired, about the walls
     Of Pandaemonium, city and proud seat
425 Of Lucifer, so by allusion called,
     Of that bright star to Satan paragoned.
     There kept their watch the legions, while the grand
     In council sat, solicitous what chance
     Might intercept their Emperor sent, so he
430 Departing gave command, and they observed.
     As when the Tartar from his Russian foe
     By Astracan over the snowy plains
     Retires, or Bactrian Sophy from the horns
     Of Turkish crescent, leaves all waste beyond
435 The realm of Aladule, in his retreat
     To Tauris or Casbeen. So these the late
     Heav'n-banished host, left desert utmost Hell
     Many a dark league, reduced in careful watch
     Round their metropolis, and now expecting
440 Each hour their great adventurer from the search

---

415. **causey:** causeway, a raised and paved highway (*OED* 3).

416. Chaos, *disparted* (divided into parts) by the creation of the bridge, is enraged by Satan's betrayal (see 2.981–87).

426. **bright star:** Lucifer, the morning star; see 5.760, 7.131; **paragoned:** compared.

427. **the grand:** the "grand infernal Peers" of 2.507.

428. **solicitous:** concerned.

431–36. **As when . . . Casbeen:** The Tartars retreat from their Russian conquerors near *Astracan*, the ancient Tartar capital. The *Bactrian Sophy*, or Shah of Persia, retreats from the crescent battle formations of the Turks (*horns / Of Turkish crescent*) to Tabriz (*Tauris*) and Kazvin (*Casbeen*), Iranian cities, laying waste to lands once under the rule of King *Aladule*. Leonard notes that both of these defeated enemies were still dangerous.

438. **reduced:** led back, drawn together, diminished.

Of foreign worlds: he through the midst unmarked,
In show plebeian angel militant
Of lowest order, passed; and from the door
Of that Plutonian hall, invisible
445 Ascended his high throne, which under state
Of richest texture spread, at th' upper end
Was placed in regal luster. Down awhile
He sat, and round about him saw unseen:
At last as from a cloud his fulgent head
450 And shape star-bright appeared, or brighter, clad
With what permissive glory since his fall
Was left him, or false glitter: all amazed
At that so sudden blaze the Stygian throng
Bent their aspect, and whom they wished beheld,
455 Their mighty chief returned: loud was th' acclaim:
Forth rushed in haste the great consulting peers,
Raised from their dark divan, and with like joy
Congratulant approached him, who with hand
Silence, and with these words attention won.
460   "Thrones, Dominations, Princedoms, Virtues, Powers,
For in possession such, not only of right,
I call ye and declare ye now, returned
Successful beyond hope, to lead ye forth
Triumphant out of this infernal pit
465 Abominable, accursed, the house of woe,
And dungeon of our tyrant: now possess,

441–55. Analogues in the epic tradition include Homer, *Od.* 7.35–145; Vergil, *Aen.* 1.579–94; and Tasso, *GL,* 10.32–50. See S. Fallon 1984.

445. **state:** canopy. See *Arcades* 14n.

451. **permissive:** permitted (by God); cp. the "high permission" of 1.212.

453. **sudden blaze:** Cp. *Lyc* 74, where the context is also a nurtured ambition ready to publicize its achievements and about to be thwarted; *PR* 3.47.

457. **divan:** council (*OED* 1b). The Turkish origins of the term fit with Satan as "sultan" (1.348). The military successes of

King Suleiman I (1520–1566) in Hungary, Armenia, Persia, and Africa caused widespread alarm in Europe, and led to commonplace associations between Turks and devils.

458. **Congratulant:** expressing congratulation.

460. The Father, when exalting his Son, was the first to use these titles (5.601), the meaning of which Satan (5.772) and Abdiel (5.840) dispute. Satan now declares the titles to be theirs not only by right but by possession (of estates formerly controlled by God).

As lords, a spacious world, to our native Heaven
Little inferior, by my adventure hard
With peril great achieved. Long were to tell
470 What I have done, what suffered, with what pain
Voyaged th' unreal, vast, unbounded deep
Of horrible confusion, over which
By Sin and Death a broad way now is paved
To expedite your glorious march; but I
475 Toiled out my uncouth passage, forced to ride
Th' untractable abyss, plunged in the womb
Of unoriginal Night and Chaos wild,
That jealous of their secrets fiercely opposed
My journey strange, with clamorous uproar
480 Protesting fate supreme; thence how I found
The new created world, which fame in Heav'n
Long had foretold, a fabric wonderful
Of absolute perfection, therein man
Placed in a Paradise, by our exile
485 Made happy; him by fraud I have seduced
From his Creator, and the more to increase
Your wonder, with an apple; he thereat
Offended, worth your laughter, hath giv'n up
Both his beloved man and all his world,
490 To Sin and Death a prey, and so to us,
Without our hazard, labor, or alarm,
To range in, and to dwell, and over man
To rule, as over all he should have ruled.
True is, me also he hath judged, or rather
495 Me not, but the brute serpent in whose shape

---

471. **unreal:** formless, the equivalent of un-reality in Aristotelian metaphysics.

475. **uncouth:** strange, unusual.

477. **unoriginal:** without origin, uncreated.

477–78. **Chaos . . . opposed:** Though the journey through Chaos was difficult, Chaos and Night hardly opposed Satan (2.910–1009); but see Chaos's indignation at lines 415–18.

480. **Protesting fate supreme:** Satan here identifies himself with supreme Fate, as usual parodying God (7.173).

481–82. **fame . . . foretold:** See 1.651–56, 2.345–76.

494–99. Like most of the biblical commentators (A. Williams 128), Satan supposes that the first part of the protevangelium (see 175–81n), condemning the serpent to grovel in the dust, applies only to the snake, whereas the second part, in which

Man I deceived: that which to me belongs,
Is enmity, which he will put between
Me and mankind; I am to bruise his heel;
His seed, when is not set, shall bruise my head:
500 A world who would not purchase with a bruise,
Or much more grievous pain? Ye have th' account
Of my performance: what remains, ye gods,
But up and enter now into full bliss."
    So having said, a while he stood, expecting
505 Their universal shout and high applause
To fill his ear, when contrary he hears
On all sides, from innumerable tongues
A dismal universal hiss, the sound
Of public scorn; he wondered, but not long
510 Had leisure, wond'ring at himself now more;
His visage drawn he felt to sharp and spare,
His arms clung to his ribs, his legs entwining
Each other, till supplanted down he fell
A monstrous serpent on his belly prone,
515 Reluctant, but in vain; a greater power
Now ruled him, punished in the shape he sinned,
According to his doom: he would have spoke,
But hiss for hiss returned with forkèd tongue
To forkèd tongue, for now were all transformed
520 Alike, to serpents all as accessories
To his bold riot: dreadful was the din

---

the seed of the woman will bruise the serpent in the head and be itself bruised in the heel, applies to him (Satan). He is about to be proven wrong. On the transformation of the devils into serpents, see Kerrigan 2004.

508–9. **universal hiss . . . scorn:** There is only one sound intelligible within the sign system of human language that both men and snakes can produce, and that is the hiss that greets a bad show. See Shakespeare's "serpent's tongue" (*MND* 5.1.433). On scorn, see Kerrigan 2000, 150–52.

509. **wondered:** ironically remembering Eve, who found the human speech of the serpent a "wonder" (9.566), as Satan now wonders at the serpentine hiss of his audience.

511–15. The passage imitates the serpent metamorphoses in Ovid, *Met.* 4.572–603, and Dante, *Inf.* 24, 25.

513. **supplanted:** tripped up, overthrown.

515. **Reluctant:** primarily in the sense of "writhing or struggling against" (Lat. *reluctari*).

517. **doom:** the judgment at lines 175–81.

Of hissing through the hall, thick swarming now
With complicated monsters head and tail,
Scorpion and asp, and amphisbaena dire,
525 Cerastes horned, hydrus, and ellops drear,
And dipsas (not so thick swarm'd once the soil
Bedropped with blood of Gorgon, or the Isle
Ophiusa); but still greatest he the midst,
Now dragon grown, larger than whom the sun
530 Engendered in the Pythian vale on slime,
Huge Python, and his power no less he seemed
Above the rest still to retain; they all
Him followed issuing forth to th' open field,
Where all yet left of that revolted rout
535 Heav'n-fall'n, in station stood or just array,
Sublime with expectation when to see
In triumph issuing forth their glorious chief;
They saw, but other sight instead, a crowd
Of ugly serpents; horror on them fell,
540 And horrid sympathy; for what they saw,
They felt themselves now changing; down their arms,
Down fell both spear and shield, down they as fast,
And the dire hiss renewed, and the dire form
Catched by contagion, like in punishment,
545 As in their crime. Thus was th' applause they meant,
Turned to exploding hiss, triumph to shame
Cast on themselves from their own mouths. There stood
A grove hard by, sprung up with this their change,

524. **amphisbaena:** mythical snake with a head at both ends.

525. **Cerastes horned:** a snake with four horns; **hydrus . . . ellops:** water snakes.

526. **dipsas:** The bite of *dipsas* (from the Gk. word for "thirst") caused *scalding thirst* (l. 556).

526–27. **soil . . . Gorgon:** As Perseus flew over Libya with the head of Medusa, drops of her blood fell to the earth and became snakes—which explains why, according to Ovid, *Met.* 3.616, and Lucan,

Pharsalia 9.696, serpents are so common there.

528. **Ophiusa:** a Mediterranean island, from the Gk. "full of snakes."

529. **dragon:** Satan had long been identified with the "great dragon" of Rev. 12.9. Cp. Fletcher, *The Purple Island* 7.11.

530. **Pythian vale:** Delphi.

531. **Python:** the great serpent born of the *slime* left behind by Deucalion's flood (Ovid, *Met.* 1.438) and eventually slain by Apollo.

536. **Sublime:** exalted, elated.

His will who reigns above, to aggravate
550 Their penance, laden with fair fruit like that
Which grew in Paradise, the bait of Eve
Used by the Tempter: on that prospect strange
Their earnest eyes they fixed, imagining
For one forbidden tree a multitude
555 Now ris'n, to work them further woe or shame;
Yet parched with scalding thirst and hunger fierce,
Though to delude them sent, could not abstain,
But on they rolled in heaps, and up the trees
Climbing, sat thicker than the snaky locks
560 That curled Megaera: greedily they plucked
The fruitage fair to sight, like that which grew
Near that bituminous lake where Sodom flamed;
This more delusive, not the touch, but taste
Deceived; they fondly thinking to allay
565 Their appetite with gust, instead of fruit
Chewed bitter ashes, which th' offended taste
With spattering noise rejected: oft they assayed,
Hunger and thirst constraining, drugged as oft,
With hatefulest disrelish writhed their jaws
570 With soot and cinders filled; so oft they fell
Into the same illusion, not as man
Whom they triumphed once lapsed. Thus were they plagued
And worn with famine, long and ceaseless hiss,
Till their lost shape, permitted, they resumed,
575 Yearly enjoined, some say, to undergo
This annual humbling certain numbered days,
To dash their pride, and joy for man seduced.
However some tradition they dispersed

559–60. **snaky locks . . . Megaera:** Her hair, like Medusa's, was serpents (Ovid, *Met.* 4.771).

560–68. the *bituminous lake* is the Dead Sea, beside which Sodom and Gomorrah were situated. According to Josephus, *Wars* 4.8.4, the ashes of Sodom grow in the fruit of the area, which when plucked dissolve into smoke and ashes.

565. **gust:** gusto.

568. **drugged:** nauseated.

575. **some say:** A source has not been found for Milton's account of the annual metamorphosis of the devils.

578–84. Fowler notes that *purchase* can mean "annual return or rent from land," and thus alludes to the annual metamorphosis. According to some authorities, Milton

Among the heathen of their purchase got,
580 And fabled how the serpent, whom they called
Ophion with Eurynome, the wide-
Encroaching Eve perhaps, had first the rule
Of high Olympus, thence by Saturn driv'n
And Ops, ere yet Dictaean Jove was born.
585 Meanwhile in Paradise the Hellish pair
Too soon arrived, Sin there in power before,
Once actual, now in body, and to dwell
Habitual habitant; behind her Death
Close following pace for pace, not mounted yet
590 On his pale horse: to whom Sin thus began.
  "Second of Satan sprung, all conquering Death,
What think'st thou of our empire now, though earned
With travail difficult, not better far
Than still at Hell's dark threshold to have sat watch,
595 Unnamed, undreaded, and thyself half starved?"
  Whom thus the Sin-born monster answered soon.
"To me, who with eternal famine pine,
Alike is Hell, or Paradise, or Heaven,
There best, where most with ravin I may meet;
600 Which here, though plenteous, all too little seems
To stuff this maw, this vast unhidebound corpse."
  To whom th' incestuous mother thus replied.
"Thou therefore on these herbs, and fruits, and flow'rs
Feed first, on each beast next, and fish, and fowl,
605 No homely morsels, and whatever thing
The scythe of Time mows down, devour unspared,
Till I in man residing through the race,
His thoughts, his looks, words, actions all infect,
And season him thy last and sweetest prey."

---

says, the devils spread stories of primor-
dial serpents in the ancient world, among
them that of Ophion (from Gk. for "ser-
pent") and *Eurynome,* the first rulers of
Olympus.
584. **Dictaean:** Jove was raised in Crete, in
the vicinity of Mount Dicte.

586–87. **there . . . body:** a brief history of sin
in Paradise: there by *power* or potential
before the Fall, then *actual* at the Fall, *now
in body,* as the character Sin arrives.
590. **pale horse:** See Rev. 6.8.
601. **unhidebound:** skin so loose that it can
hold a great deal.

610 This said, they both betook them several ways,
Both to destroy, or unimmortal make
All kinds, and for destruction to mature
Sooner or later; which th' Almighty seeing,
From his transcendent seat the saints among,
615 To those bright orders uttered thus his voice.
    "See with what heat these dogs of Hell advance
To waste and havoc yonder world, which I
So fair and good created, and had still
Kept in that state, had not the folly of man
620 Let in these wasteful Furies, who impute
Folly to me, so doth the Prince of Hell
And his adherents, that with so much ease
I suffer them to enter and possess
A place so Heav'nly, and conniving seem
625 To gratify my scornful enemies,
That laugh, as if transported with some fit
Of passion, I to them had quitted all,
At random yielded up to their misrule;
And know not that I called and drew them thither
630 My Hell-hounds, to lick up the draff and filth
Which man's polluting sin with taint hath shed
On what was pure, till crammed and gorged, nigh burst
With sucked and glutted offal, at one sling
Of thy victorious arm, well-pleasing Son,
635 Both Sin, and Death, and yawning grave at last
Through Chaos hurled, obstruct the mouth of Hell
Forever, and seal up his ravenous jaws.
Then heav'n and earth renewed shall be made pure
To sanctity that shall receive no stain:
640 Till then the curse pronounced on both precedes."

---

611. **unimmortal:** mortal; the negative of *immortal* neatly conveys the effect of the Fall.

617. **havoc:** Kings victorious on the battlefield had the privilege of shouting "havoc," a signal that no quarter should be given in slaughter and pillage. See Shakespeare, *JC* 3.1.273.

627. **quitted:** handed over.

630. **draff:** refuse, swill.

633–34. **at one sling . . . arm:** "The souls of thine enemies, them shall he sling out, as out of the middle of a sling" (1 Sam. 25.29).

640. **precedes:** has precedence.

He ended, and the Heav'nly audience loud
Sung hallelujah, as the sound of seas,
Through multitude that sung: "Just are thy ways,
Righteous are thy decrees on all thy works;
645 Who can extenuate thee? Next, to the Son,
Destined restorer of mankind, by whom
New heav'n and earth shall to the ages rise,
Or down from Heav'n descend." Such was their song,
While the Creator calling forth by name
650 His mighty angels gave them several charge,
As sorted best with present things. The sun
Had first his precept so to move, so shine,
As might affect the Earth with cold and heat
Scarce tolerable, and from the north to call
655 Decrepit winter, from the south to bring
Solstitial summer's heat. To the blank moon
Her office they prescribed, to th' other five
Their planetary motions and aspects
In sextile, square, and trine, and opposite,
660 Of noxious efficacy, and when to join
In synod unbenign, and taught the fixed
Their influence malignant when to show'r,
Which of them rising with the sun, or falling,
Should prove tempestuous: to the winds they set
665 Their corners, when with bluster to confound
Sea, air, and shore, the thunder when to roll
With terror through the dark aerial hall.
Some say he bid his angels turn askance
The poles of Earth twice ten degrees and more
670 From the sun's axle; they with labor pushed

645. **extenuate:** disparage.
656. **blank:** pale.
658. **aspects:** astrological positions.
659. A list of aspects: *sextile* (60°), *square* (90°), *trine* (120°), and *opposite* (180°).
661. **synod:** conjunction; cp. 6.156n; **fixed:** fixed stars.
668–87. Before the Fall, the ecliptic follows the *equinoctial road* (l. 672) or equator, which produces *spring/Perpetual* (ll. 678–79), and a sun always in Aries. There are two ways to modify these conditions in order to produce a result consistent with astrological observations in the fallen world. In a heliocentric (Copernican) system, the axis of the earth must be

Oblique the centric globe: some say the sun
Was bid turn reins from th' equinoctial road
Like distant breadth to Taurus with the sev'n
Atlantic Sisters, and the Spartan Twins
675   Up to the Tropic Crab; thence down amain
By Leo and the Virgin and the Scales,
As deep as Capricorn, to bring in change
Of seasons to each clime; else had the spring
Perpetual smiled on Earth with vernant flow'rs,
680   Equal in days and nights, except to those
Beyond the polar circles; to them day
Had unbenighted shone, while the low sun
To recompense his distance, in their sight
Had rounded still th' horizon, and not known
685   Or east or west, which had forbid the snow
From cold Estotiland, and south as far
Beneath Magellan. At that tasted fruit
The sun, as from Thyestean banquet, turned
His course intended; else how had the world
690   Inhabited, though sinless, more than now,
Avoided pinching cold and scorching heat?
These changes in the heav'ns, though slow, produced
Like change on sea and land, sideral blast,
Vapor, and mist, and exhalation hot,
695   Corrupt and pestilent: now from the north

---

tilted around 23°. In a terracentric (Ptole-
maic) system, the plane of the sun's orbit
must be tilted *like distant breadth* (that is,
around 23°). Milton presents both expla-
nations and does not choose between
them. *Some say* (l. 668) the one, *some say*
(l. 671) the other.

672–77. **Was bid . . . Capricorn:** Once resi-
dent in Aries, the sun now travels through
the zodiac.

686. **Estotiland:** northern Labrador.

687. **Magellan:** Strait of Magellan.

688. **Thyestean banquet:** In Seneca's
tragedy *Thyestes,* the sun turns aside in

horror from the sight of Thyestes eating
his sons. A chorus (789–881) wonders if
the sun's departure might not signal a re-
turn to "formless chaos" (832).

693. **sideral blast:** probably not malign astral
influences, as Fowler and Leonard sug-
gest, because Milton has shifted from
celestial to terrestial change; perhaps ex-
halations or vapors released from the
earth, drawn toward the stars (*sideral*) by
the sun's heat, and thought to produce
various *blasts* or explosions, such as shoot-
ing stars and comets.

Of Norumbega, and the Samoed shore
Bursting their brazen dungeon, armed with ice
And snow and hail and stormy gust and flaw,
Boreas and Caecias and Argestes loud
700 And Thrascias rend the woods and seas upturn;
With adverse blast upturns them from the south
Notus and Afer black with thund'rous clouds
From Serraliona; thwart of these as fierce
Forth rush the Levant and the ponent winds
705 Eurus and Zephyr with their lateral noise,
Sirocco, and Libecchio. Thus began
Outrage from lifeless things; but Discord first
Daughter of Sin, among th' irrational,
Death introduced through fierce antipathy:
710 Beast now with beast gan war, and fowl with fowl,
And fish with fish; to graze the herb all leaving,
Devoured each other; nor stood much in awe
Of man, but fled him, or with count'nance grim
Glared on him passing: these were from without
715 The growing miseries, which Adam saw
Already in part, though hid in gloomiest shade,
To sorrow abandoned, but worse felt within,
And in a troubled sea of passion tossed,
Thus to disburden sought with sad complaint.
720   "O miserable of happy! Is this the end
Of this new glorious world, and me so late
The glory of that glory? Who now become
Accursed of blessed; hide me from the face

---

696. **Norumbega:** a province of North
America; **Samoed:** northeastern Siberia.
697. **brazen dungeon:** where Aeolus impris-
oned the winds (*Aen.* 1.141).
699–706. The northern winds of *Boreas, Cae-
cias, Argestes,* and *Thrascias* are opposed by
the southern winds of *Notus* and *Afer.* This
system is attacked at various side angles
to the east and west (*thwart*) by winds
named *Levant* et cetera.

714–17. **these . . . within:** a beautiful effect:
the chain of bad external causes in lines
651–714 has led to the *part* (l. 716) Adam al-
ready sees, whereupon Milton shifts to
his inner turbulence, which Adam then
seeks to *disburden* through externalizing
speech. We have moved back in time be-
fore the arrival of Sin and Death on Earth
(342–45n).

Of God, whom to behold was then my highth

725 Of happiness: yet well, if here would end
The misery, I deserved it, and would bear
My own deservings; but this will not serve;
All that I eat or drink, or shall beget,
Is propagated curse. O voice once heard

730 Delightfully, 'Increase and multiply,'
Now death to hear! For what can I increase
Or multiply, but curses on my head?
Who of all ages to succeed, but feeling
The evil on him brought by me, will curse

735 My head, 'Ill fare our ancestor impure,
For this we may thank Adam'? But his thanks
Shall be the execration; so besides
Mine own that bide upon me, all from me
Shall with a fierce reflux on me redound,

740 On me as on their natural center light
Heavy, though in their place. O fleeting joys
Of Paradise, dear bought with lasting woes!
Did I request thee, Maker, from my clay
To mold me man, did I solicit thee

745 From darkness to promote me, or here place
In this delicious garden? As my will
Concurred not to my being, it were but right
And equal to reduce me to my dust,
Desirous to resign, and render back

750 All I received, unable to perform
Thy terms too hard, by which I was to hold
The good I sought not. To the loss of that,

---

729. **propagated curse:** the curses of Adam's children upon their original forefather, increased and multiplied by the act of propagation. The commandment to "increase and multiply" is now literally transformed into ramifying curses, as Milton, an author much concerned with fame, has Adam confront the terror of infamy.

740–41. **On me ... place:** When a body occupies its *natural center* in Aristotle's physics, it is weightless, but the curses of Adam's children are mysteriously *heavy*.

743–46. Isa. 45.9: "Woe unto him that striveth with his Maker! . . . Shall the clay say to him that fashioneth it, What makest thou?"

748. **equal:** equitable.

Sufficient penalty, why hast thou added
The sense of endless woes? Inexplicable
755 Thy justice seems; yet to say truth, too late,
I thus contest; then should have been refused
Those terms whatever, when they were proposed:
Thou didst accept them; wilt thou enjoy the good,
Then cavil the conditions? And though God
760 Made thee without thy leave, what if thy son
Prove disobedient, and reproved, retort,
'Wherefore didst thou beget me? I sought it not,'
Wouldst thou admit for his contempt of thee
That proud excuse? Yet him not thy election,
765 But natural necessity begot.
God made thee of choice his own, and of his own
To serve him, thy reward was of his grace,
Thy punishment then justly is at his will.
Be it so, for I submit, his doom is fair,
770 That dust I am, and shall to dust return:
O welcome hour whenever! Why delays
His hand to execute what his decree
Fixed on this day? Why do I overlive,
Why am I mocked with death, and lengthened out
775 To deathless pain? How gladly would I meet
Mortality my sentence, and be earth
Insensible, how glad would lay me down
As in my mother's lap! There I should rest
And sleep secure; his dreadful voice no more
780 Would thunder in my ears, no fear of worse
To me and to my offspring would torment me
With cruel expectation. Yet one doubt
Pursues me still, lest all I cannot die,
Lest that pure breath of life, the spirit of man
785 Which God inspired, cannot together perish

---

758. **Thou:** "I myself." Adam here addresses
himself, not his Maker, as in lines 743–55.
762. Isa. 45.10: "Woe unto him that saith unto
his father, 'What begettest thou?' "

782. **one doubt:** The same doubt reroutes
the thoughts of Hamlet in his "To be, or
not to be" soliloquy (3.1.56–88).
783. **all:** altogether, entirely.

With this corporeal clod; then in the grave,
Or in some other dismal place who knows
But I shall die a living death? O thought
Horrid, if true! Yet why? It was but breath
790 Of Life that sinned; what dies but what had life
And sin? The body properly hath neither.
All of me then shall die: let this appease
The doubt, since human reach no further knows.
For though the Lord of all be infinite,
795 Is his wrath also? Be it, man is not so,
But mortal doomed. How can he exercise
Wrath without end on man whom death must end?
Can he make deathless death? That were to make
Strange contradiction, which to God himself
800 Impossible is held, as argument
Of weakness, not of power. Will he draw out,
For anger's sake, finite to infinite
In punished man, to satisfy his rigor
Satisfied never? That were to extend
805 His sentence beyond dust and nature's law,
By which all causes else according still
To the reception of their matter act,
Not to th' extent of their own sphere. But say
That death be not one stroke, as I supposed,
810 Bereaving sense, but endless misery
From this day onward, which l feel begun
Both in me, and without me, and so last
To perpetuity; ay me, that fear
Comes thund'ring back with dreadful revolution
815 On my defenseless head; both Death and I
Am found eternal, and incorporate both,

786–92. **then . . . die:** Adam's reasoning here closely follows Milton's formulation of the mortalist heresy—the idea that body and soul die together (*CD* 1.13).

791. **The body properly hath neither:** Augustine, *City of God* 14.3.

798–801. "The power of God is not exerted in those kinds of things which . . . imply a contradiction" (*CD* 1.2 in *MLM* 1150).

815–16. *Death and I* take the singular verb *am* because they are *incorporate,* united in one body.

Nor I on my part single, in me all
Posterity stands cursed: fair patrimony
That I must leave ye, sons; O were I able
820　To waste it all myself, and leave ye none!
So disinherited how would ye bless
Me now your curse! Ah, why should all mankind
For one man's fault thus guiltless be condemned,
If guiltless? But from me what can proceed,
825　But all corrupt, both mind and will depraved,
Not to do only, but to will the same
With me? How can they then acquitted stand
In sight of God? Him after all disputes
Forced I absolve: all my evasions vain,
830　And reasonings, though through mazes, lead me still
But to my own conviction: first and last
On me, me only, as the source and spring
Of all corruption, all the blame lights due;
So might the wrath. Fond wish! Couldst thou support
835　That burden heavier than the Earth to bear,
Than all the world much heavier, though divided
With that bad woman? Thus what thou desir'st
And what thou fear'st, alike destroys all hope
Of refuge, and concludes thee miserable
840　Beyond all past example and future,
To Satan only like both crime and doom.
O conscience, into what abyss of fears
And horrors hast thou driv'n me; out of which
I find no way, from deep to deeper plunged!"
845　　Thus Adam to himself lamented loud
Through the still night, not now, as ere man fell,
Wholesome and cool, and mild, but with black air
Accompanied, with damps and dreadful gloom,

---

831. **conviction:** See 84n.

831–34. **first and last . . . wish!:** Eve later gives voice to the same fond wish (ll. 933–36). The only being with the power to realize this desire is the Son (3.236–37).

837–38. **what thou desir'st:** Death; **what thou fear'st:** Death.

842–44. **O conscience . . . plunged!:** evoking 4.75–78, and thus indeed *To Satan only like* (l. 841).

Which to his evil conscience represented
850 All things with double terror: on the ground
Outstretched he lay, on the cold ground, and oft
Cursed his creation, Death as oft accused
Of tardy execution, since denounced
The day of his offense. "Why comes not Death,"
855 Said he, "with one thrice acceptable stroke
To end me? Shall Truth fail to keep her word,
Justice Divine not hasten to be just?
But Death comes not at call, Justice Divine
Mends not her slowest pace for prayers or cries.
860 O woods, O fountains, hillocks, dales and bow'rs,
With other echo late I taught your shades
To answer, and resound far other song."
Whom thus afflicted when sad Eve beheld,
Desolate where she sat, approaching nigh,
865 Soft words to his fierce passion she assayed:
But her with stern regard he thus repell'd.

        "Out of my sight, thou serpent, that name best
Befits thee with him leagued, thyself as false
And hateful; nothing wants, but that thy shape,
870 Like his, and color serpentine may show
Thy inward fraud, to warn all creatures from thee
Henceforth; lest that too Heav'nly form, pretended
To Hellish falsehood, snare them. But for thee

849–50. **Which . . . terror:** Greville observes
that frightening hallucinations provoked
by darkness "proper reflections of the
error [original sin] be,/And images of
self-confusednesses/ Which hurt imagi-
nations only see;/And from this nothing
seen, tells news of devils,/Which but ex-
pressions be of inward evils" (*Caelica* C).

853–54. **since . . . offense:** "since it was an-
nounced that death would fall on the day
man ate the fruit." Adam forgets that the
sentence was delayed (see ll. 209–11).

867–908. The speech bristles with misogyny,
some of it standard, such as the opening
allusion to a false etymology deriving *Eve*

from *hevia* (Heb. for "snake"), the insult
terming Eve *but a rib/Crooked by nature* (ll.
884–85), or the disparagement of the act
of propagation, and some of it Miltonic,
such as the closing catalog of the ways in
which marriage will fail in the fallen
world, which echoes complaints in the
poet's divorce tracts. But it would be a
mistake to confuse Adam's sour diatribe
with Milton's own attitudes. His repre-
sentation of Adam and Eve's subsequent
behavior shows that the author did not
subscribe to the articles of Adam's vitu-
peration.

872–73. **pretended/To:** masking.

I had persisted happy, had not thy pride
875 And wand'ring vanity, when least was safe,
Rejected my forewarning, and disdained
Not to be trusted, longing to be seen
Though by the Devil himself, him overweening
To overreach, but with the serpent meeting
880 Fooled and beguiled, by him thou, I by thee,
To trust thee from my side, imagined wise,
Constant, mature, proof against all assaults,
And understood not all was but a show
Rather than solid virtue, all but a rib
885 Crooked by nature, bent, as now appears,
More to the part sinister from me drawn,
Well if thrown out, as supernumerary
To my just number found. O why did God,
Creator wise, that peopled highest Heav'n
890 With spirits masculine, create at last
This novelty on Earth, this fair defect
Of nature, and not fill the world at once
With men as angels without feminine,
Or find some other way to generate
895 Mankind? This mischief had not then befall'n,
And more that shall befall, innumerable
Disturbances on Earth through female snares,
And strait conjunction with this sex: for either
He never shall find out fit mate, but such
900 As some misfortune brings him, or mistake,
Or whom he wishes most shall seldom gain
Through her perverseness, but shall see her gained
By a far worse, or if she love, withheld

---

886. **sinister:** literally "left," figuratively "unlucky."

887. The line itself contains, in its feminine ending, a *supernumerary* syllable.

888–95. **O why . . . Mankind:** Adam's lament that God created woman at all follows Euripides, *Hippolytus* 616–19.

890. **spirits masculine:** Although, as we have earlier been told (1.424), angels (or at least fallen angels) can assume either sex, the ability to take on female form is evidently not the same thing as being female in sex. The angels of the poem are unwaveringly masculine in look and attitude.

891–92. **defect/Of nature:** as Aristotle had maintained in *On Generation* 737a28, 766a31–32, 766b8–15, 767b8–9.

By parents, or his happiest choice too late
905 Shall meet, already linked and wedlock-bound
To a fell adversary, his hate or shame:
Which infinite calamity shall cause
To human life, and household peace confound."
       He added not, and from her turned, but Eve
910 Not so repulsed, with tears that ceased not flowing,
And tresses all disordered, at his feet
Fell humble, and embracing them, besought
His peace, and thus proceeded in her plaint.
       "Forsake me not thus, Adam, witness Heav'n
915 What love sincere, and reverence in my heart
I bear thee, and unweeting have offended,
Unhappily deceived; thy suppliant
I beg, and clasp thy knees; bereave me not,
Whereon I live, thy gentle looks, thy aid,
920 Thy counsel in this uttermost distress,
My only strength and stay: forlorn of thee,
Whither shall I betake me, where subsist?
While yet we live, scarce one short hour perhaps,
Between us two let there be peace, both joining,
925 As joined in injuries, one enmity
Against a foe by doom express assigned us,
That cruel serpent: on me exercise not
Thy hatred for this misery befall'n,
On me already lost, me than thyself
930 More miserable; both have sinned, but thou
Against God only, I against God and thee,
And to the place of judgment will return,
There with my cries importune Heaven, that all
The sentence from thy head removed may light
935 On me, sole cause to thee of all this woe,
Me me only just object of his ire."
       She ended weeping, and her lowly plight,
Immovable till peace obtained from fault

925. Eve calls attention to the joint *enmity*   vangelium (175–81n).
against the serpent foretold in the prote-

Acknowledged and deplored, in Adam wrought
940 Commiseration; soon his heart relented
Towards her, his life so late and sole delight,
Now at his feet submissive in distress,
Creature so fair his reconcilement seeking,
His counsel whom she had displeased, his aid;
945 As one disarmed, his anger all he lost,
And thus with peaceful words upraised her soon.
      "Unwary, and too desirous, as before,
So now of what thou know'st not, who desir'st
The punishment all on thyself; alas,
950 Bear thine own first, ill able to sustain
His full wrath whose thou feel'st as yet least part,
And my displeasure bear'st so ill. If prayers
Could alter high decrees, I to that place
Would speed before thee, and be louder heard,
955 That on my head all might be visited,
Thy frailty and infirmer sex forgiv'n,
To me committed and by me exposed.
But rise, let us no more contend, nor blame
Each other, blamed enough elsewhere, but strive
960 In offices of love, how we may light'n
Each other's burden in our share of woe;
Since this day's death denounced, if aught I see,
Will prove no sudden, but a slow-paced evil,
A long day's dying to augment our pain,
965 And to our seed (O hapless seed!) derived."
      To whom thus Eve, recovering heart, replied.
"Adam, by sad experiment I know
How little weight my words with thee can find,
Found so erroneous, thence by just event
970 Found so unfortunate; nevertheless,

---

940. **Commiseration:** compassion for another's misery, precisely what was missing in his misogynistic diatribe (ll. 867–908).
965. **derived:** passed down by descent.

Adam's return to the question of seed prompts Eve's next speech.
969. **event:** outcome, with a rueful pun on her name.

Restored by thee, vile as I am, to place
Of new acceptance, hopeful to regain
Thy love, the sole contentment of my heart,
Living or dying, from thee I will not hide
975 What thoughts in my unquiet breast are ris'n,
Tending to some relief of our extremes,
Or end, though sharp and sad, yet tolerable,
As in our evils, and of easier choice.
If care of our descent perplex us most,
980 Which must be born to certain woe, devoured
By Death at last, and miserable it is
To be to others cause of misery,
Our own begotten, and of our loins to bring
Into this cursèd world a woful race,
985 That after wretched life must be at last
Food for so foul a monster, in thy power
It lies, yet ere conception to prevent
The race unblest, to being yet unbegot.
Childless thou art, childless remain: so Death
990 Shall be deceived his glut, and with us two
Be forced to satisfy his rav'nous maw.
But if thou judge it hard and difficult,
Conversing, looking, loving, to abstain
From love's due rites, nuptial embraces sweet,
995 And with desire to languish without hope,
Before the present object languishing

978. **As in:** considering.

979–1006. Adam has been lamenting at length his forthcoming infamy, but Eve cuts to the chase. Dread of our seed comes down to this: we can either abstain from the sexual act and have no seed, or, if such frustration seems unendurable, we can kill ourselves and again leave no seed. The speech seems to lift a veil from Adam's mind, reminding us that, as Milton emphasized at 9.1187–89, fallen men discern mistakes in others that they do not mark in themselves.

989. In early editions the words "so Death" were placed at the beginning of line 990. This is most likely an error, since otherwise 989 would be the only tetrameter line, and 990 the only hexameter line, in the poem.

990. **deceived:** cheated of.

994. **sweet:** The reintroduction of this key word in unfallen eroticism (4.298, 311, 641–56; 5.296; 8.603; 9.238, 407) suggests how severe the pangs of frustration would be and deftly reminds Adam of their mutual pleasures.

With like desire, which would be misery
And torment less than none of what we dread,
Then both ourselves and seed at once to free
1000 From what we fear for both, let us make short,
Let us seek Death, or he not found, supply
With our own hands his office on ourselves;
Why stand we longer shivering under fears,
That show no end but death, and have the power,
1005 Of many ways to die the shortest choosing,
Destruction with destruction to destroy?"
    She ended here, or vehement despair
Broke off the rest; so much of death her thoughts
Had entertained, as dyed her cheeks with pale.
1010 But Adam with such counsel nothing swayed,
To better hopes his more attentive mind
Laboring had raised, and thus to Eve replied.
    "Eve, thy contempt of life and pleasure seems
To argue in thee something more sublime
1015 And excellent than what thy mind contemns;
But self-destruction therefore sought, refutes
That excellence thought in thee, and implies,
Not thy contempt, but anguish and regret
For loss of life and pleasure overloved.
1020 Or if thou covet death, as utmost end
Of misery, so thinking to evade
The penalty pronounced, doubt not but God
Hath wiselier armed his vengeful ire than so
To be forestalled; much more I fear lest death
1025 So snatched will not exempt us from the pain
We are by doom to pay; rather such acts
Of contumacy will provoke the Highest
To make death in us live: then let us seek
Some safer resolution, which methinks
1030 I have in view, calling to mind with heed

997–98. Satan has already verified that sexual frustration is "not the least" of Hell's torments (4.509–11).

1030–40. Again the protevangelium revives and guides.

Part of our sentence, that thy seed shall bruise
The serpent's head; piteous amends, unless
Be meant, whom I conjecture, our grand foe
Satan, who in the serpent hath contrived
1035 Against us this deceit: to crush his head
Would be revenge indeed, which will be lost
By death brought on ourselves, or childless days
Resolved, as thou proposest; so our foe
Shall scape his punishment ordained, and we
1040 Instead shall double ours upon our heads.
No more be mentioned then of violence
Against ourselves, and willful barrenness,
That cuts us off from hope, and savors only
Rancor and pride, impatience and despite,
1045 Reluctance against God and his just yoke
Laid on our necks. Remember with what mild
And gracious temper he both heard and judged
Without wrath or reviling; we expected
Immediate dissolution, which we thought
1050 Was meant by death that day, when lo, to thee
Pains only in child-bearing were foretold,
And bringing forth, soon recompensed with joy,
Fruit of thy womb: on me the curse aslope
Glanced on the ground, with labor I must earn
1055 My bread; what harm? Idleness had been worse;
My labor will sustain me; and lest cold
Or heat should injure us, his timely care
Hath unbesought provided, and his hands
Clothed us unworthy, pitying while he judged;
1060 How much more, if we pray him, will his ear
Be open, and his heart to pity incline,
And teach us further by what means to shun

1053. **Fruit of thy womb:** anticipating Luke
1.41–42; **aslope:** Adam's curse (to earn his
bread with labor) glanced off him and hit
the ground (l. 201: *Cursed is the ground*)
more directly than it hit him. Earlier,

when he was in despair (ll. 720–42), his
blessings seemed curses. Now that he is
reinvigorated, his curse seems a blessing.
1062. **by what means:** The entire future of
peaceful technology is anticipated here.

Th' inclement seasons, rain, ice, hail and snow,
Which now the sky with various face begins
1065 To show us in this mountain, while the winds
Blow moist and keen, shattering the graceful locks
Of these fair spreading trees; which bids us seek
Some better shroud, some better warmth to cherish
Our limbs benumbed, ere this diurnal star
1070 Leave cold the night, how we his gathered beams
Reflected, may with matter sere foment,
Or by collision of two bodies grind
The air attrite to fire, as late the clouds
Justling or pushed with winds rude in their shock
1075 Tine the slant lightning, whose thwart flame driv'n down
Kindles the gummy bark of fir or pine,
And sends a comfortable heat from far,
Which might supply the sun: such fire to use,
And what may else be remedy or cure
1080 To evils which our own misdeeds have wrought,
He will instruct us praying, and of grace
Beseeching him, so as we need not fear
To pass commodiously this life, sustained
By him with many comforts, till we end
1085 In dust, our final rest and native home.
What better can we do, than to the place
Repairing where he judged us, prostrate fall
Before him reverent, and there confess
Humbly our faults, and pardon beg, with tears

1066. **shattering:** shaking, breaking into pieces, as in *Lyc* 5, where leaves are also the verb's object.
1068. **shroud:** shelter.
1071. **foment:** heat.
1073. **attrite:** rubbed at.
1075. **Tine:** ignite. On the theological and philosophical implication of Adam's invention of fire, see Hoerner 1995.
1086–1104. Another of the poem's many mirroring effects, this one being the only imitation in Milton's work of the extensive formulaic repetition found in Homer

(e.g., *Il.* 9.122–57, 264–99). (Lines 1093–96 are not repeated because Adam and Eve's punishment will eventually include expulsion from Paradise.) Tayler 1979, 84 remarks that "not only do the narrator's words place a doctrinal seal upon this stage in the process of repentance" but they also create "a moment of stasis in which we all [Adam and Eve, the narrator, the reader] see things the same way": this is indeed the best thing to say, the best thing to do.

1090 Watering the ground, and with our sighs the air
    Frequenting, sent from hearts contrite, in sign
    Of sorrow unfeigned, and humiliation meek.
    Undoubtedly he will relent and turn
    From his displeasure; in whose look serene,
1095 When angry most he seemed and most severe,
    What else but favor, grace, and mercy shone?"
        So spake our father penitent, nor Eve
    Felt less remorse: they forthwith to the place
    Repairing where he judged them prostrate fell
1100 Before him reverent, and both confessed
    Humbly their faults, and pardon begged, with tears
    Watering the ground, and with their sighs the air
    Frequenting, sent from hearts contrite, in sign
    Of sorrow unfeigned, and humiliation meek.

BOOK XI

THE ARGUMENT

The Son of God presents to his Father the prayers of our first parents now repenting, and intercedes for them. God accepts them, but declares that they must no longer abide in Paradise; sends Michael with a band of Cherubim to dispossess them; but first to reveal to Adam future things; Michael's coming down. Adam shows to Eve certain ominous signs; he discerns Michael's approach, goes out to meet him: the angel denounces their departure. Eve's lamentation. Adam pleads, but submits. The angel leads him up to a high hill, sets before him in vision what shall happen till the Flood.

> Thus they in lowliest plight repentant stood
> Praying, for from the mercy-seat above
> Prevenient grace descending had removed
> The stony from their hearts, and made new flesh
> 5   Regenerate grow instead, that sighs now breathed
> Unutterable, which the spirit of prayer
> Inspired, and winged for Heav'n with speedier flight
> Then loudest oratory: yet their port
> Not of mean suitors, nor important less
> 10 Seemed their petition, than when th' ancient pair

---

1. **stood:** remained; the word, which may imply spiritual regeneration, is not intended to contradict "prostrate" in 10.1099.
2. **mercy-seat:** the cover of the Ark of the Covenant, whose cherubim represented intercession in Heaven; see Exod. 25.17–23.
3. **Prevenient grace:** grace that literally "comes before" human choice.
4. **stony . . . flesh:** From Ezek. 11.19: "I will

take the stony heart out of their flesh, and will give them a heart of flesh."
5–6. **sighs now breathed/Unutterable:** Cp. Rom. 8.26, where "groanings which cannot be uttered" intercede for humankind. Cp. *Eikon* 16 (Yale 3:507).
8. **port:** bearing.
10–14. **th' ancient pair . . . devout:** *Deucalion* and his wife, *Pyrrha*, figures in Greek

In fables old, less ancient yet than these,
Deucalion and chaste Pyrrha to restore
The race of mankind drowned, before the shrine
Of Themis stood devout. To Heav'n their prayers
15   Flew up, nor miss'd the way, by envious winds
Blown vagabond or frustrate: in they passed
Dimensionless through Heav'nly doors; then clad
With incense, where the golden altar fumed,
By their great Intercessor, came in sight
20   Before the Father's throne: them the glad Son
Presenting, thus to intercede began.
     "See Father, what first fruits on Earth are sprung
From thy implanted grace in man, these sighs
And prayers, which in this golden censer, mixed
25   With incense, I thy priest before thee bring,
Fruits of more pleasing savor from thy seed
Sown with contrition in his heart, than those
Which his own hand manuring all the trees
Of Paradise could have produced, ere fall'n
30   From innocence. Now therefore bend thine ear
To supplication, hear his sighs though mute;
Unskillful with what words to pray, let me
Interpret for him, me his advocate
And propitiation, all his works on me
35   Good or not good ingraft; my merit those
Shall perfect, and for these my death shall pay.
Accept me, and in me from these receive
The smell of peace toward mankind, let him live

mythology, survived the flood in an ark.
Themis, goddess of justice, told them to
throw stones behind them, and the stones
turned into people (echoing the trans-
formation from stony to fleshly hearts
in l. 4).

14–16. **To Heav'n . . . frustrate:** Cp. the Par-
adise of Fools at 3.485–89.

17. **Dimensionless:** without spatial exten-
sion.

18. **incense:** See Rev. 8.3.

28. **manuring:** tending (by hand).

33–34. **me . . . propitiation:** "And if any man
sin, we have an advocate with the Father,
Jesus Christ the righteous: and he is the
propitiation for our sins" (1 John 2.1–2).
The repeated *me* in these lines echoes
3.178–82, 236–38. Cp. 10.830–32.

35. **ingraft:** See Rom. 11.16–24, for Protestants
a key text on the superiority of faith to
good works.

Before thee reconciled, at least his days
40   Numbered, though sad, till death, his doom (which I
To mitigate thus plead, not to reverse)
To better life shall yield him, where with me
All my redeemed may dwell in joy and bliss,
Made one with me as I with thee am one."
45   To whom the Father, without cloud, serene.
"All thy request for man, accepted Son,
Obtain, all thy request was my decree:
But longer in that Paradise to dwell,
The law I gave to nature him forbids:
50   Those pure immortal elements that know
No gross, no unharmonious mixture foul,
Eject him tainted now, and purge him off
As a distemper, gross to air as gross,
And mortal food, as may dispose him best
55   For dissolution wrought by sin, that first
Distempered all things, and of incorrupt
Corrupted. I at first with two fair gifts
Created him endowed, with happiness
And immortality: that fondly lost,
60   This other served but to eternize woe;
Till I provided death; so death becomes
His final remedy, and after life
Tried in sharp tribulation, and refined
By faith and faithful works, to second life,
65   Waked in the renovation of the just,
Resigns him up with heav'n and Earth renewed.
But let us call to synod all the blest
Through Heav'n's wide bounds; from them I will not hide

---

44. John 17.22–23: "that they may be one, even as we are one: I in them, and thou in me." Note how the symmetry of Milton's line takes shape about the central *as I*.

53. **distemper:** medical term, denoting an imbalance of the four humors. The expulsion of Adam and Eve is here presented as an automatic purgation in which immortal elements rid themselves of tainted elements.

55. **dissolution:** death, disintegration.

59. **fondly:** foolishly.

60. **This other:** immortality (l. 59).

64. Cp. 12.427; *CD* I.22.

66. **Resigns:** The subject of the verb is *death* (l. 61).

My judgments, how with mankind I proceed,
70 As how with peccant angels late they saw;
And in their state, though firm, stood more confirmed."
He ended, and the Son gave signal high
To the bright minister that watched; he blew
His trumpet, heard in Oreb since perhaps
75 When God descended, and perhaps once more
To sound at general doom. Th' angelic blast
Filled all the regions: from their blissful bow'rs
Of amarantine shade, fountain or spring,
By the waters of life, where'er they sat
80 In fellowships of joy: the sons of light
Hasted, resorting to the summons high,
And took their seats; till from his throne supreme
Th' Almighty thus pronounced his sov'reign will.
"O Sons, like one of us man is become
85 To know both good and evil, since his taste
Of that defended fruit; but let him boast
His knowledge of good lost, and evil got,
Happier, had it sufficed him to have known
Good by itself, and evil not at all.
90 He sorrows now, repents, and prays contrite,
My motions in him; longer than they move,
His heart I know, how variable and vain
Self-left. Lest therefore his now bolder hand
Reach also of the Tree of Life, and eat,
95 And live forever, dream at least to live
Forever, to remove him I decree,
And send him from the garden forth to till
The ground whence he was taken, fitter soil.
"Michael, this my behest have thou in charge,

---

74. **heard in Oreb:** A trumpet sounded when God delivered the Ten Command-ments (Exod. 19.19); see *Nat Ode* 156–59.

75. **perhaps once more:** reminiscent of the opening of *Lycidas,* which alludes to the "yet once more" of Heb. 12.26–27.

78. **amarantine:** bloodred and unfading, like the legendary flower amaranthus (see 3.353).

86. **defended:** forbidden.

91. **motions:** inward promptings of the soul; cp. *PR* 1.290, *SA* 1382.

93. **Self-left:** when left to itself.

93–98. **Lest . . . soil:** The passage is based on Gen. 3.22–23.

100 Take to thee from among the Cherubim
    Thy choice of flaming warriors, lest the fiend
    Or in behalf of man, or to invade
    Vacant possession, some new trouble raise:
    Haste thee, and from the Paradise of God
105 Without remorse drive out the sinful pair,
    From hallowed ground th' unholy, and denounce
    To them and to their progeny from thence
    Perpetual banishment. Yet lest they faint
    At the sad sentence rigorously urged,
110 For I behold them softened and with tears
    Bewailing their excess, all terror hide.
    If patiently thy bidding they obey,
    Dismiss them not disconsolate; reveal
    To Adam what shall come in future days,
115 As I shall thee enlighten, intermix
    My cov'nant in the woman's seed renewed;
    So send them forth, though sorrowing, yet in peace:
    And on the east side of the garden place,
    Where entrance up from Eden easiest climbs,
120 Cherubic watch, and of a sword the flame
    Wide-waving, all approach far off to fright,
    And guard all passage to the Tree of Life:
    Lest Paradise a receptacle prove
    To spirits foul, and all my trees their prey,
125 With whose stol'n fruit man once more to delude."
        He ceased; and th' archangelic power prepared
    For swift descent, with him the cohort bright
    Of watchful Cherubim; four faces each
    Had, like a double Janus, all their shape
130 Spangled with eyes more numerous than those
    Of Argus, and more wakeful than to drowse,

102. **Or . . . or:** either . . . or.
106. **denounce:** announce.
108. **faint:** lose heart.
111. **excess:** transgression. Cp. 3.696.
129. **Janus:** two-faced Roman god of gates, beginnings, transitions.

131. **Argus:** The hundred-eyed giant set to guard Io, whom *Hermes* (Mercury) put to sleep with his *pipe* and his *opiate rod*, then killed. See Ovid, *Met.* 1.568–779.

Charmed with Arcadian pipe, the pastoral reed
Of Hermes, or his opiate rod. Meanwhile
To resalute the world with sacred light
135   Leucothea waked, and with fresh dews imbalmed
The Earth, when Adam and first matron Eve
Had ended now their orisons, and found
Strength added from above, new hope to spring
Out of despair, joy, but with fear yet linked;
140   Which thus to Eve his welcome words renewed.
      "Eve, easily may faith admit, that all
The good which we enjoy, from Heav'n descends;
But that from us aught should ascend to Heav'n
So prevalent as to concern the mind
145   Of God high-blest, or to incline his will,
Hard to belief may seem; yet this will prayer,
Or one short sigh of human breath, upborne
Ev'n to the seat of God. For since I sought
By prayer th' offended Deity to appease,
150   Kneeled and before him humbled all my heart,
Methought I saw him placable and mild,
Bending his ear; persuasion in me grew
That I was heard with favor; peace returned
Home to my breast, and to my memory
155   His promise, that thy seed shall bruise our foe;
Which then not minded in dismay, yet now
Assures me that the bitterness of death
Is past, and we shall live. Whence hail to thee,
Eve rightly called, Mother of all Mankind,
160   Mother of all things living, since by thee
Man is to live, and all things live for man."
      To whom thus Eve with sad demeanor meek.
      "Ill-worthy I such title should belong

---

135. **Leucothea:** goddess of the dawn.
144. **prevalent:** potent.
157–58. **Assures . . . past:** Echoing the words of Agag ("surely the bitterness of death is past") just before he is killed by Samuel (1 Sam. 15.32).

158. **hail to thee:** Adam prefigures the Annunciation (Ave Maria).
159. **Eve rightly called:** Here Adam confirms the epithet *mother* first given to Eve by the voice of God (4.475); *Eve* is cognate with Heb. *chai* or "life." See Gen. 3.20.

To me transgressor, who for thee ordained
165　A help, became thy snare; to me reproach
Rather belongs, distrust and all dispraise:
But infinite in pardon was my judge,
That I who first brought death on all, am graced
The source of life; next favorable thou,
170　Who highly thus to entitle me vouchsaf'st,
Far other name deserving. But the field
To labor calls us now with sweat imposed,
Though after sleepless night; for see the morn,
All unconcerned with our unrest, begins
175　Her rosy progress smiling; let us forth,
I never from thy side henceforth to stray,
Where'er our day's work lies, though now enjoined
Laborious, till day droop; while here we dwell,
What can be toilsome in these pleasant walks?
180　Here let us live, though in fall'n state, content."
　　　So spake, so wished much-humbled Eve, but fate
Subscribed not; nature first gave signs, impressed
On bird, beast, air, air suddenly eclipsed
After short blush of morn; nigh in her sight
185　The bird of Jove, stooped from his airy tour,
Two birds of gayest plume before him drove:
Down from a hill the beast that reigns in woods,
First hunter then, pursued a gentle brace,
Goodliest of all the forest, hart and hind;
190　Direct to th' eastern gate was bent their flight.
Adam observed, and with his eye the chase
Pursuing, not unmoved to Eve thus spake.
　　　"O Eve, some further change awaits us nigh,
Which Heav'n by these mute signs in nature shows

---

185. **The bird of Jove:** the eagle; **stooped:** having swooped down to strike his prey (technical term in falconry).

186. **Two birds of gayest plume:** The eagle chasing these birds is an augury of Michael's expulsion of Adam and Eve from the garden.

187. **the beast that reigns:** the lion, who is to land animals what the eagle is to birds. Another augury of Adam and Eve's expulsion from Eden.

188. **brace:** pair.

195 Forerunners of his purpose, or to warn
Us haply too secure of our discharge
From penalty, because from death released
Some days; how long, and what till then our life,
Who knows, or more than this, that we are dust,
200 And thither must return and be no more.
Why else this double object in our sight
Of flight pursued in th' air and o'er the ground
One way the selfsame hour? Why in the east
Darkness ere day's mid-course, and morning light
205 More orient in yon western cloud that draws
O're the blue firmament a radiant white,
And slow descends, with something Heav'nly fraught."
    He erred not, for by this the Heav'nly bands
Down from a sky of jasper lighted now
210 In Paradise, and on a hill made halt,
A glorious apparition, had not doubt
And carnal fear that day dimmed Adam's eye.
Not that more glorious, when the angels met
Jacob in Mahanaim, where he saw
215 The field pavilioned with his guardians bright;
Nor that which on the flaming mount appeared
In Dothan, covered with a camp of fire,
Against the Syrian king, who to surprise
One man, assassin-like had levied war,
220 War unproclaimed. The princely hierarch
In their bright stand, there left his powers to seize
Possession of the garden; he alone,
To find where Adam sheltered, took his way,

---

196. **secure:** overconfident.
205. **orient:** bright.
208. **by this:** by this time.
209. **lighted:** landed.
210. **made halt:** came to a halt (military term).
214. **Mahanaim:** Jacob named the place (Heb. for "armies") when he saw an army of angels there (Gen. 32.1–2).

215. **pavilioned:** encamped. See Milton's version of Psalm 3, lines 17–18.
216–20. **Nor that . . . unproclaimed:** Elisha and his fearful servant also had a vision of an angelic army with "horses and chariots of fire" when the *Syrian king* laid siege to the city of *Dothan* (2 Kings 6.7).
221. **stand:** station (military term).

Not unperceived of Adam, who to Eve,
225 While the great visitant approached, thus spake.
    "Eve, now expect great tidings, which perhaps
Of us will soon determine, or impose
New laws to be observed; for I descry
From yonder blazing cloud that veils the hill
230 One of the Heav'nly host, and by his gait
None of the meanest, some great potentate
Or of the Thrones above, such majesty
Invests him coming; yet not terrible,
That I should fear, nor sociably mild,
235 As Raphael, that I should much confide,
But solemn and sublime, whom not to offend,
With reverence I must meet, and thou retire."
He ended; and th' archangel soon drew nigh,
Not in his shape celestial, but as man
240 Clad to meet man; over his lucid arms
A military vest of purple flowed
Livelier than Meliboean, or the grain
Of Sarra, worn by kings and heroes old
In time of truce; Iris had dipped the woof;
245 His starry helm unbuckled showed him prime
In manhood where youth ended; by his side
As in a glistering zodiac hung the sword,
Satan's dire dread, and in his hand the spear.
Adam bowed low, he kingly from his state
250 Inclined not, but his coming thus declared.
    "Adam, Heav'n's high behest no preface needs:
Sufficient that thy prayers are heard, and death,
Then due by sentence when thou didst transgress,
Defeated of his seizure many days
255 Giv'n thee of grace, wherein thou may'st repent,

---

227. **determine:** bring to an end.
240. **lucid:** bright.
242–43. **Meliboean . . . Sarra:** The cities of Meliboea and Tyre (*Sarra*) were famous for dyes (*grain* = dye) made from local fish.
244. **Iris . . . woof:** Iris is goddess of the rainbow. Cp. *Masque* 83, where the Attendant Spirit doffs "sky robes spun out of Iris' woof," and *PL* 11.895–98.
254. **Defeated:** cheated.

And one bad act with many deeds well done
May'st cover: well may then thy Lord appeased
Redeem thee quite from death's rapacious claim;
But longer in this Paradise to dwell
260 Permits not; to remove thee I am come,
And send thee from the garden forth to till
The ground whence thou wast tak'n, fitter soil."
    He added not, for Adam at the news
Heart-strook with chilling grip of sorrow stood,
265 That all his senses bound; Eve, who unseen
Yet all had heard, with audible lament
Discovered soon the place of her retire.
    "O unexpected stroke, worse than of death!
Must I thus leave thee Paradise? Thus leave
270 Thee native soil, these happy walks and shades,
Fit haunt of gods? Where I had hope to spend,
Quiet though sad, the respite of that day
That must be mortal to us both. O flow'rs,
That never will in other climate grow,
275 My early visitation, and my last
At ev'n, which I bred up with tender hand
From the first op'ning bud, and gave ye names,
Who now shall rear ye to the sun, or rank
Your tribes, and water from th' ambrosial fount?
280 Thee lastly nuptial bower, by me adorned
With what to sight or smell was sweet; from thee
How shall I part, and whither wander down
Into a lower world, to this obscure
And wild, how shall we breathe in other air

256–57. **one . . . cover:** 1 Pet. 4.8: "For charity covers a multitude of sins."

259–62. Varied only slightly from lines 48–49, 96–98, in the manner of Homer's repetitive treatment of messages.

264. **grip:** spasm.

267. **Discovered:** revealed; **retire:** withdrawal.

270. **native soil:** "Paradise was the *native place* of Eve; but Adam was formed out of the dust of the ground, and was afterwards brought into Paradise" (Newton).

272. **respite:** temporary suspension of a death sentence (legal term).

277. **gave ye names:** Presumably this naming of the flowers, which has no biblical precedent, entailed, like Adam's naming of the creatures, an intuitive understanding of "their nature" (8.353).

283. **to this:** compared to this.

285　Less pure, accustomed to immortal fruits?"
　　　　Whom thus the angel interrupted mild.
　　　"Lament not Eve, but patiently resign
　　　What justly thou hast lost; nor set thy heart,
　　　Thus over-fond, on that which is not thine;
290　Thy going is not lonely, with thee goes
　　　Thy husband, him to follow thou art bound;
　　　Where he abides, think there thy native soil."
　　　　Adam by this from the cold sudden damp
　　　Recovering, and his scattered spirits returned,
295　To Michael thus his humble words addressed.
　　　　"Celestial, whether among the Thrones, or named
　　　Of them the highest, for such of shape may seem
　　　Prince above princes, gently hast thou told
　　　Thy message, which might else in telling wound,
300　And in performing end us; what besides
　　　Of sorrow and dejection and despair
　　　Our frailty can sustain, thy tidings bring,
　　　Departure from this happy place, our sweet
　　　Recess, and only consolation left
305　Familiar to our eyes, all places else
　　　Inhospitable appear and desolate,
　　　Nor knowing us nor known: and if by prayer
　　　Incessant I could hope to change the will
　　　Of him who all things can, I would not cease
310　To weary him with my assiduous cries:
　　　But prayer against his absolute decree
　　　No more avails than breath against the wind,
　　　Blown stifling back on him that breathes it forth:
　　　Therefore to his great bidding I submit.
315　This most afflicts me, that departing hence,
　　　As from his face I shall be hid, deprived
　　　His blessed count'nance; here I could frequent,

290–92. Eve will make this view her own in the last speech in the poem (12.615–18).
293. **by this:** by this time; **damp:** stupor, depression.

309. **can:** is able to do, has knowledge of.
316. **from . . . hid:** a biblical idiom (Gen. 4.14, Ps. 104.27). Cp. 12.106–9 and *SA* 1749.

With worship, place by place where he vouchsafed
Presence divine, and to my sons relate,
320 "On this Mount he appeared, under this tree
Stood visible, among these pines his voice
I heard, here with him at this fountain talked."
So many grateful altars I would rear
Of grassy turf, and pile up every stone
325 Of luster from the brook, in memory,
Or monument to ages, and thereon
Offer sweet smelling gums and fruits and flow'rs:
In yonder nether world where shall I seek
His bright appearances, or footstep trace?
330 For though I fled him angry, yet recalled
To life prolonged and promised race, I now
Gladly behold though but his utmost skirts
Of glory, and far off his steps adore."
      To whom thus Michael with regard benign.
335 "Adam, thou know'st Heav'n his, and all the Earth,
Not this rock only; his omnipresence fills
Land, sea, and air, and every kind that lives,
Fomented by his virtual power and warmed:
All th' Earth he gave thee to possess and rule,
340 No despicable gift; surmise not then
His presence to these narrow bounds confined
Of Paradise or Eden: this had been
Perhaps thy capital seat, from whence had spread
All generations, and had hither come
345 From all the ends of th' Earth, to celebrate
And reverence thee their great progenitor.
But this preeminence thou hast lost, brought down
To dwell on even ground now with thy sons:
Yet doubt not but in valley and in plain
350 God is as here, and will be found alike
Present, and of his presence many a sign
Still following thee, still compassing thee round
With goodness and paternal love, his face

---

331. **promised race:** the human race.   338. **Fomented:** nurtured; **virtual:** potent.

Express, and of his steps the track divine.
355　Which that thou may'st believe, and be confirmed
Ere thou from hence depart, know I am sent
To show thee what shall come in future days
To thee and to thy offspring; good with bad
Expect to hear, supernal grace contending
360　With sinfulness of men; thereby to learn
True patience, and to temper joy with fear
And pious sorrow, equally inured
By moderation either state to bear,
Prosperous or adverse: so shalt thou lead
365　Safest thy life, and best prepared endure
Thy mortal passage when it comes. Ascend
This hill; let Eve (for I have drenched her eyes)
Here sleep below while thou to foresight wak'st,
As once thou slept'st, while she to life was formed."
370　　　To whom thus Adam gratefully replied.
"Ascend, I follow thee, safe guide, the path
Thou lead'st me, and to the hand of Heav'n submit,
However chast'ning, to the evil turn
My obvious breast, arming to overcome
375　By suffering, and earn rest from labor won,
If so I may attain." So both ascend
In the visions of God: it was a hill
Of Paradise the highest, from whose top
The hemisphere of earth in clearest ken
380　Stretched out to the amplest reach of prospect lay.
Not higher that hill nor wider looking round,
Whereon for different cause the Tempter set

356–58. **Ere . . . offspring:** As Addison was among the first to note, the idea of Adam's vision was probably suggested to Milton by the vision of his descendants given to Aeneas in the last book of the *Aeneid*. Addison also noted that the vision was necessary to console Adam, who "sees his offspring triumphing over his great enemy, and himself restored to a happier Paradise" (49).

361. **True patience:** Christian patience, which includes hope, as opposed to the apathy recommended by stoicism.

367. **drenched:** administered medicine (a sleeping potion) to. Cp. 2.73n.

374. **obvious:** vulnerable.

377. **visions of God:** visions sent by God.

Our second Adam in the wilderness,
To show him all Earth's kingdoms and their glory.
385 His eye might there command wherever stood
City of old or modern fame, the seat
Of mightiest empire, from the destined walls
Of Cambalu, seat of Cathayan Khan
And Samarkand by Oxus, Temir's throne,
390 To Paquin of Sinaean kings, and thence
To Agra and Lahore of Great Mogul
Down to the golden Chersonese, or where
The Persian in Ecbatan sat, or since
In Hispahan, or where the Russian Czar
395 In Moscow, or the Sultan in Bizance,
Turkestan-born; nor could his eye not ken
Th' Empire of Negus to his utmost port
Ercoco and the less maritime kings
Mombaza, and Quiloa, and Melind,
400 And Sofala thought Ophir, to the realm
Of Congo, and Angola farthest south;
Or thence from Niger flood to Atlas mount

---

383. **second Adam:** See 10.183n.

388. **Cambalu:** capital of Cathay (China), modern Beijing, seat of the khans. Milton's geography of imperialism to come moves from east to west, like the sun, and like history as traditionally conceived in the West (see Chambers 1961).

389. **Samarkand by Oxus:** an Uzbekistan city on the river Oxus, the birthplace and royal residence of Tamburlaine (*Temir*).

390. **Paquin:** also a name for modern Beijing, where Chinese (*Sinaean*) kings ruled.

391. **Agra:** Mogul capital, where Akbar built the Taj Mahal; **Lahore:** Pakistani city where Mogul emperors sometimes resided.

392. **golden Chersonese:** area to the east of India, fabled for its wealth.

393–94. **Ecbatan:** Ecbatana, modern Hamadan in Iran, once the summer residence of Persian kings; **Hispahan:** Isfa-

han in Iran, made the Persian capital in the sixteenth century.

395. **Bizance:** Byzantium (modern Istanbul), conquered by the Ottoman Empire in the fifteenth century.

396. **Turkestan-born:** The Ottoman Turks originated in Turkistan.

397. **Negus:** title of Abyssinian emperors.

398. **Ercoco:** Arkiko, in modern Ethiopia.

399–400. **Mombaza** (modern Mombasa, in Kenya), **Quiloa** (Kilwa, in Tanzania), **Melind** (Malindi, in Kenya), and **Sofala** (in Mozambique) are port cities in eastern Africa visited by Vasco da Gama. Sofala was one of a number of candidates for the biblical *Ophir*, where Solomon found gold.

402. **Niger:** a West African river; **Atlas mount:** the Atlas Mountains of westernmost Africa.

The kingdoms of Almansor, Fez and Sus,
Morocco and Algiers, and Tremisen;
405 On Europe thence, and where Rome was to sway
The world: in spirit perhaps he also saw
Rich Mexico the seat of Motezume,
And Cusco in Peru, the richer seat
Of Atabalipa, and yet unspoiled
410 Guiana, whose great city Geryon's sons
Call El Dorado: but to nobler sights
Michael from Adam's eyes the film removed
Which that false fruit that promised clearer sight
Had bred; then purged with euphrasy and rue
415 The visual nerve, for he had much to see;
And from the Well of Life three drops instilled.
So deep the power of these ingredients pierced,
Even to the inmost seat of mental sight,
That Adam now enforced to close his eyes,
420 Sunk down and all his spirits became entranced:
But him the gentle angel by the hand
Soon raised, and his attention thus recalled.

403. **Almansor:** Muslim kings claimed the surname Al-Mansur (made victorious by God), and ruled over *Fez*, a Moroccan city, and *Sus* (Tunis).

404. **Tremisen:** an area of Algeria.

406. **in spirit:** in a visionary extension of eyesight; the New World would have been hidden by the curvature of the earth.

407. **Motezume:** the Aztec emperor Montezuma, who surrendered to Hernán Cortés in 1520.

409. **Atabalipa:** Atahualpa, the Incan emperor slain by Francisco Pizarro in 1533; his Peruvian capital of *Cusco* fell to the Spaniards.

410. **Geryon's sons:** an epithet for Spaniards, based on a mythical monster named Geryon, who lived on a Spanish island and was slain by Hercules.

411. **El Dorado:** a mythical city in the New World that Sir Walter Ralegh among others sought in vain. See Ralegh's *The Discoverie of Guiana* (1595), 10.

412. **the film removed:** A god clearing mortal eyes is an epic convention (*Il.* 5.126; *Aen.* 2.604; *GL* 18.92f), but given the real physiological effects of the forbidden fruit (9.1011–12, 1044–51), it seems likely that this film is actual rather than metaphorical: Adam had incipient *gutta serena,* the "dim suffusion" (3.26) from which Milton suffered.

414. **euphrasy and rue:** medicinal herbs used in the treatment of eyesight. Milton might have taken salves made of these herbs in the course of going blind.

416. **the Well of Life:** perhaps the "fountain of life" of Ps. 36.9; **three drops:** a conspicuous dose in a poem that is not conventionally trinitarian.

"Adam, now ope thine eyes, and first behold
Th' effects which thy original crime hath wrought
425 In some to spring from thee, who never touched
Th' excepted tree, nor with the snake conspired,
Nor sinned thy sin, yet from that sin derive
Corruption to bring forth more violent deeds."
    His eyes he opened, and beheld a field,
430 Part arable and tilth, whereon were sheaves
New reapt, the other part sheep-walks and folds;
I' th' midst an altar as the landmark stood
Rustic, of grassy sward; thither anon
A sweaty reaper from his tillage brought
435 First fruits, the green ear, and the yellow sheaf,
Unculled, as came to hand; a shepherd next
More meek came with the firstlings of his flock
Choicest and best; then sacrificing, laid
The inwards and their fat, with incense strewed,
440 On the cleft wood, and all due rites performed.
His off'ring soon propitious fire from heav'n
Consumed with nimble glance, and grateful steam;
The other's not, for his was not sincere;
Whereat he inly raged, and as they talked,
445 Smote him into the midriff with a stone
That beat out life; he fell, and deadly pale
Groaned out his soul with gushing blood effused.
Much at that sight was Adam in his heart
Dismayed, and thus in haste to th' angel cried.
450 "O teacher, some great mischief hath befall'n
To that meek man, who well had sacrificed;
Is piety thus and pure devotion paid?"
    T' whom Michael thus, he also moved, replied.
"These two are brethren, Adam, and to come

---

426. **excepted:** forbidden.
427. **that sin:** 1667; 1674 drops "sin," spoiling the meter.
430. **tilth:** cultivated land.
433. **sward:** turf.
436. **Unculled:** not picked by design.

441. **propitious fire from heav'n:** After Abel follows the rules for sacrificing in Lev. 1–8, Heaven consumes his offering (Gen. 4.4).
442. **glance:** flash.
447. **effused:** poured out.

455 Out of thy loins; th' unjust the just hath slain,
For envy that his brother's offering found
From Heav'n acceptance; but the bloody fact
Will be avenged, and th' other's faith approved
Lose no reward, though here thou see him die,
460 Rolling in dust and gore." To which our sire.
    "Alas, both for the deed and for the cause!
But have I now seen death? Is this the way
I must return to native dust? O sight
Of terror, foul and ugly to behold,
465 Horrid to think, how horrible to feel!"
    To whom thus Michael. "Death thou hast seen
In his first shape on man; but many shapes
Of Death, and many are the ways that lead
To his grim cave, all dismal; yet to sense
470 More terrible at th' entrance than within.
Some, as thou saw'st, by violent stroke shall die,
By fire, flood, famine; by intemperance more
In meats and drinks, which on the Earth shall bring
Diseases dire, of which a monstrous crew
475 Before thee shall appear; that thou may'st know
What misery th' inabstinence of Eve
Shall bring on men." Immediately a place
Before his eyes appeared, sad, noisome, dark,
A lazar-house it seemed, wherein were laid
480 Numbers of all diseased, all maladies
Of ghastly spasm, or racking torture, qualms
Of heart-sick agony, all feverous kinds,
Convulsions, epilepsies, fierce catarrhs,
Intestine stone and ulcer, colic pangs,
485 Demoniac frenzy, moping melancholy
And moon-struck madness, pining atrophy,

---

457. **fact:** crime.
469. **his grim cave:** Cp. the cave to the underworld in *Aen.* 6.237, 273–94.
479. **lazar-house:** hospital for those with infectious diseases, especially the dreaded leprosy; *lazar* comes from the name of the beggar in Luke 16.20. There were a number of lazar houses in England (Wilson 1963, 81).
481. **qualms:** faintings.
485–87. These lines were added in 1674.

Marasmus, and wide-wasting pestilence,
Dropsies, and asthmas, and joint-racking rheums.
Dire was the tossing, deep the groans; Despair
490 Tended the sick busiest from couch to couch;
And over them triumphant Death his dart
Shook, but delayed to strike, though oft invoked
With vows, as their chief good, and final hope.
Sight so deform what heart of rock could long
495 Dry-eyed behold? Adam could not, but wept,
Though not of woman born; compassion quelled
His best of man, and gave him up to tears
A space, till firmer thoughts restrained excess,
And scarce recovering words his plaint renewed.

500   "O miserable mankind, to what fall
Degraded, to what wretched state reserved!
Better end here unborn. Why is life giv'n
To be thus wrested from us? Rather why
Obtruded on us thus? Who if we knew
505 What we receive, would either not accept
Life offered, or soon beg to lay it down,
Glad to be so dismissed in peace. Can thus
Th' image of God in man created once
So goodly and erect, though faulty since,
510 To such unsightly sufferings be debased
Under inhuman pains? Why should not man,
Retaining still divine similitude
In part, from such deformities be free,

487. **Marasmus**: consumption.
488. **Dropsies**: morbid retentions of fluid; **rheums**: mucous discharges.
496. **Though not of woman born**: Although the phrasing evokes *MAC* 4.1.80 and 5.3.13, Milton draws on Shakespeare's association between a man's tears and his internalized mother in *H5* 4.6.30–32 and *TN* 2.1.35–38.
497. **best of man**: manliness, normally impervious to tears. But Milton's Adam, apparently no exponent of tearless masculinity, weeps on his own here, and at

lines 675, 754–58, and 12.372–73; Eve weeps on her own at 5.130–35, 9.990–91, and 10.910; they cry together at 9.1121, 10.1101–2, and 12.645.
502–507. **Better . . . peace**: A commonplace of both classical literature (Sophocles, *Oedipus at Colonus* 1224–26; Theognis of Megara, *Maxims*, 425–28; Seneca, *Ad Marciam: De Consolatione* 22.3) and Renaissance literature (*2H4* 3.1.45–56; Jonson, "To the Immortal Memory . . . Sir. Lucius Cary and Sir H. Morison," 1–20).

And for his Maker's image sake exempt?"

515 "Their Maker's image," answered Michael, "then
Forsook them, when themselves they vilified
To serve ungoverned appetite, and took
His image whom they served, a brutish vice,
Inductive mainly to the sin of Eve.

520 Therefore so abject is their punishment,
Disfiguring not God's likeness, but their own,
Or if his likeness, by themselves defaced
While they pervert pure nature's healthful rules
To loathsome sickness, worthily, since they

525 God's image did not reverence in themselves."
"I yield it just," said Adam, "and submit.
But is there yet no other way, besides
These painful passages, how we may come
To death, and mix with our connatural dust?"

530 "There is," said Michael, "if thou well observe
The rule of *not too much,* by temperance taught
In what thou eat'st and drink'st, seeking from thence
Due nourishment, not gluttonous delight,
Till many years over thy head return:

535 So may'st thou live, till like ripe fruit thou drop
Into thy mother's lap, or be with ease
Gathered, not harshly plucked, for death mature:
This is old age; but then thou must outlive
Thy youth, thy strength, thy beauty, which will change

540 To withered weak and gray; thy senses then
Obtuse, all taste of pleasure must forgo,
To what thou hast, and for the air of youth
Hopeful and cheerful, in thy blood will reign
A melancholy damp of cold and dry

545 To weigh thy spirits down, and last consume

519. **Inductive:** traceable.
531. **The rule of *not too much:*** "Nothing too much" was inscribed on the temple of Apollo at Delphi (Plato, *Protagoras* 343B; see also Aristotle, *Nichomachean Ethics* 2.2.16).

535–37. The comparison stems from Cicero, *De Senectute* 19; cp. Donne, "A Valediction Forbidding Mourning": "As virtuous men pass mildly away. . . ."
544. **damp:** Cp. 293; 9.45.

The balm of life." To whom our ancestor.

    "Henceforth I fly not death, nor would prolong
Life much, bent rather how I may be quit
Fairest and easiest of this cumbrous charge,
550   Which I must keep till my appointed day
Of rend'ring up, and patiently attend
My dissolution." Michael replied,
    "Nor love thy life, nor hate; but what thou liv'st
Live well, how long or short permit to Heav'n:
555   And now prepare thee for another sight."
He looked and saw a spacious plain, whereon
Were tents of various hue; by some were herds
Of cattle grazing: others, whence the sound
Of instruments that made melodious chime
560   Was heard, of harp and organ; and who moved
Their stops and chords was seen: his volant touch
Instinct through all proportions low and high
Fled and pursued transverse the resonant fugue.
In other part stood one who at the forge
565   Laboring, two massy clods of iron and brass
Had melted (whether found where casual fire
Had wasted woods on mountain or in vale,
Down to the veins of Earth, thence gliding hot
To some cave's mouth, or whether washed by stream
570   From underground) the liquid ore he drained
Into fit molds prepared; from which he formed
First his own tools; then, what might else be wrought
Fusile or grav'n in metal. After these,
But on the hither side a different sort
575   From the high neighboring hills, which was their seat,

551–52. The first edition had only one line here: "Of rend'ring up. Michael to him replied."

553. **Nor love thy life, nor hate:** from Martial, *Epigrams*, 10.47.

556–97. Adam's third vision, concerning the descendants of Cain, derives from Gen. 4.19–22, 6.2–4.

561. **volant:** rapid, flying.

562. **Instinct:** instinctively.

563. **fugue:** from the Latin *fuga* (flight). A "skilful organist" plays fugues in *Of Ed* (*MLM* 979).

573. **Fusile:** shaped by means of melting.

Down to the plain descended: by their guise
Just men they seemed, and all their study bent
To worship God aright, and know his works
Not hid, nor those things last which might preserve
580   Freedom and peace to men: they on the plain
Long had not walked, when from the tents behold
A bevy of fair women, richly gay
In gems and wanton dress; to the harp they sung
Soft amorous ditties, and in dance came on:
585   The men though grave, eyed them, and let their eyes
Rove without rein, till in the amorous net
Fast caught, they liked, and each his liking chose;
And now of love they treat till th' ev'ning star
Love's harbinger appeared; then all in heat
590   They light the nuptial torch, and bid invoke
Hymen, then first to marriage rites invoked;
With feast and music all the tents resound.
Such happy interview and fair event
Of love and youth not lost, songs, garlands, flow'rs,
595   And charming symphonies attached the heart
Of Adam, soon inclined to admit delight,
The bent of nature; which he thus expressed.
        "True opener of mine eyes, prime angel blest,
Much better seems this vision, and more hope
600   Of peaceful days portends, than those two past;
Those were of hate and death, or pain much worse,
Here nature seems fulfilled in all her ends."
        To whom thus Michael. "Judge not what is best
By pleasure, though to nature seeming meet,
605   Created, as thou art, to nobler end
Holy and pure, conformity divine.
Those tents thou saw'st so pleasant, were the tents
Of wickedness, wherein shall dwell his race

---

586. **amorous net:** Cp. *PR* 2.161–62; nets were
conventional in erotic contexts.
593. **interview:** a mutual viewing as well as a
verbal exchange; **event:** outcome.
595. **attached:** seized. Adam too readily

warms to the sight of youthful pleasure
not lost.
607. **tents:** Jabal was the father of tent
dwellers (Gen. 4.20).

Who slew his brother; studious they appear
610 Of arts that polish life, inventors rare,
Unmindful of their Maker, though his spirit
Taught them, but they his gifts acknowledged none.
Yet they a beauteous offspring shall beget;
For that fair female troop thou saw'st, that seemed
615 Of goddesses, so blithe, so smooth, so gay,
Yet empty of all good wherein consists
Woman's domestic honor and chief praise;
Bred only and completed to the taste
Of lustful appetence, to sing, to dance,
620 To dress, and troll the tongue, and roll the eye.
To these that sober race of men, whose lives
Religious titled them the Sons of God,
Shall yield up all their virtue, all their fame
Ignobly, to the trains and to the smiles
625 Of these fair atheists, and now swim in joy,
(Erelong to swim at large) and laugh; for which
The world erelong a world of tears must weep."
      To whom thus Adam of short joy bereft.
"O pity and shame, that they who to live well
630 Entered so fair, should turn aside to tread
Paths indirect, or in the mid way faint!
But still I see the tenor of man's woe
Holds on the same, from woman to begin."
      "From man's effeminate slackness it begins,"
635 Said th' angel, "who should better hold his place
By wisdom, and superior gifts received.
But now prepare thee for another scene."
      He looked and saw wide territory spread

---

619. **appetence:** desire.
620. **troll:** wag; note the flashy rhyme with *roll.*
622. **Sons of God:** See 5.446–48n.
624. **trains:** tricks, stratagems.
626. **Erelong to swim at large:** Michael anticipates the Flood, the forthcoming punishment for this swimming in lewd joy.
631. **mid way:** Cp. 6.91n.

632–33. **man's woe ... woman:** Adam turns *man's woe* into "woe-man," an old misogynistic joke.
638–73. The fourth vision is based on Gen. 6.4, with touches drawn from Homer's description of the shield of Achilles (*Il.* 18.478–540) and Vergil's imitation of it in *Aen.* 8.626–728.

Before him, towns, and rural works between,
640 Cities of men with lofty gates and tow'rs,
Concourse in arms, fierce faces threat'ning war,
Giants of mighty bone, and bold emprise;
Part wield their arms, part curb the foaming steed,
Single or in array of battle ranged
645 Both horse and foot, nor idly must'ring stood;
One way a band select from forage drives
A herd of beeves, fair oxen and fair kine
From a fat meadow ground; or fleecy flock,
Ewes and their bleating lambs over the plain,
650 Their booty; scarce with life the shepherds fly,
But call in aid, which makes a bloody fray;
With cruel tournament the squadrons join;
Where cattle pastured late, now scattered lies
With carcasses and arms th' ensanguined field
655 Deserted: others to a city strong
Lay siege, encamped; by battery, scale, and mine,
Assaulting; others from the wall defend
With dart and jav'lin, stones and sulfurous fire;
On each hand slaughter and gigantic deeds.
660 In other part the sceptered heralds call
To council in the city gates: anon
Grey-headed men and grave, with warriors mixed,
Assemble, and harangues are heard, but soon
In factious opposition, till at last
665 Of middle age one rising, eminent
In wise deport, spake much of right and wrong,
Of justice, of religion, truth and peace,
And judgment from above: him old and young
Exploded and had seized with violent hands,

---

642. **bold emprise:** martial enterprise; also found in *Masque* 610.
643. **curb the foaming steed:** Cp. 2.531n.
644. **ranged:** arranged.
654. **ensanguined:** blood-soaked.
656. **battery, scale, and mine:** The sieging army can break through the walls of the city (*battery*), climb over them (*scale* = ladder), and dig underneath them (*mine*).
665. **one rising:** Enoch, the first of several forthcoming examples of solitary, Abdiel-like heroism (see 5.897–903).
669. **Exploded:** silenced with mockery, hissed.

670   Had not a cloud descending snatched him thence
      Unseen amid the throng: so violence
      Proceeded, and oppression, and sword-law
      Through all the plain, and refuge none was found.
      Adam was all in tears, and to his guide
675   Lamenting turned full sad: "O what are these,
      Death's ministers, not men, who thus deal death
      Inhumanly to men, and multiply
      Ten-thousandfold the sin of him who slew
      His brother; for of whom such massacre
680   Make they but of their brethren, men of men?
      But who was that just man, whom had not Heav'n
      Rescued, had in his righteousness been lost?"
         To whom thus Michael. "These are the product
      Of those ill-mated marriages thou saw'st:
685   Where good with bad were matched, who of themselves
      Abhor to join; and by imprudence mixed,
      Produce prodigious births of body or mind.
      Such were these giants, men of high renown;
      For in those days might only shall be admired,
690   And valor and heroic virtue called;
      To overcome in battle, and subdue
      Nations, and bring home spoils with infinite
      Manslaughter, shall be held the highest pitch
      Of human glory, and for glory done
695   Of triumph, to be styled great conquerors,
      Patrons of mankind, gods, and sons of gods,
      Destroyers rightlier called and plagues of men.
      Thus fame shall be achieved, renown on earth,
      And what most merits fame in silence hid.
700   But he the sev'nth from thee, whom thou beheld'st
      The only righteous in a world perverse,
      And therefore hated, therefore so beset
      With foes for daring single to be just,
      And utter odious truth, that God would come

687–88. "There were giants in the earth in   700. **the sev'nth from thee:** See Jude 14.
those days" (Gen. 6.4).

705 To judge them with his saints: him the Most High
     Rapt in a balmy cloud with wingèd steeds
     Did, as thou saw'st, receive, to walk with God
     High in salvation and the climes of bliss,
     Exempt from death, to show thee what reward
710 Awaits the good, the rest what punishment;
     Which now direct thine eyes and soon behold."
         He looked, and saw the face of things quite changed;
     The brazen throat of war had ceased to roar,
     All now was turned to jollity and game,
715 To luxury and riot, feast and dance,
     Marrying or prostituting, as befell,
     Rape or adultery, where passing fair
     Allured them; thence from cups to civil broils.
     At length a reverend sire among them came,
720 And of their doings great dislike declared,
     And testified against their ways; he oft
     Frequented their assemblies, whereso met,
     Triumphs or festivals, and to them preached
     Conversion and repentance, as to souls
725 In prison under judgments imminent:
     But all in vain: which when he saw, he ceased
     Contending, and removed his tents far off;
     Then from the mountain hewing timber tall,
     Began to build a vessel of huge bulk,
730 Measured by cubit, length, and breadth, and highth,
     Smeared round with pitch, and in the side a door
     Contrived, and of provisions laid in large
     For man and beast: when lo a wonder strange!

---

707. **receive:** Enoch is one of only two men
   in the Bible to be received into Heaven
   without dying. The other is Elijah (see 2
   Kings 2). For Milton's interest in this phe-
   nomenon, and its relation to the mortalist
   heresy, see Kerrigan 1975, 127–44.
712–53. The fifth vision concerns the Flood
   and the corruption that preceded it (Gen.
   6–9).

715. **luxury:** lust.
717. **passing fair:** both "women passing by"
   and "surpassing beauty."
719. **reverend sire:** Noah. Cp. *Lyc* 103.
730. **cubit:** a unit of length (the distance
   from the elbow to the fingertips); for the
   dimensions of the ark in cubits, see Gen.
   6.15.

Of every beast, and bird, and insect small
735　Came sevens and pairs, and entered in, as taught
Their order: last the sire, and his three sons
With their four wives; and God made fast the door.
Meanwhile the south wind rose, and with black wings
Wide hovering, all the clouds together drove
740　From under Heav'n; the hills to their supply
Vapor, and exhalation dusk and moist,
Sent up amain; and now the thickened sky
Like a dark ceiling stood; down rushed the rain
Impetuous, and continued till the earth
745　No more was seen; the floating vessel swum
Uplifted, and secure with beakèd prow
Rode tilting o'er the waves, all dwellings else
Flood overwhelmed, and them with all their pomp
Deep under water rolled; sea covered sea,
750　Sea without shore; and in their palaces
Where luxury late reigned, sea-monsters whelped
And stabled; of mankind, so numerous late,
All left, in one small bottom swum embarked.
How didst thou grieve then, Adam, to behold
755　The end of all thy offspring, end so sad,
Depopulation; thee another flood,
Of tears and sorrow a flood thee also drowned,
And sunk thee as thy sons; till gently reared
By th' angel, on thy feet thou stood'st at last,
760　Though comfortless, as when a father mourns
His children, all in view destroyed at once;
And scarce to th' angel utter'dst thus thy plaint.
　　"O visions ill foreseen! Better had I
Lived ignorant of future, so had borne

---

734. **insect:** Commentators often excluded insects from Noah's ark because they were thought to reproduce without coupling.

735. **sevens and pairs:** The ark contained seven pairs each of all clean animals and only one pair each of unclean animals (Gen. 7.2).

738–53. This passage draws from the description of Deucalion's flood in Ovid, *Met.* 1.262–347.

740. **supply:** assistance.

741. **exhalation dusk:** dark mist.

753. **bottom:** boat.

755–56. **The end . . . Depopulation:** See Matt. 6.34.

765 My part of evil only, each day's lot
Enough to bear; those now, that were dispensed
The burd'n of many ages, on me light
At once, by my foreknowledge gaining birth
Abortive, to torment me ere their being,
770 With thought that they must be. Let no man seek
Henceforth to be foretold what shall befall
Him or his childern, evil he may be sure,
Which neither his foreknowing can prevent,
And he the future evil shall no less
775 In apprehension than in substance feel
Grievous to bear: but that care now is past,
Man is not whom to warn: those few escaped
Famine and anguish will at last consume
Wand'ring that wat'ry desert: I had hope
780 When violence was ceased, and war on Earth,
All would have then gone well, peace would have crowned
With length of happy days the race of man;
But I was far deceived; for now I see
Peace to corrupt no less than war to waste.
785 How comes it thus? Unfold, celestial guide,
And whether here the race of man will end."
      To whom thus Michael. "Those whom last thou saw'st
In triumph and luxurious wealth, are they
First seen in acts of prowess eminent
790 And great exploits, but of true virtue void;
Who having spilt much blood, and done much waste
Subduing nations, and achieved thereby
Fame in the world, high titles, and rich prey,
Shall change their course to pleasure, ease, and sloth,
795 Surfeit, and lust, till wantonness and pride
Raise out of friendship hostile deeds in peace.
The conquered also, and enslaved by war

---

766. **dispensed:** portioned out (so much evil for this age, so much for that age, et cetera).

777. **Man is not whom:** No one remains.

797–807. In both his poetry and his prose, Milton often states his belief that moral corruption and the loss of political liberty go hand in hand. See *SA* 268–71.

Shall with their freedom lost all virtue lose
And fear of God, from whom their piety feigned
800 In sharp contest of battle found no aid
Against invaders; therefore cooled in zeal
Thenceforth shall practice how to live secure,
Worldly or dissolute, on what their lords
Shall leave them to enjoy; for th' earth shall bear
805 More than enough, that temperance may be tried:
So all shall turn degenerate, all depraved,
Justice and temperance, truth and faith forgot;
One man except, the only son of light
In a dark age, against example good,
810 Against allurement, custom, and a world
Offended; fearless of reproach and scorn,
Or violence, he of their wicked ways
Shall them admonish, and before them set
The paths of righteousness, how much more safe,
815 And full of peace, denouncing wrath to come
On their impenitence; and shall return
Of them derided, but of God observed
The one just man alive; by his command
Shall build a wondrous ark, as thou beheld'st,
820 To save himself and household from amidst
A world devote to universal wrack.
No sooner he with them of man and beast
Select for life shall in the ark be lodged,
And sheltered round, but all the cataracts
825 Of heav'n set open on the earth shall pour
Rain day and night, all fountains of the deep
Broke up, shall heave the ocean to usurp
Beyond all bounds, till inundation rise
Above the highest hills: then shall this mount
830 Of Paradise by might of waves be moved
Out of his place, pushed by the hornèd flood,
With all his verdure spoiled, and trees adrift

---

808. **One man:** Noah.
815. **denouncing:** proclaiming.

821. **devote:** consecrated to utter destruc-
tion, doomed.

Down the great river to the op'ning gulf,
And there take root an island salt and bare,
835 The haunt of seals and orcs, and sea-mews' clang.
To teach thee that God attributes to place
No sanctity, if none be thither brought
By men who there frequent, or therein dwell.
And now what further shall ensue, behold."
840   He looked, and saw the ark hull on the flood,
Which now abated, for the clouds were fled,
Driv'n by a keen north wind, that blowing dry
Wrinkled the face of deluge, as decayed;
And the clear sun on his wide wat'ry glass
845 Gazed hot, and of the fresh wave largely drew,
As after thirst, which made their flowing shrink
From standing lake to tripping ebb, that stole
With soft foot towards the deep, who now had stopped
His sluices, as the heav'n his windows shut.
850 The ark no more now floats, but seems on ground
Fast on the top of some high mountain fixed.
And now the tops of hills as rocks appear;
With clamor thence the rapid currents drive
Towards the retreating sea their furious tide.
855 Forthwith from out the ark a raven flies,
And after him, the surer messenger,
A dove sent forth once and again to spy
Green tree or ground whereon his foot may light;
The second time returning, in his bill
860 An olive leaf he brings, pacific sign:

---

835. **orcs:** whales; **sea-mews:** gulls; **clang:** shrill cry.

836–37. **to place/No sanctity:** One sign of the lack of sanctity for locality is the virtual absence of place names in Book II. Indeed, even proper names are withheld, as if cults of personality were as false and distracting as cults of location.

840–69. Adam's sixth and final vision focuses on God's turn to peace and reconciliation after the judgmental wrath of the Flood.

840. **hull:** drift.

845. **of the fresh wave largely drew:** Cp. the thirsty sun of 5.422–26.

847. **tripping:** softly flowing.

851. **some high mountain:** "The Ark rested . . . upon the mountains of Ararat" (Gen. 8.4).

856. **the surer messenger:** surer, because the dove represents peace.

Anon dry ground appears, and from his ark
The ancient sire descends with all his train;
Then with uplifted hands, and eyes devout,
Grateful to Heav'n, over his head beholds
865   A dewy cloud, and in the cloud a bow
Conspicuous with three listed colors gay,
Betok'ning peace from God, and cov'nant new.
Whereat the heart of Adam erst so sad
Greatly rejoiced, and thus his joy broke forth.
870   "O thou who future things canst represent
As present, Heav'nly instructor, I revive
At this last sight, assured that man shall live
With all the creatures, and their seed preserve.
Far less I now lament for one whole world
875   Of wicked sons destroyed, than I rejoice
For one man found so perfect and so just,
That God vouchsafes to raise another world
From him, and all his anger to forget.
But say, what mean those colored streaks in heav'n,
880   Distended as the brow of God appeased,
Or serve they as a flow'ry verge to bind
The fluid skirts of that same wat'ry cloud,
Lest it again dissolve and show'r the Earth?"
      To whom th' Archangel. "Dextrously thou aim'st;
885   So willingly doth God remit his ire,
Though late repenting him of man depraved,
Grieved at his heart, when looking down he saw
The whole Earth filled with violence, and all flesh
Corrupting each their way; yet those removed,
890   Such grace shall one just man find in his sight,

---

866. **three listed colors:** stripes formed from the primary colors, red, yellow, and blue.

867. **cov'nant new:** The covenant, as explained in lines 892–901, that God will never again flood the earth, which will instead be renewed by a purging fire.

880. **Distended:** expanded or loosened, as opposed to a brow contracted in anger.

881. **verge:** border, hem.

885–87. **So willingly . . . heart:** based on Gen. 6.6–7, a passage central to Milton's discussion of metaphor in the biblical representation of God (*CD* 1.2 in *MLM* 1147).

886–901. Here Milton weaves together Gen. 6.6, 9, 11–12; 8.22; 9.11–17; 2 Pet. 3.12–13.

That he relents, not to blot out mankind,
And makes a cov'nant never to destroy
The Earth again by flood, nor let the sea
Surpass his bounds, nor rain to drown the world
895 With man therein or beast; but when he brings
Over the Earth a cloud, will therein set
His triple-colored bow, whereon to look
And call to mind his cov'nant: day and night,
Seed time and harvest, heat and hoary frost
900 Shall hold their course, till fire purge all things new,
Both heav'n and earth, wherein the just shall dwell."

Book XII

The Argument

The angel Michael continues from the Flood to relate what shall succeed; then, in the mention of Abraham, comes by degrees to explain who that seed of the woman shall be which was promised Adam and Eve in the Fall; his incarnation, death, resurrection, and ascension; the state of the church till his second coming. Adam greatly satisfied and recomforted by these relations and promises descends the hill with Michael; wakens Eve, who all this while had slept, but with gentle dreams composed to quietness of mind and submission. Michael in either hand leads them out of Paradise, the fiery sword waving behind them, and the Cherubim taking their stations to guard the place.

As one who in his journey bates at noon,
Though bent on speed, so here the Archangel paused
Betwixt the world destroyed and world restored,
If Adam aught perhaps might interpose;
5   Then with transition sweet new speech resumes.
    "Thus thou hast seen one world begin and end;
And man as from a second stock proceed.
Much thou hast yet to see, but I perceive
Thy mortal sight to fail; objects divine
10 Must needs impair and weary human sense:
Henceforth what is to come I will relate,

1–5. This passage first appeared in 1674, where the long Book 10 of 1667 was divided into the current Books 11 and 12.

1. **bates:** pauses at an inn for refreshment.

7. **second stock:** Noah now takes the place of Adam, but the passage also glances at

Christ, the stock onto which we are grafted in Rom. 11.17–27.

11. **I will relate:** Adam's instruction switches from visions to narrations, and the pace doubles, since the visions of Book 11 were first described and then explained. The

Thou therefore give due audience, and attend.
This second source of men, while yet but few,
And while the dread of judgment past remains
15   Fresh in their minds, fearing the Deity,
With some regard to what is just and right
Shall lead their lives, and multiply apace,
Laboring the soil, and reaping plenteous crop,
Corn, wine and oil; and from the herd or flock,
20   Oft sacrificing bullock, lamb, or kid,
With large wine-offerings poured, and sacred feast,
Shall spend their days in joy unblamed, and dwell
Long time in peace by families and tribes
Under paternal rule; till one shall rise
25   Of proud ambitious heart, who not content
With fair equality, fraternal state,
Will arrogate dominion undeserved
Over his brethren, and quite dispossess
Concord and law of nature from the Earth;
30   Hunting (and men not beasts shall be his game)
With war and hostile snare such as refuse
Subjection to his empire tyrannous:
A mighty hunter thence he shall be styled
Before the Lord, as in despite of Heav'n,
35   Or from Heav'n claiming second sov'reignty;
And from rebellion shall derive his name,
Though of rebellion others he accuse.
He with a crew, whom like ambition joins
With him or under him to tyrannize,

---

six visions in Book 11 are structurally bal-
anced by Michael's six main speeches in
Book 12.

24. **one shall rise:** Nimrod; as in Book 11,
proper names and place names are for the
time being withheld.

27. **arrogate dominion:** In biblical history,
Nimrod is the first tyrant; see Ralegh,
History of the World, 1.10.1.

30. **Hunting:** In Gen. 10.9, Nimrod is "a
mighty hunter before the Lord."

34–35. **as in despite . . . sov'reignty:** Michael
says that Nimrod's epithet (see previous
note) means that he either brazenly defies
God or invents the blasphemous doctrine
of the divine right of kings.

36. *Nimrod* was sometimes said to derive
from the Hebrew *marad*, "to rebel." The
sense is that he is rebelling against God.

38–62. In presenting Nimrod as the builder
of Babel, Milton follows the view of Jose-
phus (*Antiq.* 1.4.2).

40 Marching from Eden towards the west, shall find
    The plain, wherein a black bituminous gurge
    Boils out from under ground, the mouth of Hell;
    Of brick, and of that stuff they cast to build
    A city and tow'r, whose top may reach to Heav'n;
45 And get themselves a name, lest far dispersed
    In foreign lands their memory be lost,
    Regardless whether good or evil fame.
    But God who oft descends to visit men
    Unseen, and through their habitations walks
50 To mark their doings, them beholding soon,
    Comes down to see their city, ere the tower
    Obstruct Heav'n tow'rs, and in derision sets
    Upon their tongues a various spirit to raze
    Quite out their native language, and instead
55 To sow a jangling noise of words unknown:
    Forthwith a hideous gabble rises loud
    Among the builders; each to other calls
    Not understood, till hoarse, and all in rage,
    As mocked they storm; great laughter was in Heav'n
60 And looking down, to see the hubbub strange
    And hear the din; thus was the building left
    Ridiculous, and the work Confusion named."
        Whereto thus Adam fatherly displeased.
    "O execrable son so to aspire
65 Above his brethren, to himself assuming
    Authority usurped, from God not giv'n:
    He gave us only over beast, fish, fowl
    Dominion absolute; that right we hold
    By his donation; but man over men

41. **The plain:** the site of Babylon; **gurge:** whirlpool.

52. **in derision:** "The Lord shall have them in derision" (Ps. 2.4).

53–54. **to raze . . . language:** In the context of *Paradise Lost*, this well-known biblical episode suggests both the original names of the rebel angels razed from the Books of Life (1.362–63) and the senseless hissing and spitting of the metamorphosed devils (10.504–77).

60. **hubbub:** reminiscent of Chaos, "a universal hubbub wild/Of stunning sounds and voices all confused" (2.951–52).

62. **Confusion named:** *Babel* was sometimes said to derive from the Hebrew *balal,* "to confound."

70   He made not lord; such title to himself
      Reserving, human left from human free.
      But this usurper his encroachment proud
      Stays not on man; to God his tow'r intends
      Siege and defiance. Wretched man! What food
75   Will he convey up thither to sustain
      Himself and his rash army, where thin air
      Above the clouds will pine his entrails gross,
      And famish him of breath, if not of bread?"
          To whom thus Michael. "Justly thou abhorr'st
80   That son, who on the quiet state of men
      Such trouble brought, affecting to subdue
      Rational liberty; yet know withal,
      Since thy original lapse, true liberty
      Is lost, which always with right reason dwells
85   Twinned, and from her hath no dividual being:
      Reason in man obscured, or not obeyed,
      Immediately inordinate desires
      And upstart passions catch the government
      From reason, and to servitude reduce
90   Man till then free. Therefore since he permits
      Within himself unworthy powers to reign
      Over free reason, God in judgment just
      Subjects him from without to violent lords;
      Who oft as undeservedly enthrall
95   His outward freedom: tyranny must be,
      Though to the tyrant thereby no excuse.
      Yet sometimes nations will decline so low
      From virtue, which is reason, that no wrong,
      But justice, and some fatal curse annexed
100   Deprives them of their outward liberty,

---

82. **Rational liberty:** the freedom proper to rational animals (but not to the subjected beasts).

84. **right reason:** conscience, innate knowledge of what is just and right. See Hoopes. Michael observes that this faculty was impaired by the Fall, so that true liberty, which is obedience to right reason, was lost in the microcosm of the human soul before it was lost in the macrocosm of human government. Cp. 6.42n.

85. **dividual:** separate.

Their inward lost: witness th' irreverent son
Of him who built the ark, who for the shame
Done to his father, heard this heavy curse,
'Servant of servants,' on his vicious race.
105 Thus will this latter, as the former world,
Still tend from bad to worse, till God at last
Wearied with their iniquities, withdraw
His presence from among them, and avert
His holy eyes, resolving from thenceforth
110 To leave them to their own polluted ways;
And one peculiar nation to select
From all the rest, of whom to be invoked,
A nation from one faithful man to spring:
Him on this side Euphrates yet residing,
115 Bred up in idol-worship; O that men
(Canst thou believe?) should be so stupid grown,
While yet the patriarch lived, who scaped the Flood,
As to forsake the living God, and fall
To worship their own work in wood and stone
120 For gods! Yet him God the Most High vouchsafes
To call by vision from his father's house,
His kindred and false gods, into a land
Which he will show him, and from him will raise
A mighty nation, and upon him shower
125 His benediction so, that in his seed
All nations shall be blest; he straight obeys,
Not knowing to what land, yet firm believes:
I see him, but thou canst not, with what faith
He leaves his gods, his friends, and native soil
130 Ur of Chaldea, passing now the ford

---

103. **this heavy curse:** See Noah's curse on
  Ham's sons in Gen. 9.25.
104. **race:** descendants.
111. **one peculiar nation:** *Peculiar*, meaning
  "uniquely favored" and used of the Jews
  or of Christian believers in phrases such
  as "peculiar nation" or "peculiar people,"
was once a common idiom sanctioned by
Bible translation (*OED* B.1.1a).
113. **one faithful man:** Abraham; Milton's ac-
  count of him derives from Gen. 11–25.
115. **Bred up in idol-worship:** See Josh. 24.2.
117. **the patriarch:** Noah lived 350 years after
  the Flood (Gen. 9.28).
130. **Ur:** a city in ancient Babylonia.

To Haran, after him a cumbrous train
Of herds and flocks, and numerous servitude;
Not wand'ring poor, but trusting all his wealth
With God, who called him, in a land unknown.

135 Canaan he now attains, I see his tents
Pitched about Sechem, and the neighboring plain
Of Moreh; there by promise he receives
Gift to his progeny of all that land;
From Hamath northward to the desert south

140 (Things by their names I call, though yet unnamed)
From Hermon east to the great western sea,
Mount Hermon, yonder sea, each place behold
In prospect, as I point them; on the shore
Mount Carmel; here the double-founted stream

145 Jordan, true limit eastward; but his sons
Shall dwell to Senir, that long ridge of hills.
This ponder, that all nations of the Earth
Shall in his seed be blessed; by that seed
Is meant thy great Deliverer, who shall bruise

150 The serpent's head; whereof to thee anon
Plainlier shall be revealed. This patriarch blest,
Whom 'faithful Abraham' due time shall call,
A son, and of his son a grandchild leaves,
Like him in faith, in wisdom, and renown;

155 The grandchild with twelve sons increased, departs
From Canaan, to a land hereafter called
Egypt, divided by the river Nile;
See where it flows, disgorging at seven mouths

131. **Haran:** a city on the Belikh, a tributary of the Euphrates, on the border of Canaan.

132. **servitude:** slaves and servants.

136. **Sechem:** commercial center in Canaan, present-day Nablus.

139–45. A precise description of the Promised Land, drawn mostly from Num. 34. Its northern border is the district of *Hamath*, its southern the *desert* of Zin, its western the Mediterranean (*great western sea*), and its eastern the river *Jordan, double-founted* because of the supposed confluence of the Jor and the Dan.

140. **Things by their names I call:** Michael calls attention to the sudden reintroduction of place names and (with Abraham in line 152) proper names, hitherto missing from Adam's second education (see 11.836–37n; 12.24n).

153. **son:** Isaac; **grandchild:** Jacob.

Into the sea: to sojourn in that land
160 He comes invited by a younger son
In time of dearth, a son whose worthy deeds
Raise him to be the second in that realm
Of Pharaoh: there he dies, and leaves his race
Growing into a nation, and now grown
165 Suspected to a sequent king, who seeks
To stop their overgrowth, as inmate guests
Too numerous; whence of guests he makes them slaves
Inhospitably, and kills their infant males:
Till by two brethren (those two brethren call
170 Moses and Aaron) sent from God to claim
His people from enthralment, they return
With glory and spoil back to their promised land.
But first the lawless tyrant, who denies
To know their God, or message to regard,
175 Must be compelled by signs and judgments dire;
To blood unshed the rivers must be turned,
Frogs, lice and flies must all his palace fill
With loathed intrusion, and fill all the land;
His cattle must of rot and murrain die,
180 Botches and blains must all his flesh emboss,
And all his people; thunder mixed with hail,
Hail mixed with fire must rend th' Egyptian sky
And wheel on th' earth, devouring where it rolls;
What it devours not, herb, or fruit, or grain,
185 A darksome cloud of locusts swarming down
Must eat, and on the ground leave nothing green:
Darkness must overshadow all his bounds,
Palpable darkness, and blot out three days;
Last with one midnight stroke all the first-born

160. **younger son:** Joseph.
165. **Suspected to:** an object of suspicion to.
166. **overgrowth:** excessive growth.
173. **denies:** refuses.
175. **signs and judgments dire:** the ten plagues of Exod. 7–12.

179. **murrain:** a cattle plague.
180. **Botches:** boils; **blains:** pustules; **emboss:** swell.
188. **Palpable darkness:** See 2.406n.

190 Of Egypt must lie dead. Thus with ten wounds
The river-dragon tamed at length submits
To let his sojourners depart, and oft
Humbles his stubborn heart, but still as ice
More hardened after thaw, till in his rage
195 Pursuing whom he late dismissed, the sea
Swallows him with his host, but them lets pass
As on dry land between two crystal walls,
Awed by the rod of Moses so to stand
Divided, till his rescued gain their shore:
200 Such wondrous power God to his saint will lend,
Though present in his angel, who shall go
Before them in a cloud, and pillar of fire,
By day a cloud, by night a pillar of fire,
To guide them in their journey, and remove
205 Behind them, while th' obdurate king pursues:
All night he will pursue, but his approach
Darkness defends between till morning watch;
Then through the fiery pillar and the cloud
God looking forth will trouble all his host
210 And craze their chariot wheels: when by command
Moses once more his potent rod extends
Over the sea; the sea his rod obeys;
On their embattled ranks the waves return,
And overwhelm their war: the race elect
215 Safe towards Canaan from the shore advance
Through the wild desert, not the readiest way,
Lest ent'ring on the Canaanite alarmed
War terrify them inexpert, and fear
Return them back to Egypt, choosing rather
220 Inglorious life with servitude; for life
To noble and ignoble is more sweet
Untrained in arms, where rashness leads not on.

---

207. **defends:** prevents.
210. **craze:** shatter.
214. **war:** soldiers.
216. **not the readiest way:** The detour was
intended to circumvent the warlike
Philistines (Exod. 13).
217. **alarmed:** called to arms.

This also shall they gain by their delay
In the wide wilderness, there they shall found
225   Their government, and their great senate choose
Through the twelve tribes, to rule by laws ordained:
God from the mount of Sinai, whose gray top
Shall tremble, he descending, will himself
In thunder, lightning, and loud trumpet's sound
230   Ordain them laws; part such as appertain
To civil justice, part religious rites
Of sacrifice, informing them, by types
And shadows, of that destined seed to bruise
The serpent, by what means he shall achieve
235   Mankind's deliverance. But the voice of God
To mortal ear is dreadful; they beseech
That Moses might report to them his will,
And terror cease; he grants what they besought
Instructed that to God is no access
240   Without mediator, whose high office now
Moses in figure bears, to introduce
One greater, of whose day he shall foretell,
And all the prophets in their age the times
Of great Messiah shall sing. Thus laws and rites
245   Established, such delight hath God in men
Obedient to his will, that he vouchsafes
Among them to set up his tabernacle,
The Holy One with mortal men to dwell:
By his prescript a sanctuary is framed
250   Of cedar, overlaid with gold, therein
An ark, and in the ark his testimony,
The records of his cov'nant, over these
A mercy-seat of gold between the wings
Of two bright Cherubim; before him burn

---

225. **great senate:** the Seventy Elders of Exod. 24.19 and Num. 11.16–30. Milton cites the Sanhedrin as a model senate in *REW* (*MLM* 1124).

232–33. **types/And shadows:** prefigurations of Christianity; cp. *shadowy types* (l. 303).

241. **Moses in figure bears:** Moses prefigures Christ as mediator between man and God.

247. **his tabernacle:** the Ark of the Covenant, which contained manna, the tables of the law, and Aaron's rod.

255 Seven lamps as in a zodiac representing
The heav'nly fires; over the tent a cloud
Shall rest by day, a fiery gleam by night,
Save when they journey, and at length they come,
Conducted by his angel to the land

260 Promised to Abraham and his seed: the rest
Were long to tell, how many battles fought,
How many kings destroyed, and kingdoms won,
Or how the sun shall in mid-heav'n stand still
A day entire, and night's due course adjourn,

265 Man's voice commanding, 'Sun in Gibeon stand,
And thou moon in the vale of Aialon,
Till Israel overcome'; so call the third
From Abraham, son of Isaac, and from him
His whole descent, who thus shall Canaan win."

270   Here Adam interposed. "O sent from Heav'n,
Enlight'ner of my darkness, gracious things
Thou hast revealed, those chiefly which concern
Just Abraham and his seed: now first I find
Mine eyes true op'ning, and my heart much eased,

275 Erewhile perplexed with thoughts what would become
Of me and all mankind; but now I see
His day, in whom all nations shall be blest,
Favor unmerited by me, who sought
Forbidden knowledge by forbidden means.

280 This yet I apprehend not, why to those
Among whom God will deign to dwell on Earth
So many and so various laws are giv'n;
So many laws argue so many sins
Among them; how can God with such reside?"

---

255. **Seven lamps as in a zodiac:** Josephus, *Antiq.*, 3.6–7, maintained that the seven lamps of the candlestick (Exod. 25.37) represented the seven planets.

265–67. **Sun . . . overcome:** Paraphrasing the words of Joshua when routing the five Amorite kings at Gibeon (Josh. 10.12–13). The episode appears among the subjects for a tragic poem listed in the *CMS*.

267. **so call the third:** Jacob, who is named *Israel* ("he that strives with God") by a mysterious wrestling opponent in Gen. 32.24–28.

274. **eyes true op'ning:** Adam alludes to the opening of the eyes Satan falsely promised Eve upon her eating the forbidden fruit (9.706–8, 985, 1053).

277. **His:** Abraham's.

285   To whom thus Michael. "Doubt not but that sin
      Will reign among them, as of thee begot;
      And therefore was law given them to evince
      Their natural pravity, by stirring up
      Sin against law to fight; that when they see
290   Law can discover sin, but not remove,
      Save by those shadowy expiations weak,
      The blood of bulls and goats, they may conclude
      Some blood more precious must be paid for man,
      Just for unjust, that in such righteousness
295   To them by faith imputed, they may find
      Justification towards God, and peace
      Of conscience, which the law by ceremonies
      Cannot appease, nor man the moral part
      Perform, and not performing cannot live.
300   So law appears imperfect, and but giv'n
      With purpose to resign them in full time
      Up to a better cov'nant, disciplined
      From shadowy types to truth, from flesh to spirit,
      From imposition of strict laws to free
305   Acceptance of large grace, from servile fear
      To filial, works of law to works of faith.
      And therefore shall not Moses, though of God
      Highly beloved, being but the minister
      Of law, his people into Canaan lead;
310   But Joshua whom the Gentiles Jesus call,
      His name and office bearing, who shall quell
      The adversary serpent, and bring back

---

287. **therefore was law given them:** It is a dictum of Christian (especially Protestant) theology, stemming from Paul, that law can discover sin but not purge it (Rom. 3.19–28, 4.15–16, 5.12–15).

288. **natural pravity:** original sin. See *CD* 1.11.

292. **blood of bulls and goats:** "It is not possible that the blood of bulls and of goats should take away sins" (Heb. 10.4).

293. **blood more precious:** "the precious blood of Christ" (1 Pet. 1.19).

295. **imputed:** attributed vicariously.

296. **Justification:** a theological term: "The judgment of God . . . by virtue of which those who are regenerate . . . are absolved from sins and from death through Christ's absolutely full satisfaction, . . . not by the works of the law but through faith" (*CD* 1.22, Yale 6:485).

310. **Joshua . . . Jesus call:** *Joshua* in Hebrew and *Jesus* in Greek both mean "savior."

Through the world's wilderness long wandered man
Safe to eternal Paradise of rest.
315 Meanwhile they in their earthly Canaan placed
Long time shall dwell and prosper, but when sins
National interrupt their public peace,
Provoking God to raise them enemies:
From whom as oft he saves them penitent
320 By judges first, then under kings; of whom
The second, both for piety renowned
And puissant deeds, a promise shall receive
Irrevocable, that his regal throne
Forever shall endure; the like shall sing
325 All prophecy, that of the royal stock
Of David (so I name this king) shall rise
A son, the woman's seed to thee foretold,
Foretold to Abraham, as in whom shall trust
All nations, and to kings foretold, of kings
330 The last, for of his reign shall be no end.
But first a long succession must ensue,
And his next son for wealth and wisdom famed,
The clouded ark of God till then in tents
Wand'ring, shall in a glorious temple enshrine.
335 Such follow him, as shall be registered
Part good, part bad, of bad the longer scroll,
Whose foul idolatries and other faults
Heaped to the popular sum, will so incense
God, as to leave them, and expose their land,
340 Their city, his temple, and his holy ark
With all his sacred things, a scorn and prey
To that proud city, whose high walls thou saw'st
Left in confusion, Babylon thence called.
There in captivity he lets them dwell
345 The space of seventy years, then brings them back,

---

316. **but:** except.

322. **a promise:** "Thy throne shall be established forever," Nathan promises King David (2 Sam. 7.16).

332. **his next son:** Solomon.

338. **Heaped to the popular sum:** added to the sins of the people.

343–47. The seventy years of the Babylonian Captivity were foretold in Jer. 25.12 and are described in 2 Kings 25, 2 Chron. 36.

Rememb'ring mercy, and his cov'nant sworn
To David, 'stablished as the days of Heav'n.
Returned from Babylon by leave of kings
Their Lords, whom God disposed, the house of God
350 They first re-edify, and for a while
In mean estate live moderate, till grown
In wealth and multitude, factious they grow;
But first among the priests dissension springs,
Men who attend the altar, and should most
355 Endeavor peace: their strife pollution brings
Upon the temple itself: at last they seize
The scepter, and regard not David's sons,
Then lose it to a stranger, that the true
Anointed King Messiah might be born
360 Barred of his right; yet at his birth a star
Unseen before in Heav'n proclaims him come,
And guides the eastern sages, who inquire
His place, to offer incense, myrrh, and gold;
His place of birth a solemn angel tells
365 To simple shepherds, keeping watch by night;
They gladly thither haste, and by a choir
Of squadroned angels hear his carol sung.
A virgin is his mother, but his sire
The power of the Most High; he shall ascend
370 The throne hereditary, and bound his reign
With Earth's wide bounds, his glory with the Heav'ns."
      He ceased, discerning Adam with such joy
Surcharged, as had like grief been dewed in tears,
Without the vent of words, which these he breathed.
375   "O prophet of glad tidings, finisher
Of utmost hope! Now clear I understand
What oft my steadiest thoughts have searched in vain,

---

348. **kings:** Cyrus, Darius, and Artaxerxes, the Persian kings under whom Jerusalem was rebuilt.

349. **disposed:** put in a favorable mood.

350. **re-edify:** rebuild, with spiritual overtones (see Coolidge 23–54).

358. **a stranger:** Antipater, whom Julius Caesar appointed ruler of Judea (now a Roman colony).

360. **Barred of:** barred from; **a star:** the star of Bethlehem, proclaiming Christ the true king.

Why our great expectation should be called
The seed of woman: Virgin Mother, hail,
380 High in the love of Heav'n, yet from my loins
Thou shalt proceed, and from thy womb the Son
Of God Most High; so God with man unites.
Needs must the serpent now his capital bruise
Expect with mortal pain: say where and when
385 Their fight, what stroke shall bruise the victor's heel."
　　To whom thus Michael. "Dream not of their fight,
As of a duel, or the local wounds
Of head or heel: not therefore joins the Son
Manhood to Godhead, with more strength to foil
390 Thy enemy; nor so is overcome
Satan, whose fall from Heav'n, a deadlier bruise,
Disabled not to give thee thy death's wound:
Which he who comes thy Savior shall recure,
Not by destroying Satan, but his works
395 In thee and in thy seed: nor can this be,
But by fulfilling that which thou didst want,
Obedience to the law of God, imposed
On penalty of death, and suffering death,
The penalty to thy transgression due,
400 And due to theirs which out of thine will grow:
So only can high justice rest apaid.
The law of God exact he shall fulfill
Both by obedience and by love, though love
Alone fulfill the law; thy punishment
405 He shall endure by coming in the flesh
To a reproachful life and cursèd death,
Proclaiming life to all who shall believe
In his redemption, and that his obedience

---

379. **hail:** See 11.158n.
383. **capital:** both "on the head" and "fatal."
393. **recure:** heal.
396. **want:** lack.
401. **apaid:** satisfied, the debt paid; see 3.246.
403. **by love:** "Love is the fulfilling of the law" (Rom. 13.10).

406. Crucifixion for the Jews was an ultimate punishment, virtually damnation (Gal. 3.13). The Romans also regarded it as the "extreme and ultimate punishment of slaves" (Cicero, *Against Verres*, 2.5.169).

Imputed becomes theirs by faith, his merits
410   To save them, not their own, though legal works.
For this he shall live hated, be blasphemed,
Seized on by force, judged, and to death condemned
A shameful and accursed, nailed to the cross
By his own nation, slain for bringing life;
415   But to the cross he nails thy enemies,
The law that is against thee, and the sins
Of all mankind, with him there crucified,
Never to hurt them more who rightly trust
In this his satisfaction; so he dies,
420   But soon revives, Death over him no power
Shall long usurp; ere the third dawning light
Return, the stars of morn shall see him rise
Out of his grave, fresh as the dawning light,
Thy ransom paid, which man from death redeems,
425   His death for man, as many as offered life
Neglect not, and the benefit embrace
By faith not void of works: this Godlike act
Annuls thy doom, the death thou shouldst have died,
In sin forever lost from life; this act
430   Shall bruise the head of Satan, crush his strength
Defeating Sin and Death, his two main arms,
And fix far deeper in his head their stings
Than temporal death shall bruise the victor's heel,
Or theirs whom he redeems, a death like sleep,
435   A gentle wafting to immortal life.
Nor after resurrection shall he stay
Longer on Earth than certain times to appear
To his disciples, men who in his life

409. **Imputed:** See 295n. In the Protestant doctrine of justification, Christ's obedience is *imputed* or "attributed vicariously" to the faithful Christian, who cannot by means of his own works merit salvation.

415–16. **to the cross . . . sins:** See Col. 2.14.

423. **fresh as the dawning light:** Although dawn as a symbol of resurrection was commonplace, Milton found great poetry in it; recall the various dawns in *Nativity Ode* and *Lycidas.*

432. **fix far deeper in his head:** The stings of Sin and Death are returned to their source in Satan's head (Flannagan); see 2.758.

Still followed him; to them shall leave in charge
440 To teach all nations what of him they learned
And his salvation, them who shall believe
Baptizing in the profluent stream, the sign
Of washing them from guilt of sin to life
Pure, and in mind prepared, if so befall,
445 For death, like that which the Redeemer died.
All nations they shall teach; for from that day
Not only to the sons of Abraham's loins
Salvation shall be preached, but to the sons
Of Abraham's faith wherever through the world;
450 So in his seed all nations shall be blest.
Then to the Heav'n of Heav'ns he shall ascend
With victory, triumphing through the air
Over his foes and thine; there shall surprise
The serpent, Prince of Air, and drag in chains
455 Through all his realm, and there confounded leave;
Then enter into glory, and resume
His seat at God's right hand, exalted high
Above all names in Heav'n; and thence shall come,
When this world's dissolution shall be ripe,
460 With glory and power to judge both quick and dead,
To judge th' unfaithful dead, but to reward
His faithful, and receive them into bliss,
Whether in Heav'n or Earth, for then the Earth
Shall all be Paradise, far happier place
465 Than this of Eden, and far happier days."
So spake th' Archangel Michael, then paused,
As at the world's great period; and our sire
Replete with joy and wonder thus replied.
"O goodness infinite, goodness immense!

---

442. **profluent:** flowing; Milton favored baptism in *profluentum aquam* (running water) (*CD* 1.28 in *MLM* 1280).

447–50. The universal teaching of the Apostles fulfills the promise to Abraham that all nations (men of faith throughout the world) shall be blessed in his seed.

454. **Prince of Air:** as in Eph. 2.2; **drag in chains:** as in Rev. 20.1.

460. **quick:** living.

467. **period:** end.

470 That all this good of evil shall produce,
And evil turn to good; more wonderful
Than that which by creation first brought forth
Light out of darkness! Full of doubt I stand,
Whether I should repent me now of sin
475 By me done and occasioned, or rejoice
Much more, that much more good thereof shall spring,
To God more glory, more good will to men
From God, and over wrath grace shall abound.
But say, if our Deliverer up to Heav'n
480 Must reascend, what will betide the few
His faithful, left among th' unfaithful herd,
The enemies of truth; who then shall guide
His people, who defend? Will they not deal
Worse with his followers than with him they dealt?"
485   "Be sure they will," said th' angel. "But from Heav'n
He to his own a comforter will send,
The promise of the Father, who shall dwell
His Spirit within them, and the law of faith
Working through love, upon their hearts shall write,
490 To guide them in all truth, and also arm
With spiritual armor, able to resist
Satan's assaults, and quench his fiery darts,
What man can do against them, not afraid,

470. **shall produce:** The subject of this verb is *goodness* in line 469.

475. **or rejoice:** See Lovejoy 1937 on the tradition of the *felix culpa* or "fortunate fall," and Danielson (202–27) for a vigorous denial of its relevance to *Paradise Lost*. Milton's version of the *felix culpa* is the central paradox of the epic. The Fall is not fortunate; the Fall is fortunate. Though Danielson may go too far in excluding the fortunate fall from the poem, he demonstrates that Milton's is importantly more subdued than some versions of *felix culpa*. Adam wonders whether his sin is the precondition of Christian salvation. But he does not rejoice in his disobedience, emphasizing instead the glorious power of God to create, even from his sin, *goodness immense* (l. 469).

478. **over wrath grace shall abound:** "Where sin abounded, grace did much more abound" (Rom. 5.20).

486. **a comforter:** the Holy Spirit.

488. **the law of faith:** Rom. 3.27.

489. **upon their hearts shall write:** See Paul's contrast between the Old Testament Law, written "on tables of stone," and the Gospel, written by "the Spirit of the living God" on "fleshly tables of the heart" (2 Cor. 3.3).

491. **spiritual armor:** See Eph. 6.11–17.

Though to the death, against such cruelties
495 With inward consolations recompensed,
And oft supported so as shall amaze
Their proudest persecutors: for the Spirit
Poured first on his apostles, whom he sends
To evangelize the nations, then on all
500 Baptized, shall them with wondrous gifts endue
To speak all tongues, and do all miracles,
As did their Lord before them. Thus they win
Great numbers of each nation to receive
With joy the tidings brought from Heav'n: at length
505 Their ministry performed, and race well run,
Their doctrine and their story written left,
They die; but in their room, as they forewarn,
Wolves shall succeed for teachers, grievous wolves,
Who all the sacred mysteries of Heav'n
510 To their own vile advantages shall turn
Of lucre and ambition, and the truth
With superstitions and traditions taint,
Left only in those written records pure,
Though not but by the Spirit understood.
515 Then shall they seek to avail themselves of names,
Places and titles, and with these to join
Secular power, though feigning still to act
By spiritual, to themselves appropriating
The Spirit of God, promised alike and giv'n
520 To all believers; and from that pretense,
Spiritual laws by carnal power shall force
On every conscience; laws which none shall find

---

501. **speak all tongues:** See Mark 16–17, Acts
2.4–7; this miracle is precisely opposite to
Babel's confusion of tongues (ll. 52–59).
508. **grievous wolves:** See Paul's warning
about corrupt priests in Acts 20.29; and
see 4.193n.
511–14. **the truth . . . understood:** Protes-
tants believe that God's truth in the
Scriptures must be apprehended not

through church tradition or the teachings
of the priesthood but by the individual
believer, whose interpretation will ideally
be guided by the Holy Spirit.
523–24. **enrolled . . . engrave:** The oppres-
sive laws binding the Christian con-
science will be found neither in biblical
writing (*enrolled*) nor in the Spirit's writ-
ing on the heart (see 489n).

Left them enrolled, or what the Spirit within
Shall on the heart engrave. What will they then
525 But force the Spirit of Grace itself, and bind
His consort Liberty; what, but unbuild
His living temples, built by faith to stand,
Their own faith not another's: for on Earth
Who against faith and conscience can be heard
530 Infallible? Yet many will presume:
Whence heavy persecution shall arise
On all who in the worship persevere
Of Spirit and Truth; the rest, far greater part,
Will deem in outward rites and specious forms
535 Religion satisfied; Truth shall retire
Bestuck with sland'rous darts, and works of faith
Rarely be found: so shall the world go on,
To good malignant, to bad men benign,
Under her own weight groaning till the day
540 Appear of respiration to the just,
And vengeance to the wicked, at return
Of him so lately promised to thy aid
The woman's seed, obscurely then foretold,
Now amplier known thy Savior and thy Lord,
545 Last in the clouds from Heav'n to be revealed
In glory of the Father, to dissolve
Satan with his perverted world, then raise
From the conflagrant mass, purged and refined,
New heav'ns, new earth, ages of endless date
550 Founded in righteousness and peace and love
To bring forth fruits, joy and eternal bliss."

---

527. **living temples:** 1 Cor. 3.16: "Know ye not that ye are the temple of God?" Cp. 1.17.

528–30. **for on Earth . . . Infallible?:** a dismissal of the idea of papal infallibility. See *A Treatise of Civil Power* (Yale 7:244).

534. Here we print "Will" (1667) rather than "Well" (1674).

539. **Under her own weight groaning:** a groaning that began with *sighing* at the moment of Eve's fall (9.783) and contin-

ued with a *second groan* at the moment of Adam's fall (9.1001).

540. **respiration:** breathing space.

546. **dissolve:** terminate. It is impossible to decide on the basis of this one verb whether Milton has here altered his opinion on the endless sufferings of the devils in Hell (*CD* 1.33 in *MLM* 1310).

549. **New heav'ns, new earth:** See 2 Pet. 3.13.

He ended; and thus Adam last replied.
"How soon hath thy prediction, seer blest,
Measured this transient world, the race of time,
555 Till time stand fixed: beyond is all abyss,
Eternity, whose end no eye can reach.
Greatly instructed I shall hence depart,
Greatly in peace of thought, and have my fill
Of knowledge, what this vessel can contain;
560 Beyond which was my folly to aspire.
Henceforth I learn, that to obey is best,
And love with fear the only God, to walk
As in his presence, ever to observe
His providence, and on him sole depend,
565 Merciful over all his works, with good
Still overcoming evil, and by small
Accomplishing great things, by things deemed weak
Subverting worldly strong, and worldly wise
By simply meek; that suffering for truth's sake
570 Is fortitude to highest victory,
And, to the faithful, death the gate of life;
Taught this by his example whom I now
Acknowledge my Redeemer ever blest."
To whom thus also th' angel last replied:
575 "This having learnt, thou hast attained the sum
Of wisdom; hope no higher, though all the stars
Thou knew'st by name, and all th' ethereal powers,
All secrets of the deep, all nature's works,
Or works of God in heav'n, air, earth, or sea,
580 And all the riches of this world enjoyedst,
And all the rule, one empire; only add
Deeds to thy knowledge answerable, add faith,

---

555. **stand fixed:** stands out clearly.
559. **vessel:** human being.
565. **Merciful . . . works:** "His tender mercies are over all his works" (Ps. 145.9).
565–66. **with good . . . evil:** "Overcome evil with good" (Rom. 12.21).
567–68. **things . . . strong:** "God hath chosen the weak things of the world to confound the things which are mighty" (1 Cor. 1.27).
581–85. **only add . . . rest:** A similar list of virtues, also emphasizing charity, appears in 2 Pet. 1.
582. **answerable:** corresponding with.

Add virtue, patience, temperance, add love,
By name to come called charity, the soul
585   Of all the rest: then wilt thou not be loath
To leave this Paradise, but shalt possess
A paradise within thee, happier far.
Let us descend now therefore from this top
Of speculation; for the hour precise
590   Exacts our parting hence; and see the guards,
By me encamped on yonder hill, expect
Their motion, at whose front a flaming sword,
In signal of remove, waves fiercely round;
We may no longer stay: go, waken Eve;
595   Her also I with gentle dreams have calmed
Portending good, and all her spirits composed
To meek submission: thou at season fit
Let her with thee partake what thou hast heard,
Chiefly what may concern her faith to know,
600   The great deliverance by her seed to come
(For by the woman's seed) on all mankind.
That ye may live, which will be many days,
Both in one faith unanimous though sad,
With cause for evils past, yet much more cheered
605   With meditation on the happy end."
     He ended, and they both descend the hill;
Descended, Adam to the bower where Eve
Lay sleeping ran before, but found her waked;
And thus with words not sad she him received.
610   "Whence thou return'st, and whither went'st, I know;
For God is also in sleep, and dreams advise,

---

587. The *paradise within* is not biblical. It is Milton's addition to the largely traditional, biblical, Pauline spiritual vocabulary of Book 12, and has behind it the entire weight of his poem; cp. Satan's Hell within (4.20). See Duncan (257–68) for analogues. **happier far:** happier than continuing, having fallen, to live in Eden (for which Adam and Eve yearned at 11.263–333).

594. **stay: go:** Note the conjunction of these words, for they will appear in Eve's forthcoming speech; see 9.372 for the first conjoining of *go* and *stay*.

604. **With cause for evils past:** "With good reason (referring back to *sad* in l. 603), in view of past misdeeds."

608. **ran before:** who had run before (to the bower); **found her waked:** In the prose Argument, Adam *wakens Eve.*

Which he hath sent propitious, some great good
Presaging, since with sorrow and heart's distress
Wearied I fell asleep: but now lead on;
615 In me is no delay; with thee to go,
Is to stay here; without thee here to stay,
Is to go hence unwilling; thou to me
Art all things under Heav'n, all places thou,
Who for my willful crime art banished hence.
620 This further consolation yet secure
I carry hence; though all by me is lost,
Such favor I unworthy am vouchsafed,
By me the promised seed shall all restore."
So spake our mother Eve, and Adam heard
625 Well pleased, but answered not; for now too nigh
Th' Archangel stood, and from the other hill
To their fixed station, all in bright array
The Cherubim descended; on the ground
Gliding meteorous, as ev'ning mist
630 Ris'n from a river o're the marish glides,
And gathers ground fast at the laborer's heel
Homeward returning. High in front advanced,
The brandished sword of God before them blazed
Fierce as a comet; which with torrid heat,
635 And vapor as the Libyan air adust,
Began to parch that temperate clime; whereat
In either hand the hast'ning Angel caught
Our ling'ring parents, and to th' eastern gate
Led them direct, and down the cliff as fast

615–20. Now the words linked at 9.372 (see note) and 12.594 (see note) are woven into a beautiful love lyric, full of internal rhymes and repetitions, in which the *paradise within* widens to include their love and marriage: *with thee to go,/Is to stay here*, in Paradise. Cp. Shakespeare, *ANT* 1.3.101–5.

629. **meteorous:** above the ground; see Hill (in Hill and Kerrigan 117–28) on the word's associations with Aristophanes, Plato, and Luke 12.29.

630. **marish:** marsh.

631. **laborer's heel:** Milton's myth spills out into everyday reality: Adam, and all after him, bear the curse of laboring, and their *heel*, in the terms of the protevangelium (see 10.175–81n), will one day feel the serpent sting of death.

635. **adust:** burnt up, scorched.

640 To the subjected plain; then disappeared.
　　They looking back, all th' eastern side beheld
　　Of Paradise, so late their happy seat,
　　Waved over by that flaming brand, the gate
　　With dreadful faces thronged and fiery arms:
645 Some natural tears they dropped, but wiped them soon;
　　The world was all before them, where to choose
　　Their place of rest, and providence their guide:
　　They hand in hand with wand'ring steps and slow,
　　Through Eden took their solitary way.

640. **subjected:** lying beneath.
643. **brand:** sword.
648. **hand in hand:** See 4.448, 689, 739.

648–49. The end-words of the last two lines
　　quietly, satisfyingly rhyme with *go* and
　　stay (see ll. 615–20n).

Acknowledgments

We are grateful to our editor, Judy Sternlight, for her numerous good turns, and to the crack production team at Random House for the superb detailing and overall beauty of the published book. We were ably assisted in our editorial work by Phillip Albonetti, Yaser Amad, Joel Dodson, Jonathan Lamb, Mary Maddox, Jennifer Nichols, Shea Suski, Natalie Tenner, Claire Fallon, Joseph Rumrich, and Amelia Kerrigan.

Works Cited

I. Editions of Milton

Bentley, Richard. *Milton's "Paradise Lost."* Jacob Tonson, 1732.

Broadbent, J. B. (gen. ed.). *The Cambridge Milton.* Cambridge Univ. Press, 1972.

Browne, R. C. *English Poems by John Milton.* 2 vols. Clarendon Press, 1870.

Bush, Douglas. *The Complete Poetical Works of John Milton.* Houghton Mifflin, 1965.

Darbishire, Helen. *The Manuscript of Milton's Paradise Lost Book I.* Clarendon Press, 1931.

Elledge, Scott. *John Milton: "Paradise Lost."* 2nd ed. Norton, 1993.

Flannagan, Roy. *The Riverside Milton.* Houghton Mifflin, 1998.

Fowler, Alastair. *Paradise Lost.* 2nd ed. Longman, 1998.

Hughes, Merritt Y. *Complete Poems and Major Prose.* Odyssey Press, 1957.

Leonard, John. *John Milton: The Complete Poems.* Penguin, 1998.

————. *Paradise Lost.* Penguin, 2000.

Newton, Thomas. *"Paradise Lost": A Poem in Twelve Books.* 2 vols. J. and R. Tonson, 1749.

Ricks, Christopher. *John Milton: "Paradise Lost" and "Paradise Regained."* Signet Classics, 1968.

Todd, H. J. *The Poetical Works of John Milton.* 6 vols. R. Gilpert, 1826.

Verity, A. W. *Paradise Lost.* 2 vols. Cambridge Univ. Press, 1921.

Wolfe, Don M., et al. *The Complete Prose Works of John Milton.* 8 vols. Yale Univ. Press, 1953–82.

II. Critical and Historical Works Cited in the Notes and Introduction

Addison, Joseph. *Criticisms on Milton.* Cassell and Co., 1898.

Aristotle. *The Art of Poetry.* Edited by W. Hamilton Fyfe. Clarendon Press, 1940.

Aubrey, John. *Aubrey's Brief Lives.* Ed. Andrew Clark. 2 vols. Clarendon Press, 1898.

———. *Aubrey's Brief Lives.* Ed. Oliver Lawson Dick. Secker and Warburg, 1950.

Auerbach, Erich. *Scenes from the Drama of European Literature,* trans. Ralph Mannheim. Meridian Books, 1959.

Babb, Lawrence. *The Moral Cosmos of Paradise Lost.* Michigan State Univ. Press, 1970.

Baillie, Robert. *A Dissausive from the Errours of the Time.* Samuel Gillibrand, 1646.

Banister, Richard. *A Treatise of One Hundred and Thirteen Diseases of the Eyes.* 1622.

Bauman, Michael. *Milton's Arianism.* Peter Lang, 1987.

Berry, Boyd M. *Process of Speech: Puritan Religious Writing and Paradise Lost.* Johns Hopkins Univ. Press, 1976.

Bloom, Harold. *The Anxiety of Influence: A Theory of Poetry.* Oxford Univ. Press, 1973.

Boone, Lalia P. "The Language of Book VI, *Paradise Lost.*" In Patrick, J. Max, ed., *SAMLA Studies in Milton.* Univ. of Florida Press, 1953.

Browne, Sir Thomas. *Religo Medici.* Andrew Crooke, 1642.

Burton, Robert. *The Anatomy of Melancholy.* Eds. Floyd Dell and Paul Jordon-Smith. Tudor Publishing, 1927.

Caedmon. *The Caedmon Manuscript of Anglo-Saxon Biblical Poetry.* Ed. Israel Gollancz. Oxford Univ. Press, 1927.

Calvin, John. *Institutes of the Christian Religion.* 2 vols. Trans. Ford Lewis Battles. Eerdmans, 1986.

Campbell, Gordon. *A Milton Chronology.* Macmillan Press, 1997.

Campbell, Gordon, Thomas N. Corns, John K. Hale, David I. Holmes, and Fiona Tweedie. "The Provenance of *De Doctrina Christiana,*" *Milton Quarterly* 31 (1997): 67–117.

Chambers, A. B. " 'Goodfriday, 1913. Riding Westward': The Poem and the Tradition," *English Literary History* 28 (1961): 31–53.

———. "Chaos in *Paradise Lost,*" *Journal of the History of Ideas* 24 (1963): 180–84.

Channing, William Ellery. *Remarks on the Character and Writings of John Milton.* Isaac Butts, 1826.

Cirillo, Albert R. "Noon-Midnight and the Temporal Structure of *Paradise Lost,*" *ELR* 29 (1962): 372–95.

Coleridge, S. T. *Table Talk.* Ed. Henry Morley. Routledge and Sons, 1886.

———. *Lectures and Notes on Shakespeare and Other English Poets.* Ed. by T. Ashe. G. Bell & Sons, 1902.

Conti, Natale. *Mythologiae.* Ed. Stephen Orgbel. New York, 1979.

Cowley, Abraham. *Poems.* Ed. A. R. Waller. Cambridge Univ. Press, 1905.

Creaser, John. "Editorial Problems in Milton," *Review of English Studies* XXXV, No. 135 (1983): 279–303.

———. "Editorial Problems in Milton" (Concluded), *Review of English Studies* XXXV, No. 137 (1984): 45–60.

Cudworth, Ralph. *True Intellectual System of the Universe.* Ed. J. L. Mosheim. 3 vols. Thomas Tegg, 1845.

Curry, Walter Clyde. *Shakespeare's Philosophical Patterns.* Louisiana State Univ. Press, 1937.

Danielson, Dennis. *Milton's Good God: A Study in Literary Theodicy.* Cambridge Univ. Press, 1982.

Dante. *Inferno.* Trans. Allen Mandelbaum. Berkeley: Univ. of California Press, 1980.

Darbishire, Helen. *Early Lives of Milton.* Oxford Univ. Press, 1932.

Davies, Sir John. *Poems.* Columbia Univ. Press, 1941.

Davies, Stevie. *The Feminine Reclaimed: The Idea of the Women in Spenser, Shakespeare, and Milton.* Univ. Press of Kentucky, 1986.

Defoe, Daniel. *Political History of the Devil.* T. Warner, 1726.

Dennis, John. *The Grounds of Criticism in Poetry.* George Strahan, 1704.

Dryden, John. *Critical and Miscellaneous Prose Works.* Ed. Edmond Malone. 3 vols. H. Baldwin and Son, 1800.

———. *Essays of John Dryden.* Ed. W. P. Ker. 2 vols. Clarendon Press, 1926.

Duncan, Joseph E. *Milton's Earthly Paradise: A Historical Study of Eden.* Univ. of Minnesota Press, 1972.

Edwards, Karen L. *Milton and the Natural World: Science and Poetry in Paradise Lost.* Cambridge Univ. Press, 1999.

Eliot, T. S. *The Varieties of Metaphysical Poetry.* Ed. Ronald Schuchard. Faber and Faber, 1993.

Emerson, Ralph Waldo. *The Early Lectures of Ralph Waldo Emerson.* Eds. Stephen E. Whicher and Robert E. Spiller. 3 vols. Harvard Univ. Press, 1959.

Empson, William. *Milton's God.* 2nd ed. Chatto &Windus, 1965.

Evans, J. Martin. *Paradise Lost and the Genesis Tradition.* Oxford Univ. Press, 1968.

Evelyn, John. *Fumifugium: or, The Inconveniencie of the Aer and Smoak of London Dissipated.* W. Godbid, 1661.

Fallon, Stephen. "Satan's Return to Hell: Milton's Concealed Dialogue with Homer and Virgil," *Milton Quarterly* 18 (1984): 78–81.

———. "'To Act or Not': Milton's Conception of Divine Freedom," *Journal of the History of Ideas* 49 (1988): 425–49.

———. *Milton among the Philosophers: Poetry and Materialism in Seventeenth-Century England.* Cornell Univ. Press, 1991.

———. "'Elect Above the Rest': Theology as Self-Representation in Milton."

In *Milton and Heresy.* Stephen B. Dobranski and John Rumrich, eds., pp. 93–116. Cambridge Univ. Press, 1998.

———. "Milton's Arminianism and the Authorship of *De Doctrina Christiana*," *Texas Studies in Language and Literature* 41 (1999): 103–27.

Fink, Zera S. "Milton and the Theory of Climatic Influence," *Modern Language Quarterly* 2 (1941): 67–80.

Fish, Stanley. *Surprised by Sin: The Reader in* Paradise Lost. 2nd ed. Harvard Univ. Press, 1998.

Fletcher, Harris F. *The Intellectual Development of John Milton.* 2 vols. Univ. of Illinois Press, 1961.

Froula, Christine. "When Eve Reads Milton: Undoing the Canonical Economy," *Critical Inquiry* 10 (1983): 321–47.

Frye, Northrop. *The Return to Eden: Five Essays on Milton's Epics.* Univ. of Toronto Press, 1965.

Galilei, Galileo. *Sidereus Nuncius.* Th. Baglionum, 1610.

Gallagher, Philip J, and Gilbert, Sandra. "Milton's Bogey," *PMLA* 94 (1979): 319–22.

———. *Milton, the Bible, and Misogyny.* Univ. of Missouri Press, 1990.

Gilbert, Allan H. *A Geographical Dictionary of Milton.* Yale Univ. Press, 1919.

———. *On the Composition of Paradise Lost: A Study of the Ordering and Insertion of Masterial.* Univ. of North Carolina Press, 1947.

Gilbert, Sandra. "Patriarchal Poetry and Women Readers: Reflections on Milton's Bogey," *PMLA* 93 (1978): 368–82.

Gilbert, Sandra, and Susan Gubar. *The Madwoman in the Attic: The Woman Writer and the Nineteenth-Century Literary Imagination.* Yale Univ. Press, 1979.

Goulart, Simon. *A Learned Summary upon the Poems of William of Saluste, Lord of Bartas . . .* Trans. Thomas Lodge. John Grismand, 1621.

Grotius, Hugo. *Of the Rights of Peace and War.* Trans. William Evats. M.W., 1682.

Hale, John. *Milton's Languages: The Impact of Multilingualism on Style.* Cambridge Univ. Press, 1997.

Hanford, James Holly. "The Chronology of Milton's Private Studies," *Publications of the Modern Language Association* 36 (1921): 251–314.

Hartman, Geoffrey. *Beyond Formalism: Literary Essays 1958–1970.* Yale Univ. Press, 1970.

Herford, C. H., Percy Simpson, Evelyn Simpson, eds. *Ben Jonson.* 11 vols. Clarendon Press, 1935–47.

Heylyn, Peter. *Cosmography in Four Books.* P. C. T. Passenger, B. Tooke, and T. Sawbridge, 1682.

Hobbes, Thomas. *Hobbs's Tripos, in Three Discourses.* Matt. Gilliflower and Henry Rogers, 1684.

Hoerner, Fred. " 'Fire to Use': A Practice-Theory Approach to *Paradise Lost*," *Representations* 51 (1995): 94–117.

Hooker, Richard. *Of the Laws of Ecclesiastical Polity.* John Windet, 1593.

Hoopes, Robert. *Right Reason in the English Renaissance.* Harvard Univ. Press, 1962.

Hume, Patrick. *Annotations on Milton's "Paradise Lost."* J. Tonson, 1695.

Hunter, William B., gen. ed. *A Milton Encyclopedia.* 10 vols. Bucknell Univ. Press, 1978.

Hunter, William B., C. A. Patrides, and J. H. Adamson. *Bright Essence.* Univ. of Utah Press, 1971.

Huttar, Charles A. "The Passion of Christ in *PR*," *English Literary Notes* 19 (1982): 236–60.

Ingram, James. *An Inaugural Lecture on the Utility of Anglo-Saxon Literature.* Oxford Univ. Press, 1807.

Jefferson, Thomas. *Papers of Thomas Jefferson.* Ed. Julian Boyd. 27 vols. Princeton Univ. Press, 1950–95.

Johnson, Samuel. *Lives of the English Poets.* Ed. George Birkbeck Hill. 3 vols. Clarendon Press, 1905.

Josephus, Flavius. *Works.* Trans. William Whiston. Armstrong and Plaskitt, 1832.

Kates, Judith A. *Tasso and Milton: The Problem of Christian Epic.* Associated Univ. Presses, 1983.

Kelley, Maurice. "Milton's Arianism Again Considered," *Harvard Theological Review* 54 (1961): 195–205.

Kerrigan, William. *The Prophetic Milton.* Univ. Press of Virginia, 1974.

———. *The Sacred Complex: On the Psychogenesis of Paradise Lost.* Harvard Univ. Press, 1983.

———. "Gender and Confusion in Milton and Everyone Else," *Hellas* 2 (1991): 195–220.

———. "Milton's Kisses." In *Milton and Heresy.* Stephen Dobranski and John Rumrich, eds., pp. 117–38. Cambridge Univ. Press, 1998.

———. "Of Scorn." In *The Wit to Know: Essays on English Renaissance Literature for Edward Tayler,* Eugene Hill and William Kerrigan, eds., pp. 143–63. George Herbert Journal Special Studies and Monographs, 2000.

———. "Complicated Monsters: Essence and Metamorphosis in Milton," *Texas Studies in Literature and Language* 46 (2004): 324–39.

Kerrigan, William, and Gordon Braden. *The Idea of the Renaissance.* Johns Hopkins Univ. Press, 1989.

Klemp, Paul J. " 'Now Hid, Now Seen': An Acrostic in *Paradise Lost*," *Milton Quarterly* 11 (1977): 91–92.

Lactantius. *Divine Institutes, Books 1–7.* Trans. Sister Mary Francis McDonald. Catholic Univ. of America Press, 1964.

Lau, Beth. *Keats's Paradise Lost.* Univ. Press of Florida, 1998.

Leonard, John. *Naming in Paradise: Milton and the Language of Adam and Eve.* Oxford Univ. Press, 1990.

———. "Did Milton Go to the Devil's Party?" *New York Review of Books* 18 (July 2002): 28–31.

Lewalski, Barbara Kiefer. *Paradise Lost and the Rhetoric of Literary Forms.* Princeton Univ. Press, 1985.

Lewis, C. S. *A Preface to Paradise Lost.* Oxford Univ. Press, 1942.

Lieb, Michael. *Milton and the Culture of Violence.* Cornell Univ. Press, 1994.

Lovejoy, Arthur O. "Milton and the Paradox of the Fortunate Fall," *English Literary History* 4 (1937): 161–79.

———. "Milton's Dialogue on Astronomy." In Joseph A. Mazzeo, ed., *Reason and Imagination: Studies in the History of Ideas, 1600–1800,* pp. 129–42. Columbia Univ. Press, 1962.

Lynch, Kathleen M. *Jacob Tonson: Kit-Cat Publisher.* Univ. of Tennessee Press, 1971.

Macaulay, Thomas Babington. *Macaulay's Essay on Milton.* Ed. Herbert Augustine Smith. Ginn and Co., 1998.

MacCaffrey, Isabel. *Paradise Lost as Myth.* Harvard Univ. Press, 1959.

McColley, Diane Kelsey. *Milton's Eve.* Univ. of Illinois Press, 1983.

———. *A Gust for Paradise: Milton's Eden and the Visual Arts.* Univ. of Illinois Press, 1993.

McColley, Grant. *Paradise Lost: An Account of Its Growth and Major Origins.* Packard and Co., 1940.

Mariana, Juan de. *De rege et regis institutione.* 2nd ed. Mainz (?), 1611.

———. *General History of Spain.* Trans. John Stevens. London, 1699.

Mather, Cotton. *The Angel of Bethesda.* Ed. Gordon W. Jones. American Antiquarian Society, 1972.

Moyles, R. G. *The Text of Paradise Lost: A Study in Editorial Procedure.* Univ. of Toronto Press, 1985.

Multhauf, Robert P. "Van Helmont's Reformation of the Galenic Doctrine of Digestion," *Bulletin of the History of Medicine* 29 (1955): 154–163.

Murray, Patrick. *Milton: The Modern Phase.* Barnes & Noble, 1967.

Nashe, Thomas. *An Almond for a Parrat.* Eliot's Court Press (?), 1589.

Newton, Isaac. *An Historical Account of Two Notable Corruptions of Scripture.* J. Green, 1841.

Nicolson, Marjorie Hope. "Milton and the Telescope," *English Literary History* 2 (1935): 1–32.

————. *The Breaking of the Circle: Studies in the Effect of the "New Science" on Seventeenth-Century Poetry*. Columbia Univ. Press, 1960.

Nuttall, A. D. *The Alternative Trinity: Gnostic Heresy in Marlowe, Milton, and Blake*. Clarendon Press, 1998.

Nyquist, Mary. "The Genesis of Gendered Subjectivity in the Divorce Tracts and *Paradise Lost*." In *Re-membering Milton*, Nyquist and Ferguson, eds., pp. 99–127. Methuen, 1987.

Pagel, Walter. "J. B. Van Helmont's Reformation of the Galenic Doctrine of Digestion—and Paracelsus," *Bulletin of the History of Medicine* 29 (1955): 564–66.

————. "Van Helmont's Idea on Gastric Digestion and the Gastric Acid," *Bulletin of the History of Medicine* 30 (1956): 524–36.

Paterson, James. *A Complete Commentary with Etymological, Explanatory, Critical and Classical Notes on Milton's "Paradise Lost."* R. Walker, 1744.

Patrides, C. A. "Milton and the Arian Controversy," *Proceedings of the American Philosophical Society* 120 (1976): 245–52.

Prince, F. T. *The Italian Element in Milton's Verse*. Clarendon Press, 1954.

Pritchard, William H. "Fish Contemplating a Bust of Milton," *New England Review* 22 (Fall 2001): 177–85.

Purchas, Samuel. *Purchas His Pilgrimage, or Relations of the World and the Religions Observed*. 3rd ed. William Stansby, 1617.

Rajan, Balachandra. *Milton and the Seventeenth-Century Reader*. Barnes & Noble, 1966.

Ralegh, Sir Walter. *The Discoverie of Guiana*. Robert Robinson, 1595.

————. *History of the World*. William Iaggard, 1621.

Raleigh, Sir Walter. *Milton*. Edward Arnold, 1900.

Richardson(s), Jonathan. *Explanatory Notes on Milton's "Paradise Lost."* John James and Paul Knapton, 1734.

Richardson, Robert D. *Emerson: The Mind on Fire*. Univ. of California Press, 1995.

Ricks, Christopher. *Milton's Grand Style*. Oxford Univ. Press, 1963.

Ricoeur, Paul. *The Symbolism of Evil*. Trans. Emerson Buchanan. Harper & Row, 1967.

Rumrich, John Peter. *Matter of Glory: A New Preface to Paradise Lost*. Univ. of Pittsburgh Press, 1987.

————. "Milton's God and the Matter of Chaos," *PMLA* 110 (1995): 1035–46.

————. *Milton Unbound: Controversy and Reinterpretation*. Cambridge Univ. Press, 1996.

Rusca, Antonio. *De Inferno et Statu Daemonum*. Milan, 1621.

Rymer, Thomas. *The Tragedies of the Last Age*. Richard Tonson, 1678.

———. *Monsieur Rapin's Reflections on Aristotle's Treatise of Poesie.* T. Warren, 1694.

Sandys, George. *Ovid's Metamorphosis Englished.* John Lichfield, 1632.

———. *Relation of a Journey.* Thomas Cotes, 1637.

Schwartz, Regina M. *Remembering and Repeating: Biblical Creation in Paradise Lost.* Cambridge Univ. Press, 1988.

Scot, Reginald. *The Discovery of Witchcraft.* Henry Denham, 1584.

Selden, John. *De Dis Syris.* Guilielmus Stansbeins, 1617.

Shawcross, John T. *Milton: The Critical Heritage.* 2 vols. Routledge, 1970–72.

Sperling, Harry, and Maurice Simon, trans. *The Zohar.* 5 vols. Soncino Press, 1949.

Stone, Lawrence. *The Family, Sex and Marriage in England 1500–1800.* Harper & Row, 1977.

Svendsen, Kester. *Milton and Science.* Greenwood Press, 1969.

Tayler, Edward W. *Milton's Poetry: Its Development in Time.* Duquesne Univ. Press, 1979.

Taylor, Jeremy. *The Great Exemplar.* Francis Ash, 1649.

Thorpe, James, ed. *Milton Criticism: Selections from Four Centuries.* Octagon Books, 1966.

Tilley, Morris Palmer. *A Dictionary of the Proverbs in England in the Sixteenth and Seventeenth Centuries.* University of Michigan Press, 1966.

Toland, John. *The Life of John Milton.* John Darby, 1699.

Turner, James Grantham. *One Flesh: Paradisal Marriage and Sexual Relations in the Age of Milton.* Oxford Univ. Press, 1987.

Voltaire. *La Henriade.* Chez Veuve Duchesne, 1787.

Walker, D. P. *The Decline of Hell: Seventeenth-Century Discussions of Eternal Torment.* Univ. of Chicago Press, 1964.

West, Robert. *Milton and the Angels.* Univ. of Georgia Press, 1955.

Williams, Arnold. *The Common Expositor: An Account of the Commentaries on Genesis 1527–1633.* Univ. of North Carolina Press, 1948.

Wilson, F. P. *The Plague in Shakespeare's London.* 2nd ed. Oxford Univ. Press, 1963.

Wittreich, Joseph A. *Feminist Milton.* Cornell Univ. Press, 1987.

Woods, Suzanne. "How Free Are Milton's Women?" In Walker, Julia M., ed., *Milton and the Idea of Woman,* pp. 15–31. Univ. of Illinois Press, 1988.

Wright, Thomas. *The Passions of the Minde in Generall.* Valentine Simmes, 1604.

Zagorin, Perez. *John Milton: Aristocrat and Rebel.* D. S. Brewster, 1992.

INDEX

This index includes names of historical persons and authors to whom Milton referred, and authors of scholarly and critical works referred to in this edition.

428 · Index

WILLIAM KERRIGAN is the author of many books, including *The Sacred Complex: On the Psychogenesis of Paradise Lost*, for which he won the James Holly Hanford Award of the Milton Society of America. A former president of the Milton Society, he has also earned numerous honors and distinctions from that group, including its award for lifetime achievement. He is professor emeritus at the University of Massachusetts.

JOHN RUMRICH is the author of *Matter of Glory: A New Preface to Paradise Lost* and *Milton Unbound: Controversy and Reinterpretation*. An award-winning editor and writer, he is Thaman Professor of English at the University of Texas at Austin, where he teaches early modern British literature.

STEPHEN M. FALLON is the author of *Milton's Peculiar Grace: Self-Representation and Authority* and *Milton among the Philosophers: Poetry and Materialism in Seventeenth-Century England*, winner of the Milton Society's Hanford Award. He is Cavanaugh Professor in the Humanities at the University of Notre Dame.

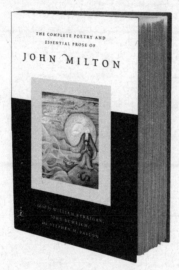